Tall Woman

The Life Story of Rose Mitchell, a Navajo Woman, c. 1874–1977

Rose Mitchell

EDITED BY CHARLOTTE J. FRISBIE

University of New Mexico Press
Albuquerque

© 2001 by University of New Mexico Press
First edition
Published with the assistance of the Amerind Foundation

Library of Congress Cataloging-in-Publication Data:
Mitchell, Rose, ca. 1874–1977.
Tall woman : The life story of Rose Mitchell, a Navajo woman,
c. 1874–1977 / edited by Charlotte J. Frisbie. — 1st ed.
p.   cm.
Includes bibliographical references and index.
ISBN 0-8263-2202-6 (cloth) — ISBN 0-8263-2203-4 (paper)
1. Mitchell, Rose, ca. 1874–1977.   2. Navajo women — Biography.
3. Navajo Indians — History.   4. Navajo Indians — Social life and customs.
I. Frisbie, Charlotte Johnson.   II. Title.
E99.N3 M66 2001
979.1004'972 — dc21
00-009014

Front cover: Tall Woman at her loom in the cookshack,
Chinle, Arizona, August 1964. Photographer, Charlotte J. Frisbie

Tall Woman

To the Memory of Tall Woman
for the example she set, her teachings,
and her willingness to share this narrative

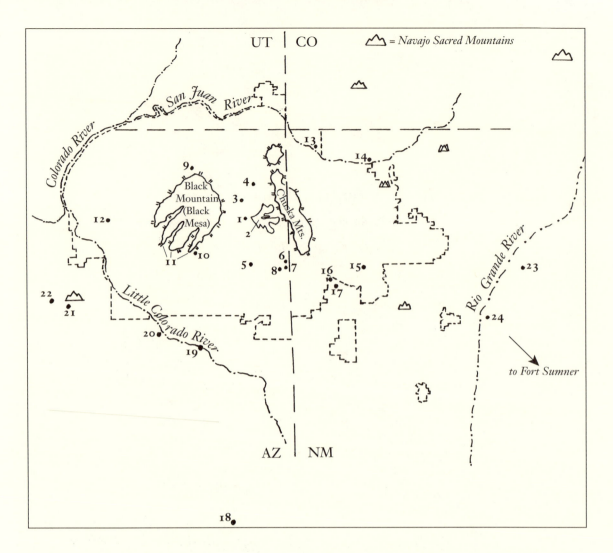

MAP 1 *Present Boundaries of the Navajo Nation and Places Important in Family History*

1 Chinle	9 Kayenta	17 Fort Wingate
2 Canyon de Chelly	10 Keams Canyon	18 Fort Apache
3 Many Farms	11 Hopi Mesas	19 Holbrook
4 Round Rock	12 Tuba City	20 Winslow
5 Ganado	13 Shiprock	21 Flagstaff
6 Fort Defiance	14 Farmington	22 Bellemont
7 Window Rock	15 Crownpoint	23 Sante Fe
8 St. Michaels	16 Gallup	24 Albuquerque

Contents

Illustrations

Acknowledgments

The list of people, institutions, and agencies who need to be thanked for assisting in some way with a project that began in 1963 and could not be finished until 1998 is necessarily long. Hopefully, the topically organized presentation that follows is inclusive; if I've forgotten someone, it is my error and totally unintentional!

For funding: The funding specifically earmarked for this project, rather than for some other, came mainly from Southern Illinois University at Edwardsville's Office of Research and Projects, Graduate School, and/or former School of Social Sciences. Via internal competitions for research funds to support approved research when I was not involved in administrative or summer teaching duties, I received various kinds of research awards from S.I.U.E. for 1971–81, 1983, 1985–86, 1988–91, and 1996. Work was also supported by sabbatical leaves from S.I.U.E. during two quarters of the 1975–76 and 1982–83 academic years, spring and fall quarters of 1990, and the 1996–97 academic year (two semesters at half-pay). Finalization of the project was made possible by a research appointment for the fall of 1998 at S.I.U.E., as part of my early-retirement agreement. Other assistance for this project during the spring of 1976 came from a ten-week Weatherhead Resident Scholar Award at the School of American Research in Santa Fe and a Grant-in-Aid from the Wheelwright Museum. The final source of direct support was a $750 NEH Travel to Collections Grant [FE 24534–90], which I used during the summer of 1990. Without this direct support, for which I am very grateful, the project would have been totally "out of pocket" and, thus, more than difficult for me to complete.

Work on Tall Woman's book was also done during research on other topics; because of that, thanks are also due to the National Science Foundation for the GS-144 Grant to David P. McAllester (1963–65), through which I began my own Navajo studies work in 1963; the American Association of University Women for a Shirley Farr Fellowship (1967–68), which supported my dissertation research on the Navajo House Blessing Ceremony; the American Philosophical Society Research Grant No. 6005 from the Penrose Fund (1971), which supported some of the archival work on *Navajo Blessingway Singer*; and the National Endowment for the Humanities for the nine-month College Teachers Award (1983–84), which supported completion of the research and writing of *Navajo Medicine Bundles or Jish*. In the same vein, appreciation is also expressed to two institutions for awards that mandated returns to the Southwest for specific purposes, thus enabling me to spend time in Chinle while trying to bring closure to the dialogues associated with Phase Two of this project. One such occasion was Colorado College's Southwest Studies Institute where I was selected as one of the faculty for the summer seminar on "Ritual Drama, Myth, and Metaphor" in 1994; in the other, I was selected by the Newberry Library as one of the participants in the "Indian Voices in the Academy" seminar on "The Teaching of Navajo History," held at Navajo Community College during June 1995.

In addition to both financial and "release time" support, needless to say, this project could not have been done without the interest, cooperation, and assistance of Tall Woman herself, and after her death, Tall Woman's family. Here the term *family* includes all of her children, her sister and half sister, and many of her grandchildren and other relatives. All of them have my deepest thanks for their continuing friendship, cooperation, and willingness to share their homes, lives, joys, and sorrows during what is now a span of thirty-five years, the time it has taken to see this project through to completion. Besides Tall Woman and her husband, Frank Mitchell (both now deceased), they include: Agnes Sanchez, the late Seya Mitchell, Howard Mitchell, Isabel Deschine, Mary Davis, Augusta Sandoval, and the late Ruth Yazzie. Additionally, the late Slim Woman and Small Woman have my gratitude, as do Ida Francis, Garnett and Ned Bernally, all of Tall Woman's grandchildren shown in Appendix A-4, Slim Woman's grandson and his wife, Leroy and Sally Mitchell, and Elsie Deschine, one of Small Woman's children. We all regret that it was impossible to finish Tall Woman's book before her own death in 1977, and those of two of her children, Ruth in 1994 and Seya in 1998.

Besides overall thanks to the entire family, certain individuals, both Navajos and non-Navajos, need to be identified for helping with specific matters:

For interpreting: the late Albert G. "Chic" Sandoval, Sr., Augusta Sandoval, Agnes Sanchez, Cecilia Sandoval, and Evonne Shirley.

For acting as true research assistants: Augusta Sandoval, Agnes Sanchez, and the late Seya Mitchell.

For sharing his own taped conversations with Tall Woman: the late Douglas Mitchell.

For illustrations: *assistance with locating photographs*: Kristie Butler, Garnett Bernally, Augusta Sandoval, Regina Sandoval, Isabel Deschine, Howard Mitchell, Josephine Mitchell, Evonne Shirley, the late Fannie John Price, the late Susan W. McAllester, the late Dr. George McClelland, Sr., Mabel Bosch Denton (for the late James Bosch), the late Father Dan Wefer, O.F.M., Father Mark Sandford, O.F.M., Father Marcan Hetteberg, O.F.M., Brother Gerald Grantner, O.F.M., Margaret Garcia Delaney, Mary and the late Carl Gorman, Ed Chamberlin, Arthur Olívas, Kim Walters, James Faris, Hal and Lucretia Ottaway, Dr. George McClelland, Jr., and Klara Kelley; *help with photo identifications*: the late Seya Mitchell, Mary Davis, Garnett Bernally, Augusta Sandoval, Brother Gerald Grantner, O.F.M., Father Cormac Antram, O.F.M., Father Mark Sandford, O.F.M., Father Marcan Hetteberg, O.F.M., the late Father Simon Conrad, O.F.M., Reverend Joseph W. Gray, and Margaret Garcia Delaney; *permission to use archival and other photographs*: Southwest Museum, Museum of New Mexico, Franciscan Archives at St. Michaels, the Franciscan Archives in Cincinnati, Margaret Garcia Delaney, Mary and the late Carl Gorman, Garnett Bernally, and all individuals so portrayed; *preparation of photographs*: the late Father Simon Conrad, O.F.M., St. Michaels; Father Marcan Hetteberg, O.F.M., Cincinnati; and Kathy Sullivan, student worker, at S.I.U.E. Audiovisual Services, Laura Million, director.

For permission to quote from Weaving a World: Museum of New Mexico Press.

For assistance with geography and place-names: the late Seya Mitchell, Mary Davis, Augusta Sandoval, Klara Kelley, and Stephen C. Jett.

For discussion of archaeological issues: Klara Kelley, David Brugge, Peter Noyes, and Dennis Gilpin.

For help with maps: Klara Kelley, Stephen C. Jett, Cecil ("Dino") Sandoval, Jr.; *for preparation of final maps:* Klara Kelley and Harris Francis.

For sketches later converted to line art: the late Tall Woman, the late Seya Mitchell, Mary Davis, and Augusta Sandoval.

For preparation of line art: Jennifer A. Frisbie.

For assistance with family genealogical matters: the following individuals, all of whom are now deceased: Tall Woman and her sister and half sister, Small Woman and Slim Woman; Frank Mitchell, Ruth Yazzie, and Seya Mitchell. In addition, others who helped included: Augusta Sandoval, Mary Davis, Agnes Sanchez, Garnett Bernally, Howard Mitchell, Isabel Deschine, Ida Francis, Lena Shirley, Evonne Shirley, Marie Shirley Lee, Mildred Yazzie Kee, Elta Yazzie, Lynn Shirley, Alfred Shirley, Timothy Shirley, Franklin Shirley, Josephine Mitchell, Jerry Mitchell, Joseph Klade, Geneva Toledo, Leroy Mitchell, Louise Davis, Doris Davis, Elsie Deschine, Shirley Beecher, Donald Mitchell, and Donna Mae Scott.

For census data and/or birth, marriage, death records: numerous staff members at the Tribal Census offices in both Window Rock and Chinle; at Trinity Presbyterian Church, Chinle, Reverend and Mrs. Clyde McDaniel, Jr. (summer 1990), and Reverend Norma McCabe (1996–97); through correspondence, Reverend Joseph Gray (1996–97); numerous Franciscan Fathers over the years, at various times and in several locations: Father Caron Vollmer, O.F.M., at St. Isabel's, Lukachukai; at St. Michaels Mission, especially the late Fathers Emanuel Trockur, Daniel Wefer, and Simon Conrad, as well as Fathers Martan Rademaker and Cormac Antram, all O.F.M.; at Our Lady of Fatima Church, Chinle, especially Father Blane Grein, O.F.M., from 1978 on, Father Hilary Brzezinski, O.F.M., summer 1990, and the rest of the staff during

1996–98: Father Pio O'Connor, O.F.M.; Sr. Margaret Bohn, O.P., Pastoral Ministry; Sr. Adelaide Link, S.F.P., Social Outreach, and Shirley Jean Britt (besides Father Blane Grein, O.F.M.); and Father Marcan Hetteberg, O.F.M., Franciscan Archives, Cincinnati, 1997–98.

For assistance with other Franciscan records: Fathers Marcan Hetteberg, Blane Grein, and Mark Sandford, and Brother Gerald Grantner, all O.F.M.

For preparation of the genealogy charts (A1–3) in Appendix A: Kerry Smith.

For help with the Hubbell Trading Post records: David Brugge, Martha Blue, Dorothy Hubbell, Ed Chamberlin (1990, 1997), Kathy Tabaha and Teresa Wilkins (1996), Klara Kelley (1997), and Kathy M'Closkey (1995–96).

For medical records: Helen Silversmith, ART, Sage Memorial Hospital, Ganado, Medical Records Department, 1976.

For extensive help with locating, discussing, and clarifying certain information: all members of Tall Woman's family; Father Blane Grein, O.F.M., and Father Pio O'Connor, O.F.M. (Our Lady of Fatima, Chinle); at St. Michaels: the late Fathers Simon Conrad, Dan Wefer, and Emanuel Trockur, all O.F.M.; Father Cormac Antram, O.F.M., Brothers John Friebel and Gerald Grantner, both O.F.M.; Father Caron Vollmer, O.F.M. (St. Isabel's Mission, Lukachukai); Father Marcan Hetteberg, O.F.M., Franciscan Archives, Cincinnati; Father Mark Sandford, O.F.M. (Louisville, Ky.); Father Murray Bodo, O.F.M. (Cincinnati, Ohio); Sr. M. Catherine Joseph (Sisters of the Blessed Sacrament, Bensalem, Pa.); Reverend Joseph Gray (formerly at Trinity Presbyterian Church, Chinle; now Duarte, Calif.); and Reverend Norma McCabe (Trinity Presbyterian Church, Chinle). Also: Grace Davis, Sybil Baldwin, Ellen Hubbard, Ned Yazzie, Alfred Taylor, Robert Tayah, Robert Martinez, Kristie Butler, David Brugge, Klara Kelley, Stephen C. Jett, James Faris, Joyce Griffen, Martin Link, Scott Russell, Robert McPherson, Alexa Roberts, John Stein, Peter Noyes, Peter McKenna, Martha Blue, David P. McAllester, Melinda Barlow, Kathy M'Closkey, Clifford Barnett, Miranda Haskie, and Margaret Garcia Delaney.

For helpful professional dialogues/supportive colleagueship during this project: the late Mary Shepardson, Klara Kelley, Dave Brugge, Jim Faris, Caroline Olin, Kay Halpern, Joyce and Bill Griffen, Steve Jett, Marty Link, Bob Young, Joyce Aschenbrenner, Suzanne Jacobitti, Sharon Hahs, Ted Frisbie, Sid Denny, David McAllester, Bob McPherson, Karen Ritts Benally, Russ Hartman, Clarenda Begay, Martha Blue, Ann Hedlund, Teresa Wilkins, Kathy M'Closkey, Peter Noyes, Alexa Roberts, Scott Russell, Dennis Gilpin, Joann Kealiinohomoku, and Father Blane Grein, O.F.M.

For "good times" and/or emotional or logistical support during 1996–97: Dave and Natalie, Inge and Loren, Jim, Hugh, Beth and Peter, Shirley and Bobby, Josephine and Manny, Klara and Dave, Paula and Danny, Caroline, Kay, Steve, Margaret, Pat N.,

Pat S., Bonnie, Phil and Faye, Audrey, Russ and Edna, Ted, Elizabeth, Jennifer, Kerry, Joann, Doug, Steve, Janet, Joyce and Bill, and all the Mitchells.

For critiquing earlier drafts of specific endnotes and/or sections of the manuscript: Garnett Bernally, Shirley Beecher, Klara Kelley, Jim Faris, Steve Jett, Kathy M'Closkey, Joyce Aschenbrenner, Margaret Garcia Delaney, David McAllester, Fathers Blane Grein, Mark Sandford, and Marcan Hetteberg, all O.F.M., Beth Hadas, and Dave Brugge.

For reading/critiquing the entire manuscript in one or more of its revised versions: Agnes Sanchez, Augusta Sandoval, Beth Hadas, Dave Brugge, David McAllester, and Klara Kelley.

For assistance with some details of manuscript preparation during 1997–98: Rhonda Harper and Heather Copple, secretary and student worker, respectively, Anthropology Department, S.I.U.E.

For assistance with proofreading: Jennifer A. Frisbie, Elizabeth B. Frisbie, and Ted Frisbie.

For editorial expertise, guidance, and production: Elizabeth Hadas, Floyce Alexander, and Dawn Hall.

CHARLOTTE J. FRISBIE
December 15, 1998

Introduction

This is the story of a Navajo woman who was reportedly born in 1874, six years after the Navajos returned from incarceration at Fort Sumner (1863–68), and who lived for "102 plus" years, reaching the People's goal of "death from old age" in 1977. Told in her words, but in English translation, and supported by anthropological endnotes drawn from a variety of sources, it is being published to fulfill a promise made to her in 1963. It was her wish that her story be shared not just with her own descendants in future generations, but also with others, so that her experiences and thoughts might help Navajos and non-Navajos alike learn more about what some of the People went through during this time period.

As a person, Tall Woman was loving, generous, quiet, hardworking, and thoroughly rooted in the beliefs and practices characteristic of many Navajos of her time. Forbidden to go to school by her parents, her education was based on teachings of and examples from her elders. Highly creative and talented, she became well known as a weaver, first of what are now called "Phase Two Chief Blankets" and later, of "Chinle-style rugs"; she was also a storehouse of knowledge about traditional plants and how to prepare them for use as food and medicine. Additionally, she was highly respected and frequently sought out for her skills as a midwife. Despite her reputation, Tall Woman remained unassuming and humble; living the life of a "traditional Navajo woman," she focused on the hogan, her children, the livestock, especially the sheep and goats, and the farm. Growing up in a family of more than twelve children, her childhood and early adult life occurred in worlds of constant motion. The family's movements corresponded to their subsistence practices of foraging and eventually horticulture, and then agriculture, which were combined with sheep, goat, horse, and cattle pastoralism to provide a substantial part of their economic base. After celebrating her Puberty Ceremony, Tall Woman met and eventually started living with Frank Mitchell, a Navajo who later became well known as a political leader, judge, and Blessingway singer. Together they produced twelve children, seven of whom survived into adulthood and also survived both of their parents.

Life History Context

Within American anthropology, life histories and other kinds of personal documents, such as autobiographies and biographies, have been a recognized genre since Franz Boas began training students. There is now an extensive literature that examines the genre from numerous perspectives, discussing methodologies involved, analyzing specific works, and considering how they illustrate theoretical concerns of various schools of thought, be these earlier "culture and personality" ideas or the more contemporary critiques of feminism and postmodernism. Building on earlier work, contemporary anthropologists remain interested in life histories as one of the numerous genres available for "writing culture" (Clifford and Marcus 1986).

However, while the literature includes many examples of the genre, both with and without accompanying anthropological commentary, life histories of women remain scarce (see Green 1980; Langness and Frank 1981; and Watson and Watson-Franke 1985). While the impetus of women's studies courses and concerns with broader gender issues have led to improvements in the recent past (of which Shostak 1981 is perhaps the best-known example), for many places in the world we still lack documents wherein women speak for themselves about their lives. For this and a variety of other reasons, a number of scholars in American Indian studies, feminist research, and more broadly within postmodern American anthropology continue to participate in active dialogues about doing contemporary ethnography and "writing culture," using life histories as well as other established genres, blurred genres, or new, experimental approaches. A number of works illustrate the wide-ranging discussions about dialogic models, collaboration and creativity, the feasibility of feminist ethnography, and other contemporary concerns. Among them, besides those appearing in the interdisciplinary *Journal of Narrative and Life History*, are works by Carr (1988), Theisz (1981), Fienup-Riordan (1990), Abu-Lughod (1990, 1993), Behar (1993), Behar and Gordon (1995), Krupat (1989), Brumble (1990), Swann and Krupat (1987), Rice (1994), Wallace (1994), Linde (1993), Frank (1995), Frank and Vanderburg (1986), Rosenwald and Ochberg (1992), Okely and Callaway (1992), Keesing (1985), Marcus and Cushman (1982), Marcus and Fischer (1986), Clifford and Marcus (1986), Clifford (1988), Geertz (1988), Gottlieb (1995), Kennedy (1995), Myerhoff (1992), Rosaldo (1993), Shokeid (1997), B. Tedlock (1991), D. Tedlock (1983), D. Tedlock and Mannheim (1995), Turner and Bruner (1986), Hoskins (1985), Harding and Myers (1994), Brady and Turner (1994), Lavie et al. (1993), Visweswaran (1994, 1997), Stacey (1991), Strathern (1987), Barbre et al. (1989), Bruner (1993), Mascia-Lees et al. (1989), Minh-ha (1989), Ward (1998), D. Wolf (1996), M. Wolf (1992), Alpern et al. (1992), and Smith and Watson (1998).

Scholars in Native American studies during the past two decades have been addressing the gender imbalance problem by publishing basic resources (e.g., Medicine

1978; Albers and Medicine 1983; Bataille and Sands 1984, 1991; Powers 1986; Bataille 1993; Vander 1988), overviews and critiques (e.g., Albers 1989), further discussions of Native American autobiographies (e.g., Carr 1988; Krupat 1989; Brumble 1990), and a number of women's personal narratives. Among the latter are those illustrating women's life experiences in the Yukon (Cruikshank 1992), and among the Haida (Blackman 1982), Lakota (Brave Bird with Erdoes 1993; Crow Dog and Erdoes 1990; St. Pierre 1991; Red Shirt 1998; Bettelyoun and Waggoner 1999), Inupiaq (Blackman 1989), Shoshone (Horne and McBeth 1998), Ojibway (Broker 1983), Salish (Miller 1990), Penobscot (McBride 1995), Cherokee (Mankiller and Wallis 1993), northern Paiutes (Canfield 1983), Comanche (Harris 2000), and Crow (Voget 1995; Snell 2000). There is also evidence now of multigenerational approaches or group biographies that stress ties with female ancestors (Boyer and Gayton 1992; Sneve 1995). Non-Navajo Native American male personal documents have also continued to be published (e.g., Seaman 1993; Emerick and Hanna 1993; Sundance with Gaede 1994; Hittman 1996).

In Navajo studies, however, the gender imbalance situation has not improved. Despite active scholarship on numerous topics, including gender (e.g., *American Indian Quarterly* 1982; Roessel 1981; Lamphere 1989; Frisbie 1989, 1993a Preface; Jaskoski 1990; Mc-Pherson 1993; Sparks 1995; Schwarz 1997), the focus continues to be on men. The first life histories were of males and they remain the classics: Walter Dyk's *Son of Old Man Hat* (1938) and *A Navaho Autobiography* (1947), and the Leightons' *Gregorio* (1949). Other, shorter histories, mostly of men, appeared in the 1940s, 1950s, and 1960s, in the Leightons' *The Navaho Door* (1944), Vogt's *Navaho Veterans* (1951), and two essays by Kluckhohn (1956, 1964). The late 1960s brought *Miracle Hill* (Emerson Blackhorse Mitchell and T. D. Allen 1967), *Black Mountain Boy* (Carlson and Witherspoon 1968), and *Denetsosie* (Johnson 1969). During the 1970s Navajo Community College Press published a number of collections of personal documents; in all, women's voices were included but hardly to the extent of men's. Examples include *Navajo Biographies* (Hoffman and Johnson 1970), *Navajo Stories of the Long Walk Period* (Johnson 1973), *Navajo Livestock Reduction* (Roessel and Johnson 1974), *Stories of Traditional Navajo Life and Culture* (Johnson 1977a), and *Navajos and World War II* (Johnson 1977b). In 1978, another male life history, *Navajo Blessingway Singer* (Mitchell 1978) became available, and in 1980, another emerged, *Left Handed* (Dyk and Dyk 1980), as a sequel to *Son of Old Man Hat*.

Although some of us tried to stimulate change through a session on Navajo Women at the American Anthropological Association meetings in 1981 (some of the papers from which appeared in *American Indian Quarterly*, spring/summer 1982), throughout most of the 1990s, gender imbalance in Navajo life histories has not been addressed. All of the personal narratives that emerged in the late 1980s and from 1990 through 1998 have been of males; they include *Bighorse, the Warrior*, as recalled by his daughter, Tiana, and told in her father's voice (Bighorse 1990), and *Lucky, the Navajo Singer* (collected by the

Leightons, edited/annotated by Joyce Griffen) (Leighton and Leighton 1992). We also have a brief biography of Pete Price (Jett 1991); an autobiographical fragment from Greyeyes (Stewart 1988); two male autobiographies (Lee 1987; MacDonald with Schwarz 1993). The future will bring McPherson's (2000) work on Navajo Oshley, a migrant worker from southeastern Utah, and Barnett's (n.d.; p.c. 5/28/97) on the late Albert G. "Chic" Sandoval, Sr. The latter, currently in preparation, will be based on tapes Chic made for Barnett in the 1960s. Its final assemblage may involve assistance from Chic's granddaughter, Miranda Haskie (p.c. 6/8/97).

Thus, even now at the beginning of the twenty-first century, if you are looking for works wherein a Navajo woman tells her own story, we have only three personal narratives of any significant length, all of which are partial. One, by Kay Curley Bennett (1964), best known to some as Kaibah, the recording artist, covers only the 1928–35 or girlhood period of her life (6/5/20–11/13/97). Obituaries (*Albuquerque Journal* 11/15/97:c-8; *Navajo Times* 11/20/97:5) noted her later contributions as an activist, author of a children's book, designer of dolls, and the first woman to run, in 1990, for the presidency of the Navajo Nation. The second personal narrative, which covers seventy years of life, is of another acculturated woman, Irene Stewart (1980), well known in the Chinle-Canyon de Chelly area of the reservation. While she gave 1907 as her birthdate (Stewart 1980:11), the short obituary notice (*Gallup Independent* 2/12/98), after her death on February 9, 1998, said she was born on July 1, 1905. The final work (Alvord and Van Pelt 1999) covers more than three decades (1959–1997) of the life of Lori Alvord, the first Navajo woman surgeon and now the Associate Dean of Student and Minority Affairs at Dartmouth Medical School. Writing with journalist Van Pelt, Alvord explains her journey into Western medicine by sharing personal life story details. While biographical, the work's main purpose is to address the crisis in contemporary Western medicine and suggest improvements based on holistic healing philosophies characteristic of Navajo medicine people.

Three other female histories are available—two of which were collected in the 1940s by Alexander and Dorothea Leighton (and published in Leighton and Leighton 1944, and 1949 as an appendix), and one of which was elicited in the early 1950s from Nancy Woodman (and included in Young and Morgan 1954)—but combined, they total only twenty pages. In the genre of biographies, the picture is similar; only one woman was included in *Navajo Biographies* (Hoffman and Johnson 1970), Annie Dodge Wauneka (pp. 292–307), who was also the focus of a biography by Mary Nelson (1972). Some additional information on Wauneka (4/10/10–11/10/97) became available in Albuquerque, Gallup, and tribal newspapers at the time of her death; Wauneka was the first woman elected to serve on the Tribal Council (1951–78). She received the 1963 Presidential Medal of Freedom for her work to improve Navajo health and health care, and was also awarded the Navajo Nation Medal of Honor in 1984, and an honorary doctorate from the University of New Mexico in 1985 (see *Albuquerque Tribune* 11/11/97:D-8; *Albuquerque Journal* 11/12/97:C-3; 11/13/97:A-16; *Navajo Times* 11/13/97:1, 2, 3; 11/20/97:2; also see Antram 1998:171–73). Other published personal data on Navajo women consist mainly of brief interviews and glimpses (Wood and Barry 1978, Bataille 1987, Witt 1981), infrequent inclusion of women's voices and experiences in collections focused on historical events, and of course, the brief references to their lives in the classic male life histories (analyzed in Frisbie 1982).

At present, some other colleagues are also focusing on Navajo women's personal documents; for example, Louise Lamphere (1995) is working with Eva Price; Joyce Griffen (1981, 1992) is editing the women's life histories in the Leighton and Leighton collection; Jennifer Denetdale (1997) is working with the children of Juanita and Chief Manuelito; Carolyn Niethammer (2001) is working with the relatives of Annie Dodge Wauneka; and Joanne McCloskey (1995, 1996, 1998), Ann Hedlund (1993), and Karen Ritts-Benally (Ritts 1989, Ritts-Benally 1993) are documenting women's lives from a multigenerational perspective. The Tenth Annual Navajo Studies Conference (1997) included, among other things, a paper by Denetdale (1997) and a session on "Doing Life History Work: Joys and Challenges," with Griffen (1997), McPherson (1997), Benally and Reed (1997), and myself (Frisbie 1997) as participants. The Eleventh Annual Navajo Studies Conference (1998) included a session organized by Louise Lamphere and Maureen Schwarz (1998) wherein five Navajo women, representing three generations, considered "Life Influences."

Thus, the context within which Tall Woman's narrative emerges is one that continues to be characterized by gender imbalance, despite active concerns and committed scholarship in Navajo studies. Tall Woman's story is that of a monolingual woman who was reared to become a sheepherder, weaver, farmer, wife, mother, and a perpetuator of traditional values and beliefs, especially those instilled by her father who was both a headman and a medicine person who performed the Blessingway and Flintway ceremonies. But it is also the account of a life transformed by colonialism, even though she herself escaped boarding-school experiences. As such, publication of her story, in addition to fulfilling a promise and a personal, professional goal, contributes to the anthropological profession in four ways. First, it helps address the continuing dearth of published women's life histories in Navajo studies by providing our *first* full-length personal narrative of a completed life of a Navajo woman. Second, it enriches our understanding of the diversity of American Indian women's experiences with colonializing forces, and of Navajo experiences during some of the critical events in Navajo history (for example, the Long Walk, the influenza epidemic of 1918–19, and the stock reduction of the 1930s). Third, it augments our knowledge of Chinle, an on-reservation community in northeastern Arizona, where the family settled in 1922. Known variously as Chin Lee, ChinLee, and Chinle until 1941, when the latter spelling was chosen, the area, like so many others, continues to lack a published community history. Tall Woman's narrative joins those of both Frank Mitchell (1978) and Irene Stewart (1980) in documenting a number of diverse developments there during the twentieth century. Finally, in Native American studies, it provides our *first* example of the "other side of the story," represented in Tall Woman's husband's autobiography, *Navajo Blessingway Singer*, which I coedited with McAllester (Mitchell 1978). Her narrative will interest scholars in anthropology, Native American studies, Navajo studies, history, ethnic studies, and gender studies; it will also have special value to Navajos and other American Indians interested in role models and indigenous accounts of life, family, local, and tribal histories.

Explanation of Particulars

In view of concerns of contemporary anthropologists, I'd like to situate "the particulars" of this project in a personal context. Acknowledgments and expressions of gratitude to those providing assistance and support for this work appear in the Acknowledgments, with appropriate dates and other information. When I first met Tall Woman, she was eighty-nine and, as she said, "in early old age." I was twenty-three, single, and a graduate student in ethnomusicology, working on an M.A. at Wesleyan University in Connecticut. For six years of the project (1964–70), I was a Ph.D. student in anthropology at the University of New Mexico; three of those years (through the period when Frank Mitchell died) I was based in Albuquerque, and three, with my husband, and later, first daughter, in Carbondale, Illinois. For the last seven years that I knew Tall Woman (before her death in 1977), I was teaching anthropology at Southern Illinois University, Edwardsville, where I was moving through various career events (including tenure, promotion, a two-year term as department chairperson, and my first "broken" sabbatical on the quarter system), and life events as well, including the birth of our second daughter (and last child), move to our farm, and death of my own father. Before her own death, Tall Woman had met my natal family during their brief visit in 1963, and my conjugal family in 1965, 1971, and 1976.

Fieldwork: I met Tall Woman in June 1963, when I arrived in Chinle, Arizona, to begin studying the Girls' Puberty Ceremony or *Kinaaldá* with her husband, Frank Mitchell, and other Blessingway singers. At the time, one of my teachers at Wesleyan University, David P. McAllester, had a grant to support work on the Blessingway. Since the Puberty Ceremony is classified by outsiders as a subceremony within it, I was hired "to work on that piece." Before the summer ended, the work had led in many directions, including the collection of Frank's life history and a small part of Tall Woman's. The following summer was also spent in Chinle doing more work on the latter, as well as initial work on Navajo medicine bundles and the House Blessing

Ceremony. That fall, I began work on my Ph.D. and thus began living in Albuquerque. From September 1964 until August 1967, I spent as much time as possible pursuing Navajo studies research and maintaining my ties with the Mitchells during weekend and school vacation visits, either in Chinle or in Albuquerque, depending on events and peoples' whereabouts. Included in the experiences we shared were Frank's final illness, death, and funeral in April 1967. Marrying Ted Frisbie in August 1965, in September 1967 I moved with him to Carbondale, Illinois, where he did his Ph.D. work in anthropology. From then until June 1970, I focused on writing my dissertation in absentia, becoming a parent for the first time in January 1968, and working for the Illinois Department of Mental Health, due to cash-flow problems. Trips to Chinle were not possible until I returned to Albuquerque in June 1970 to receive my Ph.D., although the Mitchells and I stayed in touch regularly by mail and phone during the interim. Securing a teaching job at Southern Illinois University, Edwardsville, as of September 1970 meant another move. It also opened up the possibility of competing for funds to support further research, but only during summers when it "was not my turn" (according to the department's rotational system) for summer-school teaching. I did further work with Tall Woman during the summer of 1971, with my firstborn daughter along, and also returned for five days, in December 1972, to attend a family member's funeral. My last fieldwork with Tall Woman herself was during the spring of 1976, when I was on sabbatical and based in Santa Fe. The next time that I went to Chinle from Illinois was, as is shown in the Epilogue, right after she passed away on June 29, 1977, a trip that included preparations for and participation in her funeral on July 2 and a return flight the next night, because of summer-school teaching.

From the time of her death until 1988, my research energies were devoted to Navajo medicine bundles or *jish* (see Frisbie 1987, 1993b) and other issues in Navajo studies; the cofounding, with David M. Brugge, of the Navajo Studies Conference, which met for the first time in February 1986 (see Frisbie and Brugge 1998, 1999), as well as to other anthropological concerns. Personally, in addition to full-time teaching, more administration, marriage and child-rearing, community activities, and restoration work on our historic farmhouse, I experienced the death of my mother in 1983 and the subsequent trials of finalizing parental affairs on my side of the family. However, I was able to get some more work done on Tall Woman's project during my 1982–83 sabbatical and 1983–84 NEH grant year, because for part of that time I was based in Bernalillo, New Mexico. After reaffirming family interest in the project during a spring 1988 trip, in the summer of 1989 I returned to Chinle to begin "Phase Two," which ran from then until June 1995, and included ten weeks of fieldwork during the academic summers of 1989, 1990, and 1991. A third, but double two-year term as department chairperson precluded absences for research work from 1992 until 1996, but I did manage to squeeze in two weeks of work in Chinle during the summers of 1994 and 1995, as well as brief visits before/after each annual Navajo Studies Conference. After the ethnographic research permit system (see below) was instituted by the Navajo Nation's Historic Preservation Department in 1990, and announced and discussed at the Fifth Annual Navajo Studies Conference held 10/17–20/90, at Navajo Community College (NCC), Shiprock, each time I did further work on the project on the reservation it was with an approved permit.

The work during Phase Two consisted of doing in-depth interviews with all seven surviving children, Tall Woman's sister and half sister, and other relatives, in an attempt to clarify my understanding of some things she had said, and to develop a deeper understanding of both her genealogy and the chronology of her life. It also included traveling to earlier living sites, and collecting photographic resources, copies of appropriate documents from tribal, local, and mission census records, and copies of other records from trading posts and missions. Work on verbatim transcriptions of her tapes was also done by me during this 1988–95 period. Contacts were maintained by letter, phone, and visits whenever professional conferences, court cases, or teaching invitations brought me to the Southwest, or whenever the Mitchells' lives brought any of them to the Midwest. I also returned for four days in September 1994, to participate in the funeral of one of Tall Woman's daughters, Ruth Mitchell Shirley Yazzie, who died on September 17. It was during the Phase Two period that the family reviewed examples of some new kinds of anthropological writing (at my request) and then had a series of dialogues with me about format issues. In June 1995, when I was again in Chinle, they made the format decision noted below; with it, Phase Two ended.

Phase Three, from 1995 through the fall of 1998, began with my applications for a sabbatical and grant support for 1996–97. While the latter was unsuccessful, I was granted an academic year's leave at half-pay, starting on July 1, 1996, when I finished another term as department chairperson. From then until mid-June 1997, I was based in Albuquerque in order to be near the Mitchells while assembling their mother's book. Through numerous visits, sometimes lengthy and in both directions, the eleven months were spent as follows: summer months were devoted to coding data in all typescripts and developing detailed outlines and chronologies for her text, as well as doing some additional fieldwork with her two oldest children. Actual assembly of the text began in September, and from then on polished drafts of chapters and/or entire sections were either hand-delivered or mailed by me to Chinle, and to Stockton, California, with follow-up visits in Chinle for discussions, further clarification work, and other reasons (see Frisbie 1997). The medical problems, subsequent surgeries, and complications suffered by Tall Woman's oldest son in December stymied both writing and discussions for all concerned, since concerns about him took precedence until late February. Then long discussion trips were reinstituted in a variety of locations and contexts. My sabbatical goal, of finishing a polished rough draft of the manuscript and discussing it with Tall Woman's family before the end of leave, was achieved, but with only two days left to pack and start the move back to Illinois.

Further revisions ensued during the summer of 1997, and the resulting manuscript was again returned to the family for another review. While the remainder of my work as editor was then, of necessity, once again postponed because of returning to full-time teaching in August 1997, during the 1997–98 academic year a few of the "loose ends" were addressed. These included resolving some historical and genealogical queries, and doing collaborative work with individuals hired to prepare line art, maps, genealogy charts, and photographs. After the manuscript was returned by the family with a few more requests for changes, it was submitted, with family approval, to the Navajo Historic Preservation Department (see below); their approval was forthcoming in January 1998. During the summer of 1998, when it was again possible for me to work on the book, I began the process of incorporating remaining revisions and finalizing the manuscript for submission to a publisher. Another trip to Chinle for a week in July 1998, to participate in the funeral of Tall Woman's oldest son, Seya, sadly interrupted the process, as did several other upheavals. However, thanks to a research appointment at S.I.U.E. during the fall semester of 1998 (negotiated as part of my early-retirement agreement) and another two weeks in Arizona, around my participation in the Eleventh Annual Navajo Studies Conference in October, I was able to cross-check a few remaining details and then, finally, complete Phase Three work by December 15, 1998.

Methodologies: As should be clear, work on this project, both with Tall Woman herself and on other pieces, was done piecemeal out of the necessities caused by geographic locations, life events, my own career path, and the fact that I was pursuing other interests simultaneously, both in research and service. Summers or other times when I was working with the Mitchells or in communities within driving distance, I lived with them, following what anthropologists call "participant observation" approaches while also employing nondirected and directed interviewing methods while collecting Tall Woman's story. In the beginning, I was a stranger, a redheaded white woman eventually named "Blond Woman." While Frank and Tall Woman initially labeled me their "granddaughter," before my first summer ended she changed my label to "daughter." Their children called me "younger sister," a label they still use today. But now their children's children do the same, only changing the "younger" to "older." With Frank and Tall Woman, I always used grandparent terms, out of respect; with other family members, I use sibling terms to this day, and go with however I am introduced to the next generation's new additions.

Participant observation means you fit in, help out, do whatever someone with your gender/age/marital/kin identities would do. Thus, I learned to herd, shear, and butcher sheep, milk goats, grind corn on a metate, gather wild foods and prepare some of them, card and spin wool, cook a number of "Navajo dishes," drive a wagon, reroof summer ramadas with cottonwood limbs, take livestock to water holes, and haul water. I also learned to sleep on a sheepskin on a hogan floor, to sweep and tidy up the hogan each morning, to properly dispose of fingernail clippings and hair from hairbrushes, to sit, walk, and sometimes talk appropriately, and to do countless other things, be it how to laugh the Navajo way, give directions, joke, share plans, depart and arrive, gather some plants in the right way, or appropriately contribute to ceremonies. Some skills that I needed I already possessed from camping, such as riding horseback, building fires, using lanterns and outhouses, and chopping wood. I enjoyed my life with the family in Chinle from the start; in addition to the professional and daily life work, it included breaks spent horseback riding, traveling in the wagon, visiting many people, having picnics, attending rodeos, going swimming, singing songs around a fire while roasting marshmallows, visiting famous archaeological and historical sites and nearby pueblos on occasion, and going to fairs and the like. It also included going with Frank and/or other family members to a variety of Navajo ceremonies, including Blessingways, Puberty Ceremonies, weddings, Protection Rites, Enemyways, Red Antways, Nightways, and Lifeways. Having Elizabeth, our firstborn daughter, with me in the summer of 1971 taught me many other things about fieldwork, which I have addressed elsewhere (Frisbie 1975a and b).

To explicate my own relationship with Tall Woman, I felt very close to her and saw her as a model grandmother. I admired her never-ending energy, her positive attitude, quiet humility, creativity, and her sense of humor. And, as I became more familiar with the story of her life, my admiration of her strength and wisdom increased. The solidity of her roots in the landscape and in the "traditional" sacred, Navajo beliefs, and the ways in which she expressed these in her daily life became more and more apparent with time, and, for me, awe-inspiring. I also grew to understand and recognize her central importance in the extended family, her role as *the person* who really kept everything together, even in her old age. I admired her determination and her endurance, and the fact she never whined or complained about her own physical condition, family poverty, or other worries. We joked a lot and went places together frequently, before she became paralyzed by her first stroke. And even after that, we were always comfortable around each other. I'm not saying she didn't scold me at times, because she did. Initially, it was because of my ignorance of Navajo ways, especially those concerned with the positioning of sheepskins at night in the hogan. I also did things she saw as foolish, like taking her grandchildren swimming at Many Farms Lake, or later, going to the Chinle Community Cemetery (as explained in endnotes). And when I became a parent, she didn't always agree with my approaches or my daughters' reactions to some of the daily events. But Tall Woman and I always showed each other respect, love, and concern; she felt free to ask me for help in countless ways and I felt free to provide it when I could, and explain why when I couldn't.

In the beginning, I paid room and board by the week, and hourly wages to all with whom I worked. With time, the former sometimes got converted, either totally or in part, to groceries upon request, as well as other kinds of assistance, including transportation (to stores, government offices, ceremonies, homes of relatives for visits, outings, homes of diagnosticians and other ceremonialists, and so forth); purchase of rugs, dolls, purses, jewelry, and other items being made within the extended family; purchase of other kinds of needed supplies; paying of bills and/or loans of money, which usually became gifts; and sponsoring family get-togethers and providing food, work, and transportation to make them possible.

During the project years, whenever I was based in the Southwest (Albuquerque, Bernalillo, and Santa Fe), the reciprocity of the relationship included my providing shelter and food, and whatever else was needed at the time by whomever was in town, for however long, and for whatever purpose. And when family members came to Illinois, the same was true. Over the years, we've also been able to travel together to some conference sites and other places. And when I've been in the Southwest when a serious illness and surgery were in process, I've also served as a home base, a place for food, shelter, transportation, as well as for communicating news and plans by telephone to distant, concerned relatives.

I first asked Tall Woman if she would be interested in recording her life story in June 1963, a question to which she answered, "I don't know." I already knew that although her husband favored such work, some Navajos, both past and present, opposed it, believing that to give such information was excessive and hastened, if not precipitated, one's own end (see Scott 1998). I also fully understood, given the very personal and private nature of the proposed project, that the decision was solely up to her. A day or two later, when I started to work with Frank on his life story, Tall Woman appeared at his cabin where we were working (in nondirected format), dressed in her best. He tried to shoo her out but she took a seat in a chair and stayed, making no comment. That night in the hogan, they began talking about what we were doing. From then on, they'd often sit outside during "work breaks," discussing things he was talking about, sometimes joking all over again with each other, and sometimes with Tall Woman making it clear she was learning some things about him that she had never known. After that first day, she often came in to sit while he and I worked. Never idle, she always brought wool along, and continued to card and/or spin while present; she never interrupted in any way, not even with the Navajo "um," or "uh huh" to indicate that she was listening. Two more requests from me in the next few days got the same answer from her as the first. The fourth request, however, about a week later, got a "Maybe, I'm thinking about it." That night she discussed her thinking with Frank and he encouraged her to go ahead so that future generations would know about her, too, and that everybody, even in distant places, could learn about things they had gone through together and apart. The next day, without me asking, she told me she had decided she would like to record her story and have it published, too, if I would write the last part of it, after she had passed away. Then she asked when I would like to start. Since I already had some interviews arranged with other Blessingway singers for the next several days, I opted for about a week's delay, which she said was fine.

For the first few days of nondirected interviewing, Tall Woman dressed in her best and told Frank we would be using his cabin as the location for our work together. She also told him he'd have to leave and go herd sheep, and after teasing her he did. After a few days of that approach, she said maybe we could work while she was dyeing or carding wool, weaving, or doing other things, and so the locations started to change. Throughout, however, whenever small grandchildren dropped in to listen, she shooed them out; if they didn't go, she'd stop talking until they left. She also always stopped working whenever visitors appeared in wagons, on horseback, or in vehicles. Sometimes one of her daughters would drop in to listen while we were working, occasionally interrupting her with questions or sideline comments, but never staying too long. She never told any of them to leave. Once the directed interviewing started, there was always another person present, acting as verbatim interpreter, as noted below.

Personnel

Tall Woman's text consists of narratives she recorded for me over the years (through both nondirected and directed interviewing), as well as numerous conversations we had while doing things together. They are supplemented in one place by information gathered by her grandson, the late Douglas ["Doogie"] Mitchell, who taped his late-night conversations with her when he was visiting during his Christmas vacation in December 1970. Doogie told me about these tapes and volunteered to let me duplicate them, which I did in 1971. Later analyses showed that their conversations stressed food preparation, kinship connections, and memories of her early days, and that their dialogues essentially duplicated some of my materials in content, although hardly in style, except for her comments about buffalos (now in Chapter 2). Through directed interviewing, other family members provided clarifying explanations, some of which have been incorporated in endnotes. These individuals included all of Tall Woman's surviving children: Mary Davis, Seya Mitchell, Agnes Sanchez, Ruth Yazzie, Howard Mitchell, Augusta Sandoval, and Isabel Deschine. Her sister, Small Woman or Woman at the Hard Ground Place (also called Grandma Black by some), and her half sister, Slim Woman, also known as Grandma Clauschee, also helped, as did Ida Francis and Garnett Bernally.

Although I have some training in reading, writing, and speaking Navajo, rather than relying on skills that become rusty without daily use I employed interpreters during my work with Tall Woman (1963–77). They included Albert G. "Chic" Sandoval, Sr. (1963–68), Augusta Sandoval, Cecilia Sandoval, Evonne Shirley, and Agnes Sanchez. Interpreters during my work with others included Augusta Sandoval (for Tall Woman's sister, half sister, Ida Francis, Ruth Yazzie, Mary Davis, and Isabel Deschine), and Agnes Sanchez (for Ruth Yazzie). Interviews with Garnett Bernally, Agnes Sanchez, Howard Mitchell, Augusta Sandoval, and Seya Mitchell were done in English. Interviews were taped when such was agreeable to the interviewee; otherwise, notes were taken during them, which in all cases was agreeable.

Although the project could not have been finished "after the fact" without everyone's cooperation, certain individuals need to be mentioned for helping in special ways. Augusta Sandoval became my research assistant, tracking down answers to genealogy questions raised through the mail or by phone by me at times during 1996–97 when I couldn't be in Chinle. When we started discussing drafts of the text, she also was the one who suggested "who in the family would know" about things I needed clarified and then went with me to get it done, if the person were monolingual. Seya Mitchell also became a research assistant, especially between 1989 and 1995, during my attempts to understand census information about relatives in Tall Woman's own generation, and earlier living sites mentioned in her text. He also readily shared his knowledge of early Navajo history and the landscape and geography important within the family, and became an enthusiastic travel partner when it was possible for me to consider visiting some of these places. Finally, the readings and rereadings of the various versions of the whole manuscript were done during 1996–97 by Augusta Sandoval and Agnes Sanchez; Garnett Bernally read and corrected the sections that concerned her. Discussions about revisions involved the readers, and other family members as needed.

Negotiated Decisions: Format, Content, and Possible Royalties

Life stories are not told as presented here, as monologues. Instead, fieldwork interactions, as all human conversations, consist of dialogues among speakers and listeners. In recent, postmodern times, anthropologists have become interested in presenting field data in formats that indicate the dialogic nature of conversations, and the reality of multiple voices. There has also been a shift toward experimenting with ways of writing ethnographies, and recognition that the fieldworker's affecting presence should also be incorporated.

Even though professionally I am encouraged by and supportive of such trends, this text does not reflect them. After reading and reviewing a number of the "newer ethnographies" that I loaned to the family (between 1989 and 1995) to illustrate what I was talking about, Tall Woman's children decided in June 1995 that they wanted their mother's book "done just like you did Dad's." In Frank Mitchell's life history, which was published in 1978, such questions, of course, were never raised during negotiations with the family. But even though anthropological options and interests had changed in the interim and those involved in the reading and discussing of new format possibilities understood them, they rejected them in favor of a single focus on their mother's voice. Rather than present our whole discussion here, let me just provide one quote: "Why would you put our voices and yours in there with hers? It's *her* story; keep everybody else, us, and yourself, out of it, and let her speak. Put all the other stuff in the end, in notes, or in the back of the book, where it is in Dad's. That's the way we want you to do it. Obviously we all know you and she were talking together about these things, and even some of us dropped in and out, throwing in our two cents. But tell it as her story, and keep everything else out of there. We're not saying the other stuff shouldn't go someplace; it has to; those notes are important, too. People need to understand how her words fit with other things, how her story connects with events here in Chinle, and elsewhere on the reservation, even with all of Navajo history. But don't clutter up her words by putting all the other stuff in the text. Let her speak by herself." Thus it was that the decision about format was made; that was how it came into being.

This project, which was finished after the fact, that is, many years after Tall Woman had passed away, depended from its inception on collaborative cooperation among all those involved in it. For me, after her death, it depended on cooperation and assistance from her children and other relatives. Each of my concerns was presented to them as they unfolded, so that people could start thinking about and discussing them, before we all came together to have group meetings. Between 1989 and 1995, the format decision was primary. Once text construction started in September 1996, collaborative cooperation entailed further traveling, discussions with "people who would know" in order to clarify some things I still didn't understand, and constant sharing of polished rough drafts of the text, as they emerged. The manuscript was delivered in piecemeal fashion to Chinle and also mailed in similar fashion to California. Then, through extended visits, phone calls, and letters, reactions were forthcoming. Discussions were mainly face to face, but also occurred on the phone. Suggestions were made about corrections, deletions, and rewordings. And other issues of concern to me, such as the appropriateness of including the ethnobotanical materials, were rediscussed. "Family" corrections concerned chronological orderings, facts clearly remembered by family members who went to school, or things I had misinterpreted. Their deletions concerned statements found to be repetitious, as well as those labeled "too personal" to appear in print. Sometimes, after discussions about the latter, the people involved would decide something could be left in, if it were reworded and said in a more general way. In those cases, discussions always started with, "Of course that's what happened; what she told you about that is true. But, we don't want that in there in quite that way because we're still here and there are people who don't have to know about that. So how about if you say it this way . . . ?"

Appendixes have been restricted to genealogical information (Appendix A), chronological data (Appendix B), and information on school attendance by the children born to and/or raised by Tall Woman and Frank Mitchell who were sent to government schools (Appendix C). Short introductions, which address relevant issues, accompany each appendix. Although an additional one incorporating Tall Woman's recipes for "traditional foods" was originally planned, the limits of my sabbatical and need to give priority to a family member's serious illness, between December 1996 and late February 1997, made this impossible. Perhaps that was fortuitous, given the size of the text without them. Documenting her recipes in cookbook format could make a separate, follow-up project, and perhaps will, in the future, if her daughters and I can get together with the necessary supplies and create them under "test kitchen" conditions.

Possible illustrations were assembled between 1989 and 1997. In May 1997, the family reviewed the possibilities and prioritized their choices, understanding that conversion of colored slides to black and white prints might reduce final options, and that the number of illustrations would ultimately be negotiated with the publisher. The goal was to include selected photographs of structures historically relevant in the narrative, as well as some of Tall Woman at different time periods and at least one of each of her children who survived into adulthood. While Franciscan publications made it possible to include a photograph of her father, Man Who Shouts, pictures of her mother regrettably could not be located, and those I had taken of her sister and half sister, once converted to black and white, were not of publishable quality.

Discussions about royalties were begun during 1996–97 dialogues about drafts of the manuscript. In view of Frank's book and two editions of *Kinaaldá*, the family already had experience with the process. Their decision, forthcoming in August 1998, while Agnes was still in Chinle, stipulated that any future income from Tall Woman's book would go directly into a central fund for the family.

Editorial Decisions

My job as editor of this manuscript included specific tasks and further decision making. The primary job, of course, was that of assembling Tall Woman's words (after transcribing, analyzing, and coding all field tapes and fieldnotes), and developing the Epilogue; researching and writing the contextualizing, explanatory endnotes; and creating the "front and back matter." A major challenge in the assemblage process was that of adding a chronological sense to the materials by arranging them according to Western time. Tall Woman did not speak in such terms; using retrospective and contemporaneous voices, she narrated her story in the Navajo way, cyclically around critical or significant events, without anchors in Western linear time. However, occasionally she *did* refer to an event by date, because its nature and repeated discussion within the family had engraved a date on her mind. She also sometimes used these events comparatively when indicating when other things happened. Furthermore, her approach to narration was not hit or miss. In general, when she chose to focus on stories of the ancestors, she narrated only those during those particular work sessions; the same was true for her retrospective narrations of her infancy, early childhood, and so forth. Using these clues, ethnohistorical data, and detailed work with each of her children, I was able to develop a better understanding of the overall chronology for her story, the major part of which, of course, had already unfolded before I met her. Her narrative is arranged according to this understanding (which has again been checked with her family), and according to the Navajo view of life as a walk through cyclical time, marked by infancy and childhood, young adulthood, maturity and grandparent years, and eventually, if one is lucky, old age. Tall Woman's voice is retrospective until the final section, where it becomes contemporaneous; she was eighty-nine when I first met her, and had already become a highly respected elder, grandmother and great-grandmother, and truly "an old age person." The final section includes the rest of what she wanted to say, sprinkled here and there with references to "you," that is, me. As explained below, it is followed by the Epilogue that she requested I write to account for the end of her days, constructed according to the wishes of her family.

In addition to adding a chronological arrangement to satisfy expectations of Western readers, as editor I also had the job of reducing differences in styles of interpretation, made obvious by my necessary use of multiple interpreters during the collection of her narrative. Individuals have different ways of speaking and different degrees of experience in interpreting. The main interpreter during the work from June 1963 through August 1967, was Albert G. "Chic" Sandoval, Sr. (12/27/1892–4/1/1968). Chic was a professional tribal interpreter who had already worked with many anthropologists (e.g., Barnett, above), but he was also a relative who lived in nearby Luka-chukai, Arizona. At times when he was not available to work for hire because of other commitments, various family members, standing in the relationship of daughter and granddaughter, were similarly employed. Others, including both of her sons and her husband, Frank (until 4/67), sometimes rose to the occasion on the spur of the moment, and not for hire. After Chic's death in 1968, I hired one of Tall Woman's daughters, Augusta Sandoval, as my main interpreter, working in and around her own full-time employment schedule, summer jobs, and other family commitments. And as indicated above, after Tall Woman's death both Augusta and her older sister, Agnes Sanchez, helped interpret when I was working with monolingual relatives. Since Tall Woman was monolingual, I had no sample of "her English" to follow when dealing with the translations. Throughout the text I have tried to retain the flavor of her Navajo speech as best as I understood it while presenting it in a kind of English that follows the way English-speaking members of the family talk. However, certain "professionalisms" Chic always used when interpreting, and certain "favorite" and idiomatic expressions of other interpreters have been deleted. Examples include "potteries," "materials," "Washingdon," "elderlies," and the like. Hopefully, the result is a close approximation of how Tall Woman would have spoken in English. I am fully aware of the numerous issues involved in translations; the selectivity of human vision, hearing, and recall; the unending levels of reinterpretation that all anthropological field data pass through when being processed for publication; and lots of other questions, including those of the effects of the interpreter's experience, age, gender, and relationships (kin or otherwise) with the interviewer and interviewee on the outcome. For those interested, a rich literature exists within anthropology, especially within areas concerned with linguistics, ethnographic fieldwork, and "writing culture," wherein many of these issues are explored.

In addition to adding chronological order and trying to standardize English translations or at least make them consistent, editorial work also consisted of reviewing multiple accounts of single events, choosing the fullest for inclusion and then discarding the others, and removing repetitions within the story. The latter consumed much time during the construction of "polished rough drafts" to be shared with the family, and their subsequent reviews thereof. A certain amount of repetition is characteristic of Navajo speech, and I hope the level that has been retained herein is enough to capture it.

The internal organization of the book was also an editorial decision, since within the parameters of the Navajo view of life as a walk through cyclical time, there remained the questions of where to start and end chapters, should these be grouped in sections, and how all such artificial, imposed divisions should be entitled. I finally decided on sections to mark the periods Navajos recognize in the human life cycle, but with subdivisions within adulthood, and with chapters within sections. The chronological span of the resulting sections is as follows: Part I—pre-1846 until the late 1890s; Part II—from the late 1890s until her father's death in the winter of 1922; Part III—directly after her father's death through her mother's death in August 1935; Part IV—September 1935 until 1951; Part V—1951 through Tall Woman's 1971 words to the future generations; and Part VI, the Epilogue—1971–77, Tall Woman's last years, death and funeral in 1977, and family's concluding reflections. Individual chapters bear titles that come from Tall Woman's words wherever possible; short phrases underneath chapter titles show some of the major events within each chapter.

While the organization essentially follows Western chronology, as noted above, there are three places where Tall Woman chose to talk almost in chunks, speaking extensively about a single, specific topic or event that was ongoing simultaneously with a number of preceding events, or someone whose impact was major during a number of years. In these places, I have followed the way she spoke and thus left these as blocks or chunks, noting in an endnote the simultaneity of the material with other events. The first such place appears in Chapter 2 (Part I) wherein Tall Woman foregrounds a number of her relatives, thus implicitly stressing the importance of kin relations. While some readers may find this presentation "dense" (even with the visual aids provided by the three kinship charts and one list in the four-part genealogical appendix, Appendix A), and wish she and/or I had opted to explain the people in her narrative as they appeared, Tall Woman chose to do it "up front" so (I) "would know who [she was] talking about later." I chose not to alter her presentation. Another chunk concerns life with her mother, after her father passed away; this now appears as Chapter 15 (Part III), but is simultaneous with Chapters 12–14 of that section of the book. The final place concerns the daily round from the late 1930s through the late 1950s, when Frank was often gone and the women who were home were, in large part, responsible for the farm. Her extensive discussion of this part of the daily round now appears as Chapter 18 (Part IV), but is simultaneous with Chapters 17–21 (all the chapters in Part IV and the first in Part V).

Another part of the editorial work that needs explication is the Epilogue, which both Tall Woman and the family wanted me to construct. Her text changes in Part V, where she is speaking in a contemporaneous voice, since she starts including references to me and then stipulates what she sees as her final words to future generations and asks that they be followed by an Epilogue, authored by me, to document the end of her days. Developing it during the spring of 1997 proved to be emotionally difficult for me as a writer and the family as readers, since it reawakened memories of her final sufferings and of the loss that all of us felt at her death. The Epilogue is based on my fieldnotes, field journals, letters, and phone conversations; in it I've tried to provide a glimpse of the contextual setting for her final years by highlighting some family events without publicizing turmoils, disputes, or too many of the Western medical details of Tall Woman's demise. During the discussions of the draft version of the Epilogue, the family opted for the level of detail it now contains; as one daughter put it: "People should learn what we went through when our mother started suffering; talking about all those things will show them the kinds of things they need to know and what they need to do to care for their elders in the right way. Maybe after people read how we handled that, they'll stop dumping their parents and grandparents in nursing homes, and take care of them at home, like they should." Similar comments were made about proposed descriptions of her final days, death, and funeral: "When you go through that, there's a lot to be done, there's a lot to think about, plan for. Maybe that will help teach some of the People about those things, too, so they know what's ahead before something like that comes along in their own family." The Epilogue ends as requested by her children, namely with a presentation, in the manner requested, of their comments on why Tall Woman was "an outstanding woman."

The Navajo orthography in this work follows Young and Morgan (1980), except in cases where family linguistic practices differed. The Navajo term or name appears first, *transcribed as pronounced by Tall Woman and/or family members* and in italics, followed by the interpreter's English translation, whenever available and/or possible (see below), in brackets. Subsequent references to the same term or person are done only in English. In cases where people have multiple names, they are indicated either in the text (if Tall Woman did so), or on the genealogy charts (Appendix A: 1–3); however, only one name has been chosen for consistent usage in the text; the choice is indicated by having that name appear first in any lists of multiple names in the narrative. Needless to say, when people shared names among their multiple ones, preference herein has been given to distinctive names for all, to avoid confusion for readers. In the case of the name of the narrator herself, it was a family decision to use the English translation of Tall Woman's Navajo name, *ʼAsdzáán Nééz* [Tall Woman], rather than "the name some Anglo gave her," Rose Mitchell, throughout this work. The one exception, of course, is the use of Rose Mitchell as author on the cover; the family felt this was necessary to indicate the connection between her narrative and Frank's (Mitchell 1978).

Several other decisions about names also need explanation. All family members preferred to be called by their real names in the text. However, statements quoted from them or from members of subsequent generations in endnotes carry their initials, rather than full names, with permission and as a space-saving device. Those most frequently represented in this manner are as follows: Mary Davis [MD], Augusta Sandoval [AS], Agnes Sanchez [AgS], Seya Mitchell [SM], Isabel Deschine [ID], Ruth Yazzie [RY], Howard Mitchell [HM], Garnett Bernally [GB], Ida Francis [IF], Woody Davis [WD], Sam Sanishya [SS], Leroy Mitchell [LM], Shirley Mitchell Beecher [SMB], (George) Acey Davis [AD], and Albert G. "Chic" Sandoval [CS]. Except for the initials used in a few of the Epilogue's endnotes, other times where initials are used the person's name is given first. The initials used in endnotes 18, 21, and 23 in the Epilogue are readily "translated" by consulting Appendix A-4 to find the names of individuals' spouses and/or Tall Woman's grandchildren. In a few cases, where an individual wanted a comment included but requested anonymity because of the topic, quotes are handled accordingly. Finally, herein, the full names and titles for Franciscan priests and brothers have been retained in endnotes, despite the common practice of addressing them as Father X or Brother Y (with X and Y being first names). This was done to prevent confusion, given some common, shared first names.

Some other editorial decisions also need clarification. First, the endnotes are designed to clarify the text where necessary, to anchor it in Navajo history, and to lead interested readers to pertinent literature on specific topics. They were *not* viewed as the place for comparative essays on any of the things that came readily to mind while assembling the narrative. Thus, readers will *not* find a comparison of Tall Woman's text to her husband's, although sometimes the latter is cross-referenced. As has already been noted (Frisbie 1997; Frisbie with Sandoval 1999), the texts are of a very different nature and a comparison of the two will provide future generations with data for many intriguing and worthwhile considerations. There is also *no* comparison of Tall Woman's ethnohistorical narratives to other published narratives of similar time periods or events, such as those in some of the life histories and other personal documents cited above, as well as in Johnson (1973) for the Long Walk, and Roessel and Johnson (1974) for the Stock Reduction. Finally, there are *no* comparisons of what Tall Woman had to say about either specific places or plants to the literature that respectively addresses Navajo place-names and Navajo ethnobotany.

Editorial decisions about the latter two topical areas (discussed below) have been made after numerous discussions with professional colleagues as well as family members, and after careful consideration of tribal sovereignty issues in today's world and the Navajo Nation's responses to them. The People, indeed, are the ones to decide who should be doing what kind of research about Navajos; that is a sovereignty issue in today's world that needs to be recognized, understood, and respected. In response, the Navajo Nation established an office to oversee research, and institutionalized procedures to be followed. In 1990, a system was established mandating that ethnographic research on the reservation be done by permits issued by the Navajo Nation's Historic Preservation Department (NNHPD). Among permit stipulations are awareness of culturally sensitive areas and the need to protect sites, artifacts, and items of cultural patrimony or cultural significance, as well as indigenous knowledge. Additionally, permits require authors to have manuscripts cleared by NNHPD before submitting them for publication consideration, thus ensuring review of the treatment of the above-mentioned concerns. The system also provides a mechanism whereby ethnographic as well as archaeological researchers may file data on culturally sensitive topics, places, and the like with the office through a "Confidential Appendix." Such materials are then housed at NNHPD (within either the Traditional Cultural Program or the Cultural Resource Compliance Section), where they are available for review upon request by those with appropriate credentials and motives. Rather than imposing "academic censorship," the procedures, which protect all concerned, provide a useful solution to many of the dilemmas now facing outsiders interested in Navajo studies research.

Because "culturally sensitive materials" include both geographic places and ethno-

botanical data, the editorial decisions concerning each in this work need further explication. Navajo studies scholars have active and valid interests in geography and landscape,
among other issues, and the literature already provides a base for comparative work (see
the Franciscan Fathers 1910:130–37; 1912:202–6; Van Valkenburgh 1941, 1974; Kelley
and Francis 1994, as well as Haile n.d., Reichard n.d., Linford 2000, and Jett, with
Neboyia, Morgan, and Young 2000). However, in today's world, information inno-
cently published about geographical locations may end up being used in ways not intended, be it by lawyers, outsiders bent on further appropriation during quests for
"spirituality," mining companies, or others. Consequently, data about landscape and places
have become "sensitive" in many places on the globe, including the Navajo Nation.

In view of the above, the materials that concern the landscape and specific places in
Tall Woman's narrative have been carefully scrutinized as part of the editorial process.
My own knowledge of these places is based on work and travels with family members after
her death. However, even now, I am in no position to assess their potential cultural
significance to the People. To do so would require a separate project and permit, local
field interviews, mapping of exact locations, and other methodologies, all of which are
beyond the scope of this work. Thus, the information I subsequently collected on
places she mentioned has been assembled in a Confidential Appendix and filed with
NNHPD. Additionally, the four maps used herein have been constructed to indicate the
major, basic places in her narrative and to illustrate how she grounded her narration in
landscape, rather than to locate all the places she mentions. Thus, the maps, too, have
been designed with NNHPD concerns in the foreground.

The same parameters have been used as guides for the treatment of ethnobotanical
data. While I collected a lot of information on plants from Tall Woman and augmented it, after her death, by work with the children who had learned from her, such
information does *not* appear herein. Plants are viewed as a gift from the Holy People
by the Navajos; they are used when needed and only after being approached respect-
fully and with appropriate prayers and other procedures. Thus, information concerning them is among that which is termed "culturally sensitive," for it indeed is an important part of Navajo knowledge, or "intellectual property."

Because Tall Woman was very well versed in ethnobotanical matters, she mentioned plants frequently. When I first started pondering editorial decisions, I initiated
discussions with her family to elicit their feelings about the appropriateness of having
such information appear at all in the published version of her narrative. I did so because of my own support of the intellectual property rights of the world's indigenous
peoples (the discussions of which foreground botanical knowledge) and my wish to
protect them (see *Cultural Survival Quarterly* 1991; Brush 1993; Messer 1993, 1997;
Salmon 1997; Turner 1997; Brown 1998; and Sillitoe 1998, among others). But Tall
Woman's children found my concerns "ridiculous." To share some of the responses

that my numerous explanations of concerns elicited, some quotes from our discussions follow: "Of course she told you a lot about plants; she knew about them and used them all the time. But why are you worrying about that? Everybody used to know those things; it wasn't any secret back then, so why should it be treated as a secret now? Anybody who says those things, even if it's somebody or some group in Window Rock, is just hurting the Navajo people. Those things are part of our heritage and need to be passed on. Just leave them in, like she told you." When I replied by restating my concerns and again explaining the background for and appropriateness of international concerns about protecting medicinal plant knowledge, I was interrupted with, "Sure, she used those as medicines for us, herself, our Dad, and even the animals. She knew those things. But those plants were *everyday*; all those things were just like aspirin is today. They were common. She didn't tell you how to make any of the ones we use for ceremonies, any of those mixtures of different plants that are used for washing the patient or drunk as emetics, or things like that. *Those are sacred* and maybe or maybe not things like that should be taken out of her text. But she didn't include details on those when she talked with you, even though she knew those, too. So stop worrying about it; we want you to leave those in there, just the way she told you about them. Nowadays, lots of people don't know anything about those things. But in my mother's day, everybody did. That's one way of preserving what her generation knew and passing it on. Then, if somebody gets interested in those plants in the future, they can look in her story and maybe learn something about them and start those things up again. But that probably won't happen; a lot of those plants aren't even around anymore. That's probably because the People quit using them."

Such discussions told me "we" were leaving the plants in; however, for me, they did not address what to do with the extensive information she gave me in directed interviewing, all of which augmented the text. At that point, I started considering the issues from different perspectives and discussing them with colleagues attuned to matters deemed "culturally sensitive" among today's Navajos. One of the questions I posed to myself was what did I professionally know about plants? The answer was "almost nothing," since I have no botanical expertise. While Tall Woman and I traveled to gather Mormon and Navajo tea, yucca roots (for soap), pinyon nuts, "the yellow berries used in making cheese," juniper, sagebrush, and a few other things, we undertook no other "ethnobotanical" trips. I never took her or others on journeys designed to collect botanical field specimens of the plants she mentioned, some of which have multiple Navajo names. Having no personal botanical expertise, I realized I had no basis for assigning English names to the plants she named only in Navajo. I also had no basis for classifying them according to appropriate Latin genus and species nomenclatures, no matter what botanical taxonomic system I might choose to follow, and despite the extant literature on such matters in Navajo studies (cited later, in a text endnote). To do so professionally would necessitate different training, or hiring assistants who had it, after securing a different permit for another, separate project that included field collections.

Professional ethical issues were also factored into these considerations, as were my own understandings of the sacredness of Navajo plants and the fact that they, too, are rightfully included in NNHPD definitions of "culturally sensitive" materials. The result was another set of editorial decisions: readers will *not* find botanical classifications for the plants mentioned in this work in endnotes. Additionally, *except* for those that are common, such as juniper (or cedar), broad and narrow leaf yucca, wild carrots, wild onions, wild potatoes, wild spinach, cliffrose, Mormon tea, Navajo tea, sunflowers, sagebrush, sumac, cottonwood, tamarisk, buckhorn and prickly pear cacti, pinyon, and the like, in this work plant names are *given only in Navajo*. As I was reviewing the manuscript with a focus on this issue, it became clear that the latter decision was consistent with what interpreters had already done: for common plants, they readily provided an English translation; for others, they said they "weren't sure exactly which plant she meant without seeing it." Hopefully, these decisions respect the concerns of all involved; they preserve the information about plants that Tall Woman wove into her narrative while recording her story, and thus remain true to her and her family's wishes. But they simultaneously exclude both the additional information she and others gave me, and any attempts at translation and classification of the plants named herein only in Navajo, thus respecting Navajo sensitivities and acknowledging the specialized, professional nature of accurate ethnobotanical classifications.

One other editorial decision needs explication, since it led to inclusion of another kind of information in endnotes. Working on understanding a person's life narrative leads a researcher in many directions. For me, one direction this book led to was the history of the community of Chinle, Arizona, where Tall Woman spent most of her life after the winter of 1922. While pieces of the community's history are documented in a variety of publications, especially those concerned with the National Park Service, trading posts and traders, and missions and missionaries, to date there has been no attempt to assemble these pieces, or expand them through in-depth community-history research. During 1996–97 fieldwork, it became clear that no one in the present community was engaged in collecting or documenting this history, although many Navajos and non-Navajos, living and working in Chinle, were interested in seeing it done. In the course of working on this and other projects, I began the job. Herein, however, endnotes are limited to documenting and/or clarifying events, structures, or developments in the community mentioned in Tall Woman's narrative (beginning in Chapter 4). While it has now become possible for me to explore one very small piece of Chinle's history (see Frisbie 1998), a thorough study awaits future efforts, should the idea have community support.

At present, except for the Confidential Appendix materials noted above, the field tapes, fieldnotes, field journals, and all draft manuscripts connected with this project remain in the sole possession of the editor. Their final disposition remains undecided.

References

Abu-Lughod, Lila
1990 Can There be a Feminist Ethnography? Women and Performance: A Journal of Feminist Theory 5(1):7–27.
1993 Writing Women's Worlds. Berkeley: University of California Press.

Albers, Patricia C.
1989 From Illusion to Illumination: Anthropological Studies of American Indian Women. *In* Gender and Anthropology: Critical Review for Research and Teaching. Sandra Morgen, ed. Pp. 132–70. Washington, D.C.: American Anthropological Association.

Albers, Patricia, and Beatrice Medicine
1983 The Hidden Half. Lanham, Md.: University Press of America.

Albuquerque Journal
1997 Obituaries of Annie Dodge Wauneka. Nov. 12: C-3; Nov. 13: A-16.
1997 Obituary of Kay "Kaibah" Curley Bennett. Nov. 15: C-8.

Albuquerque Tribune
1997 Obituary of Annie Dodge Wauneka. Nov. 11: D-8.

Alpern, Sara, J. Antler, E. Perry, and I. Scobie, eds.
1992 The Challenge of Feminist Biography. Urbana: University of Illinois Press.

Alvord, Lori Arviso, and Elizabeth Cohen Van Pelt
1999 The Scalpel and the Silver Bear: The First Navajo Woman Surgeon Combines Western Medicine and Traditional Healing. New York: Bantam Books.

American Indian Quarterly
1982 Special Issue: Women in Continuity and Change: The Navajo Example. Vol. 6(1–2). [Spring/summer issue] Joyce Griffen, guest ed.

Antram, Father Cormac, O.F.M.
1998 Laborers of the Harvest. Gallup, N.M.: The Indian Trader.

Barbre, Joy Webster, et al., eds.
1989 Interpreting Women's Lives: Feminist Theory and Personal Narratives. Bloomington: Indiana University Press.

Barnett, Clifford
1997 Personal communication, 5/28.

n.d. Life History of Albert G. "Chic" Sandoval, Sr., 12/27/1892–4/1/1968. MS in preparation [12/98].

Bataille, Gretchen M.
1987 An Interview with Geraldine Keams. Explorations in Ethnic Studies 10(1):1–8. [January.]

Bataille, Gretchen M., ed.
1993 Native American Women: A Biographical Dictionary. New York: Garland Publishing.

Bataille, Gretchen M., and Kathleen Mullen Sands
1984 American Indian Women Telling Their Lives. Lincoln: University of Nebraska Press.
1991 American Indian Women: A Guide to Research. New York: Garland Publishing.

Behar, Ruth
1993 Translated Woman: Crossing the Border with Esperanza's Story. Boston: Beacon Press.

Behar, Ruth, and Deborah A. Gordon, eds.
1995 Women Writing Culture. Berkeley: University of California Press.

Benally, Karen Ritts, and Paul F. Reed
1997 The Landscapes of Life: Life History and the Archaeological Record. Paper presented in session, Doing Life History Work: Joys and Challenges, at the Tenth Annual Navajo Studies Conference, University of New Mexico, Albuquerque, Apr. 16–19.

Bennett, Kay
1964 Kaibah: Recollections of a Navajo Girlhood. Los Angeles: Westernlore Press.

Bettelyoun, Susan Bordeaux, and Josephine Waggoner
1999 With My Own Eyes: A Lakota Woman Tells Her People's History. Emily Levine, ed. Lincoln: University of Nebraska Press.

Bighorse, Tiana
1990 Bighorse, the Warrior. Noel Bennett, ed. Tucson: University of Arizona Press.

Blackman, Margaret B.
1982 During My Time: Florence Edenshaw Davidson, A Haida Woman. Seattle: University of Washington Press.
1989 Sadie Brower Neakok: An Inupiaq Woman. Seattle: University of Washington Press.

Boyer, Ruth McDonald, and Narcissus Duffy Gayton
1992 Apache Mothers and Daughters: Four Generations of a Family. Norman: University of Oklahoma Press.

Brady, Ivan, and Edith Turner, eds.
1994 Special Issue: Humanism and Anthropology. Anthropology and Humanism 19(1).

Brave Bird, Mary, with Richard Erdoes
1993 Ohitika Woman. New York: Grove Press.

Broker, Ignatia
1983 Night Flying Woman: An Ojibway Narrative. St. Paul: Minnesota Historical Society Press.

Brown, Michael F.
1998 Can Culture Be Copyrighted? Current Anthropology 39(2):193–222.

Brumble, H. David, III
1990 American Indian Autobiography. Berkeley: University of California Press, paperback ed.

Bruner, Edward M.
1993 Introduction: The Ethnographic Self and the Personal Self. *In* Anthropology and Literature. Paul Benson, ed. Pp. 1–26. Urbana: University of Illinois Press.

Brush, Stephen B.
1993 Indigenous Knowledge of Biological Resources and Intellectual Property Rights: The Role of Anthropology. American Anthropologist 95(3):653–86.

Canfield, Gae Whitney
1983 Sarah Winnemucca of the Northern Paiutes. Norman: University of Oklahoma Press.

Carlson, Vada, and Gary Witherspoon
1968 Black Mountain Boy: A Story of the Boyhood of John Honie. Rough Rock, Ariz.: Rough Rock Demonstration School.

Carr, Helen
1988 In Other Words: Native American Women's Autobiography. *In* Life/Lines: Theorizing Women's Autobiography. Bella Brodzski and Celeste Schenck, eds. Pp. 131–53. Ithaca: Cornell University Press.

Clifford, James
1988 Predicament of Culture. Cambridge: Harvard University Press.

Clifford, James, and George E. Marcus, eds.
1986 Writing Culture. Berkeley: University of California Press.

Crow Dog, Mary, and Richard Erdoes
1990 Lakota Woman. New York: Grove Weidenfeld.

Cruikshank, Julie
1992 Life Lived Like a Story: Life Stories of Three Yukon Native Elders [in collabora-

tion with Angela Sidney, Kitty Smith, and Annie Ned]. Lincoln: University of Nebraska Press, Bison paperback ed.

Cultural Survival Quarterly
1991 Intellectual Property Rights: The Politics of Ownership. Cultural Survival Quarterly 15(3). [Summer issue.]

Denetdale, Jennifer R.
1997 And Then I Became Navajo Again: Stories from the Daughters and Sons of Juanita and Chief Manuelito. Paper presented at the Tenth Annual Navajo Studies Conference, University of New Mexico, Albuquerque, Apr. 16–19.

Dyk, Walter
1938 Son of Old Man Hat. Lincoln: University of Nebraska Press.
1947 A Navaho Autobiography. Viking Fund Publications in Anthropology 8. New York: Viking Fund.

Dyk, Walter, and Ruth Dyk
1980 Left Handed: A Navajo Autobiography. New York: Columbia University Press.

Emerick, Richard G., and Mark Hanna
1993 Man of the Canyon-An Old Indian Remembers His Life. Orono, Maine: North Lights.

Fienup-Riordan, Ann
1990 Eskimo Essays: Yup'ik Lives and How We see Them. New Brunswick, N.J.: Rutgers University Press.

Franciscan Fathers
1910 An Ethnologic Dictionary of the Navaho Language. Saint Michaels, Ariz.: The Franciscan Fathers.
1912 A Vocabulary of the Navaho Language. Vol. 1: English-Navaho. Vol. 2: Navaho-English. Saint Michaels, Ariz.: The Franciscan Fathers.

Frank, Gelya
1995 Ruth Behar's Biography in the Shadow: A Review of Reviews. American Anthropologist 97(2):357–74.

Frank, Gelya, and Rosamond M. Vanderburgh
1986 Cross-Cultural Use of Life History Methods in Gerontology. *In* New Methods for Old-Age Research. Christine L. Fry and Jennie Keith, eds. Pp. 185–212. South Hadley, Mass.: Bergin and Garvey Publishers.

Frisbie, Charlotte J.
1975a Fieldwork as a 'Single Parent'": To Be or Not to Be Accompanied by a Child. *In* Collected Papers in Honor of Florence Hawley Ellis. Theodore R. Frisbie, ed.

Pp. 98–119. Papers of the Archaeological Society of New Mexico 2. Norman: Hooper Publishing Company.

1975b Observations on a Preschooler's First Experience with Cross-Cultural Living. Journal of Man 7(1):91–112. [Winter.]

1982 Traditional Navajo Women: Ethnographic and Life History Portrayals. American Indian Quarterly 6(1–2):11–33.

1987 Navajo Medicine Bundles or *Jish*: Acquisition, Transmission, and Disposition in the Past and Present. Albuquerque: University of New Mexico Press.

1989 Gender and Navajo Music: Unanswered Questions. *In* Women in North American Indian Music: Six Essays. Richard Keeling, ed. Pp. 22–38. Society for Ethnomusicology Special Series 6.

1993a Kinaaldá. Repr., paperback ed. with new Preface. Salt Lake City: University of Utah Press. Originally published, Middletown, Conn.: Wesleyan University Press, 1967.

1993b NAGPRA and the Repatriation of Jish. *In* Papers from the Third, Fourth, and Sixth Navajo Studies Conferences. June-el Piper, ed.; Alexandra Roberts and Jenevieve Smith, comps. Pp. 119–27. Window Rock, Ariz.: Navajo Nation Historic Preservation Department.

1997 The Final Stages of a Life History Project [with additional comments by Augusta Sandoval]. Paper presented in session, Doing Life History Work: Joys and Challenges, at the Tenth Annual Navajo Studies Conference, University of New Mexico, Albuquerque, Apr. 16–19.

1998 On the Trail of Chinle's "Big House." *In* Diné Bíkéyah: Papers in Honor of David M. Brugge. Meliha S. Duran and David T. Kirkpatrick, eds. Archaeological Society of New Mexico Papers 24: 69–85. Albuquerque: Archaeological Society of New Mexico.

Frisbie, Charlotte J., and David M. Brugge

1998 The First Navajo Studies Conference: Reflections by the Cofounders. Paper presented in special session, History and Future of the Navajo Studies Conference, at the Eleventh Annual Navajo Studies Conference, Navajo Nation Museum, Window Rock, Ariz., Oct. 21–24.

1999 The First Navajo Studies Conference: Reflections by the Cofounders. *In* Diné Baa Hané Bi Naaltsoos: Collected Papers from the Seventh through Tenth Navajo Studies Conferences. June-el Piper, ed. Pp. 1–9. Window Rock, Ariz.: Navajo Nation Historic Preservation Department.

Frisbie, Charlotte J., with Augusta Sandoval

1999 The Final Stages of a Life History Project. *In* Diné Baa Hané Bi Naaltsoos: Collected Papers from the Seventh through Tenth Navajo Studies Conferences. June-el Piper, ed. Pp. 63–67. Window Rock, Ariz.: Navajo Nation Historic Preservation Department.

Gallup Independent

1998 Obituary of Irene Stewart. Feb. 12.

Geertz, Clifford
1988 Works and Lives: The Anthropologist as Author. Stanford: Stanford University Press.

Gottlieb, Alma
1995 Beyond the Lonely Anthropologist: Collaboration in Research and Writing. American Anthropologist 97(1):21–26.

Green, Rayna
1980 Native American Women: A Review Essay. Signs 6(2):248–67.

Griffen, Joyce
1981 Millie Joe Masden: A Navajo Woman's Story. 51 pp. MS, unpublished. Copy in author's possession.
1992 Questions of Confidentiality in the Reporting of Life Histories. Paper presented at the Sixth Annual Navajo Studies Conference, Window Rock, Ariz., Mar. 12–14.
1997 A German in Navajo Studies. Paper presented in session, Doing Life History Work: Joys and Challenges, at the Tenth Annual Navajo Studies Conference, University of New Mexico, Albuquerque, Apr. 16–19.

Haile, Father Berard, O.F.M.
n.d. Place Names. Berard Haile Papers. Special Collections, Box 5, Folder 12. University of Arizona, Tucson.

Harding, Susan, and Fred Myers
1994 Further Inflections: toward Ethnographies of the Future. Theme Issue of Cultural Anthropology 9(3).

Harris, LaDonna
2000 LaDonna Harris: A Comanche Life. H. Henrietta Stockel, ed. Lincoln: University of Nebraska Press.

Haskie, Miranda
1997 Personal communication, 6/8.

Hedlund, Ann Lane
1992 Reflections of the Weaver's World: The Gloria F. Ross Collection of Contemporary Navajo Weaving. Denver: Denver Art Museum.

Hittman, Michael
1996 Corbett Mack: The Life of a Northern Paiute. Lincoln: University of Nebraska Press.

Hoffman, Virginia, and Broderick H. Johnson
1970 Navajo Biographies. Chinle, Ariz.: Rough Rock Demonstration School.

Horne, Esther Burnett, and Sally McBeth
1998 Essie's Story: The Life and Legacy of a Shoshone Teacher. Lincoln: University of Nebraska Press.

Hoskins, Janet
1985 A Life History from Both Sides: The Changing Poetics of Personal Experience. Journal of Anthropological Research 41(2):147–70.

Jaskoski, Helen
1990 The Family of Changing Woman: Nature and Women in Navaho Thought. *In* Anxiety, Guilt and Freedom: Religious Studies Perspectives. Benjamin J. Hubbard and Bradley E. Starr, eds. Pp. 23–46. Lanham, Md.: University Press of America.

Jett, Stephen C.
1991 Pete Price, Navajo Medicineman (1868–1951): A Brief Biography. American Indian Quarterly 15(1):91–103.

Jett, Stephen C., with the assistance of Chauncey M. Neboyia, William Morgan, Sr., and Robert W. Young.
2000 Navajo Placenames and Trails of the Canyon de Chelly System, Arizona. New York: Peter Lang Publishing.

Johnson, Broderick H., ed.
1969 Denetsosie. Chinle, Ariz.: Rough Rock Demonstration School.
1973 Navajo Stories of the Long Walk Period. Tsaile, Ariz.: Navajo Community College Press.
1977a Stories of Traditional Navajo Life and Culture by Twenty-Two Navajo Men and Women. Tsaile, Ariz.: Navajo Community College Press.
1977b Navajos and World War II. [Accounts from eleven participants, three women and eight men.] Tsaile, Ariz.: Navajo Community College Press.

Keesing, Roger M.
1985 Kwaio Women Speak. American Anthropologist 87(1):27–39.

Kelley, Klara Bonsack, and Harris Francis
1994 Navajo Sacred Places. Bloomington: Indiana University Press.

Kennedy, Elizabeth Lapovsky
1995 In Pursuit of Connection: Reflections on Collaborative Work. American Anthropologist 97(1):26–33.

Kluckhohn, Clyde
1956 A Navaho Personal Document with a Brief Paretian Analysis. *In* Personal Character and Cultural Milieu. Douglas Haring, ed. Pp. 513–33. 3d rev. ed. Syracuse, N.Y.: Syracuse University Press.
1964 A Navaho Politician. *In* Culture and Behavior, The Collected Essays of Clyde Kluckhohn. Richard Kluckhohn, ed. Pp. 182–209. 2d printing. New York: Free Press of Glencoe.

Krupat, Arnold
1989 For Those Who Come After: A Study of Native American Autobiography. Berkeley: University of California Press, paperback ed.

Lamphere, Louise
1989 Historical and Regional Variability in Navajo Women's Roles. Journal of Anthropological Research 45(4):431–56.
1995 Bringing Navajo Women into History: The Personal Narratives of Eva Price, Navajo Healer. Snead-Wertheim Lecture, University of New Mexico, Apr. 4.

Lamphere, Louise, and Maureen Trudelle Schwarz
1998 Life Influences: Three Generations of Navajo Women. Presentations by five Navajo women: Eva Price, Caroline Cadman, Valerie Johnson, Mae Bekis, and Sunny Dooley, as well as anthropologist organizers, Louise Lamphere and Maureen Schwarz. Session at the Eleventh Annual Navajo Studies Conference, Navajo Nation Museum, Window Rock, Ariz., Oct. 21–24.

Langness, L. L., and Gelya Frank
1981 Lives: An Anthropological Approach to Biography. Novato, Calif.: Chandler and Sharp Publishers.

Lavie, Smadar, Kirin Narayan, and Renato Rosaldo, eds.
1993 Creativity/Anthropology. Ithaca: Cornell University Press.

Lee, George P.
1987 Silent Courage: An Indian Story, The Autobiography of George P. Lee, a Navajo. Salt Lake City: Deseret Book Co.

Leighton, Alexander H., and Dorothea C. Leighton
1944 The Navaho Door. Cambridge: Harvard University Press.
1949 Gregorio, The Hand-Trembler. Papers of the Peabody Museum of American Archaeology and Ethnology, Harvard University 40(1). [Includes life history of second wife, Nazba, as Appendix, Pp. 171–77.]
1992 Lucky, the Navajo Singer. Edited and annotated by Joyce J. Griffen. Albuquerque: University of New Mexico Press.

Linde, Charlotte
1993 Life Stories: The Creation of Coherence. New York: Oxford University Press.

Linford, Laurance D.
2000 Navajo Places: History, Legend, Landscape. Salt Lake City: University of Utah Press.

McBride, Bunny
1995 Molly Spotted Elk: A Penobscot in Paris. Norman: University of Oklahoma Press.

McCloskey, Joanne E.

1995 Family Dynamics in Three Generations of Navajo Women. Paper presented at the Eighth Annual Navajo Studies Conference, San Juan College, Farmington, N.M., Mar. 15–17.

1996 Being a Grandmother in Navajo Society. Paper presented at the Ninth Annual Navajo Studies Conference, Fort Lewis College, Durango, Colo., Apr. 10–13.

1998 Three Generations of Navajo Women: Negotiating Life Course Strategies in the Eastern Navajo Agency. American Indian Culture and Research Journal 22(2):103–29.

MacDonald, Peter, with Ted Schwarz

1993 The Last Warrior: Peter MacDonald and the Navajo Nation. New York: Orion Books.

McPherson, Robert

1993 From Dezba to 'John': The Changing Role of Navajo Women in Southeastern Utah. Paper presented at the Seventh Annual Navajo Studies Conference, Navajo Community College, Tsaile, Ariz., Oct. 4–9.

1997 Of Metaphors and Learning: Navajo Teachings for Today's Youth. Paper presented in session, Doing Life History Work: Joys and Challenges, at the Tenth Annual Navajo Studies Conference, University of New Mexico, Albuquerque, Apr. 16–19.

2000 The Journey of Navajo Oshley: An Autobiography and Life History. Logan: Utah State University Press.

Mankiller, Wilma, and Michael Wallis

1993 Mankiller: A Chief and Her People. An Autobiography by the Principal Chief of the Cherokee Nation. New York: St. Martin's Press.

Marcus, George E., and Dick Cushman

1982 Ethnographies as Texts. Annual Review of Anthropology 11:25–69.

Marcus, George E., and Michael M. J. Fischer

1986 Anthropology as Cultural Critique. Chicago: University of Chicago Press.

Mascia-Lees, Frances E., Patricia Sharpe, and Colleen B. Cohen

1989 The Postmodernist Turn in Anthropology: Cautions from a Feminist Perspective. Signs 15(1):7–33.

Medicine, Bea

1978 The Native American Woman: A Perspective. Austin, Tex.: National Educational Laboratory Publishers.

Messer, Ellen

1993 Anthropology and Human Rights. Annual Review of Anthropology 22:221–49. Palo Alto, Calif.: Annual Reviews.

1997 Pluralist Approaches to Human Rights. Journal of Anthropological Research 53(3):293–317.

Miller, Jay, ed.
1990 Mourning Dove: A Salishan Autobiography. Lincoln: University of Nebraska Press.

Minh-ha, Trinh T.
1989 Woman, Native, Other: Writing Postcoloniality and Feminism. Bloomington: Indiana University Press.

Mitchell, Emerson Blackhorse, and T. D. Allen
1967 Miracle Hill: The Story of a Navaho Boy. Norman: University of Oklahoma Press.

Mitchell, Frank
1978 Navajo Blessingway Singer: The Autobiography of Frank Mitchell, 1881–1967. Charlotte J. Frisbie and David P. McAllester, eds. Tucson: University of Arizona Press.

Myerhoff, Barbara
1992 Remembered Lives: The Work of Ritual, Storytelling, and Growing Older. Ann Arbor: University of Michigan Press.

Navajo Times
1997 Obituary of Kay 'Kaibah' Curley Bennett. Nov. 20:5.
1997 Obituary notices for Annie Dodge Wauneka. Nov. 13:1, 2,3; Nov. 20:2.

Nelson, Mary Carroll
1972 Annie Wauneka: The Story of an American Indian. Minneapolis: Dillon Press, Inc.

Niethammer, Carolyn
2001 I'll Go and Do More: Annie Dodge Wauneka, Navajo Leader and Activist. Lincoln: University of Nebraska Press.

Okely, Judith, and Helen Callaway, eds.
1992 Anthropology and Autobiography. New York: Routledge.

Powers, Marla
1986 Oglala Women. Myth, Ritual, and Reality. Chicago: University of Chicago Press.

Red Shirt, Delphine
1998 Bead on an Anthill: A Lakota Childhood. Lincoln: University of Nebraska Press.

Reichard, Gladys A.
n.d. A Dictionary of Nouns. English-Navajo. Gladys A. Reichard Collection, MS 29–52. Museum of Northern Arizona Archives, Museum of Northern Arizona, Flagstaff, Ariz. Partial notes thereon, and some Xeroxes of pages of MS provided by D. Brugge July 1996. [MS probably dates after 1945, the latest entry in the bibliography.]

Rice, Julian
1994 A Ventriloquy of Anthros: Densmore, Dorsey, Lame Deer, and Erdoes. American Indian Quarterly 18(2):169–95.

Ritts, Karen Rose

1989 Turnings: From Life History to Group Biography-Four Generations of Change in a Navajo Family. Ph.D. diss., Northwestern University.

Ritts-Benally, Karen

1993 I Was Born at Oak Spring Canyon: Life, Family, and Land-Use Histories along the Transwestern Pipeline Corridor. *In* Papers from the Third, Fourth, and Sixth Navajo Studies Conferences. June-el Piper, ed.; Alexandra Roberts and Jenevieve Smith, comps. Pp. 339–54. Window Rock, Ariz.: Navajo Nation Historic Preservation Department.

Roessel, Ruth

1981 Women in Navajo Society. Chinle, Ariz.: Rough Rock Demonstration School.

Roessel, Ruth, and Broderick H. Johnson, comps.

1974 Navajo Livestock Reduction: A National Disgrace. Chinle: Navajo Community College Press [at Tsaile].

Rosaldo, Renato

1993 Culture and Truth: The Remaking of Social Analysis. 2d ed. Boston: Beacon Press.

Rosenwald, George C., and Richard L. Ochberg, eds.

1992 Storied Lives: The Cultural Politics of Self-Understanding. New Haven: Yale University Press.

St. Pierre, Mark

1991 Madonna Swan: A Lakota Woman's Story. Norman: University of Oklahoma Press.

Salmon, Merrilee H.

1997 Ethical Considerations in Anthropology and Archaeology, or Relativism and Justice for All. Journal of Anthropological Research 53(1):47–63.

Schwarz, Maureen T.

1997 Molded in the Image of Changing Woman: Navajo Views on the Human Body and Personhood. Tucson: University of Arizona Press.

Scott, Peggy F.

1998 Personal Opinions Opposing Life History Work with Navajo Elders, expressed while serving as Moderator for General Session, Conducting Research on the Navajo Nation: Research Ethics, at the Eleventh Annual Navajo Studies Conference, Navajo Nation Museum, Window Rock, Ariz., Oct. 21–24.

Seaman, P. David, ed.

1993 Born A Chief: The Nineteenth Century Hopi Boyhood of Edmund Nequatewa, as told to Alfred F. Whiting. Tucson: University of Arizona Press.

Shokeid, Moshe
1997 Negotiating Multiple Viewpoints: The Cook, the Native, the Publisher, and the Ethnographic Text. Current Anthropology 38(4):631–45. [With CA Comment.]

Shostak, Marjorie
1981 Nisa, The Life and Worlds of a !Kung Woman. Cambridge: Harvard University Press.

Sillitoe, Paul
1998 The Development of Indigenous Knowledge: A New Applied Anthropology. Current Anthropology 39(2):223–52. [With CA Comment.]

Smith, Sidonie, and Julia Watson, eds.
1998 Women, Autobiography, Theory: A Reader. Madison: University of Wisconsin Press.

Snell, Alma Hogan
2000 Grandmother's Grandchild: My Crow Indian Life. Becky Matthews, ed. Lincoln: University of Nebraska Press.

Sneve, Virginia Driving Hawk
1995 Completing the Circle. Lincoln: University of Nebraska Press.

Sparks, Carol Douglas
1995 The Land Incarnate: Navajo Women and the Dialogue of Colonialism, 1821–1870. In Negotiators of Change: Historical Perspectives on Native American Women. Nancy Shoemaker, ed. Pp. 135–56. New York: Routledge.

Stacey, Judith
1991 Can There Be a Feminist Ethnography? In Women's Words, The Feminist Practice of Oral History. Sherna Berger Gluck and Daphne Patai, eds. Pp. 111–19. New York: Routledge.

Stewart, Greyeyes
1988 Before Blessingway: An Autobiographical Fragment (as told to James K. McNeley in the early 1970s). Diné Be'iina': A Journal of Navajo Life 1(2):22–23.

Stewart, Irene
1980 A Voice in Her Tribe: A Navajo Woman's Own Story. Doris O. Dawdy, ed. Ballena Press Anthropological Papers 17. Socorro, N.M.: Ballena Press. [Foreword by Mary Shepardson.]

Strathern, Marilyn
1987 An Awkward Relationship: The Case of Feminism and Anthropology. Signs 12(2):276–92.

Sundance, Robert, with Marc Gaede
1994 Sundance: The Robert Sundance Story. La Cañada, Calif.: Chaco Press.

Swann, Brian, and Arnold Krupat, eds.
1987 I Tell You Now: Autobiographical Essays by Native American Writers. Lincoln: University of Nebraska Press.

Tedlock, Barbara
1991 From Participant Observation to the Observation of Participation: The Emergence of Narrative Ethnography. Journal of Anthropological Research 47(1):69–94.

Tedlock, Dennis
1983 The Spoken Word and the Work of Interpretation. Philadelphia: University of Pennsylvania Press.

Tedlock, Dennis, and Bruce Mannheim, eds.
1995 The Dialogic Emergence of Culture. Urbana: University of Illinois Press.

Theisz, R. D.
1981 The Critical Collaboration: Introductions as a Gateway to the Study of Native American Bi-Autobiography. American Indian Culture and Research Journal 5(1):65–80.

Turner, Terence
1997 Human Rights, Human Difference: Anthropology's Contribution to an Emancipatory Cultural Politics. Journal of Anthropological Research 53(3):273–91.

Turner, Victor W., and Edward M. Bruner, eds.
1986 The Anthropology of Experience. Urbana: University of Illinois Press.

Vander, Judith
1988 Songprints: The Musical Experience of Five Shoshone Women. Urbana: University of Illinois Press.

Van Valkenburg, Richard F.
1941 Diné Bikéyah. Window Rock, Ariz.: U.S. Department of the Interior, Office of Indian Affairs, Navajo Service.

Van Valkenburg, Richard F., edited by Clyde Kluckhohn
1974 Navajo Sacred Places. *In* Navajo Indians III: Commission Findings. Pp. 9–199. American Indian Ethnohistory: Indians of the Southwest. David A. Horr, comp. and ed. New York: Garland Publishing.

Visweswaran, Kamala
1994 The Fictions of Feminist Ethnography. Minneapolis: University of Minnesota Press.
1997 Histories of Feminist Ethnography. Annual Review of Anthropology 26:591–621. Palo Alto, Calif.: Annual Reviews.

Voget, Fred W.
1995 They Call Me Agnes: A Crow Narrative Based on the Life of Agnes Yellowtail Deernose. Norman: University of Oklahoma Press.

Vogt, Evon Z.
1951 Navaho Veterans: A Study of Changing Values. Papers of the Peabody Museum of American Archaeology and Ethnology, Harvard University 41(1).

Wallace, Mark
1994 Black Hawk's An Autobiography: Production and Use of an 'Indian' Voice. American Indian Quarterly 18(4):481–95.

Ward, Martha C.
1998 A Sounding of Women: Autobiographies from Unexpected Places. Needham Heights, Mass.: Allyn and Bacon.

Watson, Lawrence C., and Maria-Barbara Watson-Franke
1985 Interpreting Life Histories. New Brunswick, N.J.: Rutgers University Press.

Witt, Shirley Hill
1981 An Interview with Dr. Annie Dodge Wauneka. Frontiers 6(3):64–67.

Wolf, Diane L.
1996 Feminist Dilemmas in Fieldwork. Boulder: Westview Press.

Wolf, Margery
1992 A Thrice-Told Tale: Feminism, Postmodernism and Ethnographic Responsibility. Stanford: Stanford University Press.

Wood, Beth, and Tom Barry
1978 The Story of Three Navajo Women. Integrateducation 16(2):33–35. [March-April.]

Young, Robert W., and William Morgan
1980 The Navajo Dictionary: A Grammar and Colloquial Dictionary. Albuquerque: University of New Mexico Press.

Young, Robert W., and William Morgan, eds.
1954 Navajo Historical Selections. Navajo Historical Series 3. Phoenix: Department of the Interior, Bureau of Indian Affairs. [Includes 'The Story of an Orphan,' Nancy Woodman's story, pp. 65–68, English text; pp.138–41, Navajo text.]

one

Narratives of Forebears, Infancy, and Childhood

Stories from the Old People

1

Encounters and conflicts with pre-Fort Sumner enemies . . .
Tanabah's *escape from a Ute war party.*

Way, way back before my grandparents' time, I don't know what conditions the Peo-ple[1] faced while they moved around. When I was big enough to remember things, I know the old people used to tell us about what they went through in their young days. A lot of those things were just horrible; sometimes we used to think they told us about those awful things just to scare us. But now I know they wanted us to learn from the things they went through.

The things I know about those early times are the stories I heard from the old peo-ple we used to move around with. I don't know anything about that myself, of course, because I was not around at that time. Some of the things that they told are just too fearful to repeat and I don't want to think about them. But I will tell you some of the stories my grandparents and other old people used to talk about.

I never really knew my real grandmother, my mother's mother; I never saw her. She had passed away from old age somewhere in the mountains before I was born.[2] From what we were told, my real grandmother had at least two sisters; the one who was older was the grandmother to Chee Jones; the other sister was the grandmother to *Hastiin Tsoh* [Big Man]. We called those women our grandmothers, too, because they were my real grandmother's sisters. They were all *Kiyaa'áanii* [Towering House Peo-ple], like my real grandmother and my mother; that is our clan.[3] They moved around with us when I was small[4] and they and our other relatives used to talk about these things. The man who was the husband of my real grandmother also used to move with us when I was very small. I know he was called *Hashk'aan Hobo* or *Hashk'aan na'ałjidi* [Yucca Fruit Man Packing a Burden]. That old man was my mother's father. I saw him myself only one time; he was very old at the time I saw him, and I never got to know him.

Those other grandmothers used to tell us that in their young days the People were not settled down in places like here in the Chinle Valley or in other locations. When they were young, they were always on the move because they had lots of enemies in all directions and they were trying to run and hide from them.[5] You see, the People barely had enough to eat in those times; they were nearly starved. So, I guess sometimes groups would get together and the young warriors would go out and try to steal food from others in this area. They would steal things like sheep and horses, and even crops that others were raising. Often, people would get hurt or even killed during those raids, both Navajos and others. Sometimes people were taken prisoner. The Navajos who survived would bring back animals and other food to share with their relatives. Sometimes the prisoners were just kept around and used by the People as slaves. I guess some of them were even taken to other places later and traded or sold for food and other things.

Those raids caused a lot of trouble for the People in all directions. Others were always going out looking for their animals and relatives who had been captured. My grandmothers said that because of that, in their time the People were always moving around, running and hiding in different places, like high in the mountains or in canyons they knew about in this part of the country. When their enemies saw them, they chased the People and would fight with them, killing those they could and capturing whatever animals and people they could take. And then I guess the same thing would happen. Those enemies would take the prisoners far away and use them for slaves themselves, or sell them to others in places like Santa Fe, Taos, and even down in Mexico.

From what the old people told us, I guess they had trouble with Utes and Apaches and even some of the Pueblo Indians because of all that stealing and raiding. And then too, sometimes those other Indians joined together with Spanish soldiers and Mexican soldiers. Officials in Santa Fe, where the headquarters were, would order troops to travel this way, looking for Navajos who were stealing. Sometimes other Indians who were also our enemies would help those troops. So, it was all those people who kept chasing the Navajos around in my grandparents' time, keeping them on the run. The old people talked about their own experiences during those times. They also told us stories they heard from Navajos who had moved out this way from different places in New Mexico to get away from the soldiers.

My grandmothers and other relatives had lots of stories about conflicts that took place in areas where they were located at one time or another.[6] Sometimes those stories would even make us laugh because the Navajo warriors outwitted those people. One story was about a woman called 'Asdzáán Woo'i [Tooth Woman]. Her name always made us laugh but nobody ever said how she got that name or why they called her that. They said Tooth Woman was coming from the east, moving toward Valley Store. I guess one day in the springtime, she went on top of the little hill down there and looked toward Lukachukai. Over there, she saw Ute enemies coming this way, from over by the Chuska Mountains. A lot of times, in the spring those Utes would come into the Chinle Valley from that direction, searching for Navajos. So she jumped on a horse bareback, and took off. She headed toward the top of *Tł'oh Chíí'* [Red Grass (Mesa)], that red mesa over there, just this side of old Valley Store. There's a horse trail there that goes all the way to the top. That trail has lots of rocks on it; some of them were in piles, almost like walls. But her horse knew the trail very well. It jumped over those without difficulty and took her right up there very fast. When she got way on the top, she stopped and watched those Utes coming. When they started up the trail, their horses didn't want to jump over those rocks. So she went to the edge above them, got off her horse, and gave a big war whoop and a big wave. Then she jumped back on her horse and took off toward Black Mountain. Those Utes just stopped and watched her. Then they turned their horses around; they gave up and went back. They never caught her. The old people used to laugh about her story.*[7]

Another time some of the People were trying to escape from Utes who had come out of Utah to help the soldiers from Santa Fe fight the Navajos. There was a Navajo man who knew how to cross over the Kayenta Mountain by a trail that went on top of it. That trail passed near some water on the top, and he was trying to help the other Navajos go through there by showing them where that trail was. My grandmothers said it was said that there were lots of bees up in that area. When the Navajos got up on the top, right at the edge of the mountain they found a lot of beehives. When the soldiers and those Utes started coming up the trail on horseback, the Navajos on top threw those beehives all the way down to where their enemies were coming. Those bees came out and started stinging their enemies. All those Utes and those soldiers just turned around and went back. They gave up.*

There were lots of stories about different things that happened more toward Rough Rock, too. I guess that whole area from Rough Rock and Kayenta all the way through the Black Mountain area and over to Salina and Keams Canyon, was like a stronghold for some of the People during all those troubles. The canyons here, Canyon de Chelly and del Muerto, were strongholds, too. Sometimes the stories the old people told about conflicts at those different places involved the use of witchcraft.[8] I don't know anything about how that was done and our relatives never explained that to us. But I guess there were certain places out here where they used to have trouble from witchcraft, just among themselves, too, in those early times. They used to accuse a lot of old men of doing that in the Black Mountain area and other places.

The old people said that one time a group of Navajos was being chased by some Mexicans up in the mountains around Rough Rock. The Mexicans were camped down below for the night and the Navajos were on top. The troops had chased them all the way up there, by that trail that goes up in the mountain. They held a council and asked one old man who knew how to do witchcraft things to do something. I guess he and two or three others went to the edge of the mountain where they could look down and see the soldiers who were camped there. They say this old man knew what to do to witch people. So he sang some songs and said some prayers. When the Navajos got up early the next morning, they found that the soldiers had all left during the night. They just quit, turned back, and went back to Santa Fe. That was before the American soldiers came and forced the People to go to Fort Sumner.

Over closer to Cottonwood, Salina, and Pinon there are other places, lots of places the People have names for because of what happened during those troubles with our enemies. There's Many Skeletons, and that place they call Where the Mexicans Came Over the Mountain; there's also that No Water Flat or Waterless Mesa. In those days the People just kept moving around, hiding, trying to stay ahead of the soldiers, the Mexicans. Some tried hiding in the Chinle area in the strongholds in the Canyon; others kept moving toward Black Mountain and Keams Canyon, trying to stay way up on top in places where they would be safe and not seen. Waterless Mesa is one of those places; of course, that whole mountain, all the way from Rough Rock to Kayenta, is where many of the People went. They moved up there during that time when the Mexican soldiers kept coming out from Santa Fe, looking for Navajos.

Waterless Mesa is called *Tó' 'ádin nihaaską́ą́*, No Water Mountain, No Water Flat.[9] It was a stronghold in those early times because the trail that goes up there is just for a few horses. The People moved up there to escape the soldiers. They were up there on top and the troops put their tents up and camped down below, where the water was. The People were hiding up there for a long time and they ran out of food; they also needed to get to the water at the bottom. Sometimes they would try and send someone to crawl down there at night to bring back water. Eventually, when they had nothing left to eat, the People decided to ask this man who was with them to do witchcraft on the soldiers, to go witch the General. He knew how to do those things. They asked him three times to do that but he kept refusing; he was afraid to do it. He didn't want to make a mistake because it might come back on him. The old people said that when those people asked him the fourth time, he said he would, if someone would go with him. He asked for volunteers; he didn't want to go down there alone, by himself, at night because something might happen. So one man finally volunteered. In those days, they used to have a lot of those witches.

In the evening, they did some hand-trembling[10] to see who was in charge of those soldiers and to find out what was going to happen. Then they got this man who knew about witchcraft to go over to the edge of the cliff. That night he sang some songs and did other things that he knew how to do. He and that other man went down below; they were down there and yet, they talked from on top of that mountain. I don't know how he did that.[11]

The next morning, the soldiers tried to come up that trail, one at a time. All the Navajos were lined up on the edge there, hiding. When their enemies started up the trail, they began shooting arrows at them from the top. The General was the first one they killed. Then the soldiers started running; they just turned back. The People said that was a big victory for the Navajos right there. We never heard who that man was who knew those things or who it was leading the soldiers. The things that were done over there were kept very secret; all the old people told us was that lots of different kinds of songs were fixed for that; it was a Battle Song that killed most of those soldiers. Of course, some of the Navajos got killed there, too. Those who were left kept moving to the other side of Cottonwood, west of there. That's where they buried a lot of the Navajos killed in that battle. There are lots of skeletons there at a place called *Ts'íísts'in Łání* [Many Skeletons].

There were lots of places where the People had wars with those soldiers, those Mexicans who kept coming from the west, northwest. A lot of the fighting was going on by that river, the Colorado, more toward Kayenta. But there were also a lot of our warriors fighting at a place called Tachee. At the same time they were fighting down on the Tachee side, up here they were fighting at a place called *Naakaii Haaznání* [Where the Mexicans Came Over the Mountain]. That place is about half way up on Black Mountain. There's a peak there called *Tsé łbáí* [Gray Rock]; on this side of that peak, down underneath it is where this place is. There's a trail that goes straight through there right to the top. That's the name of that place now; they call it after those Mexican soldiers who came.

Those armies kept coming out from Santa Fe to tell us to stop raiding and stealing. You know, the Navajos who used to live in what is now called New Mexico used to steal sheep from the Mexicans, even right around Santa Fe. There was a lot of trouble over that. One of the stories the old people told was about the punishment for that. I guess one time some Navajos were caught taking some Mexican sheep. After the Mexicans captured them and got their sheep back, they butchered one of those sheep and skinned it. Then they took the leader of that raid and put that sheepskin over his head, after they cut holes in it for the eyes. Then they hung him until he was dead with that over his head. After that, they put him across a horse and brought him back to where some of the People were living, with that skin still over his head. When things like that started happening, a lot of Navajos began moving out this way, to get away. That was way before Fort Sumner, and before there was any reservation out here. I guess those Mexicans and other people wanted to settle on the land, too.

A lot of the People moved to the top of Black Mountain when they came from New Mexico; they settled all over the top. There were warriors there, and women, children, and old people. There used to be lots of old hogans up there but they're probably all gone now. The old people told us that the soldiers were located from Keams Canyon all the way down, and they moved out from there, from the other side of the mountain. That's why a lot of the People stopped and settled right there on top of those mountains, between that Black Mountain and Keams Canyon Mountain. Of course, some of them settled over here in Canyon de Chelly and Canyon del Muerto. And some of them went beyond to Leupp and Tuba City, and settled over there, and also in the southern part of Arizona.

The People moved up in the mountains and the soldiers went up there after them. They fought over there at Where the Mexicans Came Over the Mountain and those soldiers killed some of the People there. A lot of Navajos gathered together right on the top of that mountain at that place, on that trail that goes up there. The soldiers came up there on horseback; it was mainly the cavalry. The fighting there lasted for quite some time. The Navajos sent for help, for more reinforcements from their Canyon stronghold to help fight that cavalry. Those Mexicans were killing the warriors and then stealing the women, children, sheep, and other livestock. A lot of people were killed there on both sides and those soldiers chased some of the Navajos down the other side of the mountain toward Keams Canyon. Finally, the Navajos who were left were able to stop the cavalry, turn those soldiers back; they went back to Santa Fe and their station in Keams Canyon. Then, after a while, the Navajos who were living up there started coming back this way. In my young days you could still see a lot of graves of people who were killed during the fighting at that place over near the Black Mountain store.[12]

There is one other story that has been passed along in our family. It is just awful but I have already told my children and grandchildren about it, so I will talk about it here. It concerns one of the women in our family during my grandmother's time; after this happened, she became known as *Tanabah* [Woman Who Returned from the Warpath].[13] She escaped and made her way back to her people. The way my mother told this story to us, I think it was the Utes who had captured them at that time. My mother said it was her mother who used to tell this story. We think this happened to one of her sisters, my real grandmother's sisters. It sounded awful fearful because she gave birth to a baby and just left it. That's awful to do a thing like that. The reason she deserted her baby was that the enemy was chasing them. They didn't have any way to save those children because they might not even be able to save themselves. My mother said that her mother thought that was why *Tanabah* left her baby behind. That was the story of my real grandmother's sister, one of her sisters. I guess my real grandmother was expecting that the same thing might occur again some day. She used to put a scare into her children by talking like that; my mother did the same thing with us.*

A group of women were taken prisoners by the Ute Indians. The Utes had been chasing the People and they had run somewhere to the top of the mountain, trying to escape by going to the west. It might have been over here, somewhere in the Black Mountain region, toward Kayenta. My mother said that my grandmother never told them exactly what location that was, just up in the mountains somewhere. It might have been the Chuska Mountains because some of the other people who escaped from those Utes used to talk about coming back this way from up there.

That woman was already pregnant when the Utes started chasing them. It was early in the winter when that happened; snow was just beginning in the mountains. The People hid on the top, watching the Utes below. I guess they finally captured those women and started driving them back over the mountain, going back to wherever they came from.

By the time they started marching them along, those Utes were pretty hungry; they were almost starving because they had run out of food. Finally they got so hungry that they killed one of the mules they were using to carry their equipment. Those Utes packed their supplies and other things on the backs of the few mules they had. They killed one of the mules right there where they stopped for the night and cut it up, with the skin and all still on there. They didn't even bother to butcher it.*

When they stopped for the night, they would build those big brush corrals, like we do for the Yeibichei Dance[14] or the Fire Dance; they made those out of juniper and pine and other trees, and moved inside to sleep. In the middle of that, they built a big fire. Even those women prisoners were driven inside that big brush corral. After the Utes killed that mule, they built a fire. Then they took those pieces of meat and stuck them on sticks and put those around the edge of the fire; they didn't have any grills or anything like that to put anything on the fire. Then they passed that meat around to different ones in the group; some of the meat was only partially cooked, but they ate it anyway. They just cut it up and ate it; they had no dishes of any kind. While they were eating, they told the women they had captured to fix blood sausage for them out of that mule. They gave them a pan to cook it in and some water, which they were carrying in those *'ásaa' yázhí* [small pot], some kind of small pot like those woven baskets, water jugs.[15]

On that particular day, before they stopped to build their brush place for the night and killed the mule, the Utes gave that woman a whole pile of old rags from some kind of very heavy material, like canvas. They told her to wrap her baby in those scraps if she had it on the way. They knew she was already very close to her time to have the baby when they were marching her along.

Whenever they stopped to spend the night, those Utes would tie their prisoners up. Their hands were all tied in the back; I guess they used one rope to tie each one's arms and legs. They also tied those prisoners to one another as they lay down to sleep. They would tell them to sleep on the ground, wherever they had space for them to spend the night.

That night this woman had her bundle of scraps, and some food she had been collecting. She also had some of the blood sausage because the Utes had told the Navajos they could keep that for themselves. She was determined not to go much further with them. I guess she had in the back of her mind somewhere that she was going to try to escape one way or another, and she was trying to make her plans.

That night the Utes drove them into that corral. They put those women on one side and tied them all up, their feet, and their hands in the back. The Utes were close to the entrance, right on the side of it. They just sat there, one against the other, and went to sleep, sitting up. That night it was clear and the moon was out; there was a lot of moonlight. Somewhere in the middle of the night this woman woke up and realized that her hands were free; they were tied when she went to bed and here, when she woke up, her binding rope was loose. So she slipped out of her rope. She said when she found that rope loose, she just thought, "I'm not going to stay here. I'll just get the binding rope loose from my ankles too," which she did. So she got up quietly and looked around; everyone else, all of those other women she was tied with and those Utes, were sound asleep. So she quietly untied her feet and crawled out of there. She did not bother about putting on her moccasins, but she picked up a little pot she was carrying for water and the little food she had saved, and walked off. She said there were quite a number of women tied up together as they slept. "When I got myself loose, I didn't want to disturb the others. I was afraid there'd be a commotion during the night."

So she quietly moved out, taking what few other things she wanted to take with her. She went a little way behind the corral, to where there was a big tree. She stood behind that for a while and nobody woke up. So, she just started walking from there. She left her moccasins off at the start and tried to walk where there was no snow. She walked for quite a distance without those shoes, trying to stay in different places where the sun had melted the snow so there would be no tracks.

She told us, "That mountain ridge was quite a distance from where I escaped that night. I walked and walked all night and after a while, that big mountain was not too far away. I just kept walking toward it. When I got into the mountain, I put on my moccasins; it was almost daylight. I just kept walking and by the time I got close to the top of that mountain, on its ridge, the sun was coming up. At daylight, just about at sunrise, I had ascended the mountain to the top, and I sat there and watched. Then I started on my journey back home."[16]

I guess after they had been captured, this woman had seen others try to escape. What the Utes did was whenever they missed one of their prisoners after the sun came up, they started to hunt them down. If they knew they had gone into the mountains, they would wait for them to come out, or to come back down. So she knew she was going to have to put herself somewhere for the rest of that day. She kept moving higher into that mountain until she came upon a thick juniper. It was the kind where the branches are very thick, growing close together. She decided no one could see through it or into it, and she crawled into it and sat there all day. She could see where she had walked from after daybreak, and she could still see the Utes.

Sure enough, after the sun came up, she saw all that dust coming from where she walked and she knew they were coming on horseback, trying to track her. So she just stayed way up on the mountain, sitting on the ground, at the base, the trunk of that real bushy, thick juniper, watching them. The mountain she had climbed was very rocky and it was impossible for a horse to go all the way up there. So a whole group of Utes only came part way up and then stopped. At noon, some of them went back down; she knew how many had come out to track her so she knew there were still some sitting there. And so she sat there all day, without moving, until late in the evening. Then the rest of them took off, firing their guns and yelling. They were saying they had found her and killed her, or something like that. All that time while she was watching them, she was saying her prayers again and again, that she would get back to her homeland out here, that she would return regardless of what happened.

A long time after they had left, she started out again. She wanted to get further, at least over the mountain on the other side before nighttime. And she did get over that one and into another mountain before it got too dark. There she found another juniper and another spot where she could hide. So she fixed her place there, built a little fire with a few twigs she found, and fixed herself something to eat with that little bundle of food and that little jug of water she carried. She never said what she used for matches, only that she fixed herself something to eat.

At the first sign of dawn the next morning, she woke up and prayed again. Then she fixed herself something to eat with the little food she had left and started out again. From the way that woman told the story, she knew where she was. It wasn't exactly the same trail the soldiers used later when they took the People to Fort Sumner, but it was near that, in that same area. The People knew the country because they moved around so much at that time; she knew when she started out that morning that she was going in the right direction to get back to her people. She wasn't lost because she knew that route would bring her back over here.

And so she left and started out; again, she wanted to get as far as she could before sundown. She walked until late that afternoon. Then she started having labor pains. They were so close together that she decided to find a place where she could get settled down. She came across another place where there were lots of junipers. So she stopped there and cleared an area out from underneath a big juniper and fixed it up. She picked up enough wood to build a fire before the pains got too bad, and broke all the branches off the juniper. That way, when she built her fire, she could keep putting those fresh junipers on top of it, and use them as heat for her back, or whatever she wanted for her pain. That's what they did in those old times.[17]

That woman said that by the time she got her little bundle of rags and the other things ready, her pains were so close that she was really crying. She was crying for her mother. She didn't know what else to do because she was out there all by herself, with no help, nobody else around. For a while she said she screamed her head off, crying for her mother. But then she realized she had no choice but to do the best she could with what she was going to go through. She didn't know if that child would come right away or whether she was going to have some difficulties. She just hoped that nothing would go wrong.

Finally, when the fire was going real good and these things were all ready, she went into labor and that baby came out, without too much trouble. It was some time after dark when the baby finally came. And so she just covered herself with the juniper she heated up. She didn't have any blankets or anything, only those rags and some other things. She put those together and tied herself together around the waist with them so she wouldn't be in too much pain. She knew she was going to have to walk quite a ways again. She just wrapped that baby up in those rags and left it lying there at her feet all night.

Early the next morning, she tied herself again around the waist real tight. That's what they used to do in those times but they used those big wide bands, sash belts,[18] and wrapped them real tight. Then she finally fixed the baby; she cut its cord and bundled it up and put it somewhere underneath a bush. She talked to that baby before she left. She said, "I don't know if I'm going to make it back to my people or not. For that reason I can't take you. I don't know how far I'll get or even if I'll get there safely. Even if I took you, I'd lose you somewhere along the way because of something that came up. So I'm going to leave you here." She talked to the baby in that way for a while, and then she left it behind, right there under that bush. When she walked away, the baby was still alive and she was really crying.[19]

From there, she wanted to get as far as she could toward the next mountain she could see. So she started walking. The wind and rain came up. Around noon, she looked back and noticed there were some crows[20] flying around, circling around where she figured she had left the baby. Maybe they had heard her crying when she left. So she just cried some more.

When she started walking again, she realized she was having trouble with her uterus coming out. She thought to herself, "This time this is going to take my life. There is nothing that I can do about this out here by myself. I don't think I am going to live through this." She stopped walking and started looking around; that's when she came across a place in the rocks where there was a split. The winds were really blowing by then and a big storm had come up. The crack in the rocks was just big enough for her to get between them. So she crawled in there upside down. And somehow, after a while, she was able to push her uterus back inside herself. But when she tried to get out of that crevice, she realized she was caught in there. She had the hardest time trying to get free; it was not until very late in the evening when she finally got herself out, after getting all bruised and scraped. I guess she was crying and screaming the whole time. But she was determined to get out, and somehow she finally did.

After she freed herself, she looked around the area and found another spot where she could spend the night. Once again, she fixed a place under a thick juniper and camped there overnight. She gathered what twigs she could find to build a fire, and as much of the snow as she could, to melt to use for her water. She also gathered more juniper and some other herbs that were around. There were lots of herbs that she knew in the mountain so she gathered them. Then she boiled them in the snow she melted, and drank that for her pain.[21] She stayed there all that night, and all the next day, too. She knew she should rest for at least a whole day before going on. She knew by then that she was far, far away from those Utes.

After she rested up, she started out again. She didn't know how many days she walked after that, but finally she got back over here, over the mountains. When she returned to her people, she was very, very thin, nothing but skin and bones. She was also very hungry, and all bruised and scratched up. Some of her relatives had moved away, but there were still some living right there. So, as soon as she came back, they did a ceremony for her and tried helping her in other ways. Gradually she came back to normal life, and later she died of old age. When she finally came back to her people, they started calling her *Tanabah*, Woman Who Returned from the Warpath. They named her that because she had escaped after all those Navajo women were taken prisoners by that Ute war party.

There are some other things from my real grandmother's time that I could tell, but I don't want to talk about them. They are too ugly. The old people had lots of stories like that but I am not going to tell any more of them. They were pursued by enemies; the Utes, the Spanish, the Mexicans, and even the Apaches were the main ones. In my grandmothers' time, the People did not stay put in one place like we do now. They were always moving around from place to place in those times because of their enemies.

My Mother's Early Times

2

My mother's early days . . . the Long Walk . . . my mother's relatives . . .
my parents get together . . . brothers and sisters before and after me . . .
I get born.

My mother used to tell us stories about her early days and the experiences the People went through at that time. Many different things happened to her while she was growing up and she used to talk about some of them with us. I know she mentioned being born some place, but I don't remember where. She didn't know when that was, and she never told us when any of us were born, either. In those days, there were no hospitals, no schools, no stores. No one kept any records like they do now. I never saw my mother's own mother, but I did see her father, Yucca Fruit Man Packing a Burden. He was an old man when I saw him. Then he passed away, so I never got to know him.

I always called my mother, *shimá* [my mother]. She had several other names she went by, like *'Asdzáán Nééz* [Tall Woman] and *'Asdzáán Nééz Nizhóní* [Tall, Beautiful Woman]. And I guess on some of the papers at the Catholic mission here in Chinle, she was known as *'Asdzáán Ntsááz* [Big, Huge Woman] and *'Asdzáán (Rose) Nizhóní* [(Rose), Beautiful Woman].[1] My mother was tall and heavyset; some people even called her Fat Woman with a Protruding Stomach in her young adulthood.* But in her family she was called Tall Woman. She died of old age after all my own children were born; some of them got to know her in her old age.

My mother used to tell us how she was raised and what conditions were like when she was small. She said that then, things were still the way they were in her own mother's time; nothing had changed very much from what her mother used to say about her own times. When my mother was growing up, the People were still on the run, always moving, trying to hide from enemies. The main things she told us about were the foods they ate and the hard times they went through when she was young. The People were poor and run down; most of the time they were starved, all skin and bones. She said you could even see the lumps on the joints of their limbs because they were in that bad condition!

In those days, the People ate anything they could find. My mother said they used to gather every thing they could find for food, like seeds, plants, and berries. Certain plants and small animals were the main ones, like *haashch'é'édą́ą'* when their berries got ripe, and wild *'ostse'* and *tł'ohdeeí*.[2] She said, "In my young days, we'd eat anything we could catch, too, like rabbits, and even rats and mice. We used to share them with one another in small pieces." That was fearful. She told us that in our ancestors' time, most of the People, even her, were skin and bones from starving. They really went through some hardships in her time. Now, it's altogether different; people waste food all the time.

It was the same with their clothes. My mother said that during her time, they didn't have any material. About all they wore were woven blanket dresses called *biil*.[3] They made those themselves out of wool from the sheep, just like we make rugs today. They had no shoes, either, so they went around barefoot.

Even though the People were in poor condition, all skin and bones, when my mother was little she remembers they were being chased all over by enemies. Those enemies were all around, and they were always trying to hide from them. Maybe the People caused some of that themselves; the old people said at that time they were always going out to steal food from others. Sometimes they took sheep and horses, and sometimes they took crops that other people were raising. I guess because of that, they had trouble from enemies in many different directions. In those times, there were many kinds of people settling in this part of the country, and more kept coming in, trying to get land to live on. Those people hunted Navajos so the People were always on the move, running and hiding out somewhere in the mountaintops all over this area. In the beginning, the Spanish and the Mexicans were the main enemies. But the People also had trouble from other Indians, like Utes, Apaches, even some of the Pueblos. My mother told me that all those things were *before* the American government took over and sent soldiers out here to round up the Navajos and march them to Fort Sumner.

Those enemies tried to capture the Navajos, even though the People were skin and bones. Some of them were taken prisoners and then taken far away and sold as slaves to other people. *Tanabah*, one of my maternal grandmother's sisters, was one of the ones taken prisoner by enemies. But she escaped at night and returned home, as I've already told you.

My mother told me when the American soldiers came and forced the People to go to Fort Sumner, Kit Carson was the General who came out from the headquarters in Santa Fe. He was joined by some Mexicans, and also some Apaches from the south and Utes from the north. So the People had a hard time at that time, too.

My mother was among those who went on the Long Walk. She told us her story about that many, many times and I want to mention it right here. That story was fearful. I guess she was afraid the same thing might happen to us. She used to say, "Maybe this will happen again, and maybe not." She told us that while she was still a child, while she was growing up, the People were notified they were wanted in Fort Defiance. Word was spread that all the People were to come in to Fort Defiance. It was just like when Jesus was born and the people were told to go home to their cities to be enrolled for the census. After a while, the People way up on top of Black Mountain got the news. That's where my real grandmother, my mother's family, and many other Towering House People were living when this happened.

When my real grandmother heard about this, she told my mother and our other relatives that she didn't want to go over there. She said she was not going to go, that she refused. When the old people told this about her, they used to wonder if maybe she already knew those officials were really going to send the People to Fort Sumner. She said she was going to remain behind, no matter what happened to her. So she went somewhere out in the mountains, far away from where they were when they got that news. We don't know where she went; she went by herself and no one ever knew. She was already up in her years when that happened, and I guess she died out there somewhere, by herself. That was my real grandmother who stayed behind and then passed away. I never heard what name she was known by among the People. She was already gone when I came to realize things.

My mother said that some others refused to go, too. The old people used to tell us that some people moved to other places in the mountains in small groups, to hide from the soldiers. Some of them passed away before the others were released from Fort Sumner. Others eventually found their relatives when they were allowed to return from captivity.

After my real grandmother did that, most of the rest of my mother's family and our other relatives came down from the mountain and started off to Fort Defiance. They spent the nights out in the open while they were traveling over there. All of them traveled on foot, except one person who rode the only horse the family had at that time. My mother told us they heard they were being called in so the officials could give them food called "rations." The officials said out there in the mountains, the People had nothing to eat, so they called them in for rations. When they finally reached Fort Defiance, my mother said it was a horrible sight. Lots and lots of people were gathered there at the place where the government built that school later.[4] All of them were skin and bones and they all looked terrible. Some of them were dying right there from hunger. When they finally arrived at that place, the first thing the officials did was give the People food. My mother said when those rations were issued, some of the People didn't know how to use them. They had never seen some of those things, like the flour they were given and the coffee beans. They tried to eat those beans and use that flour like cornmeal, and more of them died from the results of that.[5]

My mother said not long after that, the officials told them they had to go to Fort Sumner. They ordered them to start moving to that place. The soldiers started marching the People to Fort Sumner, even though they were skin and bones. She didn't remember how long after that it was before they started out on that Long Walk.[6] Lots of the People walked most of the way to that place. It was far away and it took them many, many days to get there. Some of them did not survive; they died along the way because they were in that poor condition before they started out; they were not strong enough to make that journey. My mother said on that trip they were issued food; that's how some of them managed to stay alive. After they reached the place we call *Hwéeldi* [Fort Sumner or Bosque Redondo], rations were issued to them again. That's all they had to live by.

My mother said she didn't know exactly how long the soldiers held them over there in captivity. It was either three or four years, but she had forgotten. Of course, that's natural; even now we can't remember everything that happened to us in our younger days.

While she was at Fort Sumner, my mother became a young woman; she became a *kinaaldá* [pubescent woman] and had her first *Kinaaldá* [Puberty Ceremony] over there at Fort Sumner.[7] "Right after that," she said, "a strange man came around, asking that I be given in marriage to him. That was the custom in my time and my parents did that. So I never had a second Puberty Ceremony; I just started bearing children right away." That's what my mother told us.

After some time, the People were allowed to leave, to start moving back to this area, away from Fort Sumner. Of course, many of them did not return. Some had died during their journey to that place; others had passed away from diseases or from old age, or in childbirth while the People were held captive over there. My mother said the man she had been given to after her first *Kinaaldá* did not come back. He was older and she got pregnant for him right before they were released from that place. She never said if he died over there or on the way back, but he never made it back. The baby survived, though, and came back with her. Later, after my mother started living with *Hastiin Delawoshí* [Man Who Shouts],[8] that boy became known as his son. That's how he became one of my older brothers.

While I was growing up, whenever my mother and others who went on that Long Walk got together, they'd talk about what they went through during that time over there at Fort Sumner. They'd talk about those things in front of us. That would scare me. All the sufferings and hardships they related were horrible. They wanted us to know about the awful experiences they had over there. What I just mentioned here was one of my mother's stories about that.

My mother told me when the People were released from Fort Sumner, the soldiers accompanied them back to Fort Defiance again. When they arrived there, they saw even more soldiers. The officials told the People they had to remain there for a while. I guess they were still deciding whether or not they could trust the Navajos to stop raiding and fighting with all those enemies. The People were reminded about the conditions of their release from Fort Sumner, that they had promised to stop stealing and raiding others. They were told the government would help them with rations for a while, until they got back on their feet. The soldiers were going to stay at Fort Defiance and other places, like the fort at Keams Canyon. They were being put there to protect the Navajos from the enemies who used to chase them all over. The officials also told the People various ones would be chosen to supervise things in the future; those *naat'áanii* [Navajo leaders, headmen] were to come to Fort Defiance whenever there was trouble, or when the officials needed to talk to them.

After the People were reminded about the agreements that had been made, they were told they could go ahead and move out from Fort Defiance into the areas where they used to live. They were told to go wherever they wanted. Some of the People took routes over the Chuska Mountains; some, like my mother's family, started moving back to the Black Mountain area, following trails that went back on the other side. Others moved to places like the Chinle Valley, Canyon de Chelly and Canyon del Muerto (which we call the Canyon), the Chuskas, Kayenta, and elsewhere. After a while, they located some of their relatives who had refused to go, those who had hidden in the mountains. Of course, some of them, like my real grandmother, had already passed away by the time the others came back. Later, when the government schools started and officials began to send police out to capture Navajo children for school, some of the People started moving again, down into Walapai country, or more toward Santa Fe, to escape those schools.

In some places where the People went after they were allowed to move away from Fort Defiance, enemies still kept causing trouble. And, after a while, it seemed like there was lots of trouble going on again, even among the People themselves. In certain places, like around Black Mountain, they started having a lot of trouble over things like witchcraft after they came back from the Long Walk.[9]

I was never sure how many of my mother's family went to Fort Sumner or how many came back. She only told us about a few of her own relatives when we were growing up. One of those I've already mentioned, *Tanabah*, who was one of her own mother's sisters. My mother told us that besides *Tanabah*, her own mother had at least two other sisters; they were my other grandmothers, and they used to move around with us when I was very small. One of those women was the grandmother to Chee Jones; the other one was the grandmother to Big Man and Charlie Davis; those men had different mothers who were sisters.

My mother also said her mother, my real grandmother, had several brothers. I came to know two of them when I, myself, was very small. One of those men used to move around with us when I was growing up.[10] He went by different names but about the time I came to realize things, our family was calling him *Hastiin Gaanii* [Mr. Arm]. That man lost part of his arm; it was cut off about half way up. From what my mother told us, he was married to another Towering House woman called *'Asdzáán Báyóodzin* [Paiute Woman]. She also was called Strong Teeth Woman; the People used to tease her about that name but my mother never told me how she got it.* They had two boys; *Bizahalani* [Man with Many Words] was the older. The younger one was called *Bilátsohi* [Thumb Man] because one of his thumbs was missing. One time when Mr. Arm was staying with his older son, he went to sleep. When he woke up, his arm was broken or something; he saw blood oozing out of it. They tried various things to cure it and for a while it got better. But then my mother said it started bleeding again and got infected. By that time the government had started setting up those clinics.[11] I guess when his arm got worse, he went over there. But the doctors couldn't do anything for him so he had it cut off. Later he died from a stroke; the first one left him paralyzed on one side of his body; the second one killed him. Paiute Woman ended up raising those two boys by herself; they kept moving around with us while I was growing up, even after she lost her husband.[12]

Another one of my own mother's uncles, her mother's brothers, was a man who was called *Kiyaa'áanii* [Towering House Man]. He lived in the Black Mountain area and was a Blessingway singer. After my own father started to learn Blessingway, this man, who was one of my real grandmother's brothers, was one of the teachers he had for that.

I guess my own mother had some brothers and sisters, too. We were never told very much about them, so I'm not sure how many there were or where they were living. In my early days, I got to know one of my mother's older brothers who was called *Hastiin Yázhí* [Small Man]. He lived over toward Salina, way back somewhere behind the Black Mountain, not too far away from Towering House Man. When I was very little, we used to go over there and spend the winter with him, after we finished harvesting our corn and were ready to "go back across."[13] Small Man was another one of my father's Blessingway teachers, when he decided to start learning that ceremony. Some of my mother's sisters lived with us, too, when I was very small. One of them was married to my father, just like my mother was. That was the custom in those days.

My mother never told us how long it was after she came back from Fort Sumner before she started living with the man who became my father, *Hastiin Delawoshí* [Man Who Shouts]. From what she said, he was from the Salina area and when his family came back from the Long Walk, they went back there. The man who became my father had been a warrior before the People were forced to go to Fort Sumner. He and his relatives had a taste of war in them and they all participated in lots of raids on our enemies.[14] My father belonged to the *Tó díchʼíiʼnii* [Bitter Water] clan; I don't know how many names he had, or what they called him when he was a young boy. Later, during his adulthood, he was one of the ones who started helping the headmen the officials in Washington chose to serve as local leaders for the People. Those men were to supervise how the People lived after they came back from captivity. For a while, my father was called *Hastiin* [The Man]. Later, he became known as *Hastiin Delawoshí* [Man Who Shouts]; that was after he began serving as one of those headmen. He became well known for that and he stayed in that position until he passed away.[15] My father probably had other names, too; he was a very tall man and I remember he always had whiskers and a long moustache. While I was growing up, my father learned the Blessingway Ceremony and became known as a Blessingway singer. He was also known to many people because he was a very good Yeibichei dancer and knew lots of Yeibichei songs.

My mother told me that when her family came back from the Long Walk, she brought the child she had given birth to over there with her. He survived the return trip, and after she started living with Man Who Shouts, he started calling him his son. That's how that boy was named *Hastiin Delawoshí biyeʼ* [Son of Man Who Shouts]; he was one of my older brothers, too.

I never asked my mother how she met the man who became her husband after she came back. If she ever told me, I've forgotten what she said about it. All I know is they married each other, started living together, and she started having children for him.[16]

I, myself, wasn't born until after my mother had had lots of other children for Man Who Shouts. I know I had at least two older brothers and three older sisters because they were around when I was old enough to understand things, and I remember growing up with them when I was very, very small. My mother said there were also many others before I was born. Some of my older brothers and sisters died when they were little babies. She lost quite a few of the ones she gave birth to, shortly after birth. There were also some who died in their first weeks of life, and some who passed away after they started to grow up, before I was born. She said there were also some who died after they reached adulthood, but before they reached old age. So, I don't really know how many children she had altogether for Man Who Shouts. Of course, I don't know anything about these other older brothers and sisters she mentioned because I never saw any of them. I only know what my mother told me; she didn't know when they died or why; some of them had some kind of sickness, body fever, maybe small-pox or some other illness; that's all she said.

I was already an adult and raising a family when the two older brothers I knew died; both of them died before our mother passed away. One of them was a big, heavyset man when he grew up; eventually he even grew a thick moustache, and started looking just like our father.* He was known by two names: *Yah 'i'iiníiłii* [The Jailer, The One Who Throws You Behind Bars] and *Hashké Náádááł* [The One Who Returned from the Warpath in a Bad Mood].[17] Later, other boys in the family were given that warrior name too, after him. That happens at Enemyway ceremonies; that's when boys get their warrior name. This older brother of mine, The Jailer, stayed mainly around Black Mountain, taking care of my father's cows and horses. He was the only one helping with that as my father got older. He had lots of horses and cows of his own, too, on the ridge over there, near the dump. They were scattered all over the area and they filled up that whole hill; that's why we call it *Łį́į́ Bidáagi* or *Łį́į́ Bidádí* [Horses on the Edge, Covered with Horses; Horse Blind]. This big, heavyset, older brother of mine who herded cows for my father was very well known as a Yeibichei dancer; he had his own team and they used to travel around to Nightway ceremonies. He married someone from Black Mountain and they had a boy who was given the same warrior name. When that big sickness came, that flu,[18] The Jailer lost his wife; she died in childbirth during the flu and the second baby she had just had for him died, too. I was already an adult and raising my family when that happened; we had already moved away from Houses Standing in a Line. Several years after he lost his wife, he passed away, too, right up there on the mesa. That wasn't from the flu, but I don't remember if it was from some other sickness, like measles or heart trouble, or not. He was buried there on the mesa; later, when my father died, he was buried near the same place.

The other older brother I knew was smaller; he didn't look too much like Man Who Shouts. One of his names was *Hastiin bigish hólóní, Hastiin Bigishi* [Man with a Cane]. When he was a young man, he had an accident that left him crippled. He was riding horseback, trying to rope another horse. Somehow, the rope got caught and his horse went down and landed on top of him, breaking his hip. The Fort Defiance Hospital was in operation by then, but it was too far away. So a singer was hired to do the Lifeway Ceremony over him. That man told him he'd have to use crutches in the future, but that eventually he'd be able to get around.[19] For a long time, this older brother of mine didn't do anything. But finally, he made himself a cane and started trying to go out, to sit outside the hogan, with others helping him. Later, he learned to get on his horse again, using his cane. By the time my two oldest children saw him, he was riding his horse to the store and other places, and even starting to do farmwork. Despite his crippled condition, he got along all right. The other name Man with a Cane was known by was *Hastiin bit'iis* [Man with a Cottonwood Tree]. In the summer, he farmed a place across the Chinle Wash from Houses Standing in a Line. When he first started staying there in the summer, right across the road from here, below where we had our alfalfa field, he planted a cottonwood tree. At that time, there were no trees there at all; it was the very first one. So people named him after that, too.

Man with a Cane married a woman from Valley Store and they had at least two boys; Marcus Yazzie, who was also known as The One Who Returned from the Warpath in a Bad Mood, still lives there. Walter Yazzie, who was also known as Small Man, lives in Fort Defiance. That's how we're related to Alfred Yazzie who's a Nightway singer and a police chief; Walter is his father.[20] Some of my children, Mary no. 1, Seya, Agnes, and Ruth, got to know this crippled, older brother of mine, but it was Seya who was close with him.[21] In his later years, Man with a Cane had other names, too, because of his horses; he was called *Hastiin bilįį łzhini* [Man with the Black Horse] because his favorite horse, the one he rode all the time, was black, and *Hastiin bilįį łání* [Man with Many Horses]. Man with a Cane passed away after my father died, while Seya and Agnes were going to Fort Apache Indian School. He died in the spring; my daughter, Augusta, was born that summer so she never got to know him. He was over on the mesa when he died, and his family buried him there.

I don't know how many other brothers I had but I know there were others. My mother told me that another one had died in his teens, a long time before my older sisters or I were even born.[22] She also said she lost another baby boy and a baby girl right before I was born. After I was born, she had another girl; she's my younger sister, *'Asdzáán Yázhí* [Small Woman], and she lives near here. After she was born, I know my mother gave birth to two more girls, but both of them died shortly after birth from some kind of sickness. Now [1963] the three older sisters and two older brothers I knew are all gone, and even most of their children are gone. Some of their children's children are still walking around; others have passed away. Right now, there are only three of us left—my real sister who is younger than I am, a half sister who is older, and me.

I am not sure how many sisters I had, either older or younger. I remember growing up with three older ones but my mother told me there were others. Some of them died at birth; others died while we were living at Houses Standing in a Line. I think three of my older sisters passed away there; they were in their adulthoods[23] when they died; one of them was *'oosidi*.[24]

One of my older sisters was given in marriage to *Tó'aheedlíinii Nééz* [Tall Water Flows Together Man] who was also known as Jim Mitchell.[25] That happened way before the church people came to this area.[26] That man, Jim, was a brother of the man I started living with after I became a woman, but he was much, much older than Frank.[27] I don't know how many children this older sister of mine had for Jim; he roamed around a lot and had lots of children with different women, here and there. I don't think she had any children who survived for him. That sister of mine died before my oldest child, Mary no. 1, ever saw her. She may have died in childbirth with a baby; I don't remember.[28] When she died, another of my older sisters, one called Little Woman, was given to Jim. She was married to him for a while and had at least three daughters and one son for him before she died. Later, one of those girls, the one called Gai, was married to *Hashk'aan biye'* [Son of Yucca Fruit Man]; she became the mother of Ida and Betty. Another of the daughters was called Chubby Woman, and the other one was known as Beautiful Woman; she became the mother of Garnett and others, after she married Tom Scott. The boy was known as Tom. But then those young women died. That's why Ida, Garnett, and the other small children were raised by different ones in our family.[29]

My three older sisters used to move around with us with their families, all over on the mesa and in Black Mountain. One of them married *Deeshchii'nii* [Start of the Red Streak People] and had four children for him that I know about: *Hastiin Bitsui* [The Man's Grandson], who later was the father of Ben and Philemon; a daughter, Bah, who later became known as Mrs. Joseph Ganna; a son called The Policeman or The Jailer, The One Who Puts You in Prison, and another son called Sam Sanishya. When these children were small, this older sister of mine died, and her husband died, too. After that happened, my father took those four children, who were his grandchildren, and raised them like his own. They were raised with us because he became their guardian when their parents died.[30]

I want to mention right here that my father also had another wife. She was a younger sister of my mother, and she was given to Man Who Shouts after he had been living with my mother for quite some time. That was the custom in those times; lots of men had wives who were sisters. This second wife had only one child for him and then she died; she passed away a long time before my father did. She was called *Hastiin Delawoshí be'esdzáán yázhí* [Man Who Shouts' Small Wife] but she was also known as *'Asdzáán Ts'ósí* [Slim or Slender Woman] and *'Asdzáán Nééz bideezhí* or *'Asdzáán Nizhóní bideezhí* [Tall Woman's younger sister, or Beautiful Woman's younger sister]. Some people also called her *'Asdzáán Yázhí* [Small Woman]; that was because she was like an opposite of her older sister, my mother. My mother was really tall and heavy-set; this younger sister, who was also married to my father, was very different; she was short and very tiny, and the baby she had after a hard labor was also very small.[31] That baby was a girl; she was given the same name, *'Adzáán Ts'ósí, 'Asdzáán 'Ałts'ósí* [Slim Woman], because she was small, just like her mother. Slim Woman, the one who was that tiny baby, is my other sister, my half sister, because of that. She is older than me.[32] In our family, we also call her Grandma *Tł'ááshchí'í* because she married into the Red Bottom People clan; she was married to Old Man *Tł'ááshchí'í* [Old Red Bottom Man].

We never saw too much of my father's other wife or her daughter when I was little. We didn't grow up with her because this other wife lived separately from my mother and all of us. She moved around by herself and traveled with different people, not the ones who moved around with us; usually she was at least two or three miles away from where we were. So I don't know very much about my half sister's younger days.[33] My father used to go back and forth, visiting his other wife. I know he took care of both of them; sometimes I'd hear him talking with my mother about treating both of them the same, with the livestock and other things. But he spent more time with my mother and all the children she had for him, all of us.

When it was time for Slim Woman to be born, her mother had a very hard labor. She tried to give birth to her for four days, and she almost died. That almost killed her. From what my mother told me, my father went and got some hand-tremblers to find out what was holding up the birth, why this second wife was having trouble with her labor. I guess these men were Nightway singers he knew. They told him he had abused the Yeibichei himself, that he had sewn some Yeibichei masks together while this wife was pregnant. That's why it was like she was sewn shut now, when the baby was trying to come out. My mother said after the hand-trembling, my father went and got two singers to help with the birth. They were both Nightway singers and they went ahead and did some small ceremonies from that while Slim Woman's labor was going on. They kept on doing those things for both my half sister and her mother after she was finally born, too. When my father's second wife finally had the baby, it was very tiny, just like she was. We never understood why that labor was so hard for her. This wife, my mother's younger sister, died before her daughter became a woman. None of my children ever saw her. Man Who Shouts was told the tiny baby should have a Nightway done for her when she got old enough, but he never followed through on that, as far as I know.[34]

My half sister is still living [1963]; while my mother was still alive, she used to visit her all the time. She'd always walk over to where Slim Woman lives, north of where the Chinle and Nazlini Washes meet, even when she, herself, was in her old age.*[35]

When Slim Woman became a young woman, she was married to Old Red Bottom Man. He had lots of sheep and cows, and he used to farm a large area down by Many Farms. He was a real big man, not tall, but with a big stomach. When he rode his black horse around, his stomach used to hang out, and his arms would hang way out to the side. My half sister had about six children for him, three girls and three boys, and she also raised Sam Sanishya's sister, Bah, the girl who later was called Mrs. Joseph Ganna. One of the boys who was called Big Red Bottom Man went to school in Chinle with my son, Seya; they were good friends until that boy died. Old Red Bottom Man got sick from some illness after that; he suffered for a very long time before he passed away. My husband and I tried to help out with the ceremonies they were doing for him; they tried lots of different things, but he never got better for very long. He died after my own mother passed away.[36] Another of the boys, Ralph, died after that; now, the other one, Norman, is helping take care of Slim Woman. One of her daughters lives in Parker, Arizona. Another one, the one who was the mother of Leroy, passed away when her children were small, so Slim Woman raised Leroy and all of his brothers and sisters, too. The third girl, Bartine, was the mother of Charles Mitchell and many others.[37]

I don't see my half sister, Slim Woman, very often any more. I have trouble getting around now and she no longer comes to visit. She has trouble too; she can hardly see. But my other living sister, my real sister who is younger, does come to visit me, and my children visit with her and her children, too. My mother told us that this sister is the youngest; she was born after I was. I don't know if my mother lost any between me and my real younger sister, but I do know that after her, my mother had two more girls; each of them died right away.

My real younger sister, the youngest one in my family, is called 'Asdzáán Yázhí [Small Woman] by some people. She is also known as 'Asdzáán Hahóttʼizí [Woman at the Hard Ground Place] because the area where she has lived for a long time, right across the Nazlini Wash, is very hard. Other people call her 'Asdzáán Tsʼósí [Slim Woman], and in our family, some of my grandchildren call her Grandma Zhinii [Grandma Black].[38]

My real younger sister first married Hastiin Łaashi[39]; he was also called Kee Chee Tsosi. She was married to him for a very long time and had all her own children with him. Only four of her children are living now [1976]: her oldest daughter, Helen "Chee," Jennie, Elsie, and Tom Tsosi.[40] I know she and Hastiin Łaashi lost at least seven children; two boys, the oldest one who was a grown man and another one, and two girls died when that flu came and killed all the People. Two other girls, Bah and Esther, were struck by lightning in their teenage years while they were out herding sheep. I don't remember what happened to the other one they lost.

My younger sister's husband died when my daughter, Augusta, was small. She did not remarry for a very long time but finally, she did; she married Son of Yucca Fruit Man. That man was Ida's father; as I've already mentioned, Gai was married to him first and after she died, he married her younger sister, Chubby Woman. When she died in childbirth and left Eva, Samuel, and Bobby Hashkaan, and John Brown as small children, Eva came to live with us and Son of Yucca Fruit Man took the boys over to Small Woman's place. They were both widowed by then. My younger sister helped him raise those boys and eventually the two of them got married. When Son of Yucca Fruit Man died, my real younger sister did not remarry again.

These are the things I wanted to mention about the brothers and sisters I knew about, right here, before I go on with my story. Now you'll know who I'm talking about when I mention this one or that one. As for myself, I don't know exactly when I was born because my mother never told any of us those things. In her time, they didn't write anything down. My mother had all her children at home so there were no records for any of us. I do remember the few things she told me about my own birth. She said I was born a number of years after the Long Walk, and after she had already had lots of children for my father, Man Who Shouts. The family was moving around with their animals, like they always did. When I was born, they were all living over around Steamboat. The only other thing she ever told me was that it was wintertime when that happened, when I was born.[41]

I don't know what people called me when I was small, but usually children were known by their parents' name. So, I probably was just called Tall Woman's Daughter, Man Who Shouts' Daughter. After I grew up, I became known as *'Asdzáán Nééz* [Tall Woman]; that was one of my mother's names, too, as I've mentioned. I guess they called me that because when I reached adulthood and started having my own children, I was very tall and heavyset. But now, old age has made me smaller; people shrink from old age when they get up in their years.[42]

In My Very Early Days

3

Early childhood memories . . . clothing . . . food . . . starting to herd.

I don't remember anything about when I was born or what happened in my first few years of life. Of course, that's natural; no one remembers those things.* My mother told me that our family was moving around even then; they were spending the winter over near Steamboat when I was born, and when spring came, they started moving back this way. My family did that all the time, and so did others. At that time, all the People were moving about; there were no fences and no one was really settled down in one place like we are today.

Now I hardly remember my very early days; they seem so long ago. I do remember some things, though; my mother also told me about other things that happened, when I asked her about them later in my life. So I will mention here what I know about those times, before I started living with this man here, my husband.

In my very early days, we never lived in one spot for any length of time; we just roamed about from place to place, and from time to time [see Map 2]. See that Black Mountain range over there? We had relatives living there on one side, and we used to go over and live with them, or near them during the wintertime; I remember we did that often. There were a number of places we lived in the Black Mountain area; sometimes we spent the winter closer to Salina Springs, or at a place called Salty Water, or in other places. My mother said we also moved to the Keams Canyon area; I don't remember that, but she said for two winters we were over there, instead of in the Black Mountain area. We moved around like that the whole time I was growing up and even after I became a young woman and started raising my own children. It wasn't until after my father died that we stopped moving back and forth, over there in the Black Mountain area in the winter, and then here, in the Chinle Valley and over in the Fluted Rock Mountains in the summertime.

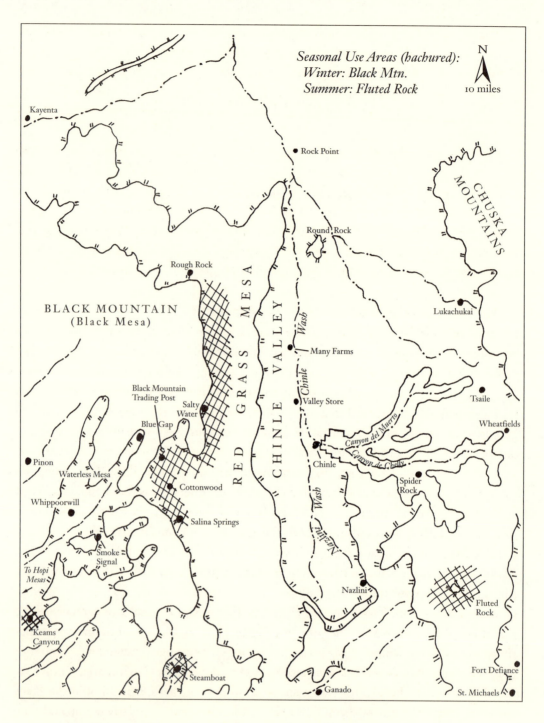

MAP 2 *Locations and Pastoral Cycle during Tall Woman's Childhood*

One of the reasons we went to Black Mountain was that when I was very small, my father, Man Who Shouts, was already learning *Hózhǫ́ǫ́jí* [Blessingway].[1] He had several teachers for that, and he used to go and spend four or five days at a time with one or another of them in the summer, and then come back here with us. Sometimes, during the winter, all of us moved over there with him because some of those men were also our relatives.

My father learned most of his Blessingway Ceremony from one of his own clan relatives, another Bitter Water person who was called *Diné T'ohi* [Tobacco Man].[2] He used to go over to his place and spend a few days before coming back home. Then he'd go back over there again for another four or five days, whenever he was ready. That's how he learned from Tobacco Man. But after Tobacco Man made the *jish* [medicine bundle] for my father and he started to practice on his own, my father decided his *jish* should be kept in the Towering House clan, my mother's clan, in the future.

My father had other teachers for the Blessingway, too. That is our custom; medicine people learn different things about the ceremonies from different singers. One of my father's other teachers was my mother's older brother, Small Man. He would visit us during the summertime and then ask us to come and live with him during the winter. So, sometimes we'd do that when I was very small; when we were ready to move back across to that area, we'd go to his place, way, way back behind the Black Mountain, out toward Salina.[3] Small Man had built several large, forked-stick hogans at his place;[4] when we went there for the winter, we would move into one of them and live there. It was a really nice place; he built it so it was away from all the cold. Even the sheep were sheltered because he made his corral in a place where they could get out of the blizzards. When we moved over there to stay with him, my father and mother took all their sheep and goats with us, and put them in with my mother's brother's sheep. We had a huge flock because both my mother and father had lots of animals. When we combined those with my uncle's over there at his winter place, it was the biggest flock I had ever seen.*

Sometimes in the winter, we would go and live with another relative, Towering House Man. He was one of my mother's mother's brothers, an uncle of my mother's. He lived near Small Man, and my father was also learning some things about Blessingway from him, because he, too, was a Blessingway singer.

Once, while my father was learning, my mother went with him way, way back on the other side of the main Black Mountain, where some other relatives lived. My father went over there many times in the summer to get together with other medicine men. Some of them were learning Blessingway; others already knew that and other ceremonies, too, so they were teaching those things to these men who were learning. My mother only went there with my father once; when she came back, she told me lots of different people had come together at that location. They all stayed over there for four or five days, and then went back to their families; that's what all those people were doing at that time. My mother said it was mainly men who were there; she never went there again. But we all went with my father when he was learning in the wintertime from Towering House Man and from Small Man. And in the summer, when he went to those men's hogans, sometimes my mother and some others in the family went along. I never did because I had to stay home and herd with my older sister.

When I was very small, we went through lots of hardships. My brothers and sisters and I barely had enough to eat and we had very little to live by. We were even barefoot most of the time. But we managed to get by. Now, nothing like that happens to any of my children and grandchildren around here. All of them can always have new shoes, stockings, anything they need. If it's a little old or has one hole in it, well then, they just throw it away and say it's no good. That's the way things are now. But when I was little, all of us suffered a lot from hunger. And, all we had to wear were garments made from that white cotton cloth.

In my childhood there were no trading posts near here; all I remember is my parents talking about the ones that had started at Ganado, Fort Defiance, and Round Rock.[5] None of those places were close to where we ever lived, either in the summer or the wintertime. So it took several days to go to those far, distant places and my father did not do that very often. The women in our family would weave rugs to be taken to Ganado and traded for the provisions we needed. That's where we got the white muslin cloth; then, it was the only kind of cloth we could get from those trading posts. Most of the time my mother, my sisters, and I would make our own skirts from that cloth; we used it just the way it was. My mother always reminded us that when she was our age, the only thing women had to wear were those woven dresses, *biil*. Sometimes, if my mother had commercial dyes on hand, we dyed the muslin some color, like black, red, yellow. In my early days, there were no different colored materials; even muslin was very scarce, at least in our family. After more white people came among us, they brought in different things for our use, and more trading posts were started in places closer to where we were living as we moved around. They had different kinds of material. But those cost a lot of money; usually our money was gone and we couldn't afford to buy any of those expensive things. So, even then, my mother kept trading for that white muslin cloth; that was the cheapest thing she could get at the store while I was growing up. Later, when things improved for my parents, my father would buy calico; from then on, we started wearing skirts like the ones I'm wearing now.

Most of the time we went barefoot, even in the winter. We had no shoes to wear. Sometimes, a few people were lucky enough to get buckskin; then they could make moccasins to wear. Otherwise, there were none. Today, of course, shoes are plentiful;

they are available and most people can afford them. When I was small, if we had any footwear at all, it was out of buckskin with a rawhide sole. That's all we wore, if we were lucky enough to have any.

As far back as I can remember, my older sisters and my mother had two pairs of moccasins each, which my father had made for them. To do that, he had to go hunting. I remember he would tell my mother that people were going hunting for deer and that he was going to go with them. They went on horseback, but I never knew where they went or who those men were that he used to hunt with. When I was small, I never saw any deer or buffalos, or other animals like that in the Chinle Valley. I know my parents used to talk about seeing buffalo around somewhere but I never heard them say what part of the reservation those animals used to roam around on. I know there must have been lots of deer somewhere because my father went hunting a lot and always came back with two of them.

My father told us there were two or three different ways to hunt deer, depending on what you planned to do with the deerskin or the meat.[6] He never explained that any further to me, so all I know is that he always took his rifle with him, and he always brought back deer. He was a very successful hunter.

First, my father would get out his hunting rifle; I remember that very well. He would make sure it was in working condition and then he'd saddle his horse and go off with those other men. They always hunted in a group. My father would get two deer in no time, and bring them back. Even though we had lots of sheep, every chance he got, he always went hunting for deer. The main reason he did that was because he wanted the skins. My father tanned the skins himself. Then he made his own moccasins, and some for others in the family—my mother, my brothers and sisters, and me, after I was old enough to be chasing the sheep around. He always tried to get as many moccasins out of those two skins as he could for his children and his wives.

My father used to make a kind of big, high moccasin for my older sisters and my mother that was called *kéntsaaí*; those were laced with buckskin all the way up the leg to the knees. He sewed those in two pieces, one on the back and the other, on the front. The skin on the back was left its natural color, but the one that was sewn on the front was dyed with natural red dye. The sole was made out of cowhide. Those knee-high moccasins, those wrap-around ones, have a purpose: they protect you all the time. They are warm in the wintertime when you're out herding the sheep in the snow. And, in the summertime, when you're out, they protect you, too. My older sisters and my mother had one pair like that and they wore them a lot. My father also made the regular moccasins, the low ones, out of deerskin; eventually he started making those for everyone in the family, and I got my first ones.[7]

When I was very little, I remember we all suffered from hunger. When my mother used to tell us about her childhood days and how they suffered from hunger, I used to think it was just the same with us. We went through lots of hardships and suffering; when I was very small, we were hungry lots of times. Food was scarce and we barely had enough to eat. That was before things started going well for my mother and father, and before they started raising crops here in the Chinle Valley. In those early times, we moved back and forth with our sheep; it was all open range then and there were no fences anywhere. The land was there for everyone's use and the People moved around, sharing the land. No one was permanently settled and no one thought any family owned any particular place.

All the People moved around with their animals, going up in the mountains in the summer where it was cooler than down in the open, in the valley. In the mountains, we could always find water and other things the sheep and goats needed. Then, in the fall, all the People would come back down from the mountains and go to other places for the winter.

In those days, we gathered a lot of what we ate. My mother and father told us those things had been put there for our use, and that we should learn how to use them for our food. They said we should pay attention to what was growing in different places as we were moving around. They also said to always look for tracks of different kinds of animals that might be around, here and there, because we could eat them, too.

When I was small, we ate rabbits a lot. I guess that was when my parents were just starting to build up our sheep. My mother cooked those rabbits whenever we'd catch them, and I've done that, too. I like to fix them as rabbit stew, with cornmeal in it so there's a thick or creamy gravy. Before we started farming, we didn't put anything else in there but later, we added potatoes, or other vegetables, with the corn to the rabbit meat.

There were lots of rabbits all around here; we saw them all the time when we were moving around, or back and forth between our summer and winter homes. In my mother's time, they used to hunt them with clubs or sticks; a whole group of people would do that together, by surrounding them. I think they still hunt rabbits that way, with those sticks, over in Hopi country. She said they also trapped rabbits.

When I was herding with my older sister, lots of times rabbits would get in among the sheep. Then one of us would come up behind them and kill them with a stick. We used to carry four or five sticks with us for that purpose. We'd haul those around in our packs, and if we were herding on a donkey or a horse, we'd pack those on them. Any kind of stick can be used, but it needs to be smooth. You don't want one that's full of splinters or one that crumbles up when you go to use it.

We also hunted prairie dogs; my sisters, other female relatives, and I always looked for those when we were out with the sheep. The easiest way to catch them is to use water if you have that available. One person pours some water into their hole while the other one stands there, ready to kill them with a stick, when they come out. We used the same sticks for those prairie dogs that we used on the rabbits.

Sometimes we also killed squirrels and chipmunks while we were herding. We'd do that mainly with sticks or clubs, but sometimes we just threw rocks and hit them. And every now and then, if any of the dogs we had in the family had gone herding with us, a dog might corner something like a badger, or even a porcupine. If that thing ended up dead, either because of the dogs or because we clubbed it, then we'd bring it home to use for food. Sometimes my father, my older brothers, or some of their children would bring those back from wherever they had gone, hunting deer or other things. My mother said they ate porcupines in her younger days, too, and she showed us how to prepare them. I don't know how many times I ate that when I was little, but it was very good. The meat under their spines is really good! All of us did those things; we gathered whatever we found while we were out herding sheep or traveling around for some other reason.

My mother also taught us about wild plants, where they grew, and how to gather them and fix them for our food. So we gathered lots of different kinds of things — nuts, berries, even wild plants with grains or seeds on them. We'd grind them and make our food that way. Even today, some people still gather some of those plants. Right here, you can see some of them growing around the edges of our cornfields.

Whenever they were available, all of us used to gather pinyon nuts. We all liked to eat them and my mother liked to cook meat with those nuts. She would shell them first; then she'd take a backbone from a sheep or some other animal, cut it up, and cook it with the pinyon nuts. That's called *haníigaii* [stew]. I never tried fixing that while I was raising my own family even though I saw my mother do it many times. Nowadays, we cook hominy with backbone meat for that stew; it's delicious.

One of the main plants we gathered in the summer was *tł'ohdeeí*. We used to gather it on top of that red mesa over there. When it had its grains on it, we'd pull the whole plant up and put it in a sack. Then we'd bring it home, grind it, and use it for food. Later, when we started growing corn, we'd mix it with corn; that has a very sweet flavor. Now, there's not much of that around here. The People stopped using it after they started cultivating fields and raising crops. Maybe that's why it doesn't grow any more. But when I was very small, the People gathered lots of wild plants and seeds for food; my mother knew all those things because in her time, the People used all of them for food, too. She taught us those things and so, in our family, we continued to do that, even after some other people stopped.

Another plant we used was *'ostse'*. That grew in lots of places. My mother taught us how to gather its seeds; you shell them with your hands, and then winnow them. Then you parch them over a hot fire. While they're still hot, you grind them up. Those seeds are very oily; you have to cultivate a taste for them because they're kind of bitter. My brothers and sisters and I really used to like them; we always used to lick the grinding stones after we finished grinding those seeds. My mother used to get after us for doing that when I was very small.* Even after we started raising crops, that 'ostse' continued to grow wild all around in our fields, and we continued to use it.[8]

Another plant we used was *haashch'é'édą́ą́'*. My mother told us to look for it while we were out herding. It was always plentiful in the Chinle Valley, but sometimes she'd take one of us and travel quite a distance, searching for it after its red berries had ripened. She and my father had eaten that in their young days, and it was one of their favorite foods.

There was another plant called *nááłtsoí*, "plant with the yellow eyes," that we used as one way of making cheese. That has purple flowers and gets yellow berries on it; we gathered the berries for making cheese, although my mother preferred to make cheese other ways. She told us that with those berries, the cheese crumbles; you can't slice it because it doesn't hold together well.[9]

We made cheese from goat's milk. We used their milk all the time when I was small because my parents had more goats than sheep, and we milked them every day. Most of the time we drank the milk. But sometimes, my mother would say it was time to make more cheese. Then we'd start saving the milk in a big container. When we had enough, we'd drop a piece of the small intestine of a young goat in there. Gradually, that made the cheese form. You let it stay there like that until all the water comes to the top. Then you pour off the water and you have the best cheese there is. Because all of us loved that cheese, whenever my parents butchered a baby goat or a lamb, they'd save that small part. Sometimes they'd get it from a newborn kid or lamb that died; other times they'd butcher just to get it. That part is called *'ats'ǫ'asis* ;[10] it's all ruffled and lots of people like to cook and eat it, either with blood sausage and other things, or by itself. We do that even now, because my husband really likes to eat that when I fix it for him. When I was very small, we'd always save that piece and dry it out for making cheese. Then, when we had enough goat's milk in our container, we'd drop it in there to make cheese.

We also used those goats for making water bags. When I was a little girl, there were no wells anywhere, no windmills. So, everyone had to dig to get water for their own use and for their animals. Later, when my father became one of the headmen, he organized the people who started to settle around us so they all made a ditch for that. But when I was small, we had to dig for water, and then haul it back to wherever we were living. That was before the stores came out here, and before we had buckets.

One of the things we carried water in was the skin of a young goat. My mother taught us how to prepare the skin for making one of those bags. You have to be very careful when you butcher, if you're going to make that. You cut the neck and then close it on that side. You butcher without cutting the belly. You have to skin down the legs; you cut just a little way on the legs, above the hoofs, and then take those off. Then you peel the skin off the rest of the body, leg by leg and inch by inch. It's hard work and it takes a long time to prepare skins that way; you can't just peel off the skin like you do with a sheep.

Those made good water containers and that's why we call it *tó 'abidí* [a water belly]. You can use either a young or full grown goat for making those. After you peel off the skin, you turn it inside out and scrub all the flesh clean with soapweed. When you finish doing that, the bag is waterproof. You tie the neck shut, and use string or rawhide to sew the opening there and the others around the limbs. When you fill it with water and close the neck opening, you have a big bag for carrying water. You can carry it on your back, or lay it across the horse's neck and bring it home that way. My mother used to prepare skins that way for us to use in bringing water home, and I've taught my children how to do that, too. But now, most people use buckets from the store. Making water belly bags is very hard work![11]

The other way we carried water when I was little was in those *tóshjeeh* [water jugs] that my mother and others used to make out of *k'ịị'* [sumac]. We used those sumac bushes for weaving baskets and different things, and then smeared them with pinyon pitch. My mother made those a lot; she learned that from her own mother, and she taught us how to make those, too. She always made them big and wide at the bottom, and narrow at the top, the neck part where the opening was. We braided horsehair to make handles for them, and she added those while she was making the basket. When she finished weaving it, she'd go and get lots and lots of pinyon and any smooth rocks she found. She'd always tell us to gather up any pebbles we saw while we were out herding, and bring them home for her. There were lots of those in the foothills and she used them when she made those water jugs.

After she had everything ready, she'd build a big fire and heat the pinyon up until the pitch started running out into some pottery container she had made for our use and put under there.[12] After she collected enough pitch that way, she'd boil it until it was almost burned. Then she put those smooth pebbles into the woven jug and poured the boiling pitch inside. Then, the water jug was rolled back and forth on pinyon boughs she had spread on the ground; she kept rolling it that way until all the holes in it were plugged with pitch. That smeared the boiling pitch all around, all over the inside, and plugged up all the holes. When it was finished, the pitch started oozing out on the outside. The pinyon pitch was what made the water jug waterproof.[13]

When we took those water jugs to get water, we'd fill them and then plug the opening with anything we could find to use for a stopper, like grass, weeds wrapped in cloth, or other things. Sometimes we'd carry those in our hands; other times, we'd put straps around our shoulders or our heads and bring those home. That way we would have water to use for a certain length of time; the big ones held lots of water.

When I was small and the People dug holes to get water, we never thought about sanitation. We drank any kind of water, and never paid any attention to whether it was good or bad. I imagine we swallowed lots of bad things with that water.* When you get water from near the surface, digging shallow holes like that, no doubt other things, like dogs, coyotes, and wild animals drink it, too. We paid no attention to that; that's the way we were in those days. Now, some of those shallow water holes have square boxes or rocks over them, like lids, to keep them covered. Now that water is clean; we know that no animals are getting into it.

We used to be careful about how we used our water because it was very scarce; we had to travel far and then dig deep for it. When I was small, my father dug a deep hole over on that hill across from here, across Chinle Wash, near the place we called *Kin Naaztí'í* [Houses Standing in a Line], where we lived many years later. We'd be sent over there to bring water back in those woven jugs and water bags, whenever we were living around here. Later, after lots of people started settling in this area and people began staying in one place more often, water became more available for our drinking and for use with our animals. My father and others put in a big ditch that ran all the way down this way. Then too, after the traders came to Chinle, they started selling buckets and other containers. Finally, my father bought several buckets and we children began using them. We'd take those to the big water hole he had made on the hill over there, or we'd go to a dry wash and dig a hole. Then, we tied a rope to our buckets, lowered them into the water, and drew it out that way. Whenever it rained, we also looked for running streams; if you put buckets in those, they filled up quickly. Sometimes, when we wanted to carry several full buckets, we'd braid horsetails and put one on each of those. Then we'd put a rope through the loops we made on the ends of the braids and carry them back home that way.

Once enough people had buckets, these woven water jugs and water belly bags went out of use. Eventually, the government started putting in wells and windmills. After those were established and lots of people had wagons, we'd take all our containers to those wells and windmills, and get all the water we needed. From then on, water was not hard to get. Now many people don't even know it used to be scarce and that it took lots of work to get it. But when I was small, there were no windmills and no buckets. Water was very scarce, and after we dug our own water holes, we had to carry it to wherever we were living in those woven jugs or those goatskin bags. That's how we managed then.

When I first started to remember things, we were moving back and forth, from the Fluted Rock area in the spring and summer, to different places over in the Black Mountain area in the wintertime. We didn't always return to the same place each time so my father would build us hogans to live in when we got to wherever we were going to settle for a while. Sometimes, he and my older brothers would build forked-stick hogans; other times, he made the round or many-sided, female kind, more like what you see around here now. It depended on how much wood was available in these different places and what other things were on hand that could be used in building our homes. In the summers, often we just stayed in these *chaha'oh*s [ramadas] that we still use; they gave us shelter from the sun but let the air come through from all the way around, and they provided all the protection we needed then. Later in his life, my father built other kinds of dwellings, too; at Houses Standing in a Line he used stones, and after that, when we moved over by the place with all the reeds, he built a log cabin as well as several round hogans. But that was later, not when I was a small girl.

When I first started to realize things, one of my older sisters and one of my older brothers were herding the sheep and goats my parents had. Together they had lots of animals, and we had a big flock that needed to be taken care of so they were the ones put in charge of that. My mother was home taking care of the small children, our home, and doing the cooking and other things. And my father was busy with the cows and horses he had, his other livestock, and also going hunting and other places. After he became a Blessingway singer, he would also be gone doing that for people when they needed him.

My mother told me that right after I started walking and running, before I was really old enough, I started trying to run after my older sister and brother who were herding. I just wanted to go with them.* Both of them always told me to stay home. When I'd start to run after them, my older brother would scold me and tell me to go back home; he said I was too little. In the winter, he'd tell me it was too cold for me to be out there with them. Sometimes they made me go back; other times, I ran away after them after they were out of sight.* Then, when I caught up with them, they'd let me stay and herd with them, until they brought the flock back.* Most of the time they herded sheep on foot.

My mother and father had a large number of sheep and goats when I was small; on my mother's side of the family there were a lot, and the same was true on my father's side. All the people in our family depended on those animals, so we had a lot to watch over. The goats they had were the real smooth kind, not the curly haired ones we have around here now. Some of them had short, white hair, and some had short, brown hair, but that hair was plain, not curly. My mother said those smooth ones produced more milk than the other kinds, and that goats of all kinds produced more milk than sheep. So even though she used sheep wool for her rugs, when I was a small child, our flock had many more goats in it than sheep; over half of them were goats. I guess another reason for that was that we used a lot of milk for our food and we made our own cheese with that goat intestine. And then, too, we used the goatskins for making those water belly bags. When I was very small, my mother and father used both the goats and sheep for meat, when we got hungry for mutton. My mother made blood sausage after we butchered, and used everything else from those animals, too. We kept those skins, and after drying them out, we used those to sleep on; those were our beds, just like some of us around here are still doing right now.[14]

Those goats were the ones that used to cause problems for my sister and me when we herded. After a while, my older brother turned that over to me, and I started herding all the time with that older sister of mine. In spite of all kinds of weather, we had to herd. Even in the winter, when the snow was deep, we had to herd and take care of the sheep. When I was very small, all of us were in good health. The other ones who were old enough to herd stayed home and helped my mother with the weaving while my older sister and I were out herding. The two of us were the only ones in the family responsible for that. She and I stuck together; all we ever did when I was small was herd sheep.[15]

What I learned right away was that once those goats got out in the open, they took off like jackrabbits or deer. And once they did that, the sheep would start following them, spreading out in all directions.* When that happened, my older sister and I would have to chase around after them, just like we were chasing a deer. Sometimes we'd get so worn out from trying to keep them together. It was so hard to get them back together once they went all over, after the goats did that.* But when you're herding, that's your job, to keep all the sheep and goats together so they aren't running all over the place and getting lost.

Water was very scarce in the summer when it didn't rain. Then we'd have to move the sheep; depending on where we were at the time, sometimes we'd take them toward the mountains; sometimes, we just went toward Canyon del Muerto from here. If you go far enough, you come to where there are some natural springs in the rocks. That's where we'd go with the sheep sometimes; then we'd take a water belly bag or a woven water jug and get water out of those springs for them. But sometimes the only water we could find would be inside one of the caves in the Canyon. It'd be too hard to try and get the sheep in there, so my sister or I would go, get the water out, and haul it back down to where the sheep waited.

Sometimes when we herded, my parents let us use a donkey. They always tried to have two of them around, and sometimes if one of those was not needed for some other purpose, they told us we could ride it. When I was small, I never rode alone; I always sat behind my sister, riding double with her. When I got older, if both donkeys were available, each of us would ride one. It was mainly in the summertime, when the weather got very hot, that they might let us use a donkey for herding. The donkeys my parents had when I got a little older didn't seem to mind hauling both of us around, riding double on one of them, even though I was a little bigger.

My father had horses, too, when I was small, but we never used those for herding; I was too small to crawl up on their backs.* After I got older, we were allowed to use the horses and finally, they said I was old enough to start riding horses alone. When that happened, my father used to tell my older sister and me to get two horses and take the sheep to where there was water. Sometimes, he'd ask us to drive his horses to the water hole on foot, and we'd do that, too. And sometimes my older sister took those horses to the water place all alone. But even after I was allowed to ride horses, the animals I rode most of the time were donkeys; they were more gentle and I never had a hard time crawling on their backs.* So I always preferred to ride one of them when I was herding.

One of the things I barely remember from when I was very small, right after I had started herding with my older sister, was being somewhere in the mountains. It was summer, and we were some place that was like a jungle, where the trees all around me were huge.* When I got a little older, I asked my mother about it. She told me that what I was describing was the timbers at a place up in the mountains around Fluted Rock where we spent many of our summers.* Even when I was a baby, they would go there with the sheep, so I guess I was there a lot with my mother.

I used to be very scared whenever we'd go up there after I realized we were in the mountains. I was always afraid to go away from our home there. When we'd get over there and my older sister would ask me to come help her herd, I didn't want to do that. Instead, I would start crying. I don't know why now, but then, those trees just looked so big; it was like a huge jungle all around me, from where I was standing and looking up. I guess everything scared me because it was so big.* The first time I remember being there I refused to go herding sheep with my sister; I was too afraid to go away from our hogan there so I just stayed right around the place. The next time we took the sheep over there, the next summer, I was still afraid. But from then on, I did go and herd around there with my older sister. Then I found out that she was afraid, too.

The reason I think we were both afraid was that we had to herd on foot over there in the mountains. It wouldn't have been so bad if we could have had the donkeys or horses to ride. But I was too small to crawl on the horse's back, even behind my sister, and those two donkeys we used for herding at other times out in the open were getting old and mean. Every time we tried to saddle them up, they'd bite and kick us.* That made my father worry about them hurting us when we were out herding. So he told us not to use them any more. He said, "Just walk, just go on foot while you herd the sheep here." Then he penned up those donkeys up there in the mountains. Nobody used them for anything because they were so mean. They even tried to bite and kick older people in the family, anytime anyone went near them. I guess they were just tired.* That's the way donkeys are; they get tired and they kick and get stubborn. I think that was one reason why I was so scared about getting out to help herd the sheep while we were there at our summer home.

Then too, my sister and I knew there were many things in that place that could come out and grab us from behind the trees, or the bushes. It was like a jungle all around us there, and both of us were scared to go out and walk around, watching the sheep. My father had come across some tracks, fresh bear tracks, around where we were living. I guess that's what *really* scared both of us. He told us that lots of times when bears got hungry, they'd attack sheep. I think that was the main reason why my sister and I were so scared. We stayed close to our hogan; we never went too far out into those woods with the sheep while we were at that place.

One time when the two of us were herding, the dogs we had that helped us herd had followed us. They were big dogs and this time that I'm talking about, in my very early days at this place, those dogs started barking and howling, and carrying on when they were near us. I guess they smelled a bear, even though it was somewhere off in the distance. They must have come across bear tracks or a place where bears had been lying. They probably smelled the odor the bears had left and that's why they started barking and barking. My sister and I looked around but we saw nothing. But even though it seemed like there was nothing around, the dogs kept barking.

So when we got home that day, my older sister told my father about the way the dogs were carrying on while we were herding. She told him where we had gone and that even though we had looked all around, we didn't see signs of anything. But despite that, the dogs kept barking and barking. The first thing my father told us was that it was that thing that roams the mountain. That's the bears.* That's the way he put it, "the thing that roams the mountain." And my sister and I didn't know what he was talking about. So she asked, "What is that?" I guess my father didn't want to say *shash* [bear] so the next time he said it was those people, those men who roam the mountains.[16] We still didn't understand, so she asked again. This time he didn't say anything. And so she repeated her question; finally he said, "It's a bear." Then, we were really scared; that *really* scared us.*

Then my father said that besides bears, there were other things up there in those mountains, like coyotes, wolves, mountain lions, and other animals. But he told us that as long as we didn't bother them, and as long as they weren't hungry, they wouldn't attack or do anything like that. He also said we should never use the word *shash* when we were angry at the sheep or anything else, or for any reason in the future. He told us not to use that word when we were out herding because the bears would hear us and be offended. He said we shouldn't be scared of them. "As long as you're not scared of them, and as long as they're not hungry, they're not going to do anything to you or our sheep." That's what he told us right there. But, who wouldn't be scared when they were told about all those things roaming around up there in the mountains? That made both of us even more scared.* And so, even though my father told us not to be afraid, my sister and I were still very scared about herding the sheep every time we went up there in those mountains in the summer.

Starting to Get Older

4

Later childhood . . . my father's peach trees . . . starting to plant corn and other things . . . seeing white people . . . trading with Hopis . . . weaving . . . trading at Ganado.

During my childhood times, we kept returning to Fluted Rock in the summer. We'd always go across from Black Mountain and take the sheep up there to spend the summer. It's cooler there in the summertime and there was always plenty of grass for the sheep and goats to eat. There were no roads or anything like that in those days, and that was before any of the People had wagons.[1] So, when it was time to move with the sheep, we moved mostly on horseback. We'd pack everything on the horses my father had at that time. I remember one of my older brothers packing all the things we were going to move on the horses' backs. Then he'd take lots of them packed with those things over to wherever we were going to be staying for a while. The rest of us would follow, herding the other horses, donkeys, and all the sheep and goats. We used some of those horses to ride on when we were moving. My older sisters and I used to take turns taking care of the sheep when we were traveling along, moving to the different places we lived.

Later in the fall, usually sometime in October, we'd start moving back toward Black Mountain. My parents said it always snowed a lot in the Fluted Rock Mountains in the wintertime; if we didn't move, we'd be stuck in there for the whole winter. At that time, only one or two trading posts were established and none of them were close to Fluted Rock.

Sometimes when we were moving, we'd come through this area or near it, and maybe spend some time here before going on. At that time, the whole Chinle Valley was open range and the People were using the land as pasture for their animals. A bit later, some of them started planting different kinds of things here, like corn and beans. We weren't doing that when I first remember things, when I was very small; but after a few years, my father decided to start trying to grow some crops. I think that

41

was about the time when a few more trading posts were getting started right around here, and elsewhere in the Chinle Valley.[2]

After crossing through here with our animals, we'd go back to Black Mountain. Lots of times we went to a place we called *Tó díkʼǫ́ǫ́zh* [Salty Water], way, way back in there at the foot of the main, the original Black Mountain. We had a place there in a canyon where we spent many of our winter months when I was a child because there we were protected from the cold winds on all sides, and from the deep snow. My father built our hogan and the sheep corral back in there, underneath where some rocks jutted out, in a huge cavelike place. Even our sheep were protected from the cold winds and the snow in that nice place he fixed for them.

Then in the spring, we'd start moving back over to Fluted Rock, taking our sheep to spend the summer months up in the mountains. When the People were moving around like that with their animals, there were not too many permanent hogans. If we were at Fluted Rock, we'd be in a place where there was plenty of wood. Then my father and my older brothers would build two small, round hogans. We'd use one of those for ceremonies and live in the other. But in places where wood was scarce, he'd make the old kind, forked-stick hogans, and use those for everything, even for ceremonies.

Sometimes in the summer when we were at Fluted Rock, my mother and father would leave all of us at home with one of my older sisters while they went visiting in the Canyon[3] for a short time. My mother told us that lots of people were living down in there. She and my father knew some of them and visited them once in a while together. Most of the time, however, just one of them went into the Canyon for a short visit. When I was very small, I never went there; they never took any of us with them. Even when I got older, I never went into that place. All the years our family was moving around, we never lived in there. We just stayed up on the top, on the Fluted Rock Mountain, in the Black Mountain area, and in between those places. Since I never went there myself in those days, I don't know anything about how those people were living down in the bottom of the Canyon. I never started going there until later in my life, after I married my husband. Then I went there many times when the peaches were ripe.

My mother told me my father had a place down in the Canyon where he had lots of peach trees. It was way, way back in there, and he had all those fruit trees for many years. When they went there, they'd always bring up some peaches for us. We ate some, of course, but my mother dried most of them in the sun so we had them for our wintertime use.

When I was a little older, maybe around eight or ten, one time my father and mother went down there hoping some of the peaches would be ready. But when they got there, there were no peaches left on the trees; the People who lived down there had already taken them. My mother told me my father got very upset about that; he started looking around under the peach trees and saw lots of footprints, all over the ground. It looked like the People who lived there had just gone back in there and helped themselves to all his peaches. My mother told me he got very angry; he started cussing everybody out and yelling, "*Ch'įįdii! Ch'įįdiitah deeyá Tséyi'niis!*" ["Go to Hell, you Canyon dwellers."*][4]

After he discovered the peaches were gone, they went and talked with a lot of the People who lived near there. For a while after that, no one bothered his trees. But later, that started happening again. Every time he and my mother went down there to get our peaches, there'd be none on the trees. The People who lived around there, or others who came through that area with their animals, had helped themselves to the fruit. Of course, the trees were standing right out in the open; they weren't fenced. In those days, no one had started fencing anything.

Even though he talked to the People again, that kept happening. Every time one of them went down there to check on the trees, there were no peaches left. So finally, my father decided to forget about those peaches, to give up on them. I remember hearing him talking about that with my mother. He decided it'd be better to forget those trees, and instead, try planting some crops here in the Chinle Valley area. He wanted to start working up the land, farming it, and getting something out of it that way. That would be better than having those peach trees when everybody down in the Canyon was stealing the fruit. So after that, they never went back down there to check on the trees. I guess the People who lived there just helped themselves to everything after that. Then gradually, the trees got old and died. Peach trees are like that; you have to replant them at the right time, or that's the end of them. So that was how our fruit trees down in the Canyon came to an end, and that's when my father decided to start farming.

From then on, in the early spring when we were moving from the Black Mountain area over to Fluted Rock and passing through this area, crossing the Chinle Valley, we'd stop and my father would do some planting. In the beginning, we all stayed here while he prepared the ground and then planted some seeds. At first, he raised only a few things—some squash, beans, and corn. Later, when different kinds of seeds became available, we started growing other things, too, like watermelons and other kinds of melons, peppers, potatoes, onions, carrots, and other things. He even tried raising alfalfa later, but eventually a flood ruined that.[5]

My older brothers helped my father with the planting in those days. When that was finished, we all moved on with our sheep, up to Fluted Rock. After a month or two had passed, my father would come back down here to the Chinle Valley on horseback to check on the crops. I guess he wanted to see that nobody was getting into the fields with their sheep or horses. The fields people were starting to plant were all just out in the open. At that time, there weren't as many horses around here as there were later.

People took good care of the animals they had and most of the horses were out on the mesa, or way up in the mountains. Some of those were even wild; they didn't come down to this Valley and get into the cornfields or anything like that.

Once the plants started coming up, my father would tell my older brothers to saddle horses and go down to the Valley with him to hoe the weeds out from the crops. Just my father and my older brothers went down to do that. The rest of us were told that every so many days we should bring food down to them. And so, that's what we did. All the women and girls stayed up there in the mountains with the sheep. Every now and then, one of my brothers who had stayed behind would ride down there to check on them and see how their food supply was. If they needed more food, then several of the boys would come back to get the food we had fixed for them, like mutton and other things. They'd take that back and then stay there, helping hoe weeds and do other work. When that was finished, they all came back to the mountains.

After that, my father would go back down there by himself once in a while to see how soon it would be before the corn would be ready to harvest. As soon as the corn got ripe, he'd take my brothers back down there, and sometimes one or two of my older sisters, too, to help gather the corn and other things. Some of it would be brought back up to the mountains where we were with the sheep, for our use in making different kinds of food, like kneeldown bread and tamales. We'd also start grinding some of the corn to have cornmeal ready to use while we were moving again. Some of those things were also left right there, stored in big holes or pits we dug in the ground for that purpose.[6] We always left some melons, corn, and other vegetables stored in the ground so there'd be some food ready for our use when we returned. Sometimes, my father also dug other pits for storing wood to use for our cooking fires when we came back. He'd do that in the Black Mountain area, too, if we had anything to put away for later use, when it was time to move back in the spring. The rest of the crops that were harvested were put into sacks to be hauled back by the donkeys and horses. When everything had been harvested, when all of that was done and everything was put away, then we'd all help load the donkeys and horses. Once everything was packed up, we'd start moving back across the Chinle Valley with our animals to wherever we were going in the Black Mountain area.

Sometimes in the summer, when my father came back up to where we were living in the mountains, he'd tell us he had seen a *Bilagáana* [white person] coming through the Chinle Valley while he was checking on his crops.[7] Every now and then, one or two of them would come along on horseback, leading a pack horse. These people would stop at the little ramada he had built there near the fields for his own use, and try and talk with him.*[8] Then they'd go on. My father never said what their purpose was. Up there in the mountains, we never saw any white people; none of the women ever got a chance to talk with any of them.

It was a few years after my father started seeing white people that my older sisters and I saw them for the first time. We were out herding in the Chinle Valley when the family was moving across through that area. The first time that happened, we were afraid of them.* A few men were coming through the Valley; each of them was riding one horse and leading another with lots of things packed on it. We didn't know what they were doing. They were just all full of hair, and their beards were *big*.* That scared us and we told our parents about it when we brought the sheep in. My mother and father didn't know what they were doing, either. Maybe they were trading, but I don't think so. Some of the People said those white people were spies or something like that.

The others who traveled through the Valley in those days were Indians who came to trade with us. I remember that very well from my childhood days, and my mother told us that had been going on for a very long time, even before I was born. She told us to get to know those people and learn how to exchange things with them because that would be important to us in the future. She was right about that; my husband and I continued doing that for many years; even now, once in a while one of those people comes by with something to trade with our family.

The only ones who used to come around while I was growing up were Hopi Indians; my father and mother knew some of them, and they'd come to trade with my parents and some of my other relatives who lived near us. Those Hopis always came on donkeys; they'd ride some and pack others full of things they wanted to trade. Those donkeys hauled sacks and sacks of ground cornmeal and stacks of bread that was already made. The Hopis would load all those sacks on their donkeys, drive them over to where we were, and trade.

Most of the time they'd bring ears of corn from their fields, whole shelled corn, cornmeal that was already ground, and different types of bread they had already fixed. Some was their blue bread, but they also brought bread they make in the ground that's like our *'alkaan*[9], and their paperbread, the one that's called piki bread. Those Hopis always wanted to trade those things for mutton. My mother and father were always glad to see them; they'd give them a sheep or goat in exchange for some cornmeal or ready-made bread. Most of the time the Hopis would butcher right at the place where we were living. Then they'd take the meat back to where they lived in villages on top of those mesas west of here. Sometimes they'd load the meat on their donkeys and start back the next day. Other times, they stayed for several days or even a week, and dried their meat before packing it and going back. The main thing they always traded was corn for meat.

We kept moving back and forth like that while I was a child. As I started to get older, I began to learn about some of our relatives. That's when I found out my father had another wife who was my mother's younger sister. One time when we spent the winter with Small Man while my father was still learning the Blessingway, a young girl was there who I had never seen. She was about five or six years older than me, and I asked my mother who she was. That's when I discovered I had a half sister from that other wife. My real younger sister had already been born by then and was starting to grow up. Soon after that, my mother lost two more babies, each time shortly after birth. Both of those were girls and as far as I know, those two were the last babies she ever had. At the same time, my older brothers were becoming men, and some of them were marrying women from Black Mountain and elsewhere and going to other places to live with their families. That is the custom among us.

My older sister and I kept herding the sheep all during my childhood years. When we came back home in the afternoon with the sheep, the first thing we did was grind something to use as our food. When I was very small, my mother and older sisters were the ones who did the grinding, fixing up the wild seeds or whatever else we had gathered to eat. In those days, food was scarce. But after we started growing corn, we always had that around; it became our main food. As soon as we brought the sheep back in the afternoon, my mother would tell my older sister and me to start grinding corn. We were never too lazy to do that; we didn't mind because we were used to that kind of life.* By then, I was starting to get older; I was old enough to use the grinding stones and I knew how to help fix corn for our food.

My mother showed all of us how to fix the corn in many different ways; we had different colored corn and there's different things you make from each. As soon as I was old enough, I started watching her do those things and trying to do them myself. Pretty soon all of us, even my younger sister, learned how to fix things for the whole family to eat. Some of the corn we made into cornmeal mush and then fixed that in different ways. Some of it we used for making different kinds of bread, like *náneeskaadí* [tortillas], fry bread, the big and small tamales, dumplings, paperbread, the corn cake we baked in the ground, that *'alkaan*, and other kinds. Some of it we fixed with meat for stew. We learned how to fix the blue, yellow, and white corn in many different ways. There are also some special foods that must be made when you have certain ceremonies, because they go with those. My mother started to show us how to do all those things.[10]

Even after trading posts were established around where we were living and flour became available from the stores, my mother didn't buy that very often. She preferred to use corn, and she had us grind it, day after day after day. We did lots of grinding after we came in with the sheep, because we used corn every day. Even later, after my mother started using flour now and then, she always mixed cornmeal in with it. She never made tortillas just out of flour; instead, she stretched the store-bought flour by adding ground corn.

I think another reason we started raising lots of corn was that it was important in my father's Blessingway. Its pollen is used ceremonially and when the time was right, we used to gather it for use in ceremonies and also around here, in our daily prayers. That's called *tádidíín* [corn pollen]; you gather it from the tassels when the time is right to shake off the pollen.

At night, after herding the sheep, we'd grind corn. All of us did that, including my mother, but at night, she was usually busy weaving, or taking care of the younger children who were around. She taught all of us to use the grinding stones. My father used to watch us; he'd tell us to grind it up real fine, and to make sure we fixed enough of it. He liked the foods my mother fixed, and he encouraged us to learn all those things from her. Some of them he even knew how to make himself; it was just like the weaving. He knew things about that, too, and later, when I was raising my own children, he taught my oldest daughter, Mary no. 1, lots of things about weaving. I, of course, instructed her in that too, by telling her to watch me. But my father actually showed her how to put up the loom and start making rugs.

After we fixed something to eat, we got out the wool my mother kept in sacks in our hogan. The wool had been sheared from our sheep. Every night, all of us would sit and work on the wool, carding and spinning it for the rugs my mother and older sisters were making. And so, in that way, we kept going along while I was growing up as a young girl.

In my family, in our time all of us—my mother, my older sisters, and the rest of us—did lots of weaving. That's about all we did; my older sister and I were always carding wool or weaving when we were not out herding sheep. My mother and my other older sisters stayed home weaving all the time. All my older sisters were very good weavers; that was about all they did. They stayed home, preparing the wool and then weaving rugs. Sometimes each of them would put up two looms. After they'd get the yarn and wool ready, they'd start on those and in no time, they'd be finished with the first one and started on the second. The other sisters sitting there would be preparing more wool for other looms that were going to be put up. There was no end to our work as far as carding the wool, spinning it, and then putting up the looms. The thing I guess my older sisters liked the best about it was that they'd always get a reward from it. When our rugs were ready, my father took them to the trader in Ganado and got lots of things, food and whatever else we needed, in exchange for them. That was the happiest part of it for my older sisters; I think that's why they were willing to do it all those years.

When I was a child, the trading post at Ganado, Hubbell's, was the store closest to where we were living, even though it was a great distance away from whatever areas we were moving around in with our sheep. When my father went over there, we always packed our rugs on two donkeys or horses; we didn't have a wagon or any other means of transportation, so we just used horses and donkeys for hauling things to

Hubbell's. He also took wool to Ganado after we sheared our sheep. We used to have *lots* of it; after we set aside what we needed at home for weaving, we'd pack the rest in big sacks to be taken to Hubbell's in the same way.

My mother and my older sisters never made only one or two rugs, and that was the way they taught me, too. I kept watching them weave while I worked on the wool, carding and spinning it at night, and after a while I started doing that, too. I, myself, liked to weave. Soon I started learning some of the different ways of doing it. Every time one of us finished a rug, we'd put it away and make another one. We made lots of them, some huge, some small. My older sisters were the main ones who made the big-sized ones. Two of them would team up on a big rug and work on it together. The smaller ones we all made were the single saddle blankets or the double saddle blankets.[11] We would make a whole pile of rugs. When we had made enough to load up two horses or two donkeys, we'd stop and pack up our rugs. Then we'd load them onto two donkeys or two horses, whichever were available, so my father could take them to Ganado and trade.

The trader over there was really nice to my parents and my older sisters. Whenever they went over there, they'd come back with *lots* of groceries and whatever else we needed here at home, like new blankets, quilts, and other things. When the horses or donkeys came back, you couldn't even tell it was those animals.* All over, in every little place available, things were tied onto them. All you saw in the distance was these big things, all covered with bundles.* You couldn't even tell where the horse or the donkey was.* It was just one big thing that came back, all packed with food and other things; it just looked like a great big bundle coming back.*

While I was growing up, flour was the main thing my parents bought at the store, and Hubbell's [see Fig. 1] was the only place they went.[12] That store was very far away and they didn't go there very often. So when they did, they bought lots of flour; sacks and sacks of it would be packed on the donkeys or horses, coming back. Now we have flour right here in the stores and it seems like nobody ever buys enough to have on hand. My parents never bought any lard from the store while I was growing up because we used animal fat. That came mainly from the sheep but if someone killed a cow, its fat would be saved for cooking, too. Nowadays, I don't know what kind of grease it is that people buy at the stores or where it comes from. Some people say it's not even animal fat in those cans. Around here, even now, most of the time we use animal fat instead of canned things, lard, shortening, or whatever you call it, when we make fry bread and other things.

The only place my family went to trade rugs for food was Ganado.[13] Until I was about ten, I never went with them; I was too little at first, and then later, I had to stay here and take care of the sheep and my little sister, while my mother and my older sisters went over there with my father. They always told me about what they saw each

FIG. 1. Wagons loaded with wool, in front of Hubbell's Trading Post, Ganado, Arizona, ca. 1906. Photographer, Joseph Amasa Munk. Courtesy of the Southwest Museum, Los Angeles. Photograph no. N.42457.

time they came back, so I already knew there were all kinds of things at that store. When I finally did go with them to see what the place was, when I first walked in there I wasn't too surprised. But then I came to where they had the flour sacks stacked all the way up to the ceiling, and all the blankets[14] and quilts piled up on shelves right to the top of the building. I just kept staring and staring at those; I couldn't believe there could be so much flour and so many blankets all in one place.*

The trader at Ganado was one of the Hubbells, Old Man Hubbell himself. He was so kind to us. He and my father used to be very good friends and that man was really nice to my father even when I was very little, before my father became one of the headmen among the People. Sometimes my father would go there without anything to trade, and with very little money to use in buying anything. That man would help him out with lots of things anyway. He was the nicest person we ever knew there. He always went out of his way to help the People. My father used to call him *Nák'ee Nezyeli* [Man with the Eyeglass]; I think all the People called that old man by this name.[15]

In those days our rugs always brought a good price. Nowadays [1970] it seems like rugs aren't worth anything. Despite all the work and time you put into making them, it seems like you don't get what they're worth. Because of that, some people say that it's not worth weaving anymore. But during my girlhood and even in my young adulthood, while I was raising my own family, to me it was always worth it. Even if we went to Ganado with only a few rugs, it always seemed to me like we came back with the whole store in exchange for our rugs.*

Of course, nowadays not too many people make lots of rugs to trade like we did in my time. Now, when women make a rug, it's just one; as soon as they're through, they run off to the trading post with it. If you go to the store with only one, you don't get very much for it. It takes a long time to make another one and between the time you trade one and finish the next, lots of people run out of food and other supplies. In my time, we never made just one. We kept weaving and putting each rug aside when we finished it, until each of us had made maybe fifteen or twenty. Then my father and others would take them to the trading post at Ganado all at one time. He had to go a very long distance when he traveled over there so he never did that until each of us had finished lots of rugs. That way we got lots of things in exchange for our rugs.

Of course, it's true that now the People don't have as many sheep and goats as in earlier times. All of those had to be cut back because of overgrazing. That's what we were told; that's what we were ordered to do after I had my last child, Isabel.[16] Before that, each family had lots of sheep and plenty of wool for themselves. There was also enough wool for some of it to be taken to the traders and exchanged for food and other things. But now, wool is scarce. Maybe that's another reason why there is less rug-making for trading now.

Old Man Hubbell always had a place for the People to stay when they came to his store from long distances, like from here in Chinle, or down in the Valley, or the Canyon, or other places. If they needed to stay overnight, he always furnished them with food, a place, and anything else he could to help them out. Then the next day, the people would do their trading. Sometimes they started back right after that, and sometimes they spent another night at Ganado before starting back early the next morning. Man with the Eyeglass always treated the People kindly. Even after my father got his wagon and went over there with all the rugs we had finished making, that old man would always tell him and whoever went with him to stay a few days before starting back. And so they did; they used the place he had there for that purpose.[17]

I guess that store was a good gathering place for all the Navajo people, too. After my father, Man Who Shouts, became recognized as a headman, he was quite well known. He used to go over there and visit with other leaders who came there, as well as whoever else happened to come in from other places.[18] My mother went with him most of the time then because she knew a lot of women from all those areas, too. We always felt that Hubbell's store at Ganado was the best one around; it was a good place to trade and do all your visiting at the same time, and that trader was always kind to all the People. Many people said they knew they would get a fair trade there for their wool, their sheep, horses or other animals, and for their rugs.

My father and mother went there more after he had a wagon; they'd haul our rugs over there and come back with the wagon loaded up with everything we needed. They said they saw that old man with many Navajos and that he was very kind and thoughtful to everybody, no matter who they were or where they came from. It seemed like he went out of his way to treat everybody alike, and to help the People all he could. That trader knew my father had another wife, my mother's younger sister. Sometimes he went there with both of them; they rode horses over there together. When my father went over there just with my mother and left his other wife behind, Man with the Eyeglass always asked about her and gave my father something to bring back for her. That old man knew lots of men had two wives at that time; almost everybody did because there was no law against it. Most of the time the wives were sisters or other relatives to each other. No matter who my father went over there with, Old Man Hubbell always asked him how many children he had now, with each wife. Then he'd put something in the sacks for each of my father's children. That's how nice he was. Everybody thought a lot of him and really liked him.

The People said that Man with the Eyeglass always gave them something extra during their trading. My father and mother, and my older sisters said that was true, too, even before I went there for the first time and saw that myself. Even though we gave him all the rugs we had finished weaving and traded on the basis of them, he'd always give us something extra, something we didn't pay for or trade anything for. He did that with all the People, not just us. He'd ask the women what they needed and then give them things like coffee pots, buckets, dishes and cups, big mixing pans, or other things to use around the hogan for cooking. That was one of the reasons all the People really liked him and went over there to trade, even though they had to travel long distances to do that. In my childhood and early adulthood, it seemed like *everybody* we knew went over there to Ganado. That was true even though there were a few other stores here and there around the reservation, like at Fort Defiance and then here in Chinle too, with the one Sam Day started, the one we now call the Thunderbird [see Fig. 2]. Even now, when the old people get together and talk about things, somebody always brings up Man with the Eyeglass and talks about how kind he was. He had a good reputation among the People.

FIG. 2. Sam Day's Trading Post, Chinle, Arizona, ca. 1902–3. Photographer, Ben Wittick. Courtesy of the Museum of New Mexico, Santa Fe. Negative no. 16032.

Late Girlhood and End of Childhood

5

*Farming and settlement patterns change . . . learning to use corn for food
. . . I begin to notice ceremonies . . . my father becomes a headman and gets
a new name . . . we hear about schools . . . becoming a woman . . .
my older sister's wedding to Jim Mitchell*

We continued moving back and forth across the Chinle Valley with our animals as I was getting older. Gradually my father started farming more areas here in the Chinle Valley. He'd get other relatives to help him prepare the ground and plant the seeds. With time, these others got interested in planting and trying to raise their own food, too. My father helped them and they helped him. With time, it seemed to me that the number of people who were moving around with us started getting larger.

A lot of my father's sons, my older brothers, were already married to different women by then, and had started having children. All those people were very close, like the old pioneers way back. It was just like one big family all the way down the line to another, and they stayed close together. My father was always really close with his sons, and later, with their sons, too. He'd always tell my brothers and their families to come and help plant corn and other things here in the Valley. Later, he'd get all of them to help hoe the weeds. Some of the children of my older sisters who I never knew helped with that, too.

As more and more people started planting in the Valley, the areas my father and our relatives were farming started spreading. Eventually those fields went from the other side of the place where they later built the first school in Chinle[1] all the way down, at least to Valley Store. They'd come and work up that whole area. Other families came too, from my mother's side and also my father's side. Some of them had married into our family; they came on horseback to help, before anyone out here had wagons.

Somebody in that group, I don't recall who it was, had gotten one of those plows from the tools the government was issuing to the People at Fort Defiance and a few other places where there were warehouses and some trading posts getting started. That plow made it possible to work lots of ground. So the People would round up all the horses that were available and bring them down to the Valley to use them in plowing up the land. When they were finished, they'd plant the whole area with different kinds of seeds. Then they'd go back home until it was time to hoe the weeds and later, harvest the crops.

My father was the one who came down from Fluted Rock to check on the fields everyone had planted. As more and more of the Valley started being planted, he'd bring others with him, like my older brothers' and older sisters' children, to check on the crops and see how much the plants had grown. Then he'd ride his horse to the homes of different ones and tell them the condition of their fields. If it was time to hoe weeds, he'd spread that news, too, and then come back to Fluted Rock to get some of the ones who were there with their animals to come and help.

The men started staying down in the Valley, close together, while they were working in the fields. They always helped each other, and stayed there until everything was finished, everybody was done planting, hoeing, or doing whatever else needed to be done. Different families planted in different areas and they would help each other. They never went back when just one area was finished; instead, they stayed and helped each other. That meant they were down in the Valley for long periods of time. They didn't go back to Fluted Rock or wherever else they were living in the summer with their animals until the whole Valley was planted, or hoed. The same was true when it was time to harvest. When the corn ripened, when the melons and other things were ready, the People always knew because my father was watching the crops. Then they all helped one another again with the harvest. All this time, those of us at Fluted Rock or in other places would go back and forth on horseback every few days, to check on their food supplies.

I think it was about this time that my father started thinking about how to get water one could depend on down in the area near his fields. After talking about it for a while with others, he started digging a small well on the little hill on the other side of the Chinle Wash from here. The Wash was closer to the hill when I was growing up than it is now; he always told all of us that whenever we needed water for the animals or our own use when we were herding, if we went near the banks of a wash and dug down only a few feet with any kind of stick, or even our hands, pretty soon water would come into that hole.

So he started digging in a few places along the banks of the Wash and getting water. Then my older sister and I could take the sheep there to drink when we were herding, while we were moving through here either to Fluted Rock or back across to Salty

Water or other places in the Black Mountain area. My older brothers used to take my father's horses there, too; when my older sister and I started being asked by my father to take care of some of the horses, we did the same thing.

At first, when he started digging holes along the Wash, on the other side, close to that hill, he did it alone. Every year when we'd move through here, he'd check on those places so we could use them as water holes for the animals. I guess the men hauled water for their own use from there, too, while they were planting and hoeing. After a while, the People who were planting in this Valley saw that this was a good idea for their sheep and horses. So, up and down the Valley, they started helping my father dig those holes.

About that time, one of my older brothers and my father started using a team of horses with a big scraper, an old tublike thing with a handle on it, to do the work. I don't remember where they got that thing, but they worked together when they used it. After hitching it up, they'd go around and around, taking off most of the top layer of dirt. They'd pull that thing so far, maybe fifty feet, before turning and coming back. In that way, they kept going deeper and deeper and it wasn't too long, too far down, before they hit water. When the water came up to the surface, it was more like a pond.

They started doing that along the Wash a little ways from where the Chinle Boarding School was finally built, on that side, and kept doing that all the way down, just a short distance from the Wash, beside where the main Wash runs. They took the scraper along there and made huge holes in the ground. Then water would come and fill them and people would have plenty of it. The People in this Valley at that time started helping my father and my older brother do that in order to get water for their livestock. Pretty soon, there was plenty of water beside the Wash all the way down for everybody to use for their animals while they were living around here, working in their fields or doing other things.[2] Later, when my father decided we were going to live in this area during the summertime instead of going to Fluted Rock, that's how the sheep and horses survived in the summer, when we didn't get enough rain. Of course, the horses and cows out in the mountains or on the mesa could find water at natural water holes, or crevices in the rocks where water stays when it rains, or at the places where there are natural springs.

When my father and my older brother were using the scraper to dig all those holes, that was *way before* the government sent those soil conservation people out here, that CCC or whatever it was called. Those people were the ones who started building reservoirs, dams at various places, little ponds, and other things so there'd be water for the livestock in areas near Black Mountain, across Snake Flat, and in other places. After they built those, when it rained water was caught in those places and held there for a while. But then some of them went completely dry after so many months, and again, the animals had no water. All those government projects happened a long time after my father did this; both he and my older brothers had passed away before those things started happening out here.[3]

After my father starting farming more ground and others began planting in different places in the Valley, he started talking about settling down in this area. Later, after he got a farm wagon from Fort Defiance, he went up in the mountains at Fluted Rock and started cutting timbers to use in building a hogan here in the Valley so we could be closer to the areas he was farming. Later, he also cut timbers for fences and others started doing that, too. And so, from then on, different ones in our family started building hogans around here in this area, and putting up a few fences. But nobody really worried about fencing where they were raising their crops until later, when many more people moved into this area and settled around here, too.[4]

I think it was around this time that my father decided to start raising alfalfa. Eventually he had a huge alfalfa field somewhere here in the Valley; I don't remember exactly where, but I know he was the only one who planted that here. The alfalfa grew very well for years; our relatives started cutting it with long knives, like scythes, tools they got from the government. The livestock liked to eat it in the winter; even my father used it for his horses. But then, after many years, one time early in the spring, it rained and rained. It rained so much that lots of water came out from the Canyon. It rushed down through this Valley and flooded out the whole area where my father had the alfalfa planted. That was the end of his alfalfa; he never tried raising it again, although my husband and I did, for many years, over near the Chinle Wash.

As we were going along like this, we planted more and more corn; it became our main food. As I got older, in my late girlhood, my mother started showing me how to make lots of different things out of corn; my older sisters already knew those things. Many of those foods depend on you grinding the corn into cornmeal first. Of course, nowadays, many people don't want to bother to do that; they just depend on store-bought flour. But back then, every afternoon, late, after my sister and I came back with the sheep, we'd grind corn for use in the evening meal.

We used to make various kinds of food from cornmeal. Some of those were tamales, *łeeh yilzhoozh* [big tamales] or *taajilehíí* [little tamales].[5] Both of those are made out of cornmeal mush and corn husks. You fix the mush first and then put it in the husks; then you tie those together with strips of corn husk and cook them. The little ones are boiled in water; the big ones are baked in the ground, or some other kind of oven.

When I got more grown up, my mother showed me how to make *tsé'ást'éí* [paper-bread], the really thin piki bread. To do that you need a flat rock that's smoothed all over to use as your grillstone. You have to find one of those first, and then bring it home and make it smooth. My mother used to go and get those stones; I don't know where she went because she always went by herself, somewhere in the Black Mountain area. She'd go way out there into the mountain and then bring back usually about two slabs of it. That was some special kind of stone, but I don't know exactly what. She'd fix the surface, chip a piece of that, grind it down until it was nice and round. Then she'd take some stones that had been made really smooth in the water and rub the top of it over and over. She sanded it that way, polished it until it was smooth. The top of the grillstone has to be perfect, as smooth as glass. Then she'd treat it with pitch by heating some of that on there and letting it cook into the surface. After it cooled off, it was ready to use.[6] My mother was the only one who ever went to get those stones. She'd fix those herself and that is what we used. Now, nobody knows where those rocks are; you have to have that grillstone if you're going to make really good paperbread.

When you finish fixing the grillstone and it's ready for use, you put it on hot coals and let it get hot. Then you take some cornmeal and make it into mush. After that's ready, you dip some out and with your bare hand, you spread it all over that hot rock. That's why that bread is called *Tsét'ees*, "stone cooked."

You have to practice and practice if you're going to learn to make that. The grill gets so hot that at first you can't touch it. But, if you keep practicing, after a while the palm of your hand gets used to it, and you don't feel the heat anymore. That's the hardest part, getting your hand used to the heat.* And then, the other thing is learning to put it on the grill evenly. After you've learned, you can put the batter on there quickly. You put it on in a thin plaster, really smoothly. You only go over that once, and you have to do it perfectly. If you don't move your hand right, it'll have lumps in it, here and there, and not come out right; in some places it'll be too cooked and the other places, not cooked enough.

When the bread is done, you take it off the griddle with a stick. You fold it up with that. We fixed all those sticks ourselves. You don't use the stirring sticks you use for making cornmeal mush for that; instead, you make a different one. For the paperbread, one end has to be flat, shovel-like. You use that end like a turner but you don't turn the paperbread over while it cooks. You use the flat end of the stick to loosen it, so you can roll it up. My mother always folded it this way [vertically] first, and then again, in half [horizontally]; she kept doing that, using the stick and folding it right over the stick itself. We used the smooth, round end of the stick for that. Those sticks get worn out quickly; after you first start using them, they shape themselves up nicely before too long. You can use the flat end of that stick for turning other things too, the ones that are more like pancakes.

That's how you make paperbread. My mother used to make it and she taught all of us how. Even my father learned to do that. Paperbread is delicious; everyone in our family really liked it and it was the same way with all the children I had. After I started raising my own family, I used to make that a lot because they all liked it, too. Now I haven't made it for some time. I had a flat stone I used for that; I got that over there and fixed it up, like my mother taught me when I was in my late girlhood. I think that stone is over in the cookshack; I haven't seen it for several years and I'm not sure where I left it. But I'd like to get it out and use it once more before putting it away for good. I haven't done that yet.[7]

There were other foods from corn that my mother taught us, too. When we raised blue corn there were certain ones made from that, like *bááh dootł'izhi* [blue bread] and also the blue cornmeal mush. With the white or yellow corn, there's the regular tortillas and *dah díníilghaazh* [fry bread].[8] That's the same thing, but you cook it in hot fat. Then, too, there's the one that's like a pancake; it's called *'abe'bee neezmasí* [literally, milk with it it gets round] because we made it with fresh goat's milk or sheep's milk. And there's also the cake we cook in the ground, the *'alkaan*. That's made out of regular cornmeal. It takes a lot of corn; you have to grind up lots to make even a small one. That's a lot of work, and nowadays, most people don't want to do that work anymore. So, you see, we learned to make many different kinds of things with corn; even cornbread was made in different shapes and fixed different ways.

As far back as I can remember, even when I was very, very small, we were having ceremonies at our hogan for somebody in the family. Sometimes they were small ones, a one-night prayer or something like that. Other times, they were big ones like five-night or nine-night ceremonies. It seemed like there was always something going on for somebody at our place. That was true even though my mother, my older sisters and brothers, and the rest of us were all in good health when I was in my girlhood.

After my father started practicing Blessingway on his own, after he finished learning, had that *jish* prepared for him and was blessed with that, he was always involved in helping others with those things. If someone in our family wasn't feeling well or was being bothered by bad dreams or something, he'd get people, like hand-tremblers or star-gazers, to help decide what was wrong and what should be done. Then, if it pertained to his Blessingway Ceremony, he'd do that himself for whoever needed something done. If it concerned something else, he'd go and get someone who was trained in that ceremony for the one who was sick. The only person he could not do his Blessingway for was my mother, and his other wife, too. He always told us his teachers said husbands could not sing over their wives; if they ignored that rule and did that, they would no longer be married to each other. Usually, when people came because they needed my father's ceremony, he'd go back with them, on horseback, to do it. But sometimes, people would ask if they could use one of our hogans for the ceremony he was going to do. When that happened, sometimes some of us would help out with different parts of it. In that way I guess all of us started to become familiar with some of the things involved in his Blessingway.

From the time we were little, we were instructed to offer a prayer to the east at dawn, and to take care of our sheep, the hogan, and other things according to what my father had been taught about the Blessingway, and to follow other restrictions, too. One of those was not to make fun of any of those things. We were told never to touch his medicine bundle, or fool around with the corn pollen, the deerskins, or other things. Those are sacred and have to be respected. They also told us never to make fun of the songs or prayers, never to play at that. We were not supposed to joke about any of the medicine people who knew the ceremonies or make fun of anyone who knew how to diagnose someone's illness. Making fun of any of those, or playing with those things, or in that way was not permitted. That's what they told us. I remember I did that once, and I think the rest of my brothers and sisters did, too. But both my mother and father scolded us for that. They said, "Those things are holy; you have to be very careful with those things, and respect them. Those things come from the Holy People. They have given us instructions to live by, and we have to respect them. Only people who have been trained in the proper use of those things can handle them in the right way." They said even little children were supposed to respect those things. Otherwise, bad things would happen to the whole family.

When I was small, my mother told me about my half sister, where she came from. She also told me that when her sister had that baby, a number of people had gone over there to where she was living, to try and help with that because that almost killed her. She said my father got some Yeibichei singers to help because of what he was told by the hand-tremblers. I think that was the first time I ever heard about a Nightway Ceremony, but of course, I didn't see what they did because that happened before I was born.

As I was growing up, I heard people talking about Enemyways they were planning to have for their relatives. No matter where we were living, they'd always come around and tell my parents about it and ask them to help, even if it was being held for a neighbor or a friend. So that was how I started hearing about the ceremonies called Enemyways; lots of times people just said "Squaw Dance," when talking about that. That's what many Navajos called them, even when I was small, just like they do now. So I knew there were things going on that were called Squaw Dances or Enemyways in my young days.[9] But I never went to one of those or any other kind of ceremony being held elsewhere when I was small. Of course, we all went to the ones that were held right here at home for somebody in our family, because we were all helping with them. And later, when we had an Enemyway Ceremony at our place for my older sister, when she was very sick and about to pass away, we all went to that.

My father was always asked to help out because people knew he had lots of sheep and goats. That was the main way he could help people when they were doing ceremonies. Of course, my mother would go and help with the cooking, and also take different types of food and other things to contribute, if those things were available around here. Sometimes my mother or my father would contribute two or three sheep, or they'd butcher here at home and take the meat over to where the ceremony was going on. Nowadays, we have lots of different kinds of food at the stores; you can help someone having a ceremony by just buying some groceries and taking them over to that place. But in my young days, we didn't have stores around here. All my father offered was mutton, meat for the People to use.

In those days, things were very different as far as children were concerned. In my time, my older sisters and I never went anywhere without permission. If we wanted to go somewhere and we were told no, then we stayed home. That's the way my mother and father raised all of us; we were not allowed to take off, just go anywhere. We also never went places by ourselves, without someone with us. While we were young and growing up, we were not permitted to do that. Now [1963] it seems like girls just run wild; they decide to go somewhere and just go, without anyone looking after them. That's especially true of school-aged children. They go all over to those Squaw Dances and other things. They go to gathering places where there are lots of people, even though that's dangerous with so many drunks running around. We try and talk to them about these things, but they don't seem to pay any attention to us; they just go ahead their own way, no matter what we say.

My father and my mother, both of them talked about these things a lot with my older sisters and me, as we were growing up. For myself, I remember they started talking about these things with me as soon as I was old enough to start going out away from home with my older sister to herd our sheep and goats. My parents used to tell me, "If it happens that a man should come up to you and start talking with you and asking you questions, always answer him. Do *not* hesitate to talk to anyone. You must always talk to a man, especially an old man. If you don't talk, don't answer, he may wish bad things on you. He may be a witch. Therefore, you must talk to anyone who starts talking to you. Even if you're out herding sheep, don't hesitate to answer, if someone comes along and starts talking to you and asking you questions." That was the way my father and mother instructed us all the time. They warned us not to hesitate to talk to anybody. If you did not speak up, that man would be liable to do something to you.[10] And so, we acted according to that. When we were out herding, lots of times men would come along looking for horses, cattle, or other animals. They'd ask us things, and one of us would always answer right away. We remembered what our parents had said about that.

My mother and father also told us to stay out of places where lots of people gathered. They said that many times, somewhere in those groups, there would be people who did harm to others, people who practiced witchcraft. It was for those reasons they didn't want us going all over to Enemyways, other ceremonies, or gatherings for other reasons. I didn't understand what they were talking about at first, when I was very small, but I followed their instructions. As I got older, I began to learn about those things. And, as each of us got older, my mother and my father started taking us places with them. Most of the time, whenever they went to an Enemyway or another ceremony, even if they were only going for a short time to contribute food to the People, they'd take one of us with them. Sometimes my older sister would go, and sometimes I was the one who would ride with my mother and father, either on my own horse or donkey, or sitting behind one of them. Of course, sometimes they'd go by themselves and stay there, helping out while we took care of things at home. But the whole time we were growing up, I never remember any of us going anywhere on our own accord or going anywhere alone.

While I was growing up, after I started realizing things and learning how to do things, I began noticing that my father was always talking with other people, men who I knew were called leaders in the areas where we were living. Then too, when we went to Hubbell's or other places, like ceremonies, people would ask my father to give talks about different things. My older sisters and I used to talk about this, wondering what it was about. Then too, it seemed to us that my father was gone more and more. For a while, all we knew was that he had to go here or there, to take care of something.

Finally, one time when he was gone again, one of us asked our mother about it. We were wondering where he was and why it seemed like he was not around much any more, like we were just there alone with our mother and other relatives, taking care of things. That was when my mother told us that he had been appointed to be one of those *naat'áaniis* [headmen][11] around here. That was why he had to travel around more, and people often came to wherever we were living to talk things over with him and to ask his advice. Sometimes, he had to go to places where the leaders gathered to discuss things that were going on in Navajo country and causing problems for the People. Sometimes, the problem just concerned one particular place or one group. Then my father would have to go and listen to the People involved in that and try and straighten things out, solve things like a family dispute or a problem over land. But other times, it seemed like the problem was happening all over the reservation. Those leaders had to go to Fort Defiance every now and then, to meet with the white officials there that Washington had put in charge of the Navajos after we were released from Fort Sumner. My mother told us the officials were called agents, and that there were agents all over, in different parts of the Navajo country. My father and others had to go and talk with them every now and then, to report on how things were going in places around the reservation. And sometimes, the leaders just went to see them on their own accord, when they felt a problem needed to be brought to the attention of those agents.

It was after my father started having that job as a leader that people started calling him *Hastiin Delawoshí* [Man Who Shouts]. From what my mother told me, I think he got that name because of his big, loud, deep voice. I guess the People in the Chinle Valley started calling him that because of what happened when it was time to irrigate all the fields they planted. In the early springtime, usually about April when the water came out from the Canyon, he'd saddle his horse and use the trail to go around to all the People living in the Valley, and tell them it was time to start irrigating. He rode along, yelling to all the People, "Let's go and start irrigating." And then, all the men would show up to start working on the irrigation ditch. All my father did was ride along on his horse, yelling, "Come on, let's go get the water, get the ditch ready and get the water going for the fields. It's time to get ready to plant." They'd make a plan to meet and each one would bring tools to help with that. After everybody showed up to help, he'd ride back and forth, supervising, telling them what to do and how to do it, how to make the ditch all the way down the line, and those that branched off from it. They all helped each other up and down the Valley. The same thing was true when it was time to plant. He'd ride along, yelling to the People, and then they'd show up with horses and whatever tools they had. Lots of times they'd gather at our hogans and start from there, and go down the Valley helping each other. All of us would butcher and make lots of fry bread to feed the People who came with their horses and tools to help. And then my father would ride around, supervising the planting. The whole time he'd be yelling in his loud voice, telling the People what to do. Every time he said something while they were working, he'd just yell.* My mother said that's why the People gave him that name. She said he even yelled like that when he gave talks to the People at ceremonies or other gatherings, or when he spoke in the meetings with other leaders, even with the agent. So that's how he got his name.

One of the things I remember hearing the People talk about while I was growing up was schools that were being started. I guess when we were released from Fort Sumner, our leaders agreed to putting Navajo children into school in the future. For a while, nothing was done about that. But then we heard that Washington was building a school in the Fort Defiance area and that children would be expected to go there, once it was open. Most of the People who were moving around with us at that time just ignored the news; they said it was only rumor. That place was too far away and we never heard much about what was going on over there, unless my father or mother went to Ganado or some place else where people were talking about those things. Then they'd come back and talk about it among themselves around here. Sometimes we'd hear what they were saying and then my older sisters and I would talk about it among ourselves. But we never really knew what "school" was, or what that meant, at least at first.

Later we heard the school at Fort Defiance had been opened and the agents were sending out police on horseback to locate children to enroll there. The stories we heard frightened us; I guess some children were snatched up and hauled over there because the policemen came across them while they were out herding, hauling water, or doing other things for the family. So, we started to hide ourselves in different places whenever we saw strangers coming toward where we were living. My father and mother knew we were doing that, but they didn't say anything to us about it right away.

Soon after those policemen started rounding children up like that, we heard there was trouble over at a place called Round Rock. My father had already been appointed as a leader for the People in this whole area by then, and I know he heard about it from lots of the other leaders, too. Many of them traveled over there to find out what that was all about. They weren't sure if those were just rumors or if something had really happened. When my father came back, he told us it was true that a man called Black Horse had caused trouble over there because of the way those policemen were stealing children for school.[12] He also told us that Washington had passed a law requiring us to go to school.[13] That was what was promised when we were released from captivity at Fort Sumner, and now Washington was going to enforce the promise our early leaders had made.

As far as my mother and father were concerned, they did not want any of us going to school. They objected strongly to it and they told all of us they did not want any of us going far away to some place like that for that purpose. They were opposed to those white agents who were sending policemen out to recruit children for school because they said lots of times, those children were taken away, without any notice to their parents. They told us to watch for those policemen and to try to hide ourselves if they came around where we were.

Not too long after they told us those things some policemen came, recruiting children for school when we were living over in the Black Mountain area but more toward Salina. Those men came, and after a while, they went into our hogan and talked with my father and mother. My oldest sister was there at the time, too, with her children. They talked a long time, and kept asking my father and mother to enroll some children in school. Finally, it was agreed that my niece, my oldest sister's daughter, would be the one from our family to go to school. I guess that oldest sister of mine was not totally opposed to that like my parents were.

After those men left, I asked my mother and father if I could be allowed to go with my niece to the school at Fort Defiance. But both of them said, "No." Right away they told me, "If you went over there, there would be no one around here to tend to the sheep." Because my mother and father had lots of sheep, a big flock, they were depending on me to stay home and take care of those animals. That's why my parents objected to me going to school. They said, "Who will herd if you go over there? Just let your niece do that." I even cried to go with her, but they refused me.[14] That's why I never went to school.

I guess some others in our family also asked if they could be enrolled in school, too, after they heard my niece had been recruited to go there. But every time my parents were asked, they both said, "No, we need you here to take care of the sheep or the horses, or other things." That was their excuse for not wanting any of us to go to school. And now, look at me; I never went to school because my parents didn't want their own children going there. But now, what has happened? I don't have many sheep left to herd at all anymore.

A lot of my older sisters were much older than me so they grew up before I came to realize things. Because of that, I don't remember the ceremonies held for them when they became young women; I was too small and they were much older, too far ahead of me, for me to remember any of that clearly. That was before my time, before I began to realize things, so I can't tell you anything about those. But I do remember my older sister's *Kinaaldá* because she was the one I herded with all during my young days. When she became a *kinaaldá*, I remember we had lots of corn available, so we made the cake, the *'alkaan*. My father was already practicing as a Blessingway singer by then, and so, of course, he sang that ceremony for her. He knew how to do that, and could lead off with the Hogan Songs, just like my husband does now. Of course, on an occasion like that, all are welcome. Anyone wishing to sing their songs at a *Kinaaldá* is welcome to come and contribute them. When they help like that, by contributing their Blessingway songs during the night, then they receive a piece of the *'alkaan*. I remember during hers, many people came to our hogan to help. My father was the main singer for the final night; he was leading it. After he finished the Hogan Songs, then others who knew Blessingway songs took over and contributed what they knew. That way, the songs went on all night until dawn, when her hair was washed and she ran her last race. I remember we all helped with that, and I remember running with her when she raced.

Some time after this older sister of mine became a *kinaaldá*, that happened to me, too. I don't remember how old I was but I believe that in my young days, girls were older when they became *kinaaldá* than they are now. At present, some girls become young women when they are ten, eleven, or fourteen. But in my girlhood days, we were older when this happened. I think my older sister was older than that, and I was older than that when we became young women, but of course, I don't know for sure.

I remember it was wintertime when I became a *kinaaldá*. At that time we were making our winter home at Salina Springs Mesa, and the snow was already about three feet deep when that happened. We still had lots of corn available for our use, so we went to work and ground corn for the *'alkaan*. I know my father was the main singer, and we made the cake we cook in the ground during the final night. I remember we cleared away the snow so we could dig the pit for my cake.* After my father had finished the Hogan Songs, then he gave others a chance to sing their Blessingway songs. Lots of people came to contribute their songs and to help in other ways. I don't know how many songs were sung that night, but they lasted all night long until dawn. And then the singing was turned back to my father because he was the leader, the main one conducting the ceremony for me.

Of course, when dawn appeared, it was time for me to wash my hair and so I did. Even though it was wintertime and it was bitter cold, I still had to do it. My ears, especially my ears, were almost frozen by that.* After that, I ran my last race and others ran with me, in the snow. When we returned, the cake was cut up and distributed to the singers who had helped. Of course, my father was included in that; he was given part of my cake. The other daughter he had by his other wife, my half sister Slim Woman, also came over to our hogan for that. She got a piece of the cake my father had received and took that back to her family on horseback.

So that was what happened at my first *Kinaaldá*; that was the first ceremony ever done for me. As I've already mentioned, all of us were in good health during my girlhood years. In the early days, there were many things you were told not to do when you were in that condition, when you became a *kinaaldá*. One of those restrictions was never to lie down all curled up; they said that would make me humpbacked. I was supposed to lie flat with outstretched limbs, and not use any pillows. I was also told not to eat anything sweet, anything with any kind of seasoning, or anything hot. If I ate things like that, my teeth would cause problems and my flesh would become wrinkled before my time. That's what they always said. But, even though I observed all the restrictions during my ceremony, I still had trouble with my teeth later in life; I got an awful tooth sickness that almost killed me.

Now those things are not observed very much. The People don't bother to tell girls about these things anymore. A *kinaaldá* girl just goes ahead with her business like at any other time because now nobody pays any attention to those restrictions. The girls eat candy and other sweet things; it's no wonder their teeth get decayed and they lose them later in life. In my youth, even our coffee was drunk unsweetened.

After my first *Kinaaldá*, we stayed at our winter place there at Salina Springs Mesa. When spring came, we started back across with our sheep. At that time, our cornfields were on the west side of Nazlini Wash, here in the Chinle Valley. When we reached that place, we stopped and planted our fields, before we moved on to our summer location in the mountains. That was one of the last times we went to Fluted Rock because my father was already talking about settling here in the Valley in the summertime by his fields.

After we went back to the mountains, my second *Kinaaldá* happened. This time we had no corn for the cake. So my mother and father decided we would give goods from the trading post to those who helped. My father went and got lots of material, like calicoes and other things. And that's what I did; because we had no corn, I had no cake.

Instead, I gave different kinds of material to the singers who participated in the final night of my second ceremony. My father did that again for me; once again, he was the main singer in charge. Again, lots of people came to help and their songs lasted all night, after he finished leading off with the Hogan Songs. Since my father was a Blessingway singer, we never had to ask anyone else to do those things for us. He was already trained to do that, so of course, we asked him.

When my second *Kinaaldá* was over, of course that was it. Right there, my girlhood ended; that's when I became a young woman. It's customary to have this ceremony only twice for a girl. People still observe this today, and try to have two for a daughter who becomes a woman. There's no change in the way that ceremony is conducted now as far as I know, except for what I've already mentioned: lots of people ignore all the restrictions we had to follow in my young days when we were in that condition.

After my second *Kinaaldá*, I went back to what I was always doing while I was a young girl; I continued herding the sheep and goats with my older sister, like before. I don't remember how many years passed from then until that man came asking to marry her. We just kept herding sheep, grinding corn, and working on the wool for my mother. By then, I was carrying wool around while we herded, and she was carding it as we followed the sheep, whenever we sat down while they grazed. That was our job and we worked on the wool that way, especially in the summer when the weather was warm like it is now [July 1963]. My older sister carded; then, when we brought the sheep in, late in the afternoon, my mother would ask us to spin the wool into yarn. Sometimes we did that after we ground corn for our evening meal; sometimes we did it later in the evening. My mother kept weaving, and sometimes we'd weave, too, at night, after we finished spinning. We just kept making rugs for my father and others to take to Hubbell's, to trade for food and whatever else we needed.

That store was still far away and my parents didn't go there very often. In those days, we didn't have any fast transportation. We still only had horses, and they were not always very strong. Sometimes they were not in condition to withstand trips to long distances, like Ganado. At that time, it took a long time to get there, especially leading the donkeys or other horses packed with our rugs, wool, and whatever else we were going to trade. It would be two or three days most of the time before anybody came back home from there with food for us. So, those of us who stayed here had to make the best out of whatever was left around home in the meantime. Even after I became a young woman, lots of times we barely had enough to eat. That's the way we were raised; all of us had to endure a lot of hardships and sometimes it was very hard to get by. But my mother taught us that if we kept weaving, if we were good weavers, we could manage to live by that. And so, that's what we did. Later, of course, the stores came closer to where we were living. But even then, it was not always easy to get food. You had to have something to trade for it. Once in a while, after other stores were established, one of us would make one or two small rugs and go to one of the stores around here to trade for food when we barely had enough to eat again.

After some more time passed, I don't know how many years, my older sister, the one I herded with, got married in the Navajo way. For a wedding, it's our custom to eat out of a basket and do other things that come from the Blessingway. It was wintertime and we were over around Salina when this man, John Mitchell, and some others came to our hogan. They asked my mother and father if my older sister could marry their brother who was called *Tó'aheedlíinii Nééz* [Tall Water Flows Together Man], Jim. They came asking that they be permitted to have their brother marry my older sister. They pleaded and pleaded with my mother and father about it, and said their whole family wanted Jim to do that. And so, after they talked that over for a *long* time, they all agreed on it and set the date. I think it was for three days from then, but I really don't remember. When my older sister and I brought the sheep back that afternoon, we were told she was going to be given in marriage to this man, Jim Mitchell. That man, of course, turned out to be the oldest brother of Frank, the man who later became my husband. My sister didn't say very much. She knew she was old enough to start having children for someone. We didn't know that man but I think my parents knew some things about his family, even though they moved around with their animals in different places than those we lived in.[15]

When the time arrived, all the people from his side came over here on horses. In those days, it was the practice for the man's side to give presents like horses or other property to the woman's family at the time of the marriage. So when they came, they brought lots of horses. They had plenty of those so they contributed them at the wedding to my father and mother. Sometimes it wasn't horses that were given. The custom was that all the People on the man's side would contribute to his gift to the woman's family. So, sometimes it would be cattle, or if no animals could be given, they'd give a belt or some other jewelry, things of value. In my older sister's case, they brought horses. I don't remember how much money horses were worth at that time. I think they gave three horses to our family. I remember those were riding horses, not the kind used for farming. That happened a long time ago, before any of the People out here had wagons or used horses to pull buggies or other vehicles.

When Jim's family arrived at our place, his relatives came, too.[16] Of course, on our side, we had everything prepared for them. It's the woman's side that prepares the meat and other available food for the man's party to eat during a wedding. You are also supposed to prepare a special cornmeal mush for that, and pour it into a good woven basket.[17] The woman who is getting married then takes that into the hogan to the man, and they eat it together in there. She is also supposed to carry a jug of water in there. They use that to wash their hands before they eat. The practice is that they pour water over each other's hands. My older sister did all those things.

After they ate the mush, all the older People who were gathered in the hogan talked to the couple about how to live together in harmony and raise a family in good ways. My father did lots of talking to both of them and offered a prayer for them in the Blessingway manner. Some other headmen who were there with us in the hogan also talked, and some of the women spoke, too. My mother didn't do that; she was not in the hogan with the rest of us because of our rule about women avoiding their sons-in-law.[18] When the speeches were over, we brought in all the food that had been prepared for the feast that goes with that ceremony.

Lots of people from our side came to that, too. Our neighbors and our relatives contributed food and other things that were available. Some of the women brought cornbread and other foods they had already prepared to help feed the visiting group. At my sister's wedding, there was lots of food because many people helped us with that. It is the practice that if any food is left over after the feast, the visiting group takes it back home with them. And, according to our customs, the basket that is used during the ceremony, the one we call a "Wedding Basket," is kept by the visiting party. But when that group came, there were no women among them; only men came. What Jim's brother, John, told my mother and father and the rest of us was that Jim's mother, their mother, was very sick at that time. For that reason, she was not able to come and the other women had stayed behind too, to take care of her. So I don't remember who took the basket. It may have been John Mitchell who did that; I don't remember that part.

That's how weddings are conducted in the traditional way. I saw that when my sister got married. Today, I know some people don't want to go through with those things because it's a lot of work to do it that way. Sometimes they say they have no room in their hogan for people to gather, or they say it's too cold, or that the People have no transportation. Some people put up lots of excuses like that so they can avoid having a wedding in the traditional way.[19]

two

Young Adulthood, Early Married Years

Getting Together with My Husband

Man Who Shouts gets his wagon and buggy . . . trouble comes to Chinle
[1905] . . . I start living with Frank Mitchell.

After my older sister was married, she continued to live with us. Her husband brought some sheep with him and so after they built their hogan, my father separated out the few sheep that belonged to my sister, and she and her husband put their animals together and started taking care of those things, too. The man she married traveled a lot, going here and there, doing different jobs. When he was around, he started helping my father and mother with the planting, hoeing, and other work here. My sister and I kept on the way we had been living earlier, before her marriage. Every day we took care of the sheep and worked on the wool. We also helped grind corn and prepare things for everyone to eat. And all of us kept weaving rugs to be sold in Ganado.

I'm not sure, but I think it was right around this time, shortly after my sister was married to Tall Water Flows Together Man [Jim], that my father got his first wagons. He was already recognized as a leader and was working in that capacity when that happened. Of course, he was also performing his ceremonies for the People and farming, too, when he acquired those vehicles. Once he had them, we had faster transportation around here.

Most of the first wagons that came into use among the People were acquired by working. The government had lots of those and let the People get them by working out their value on different kinds of projects, like building roads, schools, and other things. But the People who had been appointed to serve as leaders from different parts of the reservation were given those things. I don't remember exactly how my father got his, but I think after he was appointed to be a leader, he went to see the agent in Fort Defiance and came back with the news that he would be given those vehicles. So, he made plans to go back over there; first he brought back a buggy, and then he went and brought back a big wagon.[1]

Once he acquired those two vehicles, he started using the *tsinaabąąs* [farm wagon], the heavy one, for trips to the store, and for hauling lots of different things. The other one was a lighter one, a buggy; we called that one *tsinaabąąs dijádí,* "speedy wagon" [buckboard, light rig, buggy]. My father really liked driving the buggy, the light weight one. He started using it whenever he traveled around to meet with other leaders or to go to other places. He had two white horses he started using with the buggy, and he became well known for driving it around. My father's buggy had four wooden wheels with a piece of metal in the rims, and wooden spokes; there was one black seat in it and a black top. That was flat where it went over the seat and then it curved in the back and came all the way down to the bottom behind the seat. There was room in the buggy for one other person on the seat, and maybe one or two children in the back, where there was a place big enough to haul a bale of hay, if you put that in there crosswise. My mother used to like to go with my father in that buggy; I remember they used to take it to Fort Defiance to visit their friends, the Damons. That man's wife was from the Chinle area and my mother and father had known them a long time. They were close personal friends, and they liked to visit each other a lot. I don't think those people had a trading post or anything like that over there, although my parents did go to the store in Fort Defiance a few times when they went to see them. I don't think they were relatives by clan or any other way, either. I just know the Damons were very close friends of my parents and they visited back and forth a lot, whenever they could. And when my parents went over there for that reason, they always traveled in that buggy with the two white horses. Later, some of my own children, especially Seya, rode in the buggy a lot with my father. He used to like to take Seya and another of our relatives, Sam Sanishya, to Yeibichei dances with him. When he did, they'd go in the buggy, with the little boys sitting in the back together. Even my mother learned how to drive the buggy; sometimes she'd take it by herself and use it for her own purposes, if it were available. After my father passed away, she continued to use it while she was still strong. I don't know what happened to it after she died; it's no longer around here.

At the time my father became known for his buggy, he was the only Navajo in this area with such a vehicle. We only ever saw one other one like it; that belonged to Father Leopold, one of the priests who started visiting around in this area.[2] When he first was seen going here and there every now and then, he was riding a horse. Then after a while, we heard Father Leopold had settled here. First, he and a Brother were staying in a stone building where Garcia's Trading Post is now. I think that place had been abandoned by some early trader [see Fig. 3]. Then they built that residence for the priests and used part of that as a church [see Fig. 4]. Later, they put up the Catholic Church here in Chinle.[3] It was *after* those things had happened that we saw Father Leopold had acquired a buggy like my father's. He used to like to drive around in his buggy, too, coming over here and going other places in it.

FIG. 3. The Franciscans' first mission/residence in Chinle, Arizona, used part time from August 15, 1904, until January 1906 (and later incorporated into Garcia's Trading Post). Photographer, unknown. Courtesy of the Franciscan Friars, St. Michaels Archives. Reproduced from Ostermann (1914:28) by the late Father Simon Conrad, O.F.M.

FIG. 4. The Franciscan residence/chapel in Chinle, Arizona, ca. 1906 (before adding the porch). Photographer, unknown. Courtesy of the Franciscan Friars, St. Michaels Archives. Reproduced from Ostermann (1914:30) by the late Father Simon Conrad, O.F.M.

The other vehicle my father got was a heavy farm wagon; it was long like a box, and was made all out of wood. Even the wheels were wood. That was before there were any cars around, and before anyone started using rubber tires on wagons. People said those farm wagons were available in different sizes and that my father's was a large one. You had to hitch up a team of four horses to pull it before you could drive it. My father understood how to harness the horses but it took a while for the rest of us to learn how to put those pieces of harness together the right way so we could use the wagon. Once my father got it, he started hauling our rugs or the wool we didn't need here over to Ganado with that, and then bringing back whatever we needed from there. We also used it to load up the corn, melons, and other things we harvested in the fall from our fields here in the Chinle Valley. He and others in the family also took that big wagon up into the mountains and used it to haul wood down from there, whenever we needed some for our fires, or for building hogans. Later, when people started putting up a few fences, they also brought wood back for that purpose, too. And, when we moved from our summer homes in Fluted Rock to our winter places in the Black Mountain area, and back again, we'd load some of our things in my father's big farm wagon.

Sometimes that big wagon got used for going to ceremonies, too. When my father and some of my older brothers were going to help out with a Nightway that was being held in the area, they'd use that wagon for traveling to it. They liked to go to those together; I guess that was because my father and some of my brothers knew lots of Nightway songs, and they all were very good Yeibichei dancers. My father was really well known for that, too; he was a well-known Yeibichei dancer, just like three of my older brothers, the ones called Son of Man Who Shouts, The Jailer, and The Judge. Later, some of their children, their sons, did that, too. I guess my father's real strong voice helped with those things; he was a leader of a Yeibichei team and they used to travel around a lot, going to those ceremonies together and staying there, sometimes for all nine days. It seemed like someone was always coming around and asking my father to bring his team and help out by dancing during those ceremonies.

After my father got his buggy and the farm wagon, our donkeys got more of a rest, but he still kept them around and kept using them to haul things, too.* And, of course he kept traveling around on horseback, too; lots of times when he went to meetings or rode up and down the Valley, telling the People it was time to start irrigating, planting, or hoeing, he'd take one of his horses, saddle it, and travel that way. He kept riding horses even when he got up in his years; he was very experienced in that. So, we never understood what happened the day he got hurt, when he got the injury he never recovered from, the one that killed him. That happened because of a horse and we never learned what made his horse throw him that day, what caused that.[4]

Another one who was injured by a horse was my older brother, Man with a Cane.

Shortly after my father got his wagon and buggy, this brother of mine was hurt while riding and trying to rope another horse. Lots of ceremonies were done for him but for a long time, his injuries left him crippled. It wasn't until many years later he learned to get around with a cane.

When my father began traveling around in his buggy and going more places for meetings and other things, we started hearing about what was happening in different parts of the reservation. And sometimes we'd see things for ourselves while we were moving back and forth across the Chinle Valley with our sheep and other livestock, to our summer or winter homes. More and more people were moving into the Valley; more of the People were acquiring wagons, and there were more trading posts being established. Certain men started hauling freight for those stores from Gallup and other places; we heard that a railroad now passed through there and went on to Flagstaff and all the way to California. I guess stores from the east were shipping things out here for our use by means of that. My father and mother used to talk about the new things that were becoming available at the trading posts. Every now and then they'd trade for something new, like a few buckets to use in hauling water, or different kinds of material for us to use in making our own skirts or other clothing.

My father told us that many new things were being established because of the Fort Sumner Treaty.[5] Here and there church people, priests and others, were coming onto the reservation and asking Washington for land on which to build churches and other buildings. The government was starting to build schools in other places besides Fort Defiance, and a few hospitals were being established. And because more and more officials and others were trying to travel around in different parts of the reservation, the government started trying to build some roads. Buildings called post offices were started in a few places and certain ones were hired to haul the mail. I remember the first time we saw a man who was bringing mail to Chinle; he had a different kind of a buggy with just two wheels and he used two big mules to pull it. Of course, sometimes they used a four-wheeled vehicle while hauling the mail, too [see Figs. 5 and 6].[6]

I guess not everybody was happy about the things that were happening in those years so now and then, in different places, there'd be trouble among the People themselves or between them and outsiders. Some of the People still objected to putting their children into school, even though by then more were enrolling their children in those places. Some were not happy about the missionaries who started coming around. It seemed that there were more and more different kinds of those, and some of them talked in bad ways about each other and also about our own beliefs and our Navajo ceremonies. And then, too, in some places the officials from Washington, those agents, and even some of the traders who had licenses to sell things on the reservation were not treating the People fairly. Because of all those things, every now and then there'd be trouble in different parts of the reservation.[7] When that happened, if

FIG. 5. The mail arrives in Chinle, Arizona, probably ca. 1920. Post office building at Franciscan complex. Driver, unidentified. Photographer, unknown. Courtesy of the Franciscan Friars, St. Michaels Archives. Photograph no. C539.24–3, R6978.

it concerned something from the areas my father was responsible for or if it concerned lots of the People, the leaders were called together and told to help the agents settle the trouble.

One of the incidents we heard about, that lots of people talked about, was when some men got angry and caused an uprising right around Chinle. That happened shortly after we had moved back to the Black Mountain area for the winter; we had just settled ourselves over there when my father got word that he was needed right away back in Chinle. So, he took his fastest horse and went back; lots of leaders were notified they were needed over there, to settle troubles in that area. I was still living with my mother and father when that happened; I hadn't yet met the man who I married. I don't think he was even around in this area then because he was off working some place else, probably with the priests at St. Michaels. I know after we started living together, he talked with my father about what had happened in Chinle, because he had heard other things about it from another leader, Son of the Late Little Blacksmith.

That man wasn't really a headman like my father; he was more like a policeman because he and some others had been appointed to help keep the peace in different places. From what I remember, Son of the Late Little Blacksmith was sent to this area after the trouble in Chinle and then he was stationed here. He stayed at the Catholic mission, and when my father and other headmen used to meet with him, they'd go there for the meetings. The church let them turn their horses loose in a big field they had there for that purpose, when they came together for the meetings. If the weather was warm, all the headmen would gather and have their meetings right near the mission, under the trees that were planted around there after a while. I guess that Son of

FIG. 6. A two-wheeled mail buggy in Chinle, Arizona, probably ca. 1920. Post office building at Franciscan complex. Driver, unidentified. Photographer, unknown. Courtesy of the Franciscan Friars, St. Michaels Archives. Photograph no. C539.87–6, R6662.

the Late Little Blacksmith and the man I later married got to know each other when Frank was working around the Chinle mission, helping Father Leopold. They became pretty good friends and for a while after we were married, Frank used to travel around with that peacemaker, Son of the Late Little Blacksmith, helping him with his talks to the People.

What we heard from people around us was that a man called *Hastiin łizhinii* [Black Man] gathered all his close relatives together and armed them. They were all living in the Canyon, in Canyon de Chelly, when they did that. We never were told where they got those weapons, the guns they had. We heard they tried to ambush the agent when he was traveling through there; I guess lots of them surrounded him, waving their guns around and threatening him. So, they caused an uprising. I don't think anyone was hurt during that because others stepped in to stop them. I'm not really sure what caused those men from the Canyon to do that; it seemed like everybody who talked about it had a different way of explaining why that happened. Some people said it was because of the police who were recruiting children for school. But some said no, that happened because the agent had tried to outlaw our practice of having more than one wife. And others said the trouble really happened because of drinking at a Nightway Ceremony that was going on in that area. Drinking, using alcohol, was outlawed in that treaty, too, when the reservation was set up and the People were released from Fort Sumner. I don't remember now what my father said caused it when he came back, but somebody probably wrote all those things down in a book some place. After causing that trouble, Black Man and the men who were with him went back and hid some place in the Canyon, in one of the caves. But then the officials came, even the army I think, and with the help of my father and other leaders, picked up all the men involved in that and took them to Fort Defiance for punishment. No one in my family, not even any of our relatives, knew any of the People who caused that, but it happened right near the hill by the place we call the Thunderbird Lodge.[8]

Some time after my older sister married Jim Mitchell and after that uprising, there were some people who came around to talk with my parents, trying to arrange for me to marry one of their relatives. That happened twice that I know about, but nobody talked with me either time, and now I don't remember who came the first time, or the next time, either, wanting me to marry somebody in their families.* I just heard about it later from my parents, after I came back in with the sheep in the late afternoon. Each time I guess my parents told those people, "No, we're not going to do it." My father used to give me talks about the kind of man I should settle down with; he had lots of ideas about that, and he didn't want me getting married to just anyone.

After that had happened, I started noticing one of the younger brothers of the man who had been married to my older sister, one of Jim Mitchell's younger brothers, Frank. That man used to come around to visit his brother; he'd stay with him for a short time, and help with things his brother was doing. Sometimes he'd go into the Canyon and get his brother's horses and bring them out in the spring, when it was time to start plowing and planting. Sometimes he helped with the planting, too, or even the herding. And sometimes he and Jim, and others in their family, would saddle horses and go to some of the Enemyways that were being held in the Valley.

While he was doing that, he started getting to know other people in our family. I guess he started noticing me, too. When he'd come around, we'd see each other, and just talk together when I was over at my sister's hogan, or when I was outside with the sheep, or doing other things around where we were living at the time. We were here in the Chinle Valley, passing through here and staying here for a while with our fields and our animals, when I noticed he was starting to come around. I think he was still helping the priests over at St. Michaels when he started visiting his brother like that. Sometimes he didn't stay more than a day or so, before he rode the horse he was using on toward Tsaile, where his mother had her home in the wintertime. In the spring, she and some of the rest of their family moved more this way, out on the rim of the Canyon; then she was closer to Jim, who had married my older sister. Sometimes my sister's hogan was close to the rest of the family; sometimes Jim would build it more apart, closer to where we are living now. That was starting to happen; as my older sisters had children, and more and more people started moving around with us, the group spread out more in whatever area we were living in. We were all still traveling together but sometimes the hogans different ones built were farther apart, not right next door like around here now.

After a while, that man, Jim's younger brother, and I just started getting together, staying together. It was in the summer and we were living across from here, across the

Chinle Wash, over against that hill you can see from here. Even though there's lots of sand there now, at that time the land was very different. There were no trees anywhere and no fences, and that area was a very good place to farm. So my father had planted lots of corn and other things over there and we were all there. That was near where he and other men had made those water holes all the way down the line with that big scraper so we could always get water for the sheep and our own use. That particular time, my father had decided the whole family would stay right there; we didn't move on up to the Fluted Rock area that summer after my father, brothers, and others had planted the crops; instead, we stayed here with the sheep. After that, sometimes in the summer we'd stay here; sometimes we'd go on to Fluted Rock after the fields were planted, and only the men would go back and forth to check on the fields. And sometimes, after the hogans and the ramadas were built in the mountains, some of the family would come back here and stay near the fields, while the rest of us stayed up there in the mountains with the sheep, in the place where the giant trees scared me in my girlhood.* Five or six years later, my father stopped going up in those mountains altogether, except when he and other men took the wagon up there for wood. That was around the time my third child, Seya, was born; he never went up there with us, but the first two girls did. I remember they were scared to be up there with my father and mother and me and our sheep; that place scared them just like it had scared me when I was little.*

So gradually, across the Chinle Wash from here became the area where my father would build our summer homes. He and the rest of our relatives kept farming this whole Valley. Gradually we were all settling in this area in the summertime, even though he still kept his horses over in the Black Mountain area, around Salty Water, or Thin Rock, or closer to Fish Point [see Map 3]. My father's cattle and horses also roamed around in other places, too, like along the ridge you can see from here, the edge of that little mesa to the west. He had lots of livestock in those days, and when those animals were on the ridge over there, that's all you could see. The horses spread out, but even though they were scattered, they filled up the whole area. That little mesa there where the dump and cemetery are, and all the way down to where they are talking about building a new hospital, the whole area would be covered with his livestock. My older brother, the heavyset one called The Jailer, also had lots of horses and cattle. He took care of all my father's livestock the whole time, going back and forth from where he was living over in the Black Mountain area, while the rest of us were over here, or in Fluted Rock. He put his animals in with my father's, and took care of all of them together. When it was time to brand them, he and some others would round them all up and drive them over to wherever they had fixed the corrals they were going to use for that purpose, like at Fish Point or other places. Because that mesa was filled up with those animals from my father and my older brother, the People

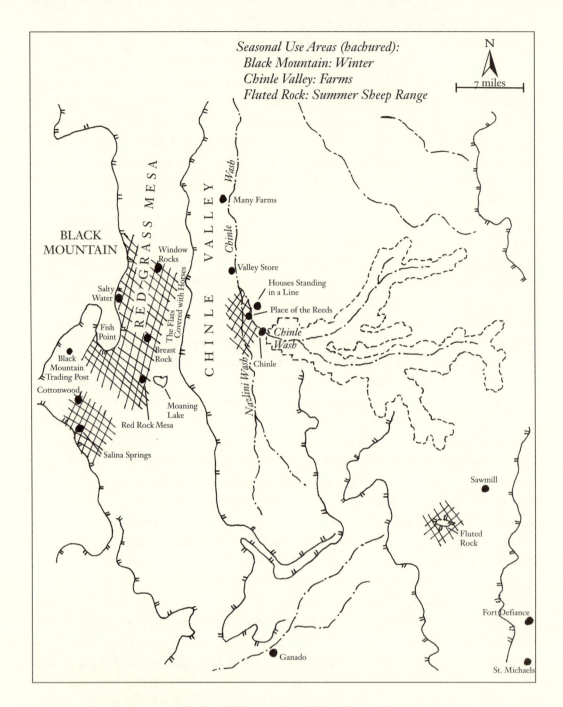

N

7 miles

BLACK
MOUNTAIN

RED GRASS MESA

CHINLE VALLEY

Chinle Wash

Many Farms

Window
Rocks

The Flats Covered with Horses

Salty
Water

Fish
Point

Valley Store

Houses Standing
in a Line

Place of the Reeds

Chinle
Wash

Black
Mountain
Trading Post

Breast
Rock

Nazlini Wash

Chinle

Cottonwood

Moaning
Lake

Red Rock Mesa

Salina Springs

Sawmill

Fluted
Rock

Fort Defiance

Ganado

St. Michaels

MAP 3   *Locations Important in Tall Woman's Adulthood*

around here started calling that ridge Horses on the Edge or Covered with Horses. It had that name even after those animals were gone and after The Jailer and my father both passed away; but then, after a while, people stopped calling it that. I don't know if that ridge even has a name now; maybe it's just Covered with Trash.*

Eventually, some of the People who had been moving around with us stopped going to other places in the winter; they just stayed here in the Valley the whole time, and when we'd come back through this area, we'd all live near each other again. My father never stopped moving back and forth with his animals, so we kept moving back to the Black Mountain area in the fall until he passed away.

I don't remember exactly when Frank and I started staying together; we didn't write it down so there are no records of that.[9] We didn't have a ceremony like my older sister did; and, even though the priests were already living here in Chinle, we didn't have them marry us. We simply started living together. One of the reasons we did it that way is that at that time Frank had no one to come and ask my family for me. His mother was very sick and there was also sickness, I think tuberculosis, among some of his brothers and sisters. When we got together, Frank had no one to speak on his behalf. It's our practice that a close relative does that for you, but for some reason, neither of his older brothers, Jim or John, was available to do that for him. So, Frank just came over here and started living with me; we started living together that way. From what I remember, his brother John was off working somewhere, like at the sawmill that was operating a ways from here, or over at the store in Fort Defiance. And that other one, Jim, just went back to running around after he married my older sister in that Wedding Ceremony we had for her. From what my parents and others told me, he had lots of women in many different places, and he kept running around, doing that, even after he had married my older sister, the one I used to herd with all the time. When he was around here, he helped with the farm; he also had lots of fields where he was raising things, too, and lots of horses he kept down in the Canyon. But lots of times, he was gone, just running around.

After my parents noticed Frank was coming around our place to see me, and staying here, they decided they should talk with us about that. They waited until one time when he didn't go back to his own place, when he was still here, staying around. Then my father came over to where the two of us were sitting and said he wanted to talk with Frank, who was called Big Schoolboy at that time. Frank was a big man and he had been enrolled in the Fort Defiance School for a few years, after they started rounding up children for that; so, he had some education.

After my father came and said that, he and Frank went over to my parents' hogan. They stayed over there quite a while. My mother was in there weaving, and I guess she talked to him too, about some of those things. After a while, she came out and told me to come over there, too. And then, they talked to both of us together. I don't know if they ever said anything to each other or anyone else in the family about us starting out that way, not having a ceremony to get married in the traditional way; I never heard.

I remember they both talked to us together for a long time. Their words stayed with me even after they passed away; even now I can remember what they said to us. They talked about how to live together in peace and harmony, in a good way, without abusing each other or being jealous, or chasing around after other people. They also told us we had to plan ahead, make a plan for our lives together so we would have some things to go by, something to live with, and things to use in caring for any children we would have together in the future. They told us only a few of the sheep and goats that I was taking care of and herding all the time, belonged to me. My father asked Frank what property he had; at that time, Frank was using a horse that belonged to his older brother, John, and he had no sheep or other things, just the clothes he was wearing. He said his mother had lots of sheep, but many of those had already been used up, in the ceremonies they were doing for her and some of his brothers and sisters, because of the sickness in their family. My father said that even though he and my mother had cattle and sheep, and horses and wagons, and even though they had jewelry, none of that belonged to me, except for a few sheep. But he said if Frank started acquiring some animals, we could put those together and start building up our own herd that way.

My parents knew that Frank had already been to lots of places, doing different kinds of work to make a living. My father said he was glad to know Frank knew how to work, and how to help his mother and his own brothers and sisters. He said it was good he had gone to school and learned some things about English, and had worked in the store for traders and for the priests. But then he said all those things were temporary, they wouldn't last throughout our lives. He said we shouldn't plan to raise a family on the basis of those things. I guess the whole time he was planning to say he thought Frank should learn to be a Blessingway singer, because that's what he finally said. He said if Frank did that, he'd have something to go by for all his life. I guess he already knew Frank's father was a singer, and some of his other relatives were also trained to perform various ceremonies. So he added his encouragement about that when he talked with us.

They told us we could live right there with them, that we could use one of the hogans as our own and stay in it until we built our own place, right there with the rest of the family. My parents said we could put our sheep and goats in with theirs, and take care of them that way. But my father told Frank that from here on, it'd be up to him to start providing for me and any children I might have in the future. If we were going to be living together, my father said we shouldn't be looking to him to support us and provide food and other things we might need. He said we needed to establish ourselves on our own because only in the very beginning, when we were starting out, could we depend on them to help us. He also told Frank if he and I were going to be together, Frank should plan on helping with the sheep and other livestock, and with the plowing, planting, hoeing, and the other farm work, too.

They also talked to us for a long time about having a family, and taking care of your children. My father said over and over that we had to learn to plan ahead, think about things, and make plans about how we were going to support any children we might have. He said, "In time, you'll start having children; you must plan for them. If you don't do that, if the two of you don't plan for their future, who will do it? No one. They'll be your own children; therefore, you must provide something for them. You'll need to set aside a few sheep and goats for them, when you build up your herd. And you'll need to establish your home and do all the work around the place. You two are the ones who will have to do those things. No one else is going to do that for you. Only in that way will your children be taken care of." He also said it'd be up to us to raise our children in the right way, to instruct them as they started growing so they learned to work hard, taking care of the sheep and whatever other animals we acquired, and raising corn and other things to eat, and to fix the different kinds of food we used. He also said children needed to learn to help their relatives, and not run here and there, drinking wine or getting in trouble, and having babies and deserting their children. Those were the things my parents talked to us about; those were the instructions Frank and I were given from them when we started living with each other. We each remembered their talks through our whole lives; now I realize the things they told us were correct. As the years went by, we had most of the experiences they said would happen to us.

When we were in there, in the hogan together, it was my father who did most of the talking. He gave us a real stern talk about those things in his loud, deep voice. Every now and then, my mother just added some words to what he was saying. Later, when Frank was spending a few days with his own mother who had moved near us, my mother talked to me by herself. I was sitting some place, carding wool, and she came over there with the wool she was spinning. She talked to me some more about being married and raising children. She said I'd learn it was hard and that many hardships would come along. She said I'd have to be very strong to bear the things that would happen to me as a married woman. She also said I should never leave my children and take off to Squaw Dances or other such places. And never once did I do that in my life; I'm not lying about that, either. Of course Frank went to all those things, but men can take care of themselves. If you're a woman with a baby, why would you want to be running around, carrying your baby to those kinds of places? My mother reminded me of those things; she said my duty was to take care of the home and my children. I've done that right up to the present time. She also reminded me I had been raised with my father's Blessingway and that it would see me through all kinds of difficulties, if I continued to follow along in the ways I had been raised.

At that time, she also talked to me a long time about jealousy. I guess lots of times men run around, even right after they settle down and start living with someone and raising a family. They keep running around, finding other women, and even sometimes having children with them. She said I should never get mad if Frank did that. She told me to always keep quiet about it. She said, "You should just stay home and take good care of your children, your home, and your sheep." She said not to fight about anything like that, because a man would always come back when he was through running around, if you made a good home for him and were raising his children in the right way. She also told me that some women ran around, too. I, myself, never did that; Frank was the only man I ever picked up with, and once I started living with him, I stayed with him from then right up to the present time. Even though at times he'd take a notion to get careless, I, myself, never ran around. I tried to follow my parents' instructions.

When my mother talked with me that time, she said I should keep working hard, always prepare meals in the right way, keep the hogan swept out and any property we might acquire in good condition. She also encouraged me to keep weaving. She said, "I've taught all of you to weave, and all of you are good weavers. You will find you can support yourself with that. You can feed your children with it, even if there's no other way to acquire food." She reminded me when I was small, and growing up with all my brothers and sisters, lots of times the only way she and my father could trade for things to eat before he started farming was with the rugs she and my older sisters were always making. And even now that he was a well-known stockman, a singer, and a headman, our rugs continued to give us something to trade on for what we needed from the store.

My mother, during her talk, also told me that sometimes men would be gone for long periods of time, like my own father was. She said some went off because they were working in different places to help support their wives and children. And some went off for other reasons, even gambling. She said never to chase after Frank or worry about what he was doing if he was gone in the future like that. She said over and over my job was to stay home and take care of all the things there — the children, the sheep, the home, and the fields. She said it was up to me to raise the children so they always had something to eat and something to wear. Finally, she stopped talking like that and we just sat there. I didn't say anything about any of her words. A lot of them scared me.[10]

Even though my parents had talked with us, for most of the summer Frank kept going back and forth, to his mother's place, to where his father had moved, and then back here where we were staying, across from here, across the Chinle Wash, where my father had planted corn. And sometimes he'd be with Father Leopold, helping around at the priest's house because he had a small job there. I guess my father just watched

Frank in the beginning; maybe he was wondering why he didn't settle down with me and stay here all the time. So, after a while, near the end of the summer, my father took a horse and rode over to see Frank's father so they could talk about those things together.

A short time after that, that man came over here one time when Frank had been here for a few days again. He was called Water Edge Man, but I called him my brother because his father belonged to the same clan as my father, the Bitter Water People. After Water Edge Man went in the hogan to see my father and mother, he came over and told us both to come over there. And then both Frank's father and my father talked with us about getting started in the right way. Frank's father talked differently; he didn't scare us and he didn't shout or yell.* Both of them told Frank he should stop going between the two families, even though he was worrying about all the sicknesses on his own side. They told him to stay right here all the time. Then, too, they both encouraged him again to start learning about the Blessingway. I guess his father knew Frank was already starting to ask him some questions about that. I didn't say anything during their talks, and after a while, Frank didn't, either. We just sat there and listened. When they finished, they said they were both giving us to each other, and that we should start living together out in the open from then on. My older half sister, Slim Woman, was already doing that with Red Bottom Man; they, too, had started living together.

The summer was almost over when those men talked to us; the early corn was already picked and we were making the different kinds of foods we make from corn before it's fully ripe, when the ears are tiny or a bit later, before those kernels are fully formed. My father had already starting making plans about harvesting the other things he had raised and moving back to the Black Mountain area. So after that, Frank and I stayed together out in the open. Of course, everyone in my family already knew we were together, we were married. And, when we started going places together, others began calling me 'Ółta'í Tsoh be'esdzáán, Big Schoolboy's Wife, because of that.* I guess it was pretty well known by the time we started moving back to our winter location with the wagon, the buggy, and all the animals. And of course, even though I was now married, I kept living with my parents, my sisters and their husbands and children, just like before, and we all kept moving around together in the fall, and then again, in the spring.

Starting Out Together

Early years of marriage . . . births of Mary no. 1 and Mary no. 2 . . . Frank works at the sawmill and earns a wagon . . . first buildings at the Chinle Boarding School . . . Seya is born . . . Annunciation Mission is built and dedicated . . . Frank leaves to work as a freighter.

After Frank and I married each other, for a while he stayed right here with my parents and the rest of us. He helped with the farming and the horses, and he and my father started to get to know each other. I know for a while Frank was scared of him, but gradually he got used to his big loud voice and realized that was why he was called Man Who Shouts. Sometimes Frank didn't understand the way my father talked to the People who were moving around with us, following him as a leader. He said it seemed like the words were strange, maybe even some old kind of Navajo.* He used to notice it a lot whenever he'd come back from going some place with Son of the Late Little Blacksmith. That man became a good friend of my husband's, and kept asking him to go with him to different places where he had to investigate troubles that were reported. Frank heard him talking to the People a lot because of that; he used to understand his talks clearly, but when he heard my father talking, it'd be hard for him to follow his words. Finally, he asked my father about those things. I guess all he learned was that there were different ways of talking to the People. The peacemaker, Son of the Late Little Blacksmith, used to call the headmen together so they could discuss problems and he could explain some of the government's policies to them; that was part of his job, too. Then the leaders would make plans about how to tell the People who were settling in all these areas about those things. Frank used to go to some of those meetings, too. Every now and then, he'd come back home and tell me about them. Sometimes he'd even imitate how different leaders talked; that used to make me laugh.* But now I realize that by learning those things, he, himself, was starting to learn how to talk to the People, too.

Frank kept traveling around with the peacemaker, even though we were married. So, almost right away, I knew what my mother had told me about men who were gone a lot was right. I remembered not to worry about it, so I kept busy, helping with things around here. My parents were quite well established with everything by then, and it seemed like there was always something that had to be taken care of. Then, too, my own father was gone lots of times, doing his ceremonies, going to meetings, or traveling around for other reasons.

A while after we got married, I gave birth to our first child, a girl. We called her "Being a Woman" and "Billy Mahi" when she was small; we usually have pet names like that for our children. When she got older, she got an English name, Mary; now she's Mary Davis, as you know. It was wintertime and we were over in the Black Mountain area when that happened, but there are no records of it so I don't know exactly when she was born.[1] When I realized I was pregnant, I told some of my sisters. Later, I told my mother, and she got after me about it. She always did that, whenever she found out my sisters or I were going to have a baby; she got after us about those things. I guess that's why we always waited a long time before we told her.* I had that baby right in the hogan; my mother and father arranged for me to have a Blessingway because of that; they got an old man, Silent Man, to perform that over me when I was due. That is our practice, and so each time, right before I gave birth to a child, I had a Blessingway. Silent Man passed away shortly after he did that for me; that was the first ceremony I had after my puberty ceremonies, when I became a woman. My mother knew how to help other women give birth, and so did some of my sisters. So, my mother was in the hogan with me, with that old man who was singing, and a few other people, who helped my mother get the things ready that we use, like juniper or cedar, the sash belt, a sheepskin, and other things.[2] I didn't have any trouble that time, and that baby lived to grow up. Frank was not here when that happened, so when he came back from wherever he had gone, he found out he was a father.*

It was the same way with some of the other children I had; sometimes he wasn't around to participate in the Blessingway and other things we do at that time. After I'd gone through that a few times, I started learning from my mother the things she knew about that; her mother had taught her those things, and she passed the ways of doing that on to my sisters and me, after we became women and started having our own babies. So, eventually I started helping other women who were about to give birth, too. I guess I became known for that, after we settled down permanently here in Chinle. Eventually, people would come looking for me to help someone in their family go through that, when it was time. Even though it was the middle of the night, they'd come for me to help with that.

The second child I had was also a girl; she was born about two years later and we used to call her 'Aheejabah. I don't remember who did the Blessingway Ceremony for me when I was ready to give birth to her; over the years, we used different Blessing-way singers for that, including Jake Brown and even Old Man Curly Hair, who's one of our relatives on Frank's side. Of course, Frank never did that for me, once he became a Blessingway singer. You can't perform your ceremony for your wife or your husband; that ends the marriage, if you do that. When *'Aheejabah* went to school, she got named Mary Mitchell. So she became Mary no. 2.* She died when she was still in school at the Albuquerque Indian School. But that was later. Even with her, there was no record of her birth.[3] I had her at home, and we didn't write that down. But, by the time she died, they were keeping records on those things; that happened in the winter of 1931.

We didn't put our first child, Mary no. 1, into school when those officials came later, asking for children for the schools. She was born in a crippled condition and it took her almost three years before she could stand up and start walking around. At first, we didn't realize she had that problem; I carried her around on the cradleboard that had been made for her, like we do with our babies. My mother told me the *'awééts'áál* [cradleboard] that was made for my first child was not like the ones she had used for me or the rest of her children; those had a hole, made like a square, under the baby's bottom. You put the *'azhííh* [cliffrose bark] we used like a diaper right there and that way babies never got wet, or anything like that. I used the cliffrose bark with all of my children, but their cradleboards didn't have that hole.[4]

As my first child started to get older, I realized she should be trying to stand up, walk around. When she didn't, we realized she was born with that problem. We asked different singers about it, to see if there was some ceremony we could do for her, to heal her crippled condition. But they all said there was nothing that could be done. Because of her physical condition, we never put Mary no. 1 into school. Later, when she started walking, she learned how to get along like that; she's been that way all her life, and she learned how to make the best of it.[5]

When we started out together, Frank stayed here, helping around the place for a while. Sometimes he'd go various places with the peacemaker, the head policeman. Or, he'd go off to different ceremonies with his brothers or people in my family, like Enemyways in the summer and Nightways in the wintertime. My parents went to lots of those, to help People out by contributing sheep and doing other things. And then, too, some of my brothers knew lots of Yeibichei songs, like my father did. Some of them put teams together, so that groups of men traveled to different ceremonies and danced as Yeibichei dancers. Some of them became well known for that, and it seemed like there was always a Nightway going on that somebody was involved with in one way or another all the time in the winter, no matter where we were living. I never went to those things at that time in my life. I don't think Frank ever danced with the Yeibichei dancers, but he knew some of those songs, and other songs, too. I know he was already interested in learning more things about the Blessingway and was talking with his own father about it. He had already learned a few things about the ceremony when we started living together, and he kept doing that, now and then in our early times together. Years later, he got serious about it; then he learned from his own father. In our early years, when we were starting out together, my father kept asking him about it, kept encouraging him. Eventually, after he got serious about it, he learned other things about the Blessingway from my father, too. So he really got his ceremony from both of those men, his own father and mine.

Even though Frank was here helping out and nobody was complaining about his work, he used to tell me he wanted to find a different kind of job. He wanted to be able to support any children we might have, and acquire some animals. He said his own father had preached to him that he should follow my father, Man Who Shouts, and try to become well-to-do with livestock and wagons, and also respected as a leader. Of course, his own grandfather, his father's father, Man Who Speaks Often, was like that, too; he was a Blessingway singer and a respected headman in the Wheatfields area. And he was well-to-do, with lots of sheep and horses. Frank told me that man had taken all his animals to Fort Sumner, when the People were forced to go over there on the Long Walk. And he had brought those animals back from there, without losing too many of them. So lots of people respected him for that reason, too.

Frank thought about the things his father had said to him and also about what his mother had told him about Man Who Speaks Often. We used to talk about those kinds of things when we were starting out. I thought we could go along as we were doing, but he kept saying it'd be better for our future if he found some other kind of work that provided him with an income.

So, eventually, one time when he came back he said he had heard there was work available some place over near Fort Defiance where they had just opened a sawmill. He wanted to go over there and try and get a job, even though he knew I would be staying here with my parents and other relatives. So, he borrowed a horse from one of his brothers and went there and got a job. He was over there for a long time, probably several years.[6] But he always came back here on the weekends; whenever they dismissed him on Friday afternoon or on Saturday, he'd saddle that horse and head to wherever we were at the time. He started getting an income from that and gradually, he'd bring a few things from the trading post with him when he came home. I remember that was where he was working when our first two children were born, the first two girls. I don't know if he ever fooled around with other women while he was away working like that; I never asked about those things. When we were starting out, I just kept quiet and listened to what he told me when he came home, about the work he was doing there, and the people he was working for. Once he started having children, that kind of tied him down. He had to care for his children and help support them. So he was always looking around for different kinds of jobs by which he could earn some kind of income to provide for his family. I, of course, was helping too, because whenever I wasn't busy with the little ones, or the sheep, or preparing things to eat, I kept weaving rugs for my father to take to Ganado and trade for the things we needed.

When we were starting out, Frank was facing many problems from sicknesses in his own family. His mother kept getting worse as did one of his sisters, and so part of his income from the sawmill and whatever other jobs he found was going to help out with the ceremonies being done for them. He even tried having them live right near where I was, when they got really bad and nobody else was available to care for them. But shortly after that, they both passed away. It was hard for him to go through those things, and I remember my father trying to console him, and talk with him about those hardships and how to face them.

As for me, I hadn't had those experiences yet; everyone in our family was in good health in those years. I hadn't had any trouble losing any of my babies yet, and things were going along very well for all of us at that time. Of course, we followed my father's Blessingway teachings, and had the Blessingway done for different people in the family when it was needed. My father always had himself blessed after doing his ceremony four times, and each year, at the right time, he had his *jish* renewed, too. He always said prayers and did other things when he went hunting, or before traveling to the store or to meetings and other places. And he always blessed whatever new hogans were built for people in the family wherever we were living. We all tried to follow all the things we had been taught, like praying at dawn with our corn pollen, and living in harmony, without fighting or abusing each other.

Frank and I had been married for several years when he finally earned a wagon for our own use. He kept working on that for a long time, doing different jobs here and there. Even before he went to work at the sawmill, he used to borrow horses and help other men drag logs down from the mountains with chains, for the bridges the government was building in various places around the reservation. They were making bridges so they could build more dirt roads for people to use in traveling around. I know he worked on the bridges for the early road to Lukachukai, and also other bridges, too.

Most of the People acquired wagons by working for them, helping build roads, haul wood at the sawmill, or doing other things to earn those vehicles. From what Frank told me, the government also had other things available, if you worked for them, like tools, harnesses, shovels, and plows for farming. They kept those stored in various places around the reservation and you could get those if you worked for them in those days.

I knew, from what Frank told me one time when he came home from the sawmill, he was going to try to finish earning a wagon for our own use over there. But I didn't say anything about it; I didn't know how long it was going to take him to accomplish that plan. All he said was he had found out how to apply for a wagon and some others were going to help him work to finish earning one. And so after some more time went by, after he did more work, I guess they told him he had earned one; that's how he got one of those farm wagons for us to use for our own purposes.

Because he never said anything more about it after telling me about his plan, I was really surprised one time when he came back over to where we were, driving a wagon.* Until then, he always went back and forth on that horse his brother, John, was letting him use. I looked up from where I was taking care of my first baby, and saw this wagon coming and wondered who that was traveling in that. Then I saw it was him.* That made me very happy.

I remember how proud he was when he was finally able to drive that home to us, leading John's horse along side of it. It was a big, heavy farm wagon. Someone had loaned him two horses to use the first time he drove it over here, and they were hitched up to that with harnesses. Frank said that soon he would earn two horses to use on that wagon, and also the harnesses to go with them. And, it wasn't very long before that happened, too, and he acquired those things. He even earned a cover for our wagon, like the one we have around here now [1963]. That's his wagon standing out there and we still use it to go places, especially when it rains and the mud is deep.

After cars started coming out here on the reservation, the People learned they broke down lots of times.[7] Sometimes something went wrong with the motor; sometimes the tires blew up or lost their air. And when the weather was bad, those cars got stuck in the snow or mud. In the summer, they got stuck in sandy places, when the sand blew all over and covered up the roads that had been built. So we just kept using our wagon all through the years; the horses could always get in and out, no matter what kind of weather we had. You can haul lots of things with that, even sheep and goats, hay, corn, and things from the trading posts, like food, material, and other things. And lots of people can fit in there too, not just a few like in your car.* The only thing that's different now on our wagon that I know about is the tires. At first, Frank had wooden wheels on his wagon, like my father did. But eventually, those wore out. After there were lots of cars around and it didn't cost too much money to get those tires and those things weren't so scarce, lots of people started putting those on their wagons. That's why ours now has rubber wheels; it's wearing those car tires now.* So, just look around and see all the ugly things we have around here.* And think about the other ones I've already told you about, like those water belly bags.*

My father was pleased when he saw the wagon Frank had earned for us and those other things; he said it looked like Frank was starting to plan for the future, like he was learning how to support his wife and his family. I think he got our wagon right before our second baby was born. He brought it home and then went back to the sawmill, driving it and leading John's horse. The baby came after he went back, while he was over there again.

Once Frank started working at the sawmill, whenever he was home my father said he should take a rest, and not worry about helping with the plowing, planting, the shearing, or other things being done by the rest of the family. Sometimes, though, Frank did try and help out when he came back on the weekends to see us.

I don't remember how long he worked over there at the sawmill. After a while he told us he was going to leave that job and start helping with a bridge the government wanted to build between Fort Defiance and Chinle. He got asked to do that because he already had a wagon and knew how to haul things in it, using various kinds of chains and other things they worked with at the sawmill. The government wanted to put in a road between that sawmill and Chinle, but without the bridge, that couldn't be done. So he helped with that, too. I don't know if the pay was better for that or if he started trading things, or what. But when they finished the bridge, he came back with a team of mules and a few other horses besides the two he used on the wagon; he also brought some food and some new clothes. Our third child was on the way by then; I remember that.

Because he had those things and was known as a good worker, he was asked to help when they started building the school here in Chinle. That was shortly after they finished the bridge I just mentioned. I think Frank was put in charge of the men who were using their wagons to haul stones for that purpose. He was like a foreman for that, but he helped with the hauling, too. The government people hired some company to do the building, and the People around here who were hired all worked at different jobs.

Once that started, Frank told me he wanted to build a home close to where the construction was going on; he wanted to live with his children, close to where he was working, instead of only coming to see us on weekends. I went along with him on that and so, he got some of our relatives and other men to help him with that.[8] Once it was finished, he came over to where I was living with my parents and other relatives in the summer, at the place we called Houses Standing in a Line. We loaded up our few belongings and moved over there in our wagon, with our two small girls. So, during that time, I lived over there, very near where they were building the school. Frank built our home near where the jail was put later. It wasn't too far from the rest of my family since my father had already made all those houses in a line at the place we called *Kin Naaztí'í*, and my family was living there in the summertime.

I went back to where my mother and father were when it was almost time for our third baby to be born. My Blessingway Ceremony was held over there, and Frank was able to help out with it, although he wasn't trained in that yet. The third baby was a boy, and we named him Seya, as you know. Once again, my mother and some of my sisters were in the hogan, helping me, and once again, I had no trouble having that baby. Later, when his sister, Mary no. 2, and he got old enough, it was decided they should be put into school here in Chinle.

After I gave birth to Seya, I moved back to where Frank had built our home and went on taking care of things for my children and my husband. The few sheep we had then were in with my mother's and father's, and others were taking care of them for us. The few horses and mules Frank had acquired were roaming around in the Canyon with the animals his brother, Jim, had. We only had a place to keep the horses Frank used on the wagon over there by the home he built at that time.

I can't remember exactly when Seya was born, but it was around the time they were building the government boarding school here in Chinle. I don't remember how long they worked on building that; they kept adding to it, putting up more buildings over there for many years. Frank just helped with the beginning of that. At that time, they only put up about three buildings for that school [see Fig. 7].[9] I think that took them almost two years because Seya had already started walking around and another baby was on the way by the time they finally finished those first few buildings. Later, they started adding to those, with a dormitory for the boys and girls [see Fig. 8], and then, other buildings.

There were some other things I remember happening around here at that same time. Near where we had our home, but behind there to the east, the Gormans established a trading post [see Fig. 9]. That was Nelson and Alice, the parents of Carl and some of the other Gormans you know. I think Nelson had other stores before they started the one in Chinle, maybe at Old Sawmill, and Nazlini, too. He was a close relative of ours, another Towering House man, and he was a good business man. I guess he figured with the school being built in Chinle, it'd be a good place to have another trading post. They built that near where the Presbyterian Church was put later. That

FIG. 7. The first buildings at the Chinle Boarding School, ca. 1909–11. Foreground, left: Classroom building; right: Auditorium. Photographer, unknown. Courtesy of the Franciscan Friars, St. Michaels Archives. Photograph no. C539.9–6, R6826.

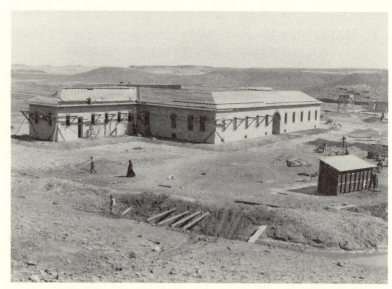

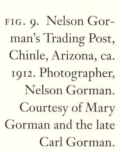

FIG. 8. Dormitories under construction at the Chinle Boarding School, ca. late 1912–early 1913. Friar in foreground, either Father Marcellus Troester, O.F.M., or Father Anselm Weber, O.F.M. Photographer, unknown. Courtesy of the Franciscan Archives, Cincinnati, Father Marcan Hetteberg, O.F.M.

FIG. 9. Nelson Gorman's Trading Post, Chinle, Arizona, ca. 1912. Photographer, Nelson Gorman. Courtesy of Mary Gorman and the late Carl Gorman.

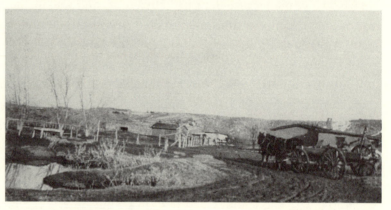

store did very well for many years. But finally, they gave it up and gave that place to the Presbyterians; I think that was because the flu came and killed so many people.[10]

The other thing I remember that was built about that time was the Catholic mission [see Fig. 10]. I think the company Frank worked for, the same one that built the Chinle Boarding School, was hired to build the mission, when they finished putting up the first few school buildings. That's the old stone church that's still standing up there, even though they don't have church services in it anymore. When the mission was finished, the priests had a dedication service for it. Lots of officials participated in that. Some of the priests from St. Michaels came out; the headmen went over there and the different peacemakers assigned to the areas around here, and the agent from Fort Defiance came, too. My parents were just starting to move back from the Black Mountain area when they had that ceremony early in the spring; they were beginning to move through the Chinle Valley area again, to get the fields planted before moving

FIG. 10. The Franciscan complex, Chinle, Arizona, 1912, soon after its dedication on March 25, 1912. Left, stone building used as the Chinle Post Office from 1911 at least until 1925, with Father Leopold Ostermann, O.F.M., postmaster. Center, Annunciation Mission. Right, Franciscan Fathers' residence. Courtesy of the Franciscan Friars, St. Michaels Archives. Photograph no. c539a1–1, R490. Also available in Ostermann (1913: n.p.).

to their summer homes at Houses Standing in a Line. I remember my father took my mother to the dedication of that mission in his buggy; Frank and some others in the family went, too, and so did lots of other Navajos. The priests invited everybody to the celebration. Of course, by then some of the Navajos had signed their children up for religious instructions from the priests, when they put them into school. Even though Frank went over there, I stayed home, with our children.[11]

After the workers finished building the stone church for the priests, the company moved away. Frank was hired to help haul their equipment to wherever they were going next, to build something for the government or someone else. They wanted Frank to keep working with them. But at the same time, some of the traders were talking to him about hauling freight in his wagon for the different stores. After he finished hauling the equipment for the building company to their next location, he came back home and told me about those things. He said the pay would be better working as a freighter, but that he'd be gone most of the time, since lots of those things had to be hauled out from Gallup to many different places. He was worried about supporting his family, and so, for that reason, he decided to take a job as a freighter.

Because we had another baby on the way, when he was ready to leave to start hauling things as a freighter, he took me back to where my family was living at Houses Standing in a Line. Mary no. 1, Mary no. 2, Seya, and I started living with my parents again, and moving around with them. And, for a number of years after that, it seemed like Frank was gone most of the time. Every now and then, he'd come back in his wagon to wherever we were living, after delivering things to the traders in Nazlini, Chinle, Valley Store, Round Rock, or other places. He never was home very long during those years because every time he was around, he'd be asked to haul wood for the Chinle Boarding School. So he'd take off again, and go up toward the mountains, either toward Fluted Rock or Tsaile, or on the other side of Houses Standing in a Line, to get wood for them.

During the years Frank was freighting,[12] I had some more babies. Some of them died and I, myself, started going through some sicknesses. But I wasn't alone in experiencing hardships because lots of things started going wrong for my mother and father, my sisters and brothers, our whole family. It wasn't the flu that caused the troubles we had then; these things happened *way before* the flu came through. Eventually we learned those things were happening because we were living at Houses Standing in a Line in the summertime.

Houses Standing in a Line

8

Spending summers at Houses Standing in a Line . . . troubles begin . . .
we finally move away.

Quite a few years after my father had started growing crops in many places in the Chinle Valley, he decided we should spend the summer right here in Chinle, instead of taking the sheep over to Fluted Rock. So we were spending our summers right across from here, across the Chinle Wash, where there used to be good farm land. Sometimes we'd all stay there; other summers, part of the family would go to Fluted Rock with the sheep and goats, as I've already mentioned.

One year my father decided to build our homes in a different place. If you look across the Chinle Wash from here and then north, that's where he did that. There was a little hill there that sloped down toward the west and he built our homes up there; that was near but above where we had been earlier, where he had found the good farm land that's now all covered with sand. Even the place on the hill where he built at that time is covered with sand now; there are lots of dunes over there. But at that time, there was no sand; the ground was good for farming in that whole area.

To the east and slightly north of there, there were places where you could get wood in the wagon. My father used to do that, and many years later, Frank and I, and our children used to go over there for wood, after we had settled here where we're living now. Even when the sands started blowing into that area and covering things up, after it rained in the summer, you could go there in the wagon for wood. But you had to go around the other way, around that hill, when you came back. It was too steep to come back down with a wagon full of wood on the dirt road that used to go by the place Bartine had over there. And even using that other way, the one that was flatter but went way around in a crookedlike fashion, unless it had rained it was too hard for the horses to pull a load in the sand. Besides that wood, to the north of the hill where we had our homes at that time, my father said there were places where large water birds gathered, like different kinds of geese and ducks; even sandhill cranes lived there at certain times of the year in large numbers. I remember when I saw those for the first time, when I was out with the sheep and those big cranes flew over, going in that direction.

My father decided to build our summer homes at that place soon after I started living with Frank. So, when we came back from the Black Mountain area, we all settled over there. We lived there for quite a few summers before anything started going wrong, and lots of people settled over there near us. There were always people who moved around with us; many of them were our relatives, but some just did that because they were following my father who was a headman.

Before we lived over there, my father had come across some rocks in that area, one time when he was traveling around on horseback. He told us he was going to try to build a house out of those because they looked like they had already been cut into squares. So, the next year, he and some of my older brothers, and some of our other relatives did that. They used those rocks and built our house all out of stone. At first, he built a nice little one, a small place; he just started with that. It was out of stone, not adobe or logs; it was not a hogan. When he finished that, he started adding to it. He kept adding on and on to it, making all of those houses in a row, all out of stone. That was really like one, long house; it was huge, when he finally stopped adding on to it. Right away, the People around here started calling that place *Kin Naaztí'í*, Houses Standing in a Line[1] because of the way he had built that up there.

After my father built all those houses standing together in a line out of stone, he also made a huge corral out of more of those same stones. My older brother and my mother's brother helped him build it. My father used that big stone corral for our sheep and goats, and sometimes, even for the horses and cattle. In the spring, when we'd round up the horses from the mountains and bring them back down, that's where we'd take them. That's why the walls of the corral were so high, to keep our horses or cattle in there, too. They built that in a circular manner and the walls were almost six feet high, all the way around.

A short distance from where he built our corral, my father also built several hogans. As I remember it, he made one or two round ones, and one forked-stick hogan. Those were mainly for our ceremonial use, and he hauled the timbers for them down from the mountains. He used his big, heavy wagon for that and some of the timbers came from Fluted Rock. I remember Frank helped him haul some of those, and others in the family did, too. Frank didn't use our wagon because my father built that place before Frank had earned a wagon for our own use.

We lived there at that long house in a line my father built for many summers. In the beginning, probably for four or five years, everything went well. All of us were in good health, and things were going well for my mother and father. Of course, during that time, all of us women kept working on the wool and weaving rugs. My father kept taking those to Ganado; he'd harness the horses he used on the wagon and haul all our rugs over to Hubbell's, and then trade there for what we needed. Sometimes, my mother or others in the family would go with him, when he traveled in the farm wagon over there. My mother knew lots of people in that area and she liked to visit with them at the store or at their homes, when they traveled that way. They'd be gone for several days when they did that, and when they came back, they brought whatever we needed, using the wagon to carry those things back here to Houses Standing in a Line.

My father had already started raising cattle and horses, along with our sheep and goats, before he built our summer homes in that place. We had *lots* of those roaming around the country because he had started doing that a long time before things started going wrong for all of us. He got all those things going really well for the whole family. We had *lots* of sheep and goats, and cattle and horses. When we put all the sheep we had at that time in the huge stone corral, it filled the whole thing right up. There was no space left in there; it was just packed with all our sheep.* That's how many sheep my parents had at that time. And when we'd move back to our winter area over by Salty Water, where he had fixed up places in that cavelike place, we had to divide that huge flock into two groups so whoever was herding them over there could control them. Otherwise, they spread all over the place and wandered off while we were moving back across from here.[2]

I guess that was one reason the People were always asking him to help them out whenever there was an Enemyway, or any other kind of big ceremony like that, going on. Sometimes, someone would even have a Nightway before we had moved back to the Black Mountain area for the winter, and they'd ask for help with that, too. Wherever we were living, people always asked my parents to help them because of all the animals they had. Because people would come and ask my father for help, we used to know what ceremonies were going on in this whole area. But then, too, most of the leaders like my father would go to those things; that way, they could talk to the People when they were gathered in one place because of a ceremony.

My father had lots of cattle and lots of horses out there on the mesa, on the other side of Salty Water at that time. From time to time, my older brother, The Jailer, would ride out there on horseback to check on those animals for my father. He was the only one who ever did that. It was all open range in those days so every now and then, someone had to go and check on the animals. He'd often be gone for several days when he did that because he'd have to locate all of them, find out how many calves or colts had been born, and then get them all back together again, so we knew they were all in one location. Sometimes, my father would tell this older brother of mine to round up those cattle and bring one or two of them back. Then he'd put them in the corral so we could butcher them for meat. Whenever anyone in the family needed that kind of meat, he'd use those cows for that purpose, and then he'd use their hides for the bottoms, the soles, of the moccasins he made for the family. But most of the time we lived on the sheep, their meat. We always kept them with us, wherever we were living, because they needed to be herded. Those horses and cows could take care of themselves out there on the mesa.

After we'd been living at Houses Standing in a Line for many summers, things started to change. It seemed like even though things had been going really well for my mother and father, lots of troubles started coming their way; everything started going wrong. Those things started *way before* the flu came through here and killed so many people. So, our troubles at that time were not from the flu. Eventually, we found out what was causing these things to happen to our family. And, after my father decided to believe what different ones were telling him about it and to do what others said, those things finally stopped.

When we moved over to Houses Standing in a Line, everybody in our family was well and healthy. But after we had lived there for some time, things started to not go right. My older sisters starting getting sick. As I remember it now, three of them and one of my older brothers passed away over there. There had been others who passed away before I was born; I'm not talking about them because that had happened long before we lived over there. These three sisters were all older than me, but not too old. They were women already, in their late twenties or maybe early thirties, somewhere right around there in their age. Two of them were already married and had children when they died; one of them had all boys, and the other, all girls. The other of my older sisters who passed away at Houses Standing in a Line didn't yet have any.

One of my older sisters was the first person to get sick after we had lived at that place for many summers. She kept getting worse so my father starting doing some small ceremonies over her, and saying some special prayers he knew. But she just got worse and worse. So, finally my parents decided to get a star-gazer to come, to see if they could learn what was causing it. My own father was a hand-trembler and he used to do that for people, when they asked for his help in that way. But he had already done that for my sister, and then had tried doing some small ceremonies because of the results of that, like Blackening and some prayers. I remember my mother kept asking him to get someone else to help find the cause of my older sister's sickness. My mother told me she was worried about him doing that hand-trembling for my older sister; she was afraid maybe it wouldn't work because the one who was sick was his own daughter. But he kept telling her that didn't matter with those kinds of things.

Finally my father agreed to go get a star-gazer he knew. The man couldn't come right away. By the time he finally rode his horse over to Houses Standing in a Line, my sister was very, very sick; she was already dying when he finally came. After he finished doing his star-gazing, he called the whole family together to explain what he'd seen. The way he saw everything during his star-gazing, the way he explained it to all of us, we were living right on top of a ruin. Where my father had built that place, Houses Standing in a Line, was practically right on top of a ruin. He told us we were not supposed to be living in an area like that; that's what he said was causing my older sister's illness. She was really sick; she was already too far gone by then, and he said she'd never get well.

After he told us that, he asked if we had noticed any pottery or other things around there. Several summers after my father finished building that place and we had all moved up there, when we'd be out with the sheep or out looking around for some of the wild plants we used for food or for dyeing wool for our rugs, my sisters and I used to see those things. Sometimes we'd come across all kinds of pottery; some were big, some, small; some had designs on them and others were plain, like the kind we make. Here and there, in some of the places we moved around in over in that area, there'd be pieces of that, lying around. Sometimes, when we'd start seeing lots of it, we'd dig around a little, too; then, we'd find other pottery, with lots of things still inside them. Those pots were always all smashed up before we uncovered them, all broken up with whatever those things were that were inside of them. My sisters and I never said anything about that to anyone; we just talked about it among ourselves, wondering what those things were we kept finding here and there in that area.

But after the star-gazer told us what he saw, we told the rest of the family about those things. My father was very quiet while that man was talking and while we were telling him about that pottery. After we mentioned those things, the star-gazer told us he was sure there was a ruin there and that it was causing all these troubles; that was the reason we were having this illness in the family all of a sudden, and that was why my older sister was dying. He also told us we should all move away from there and go to a different area. Everybody in the family heard him say that because we were all gathered there, in one of my father's big hogans, to hear what he had seen during his star-gazing.

My mother wanted to move because of what the star-gazer told us. But at first, I guess my father didn't really believe what that man said. We went ahead and had different ceremonies for my older sister; he got some singers he knew to do some more prayers for her, and we even had an Enemyway for her, shortly after the star-gazer had gone back to wherever he was living. Lots of people helped us with that, but my sister never got better. She passed away shortly after we finished the Enemyway for her. Before she died, they had moved her out of the house to a separate place where they made like a small sweathouse for her. But I don't think she was even aware she'd been carried over there; she was so very sick it seemed like she was unconscious before she passed away.

A short time after she died, two more older sisters of mine and one of my older brothers also got sick; it seemed like their sickness was the same as my older sister's because they, too, just kept getting worse. My father did the hand-trembling for all three of them, too; then he went ahead and did the same small ceremonies he had done for my sister who had already passed away. But the same thing happened; all of them kept getting worse. Then my father started going to get medicine men for them; he kept trying all kinds of ceremonies for those who got sick at Houses Standing in a Line. And he also went and got several other star-gazers to see if the first one was telling the truth. Each of them told him the same thing, that a ruin was causing that sickness and we should move. Another of my sisters died shortly after those other star-gazers had come to find out what was causing the sickness that was affecting those three.

After she passed away, we kept doing different ceremonies for the two who were left, because every day they kept getting worse. At the same time, my father also hired several hand-tremblers. Each of them came, and each of them told us the same thing, too — that we were living on a ruin and because Navajos aren't supposed to do that, people in our family were dying. And shortly after the last of those hand-tremblers had been there, the two who were still sick, another of my older sisters and one of my older brothers, passed away, one right after the other. Even though we wanted to have some more ceremonies for them, it was too late. In spite of all the ceremonies we had done, they passed away. So that was three more, right there, who died while we were still living at Houses Standing in a Line that summer.[3]

My father used up lots of cattle and sheep while those ceremonies were being done as payment to the singers who tried to help us during that time. Before that summer was over, he told my older brother, The Jailer, to round up lots of his cattle and help him take those over to Ganado. During that time my father sold lots of cattle to help with all the ceremonies that were being done here for people in the family. Of course, he didn't sell all of them; there were still quite a few up there on the mesa at the end of the summer, after the troubles we were having stopped.

Even though the priests were already established in Chinle, my father didn't ask them to bury my older brother or my older sisters when those things happened. Various people in the family helped fix them up, and take them to the places where they were buried. For four days after each of them died, we didn't wash and we didn't eat; that's our custom when someone dies.[4] It's the same way with names; when someone passes away, we don't mention that person's name again after that. My parents reminded us about all those things and told us to respect them so the deceased wouldn't get angry and bring on ghost sickness. All of us listened to what they said, and tried to keep quiet about everything that had been happening. But it was very hard; we were all very, very sad; some of us kept crying, even though my father told us we weren't supposed to do that, either.

Both my mother and father tried to console the rest of us; they said these kinds of things happened in life and we were just going to have to be strong enough to withstand them. We were all going to have to learn that these kinds of hardships could be expected; that was part of what was going to happen to all of us. They said we would learn that people died, just like new ones got born. That was the way things were planned for us by the Holy People. They said that would happen to all of us and that sometimes that happened before people got up in their years, before they died from old age. They said sometimes that happened to children, or even newborn babies, and that some day it would happen to them, too; even they, themselves, some day would leave us, and we were going to have to be able to bear that, too.

During the times when we were observing the four days after someone passed away, none of us went anywhere, like to the store or to visit other people. Of course, some of us had to go out each day to herd the sheep and goats so they had something to eat and water to drink. Even though my mother and father had used lots of those for all the ceremonies we did that summer for my three older sisters and one older brother who passed away, there were still lots of them left, and they had to be taken care of. But even with the herding, we didn't go very far from Houses Standing in a Line during that time.

I remember, too, that my father had been hired to sing a Blessingway for someone when the first of my sisters got sick; she was already very, very bad when it was time for him to do that so he told those people he was going to have to postpone the ceremony because of my sister's condition. He finally told them to ask someone else, since it seemed as if one after another of us was getting very sick, and he didn't yet know the cause of it. When you're a singer, you're not supposed to perform your ceremonies when your relatives are dying; if you have already started to do one, you have to stop, if someone passes away.

After the last of those four days was up and we had washed and eaten some food, my father called all the family together, and also all the People who moved around with us and were living over there at Houses Standing in a Line. Everyone gathered out in the open, sitting here and there on the ground to hear what he was going to say about all the things that had been happening. Frank was not there because he had already started hauling freight for the traders and was gone most of the time. I remember I was already starting to help my mother look after the children two of my sisters had left behind when they died. I just added some of them in with my own children and my mother was taking care of the others; we had already started to go along like that.

After we gathered together, my father gave a long, long talk. Even though he'd been very quiet during most of the time these things were happening, he used his big, loud voice for his talk, at least in the beginning. But as he went along, his voice got softer, almost shaky, and he started talking slowly; we all knew he was very, very sad, too, about losing so many in our family.

He told us even though he hadn't believed the first star-gazer, now he knew that man and the rest of the people who had done star-gazing and hand-trembling for us were right. He said he now believed we were living right on top of a ruin. He told us he didn't know that while he was building the stone houses, adding on to the first small one to make one huge house, making all of those together right there in a line. But he said he started to wonder about those things when he was building our big, high corral. I guess when he found the place he wanted to use for that, he decided to start building it from underneath the ground. So he dug around and came across a whole ruin right there, down under the ground, with pottery and everything else in it. He said he'd even found some bones there, too. Those were probably burials or something like that. My father said he'd never mentioned that to anyone; that was just like what my late sisters and I had done when we never said anything about the different kinds of pottery and other things we saw while we were out herding.

He said that because of everything that had happened and because of what all the star-gazers and hand-tremblers said, he now knew what he had found under the ground where he built the corral was an Anasazi ruin. He said now he understood the whole place there, the place we called Houses Standing in a Line, was on top of an old ruin. He said that thing was just like in the Canyon where you can see those ruins way up there in the cliffs. The Navajos always say that you're not supposed to live in areas like that; it's forbidden for us to live near anything like that. My father told us all the people he had hired to determine the cause of my sisters' and brother's illness were right. Each one of them, every one of them, had said only one thing and it was the same: we weren't supposed to be living in an area like that, or near it, or on it. We're *not ever* supposed to do that. They said the area was not the right kind of place to be living because the Anasazi had lived there long ago and most of them probably died and got buried there, too. That pottery was from the Anasazis; even the stones we had used to build the houses and the corral with, those stones that were already cut for that purpose, were from the Anasazis, too. Of course, we never found out how long they had been there. Navajos are never supposed to have anything to do with Anasazi things. If you do, even if it doesn't harm you right away, sooner or later it will cause trouble for you. That's probably why so many of the people who live down in the Canyon try to live as far away from those ruins as possible, even now.

My father said he believed this was why we had started having trouble; even though we were doing very well when we first started living at Houses Standing in a Line, after we'd spent a few summers there, lots of people in the family started getting sick and dying off. He said that was happening because we were living in a place like that. As I listened to my father's words, I believed he was right about those things; even though I don't really know what killed those older sisters and that older brother of mine, we had never had those kinds of troubles in our family until after we had spent several summers in that place; then people started dying.

After he said those things, my father talked about those Anasazis. He said he'd heard about them at other places but neither he nor my mother had ever seen what those creatures looked like. They had just heard about them from stories they were told while they were growing up. What he told us was that it was like in the story we have about that monster, *Yé'iitsoh* [The Big Giant]. In the old stories that many of the People tell about *Yé'iitsoh*, my father said they never knew what a *Yé'iitsoh* looked like; they couldn't even imagine it. So both my mother and father thought the stories told about *Yé'iitsoh* were like those that were told about the Anasazis. That's the way my father explained it to all of us. He said it was like the same story because nobody had ever seen the *Yé'iitsoh* or what it really looked like, and it was the same way with the Anasazis. All those things have stories about them that have been told over and over, and passed down for many, many years. He said it was just like that. He also said he and my mother had never heard of anybody who remembered seeing those Anasazis, either. But they knew all of them died; he said he'd been told the Anasazis came to their end because they were destroyed in a tornado or a whirlwind, something like that.

After he talked about those things, my father said that because of everything that had happened and because of what all the star-gazers and hand-tremblers had told us, he believed we should move away. All those people had said that, too, that we should move away from there right away. My father said we should leave that place and never live there again. He said even though it was only late summer and the corn wasn't fully ripe, we should start moving back to the Black Mountain area where we had our winter homes. Unlike other times, when we moved away from Houses Standing in a Line that summer, we just left everything the way it was. We didn't take anything except our own personal belongings, what was in the hogans and in that long house in a line. We didn't take any of the rocks or things like that. The house in a line, the hogans, the corral, and everything else were left behind when we moved away from there.

After we moved away, we went back to the Black Mountain area. Some of the family came back in the wagon to help my father harvest our fields near Houses Standing in a Line, when it was time to get the corn, melons, squash, and other things we had planted there. But my mother and I, and what was left of my sisters didn't come back; we stayed over at our winter homes, taking care of our own children and those left behind by my older sisters who passed away at that place.

For many years after that, when you looked over there from here, where we live now, you could see the whole thing; all the buildings at Houses Standing in a Line were still standing up. The long house my father had built out of stone by adding to the first, small one over and over, and that huge, high, stone corral he made on the side of the long house stood there for a long time. I know after Frank and I moved over here and our own children were starting to grow up, when Augusta and Isabel were small I could still see the walls of that house in a line from here. I used to be able to stand right here and see all those things still standing up when I looked over in that direction. Even into the late 1940s, you could still see those standing over there. I used to look over there every now and then, and think about those things.

But years later, people started going in there and taking the rocks out, little by little. The house started getting torn down by different people who came, who were moving in from other areas. I guess people started taking away those rocks because they were already cut and ready to build with. Probably none of them knew what happened to us when we used those stones over there. For a while after that started, you could still see the ruins; but then, the sand started covering those up, too. Now there's nothing but dunes all over that area.

Place of the Reeds

9

Our new summer location . . . my father gets a Flintway jish *assembled . . .
I lose a baby and start having some small ceremonies . . . moving around
and living with my parents and relatives while Frank was gone freighting.*

During the winter after we left Houses Standing in a Line, my father talked with my mother and a lot of other people about where to settle when it was time to move back across the Chinle Valley with the animals in the spring. He wanted to keep farming near the Chinle Wash so he wanted to settle in that area, but not at Houses Standing in a Line. He said we could keep taking the sheep and goats up to Fluted Rock; some of the family could live up there with the animals while the rest lived near the Wash and took care of the fields. Finally, he told us and all the People who moved around with us when we moved back he was going to settle across from where we had lived before, across the Chinle Wash from Houses Standing in a Line. He said on the other side there were lots of reeds, the kind used in ceremonies for making prayerstick offerings and other things. He knew the land around there wasn't being used by anyone else for any purpose, and that it'd be a good place in which to plant our crops.

So in the spring, when we came back over here, my father built our summer homes on the other side of the Chinle Wash. That was when we moved to this side, and started living around in the area where we are now. When we started spending our summers on this side of the Wash, my father built a log house for himself and my mother; he and other family members also built hogans and ramadas here and there in the area. Some of the family stayed in those; others took the sheep and goats to Fluted Rock and lived up there, traveling back and forth to bring mutton from there to those living in this area, and to take back the crops being raised in the fields, whenever different foods were ready to eat. We continued living like that in the summertime for a number of years; sometimes my children and I were in Fluted Rock with others who were herding the sheep right around our hogans up there. Sometimes my father and mother were there with us, too. Other times I lived down here, in one of the places my family had built near the Wash. Whenever Frank came to visit, whenever he was haul-ing freight to stores in this area, he'd stay with me and our children. Sometimes he was around long enough to help with some of the plowing, planting, or hoeing. But many times, he had to deliver things for the stores and then take off again, to pick up something else with our wagon and haul that to some place else.

The first time my father built on this side of the Wash, all along there in that whole area the land was covered with huge reeds. They were thick, just the way my father had described them to us before we moved there. A few of those had to be cleared away by my father and other men, when they started to put up the hogans that were closest to the Wash. The roots of those are long and go straight down; they spread themselves very quickly. In the spring, when the winds blow, the reeds help to shelter things; they're like a windbreak. But of course, when the winds are blowing other things around, like sand, then those things catch in them. Over the years, as more people settled in that area and started farming closer to the Wash on this side, the reeds started dying out. But even now [1963], in a few places you can still find them. Now the reeds that are left are sticking up in big mounds of sand, like dunes.

The place where we lived the first time my father built on this side of the Wash was the same place my husband, Frank, used later for planting alfalfa. It was past where he and I put our cornfields, east of that, right near the Wash, much closer than we live now. After Frank stopped freighting and settled down with us, he built us a round, log hogan at the same place. For many years, we had our own alfalfa field in the same place where my father moved all of us when we came back the next spring, after we left Houses Standing in a Line.

When my father and my mother, what was left of my brothers and sisters and their children, and my children and I first settled there, there were no fences anywhere. The whole area was covered with huge reeds and that's why we started calling it *Lók'aa'tah* [Place of the Reeds]. Others in the family settled there, too; that's why the land over there is still in our family. My younger sister, Small Woman, was there, and others, like Gai and her sisters and brother. Sam's older brothers, the ones called The Man's Grandson and The Jailer, and his older sister, Bah, were there, too. As I remember it now, Sam was only around in the summertime because he had already been put into school here in Chinle; he was in the first group of children enrolled there.[1] So, the whole family settled in that area once my father decided we should move to this side of the Wash and stay on the side where we are now.

Before then he had farmed on the other side in that huge area, even while we lived on the top at Houses Standing in a Line. After we located at the Place of the Reeds, the land there became known as my father's farm land, right along the Wash there all the way down, even though there were no fences or trees. Finally, my father gave that land to his grandson, Sam's brother, The Man's Grandson. He farmed it after my father passed away while my mother was still alive. But after a while, he got married and moved to the Black Mountain area. Then no one used the land until Ida's husband started working it. Finally, their son James came back and started farming it. That's how they ended up with it, after The Man's Grandson passed away. For many years, James raised alfalfa, corn, and melons over there where my father used to have his fields.

One of the summers my children and I were living with my parents and others along the Wash where the reeds were thick, my father shot some cranes. Farther north of Houses Standing in a Line, lots of water birds used to gather from time to time. You just had to travel a small distance to the north to see those big birds when they passed through here; we used to hear the calls of the snow geese as they flew over where we were living. Sometimes we saw sandhill cranes and other big birds like that, too. I never was sure why those birds stopped there, behind the rocks to the north of Houses Standing in a Line. I don't think there was water in that area. Maybe that was where they gathered to take a rest when they were traveling to some other area. My father said the sandhill cranes and other big birds always returned there each year.

My father had been learning the Flintway Ceremony from some older men who knew how to perform that.[2] When he finished his learning, he wanted to get a medicine bundle assembled for his own use. So he went hunting for a female and a male crane; you need those to make that kind of *jish*. The heads of those, cut off at the neck, are decorated with beads and other things, and then put together with other things when you assemble one of those. And each time you perform that for someone, if that person wants to add something to those decorations, that can be done if the right things are used and tied on the right cranehead. After my father shot the two he needed, a big ceremony was held to fix those for him. People who knew how to assemble that medicine bundle gathered together and did that for him. My father and mother took the wagon and went over there with some other people from here. They even took Seya with them, even though he was very small and barely walking around then. My two girls and I didn't go with them; we stayed here to watch the place and the animals. After that was over and he was blessed with the *jish* that was made for him with the heads of the cranes he shot, he started doing the Flintway Ceremony for people, too.

Once he had that *jish*, others wanted to borrow it from him, and so sometimes, he'd loan it out, if he knew the singers knew how to conduct the ceremony correctly. You can also use that for a Shootingway, if you know how to do that, and so sometimes singers who were trained to perform that wanted to borrow it, too. I remember my father had trouble with that one time; he loaned it to an old man, and I guess that man passed away before returning the *jish* to my father. Finally he tracked it down and brought it back. Then he had to have another ceremony to renew himself in the use of it. That was because when he finally located it among the relatives of that old man, one of the crane beaks was slightly damaged. So that had to be repaired and the whole thing reblessed.

Later my father decided to teach me a few things that went with having that *jish*. That was after the flu came through here and killed so many people in our family and in other places. I guess he was trying to make plans for the future of those craneheads; you can't keep that *jish* if you don't know some things about it. When my father passed away later, that *jish* was first given to one of his grandsons who had started learning. Later, he passed it back to me for safekeeping. I didn't learn the whole ceremony, of course, but I was able to take care of it in the right way because my father had taught me some things about it.

Over the years, different ones would come around asking to borrow it from me. Whenever that happened, I always discussed it with my husband. Lots of times, Frank knew things about the people who came, asking to borrow it for ceremonies. But he never loaned that out; he always told them it belonged to me and it was up to me to decide. I only had trouble about it once that I remember. I loaned it to somebody and they never brought it back. It disappeared for a while but eventually I heard that some man in Cottonwood had it, and was using it. He wasn't the one who had asked to borrow it from me. So Frank and I went over there in our wagon to get it. That man was home. After we talked about it and he understood it didn't belong to the man who had loaned it to him, we brought it back over here. For a while after that, I didn't loan it out again. But then I did, and each time the person has brought it back in good condition after using it, just as promised. Now I'm thinking about it a lot, because there's no one in my family who has learned the things that go with having that kind of a *jish*. I know I need to make some kind of plans about it for the future.[3]

As I remember it now, only one hardship came my way right after my father located all of us at the Place of the Reeds. I think that happened then, but I'm not certain. I don't remember that very clearly now. I gave birth to the baby I was pregnant with when Frank left to begin hauling freight for the stores and took me back to Houses Standing in a Line, where we then had all those troubles. That baby was almost due when we moved back the next spring and settled along this side of the Wash. It was the one I had after Seya. When it was time, my father hired a Blessingway singer from around here to do the one-night ceremony for me. I gave birth to the baby in the same way as before, with my mother helping right there in the hogan. Just like before, I didn't have any trouble while giving birth. The baby was a boy. When Seya saw it, he sure was excited to have a brother; until then, he was the only boy around, with his two older sisters. But then, something happened to the baby; he got sick with something before he was even two weeks old, and he passed away very soon after I noticed he was sick. I don't think we had even named him when that happened.

That was the first child I lost and it made me very sad. It seemed like some of the things my father had said to all of us before we left Houses Standing in a Line, about losing even little babies, were already coming true. The three children of mine who were living then were sad, too; their new brother hadn't even lived very long before he left us. Both my father and my mother talked with all of us about it, telling us those things just happened as you went along in your life. I guess it must have been my father who contacted the Franciscans about it; I remember Father Leopold came in his buggy to get the baby. I guess he buried him in the old cemetery that the priests had for a while behind the mission.[4]

After that happened, I started having trouble with some sicknesses. It seemed like it was indigestion because my stomach, right below my ribs, would ache lots of times after I ate something. Those pains would just come and go. My father did hand-trembling to learn the cause of it; sometimes as a result, he'd do small ceremonies for me. Some of those had small sandpaintings; other times, he'd do things that involved cutting and making prayersticks. One of the bundles he had went with the Cutting Prayersticks Ceremony so he knew those things, too.[5] Of course, sometimes he'd go and get another singer to do something else, some small ceremony that he didn't know after he did the hand-trembling when my pains got bad. That trouble seemed to last my whole life; it was always small ceremonies that were done when I got like that, not any major five-night or nine-night ones. The first major ceremony that was done for me was after Howard was born, but that was for some other troubles I had. After Frank finished working for the freighters and settled down with us, he used to go and get hand-tremblers for me, when those pains came back. Then he'd find someone to do whatever small ceremony was suggested because you don't use Blessingway for those things. Now I wonder if maybe that wasn't my gall bladder, even way back then, after my fourth child. It wasn't until a few years back that I had surgery for that; that's when those pains finally stopped.

As I remember it now, we lived along the Chinle Wash at the Place of the Reeds for three or four summers. And, during that time, except for losing at least one baby[6] and starting to get those pains, most of the time things went along in the right way, without too many other hardships. I, myself, worked very hard trying to support our three children by weaving rugs so my father could take them over to Ganado and trade for what we needed. Frank was gone most of the time because he was hauling freight. Every now and then, he'd bring us things from the store to help out, like food or some clothing for our children. He'd use some of his paycheck to buy things like that. But lots of times, he wasn't around, and I knew if I didn't keep making rugs, my children and I would face difficulties. I don't know what places Frank traveled to during those years, or what he did. He never mentioned those things when he came by, so I don't know if he was fooling around during those years or not. I tried not to think about those things; I tried to follow my mother's words, what she had told me when we first started out. Because of that, I kept thinking about my children, my home, how I was going to support my children, take care of our animals, and things like that, instead of worrying about what he was doing. I know I heard from different ones who traveled around that Frank had taken up gambling and was kind of running wild. But I never asked about it when he came to see us. I think he already told you about those things when he was recording his story for you. I remember one day, a few years ago, when I was sitting in there with you while he was working on that. He was talking about that time of his life; that was when I finally learned about some of the things he did while he was freighting. I guess that was his foolish time; that was before he finished learning the Blessingway Ceremony, before he settled down.

In the years when Frank was gone most of the time and my first three children were starting to grow up, I lived with my parents, Small Woman and her children, and others who moved with us, like Little Singer and Long Moustache. While my father was alive, all of us continued moving around, back and forth across the Chinle Valley. In the spring we'd start moving back so that by summer, we'd be somewhere near our fields, where the corn was planted, and the squash, beans, and other things. And some of the family would be in cooler places with the sheep. Then in the fall, when it started to get cold, we'd move back toward the Black Mountain area, and stay over there until it started to get warm again.

We lived in lots of different locations in the Black Mountain area in the wintertime. One place in particular I think I've already mentioned; that was at the foot of the mountain near Fish Point, where my father put the corral in a cavelike place, so the walls of the corral on three sides were rocks. When we were there, he'd use brush across the front to keep the sheep and goats in; it was like a fence, but he made it out of brush, not wire. That whole area was full of rock formations. Some of them had names and others didn't, as far as I knew. I know that here and there in that area, there were pictures on the walls of the rocks; my parents said people had drawn those a very long time ago. Some were pictures of animals, and some were more like people, but just sticklike. Because there were so many rock formations there, there were also lots of rattlesnakes. We used to warn the children about those things, and tell them to leave them alone if they came across them. My father and my mother knew different herbs to use for various kinds of injuries and illnesses; I know my father knew how to make the medicine that was used if someone was bitten by a rattlesnake but I don't think that happened to anyone while we lived over there. Later in my life, it happened to me but that was after my father passed away and we had settled down where we are now.

We lived at the foot of the whole Black Mountain area. Sometimes we were toward the west, by Red Rock Mesa; other times, we were more to the east or north, and sometimes more this way, on Red Grass Mesa. One place we called Standing Rock, and another one was known as Rock Bridge. There was another place we called Window Rock; there were rock formations over there that had holes, windows in them like the one at Window Rock where the Tribal Council meets now. Another place we called Red Rock or Red Hill. On the top of that place, there's a big, cavelike place and toward the west end, there's a canyon. Back in there, in the back of that cavelike place, there was a spring. We used to bring water down from there, from the spring and pools that were in the rocks in there. Even in the early days, we got water from that spring. We used to go up there with our goatskin bags, those water belly bags, and fill them and then drag them back down. Because lots of people did that, the place was called *Tó dishood* [Drag the Water Off, Drag the Water Out, or Drag the Water Down].* After I started raising my children, when we were living over there, Sam and Seya would haul water down from there for us; Sam rode the horse, but Seya was still too small, so he'd go up there on the donkey.

My children used to play around in different places, and sometimes make up their own names for them. I know Seya used to go to one place he and Sam called Play Hill; when we lived west of the hill, they'd go on the east side to play, when they weren't busy herding or doing other things. That way, of course, they were out of my sight.* But I didn't worry too much about that, because I could hear them from the hogan. When they started hunting, they had another place they called Rabbit Hunting Rock. There was a flat rock east of Red Rock where lots of rabbits used to come around. When they went there, they always came back with rabbits for us to eat. And near there were other rocks; on the top of those were little ponds that were full of salt. We used to go up there and gather salt to use in our cooking. That place has nothing to do with the one called Salty Water [Bitter Water] which is much further west, near Fish Point at the foot of Black Mountain, right under the gap. The water there is too salty; you can't drink it, even from the springs.

The children had other places they called by different names; one was a little gray hill that everyone called Porcupine Sitting on the Hill, Porcupine Hill. And there was Prairie Dog Flat, where they hunted other animals. All those are over there in the area where we were living when my father passed away, by those window rocks. There's a flat there called *Tse'abe'* [Breast Rock]. I guess whoever named it thought the flat rock there that stands on its side looked like a mother's breast, where milk comes from, so they named it Breast Rock and then the whole flat through there started being called that. Even after Sam was put into school here in Chinle, Seya would go to those places, taking others with him. I guess he taught them how to hunt, too, just like Sam taught him [see Map 3].

Sam was put into school first, because he was older. When we put our girl, Mary no. 2, into school, we were still traveling around like that with my parents. We moved around all over this whole area wherever there was grass; we didn't just go to one place over and over in those days. Even when we started moving across, we'd live in lots of places in this whole Chinle Valley, all over that mesa up there by the dump and then down here. In the summer, before the troubles at Houses Standing in a Line, we went as far east as that place, across the Chinle Wash. After that, we stayed on this side. My father used to plant as far north as where Mary's fields go now, and then our other relatives planted north of there. And then sometimes, some of us would go on to Fluted Rock with the sheep. When my father got sick, we moved from Black Mountain over toward Whippoorwill and then back, more toward Red Rock and the Window Rocks.

When Seya was three or four, and then again later, right after the flu came through this whole area, we spent the winter near the foot of Black Mountain at Fish Point. My father and other men used to hunt deer and wildcats on top of the mountain. There were lots of horse trails that went up Black Mountain in different places, and there were also trails across on the top. Some of those were the same ones our ancestors used when trying to escape from their enemies in the days before the People were sent to Fort Sumner.

I know one winter when we stayed at Fish Point, my father built three forked-stick hogans, *'ałch'į' 'adeez'á*, for our family to use. Those were covered with brush and dirt. Other times, he made *hooghan nímazí*, the round ones. But there were also some old stone hogans in that area and old sheep corrals that others used. Sometimes it really snowed when we were over there; we used the snow for water for the sheep and ourselves. Sometimes it'd melt by itself; sometimes we'd melt it over the fire and then carry it through the deep snow over to the circular corral my father had fixed for the sheep in that cavelike place there.

We always spent our winters some place in the Black Mountain area while my father was alive. The landscape over there then was different than it is now; years later, the winds started blowing sand around, near Fish Point and in other places. But when my first three children were small and we were over near Fish Point with my parents, there weren't any dunes. Lots of buckhorn cactus and big, prickly pear cactus grew there and there were lots of prairie dogs, porcupines, rabbits, and coyotes in that area. The men used to hunt porcupines and rabbits, and we'd fix those for our food. They also hunted prairie dogs and we ate those, too. Of course, most of the time we ate mutton; my father had lots of animals so whenever anyone wanted mutton, we'd butcher one or two sheep for our own use. And too, every now and then, he'd decide to round up one of the cattle he had over near Thin Rock, and use it for meat and making moccasins. At that time, it was not hard to find water for the animals to use in that area. There were no water tanks there when my first three children were small and we were living there with my parents. Later, the government started putting in shallow wells and dams, like the one at Salina. But those things dried up after only a little time had passed, and now, as far as I know, there's no water at any of those places the government built for that purpose.

The children used to say there were lots of rocks with holes in them; probably the winds made them that way. I knew there were lots of caves in that Black Mountain area, before the gap, and I used to warn them not to take off and go exploring in them, or in the canyons over there, either. I always worried they'd get lost, or fall and get hurt. And at night, we'd hear coyotes howling; I always told the children to come inside whenever I heard them. Lots of times it seemed like they howled every night. We tried to build fires only at night when we lived over there. We never returned to that place after my father, Man Who Shouts, passed away, even though that wasn't where we were living when he died.

There were also places in the Black Mountain area where it was cool in the summer. Sometimes, after Seya and Sam were old enough, they'd stay over there with the sheep even in the summer, while others in the family moved over here by the Chinle Wash to farm. Red Rock was one of the places where they stayed with some of the sheep, sometimes. Of course, a few grownups stayed with them when my father decided to do things that way. So sometimes I was over there with them in the summer, and sometimes, Sam's sister, Bah, was in charge of them. Usually there were other ones too, like Beautiful Woman and her sister, Chubby Woman, and their half sister, Gai, in the group that stayed together in the summer and helped herd. I remember being over there several summers, when Seya was too small to climb on a horse; he used a donkey for herding while Sam used a horse.

Whoever stayed over there to watch the children who were herding used to prepare mutton and goat's milk for the family members who were over here doing the farming right by the Wash, or farther north toward Valley Store. After we butchered, we'd put the meat in sacks, and the milk in small wooden kegs my father got at the store. They were only about two feet long, and each donkey could carry two kegs besides the sacks of meat. The boys would ride across the Chinle Valley, taking those things to the others. In those days, there were no fences in the way of their traveling. The Chinle Valley was a big, open area and people just moved around, settling where they wanted to, not in the same place over and over. About the only thing that grew in the Valley was greasewood, here and there. There still were very few trees at that time. For a while, for a great distance there was only one, the cottonwood that my crippled brother, Man with a Cane, planted where he settled across the Chinle Wash. That's why he was also called Man with a Cottonwood, Man with a Tree.

After the boys stayed over by the field for a few days, they'd start back. Then, whoever was farming would send back kneeldown bread, lots of corn, and other things to those of us staying near Red Rock or at some other place. Sometimes the boys would even bring back peaches. Even after my father gave up on his peach trees at the bottom of the Canyon, we still had relatives who had orchards there; they'd give us peaches after they got ripe.

Other summers, my father decided the sheep should go to Fluted Rock. I know when I took my children there when they were small, they were frightened by all the trees that were so big up there in the mountains, just like I had been scared of them when I was little.* They didn't see many trees in other places in those days. My father used to try to stay at Fluted Rock, if he decided the sheep should go there in the summertime. He always worried about the wild animals that lived in the forests up there. He didn't want the wolves or the bears hurting any of his grandchildren or any of the sheep or goats. So he preferred to do the herding up there himself on horseback. When we'd be up there with my mother and him, he'd always warn my three children about the things that lived in the mountains and tell them to stay right around home with me and my mother. He told them not to wander around at all while we were up there because it was easy to get lost in the woods. He said that happened to children when they went too far out from summer locations up in the mountains; all the trees looked the same, and they got turned around and didn't know how to find their way back. So my three children stayed right around wherever we were living when we were up there with my father and mother. They helped work on the wool while my mother and I kept weaving and my father did the herding. Frank was not there with us; he was gone, hauling freight.

In those days when we kept moving around, we lived in lots of different shelters. In the summer, many times we didn't stay in hogans; instead, we used ramadas or we might use tents. Some people in the family had tents from the stores; those had two end poles and a cross pole. You just threw a piece of canvas over those and then maybe pegged it down on the ends, if the winds came up. Sometimes we made shelters that were more like the circular, brush enclosures you see now at Nightways. You could put tarps, or big pieces of canvas over those, too, during the summertime and stay in them as your shelter. Of course in the wintertime, our houses were more substantial because of the snows and the winds. My father would always put up two or three hogans in the Black Mountain area, either the forked-stick ones or the round ones.

At least one summer after my father settled all of us at the Place of the Reeds, he decided there was enough grass for the sheep to the north of where we used to live at Houses Standing in a Line. Sometimes he'd ride around on horseback checking on the condition of the grass and other vegetation the animals liked to eat. He'd do that before deciding where the animals should spend the summer, after we moved across the Chinle Valley from our winter locations. That one summer, my two oldest girls lived with my parents at the Place of the Reeds, while Seya and Sam, and now and then some others too, took the sheep and went across the Wash, to the north of where we used to live. They herded north of there, staying in tents they carried over there on donkeys. Every other day or so, someone from here would ride over there to check on them and their food supplies. Sometimes that person would watch the sheep for a while, while whoever was in charge of herding rode or walked over to the store we now call the Thunderbird. That was way before they established the Park Service or the national monument at Canyon de Chelly. My father always said Seya and Sam were responsible about the animals; he never worried about the sheep when they were herding away from the rest of us like that. And because I knew someone would check on them at least every other day, I didn't worry too much, either.

During the years Frank was gone and we were moving around with my parents, my children, the three who were living, were starting to get older and learn things. By then, my father's second wife had passed away so he was with us all the time. I don't remember exactly when she died, but by then, that had happened. My father and mother helped show my children how to do lots of things; they were there to help me with instructing them. I know the children I had at that time all learned how to help with the sheep and the goats, and when they got old enough, they started to help with the herding. We had lots of animals in those days and there was always plenty of work to do on account of them.

The two oldest ones, the girls [Mary no. 1 and no. 2] started learning how to weave, too. My father and my mother both kept encouraging them, even when they were small. I think the oldest one was probably around eight or nine when she really started understanding things about setting up the loom and weaving. When we lived near the foot of Black Mountain, of course there was little wood in that area. So, my father made our looms by using the main beam of the hogan. He'd put the strings or the wool around that and then bring them down to the ground, the floor of the hogan. At the bottom, underneath there, he'd dig a hole. Then he'd take the outer bark from a piece of cedar he'd saved and roll that up real tight and then put a wire inside there. Then he'd pound the whole thing into that hole in the ground. That was like a roller; as we worked on our rugs, we'd roll up the finished part using that. The main beam of the hogan supported the rest of it, because there was no wood to use in making a frame, either the side pieces or those that went across. But when we lived in places where wood was available, well, then my father made the looms just like we do now.

My father started making small looms for the children, and he and my mother showed them how to set those up and how to start a small rug. He even made looms that were little enough for them to carry them around while they were herding; he did that for my children and also for all of their cousins who were moving around with us at that time. And he made small battens and combs, the other things you need if you're going to use a loom. He made all those in small sizes, to go with their small looms.* My father as well as my mother did lots of weaving in those days. A lot of the old men used to do that, but then it died out and only the women kept it up. Of course, I was weaving too, whenever I wasn't busy with other things. In the years Frank was away freighting, I worked very, very hard at weaving lots of rugs. It was the main thing I was using to support my children; it was the only way I had of raising them in those days. And the other women who were living with us were also weaving all the time. So, all of us kept encouraging the children to watch and learn how to do that.

My father, especially, was very, very patient with both of my oldest girls. He always sat down near them; maybe he did that because he was so tall and didn't want to be scaring the little ones by towering over them like the trees at Fluted Rock.* He never used his loud voice about those things, or scolded them; instead, he'd always try to be smiling when he was with his grandchildren, and he'd tell them funny stories, even jokes, to make them laugh, too. Many men who were like my father, who had lots of livestock and were singers and leaders, weren't like that; they were very stern all the time and almost never smiled for any reason. But even when my children did something wrong with the yarn, my father would be patient; he'd just take that back out, undo it, and quietly show them again how to do it right, always praising them for trying. They both got interested in weaving because of that.

As they got better, he made bigger looms for them to use. He kept encouraging them and finally, he said he thought their rugs were good enough to take to Ganado to trade for things we needed. I remember the first time that happened; he and my mother went over there and did the trading. They kept the things separate so each of my girls could see what their rugs had been worth in the way of food when they came back. And eventually, they even took the girls over there in their buggy, so they could learn some things about that place — how to trade, count money, and other things. My oldest girl, especially, really started working on her weaving because of those things. My father and mother really encouraged her in that; they said even in her crippled condition, if she became good at weaving, she could support herself and any children she might have later in life by means of her rugs. So, even before she became a *ki-naaldá*, she had learned a lot about weaving; today, as you know, she's known as a really good weaver in this area.

I remember my mother was still making pottery in those days; sometimes my father and mother would let my girls come into the separate hogan they used for that and sit and watch them do that, too. They also helped me gather the sheep dung used to fire those. So they started learning how to do all the things involved with making pottery, too, during that time.

Another thing my children started learning about was how to fix different things as food. As soon as they were old enough to herd, they started going places with me, my mother, and some others in the family, when we'd gather different wild plants and other things we used to fix as food. Even Seya and Sam, and the other little boys around here learned those things; my parents said they should learn too, so they could always fix something to eat for themselves, if there was nobody around to do that for them. We always took them with us to pick *haashch'é'édą́ą́'*, wild carrots, wild onions, wild potatoes, yucca fruit, Mormon tea and the other kind, and the other things we gathered. We showed them where to find them, what they looked like, and how to prepare them for use, either right then or later. And we also started showing them how to use the grinding stones and prepare a few of the traditional foods everyone in the family liked to eat.

My father and mother liked paperbread. So one time when I was fixing up a new grillstone, I showed my oldest daughter everything I knew about doing that. That's a lot of work, as I've already mentioned. After she learned, I showed her how to make paperbread without getting her hands burned. I think I taught Mary no. 2 about making it, too. My mother and father were in there, adding in what they knew about it, so I guess they learned from all of us. But it was the oldest girl, Mary no. 1, who got very good at making it. Later, as my other children came along and she started having her own family, we used to get together to make it. My parents were always like that with all their grandchildren; they were always willing to show them how to do things they knew about.

But with basket-making, it was different. My parents kind of discouraged them from learning that, telling them it was too much work and there were too many restrictions surrounding it for them to start making those. They let them watch when they were making baskets but they discouraged them from trying to learn. On account of that, I don't think they ever learned much about basket-making.

With the boys, it was different in some ways. My father used to spend time with his grandsons, teaching them about the animals, getting them started riding the donkeys and then later, when they got bigger, the horses. Of course, to teach them to take care of the livestock, he started them out with the sheep and goats. He used to talk to them about not playing around while they were herding and not acting the way billy goats do. I know he said a lot to them about billy goats, because we used to hear him.* He also asked them to help do different things in the fields; he showed them how to plant corn, beans, and other things when they were small, and later, how to hoe, and then plow, and harness the horses up to the wagon. Of course, in those days, there were no trees around here anywhere, just the lone one my crippled brother planted over by the Wash. Nothing was fenced, even where different ones put their fields. There were no paved roads going anywhere, just wagon trails, horse trails, and paths the sheep and goats made as they moved around.

My father also used to take the boys around in his buggy; that was especially true with two of his grandsons, my oldest boy, Seya, and the one we called Sam. He was older than Seya, probably by five or eight or more years, but the two of them always played together and herded together. And they went places in the buggy with my father. Everybody always said Sam and Seya were my father's favorites. As soon as they were old enough, almost every time he went somewhere, he'd take them along; he even started taking them to ceremonies. He was the one who took each of them to see the Ye'iis the first four times. Sometimes it seemed to me all those two boys were doing was riding around with my father, going somewhere with him in his buggy.* But I guess they were learning the whole time.

The main reason he took them to Nightways was so the Ye'iis could whip them; you have to be initiated four times that way so you can dance with the teams. One of the times they were whipped was at the Nightway for Long Moustache; another was at one being held for Yucca Fruit Man. I know he took them to Nightways over by Garcia's store and by the Thunderbird, and over where the low rent housing is now; at that time, there was nothing over there. I think Seya first saw the Ye'iis at a ceremony this side of where the Mormons have their church now. I remember when he came home from that and ran into the hogan, telling my mother and me about what had happened and what he had seen. We got after him right away because you're not supposed to talk about those things in front of others who haven't been initiated. There were some little children in there with us when he got back. As I remember it, he got whipped by the Ye'iis five times, even though only four is required, because that happened again when my father took him to another one down by Valley Store. Those ceremonies always started before we moved back toward Black Mountain for the winter, and my father, some of my brothers, and their children always went to them. They went to *lots* of Nightways. Lots of them were Yeibichei dancers with teams, as I've already mentioned, and Seya did that, too, later. He was able to dance because my father got him initiated like that when he was little. You can't dance, you can't even fill in for one of the dancers, unless you've been initiated like that. Lots of men around here, like Howard Wilson and Woody Davis, danced at those ceremonies and established teams to do that with them.

Another thing my father did was tell his grandchildren about his own childhood, and the things the Navajos faced way, way back, when the Spanish and Mexicans and others, like the Utes and Apaches, and different ones were chasing them all over the place and having battles. My mother didn't talk very much about those things in front of my children, or about Fort Sumner, either. But my father said he wanted his grandchildren to know those things and learn from them.

Both of my parents tried to teach the grandchildren who our relatives were and how people were related to us. When different ones would come around, my mother or father would explain who they were to my children and the others who were here. They said it was important to know those things, like who was in their own clan and the one they were born for, and who the other people were who moved around with us. I know that's how my oldest daughter, Mary no. 1, learned about my father's other wife, my mother's younger sister. She never saw that woman, of course, because she had already passed away before Mary no. 1 was old enough to realize things. But the one child she had, my half sister, Slim Woman, came around a lot. She was already living with Old Red Bottom Man by then and had some children for him, too. Sometimes we lived near them. One time when Slim Woman was here visiting, my daughter came right out and asked my mother and father who she was. My father told her he had a daughter by another wife who was my mother's younger sister. My mother explained that lots of men had two wives, but that Man Who Shouts' second wife, the mother of Slim Woman, had already passed away. She was the only child that wife had for Man Who Shouts. That's how Mary no. 1 learned Slim Woman was my half sister.

My father and mother acted the same way toward their grandchildren as they did when they were raising us. Not much of that had changed from when I was little. They expected them to learn the things they had taught us and to be raised in the same way. So I just went along with that, following what they said about those things. I don't remember that my children got into much trouble during the years we lived and moved around with my parents, while Frank was away working as a freighter. Of course, sometimes one or another of them would do something that worried me; but even then, I tried to talk nicely to them and explain why I didn't want them doing that again.

One time I remember in particular was when Seya was little; I think it was the first summer we lived at the Place of the Reeds where my father had built a log house for himself and my mother. I guess they had gone somewhere and Seya and somebody else, maybe Philemon Bitsui, were playing around by that house. For some reason, they decided to climb up on the roof and jump off, to see if they could fly. They only got bruised doing that, so they were lucky. Even though I'd already talked to them about why they shouldn't do that again, my father talked to them too, after he got back and heard about it. That was one time he scolded them. Nobody used that log house after my father passed away years later. Eventually people in the family took it down and brought the logs over here where we're living now. You can see some of them here and there in the outside walls of the old log house over there. When that was first built, it was used by my daughter, Ruth, and her family, but now, no one has used it for a long time.

Another time I remember was when my oldest girl, Mary no. 1, and her brother, Seya, were out playing along the Chinle Wash. They were probably herding at the time. I guess they found a little puppy there in the reeds and started playing with it. Both of them wanted the puppy so they started arguing about it. They were fighting over it and they almost killed it by pulling it every which way between them. Seya started crying because he wanted the puppy, but Mary no. 1 wanted it, too. I guess my father heard them because he was outside, doing something while I was in the hogan, weaving. Later he told me he walked over to where they were fighting over the puppy. He told them to stop it and get back to herding the sheep which had started to wander off all over the place. He got after them about it and that was the end of their tug of war.* He told me he reminded them that playing was not going to get them anywhere. They needed to learn to take care of the sheep, card and spin the wool, and work with the loom, weave, and do other things like that. I didn't say much when he told me about it. They were both old enough to herd but I knew children sometimes played when they were out with the sheep and goats; my sisters and I used to do that, too. So I never said anything about it to the two of them when they came back with the sheep later that afternoon.

Another thing I remember was that when Seya was very small, he had trouble getting his words out. Sometimes he stuttered; other times he'd be talking but it was hard to understand what he was trying to say. I knew I had to try to figure it out, but sometimes I couldn't. One time right after we had started living over by the Chinle Wash, one evening it was just starting to get dark. Most of the children were already inside, but he was still over by the Wash, playing. I could hear a dog howling from somewhere down that way. He came running in, all of a sudden, saying, "Mama, Mama, there's a dudi saying something over there, down there in the ditch. Let's go find the dudi." I had no idea what he was talking about.* I guess maybe he thought it was a screech owl making that sound. Sometimes we used to hear those and maybe he heard us talking about them, those *tsidiłdǫǫhii*, or explaining to the children what made that sound. But here, it was only a dog.* That was the first time my mother said something about the way his words came out. She said we should do something about it. But at that time, I didn't say anything to her; I just told him to stop playing and come inside.

There were other things my first three children did while they were playing around the Place of the Reeds. I remember once they were playing sheep; one of the Marys tied Seya's hands and feet up, like she was going to butcher. And then, one of them found a corn leaf and used that as a knife, not knowing those are sharp. Seya got cut and started crying. That scared the two Marys and they ran home. Don Nez was outside doing something; he heard Seya crying and went over there and untied him. When he brought him home, I heard what had happened. But by then, all three children were laughing about it, so I didn't say too much.

My father always had lots of visitors, like other headmen and other singers. Because of that, sometimes the three children I had at that time got teased by people they didn't know. One man who was called The Skinner used to tell Seya he was going to cut off his ears, whenever he'd see him. Seya was scared of him and always tried to run off and hide whenever he came to see my father. Another one who came around a lot was one called The Old Man; he used to ride along on his donkey looking like he was asleep. I guess Seya and Sam used to try to scare his donkey because of that, if they were out picking watermelons or something else in the fields when The Old Man came along. He didn't scare them.* But Curly Hair Water Flows Together Man, the one we called Old Curly Hair, did scare them. He was a singer and a leader, and he came to see my father a lot; they'd get together, smoke, eat, and tell stories. And at night, sometimes they'd practice their songs, going over parts of those or places in the stories some had forgotten or comparing where their teachers had different versions. Whenever Old Curly Hair was around, he always ordered Seya or Sam or the others around, saying, "Unsaddle my horse, feed my horse," or do this or that. They were scared of him, too.

All during my early married life, my father had the job as headman for this whole area. Of course, he wasn't one of the first leaders of the People; he was too young when those were appointed when the People were released from Fort Sumner.[7] Being a headman meant he had to travel a lot, to settle disputes when troubles came up, and go to meetings with other headmen or the officials at Fort Defiance. Sometimes the Franciscans here in Chinle would tell the leaders they could meet at the mission, and turn their horses in the pasture that was near that place. I remember sometimes when the weather was warm, a number of headmen from different places would gather over there, and sit out in the open, under the shade trees that had been planted there by the Fathers. My father also was asked to give talks to the People whenever they gathered at ceremonies, so he usually went to those being held around where we were living. Depending on the weather and how long he might be gone, sometimes he rode his favorite buckskin horse to those; other times he went in his buggy or the farm wagon. After the schools started opening, the headmen were also asked to come and talk to the children about the importance of getting an education, and how to behave in school and listen to the teachers.

We used to have some pictures of my father around here, taken when he was a headman, but I don't know what happened to them after my mother passed away. We used to tease him, saying he looked just like the man that tea company, Lipton, puts on its boxes of tea bags that are sold at the trading posts. He really did.* He had white hair and whiskers, and a long, white moustache. But he always kept his hair short; he never wore a *tsiiyééł* [hair bun, hairknot] like some of the other, older men did. The one picture that still exists is the one taken with Father Anselm, when my father was over at St. Michaels, probably doing some work with the priests in conjunction with his Blessingway Ceremony or going to a meeting there for some reason. That one was published in the Fathers' magazine [*Padres' Trail*], and then again, when they had their Jubilee celebration a few years ago at St. Michaels [see Fig. 11]. There were other pictures, too; I remember one we had showing him up at the Chinle mission, standing by himself in front of a Navajo blanket, holding a horse whip in one hand and his big,

FIG. 11. Man Who Shouts, Tall Woman's Father (front row, second from left, with white moustache and large hat), and other, unidentified Navajos with Father Anselm Weber, O.F.M., center, at St. Michaels. Photographer, Simeon Schwemberger, ca. 1902–8. Courtesy of the Franciscan Friars, St. Michaels Archives. Reproduced from the Schwemberger Collection by the late Father Simon Conrad, O.F.M. Photograph also appears in Franciscan Fathers (1949: n.p.) and *Padres' Trail* (Oct.–Nov. 1973: n.p.).

black hat in the other. There were some horses and other people way in the back of that picture, off to the side. That picture got lost a while back, so we no longer have it. That's true of another one showing him from his concho belt up to his hat; he had his beads on and some kind of suit coat someone had given him to wear. Somebody took that when he was on his way to some meeting. That one was around a long time; then it disappeared. Somebody probably threw it out while they were cleaning.

Because he was a headman, he was well known in many places on the reservation. Of course, he originally came from the Salina area, and so they knew him over there, and all around Black Mountain, and then down in Ganado and Fort Defiance, and throughout the Chinle Valley, and here in Chinle and in the Canyon. Other people knew him because he sang Blessingway and Flintway; years after he passed away, we were still running into people, even way over by the Grand Canyon, who had hired him to sing over their family and remembered him very well. And some people knew him because he was a big stockman who had lots of sheep and goats, and also cows and horses. And then others knew him because he sang Yeibichei songs and went to those ceremonies with his sons, many of whom were Yeibichei dancers. One of his sons, The Jailer, the big, heavyset one, looked just like him; he had a long moustache, too. My father had lots of friends, too, like the Damons and Hastiin Buckinghorse, and others he met through the trader in Ganado, when he'd be over there. And then, of course, there were all our clan relatives; on my mother's side it was Towering House People, and on his side, it was Bitter Water.

My father was known for his loud voice; even though he was called The Man when he was younger, once he started serving as a leader, he got the name Man Who Shouts. His voice scared some people, even some of his own grandchildren and in-laws.* But he really wasn't mean as a person. My own children used to talk about that, especially the ones who got to know him before he passed away. After they reached their adulthoods, they'd talk about how different he was from other men who were leaders. He knew so much about setting up looms, starting and finishing rugs, and weaving in different ways. He taught my two oldest girls and was already showing the next two girls a few of those things, even though they were still very small, when he got injured and then passed away. He also taught them about some of the plants and how to use them for food. He knew those things and wanted to show them all the things he knew. They also said he was a really nice old man, that he was very friendly to everybody, and also very, very patient. He never got after them too much when they were little, never yelled at them, or scolded them with harsh words. He was patient about everything he tried to teach them. He'd sit down with them and talk to them in a nice way when they did something they shouldn't have done. He'd explain why that was wrong and tell them not to do it again. He always was concerned about their safety and well-being, and he wanted them raised in the right way. Then, too, he always helped out when tragedies came along and children were left without parents; that's why he and my mother ended up raising several other children along the way, like Sam and the rest of those children.

Despite his big, loud voice, lots of people who were not our relatives said the same things about him; they said he was always patient when he talked to the People at meetings and ceremonies or other gatherings. They said he'd explain things clearly and in different ways, until everyone understood what he was saying, and what the agent was up to, or what the government had planned next for the People. Many of those things were confusing, and there were always rumors going around about things that mixed people up even more. So when the People gathered together, he always had to straighten things out and explain things over and over, until everybody had no more questions. That was the job given to the leaders who were chosen to work with the agent in different parts of the reservation. They had to work with him and with each other. They also had to help the policemen who were assigned to different areas to make sure no more troubles broke out, like in the earlier days. Once they started the Tribal Council, those things changed, of course. But that didn't happen until after he had passed away, so he was not part of that.

Because he was a leader, people liked to get my father's advice and hear what he had to say about different things, even when to start plowing, or when to move back to winter locations. In those days, people moved around constantly, but they didn't go by themselves. They moved in large groups; usually part of a clan that was closely related would travel together. So there were always lots of people living around us and moving with us. Then, as different ones got married, they might move elsewhere and start living with others, and moving with their families. And, others joined in with us. So, the group moving with us changed from time to time. And then too, some people decided to settle down in the Chinle area, instead of moving back and forth, in the fall and in the spring. My father didn't want to do things that way, so we kept moving until he passed away. When we'd get back over here in the Chinle area, then the people who used to move with us who had decided to settle down and stay here all the time would be near us again, while we were living here in the spring and summer.

I remember some of the people who were moving around with my parents and me when my three children were small. My younger sister, Small Woman, was there with Jennie and some of the rest of her children; she hadn't settled over where the ground is hard so she wasn't known as Woman from the Hard Ground Place yet. My older, heavyset brother, The Jailer, was with us, too, because he wasn't married then. And then there was Sam's sister, Bah. She was married to Woody Davis's older brother who was called *Diné Nééz biye'* and she already had Irene, Don, and Elsie Nez for him and some others. Later Bah remarried; she and Joseph Ganna had no children together. And there were others, like Gai, Beautiful Woman, Chubby Woman, and Tom; they stayed with us after their parents died at least until they got married. Red Woman, Woman with a Hunchback, and Big Woman were also in that group until they passed away. And so was Yucca Fruit Man and Slim Red Running into the Water Man. That one belonged to the Red Running into the Water clan, not our Towering House clan. The same was true with Long Moustache and his family; they were from a different clan but they still moved around with us. By then, others in our clan had decided to settle elsewhere. One of those was my crippled brother, Man with a Cane. He had married a woman from around Valley Store and settled by the Chinle Wash where he planted that cottonwood tree; he stayed there with his wife and two boys, Marcus and Walter. Sometimes Mr. Arm was with us with his wife, Paiute Woman, and their children; other times, they lived elsewhere in the Chinle Valley. Gai did that too; she got married around the time I had Seya or shortly thereafter and then sometimes, her family moved around with us and other times they lived with others. The Joneses were also part of our group by the time Seya was walking around; Towering House Woman had already married Squinty Jones by then. We were all like one big family, moving around and staying together, under my father as headman.

My husband, Frank, wasn't with us during those years because he was working as a freighter. He really didn't come back to settle down with us until he finished that job. That was when he got serious about learning the Blessingway. After that, his own father, who was also one of his teachers, used to come and stay with us, and move with us from time to time. Frank started learning some things from my father before he got injured and passed away. Then he settled down; that was pretty much the end of his running around years. After that, he didn't gamble very often. Once he became a Blessingway singer, he settled down and started making plans for the future. I guess that's when he turned into a grown-up man, and became responsible for his family and other things. I know later, when he used to talk to me about it, he said it was the Blessingway, learning that ceremony and starting to perform it for others, that helped him stop being wild and foolish. He said that straightened him out.

The Flu

*A terrible sickness comes . . . Agnes is born . . . the flu almost kills me . . .
how my father helped the People . . . winter at Nazlini Wash . . . Mary
no. 2 starts school . . . The Jailer dies and my father's cows get sold.*

After we had spent several summers at the Place of the Reeds, in the hogans my father
had built near where he and my mother had the log cabin, a terrible sickness started
spreading through the reservation. It was in the fall; the crops had ripened and we
were almost done harvesting them, drying some for our winter use, and putting some
into storage for the next year. We had not yet moved back to the Black Mountain area
but it was almost time to do that; my father had already started talking about it when
this sickness started.

That sickness hit us in the fall; it started spreading across the reservation almost
overnight and lots and lots of people died from it. People would feel fine during the
day, get sick in the night, and by morning, they'd have all passed away. It was like that.
It killed whole families overnight; up to about twenty people in a family would die in
one night. It seemed to really hit the young children; little children all over the area
were dying day and night, night after night. People died right and left. No one knew
what it was; it seemed as if people would break out with sores that looked like measles,
or chickenpox, or something like that. But then, right there, in most cases those
things didn't really come out on the top; they just turned back into the inside of them;
they went inward, inside their bodies, and from there, spread and killed them. Because
no one knew what it was, no one knew what to do about it; even the people trained to
find out the causes of illnesses—like the star-gazers, hand-tremblers, or listeners—
even they couldn't determine why that was happening or what should be done about it
by those trained to perform our different ceremonies.

My father, Man Who Shouts, got very worried when those things started happening. He and my mother never got sick from it, but in our family it hit the younger
children, and me, too. I don't remember how many people we lost during that time; I

know my younger sister, Small Woman, lost at least four of her children to it, two girls, the oldest boy, and another boy, and maybe others, too. It was the same with lots of others who were moving around with us at that time. One of my older brothers, The Jailer, the one who took care of my father's cows and horses, had married a woman from Black Mountain by then and was living over there with her family. That woman had already had one boy for him, the one called The One Who Returned from the Warpath in a Bad Mood; that was another of the names my older brother was known by. When the flu came, that boy lived but his mother and the new baby died. Long Moustache lost his wife, too; she was a Coyote Pass clanswoman and had just had a baby girl for him. When she died from the flu, they buried the baby in the sand with her; they knew she wouldn't survive without her mother. Long Moustache was living on the mesa, Red Rock Mesa, when the flu came. I don't remember who else we lost at that time; when people die, we don't talk about them ever again. We don't speak about those things, mention their names, or think about it. Those are our rules about that; we just try to stop thinking about it after they've been lost like that. So, for that reason, too, I don't remember who else passed away at that time. But the rest of my brothers and sisters, except for my crippled brother and my younger sister and my half sister, had already passed away before this sickness came through here. From what my parents told me, I guess I, too, almost passed away from it.

I don't remember too much about the flu; I remember getting sick and telling my parents something was happening to me. At first, I thought maybe it was related to the baby I had had several months before that; that was my daughter, Agnes. I gave birth to her late in the summer and was taking care of her and my other three children who were still living when that sickness came around.[1] My father got someone to sing the Blessingway for me when it was time for me to have my baby, and just like before, my mother was there to assist me. I didn't have any trouble and this time, the baby lived; it didn't turn out like the little boy I lost before Agnes was born. Agnes was only about two months old when the sickness started spreading through the reservation; because she was a little baby, I was worried we'd lose her. But she never got sick from it; instead, it was me.

Because of that, what I'm telling you about this is what my parents and my oldest daughter, Mary no. 1, told me after it had passed and I had recovered. All I remember is getting sick and starting to go downhill. I got so weak I couldn't get up, and people started carrying me outside in a blanket when I needed to go out. After I got too weak to stand up on my own, I don't remember much; my mind seemed to go some place else and everything started getting confused. Later, people told me I was unconscious for a while because of that sickness.

When that started, my father talked to different leaders right away, and also to different medicine people he knew, to see what others thought about it. From everything he heard, he knew the sickness was all over the reservation, in different places, and it was killing lots of people. Some people were calling it an epidemic because it spread so fast, and killed so many people. It even killed people living far away, who weren't Navajos, too. Later, we learned it was influenza. Now I know that happened to us in the fall of 1918. But it stayed around, here and there, into the next spring. So, some of the People who died from that died later, the next spring, when it seemed to come back. That happened to them, even though they survived it in the fall.[2]

My father made a plan about what to do. He was a headman, and people looked up to him to help them get through this sickness, to tell them what they should do about it. After listening to different ones talk about what was happening in other parts of the reservation and what they had tried to do to cure people who were sick, he decided we should all move closer together, so we could help one another get through it. So he rode his horse around, visiting all the People who moved with us, checking on them, and telling them we needed to come together closer, so we could help one another if that struck our families. So, a number of our relatives who were living farther north in the Chinle Valley moved over closer to where we were, at the Place of the Reeds. As I remember it, my husband, Frank, was gone during this whole time. He was still hauling freight for the stores. I don't remember if he came around at all during the time we were going through this, or if anyone notified him when I, myself, got so sick and almost passed away. I just don't remember now; maybe he said something about that in his own story.

It was really my father's work that pulled us through those times. He told us to stay close together, to help one another, and to comfort each other. He said that way we'd keep each other strong, and withstand the suffering and hardships we were facing because of this sickness. The People really listened to my father when he said those things; the young ones, the old ones, all the People listened to him and followed what he said to do. He had good ways of talking to the People, even during hardships. He was always very good at doing that in the right way.

My father started gathering different plants and making medicines for the People to use. He knew lots of things about the plants we use for different sicknesses, injuries, and ailments so he started preparing medicines. Some of those were to be mixed with water and drunk, like an emetic; other herbs he said should be heated and then applied to your body, like the heating pads some people have today. Some of those medicines he gave people were for use in the sweathouse, when they took sweatbaths to sweat that sickness out of themselves. My father told all the People *not* to wash themselves with water, either plain water or herbs mixed in water. He said that would make them catch cold and help the sickness spread. He had learned from others that using water in that way made it spread. The People had no resistance to anything because those sores had turned inside, instead of really breaking out on the skin. If they got wet, or used water like we do when bathing patients during different ceremonies, they'd be apt to catch pneumonia overnight and that, too, would kill them. So, instead of using water in that way, he said to use some of those medicines mixed with sheep fat or horse fat to make a paste, and then to rub the paste over their bodies after taking a sweatbath. Some of the People made big pieces of that, and used it like those things you call poultices. He also told people it'd be all right to mix those herbs with the *chííh* [red ocher] we use for other purposes. My father gave those herbs, those different medicines, to anyone who asked for them; he didn't ask for anything in return for doing that, and lots of people got medicines from him for their own use during that time. He just kept going out and gathering the plants he needed to make those things for the People; he was trained in those things, too.

My father also told the People none of our ceremonies would help cure us from that. He said this kind of sickness, this epidemic, had nothing to do with any of our ceremonies, not even the small ones. Instead, he said the best thing we could do was to use our Blessingway prayers, to ask that the sickness stay away from us and all our relatives, and all other Navajos, or to ask that it only touch down lightly, if we were already sick. He, himself, prayed night and day, and even at different times during the day, using his Blessingway prayers to protect his own children and all the others around us, and to get the flu to leave the Navajo reservation. He just kept praying and telling other people to do that too, in the Blessingway way; he prayed day and night, and the rest of us did, too. And he used his prayers alongside those herbs, the medicines he made for the People to use. He never used the full Blessingway Ceremony for that, or sang any Blessingway songs; he just used the prayers.

Another thing my father did was to butcher lots of his horses so people could use the meat, the broth, and the fat from them. He still had a lot of horses at that time; he hadn't sold those off because he kept telling us horses were good for many things. You can do a lot with horses; they always give you a means of transportation, and you can use them in other ways, too. He started rounding up his horses for people to use before I, myself, got sick. He had my older brother bring a lot of them down from the mesa, where they were roaming around. Then he started butchering them, day after day after day. All his horses were in good condition; there was plenty of grass for them to eat in those days out where they had been roaming around, so they were all well fed; they were nice and fat. After he butchered one, different ones around here would help cut it up. Then he'd pass the meat around to anyone who wanted some, or he'd take it to places where the families were too sick to move around on their own.

I remember Paiute Woman was one of the ones who was like that during the flu; she was very old and already kind of sick because of that. She had moved back close by us and one day she came over to my parents' hogan and told us her children were sick with that, and she, herself, was worrying because she was starting to get a few of those bumps here and there on herself, too. She said her children had all quit eating and couldn't get up; they just lay there, refusing to eat, and they were swelling up with fever. So my father gave her some meat and told her to boil it and give the broth to her children and use that for herself, too. He also gave her some herbs and told her how to fix them. After a few days, he went over to check on them and took more meat for their use. We tried to take care of her and others like her while they suffered from the flu. It killed her oldest child, her only girl, and some of her little ones, too, before it lifted up. But The Man Who Talks A Lot and his younger brother, Thumb Man, those two out of the boys she had, made it through and so did old Paiute Woman. Their father, Mr. Arm, never got sick from it; he died several years later. Then she had to raise those boys by herself, even though she was up in her years.

Everyone who was not sick was trying to help those who were suffering during those times. The flu kept killing people; as I remember it, it was mainly the young children and the old people who passed away from it. But even some of the People who had just started raising their own children, the young women and men, got sick from it and passed away, too.

My father told all the People to cook the horse meat, boil it, and drink the broth. He also cut up the fat parts into slices, like the bacon we have now. He told the People to cook the slices of fat and then mix some of the herbs he gave them with the fat, to make a paste to use on their bodies. He taught different ones how to make the paste and told them to put it all over themselves, on whatever body parts were already aching, or swollen, or burning up with fever. He also said it'd be a good idea to put that paste on all the young children, even if they weren't sick, to protect them from the flu. I know he did this for all the ones in his own family, his children and his grandchildren. He even put that on my new baby, Agnes. But, for some reason, it didn't protect me from getting sick.

My father was the only one who kept riding around, visiting the People living near us to check on them and to see what he could do to help them during that sickness. He helped whoever was in need of help, and kept using up his horses for that purpose. He said he had learned that drinking the broth from the horse meat would give you strength to withstand that sickness, and that making the paste with those herbs in it would also help. So, for that reason, he killed lots of his own horses to help the People during that time. My mother and the rest of us womenfolk helped with the butchering and the cooking; I was doing that and taking care of my children when I, myself, got sick from the flu.

Another thing my father did to help people was to bury those who passed away. Lots of people were dying overnight, and sometimes there was nobody left in the family to bury them. Or, if there were still some left, they were barely breathing, or they were too weak to stand up because of the flu. So he went around and got whoever was strong enough to help with that; I know my older brothers, the one who was crippled, and the other one who helped with all the cows and horses, those two helped my father bury people. My crippled brother had started to learn how to move around and do things again by then, in spite of his condition. That took him a long time, but he finally started riding his horse again and doing a little farming, too. So, he was available to help my father with that. They put those who had died in the sand along the Chinle Wash. Sometimes, when lots died during the night, they'd make one big hole, and then wrap up the dead and put them all in there together. Later, after the winds started blowing the sand around, most of the places they used for that were covered up with sand dunes. From what we heard, the People who were living out farther from us, closer to the Canyon, buried their dead in there; they took them into the Canyon and packed rocks against them to cover them up. The priests from the mission probably helped some people with that, too, but I don't think my father ever asked them to help anyone in our family while we went through that.[3]

From what I heard, when some of the children who were at the Chinle Boarding School, and at Fort Defiance and other schools, got sick and passed away from the flu, they got the students who were strong to help with burying them. Just like what my father and other men did around here, they'd dig big holes and wrap them up and put lots of them in there together. At the schools, they used tractors for that; they made one big ditch when lots of children died overnight, put them in there, and then covered them all up like that.

As I said, I don't remember too much about my own sickness because when I got so sick, I just lost my awareness. I know my body started swelling up all over, even though my father had used that paste on all of us, his children as well as his grandchildren. I just kept swelling up and getting weaker and weaker, and after that, I don't remember what happened. From what I was told later, everyone thought they were going to lose me. I guess I got some kind of sores; those started breaking out all over my body, after I had already lost my awareness because of the fever. But then they went inside; they didn't stay on the outside. Everyone who was not sick started feeding me broth made from horse meat, and strips of fat. My father kept mixing herbs up in the fat, and using that like an ointment; he rubbed that all over my body, and he also mixed up the herbs with sheep fat and with *chííh*, and used those things on me, too. Later, they told me my whole body swelled up—my face and hands, and even my toes swelled up; they bundled my feet up in old gunny sacks to keep them from touching the ground when I needed to go outside. In the beginning, I was able to get around, even though they said I looked bad with those sores starting to come out, and different parts of me starting to swell up. Eventually, when I got worse, my face was so swollen I couldn't open my eyes; they said even though they kept talking to me, it was as if I didn't hear them. I couldn't speak or even shake my head or move my hands.

When I got like that, too weak to get around at all or go outside by myself or with others helping me, they carried me out in a blanket, now and then. Sometimes, when they took me out, they took me to the sweathouse and gave me a sweatbath, using those herbs, medicines my father had gathered, mixing those into something for me to drink, and also with the horse and sheep fat, or with *chííh*, to rub all over me. From what they told me, I was like that for a very long time.

When the flu lifted up a bit and people stopped getting sick and passing away from it, my father said we should leave the place where we were living, the one with all the reeds. He said we needed to move away from there. But lots of people were still weak from the flu. And those who hadn't gotten sick were affected in other ways; everyone had lost lots of their relatives and friends. And they were tired out from taking care of those who had gotten sick and trying to comfort those who had lost family members — wives, husbands, sisters, brothers, children, and grandchildren.

Because the People were in that condition, my father decided it was too far to go back to our homes in the Black Mountain area for the winter. It had already turned very cold and I think he was afraid some of the People didn't have enough strength to survive the move. In those days, it always took us many days to move across the Valley, taking all our animals and herding them as we went, while others hauled things in the wagons or on the horses or donkeys. So that winter our family moved only a little ways toward the west; that year, we spent the winter over where Mary no. 1 lives now, close to the Nazlini Wash. My father kept on with his Blessingway prayers every day during that whole time. I guess no one was certain that the sickness that had killed so many people was over. That turned out to be right, because in some places it came back in the spring, and more people died from the flu, again. But my father kept trying to help people, day and night, day after day after day, and he kept saying his Blessingway prayers, asking that this flu would lift up and go away for good, and never bother the People again.

After we had moved away from the Place of the Reeds and resettled ourselves for the winter, for a long time whenever my father talked to the People, he'd talk about that terrible sickness and how it had spread so fast and killed so many of the People all over the reservation. He tried to use consoling words in his talks, and he used his big, loud voice, so everybody could hear what he was saying. He talked about those things to all of us here in the family, too, almost every day, for a very long time after that. He kept saying we should learn from what had happened during that time. That showed nobody ever really knows all the things that are going to come their way as they go along with their lives. He said we needed to learn life could be hard, that hardships and suffering were part of what we would experience while we were living. And he kept telling us we needed to be prepared for whatever was coming our way. What he believed was that the Blessingway was our main guide, and where we could get strength to withstand all the hardships we would face every day and also, in the future. All of us understood those things already because we were his children and had been raised according to those things and with his Blessingway Ceremony. But at that time, he really stressed those things to his grandchildren, the ones who hadn't passed away during the flu. He wanted them to learn right then that life would be hard, and they needed to be prepared. He wanted them to be strong so they could withstand those things. Part of that, he said, came from getting up early in the morning and doing our prayers, and then running races, even in the snow. Those things built up endurance. The same was true with learning to work around the home, and do the things that needed to be done, like gathering wild plants for food, taking care of the crops, gathering wood, hauling water, taking care of the sheep and other livestock, and learning to cook different kinds of food, or weave, and other things like that. He believed learning all those things was important; they made you strong and prepared you for your future life. My mother supported him in his teachings to his grandchildren; she said even though they needed to play now and then, it was better if they spent their time learning these things and following his teachings while he was still around to talk with them and show them things.

I know after some of our relatives recovered from all the things that happened at that time, they started having ceremonies done for them. Of course, those who had helped bury the dead or had any contact with dead people had to have ceremonies to cleanse themselves from the effects of that. So they used Ghostway and other things.[4] My father and others in the family had that. And then, too, lots of people had Blessingways done for them. We had one for ourselves, too, to keep everything going in the right way for our family in the future. We knew we had been very fortunate during the flu, because we lost only a few people. In other places, entire families passed away. My father did some of those Blessingways for different ones; of course, he, himself, had one to renew himself, his songs and prayers, and his medicine bundle after he got cleansed from burying those who had died. He got another singer to do the Blessingway Ceremony for us. I don't remember now who that was; it might have been the one called Curly Hair Water Flows Together Man, Old Curly Hair; he was a clan relative of my husband's, and he was a well-known Blessingway singer, just like my father.

The next spring, after the flu had finally left the reservation, we started preparing the fields for planting. That year we didn't have to move back from Black Mountain because we had stayed right here for the winter. In the spring, the school officials started coming around again, trying to recruit more children for the Chinle Boarding School. They did that all the time; wherever we lived, the school officials kept sending people out to tell us to put our children into school. Different ones in the family were going through that. So, we used to talk about what we heard about that school and the things the children were learning from that experience. Even though my father and mother were very opposed to that when I was a small girl and wanted to go to school, they changed their minds as the years went on. Of course, my father had acquired some direct experience with those things since he had to visit the Chinle school and other ones, too, to give talks to the children because he was a leader in this area. He decided it might be a good thing if some of the children in the family, some of his grandchildren, were put into school. I think Sam was the first one who was enrolled over there; he was older than Seya and I know he was in the first group in Chinle; some of the others were Stephen Bizadi, Adelle Brown, Rachel Jones, Ben Gorman, Henry Draper, and Joe Carroll. Most of the children seemed to like that school; they always said they were well fed and taken care of. They were given clothes to wear, and shoes, and even coats for the winter. And they were starting to learn some things about English, how to talk in that way.

The school officials kept sending people out to recruit more children. Frank knew the government had a rule about our children going to school, and my own father knew there was such a rule, too. Frank, himself, had gone to school at Fort Defiance for a few years, before we had started out together. He was glad he had done that and he wasn't opposed to sending his children to school, at least at that time. During the years he was away hauling freight, whenever he came around he'd ask if the recruiters had been here. So, we had already talked about those things and decided to enroll our second daughter, Mary no. 2, in the Chinle school. That was an elementary one and it was a government boarding school. There were others from our family who went there, too, at that time, like Ben Mitchell. Mary no. 1, our oldest girl, of course was not among them. I remember she cried to go with her sister when the recruiters came and she learned we had enrolled her younger sister. She begged to be allowed to go to school with her. But we had already decided to keep her home because of her crippled condition, so I stuck to that with her. That's why for part of the time until Seya was sent to school too, only she and Seya were around here with me and the baby, Agnes. Their sister, Mary no. 2, was already in school and didn't come back until summer vacation. That was the rule the schools had about that.

Mary no. 2 started late that summer when it was time for children to go to school. Mary no. 1 still really wanted to go; she was still begging and begging to be allowed to go with her younger sister. But my father and mother, and I, too, told her again we were not going to do that. We really needed her to stay here to help me since I was busy trying to weave and support the children and take care of them. I was also trying to help my parents; we were living with them and moving around with them all the time. My mother told Mary no. 1 if she went over there, who'd take care of all the sheep and goats, or help with the grinding, or working with the wool? After a while, she stopped begging to go, but when her younger sister actually left, she really started crying and crying, asking again to be allowed to go. And so we had to say those things all over again to her. She cried about that for days. And I guess she kept thinking about it now and then, even after she became a *kinaaldá* and reached womanhood. Sometimes she'd say to me she wondered what kind of life she would have had if we'd let her go to school. I guess I understood how she felt, because the same thing happened to me, when I was a little girl and my parents refused me on that, too. But I never said anything about that to her. After a while she stopped crying over it, and when Seya and then other ones were put into school, she never again asked about going over there with them.

Mary no. 2 was still at the Chinle Boarding School when we sent Seya a few years later, after my father had passed away. When she finished there, she left for Fort Apache. Eventually Seya and his younger sister, Agnes, went over there, too.[5] Some of the other children we had were also sent to school later, like Augusta and Howard. But others, like Ruth, David, and Isabel, we kept home with us. Sometimes we did that because we needed help around here with the animals, the farm, or other things. But sometimes, it was because we didn't like the things that were happening in the schools. We lost Mary no. 2 when she was in high school in Albuquerque, and we also lost another girl, too, Pauline, at the Chinle Boarding School.

Right before Mary no. 2 left for the Chinle school, they were branding animals over near the Nazlini Wash. My older brother, The Jailer, was there, helping my father. Even though he had lost his wife and new baby to the flu, he stayed in the Black Mountain area taking care of his own livestock and the ones my father had. The cows and horses were roaming around in that area and sometimes closer this way, on the ridge over there. This brother of mine would come to visit my father every now and then, to tell him about the cows and other things he was taking care of. And when any of those animals needed to be rounded up, he was the one who always did it. I remember after we moved over near the Nazlini Wash, away from the Place of the Reeds, he did that when it was time for the animals to be branded. He brought them all over there, and put them in the corral he and my father made in a place near the Wash where there was a gulley. Then they helped others brand the new ones, so they'd know whose cows and horses the little ones belonged to. Every person with stock had a brand; my father's looked like this:[6]

FIG. 12. Man Who Shouts' Brand. Originally sketched by Tall Woman, August 1964; redrawn by Seya Mitchell, Aug. 15, 1989. Professionally drawn by Jennifer A. Frisbie.

When they started branding at that time, Seya went over there to watch how they did it. When he came back he told me my older brother had given him a buckskin mare; it was just a colt at the time. That made Seya very proud; it was the first time someone gave him a horse. We kept her for a long time. Eventually my husband got some other colts from her and started using her with his wagon.

After those animals were branded that year, my brother, The Jailer, went back to the Black Mountain area. One or two years later, he passed away. I'm not sure when that happened but I know we were traveling across, either to our winter home or our summer one, when we learned he had died. We started moving back and forth again the next fall, after the flu was gone. I don't think I ever heard what happened to him; it was several years after the flu so I don't think that killed him. He wasn't an old man at all when he passed away; he was in his manhood, probably in his thirties or maybe early forties. Someone told me later they thought he had heart trouble, but someone else said maybe it was something like measles that killed him. My father and mother went over there after we got that news. They told us later he'd been buried in the Black Mountain area.

After this older brother of mine died, nobody ever went to check on the horses and cattle that were roaming around on the other side of Salty Water, sometimes all the way down to Fish Point. My father was starting to get up in his age by then and he was busy with his ceremonies and his job as headman. Nobody else was available to do that, either. So nobody went to find out if they were still all together, or how many had little ones, and things like that. Nobody really took care of them anymore, and I guess those animals started going wild out there.

After some time had passed, my father started wondering about his livestock and worrying about them. So he finally rode over there. What he found was that the People around there were stealing our cows right and left because they were all up there on the open range where anybody could go and take a couple of head and drive them off. Those Many Goats clanspeople who lived up in the Black Mountain area were the worst thieves this side of Chinle at that time.* The older ones who were living then are most likely all gone now, but their younger generation is probably no different; they're probably still stealing, just like the older ones did. All of those Many Goats are from right there in the Salina Springs area. They're the ones my father said were taking his cows.

When he came back from there, he told us what he had learned. He decided he wasn't going to put up with that anymore and that he was going to sell all the cows he had left. He said if those people weren't stealing them, probably we could keep a few in the family and let them reproduce themselves. But the People around there were stealing from the herd, and there was nobody from here who could keep going over there to watch those animals. So he had to get rid of them. My other older brother, the crippled one, was still living at that time. Even though he had learned how to walk and get on his horse by then, he was still suffering from his condition and he couldn't take over those things for my father. Eventually he started riding again and going places, but that was later.

So my father and some of his sons-in-law and his older grandsons went back over there and rounded up all the cows. They brought them back over here and penned them up overnight. Early the next morning, he and another man drove them to Hubbell's where he traded them all off. None of the women in the family went along. It took them all day because they had problems on that trip. The cows didn't want to go. You know, cows can get stubborn. You can drive them so far and then, they don't want to go any farther. Some turn back and start running. One of those did that on that trip; it ran almost all the way back here that day, so my father had to stop right there. Someone waited there with the other ones while he chased that one back to where the rest of the cows were. So, by the time they got to Ganado, it was late in the evening. They stayed there overnight and waited until the next day to do their selling. That was the end of the cattle we had in our family.[7]

My Father Comes to His End

11

Frank returns but keeps gambling . . . Frank has a Beautyway . . .
Ruth is born . . . Man Who Shouts gets injured . . . our new hogan . . .
Pauline is born . . . Frank learns Blessingway from my father . . . my father
gets worse . . . more ceremonies . . . my father dies.

After the flu had passed through here and lifted up for the last time, Frank gave up his job as a freighter and came back to where we were all living together, and started moving around with us. He had learned many things from his experiences in that job, and met many different kinds of people, some of whom had become close friends. After he came back, there were two in particular he ran around with. I heard the three of them went gambling and other places together, and that some people called them the "Three Musketeers." They were always together, going some place, if they weren't busy doing things around home. One of those was his oldest brother, Jim, the one who had been married in a ceremony to the sister I herded with when I was little. She passed away, I think in childbirth, with the baby. After that, another older sister of mine, Little Woman, was given to him. She had at least four children for him before she died: Gai, Chubby Woman, Beautiful Woman, and a boy known as Tom. Little Woman had died many years before Frank came back to live with us again. Her husband, Jim, ran around all the time, even while she was living; he ran around with women, and he gambled a lot. My husband was like that, too, with gambling in those days. He traveled around with Jim and another man called Jake Tom, gambling in the Canyon and other places. Those were the ones called the Three Musketeers. Even after Frank stopped freighting and came back home, he did that for a while. So even then, my weaving continued to be the main way I had of supporting all our children.

In those days, it seemed like lots of gambling was going on; of course, some of it wasn't with cards. They had places over by the Chinle Boarding School and then in other areas where people would gather for different kinds of contests. Sometimes they'd have footraces, and sometimes they'd race horses to see who had the fastest one. I guess people bet on the outcome of those things. And in those days, they also had arrow contests; they'd get together to see who could shoot the best with a bow and arrows. From what I heard, even the children at the Chinle Boarding School sometimes got to participate in the footraces and the arrow-shooting contests. But, of course, they weren't allowed to gamble.[1]

When all those things were going on, lots of men used to gamble; even some of those we moved around with gambled. So Frank wasn't the only one who did that; people from Black Mountain would even come over in their wagons and stay for days, just gambling. Sometimes they'd do that after they finished getting the fields ready for planting, or after the hoeing was done. But other times, different ones would come around just to gamble. I know my father and mother were really opposed to that; they always told us *not* to do those things, never to gamble, because that's how you lost things you needed, like clothing, jewelry, even blankets, saddle blankets, saddles, and other things. Sometimes people even gambled with cows and horses. I guess they got carried away at times and even made wagers based on livestock. So my father was really opposed to it; almost every time he talked to the People at gatherings, he'd bring that up and tell them gambling would bring them harm, and bad things would result from it. But still, people did it anyway. In those days, I don't remember very many women gambling; it was mainly the men. And, I don't think there was much of it going on wherever they were having ceremonies. I know my father and lots of other singers used to tell the People if they had come around only to gamble, they should take their cards or whatever they were going to use for that to some other place, away from where a ceremony was being done to help someone who was suffering. But now, as you know, that has changed. People gamble during ceremonies, right outside the ceremonial hogan; women join in, too, and sometimes it's only women gambling. And now, of course, people are often drinking at the same time. Sometimes, that's why they start arguing and fighting when they lose things from gambling.

People used to play the Moccasin Game in the wintertime.[2] That goes way, way back, and my parents taught us how to do that in the right season. There are lots of stories that go with that, and lots of songs for the different Holy People involved in it when it started in the beginning. We used to play that game with my parents sometimes at night in the hogan; that's how we learned about those things. But I know by the time I had four or five children, sometimes when people would gather to play the Moccasin Game, they'd start gambling with that, too. That's not why it was started back in the beginning, according to what my father taught us.

When Frank was running around and gambling with others, they used mostly cards. I don't know what kind of cards those were; they had pictures, not numbers, as I remember. I guess there were different card games those men played; one was called

Coon Can; one was Monte, and another was Casino. There were others, too, but I don't remember what they called them. I never learned how to play any of those.[3]

When people gathered around where we were living to gamble like that, the children always seemed to know about it. It seemed like every time something like that went on at night, the children would get up really early the next morning. Then they'd go over to the hogan people had used for that, and go in there, really quietly, and look around. Sometimes they found dimes or other money lying on the floor. They always ran back to where I was, and showed me whatever money they found. My mother and father told me to let them keep it, so I told them that and never said anything about them doing that. But we told all the children over and over we didn't want them doing those kinds of things when they got older, no matter what they saw. I don't think any of them ever really got involved in that very much, even though Frank gambled for some time after he came back here to start living with us for good.

Right around the time Frank told me he was going to give up freighting, he started having trouble with his back. He thought he had injured himself from heavy work. The people who hauled freight for the stores had to load all those things on their wagons, and then unload them when they got to where they were supposed to take them. Some of those things were very heavy and when Frank started having problems with his back, when that really started hurting and causing him difficulty in moving around, he figured it was because he had sprained some muscles or hurt himself in some other way while freighting. He told me that was one reason he wanted to stop doing that, even though he said the pay he earned from it was good.

When those things didn't get any better, he started going to hand-tremblers, to see what was causing it. I don't remember how many he went to see, but those people told him he was having problems because he had done something to abuse snakes. He said he knew that was true because many times, whenever he'd run into snakes either around where we were living when he came to visit me and our children, or in other places, he'd chop off their heads. We're not supposed to do things like that; we're supposed to leave them alone.

So, finally it was decided that he needed to have a Beautyway Ceremony to cure himself.[4] That's a five-night ceremony and we decided to ask Curly Hair Water Flows Together Man, Old Curly Hair to do it for him. He was well known as a singer of Blessingway, Beautyway, and some other ceremonies too, and he was a clan relative of my husband's. Everyone around here helped us prepare for that ceremony; as I remember it now, that was the first major one Frank had after we started living together and raising our children. But he may have had others I've forgotten about. For a while, maybe three or five years, that seemed to help Frank. But then other ailments came along and he started having other ceremonies.

As for myself, at that time I was in good health. The only ceremonies that were done for me were the Blessingways right before my children were born. I had one of those again when my daughter, Agnes, was born in the late summer, right before that flu swept through the reservation and killed so many people. We called her "Girl with a Light Complexion" when she was small. And I had another Blessingway when it was time for me to have my next baby, about two years after Agnes. We do that to ensure a safe delivery and also to bless the woman and the child in their new life. The next baby was another girl who we called "Woman with a Light Complexion," even when she was little.* Later she became known as "Mama Ruth," after she started having children. That's Ruth.[5] I don't remember who did those ceremonies for me when those children were born; that was a long time ago. But I had no trouble during those births, and both of those babies lived to grow up, as you know.

Shortly after Ruth was born, not quite two years after the flu killed everybody, we were starting to gather our things together to move back to the Black Mountain area for the winter. It was late in the fall and we were still down here in this area, close to the Chinle Wash, but a little to the west of the Place of the Reeds, near where we had our cornfields. That's where my father had built our hogans that spring. We had finished harvesting the crops, and the family members who were herding the sheep and goats had already started moving across the Valley with them, toward Black Mountain. My children and I were still over here, with my father and mother. Seya was outside, playing around with somebody, so he saw what happened. My mother and I were in the hogan, gathering up our belongings to get ready to move to our winter locations. Frank was gone somewhere. I think some people had hired him to haul wood for them and he was off in the wagon doing that.

One reason we were still here was that my father had to go to a meeting some place in Chinle. He was right outside the hogan and had saddled the horse he always used. After he got on it and was ready to take off, he whipped it. For some reason, his horse started bucking when he did that. Even though my father had lots of experience with horses, when that happened, he was thrown off. That fall injured him inside somehow; he couldn't get up. Seya ran in and told my mother and me what had happened and we hurried outside. Together we carried my father back inside the hogan and laid him down on the sheepskins that were still spread around for our beds. My mother started fixing some herbs for him to use as medicines for his injury; my father knew about those things and because he was trained in performing Flintway Lifeway ceremonies as well as Blessingway, all of us, after we got up in our adulthoods, had learned some things about the medicines to use for different ailments. There was no hospital here at that time; I guess there probably was some place over at the Chinle Boarding School where they kept medicines for the use of the school children and the employees who worked there, but there was no place others could go, if they wanted to see a Western doctor. It was way before they established the hospital here in Chinle.[6]

After a while, my father said he thought he had recovered. But when he tried to get up, he just sank back down because of his injuries. Finally, he told somebody who was around here to take his horse and ride over to where the meeting was being held and tell them he'd been injured and couldn't go over there. I don't remember who did that, but when that person returned, we started loading up the wagon and the buggy for our move. My father wanted to ride his horse but he wasn't able to do that, so he went in the wagon. He tried to drive his team, but after a while, he lay down in the back, among the things we were hauling back to the Black Mountain area. At that time we were living near one of the rock formations that has a window in it. I can't remember if it was Window Rock no. 2 or no. 3 where we went that winter, but it was near the base of one of them. The hill my children named Porcupine Hill was near that Window Rock, too. We all knew the area pretty well because we lived there from time to time. The People who had gone ahead had already built hogans at that place because that's where my father had decided we'd spend the winter. Those things had been talked about before the others had left to move across the Valley for the winter.

I guess Frank heard about what happened to my father from somebody else while he was hauling wood and doing whatever he had been hired to do. He finished that work and shortly after we reached our winter homes, he came over there in our wagon. After that, he started staying around more often, spending time with us and helping do things my father had been taking care of before he was injured.

For a while after that happened, my father was able to get around. Sometimes he'd still herd the sheep in the winter. He didn't like the little children doing that in the deep snow and the cold winds; he always said they should stay inside and help us with the wool and the cooking when it was wintertime. By then, Ida was about a year old; her mother, Gai, had her after the flu lifted up and went away the second time, and I think she was pregnant again, for Son of Yucca Fruit Man. Gai's sisters, Chubby Woman and Beautiful Woman, hadn't reached womanhood yet and they were moving around with us with their brother, Tom. I remember many times that winter when my father would come in from herding, he'd tell my mother or somebody else who was there watching the children, to go and butcher because he was hungry for mutton. He used to say that, even if he had already been well fed before he took the sheep out. Sometimes my mother would remind him he had already eaten. But he'd tell her there was no point in having all those sheep and doing the herding if he couldn't eat mutton when he wanted to. So, we'd just go ahead and butcher for him and fix him some mutton and other things to eat. Sometimes it'd be late at night when we were still trying to get those things cooked for him; the little children would already be asleep.

For one or two years after his injury, my father kept going to meetings when he was able and performing his ceremonies for those who needed them. But he kept telling us something was injured inside of him. And he started getting different hand-tremblers and star-gazers to find out what he should do about it. Because of that, we started doing lots of ceremonies for my father. I remember we had many major ceremonies for him in his last two years; he had a Male Shootingway, Flintway, Mountainway, Nightway, and a Big Starway in the Ghost Chasing and Evilway forms, and some other ones, too, I think, during that time.[7]

The next spring my father and all the rest of us moved back to the area near Nazlini Wash. Frank and some others in the family built their hogans over near the Chinle Wash, near where my father had built the log house at the Place of the Reeds. So some of us were living in that place, and others across from there, closer to the Nazlini Wash. The fields were between those two places. Frank built us a round, log hogan at that time, like the ones we use today; it wasn't the forked-stick kind my father built in lots of places. People were already using those and log cabins, too, when Frank built that for us. As I remember it, that was the next time he built us a home, after the temporary one we had near where they were building the Chinle Boarding School. The five children we had at the time and I were very happy to be in our own hogan by the Chinle Wash.

After Frank helped my father and others plow and plant the fields, he left to go somewhere. One day while he was gone, my mother came over and told me to take the sheep out because no one else was available to do that. She took my two little ones, Agnes and Ruth, back with her to where my father had built their hogan close to the Nazlini Wash. I left my oldest girl, Mary no. 1, to watch Mary no. 2 and Seya while I took the sheep out a short distance from there. She was about twelve then; Mary no. 2 was home from school for the summer and Seya was probably seven or eight. I don't know what those older children did while I was gone with the sheep. I guess they were playing around in our new hogan and somehow pulled the door shut so the latch came down and locked them in. I guess they tried from the inside to get out, but couldn't. From what I heard later, Mary no. 2 started crying, getting scared. Mary no. 1 said she just sat there, not worrying about it. She knew I'd be home soon. But her sister got really upset about it and started pulling on the harnesses Frank had hanging in there, from one of the logs. Maybe she was going to try to climb out by means of that; I don't know.*

I guess Seya finally decided to take some other things that were lying around in there, and pile them up so he could crawl out through the smoke hole. After he jumped down from the roof, he pushed the latch up from the outside, and opened the door. Mary no. 2 was right there, crying, all scared about not getting out. When he opened the door, she stopped crying and then started laughing and laughing. I came back with the sheep and found her laughing, so I asked what they'd been up to. When Mary no. 1 told me what had happened, I got after them. I told all of them they shouldn't be playing like that, slamming the door, and trying to climb around on things we kept inside the hogan. But nobody was hurt so I didn't really get too upset; I just told them not to do things like that anymore. I don't think any of us ever mentioned it to Frank, when he came back late in the afternoon.*

Before we moved back to the Black Mountain area that fall, I gave birth to another baby. That next one came right after Ruth; Ruth had just started walking around when I had another girl. My mother got after me about that, saying it wasn't good to have babies so close together like that. But again I had no trouble. I forget what we called that one when she was little, but when we enrolled her in the Chinle Boarding School, when she was about five, they named her Pauline, so she went by that name. When she started school, Mary no. 2 was in school in Albuquerque; Agnes and Seya were already going to school at Fort Apache and Mary no. 1 had already started raising children of her own. For that reason, a lot of my children didn't get to know her. And then too, Pauline didn't last very long after we put her in school. But that was later; I'm not to that part of my story yet. She was just a baby, hardly even sitting up, when my father passed away.[8]

It was during this time, after my father was injured and Frank came back and settled down with us, that Frank started learning more about the Blessingway from my father. He still hadn't finished learning from his own father, but there were other things he wanted to learn from my father and his father encouraged him to do that. So Frank started going with Man Who Shouts when he performed his ceremony, and asking him about various parts of it when they were traveling together, or doing things around here. I guess for a while my father didn't know if Frank was serious about it, or not. He'd been gone for so many years, and sometimes he still ran around gambling with others in this area. So, he didn't know if he could depend on him to settle down and put his mind on learning about those sacred things. But Frank kept asking questions and helping my father with all the work around where we were living, with the fields, the sheep, hauling wood and water, and even with the horses. Finally, my father told him if he was really ready to settle down, stop running around and gambling and going here and there, he'd teach him some of the things he knew. But he said he'd have to get serious about his life, raising his children, and providing for us. And so they agreed on it. I wasn't there when they agreed to that, but I noticed Frank was spending more and more time in the hogan with my father, and that he was helping him with it, traveling with him whenever my father went somewhere to do his Blessingway. Finally Frank told me my father was teaching him. That made me very happy. After that, sometimes they'd talk about those things in our hogan, too. Some nights, while I was lying there going to sleep, I'd hear them discussing certain things. My father always started with a part of the Blessingway story, like the one where the Holy Twins went in search of their father. He'd tell that first and then explain the songs that follow it. The songs go along in the same way, just like the story.

Lots of times, my father would drive the buggy to where he had been hired to do a ceremony. Sometimes, if he and Frank went toward Fort Defiance, they'd stop near Sawmill and spend the night with relatives of ours. There was one place in particular where lots of people always gathered to talk about the Blessingway and different songs and prayers. That was at the hogan of He Who Seeks War; he was one of our relatives, and he, too, was a Blessingway singer. I think his younger brother also learned that, too. He Who Seeks War and my father used to talk about those things whenever they'd get together. So, my husband started learning that way, too, from hearing what those men said and then asking about it later, when he was traveling with my father in his buggy, coming back to where we were living. Sometimes, others would be there too, who were trying to learn the Blessingway from that man.

When Frank started learning the Blessingway from my father, he built a sweat-house and started using it to cleanse himself on a regular basis. He'd always tell me he was going over there for that purpose. Sometimes I could hear him calling, "*Táchééh Haashch'ééh*" after he carried the hot stones in there and covered it all up to take his sweatbath. They did that in the beginning, when the first Holy People established the sweathouse. That's how they called all the others to join them in the sweatbath. Then, too, sometimes, I'd hear some of the songs way in the distance that he'd sing while he was in there. We have special songs that are used in the sweathouse. Sometimes, Seya would try to follow him; whenever he'd go in, he'd always come right back out, saying it was too hot for him.* I know he really liked to hear his father singing those songs; sometimes he used to try to imitate those or that call when he was playing around with Sam and others. But when he was small, before we enrolled him in school, he seemed to have trouble getting his words out right. Sometimes he'd stutter; other times it was hard to figure out what he was trying to tell me. One time when Frank was over in the sweathouse, he came running back over here saying, "Daddy is yelling *Sha'hajee-ee-ee* again." That just made me laugh.* But we're not supposed to do that, poke fun at the sacred songs or prayers or other things, so somebody always got after him whenever they heard him imitating any of those things.

In the fall when we moved back to the Black Mountain area, we settled near the Window Rocks again. Frank built his sweathouse on the top of a little hill near the lake that used to be there on the flat we called Breast Rock. One day the children were outside playing somewhere; when they came back, Seya wasn't with them. So I went looking for him, to all the places I knew he used to play. But he wasn't anywhere. So I started walking over toward the lake. That's where I finally found him; he was fast asleep right by the edge, in the sunshine. And here, there were cows all around, and some of them were sniffing him over and over.* It's a good thing they didn't step on him, or he didn't roll into the water and drown over there. That really scared me that time. When I woke him up, he said he had gotten tired while listening to Frank singing in the sweathouse and had lain down there to take a nap. Even though Frank used to bathe in the lake when he finished his sweatbath, he hadn't seen Seya there, in with the cows. When I came back and told him where I'd found him, Frank was really surprised. And Seya was surprised too; when I woke him up he found out the rest of the children had gone back, and left him over there by himself with the cows.*

Frank kept learning from my father. Of course, he already knew many things from his own father, Water Edge Man; he had already started learning the Blessingway from him before he left us to work as a freighter. But no one teaches everything they know about ceremonies, and people have different versions of those things. So Frank wanted to learn from my father, too, and he did. Finally, my father and Water Edge Man told me he had finished. His father was with us then and together, he and my father planned to have a Blessingway Ceremony for Frank, to announce he was qualified to start doing it on his own. We had that right before my father really started going downhill.[9]

My father never recovered from the injuries he got when that horse threw him. He was never able to ride a horse again, even though he had done that for many, many years and was experienced in all the things you have to learn about horses. He went on like that for a while, and we kept trying different ceremonies to cure him. The hand-tremblers and star-gazers he told us to bring in suggested different things that should be done, and we started finding people trained in those ceremonies to do them for my father. Everybody in the family helped out with all those things because they were worried when my father didn't recover from his injuries.[10]

After we'd gone on for more than a year that way and had moved back to the base of the Window Rocks, my father started getting worse. No matter what ceremonies were done for him, he just seemed to get worse. Finally he said we should move over to Whippoorwill. A lot of his clan relatives, other Bitter Water People, lived in that area, and he thought maybe they could help us with all the ceremonies we were trying to do for him. Of course, there were others we knew living over there, too; some people had moved there to escape the officials who were looking for children to enroll in school. There was a spring near Whippoorwill and different kinds of reeds grew around it in great numbers. Those were needed for one of the ceremonies that had been suggested for my father, and there were none of them where we were located near the Window Rock formations. There was also a singer over there who had been suggested by someone, and my father wanted to see if that man's ceremony would help him. So we moved over there for part of that winter. Even though his relatives didn't help us, we had some more ceremonies done for him, using those reeds. But even those did no good; he didn't get any better. So he decided we should move back to be near the rest of the family again; some of our relatives had stayed by the Window Rocks when Frank and I and our children went to Whippoorwill with my father and mother. The animals were in corrals with the rest of the family's. Of course, our herds had already started going way down because we were using up lots of the sheep for the ceremonies we were doing for my father.

When we came back from Whippoorwill, my father started having trouble getting around. Sometimes he felt well enough to go places, but more and more, he stayed home, lying down on the sheepskins and asking others to do what needed to be done. He always tried to save his strength so he could take care of the things that went with his job as headman. Once in a while he was well enough to go places in his buggy or in the wagon, if someone else managed the team so he could rest while he was traveling to wherever he needed to go.

As he started going downhill, my father began worrying about who would be appointed headman in his place when he could no longer do the job. He started saying he was an old man, up in his years, and now he realized his injury was very serious. He told my mother and different ones in the family he was beginning to think he wouldn't recover from the injury and that he was coming to the end of his days. Of course, we kept on doing different ceremonies for him, getting different ones to do whatever the hand-tremblers and others said needed to be done. But he kept getting worse. That was when he started encouraging Frank to become a headman, to carry on in his job as headman, too. Frank told me Man Who Shouts had started talking to him about that, saying he was going to inform the agent of his wishes about it.

Of course, Frank already knew how to talk to the People. He had some education from the Fort Defiance Boarding School and had traveled around, helping the Son of the Late Little Blacksmith when he was a policeman stationed at the Chinle Catholic mission earlier in time. Frank had also traveled with my father, and listened to him and others talk to the People. He knew how to do that, and he had those experiences. He had also helped with interpreting at different stores where he had worked earlier, and at St. Michaels and the mission here in Chinle, and other places, too. My father told me he believed Frank would be good at those things, now that he had finished learning the Blessingway. He said it was important for leaders to know that ceremony; it helped improve their words to the People. I know there are certain songs leaders use before giving talks so their words are clear. From what my father and Frank told me, those songs sharpen their minds, help them plan out their talks. It's because of those that their words come out right, not all confused. My father always used those before going to meetings, just like he used the songs and prayers for traveling and other reasons, like to help our crops grow or our animals stay healthy and have little ones. We all took those things seriously during our lifetimes; I still do.

After we had moved back from Whippoorwill Frank was asked to haul something for someone in the Black Mountain area, so he left in our wagon. He came back again on the last day my father was alive, early in the afternoon. He went over to the hogan where a man from Wheatfields was doing a ceremony for my father. There were other singers there, too, who knew different things. Early that morning my father had told my mother he knew his end was near and he wanted to talk to different ones in the family while he still was around to explain his wishes. So some were in there with him and others were going in, whenever there were breaks in the ceremony. Frank went in at one of those times and stayed there a very long time. It was already late in the afternoon when he and my father finished talking. When he came out, he told me things were very serious; my father felt his end was very near and he was not going to live much longer.

When Frank came out, different ones in the family asked him to take a fast horse and go over to where they kept the medicine for the children at the Chinle Boarding School. They wanted to see if there was anything that would help my father recover. So Frank agreed and saddled the fastest horse around the place, and took off at a gallop to go to Chinle. He returned late at night, again at a gallop, but by the time he got back, it was too late. My father had already passed away.

Shortly after Frank left, the singer started in again with the ceremony. We all went back into the hogan to be with my father and to help out in different ways. Only the adults were in there; we never let children go into a hogan where they're doing ceremonies for someone who is very sick. It's the same when a woman is having a baby; children aren't supposed to be in the hogan during that time, either. Because of that, none of my children were in there with me; someone was watching them in another hogan, taking care of all the children who were around at that time. My children really wanted to come in to be with my father; they begged to be allowed to do that, to see their grandfather, but I told them no. We sent them over to another hogan and told them to go to sleep.

Near sunset, the singer stopped his songs, prayers, and the other things he was doing. He told us it was no use, Man Who Shouts was coming to his end, and we should move him outside to a small ramada, a little shelter that had been built near the hogan. At first, we didn't want to believe what that man told us, but after a short time, it was clear he was right. So we moved my father into the small shelter. We always do that so the hogan doesn't have to be burned down or destroyed in some other way because a person has passed away in it. My father was still breathing and talking with us at that time; he told us to do what the singer said. He said he knew he was near his end and he didn't want the hogan to become a house of death so we couldn't use it in the future. He also told us not to be afraid about what was happening and not to worry about him returning to harm any of us in the future. He said he was dying from that injury, but he was already an old age person and we shouldn't be afraid of people who die because of that. The singer went over there with him but he left his *jish* in the hogan. A few others went there, too, but they stayed outside, near the opening of the little place that had been built for him. At that time, the singer told the rest of us to go back to the hogan where our children were; he said there was no hope and there was nothing more to be done. The other singers said the same thing, too. Even though we didn't want to go, we went back after they said that to us.

A short time after my father was moved, he passed away. It was already dark, probably close to midnight when that happened. The singer and others who were near the shelter came over to the hogan where we were waiting, and told us he was gone. It was decided we would wait until morning to fix him up since it was already late. Right after that happened, Frank returned on the fast horse. He brought some kind of medicine a doctor had given him to try for my father, but it was too late. He told us the doctor didn't know if the medicine would help him anyway. He went into the shelter to see my father. When he came out, he said it was no use; he knew Man Who Shouts had passed away. So he threw that medicine away.

Early the next morning, some of the family washed my father and fixed him up, dressed him in clean clothes and then jewelry—his silver beads, bracelets, rings—all the things he had specified. They also put on his headband, and his *dah na'ayizii* [shoulder pouch]. Then they wrapped him in blankets and tied those around him with a rope. Someone had already gone and rounded up the horse he always rode, his favorite one. They put the saddle blanket and saddle and bridle on it; then they laid him across it, like he wanted done. He had already told us what to do when he realized his end was near. It was the same with his medicine bundles; he had already specified in front of others the last day what was to happen to the craneheads he had for Flintway, the Cutting Prayersticks one, and the others he had, too. And when Frank had gone in there to talk to him in the early afternoon, he had given him his Blessingway bundle, and blessed him with the use of it. That's when he told him to make sure it stayed in his wife's clan, the Towering House People, in the future. He didn't want his own relatives, the Bitter Water People, to have those things. Those were his words and since he said them in front of others, no one caused a dispute about any of those things later.

As I remember it now, two men were appointed to take my father across to where he was buried. After they dressed him and wrapped him up, they put him on a blue horse, the buckskin that was his favorite at the time. Then they led the horse over to a ridge, south and then north from where we were living, to a place with lots of rocks. On the top of that ridge, there was a spring, and water from it used to collect in pools on those rocks. Sometimes we drank the water from there but sometimes it was too salty to use. There were no trails that went that way. Nowadays, I think it's still the same over there; no roads of any kind pass through there. Later, after we moved away from there, some people did build those old style hogans and corrals a ways from there. There are some dirt roads that go to those but they aren't too close to where we were living when my father passed away. From what I've been told, now that whole area by those Window Rock formations is covered with sand; later, the winds blew through that area, too.

When those men left, leading my father on his horse, we were all told not to watch them, and not to look over there. We told all the children to obey those words so no harm would come to them. After quite some time, those two men came back; I saw them coming in the distance, when they were still far away, because I had gone outside to take care of something. Even from a distance I could tell those men were respecting all the rules we follow when someone passes away. They had stripped down to just G strings, and had taken their hair down so it was hanging loose. As they came back, they kind of ran and skipped and jumped over the grasses and weeds in their path, and just motioned to each other, without speaking. We have lots of rules surrounding those things, and they were moving in the required way and covering up their tracks, brushing those away, too. They left the shovels and the axe there and they had killed his horse over there, as my father had requested, and sent it with him, like we do when that happens. I remember that Ida's father, Son of Yucca Fruit Man, was one of the men who helped bury my father. The Man's Grandson, one of Sam's older brothers, was the other. I don't think Frank helped with that, but maybe he did, too. Eventually we heard they had buried him near the base of the rocks, some place over there where there was a ledge nearby. They said it was near where my older, heavyset brother had been buried only a few years before. After I knew those two men were coming back from that direction, I went back inside and didn't look over there again.

For four days after Man Who Shouts died, we stayed around here. During that time, we observed all the rules we practice when someone dies. We didn't mention his name, and we went without food and water, and without washing. We all stayed quiet and we told the children not to run around playing. Those two men stayed apart from the rest of the family, in a different hogan, until the four days were up. Then we all washed. The singers who were there told us that from then on, we should resume the ways we were following, everything we had been doing before my father passed away. I remember Long Moustache was one of the ones who talked with all of us about how to go on from there, after the singers gathered up their things and started back on their horses. He was still in the group that moved around with us and he knew some things about talking to the People, too. And so for many days, he talked with us about how to go on from there with the farming and the livestock. He tried to console us with his words and his talks. For a very long time we were very, very sad. We barely went anywhere or took care of anything. Man Who Shouts was always the one who made the plans for us and when he passed away, for a long time it was as if we couldn't figure out how to do that for ourselves, without him. My mother came right out and said that to Long Moustache one day when he was encouraging us to start moving ahead with things again. She took my father's death very hard and she missed him for a very long time. But eventually, even she started doing things again. Once she pulled out of that, she became very strong again; she started making plans and she kept encouraging all of us to do the same.

After we passed through that, different ones in the family started talking about moving. Even though my father had passed away in the little shelter we built for him outside the hogan, everyone in the family wanted to move away from that place. They also wanted to burn down the main hogan because we had used it for so many ceremonies for Man Who Shouts, after he was injured when he was thrown from his horse. So we did. We didn't travel very far when we moved; we just went across to the other side of the same mesa. We built new hogans right across from where we had been when that happened, and put up new corrals for the few animals we had left. My oldest daughter, Mary no. 1, was put in charge of herding the sheep over there; she rode on horseback with them because by then, she already knew how to ride horses very well. The rest of my family went in our wagon and my mother drove the buggy. My father had left it to her for her use. It was winter when we moved but there wasn't much snow then. We resettled ourselves more to the east and below where we had been, in the area we call Red Mesa. That's the mesa you see over there when you look toward Black Mountain from here. At that time, we moved closer to another place we had been earlier, the one Seya always called his rabbit hunting place. In that area, toward the west end, there's a canyon and in there, way in the back, there are some springs. One of those was the one I told you about earlier, the one we called Drag the Water Off, Where You Drag the Water Off. That's where lots of people got water, even way back, in those water belly bags.

Others moved over there with us; I remember the one called Towering House Woman was still with us when my father died.[11] There were also some children, like Sam Taliwood and Howard Jones. They were older than Seya, but their parents were moving around with us, following my father as headman. Sam was not with us when my father passed away; he was away in school at Fort Apache, and they wouldn't let him come home, even though my father and mother had raised all those children after their parents died. I remember we sent word to Sam about my father's injury. Later, he told us he had tried to get permission to leave school and come home during that time. But that failed so he wasn't with us. His brother, the one who was called The Man's Grandson, helped bury my father, as I've already mentioned.[12] He was married at that time, but he and his wife were still moving around with us with their two boys, Ben and Philemon. My father had already given him some of the land he used to farm, the land over near the Chinle Wash. After that man, himself, passed away, Ida's son, James, started farming that ground.

three

Middle Years,
The Rest of My
Childbearing Years:
Supporting and
Raising Our Children

The Flats and Settling in Chinle

*Changes after my father died . . . Seya's stuttering cure . . . Seya starts
school in Chinle . . . Puberty ceremonies and David's birth . . . Frank's jobs
and his Ghostway, Evilway . . . I lose another baby, get bitten by a
rattlesnake, and have a Beautyway . . . changes in weaving.*

After my father died, we never again moved back to the Black Mountain area to spend
the winters; we never lived at Salina again, or below the Black Mountain store, or at
Salty Water, Rock Bridge, Rabbit Hunting Rock [or Thin Rock], Standing Rock, the
Window Rocks, or any of the other places we used to go when he was alive. Some of
the others continued to move back and forth for a while, but we never did that again.
Of course, we did go over to Black Mountain to visit people; both Frank and I had relatives who were living around Fish Point and in other places. And the children and I'd
go over there sometimes on horses or in the wagon to gather *haashch'é'édą́ą́'* and other
wild foods growing in that area. And even though we stopped moving back and forth,
we'd still take the sheep and goats to places that were cooler in the summer, wherever
there was grass for them to eat. And the horses in the family stayed out on Red Mesa;
people went and checked on them now and then.

After we moved away from where my father had passed away, we stayed on The
Flats in the Red Mesa area until it was spring. Then we moved back this way, across
the Nazlini Wash to around where Mary no. 1 lives now. From then on, we settled
around here, where we live now. Of course, we weren't always in exactly the same
place; sometimes we were closer to the Chinle Wash. We didn't really settle where we
are now until after my mother passed away. But after my father died and we came
back, we stayed right here in this area from then on.[1]

Seya really helped with the herding while we were on The Flats right after my father
died, over there by the Red Hills. Sometimes we herded on The Flats; other times, we
took the sheep more on the top of the mesa. The hills over there are full of bubbly rocks

and those shiny, glassy ones that come from volcanoes.[2] Because of the rocks, rattlesnakes really liked that area, too, and there were lots of them living there. Whoever was herding used to water the sheep at Red Lake; that was northwest of where we lived at that time, but it's gone now; it dried up. There was also a spring about half way up the mesa we used; we called it Hummingbird Spring and there was a sheep trail that went there. There were other trails, too, going up that mesa; some of those were made by the sheep, and others were horse trails. People told us Tooth Woman used some of those trails way, way back when she was being chased by enemies.

The Flats were also full of prairie dogs. After my father died and we moved over there, Seya and the others hunted prairie dogs there. They used to come back with lots of them for food. They were easy to catch on The Flats, especially if you poured water down their holes and watched for bubbles. They just grabbed them by the neck when they came out and then hit them with a stick. We all liked to eat prairie dog meat.

My crippled brother was moving with us then. He had moved over to where those Window Rocks were to help us when my father started going downhill, so he was still with us. By then, he had learned to ride a horse and he had a favorite, black one. Soon he started being called Mr. Black Horse because of it. His boys were already growing up, and the one called Walter was moving around with Jim Mitchell, helping him with his livestock. When we were on The Flats, in the red rocks area near the mesa, we were near them, but other times, those two were in the Black Mountain area. Most of the time, Chubby Woman, Beautiful Woman, and Tom moved with us rather than with their father, Jim Mitchell. He still had women in lots of places. Their sister, Gai, was already living with Son of Yucca Fruit Man, having children for him. Sometimes they moved with us and sometimes, not.[3] Sam's sister was also moving with us, with her children. That's the one who was first married to Woody's older brother; I know she had already had Irene and Don Nez for him because they were living near us, too, over there on The Flats, after my father died.

My younger sister, Small Woman, the one who eventually settled where the ground was hard, was also moving with us with her children. It was over there, while we were on The Flats, that she lost two of her girls, Esther and Bah. I think they were both up in their teens by then. They were out with the sheep and got struck by lightning while they were herding. Later in the day, someone saw their sheep wandering around and went looking for them on horseback. When they were found, it was already too late; lightning had already killed them. Sometimes lightning does that; it strikes whatever is sticking up from a flat surface. I guess that's what happened to them; there were no trees in that area, nothing else standing up.

In the spring, we came back over here. Some of the family settled very near the Nazlini Wash, but Frank and I went closer to the Chinle Wash, where he'd already built a round, log hogan for us a year or two before my father died, near my father's log cabin. My mother settled with others, closer to the Nazlini Wash in her own hogan that others built for her. But even over there, she was near me and my children; she always stayed near us after my father died. Frank planted corn, melons, and other crops close to the Chinle Wash, and he also planted alfalfa for the horses.[4]

Before the school year was up at the Chinle Boarding School, Frank decided to get Seya started over there. We had discussed that earlier and Seya wanted to go. My father had also told us during his last days to make sure we did that. He said Sam was already doing very well in school and he wanted Seya to follow after him, first at Chinle and then Fort Apache. So we told my father we'd do that, and after he passed away, we remembered that.

My mother said before Seya was enrolled, he should learn to talk right. He still had trouble getting his words out. Even after he got older, he still stuttered. My mother wanted to cure him of that by breaking a pot over his head. That's what people did way, way back when children were like that. So she and I told Seya we wanted to do that before he went to school. I guess that scared him; he started crying and said no, he didn't want that done. But he kept stuttering. My mother said even though we knew how to figure out what he was trying to say, once he got to school that would cause problems for him. Frank said the same thing. So my mother and I talked about it some more, and decided to go ahead with it, even though he had said no.

One day, after the fields were planted, my mother and I were in the hogan together, fixing some food. She got out one of the clay pots she had made and told me we should do that when Seya came in. Pretty soon he came inside and I asked him if he wanted something sweet, some sugar to eat until the food was ready. The children always liked sweet things; we rarely gave them anything like that, so of course he said yes. While he was standing there with the sugar in his hand, eating it with his fingers, my mother came up behind him and hit the clay pot with a stick right over his head. She hit it hard enough so it cracked and broke. The pieces of the pot fell all over his head and then down toward the ground. That really surprised him. He jumped and then started crying. But that fixed it. Just like she told us, after she did that, his stuttering was fixed. He never again had trouble with his words from then on. I know that was an old time cure; my mother said the People used that when she, herself, was little, whenever children stuttered. I don't think my mother had ever used it on any of us and I don't remember seeing her do it for anyone else's children. None of the rest of my children had that kind of trouble, so she only did that for Seya.[5]

Shortly after my mother cured his stuttering, Frank took Seya over to the Chinle Boarding School in the wagon and enrolled him. They told him the school year was almost over, but he could get started. So the first time he went, he was only over there for about two months before the school let the children out for summer. By then they had already added some more buildings to the school [see Fig. 13].[6] Seya came back over here to help with the fields, the herding, and other things when school ended.

That spring, right after Seya started school, lots of girls in our family became *kinaaldá*s so we had *Kinaaldá* ceremonies for them. Mary no. 1 was the first one to have her *Kinaaldá*, and then Mary no. 2, when she was home from the Fort Apache School that summer. Each of them had two *Kinaaldá*s, like we do; the first one is held when they first reach womanhood and the second, the next time that happens. Old Curly Hair sang those for Mary no. 1, but I don't remember who did that for Mary no. 2; it's a long time ago, now. The others I remember who had *Kinaaldá*s around the same time were Chubby Woman and her sister, Beautiful Woman. When Chubby Woman had hers, Agnes really wanted to run the morning races so I warned her not to get ahead, not to come back before the *kinaaldá* did. They took off toward the windmill and I was watching them [see Map 4]. And sure enough, lots of the runners came back before Chubby Woman. But they must have remembered what we told them because all of a sudden, I saw them drop out of sight; they hid themselves in the big ditch that

FIG. 13. The Chinle Boarding School (as viewed from above, on the clay butte, looking east), ca. 1920. View includes outhouse and buggies, foreground; group of children by dormitories, center; power plant, right; and Employees Club, back row, left. Photographer, unknown. Courtesy of the Franciscan Friars, St. Michaels Archives. Photograph no. C539.9–3, R450.

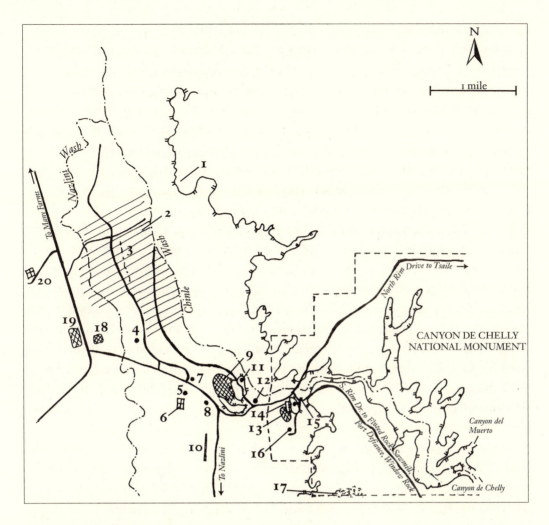

MAP 4   *Home Place and Community of Chinle, Arizona*

Home area is shaded zone

1 Houses Standing in a Line
2 Place of the Reeds
3 Big Ditch
4 Windmill
5 Franciscan Mission
6 Catholic Cemetery
7 Former Big House Trading Post
8 Former Chinle Chapter House

9 Former Chinle Boarding School
10 Airstrip
11 Former Gorman Trading Post/Presbyterian Church
12 Former Garcia Trading Post
13 NPS Campground
14 Cemetery
15 Canyon de Chelly

National Monument Headquarters
16 Former Day (McSparron) Trading Post/ Thunderbird Lodge
17 Dunes
18 Former Rodeo Ground
19 Tseyi' Shopping Center with new Chinle Post Office
20 Chinle Community Cemetery

used to go north for a long way across from here, and they stayed in there until Chubby Woman came back and got ahead of them. And then they popped out again.* I never said anything about that. I knew they used to hide in that ditch a lot when they were playing. That was the first Puberty Ceremony Agnes saw, I think, when she was old enough to remember things. She was very small when the two Marys had theirs, and of course, with Chubby Woman's, she was too young to understand what being a *kinaaldá* was. When Beautiful Woman had hers, lots of children raced with her; one morning someone played a trick on them and put up a string, a rope, or something, right outside the hogan door. When they started off running, they fell over it. My mother and I got after all of them but we never learned who did that.

Shortly after Beautiful Woman became a *kinaaldá*, she got married to Tom Scott. About a year later, she had a daughter, Garnett, for him. Chubby Woman started staying with my mother after my father died, to help with things she was doing. She and her brother, Tom, were among the children who helped herd sheep; Agnes did that too, because she was old enough by then. My mother let her use her donkey for that; she was the only one who had a donkey around here then, and she still had that donkey when she passed away. I don't remember who got it. Agnes used to really like to go out with Chubby Woman and Tom and the sheep. Sometimes she also herded with Irene Nez; she was older than Agnes but they kept their sheep here, and all the children herded near each other. We always did it that way so they weren't out somewhere by themselves.

We knew the children used to play when they took the sheep out. That never bothered us as long as they kept track of all the animals. That's what we always told them, to pay attention to how many sheep and goats they had with them and where they went so they didn't wander off and get lost. I guess when Agnes went out with Chubby Woman and Tom, he used to make lots of mud toys for them to play with. One time they were really laughing when they came back so I asked Agnes about it. She said he always made all kinds of toy people, Indians, horses, even little cradles for them to play with. I guess that day they were catching lizards and putting them in the cradles. She said they were trying to figure out which ones were the girls and which ones were the boys.* I used to laugh about those things to myself; of course, my sisters and I used to play with mud toys, too, or with sticks and rocks and other things, pretending they were people, hogans, or animals when we were herding sheep in our childhood. Probably all Navajo children do that.

At the same time we were having all those *Kinaaldá*s in the family, I had a Blessing-way because I was about to have another baby. My mother assisted me again; this time I had a boy, and we named him David.[7] He was the one born after Pauline. When he got old enough, we didn't enroll him in school. He was the only boy around here because Seya was in school, and we needed his help with the livestock. And then, too, when it was time to enroll him, we had lost his sister, Pauline, to that school so we didn't want to send him over there.

As I've already mentioned, by the time my father died, Frank was qualified to do the Blessingway Ceremony by himself and he had the medicine bundle my father had given to him. So, Frank started becoming known for his ceremony, and because he was careful with it and really knew the songs, prayers, and the stories, lots of people were starting to come around to ask him to do it.

Frank was also trying to help his father, Water Edge Man, perform that. His father was up in his years by then but people still asked him to do his Blessingway. Because he had been Frank's other teacher, Frank knew how he performed Blessingway and could help him with it. A short time after my father died, Frank's father started getting sick. He was living near us then so we helped with the ceremonies he wanted done for himself. He used up most of his livestock and other property on those ceremonies, but he didn't get any better. Finally, he told us he wanted to go back over near some relatives in Steamboat, to see if they could help. He wanted to leave his beads, his Blessingway bundle, and some other things here with Frank, but Frank told him no, he'd probably need those things. I guess he had more ceremonies done over in the Steamboat area, too, but it was hopeless. He passed away shortly after he went back over there; I think that happened the next summer after Man Who Shouts died.

Frank also started talking to the People after my father passed away. Of course, my father had encouraged him in that and had sent word to the agent that he wanted Frank to take over as leader for the area when he was no longer around. Lots of people liked the way Frank talked and they encouraged him to get it straightened out with the agent. After a while, Frank was given a paper saying he was the new headman, in my father's place.[8] So, he started going to meetings like others did, either on horseback or in the wagon.[9] In the beginning, he used to tell me he was kind of scared to get up and talk to lots of people. But then, the more he performed his Blessingway, the less scared he was. Finally he told me knowing the ceremony helped him talk to the People. He no longer was afraid; he no longer hung back waiting until people insisted he get up and do that.[10] So, that was when Frank put those two things together; those were his main jobs—talking to the People, being a headman for this whole area, and being a Blessingway singer. He was a headman for probably about fifteen years before they put him into the Council in Window Rock. I think they started the Tribal Council right after Frank was approved as a headman. But in those days, it was mainly concerned with oil or gas companies; those things had been discovered on our reservation and I guess the agent appointed a group of men to discuss leases for that. The kind of Tribal Council we have now didn't start until later, after Frank had been put in there. He got to know Chee Dodge when he started working as a headman and it was Chee who encouraged him to get involved in those things; they were good friends.[11]

Even though Frank was now living with us and working as a headman and a Blessingway singer, lots of times things were difficult. Even though we planted corn and other food, and gathered wild things, too, sometimes food and the other things we needed for our children were scarce. Frank did what other work he could find as it came along. Because he had a wagon and a team, he got hired to haul things for people and places like the Chinle Boarding School. I know before my father passed away, at one time he even worked in the Canyon with people who were digging around in there.[12] That put him in contact with Anasazi things, which we're not supposed to do. And then too, when different ones died, sometimes he had to haul the deceased to where they were going to be buried.

Eventually those things made him sick and the hand-tremblers he got for himself told him he needed to have an Evilway, a Ghostway Ceremony. That was because he had done lots of things he shouldn't have concerning dead people, like handling them, hauling wood from hogans where someone had died, and working on Anasazi ruins way back. So we had that five-day ceremony for him. Shortly after Frank's ceremony was over, I had another baby; it was another boy and it followed David, probably by two years.[13] But this one didn't live very long, maybe a week. We hadn't named it when it passed away. Frank had to help bury him because there was no one else available when that happened. Some people told him to ask the priest; Tom Scott and Beautiful Woman had a priest bury a little girl they lost a short time before I lost this baby. She didn't even live two weeks.[14] When those things happened, the priests were willing to help out and bury people, even little babies, in the cemetery they had behind the mission. But Frank said no, he'd take care of it himself. So he went ahead, even though you're not supposed to do that once you have an Evilway Ceremony. When he got sick again later, I wondered if it was because he broke the rules about that. But I just kept my thoughts to myself.

I think it was later that same summer we had another expense because I was bitten by a rattlesnake. That was the first time that happened to me and it was an accident. I was over in our alfalfa fields by the Chinle Wash. That morning, someone had gone to bring a few of our horses back and we needed to have some alfalfa for them to eat when they came in. So, I went over there and started cutting it like I always did, with a scythe. I guess there was a rattlesnake in there and somehow I must have gotten near it. When it bit me and I saw it was a rattlesnake, I dropped the scythe, came back over here, and told Frank. When things happen that concern snakes, we use the Beautyway Ceremony but we wait until the wound starts to heal. First we use herbs. My father knew what kinds of herbs to use when poisonous snakes bite you. We only have rattlesnakes and sidewinders around here that are like that; our other snakes aren't poisonous. So the first thing we did was mix up the right herbs; my mother helped me because my arm was already starting to swell up. After the wound began to heal, Frank went and hired Fingerless Man to come and sing the five-night Beautyway Ceremony for me. That removes the effects of snakes; from then on, the snakes respect you and you respect them; they don't bother you, after you've had a Beautyway.

For a short time while my arm was swollen, I had to stop weaving. But then I started again. Of course, all of us kept on weaving after my father died. I always had several looms up and I worked on weaving whenever I wasn't busy with the children or fixing things to eat or doing other things. I knew that even though Frank was working as a leader and a Blessingway singer, those things didn't bring in much in the way of income to support our children. So, even though he was now living with us and helping take care of things, I needed to weave to keep us from suffering from hunger or other hardships.

After my father died, even though my mother knew lots of people over in the Ganado and Fort Defiance areas, she didn't want to go all the way to Hubbell's with our rugs anymore; there were stores right here in Chinle by then, close at hand. Shortly after my father died, I think a group of men involved in trading in this area decided to buy up the stores here in Chinle; Cozy, The Mexican, and somebody else did that because they were the ones managing the stores here at that time.[15] Nelson Gorman had already given his post and the land to the Presbyterians by then, so there were only three stores where you could trade—the Big House, across from the mission [see Fig. 14]; Garcia's, at the foot of the hill where the Presbyterians built their church [see Fig. 15]; and the Thunderbird [see Fig. 16]. We called the Thunderbird "The Upper Store" because it was above Garcia's. Sometimes I'd take one of the children and walk over to *Kin Ntsaaí* [the Big House] when we needed something. That place was a little closer to where we were living, so we went there for small things until they closed the store part of that big building.[16] My mother started taking her rugs in the buggy to Garcia's; she liked going over there. Sometimes I took rugs there, but I

FIG. 14. The Big House (Hubbell-Cotton two-story Trading Post), Chinle, Arizona, from the front (northwest side), ca. 1920. Store entrance was through door on right, closest to the hitching post. People, unidentified. Photographer, Camillo or Pauline Garcia. Courtesy of Margaret Garcia Delaney.

FIG. 15. Garcia's (or Canyon de Chelly) Trading Post, Chinle, Arizona, ca. 1960 (just after renovation). Photographer, R. Montoya. Courtesy of Klara Kelley.

FIG. 16. Cozy McSparron's Thunderbird Lodge (originally, Sam Day's Trading Post), Chinle, Arizona, 1949. Photographer, Milton Snow. Courtesy of the Museum of New Mexico, Santa Fe. Neg. no. 46028.

also went to the Thunderbird. The McSparrons were running that store by then and I started getting to know them. Mrs. McSparron said she really liked my rugs.

When my father was still alive, we were weaving rugs called Chief Blankets. That was the only kind my father and mother ever made, and that was what he taught my older two girls to make. Those were plain with some stripes in them. We used sheep wool for those, and made them in lots of different sizes. When we were moving around all the time, the sheep wool and goat hair stayed clean. You could spin it right after you sheared; you just had to shake it once or twice and then you could start spinning, without washing or carding it because there was no dirt, burrs, sticks, or other things caught in it. But when the sheep started spending more time in the same places, it seemed as if the wool was always dirty. We washed it with soapweed, the soap we make from yucca root, and then carded it with those combs we bought at the trading post. Those wool carders wore out fast so we'd have to keep buying new ones. After we settled in this area, we kept those with our other weaving tools, like the oak battens, the combs, and our spindles.

When we made rugs, we didn't put any borders on them on either end. They were plain for however much you wanted to make that way, before you added stripes. Sometimes we made the stripes wide, sometimes narrow. Sometimes we did those in groups; sometimes we'd put a double set of stripes across the middle. There were different ways of doing it. My father used to tell both Marys how they did it was up to them. He told them to use their imaginations about it; my mother and I told them the same thing, because that's how we did it. Sometimes we bought red and black dyes to use on our own sheep wool. At first, a lot of our rugs were red with the stripes in black, white, blue, gray, or even brown. Sometimes we'd alternate the colors between large red areas; sometimes we'd make double or even triple bands of stripes in one color before changing it. How you did it was up to you. Most of the colors came from the sheep because sometimes we had a few with black or brown wool; but the red was a commercial dye and the blue was an indigo we bought, too [see Fig. 17].

Shortly after my father passed away and we settled in this area, I got interested in weaving designs. My father and mother mainly did the plain kind of weaving, but my mother knew double weaving and other things, and had already taught me those things. Then too, both of them knew how to make a design and they showed us how to make it. When I started making designs, I put them in the area where I was already making a wide stripe. Sometimes I'd only put one design in the center of the stripe, and sometimes I'd make two or three, alternating stripes with and without designs. I finally started putting a big stripe in the middle of the rug and any designs right in there. When I showed that to Mrs. McSparron, she really liked it. When I think back on it now, I think that was about the time Mrs. McSparron was trying to help more women here in Chinle become better weavers. Different traders were doing that and they were also encouraging different kinds of designs in different parts of the reservation.[17] Here in Chinle it seemed like everybody started making the one my father had shown all of us years earlier; when everybody started doing it, someone started calling it *tsiiyééł* [hairknot] [see Fig. 18].* I don't know who named it; I guess the design, the way it's done, reminded somebody of the hair bundle,* the way Navajo women wear their hair tied up in a bun with white wool.*

Once I started making designs, I realized there were lots of different ways to do that, too. I got interested in figuring those out for myself and trying different things as

FIG. 17. One of Tall Woman's Chief Blankets (Phase II), as sketched by Augusta Sandoval and Mary Davis, October 1996. Professionally drawn by Jennifer A. Frisbie.

KEY: Background color, red

Stripes of different colors and varying widths

FIG. 18. The *Tsiiyééł* [Hairknot] Design, as sketched by Mary Davis, October 1996. Professionally drawn by Jennifer A. Frisbie.

I was weaving. It was always easy for me to remember how I made the different ones, what I did to make the designs come out in different ways. I never wrote any of that down; even now, I have all those things in my head. When anybody asks me about how to make a certain design, I can still show them. Even my younger sister, Small Woman, and my half sister, Slim Woman, say that about me. Whenever we visit each other, they often ask me about a certain design, because they've forgotten how it's done. It's the same way with the different ways of fixing traditional foods. I still remember all those things, too. In those days, sometimes, when Frank would watch me weaving, he'd try to figure out how I made the patterns.* He'd always give up and then tease me about remembering them. He said my mind was best on those things and that he could never learn anything like that. I told him I'd show him; he used to knit the black stockings the Nightway dancers use, the ones that are something like knee socks. And he knew how to make moccasins, too. So I told him I thought he could learn to weave and even make rugs with designs. But he'd always laugh and say, "No, I'm too stupid to learn those things." Then he'd just go back to sitting beside my loom and watching me.

After a while, I stopped making Chief Blankets to take to the traders and only made rugs with designs in them.[18] Until then, I mainly made Chief Blankets, the same kind my mother made; they'd always buy them at the Thunderbird. Eventually, Mrs. McSparron told me I was the only one she knew in Chinle who was still making them and who knew how to do it right. That's when she asked me to make some for her own use, not to be resold at their trading post. She wanted those to be large and of course, she bought them from me, when I finished them. I know she put one of them in the living room of their home there at the trading post, but I don't know what she did with the others.

I never made sash belts; I knew how but I never had time because I was always weaving rugs. Some of my children and others in the family learned to make sash belts in school. Garnett really got good at making them. I think she learned that at the Albuquerque Indian School. I remember she used to bring the loom you use for that home with her when she spent summers with Frank and me, after her mother died. She'd work on those belts beside me, while I was weaving a rug. Sometimes I'd stop and watch her; she used to make me laugh the way she'd lie on her side to string up the loom, start a belt, or count her stitches. I teased her and we'd laugh together about that while we were both weaving.*

Besides rugs, I made lots of saddle girths and saddle blankets for Frank and others in the family who needed them. Most of the time I'd use natural gray wool or white wool for them. Sometimes I'd make a double one and put steplike designs in the corners, and maybe tassels on the corners, too [see Fig. 19]. I'd make the designs in black or white; sometimes we had sheep with black wool; the white you got from adding *dleesh* [white clay] to the wool when you washed it. You boil that in there, let it bubble up, and the wool turns really white. There was a hill near Valley Store where there was

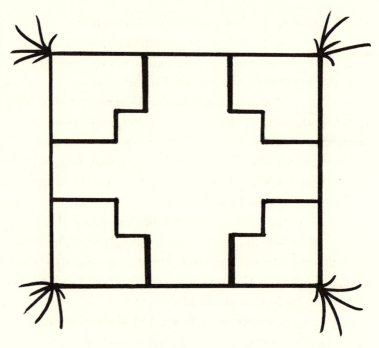

FIG. 19. One of Tall Woman's saddle blanket designs, as sketched by Mary Davis, October 1996. Professionally drawn by Jennifer A. Frisbie.

lots of that clay. My mother and I used to take horses and ride over there when we needed it. Then we'd dig it out and bring it back in sacks. Later, some of my children helped me get *dleesh* from there, too, and from other places like on the road to Nazlini near where they put the rodeo ground, and around Many Farms Lake, or behind Salina Mountain near Paperbread Mountain. There's several different kinds of *dleesh* and we use them for different purposes. Depending on what kind you need, you go to where it is and dig it from the ground.[19]

As my children grew up, I told them to sit and watch when I was weaving. That was after they were old enough to herd the sheep and had learned to help wash the wool, and do the carding and spinning. I tried to teach them all the things that go with making rugs, everything you have to do to get the yarn ready to start weaving, even making dyes from plants. And when they got old enough, they helped the adults shear. Frank knew how to put up looms and he used to do that for me, and my mother, too. We, of course, knew how to make our own and sometimes we did that, too, when he was gone somewhere.

The two Marys learned while my father was still living so they learned a lot from both my father and mother about weaving. When Agnes was small, I used to have her sit beside me in the mornings and watch; I'd try to show her how to go around the different threads to make different kinds of designs. I remember trying to teach her and also her sister, Ruth. Ruth used to sit and watch my mother, too. Lots of times both of us would be weaving at the same time and so they could sit and watch one or both of us. When Ruth sat next to my mother, she'd often tell her to sit on the other side of the loom. Every now and then she'd stop and tell Ruth to take over and do it from the other side, to bring it up from that side. Garnett did that too, when she was living with us after her mother died. But she learned sash belt weaving in school. Augusta was the same way; she learned most of what she knows about weaving in school; they used to teach that to the girls at the Chinle Boarding School and also at St. Michaels. They'd have different Navajo women come and instruct the girls in those things. Isabel learned from watching me; she didn't go to school. Right now, it's mainly Isabel and Mary no. 1 who are weaving like I am. [See front cover].

FIG. 20. Tall Woman, between 1939 and 1941. Photographer, Garnett Scott Bernally. Courtesy of Garnett Bernally.

Marriages, Births, Deaths, and Ceremonies 13

Mary marries Woody . . . Seya and Agnes go to Fort Apache . . .
Howard's birth . . . we become grandparents . . . filming of "Redskin" . . .
Pauline starts school . . . another snakebite . . . I have a Navajo Windway
. . . Pauline dies at school . . . Man with a Cane and Gai die . . . Augusta's
birth . . . trouble with my face . . . more ceremonies.

After a while, I noticed our oldest daughter, Mary no. 1, was spending time with one of the Nez boys. Of course, Sam's sister had married one of them and was living near us, so the family was around often, visiting their older brother. And then, too, some of them had been around earlier. Woody, the one Mary no. 1 married, had learned to be a Nightway dancer; he danced with the teams those two boys, The Jailer and The Man's Grandson, had when my father was still living. So he'd be around when they were practicing those things and he'd go with them to Nightways, just like my father did.[1] Woody's father's name was *Diné Nééz* [Tall Navajo] and his mother was called *Nabah*.[2] They had lots of sheep, and many times their children and mine would herd and play together. That family's name was *Nééz* so Woody was really Woody Nez. But when he went to school in Fort Defiance, the officials changed his last name to Davis. That's why you know him as Woody Davis. When Mary got interested in him, he already was a good moccasin maker and he was learning to perform Evilway. Later he also learned Shootingway, hand-trembling, and star-gazing, and became respected for those, too.

After I noticed Mary was spending time with Woody, I mentioned it to Frank and he decided to talk with them. They told us they wanted to marry each other and live together. So we had a traditional Wedding Ceremony for them, right here in the hogan. Then they started out together in their own hogan, right here with us, like we do. Frank really wanted them to get married by the priest, too, so later, after the first child they had who lived had started to sit up, they went up to the mission and got that done, too. Before that child, Mary miscarried one.

Seya spent maybe three years at the Chinle Boarding School, coming home for the summers and helping herd sheep and do other things. He told us he really liked that school.[3] I know Frank used to go over there to watch things the children were doing or to go along when they took the children to other places. Sometimes in the winters he'd pass by there when he was hauling wood for our use. At that time, the winters were really hard; we had lots and lots of snow for many years. When that happens, of course you can't go places in the wagon. So Frank made a sled and we used it for hauling wood in the snow. He got some metal wagon wheels and flattened them out, like runners, and then built like a wagon with two seats on that. He used two horses to pull the sled, and sometimes he and I went places in the snow in it. When he was hauling wood with that in the winter, he used to say when he passed by the school, the children would be sledding down the hill on the other side of the Thunderbird. I don't know where they got those sleds; maybe the school provided those for them, just like shoes.*

Sometimes the school had picnics and games for the children, or arrow-shooting contests, or footraces. And at that time there was a small racetrack here in Chinle where people could race their horses against each other.[4] Of course, some of the men gambled on all those things. While Seya was at that school, he had made friends with a white man we called Small White Man; his English name was Howard Wilson, and he was running the Big House and living upstairs while they used the downstairs for a store. That man owned a very fast race horse and people were always coming around, bringing their horses to race against it. He was known for that horse, and because he was a good Yeibichei dancer. Seya used to go over there evenings to help him with his horses and to take horses over to the Chinle school for different teachers to use.[5] That man encouraged him in horse racing and in riding like a jockey for races. He also used to encourage him in footraces the school had.[6] I remember one time Frank told me he was going over there to watch a footrace; here, when he came back, he said Seya had won. I guess he outran a tall Cherokee girl who was also at the school and was a very fast runner. He won a credit slip at the store for that race, and Frank was really proud of him. I guess all those things made Frank think the school was a good place.

After Seya had spent about three years here at the Chinle Boarding School, the officials told us he was ready to go to Fort Apache. The Chinle school here only covered the first four grades so children had to leave and go far away for any further education. Frank really wanted his children to get educated. He kept stressing the importance of that to all of us, and whenever he was asked to talk to the People. He believed things were going to change quickly and if you didn't know English, you'd be left way behind. So he wanted our children to go to school. Of course, we didn't enroll all of them. But when the Chinle officials said Seya was finished, Frank said he should go to Fort Apache for more schooling. Mary no. 2 was already over there and had told us good things about that school. So we decided Seya should go there, and we also decided to send Agnes. She never went to the Chinle Boarding School; you could start at Fort Apache too, and so that's what we did with her.

When it was time for the children to leave, Frank went over there with them. They let parents go with children who were being enrolled; they traveled in trucks covered with tarps. Frank wanted to go and see the place so he went while I stayed here. In those days, it took two whole days to go there; Frank said the first day they went past Ganado and on to Sunrise, and slept there in the trading post, before leaving in the morning. He stayed at Fort Apache one or two weeks; then he told them he was ready to come back and they brought him home. He told me lots of things about the place. I guess when he got ready to leave, Agnes really started crying about being left behind. She was still small, but Mary no. 2 was already taking care of her over there. Her brother, Seya, and her sister, Mary no. 2, were there with her, so eventually she got over that. She went there through the seventh grade and then they told us she could skip eighth. So at that point, she went on to the Albuquerque Indian School, like Mary no. 2 and Seya. Those three kind of followed each other in their schooling.

When they left for Fort Apache, Ruth, Pauline, and David were the ones who were home with me. Of course Mary no. 1 was still here, too, but she was living with Woody by then. We had already decided to keep Ruth home to help me with the children, the sheep, the farm, and other things. My mother was up in her years, and even though she lived right near us, she always needed help, too. Frank was still undecided about whether Pauline should be enrolled but she wasn't old enough yet anyway. And David had just started running around; he was still very small.

Before Agnes and Seya came back for the summer after their first year at Fort Apache, I had another baby. My mother was there to assist me and like before, I had no trouble. When it was time, we had another Blessingway Ceremony for me because the baby was due. That was another boy; he was born in the late spring and we named him Howard. When I had him, my daughter, Mary no. 1, was pregnant again for Woody; late that same summer, she had a boy who lived and they named him George Acey. So Howard and Acey were almost like twins; they were just a few months apart.

When it was time for Mary no. 1 to have her baby, they notified me she was having trouble and asked me to come over to help. I was already known for doing that because my mother had taught me those things. My mother decided I should go there alone. She said she'd already taught me everything and I didn't need her help anymore. So, I went over there by myself. Mary no. 1 had already been trying to have the baby for two days and she was worn out from that. I turned her almost upside down and started feeling her stomach, like my mother had taught me. And sure enough, I felt that her baby was turned around. Its head was facing up, not down, and that's why it wasn't getting born. So I used my hands to push on her stomach and slowly turn the baby around into the right position. I knew how to do that by then. People were coming to get me if someone in the family was having trouble with their labor. Then I'd go and do what I could to help different ones.

After I did that and told Mary no. 1 the baby was ready to get born, in about an hour, she had her baby. When he finally came out, I started scolding him, asking him why he had given his mother so much trouble? And we were joking about piercing his ears in two places, so he wouldn't be so ornery next time.[*7] That's the one we call Acey. Later, we laughed about that together and she thanked me for helping her. She said she was in lots of pain the first two days, but once I started working on her and helping the baby get turned around, it didn't hurt anymore. I told her if a woman knew how to do that, then her hands would do it right, in a gentle way, and she wouldn't cause pain for the one who was in labor. I had already done that for lots of women by then, but Mary no. 1 was the first time I did it for my own daughters. She was the first of my children to get married and have a baby, and so when Acey was born, Frank and I became grandparents.[*] I was still having children for Frank when that happened. After Howard was born, I had two more, Augusta and Isabel, before I stopped having children.

Later that summer, almost when it was time for the children to go back to school,[8] we heard some people were coming to Chinle to make a movie in the Canyon. People were starting to do that and we'd always hear about it. Lots of times, they'd send men ahead to hire Navajos to be in those, in the background. Frank heard about it at a meeting he went to so he told us and others, too. Lots of men were interested in getting some income by working for the movie people even for a few days. So, people were talking about it whenever we went over to the Big House, Garcia's, or the Thunderbird. That movie was made near the Thunderbird, and I think they even put some pictures of the store in it.

Once the movie people arrived, at night the men used to go to the Thunderbird and also closer this way, to where they set up their camp in the fields near where the laundromat is now. They put up some temporary buildings there, and on certain nights, they showed black and white, silent movies without charging people to see them. So the men always wanted to take off and go there and see those. I don't think Frank tried to get hired for that movie, but I know later, he did get parts in some of the others made around here.[9] Both Seya and Woody really wanted to be in that, and they got chosen to ride in a group of Navajos who were supposed to come over the hill on horseback or something. So, they got all ready and went over there on the right day. But just then, an official from Fort Apache got on the loudspeaker and told everybody the trucks were leaving for school the next morning, and children who were supposed to go back to school had to leave; they couldn't be in the movie. So Seya had to give that up and he was very disappointed. Woody went ahead and did it. Eventually some people in the family saw that movie, but they couldn't figure out where Woody was.* Of course, he was a young man then and he was in a big group on horseback in several places in that movie. He said they named it, "Redskin."[10]

Seya went back the next day, along with Agnes who was starting her second year. Pauline wanted to go with them, but Frank and I thought she was too small to go that far away. So we enrolled her here in Chinle. Frank took her over there and told her maybe after a year or so, she could join her brother and sisters at Fort Apache. But that's not what happened because she didn't survive her first year there. Ruth was here helping me and my mother; she really cried to go with Pauline to the Chinle Boarding School. And when others were enrolled, like Woody's niece, Nora Tsinijinnie, who herded with Ruth, Ruth cried to go with them, too. But we told her no; I needed her to stay here and help me and my mother, who was getting up in her years. David was still a small boy then, and Howard, of course, was only a few months old.

Early that fall, shortly after Acey was born, I got bitten by another rattlesnake. That shouldn't have happened because I had already had a Beautyway and was supposed to be immune from that. Howard was still a little baby and we were living where Mary does now. Lots of times in the summer when it was hot, the children and I would sleep outside on sheepskins. Of course, my mother had taught me to sprinkle an herb *nábįįh* around the outside of the hogan, the ramada, and any other place we were going to be staying, to keep poisonous snakes away.[11] She had taught us the things she knew about herbs, and I was already doing that. Even now I follow her teachings about those things. When my children were small, whenever we slept outside like that, sometimes in the morning we'd find little bull snakes or water snakes under the sheepskins. But those don't hurt you.

When this happened to me, we were all sleeping in the ramada, where it was cooler. I had a loom set up not too far from where I was sleeping near the baby. Of course, I was weaving whenever I wasn't busy taking care of other things and the night before, I had stayed up late, working on a rug. We had kerosene lanterns we used for light at that time; we didn't get electricity or any of those other things until after you met us, as you know.[12]

While I worked on my rug, Frank was over in the hogan. I think his brother, John, who lived down the road from us, had come over. He was by himself again, and he, too, was a Blessingway singer. Every now and then, the two of them got together to compare things about the ceremony, and talk about the songs and some of the things different teachers had to say about the stories and other parts. I think that's what Frank was doing over there, after we ate here with the children. I was here weaving and watching the children, and they eventually went to sleep. When Frank came in, I was still weaving and I had Howard next to me on his cradleboard. So Frank lay down on the other side, with the other children.

Early in the morning it got cold and I got up to start the fire. It was still way before dawn. That's when the baby woke up, so I went and lay down next to him and started nursing him. I used to take the babies off their cradleboards and let them rest on my arm, if I was going to lie down while nursing. After I put the baby on my arm, I stretched my hand out toward where the loom was set up. At the base of that, I had dug a hole so I could put the bottom crosspieces of the loom down in there.

I guess there was a snake in there because when I stretched my hand out in that direction, all of a sudden I felt something bite me. I immediately sat up and saw a rattlesnake, so I picked up the baby and called to Frank to wake up. He ran outside and saw the snake crawling out from underneath the ramada. I guess he was so mad he grabbed a shovel and killed it, almost splitting it in two. We're not supposed to do that, abuse snakes in any way. But since I had already had a Beautyway Ceremony and had respected everything the singer, Fingerless Man, told me to do after it was over, Frank said it was not right I had been bitten again. Snakes don't usually act like that. For that reason, he didn't want to have another Beautyway done for me. Instead, he went and got Slim Bottom of the Mountain Man to do a Navajo Windway for me. That's a five-night ceremony, too. That man and his brother, Ugly Bottom of the Mountain Man, were both qualified to perform it; they lived around Many Farms at the time. Of course, once again we waited until my wound had started to heal, before I had that ceremony done.[13]

Howard wasn't even a year old then. Because I was nursing him when I was bitten and couldn't continue that, I asked Mary if she would nurse him along with her baby, Acey, until I recovered. She said she would so I took Howard over there. Shortly after that, I got some kind of infection. Maybe it was related to the snakebite; I don't know. But when it kept spreading, Frank wanted me to have one of the doctors at the Fort Defiance Hospital try to help with that. I finally agreed to go over there with him in our wagon. They kept me there for a while because of the infection. I don't remember how long I had to stay there, or if they ever told us what caused that. It was some kind of infection on the inside of me and I think they kept me there almost a month.[14] Finally it healed and they told Frank I could come home.

When I got back, I went over to Mary's to get the baby. Howard was doing really well, just like Acey; they were both really fat and almost ready to start trying to sit up. That made me happy and I really thanked my daughter for helping me out. She said she just slept between them and nursed both of them like they were twins. They were both in good health; they didn't starve.* I remember apologizing to her for making things even harder for her; here, she had her first baby and she was crippled, too, and then she had to take care of both of them. She said she didn't mind. I sure thanked her for doing such a good job with nursing both of them. Frank thanked her too, for helping out with that. I had already brought Howard back home and started weaving again when Slim Bottom of the Mountain Man came to do the five-night Navajo Windway for me. After that, I never again had trouble from rattlesnakes.

Frank had already talked to the priest about marrying Mary no. 1 and Woody with a church ceremony, since they had only had a traditional ceremony. I guess the headmen were starting to say the People should do that; that way, there'd be a record of those things, and they'd have a license showing they were married. Frank kept saying the officials were starting to keep records on everything and to use a calendar to plan things. Finally he brought a calendar home and hung it up in the hogan. I guess one time when Frank was up at the mission for some reason, Father Emanuel told him he could marry Mary no. 1 and Woody pretty soon. So they got dressed up and went up there with Frank in the wagon, and had the ceremony done. Frank was their witness; headmen had started doing that, too, and signing the records the priests made when they married people.[15] Mary no. 1 told me about it when they came back; she took Acey with her because he was about six months old when they were married by the priest and she was still nursing him. I guess at that time the priests were also trying to write down who belonged in different families and when they were born. When Mary no. 1 came back, she said Acey had been written down at the mission, too, so there was a piece of paper over there about both of those things.[16]

Soon after that, maybe just a few weeks, the school officials came over here in the school truck. The man who got out first told Ruth, who was outside, they needed to see Frank and me, and she told them we were in the hogan. I was weaving and Frank was working on something, too, when they came in. I remember Howard was just starting to sit up at that time; I had taken him off the cradleboard right before those men arrived and put him on a sheepskin, next to my loom. He was there, trying to sit up again, when they came in. Mary no. 1 had told me Acey was trying to do the same thing over at their hogan. She used to come over here a lot with her baby, and we'd work on wool together, or cook different foods, or do other things. Of course, we lived right nearby at that time.

When those men came in, I knew right away something must be wrong from the way their words sounded, even though I couldn't understand them. Frank immediately got upset and started asking lots of questions. I thought because they were from the Chinle Boarding School, it must be something concerning Pauline. Finally Frank started to translate what they were saying. It turned out *it was* about Pauline; she was already gone! I just stood there stunned. I didn't even know what to do.

We had heard there was a sickness over at that school. It had started around the time Mary and Woody went up to the mission to get married, I think, and lots of children were sick from it. But because we had gotten no word, we thought our daughter, Pauline, wasn't one of the ones affected by that. Here, these men had come to tell us this sickness had already killed her and some of the other children. We didn't even know she was sick since they didn't let the children come home on weekends. At that time, even if they lived right here in Chinle and their parents could come in the wagon to give them transportation, they didn't allow that. The officials had never notified us about any of it. The same was true with the other parents whose children passed away at that time; they weren't notified, either. So, lots of people got angry and came to see Frank because he was a headman. That's when they learned we were suffering too, because it had killed one of our daughters.

The officials told Frank the sickness acted like some kind of epidemic. It wasn't the flu like before, but instead, something that caused sores on the outside, like chickenpox or measles. I think it was one of those two, but now I don't remember. We never saw Pauline again because of that. The officials said they had already buried the children who had passed away. That, too, upset us. We should have been asked about it, to see if we wanted to do it according to our own ways. But it was too late. They said the priests had helped and had put those children in the cemetery behind the mission. So, maybe the mission has a record of that.[17]

After those men left, Frank and I talked about what had happened. That made both of us very sad, and also angry at the schools and the way they treated parents of the children who were enrolled there. We had already had trouble with Fort Apache, too.[18] Right then, Frank said he wasn't going to send David to school and maybe none of the rest of the children we might have would go, either. Later he changed his mind on a few more of our children, but David never went.

After we were given that news and those men left, my mother came over to see what they had wanted. She, too, got very upset. Ruth started crying, and when I walked over to tell Mary no. 1, she, too, got upset about losing one of her sisters that way. So we decided to go ahead and observe the four days we usually do after someone dies, since we had just been notified about it. And we did. When the four days were over, Frank went up to the mission and got help sending a letter to notify our children who were at Fort Apache about what had happened here with their younger sister. So when they came home for the summer, they already knew Pauline wasn't going to be with us.

That was the first of my children who was lost to the schools and it took me some time to get over it. Of course, I had already lost two babies by then, shortly after birth. But this girl had already started to grow up; she was probably six when that sickness killed her, and something like that had never happened to us before.

Some time the next spring, after we had finished planting our fields, someone came on horseback to tell me my brother, the crippled one, had passed away. He was up on the mesa at the time with his animals. After he learned to ride his horse again, sometimes he'd go and stay in that area with his wife and two boys, Marcus and Walter. Other times, they'd be down here by the Chinle Wash, where he'd planted the lone cottonwood tree. That year, Man with a Cane had finished planting his fields along the Wash and had already gone up on the mesa. After he learned to get around again, he was able to do a lot of farmwork using his crutches and the horses. Of course, his boys and others helped him a lot, too. In those days, people still helped each other with plowing, planting, hoeing, and harvesting; they still moved around in groups, doing the farmwork that way and not stopping until every field was finished. I don't remember when people stopped helping each other like that, but it seems like a long time ago, now. Nowadays, we have the Ten Days Projects for some things, but most of the time, people just do their own work. They don't even help their relatives like we used to do.

When I got that news, Howard was about a year old and Acey hadn't quite reached one year yet; that's how I remember when that happened. By the time Man with a Cane died, even though it was still open range down in this area, more and more people were settling in the Valley, and more people were starting to plant trees and then live under their shade in the summertime. I think it was one of his sons who came to tell me about it. He had already passed away and his family had already buried him some place up there on the mesa when I got the news. Since they did it that way, there are no records of that.

That was the last of the brothers I had. After I was given that news, I went over and told my mother. After we had talked for a while, she wanted to go over to my sister's, Small Woman's, and also to my half sister's. She asked me to go with her, so I went back and got Howard and took him with me. Ruth watched David while my mother and I traveled to those places in the buggy, the one my father left for her. She used that for going places but she also walked a lot; she always said she liked to walk. She went over to Garcia's on foot, and sometimes, she also walked over to see Small Woman and Slim Woman, too. As she got older, I started worrying about her walking by herself, and I started telling one or another of my daughters to go with her when she started out like that to go somewhere. But that day, I went with her in the buggy. It was in the afternoon so we didn't stay too long at either place. Small Woman was already living at the Hard Ground Place with *Hastiin Łaashi* and the children they had left at that time, so we went over there first. And then we came back this way and went down toward Valley Store, where Slim Woman was living with Old Red Bottom Man. Both of those men were still alive when my last brother, Man with a Cane, passed away.

We lost another one out of our family right after that. Gai, who was older than Mary no. 1, was pregnant with her next baby. She had already had Ida right after the flu lifted up for good, and another one, Betty. She was ready to have another baby so my mother went over there to help. Gai's sister, Chubby Woman, had gone over there several days before they sent for my mother. Her other sister, Beautiful Woman, hadn't gone because she had small children to take care of.

My mother didn't come back until much later. When she did, she was driving the buggy slowly, not like she usually did so the horses moved along. So I went out to meet her and unharness the horses. She started crying when she saw me. Right away she told me Gai had passed away in childbirth. I guess she was already having trouble when they sent for my mother; even though my mother got the baby turned around so it could be born, something went wrong and Gai didn't survive. The baby was a girl and she passed away, like her mother. I guess the family was already talking about what to do with Ida and Betty; Ida was about ten when she lost her mother like that. Someone suggested Gai's sister, Chubby Woman, be given to her husband, Son of Yucca Fruit Man. My mother said that's probably what they were going to do, after the four days were up.

At that time, Chubby Woman was staying with my mother, helping her with things. She'd started doing that after she became a woman. She herded my mother's sheep by herself unless Agnes was home from Fort Apache; then they'd herd together, with Chubby Woman's brother, Tom. Chubby Woman was already known as a good weaver; she was always weaving and making lots of rugs. My mother was the same way, of course. So, many times, when my mother used the buggy, she and Chubby Woman were going to Garcia's because they had more rugs ready. That's where the two of them liked to trade; they told us The Mexican, the trader there, really liked their rugs and gave them good prices for them.

After I talked with my mother, I came back and told Frank what had happened. I said I wanted to go over there to help out. At first he wasn't sure about me doing that because I was pregnant and the baby was going to come soon. When you're pregnant, you shouldn't have contact with those things because that will harm the baby.[19] He reminded me of that. But I told him I wouldn't help fix Gai or her baby up, that I'd help in other ways. When we got finished talking, I walked over to tell Beautiful Woman what had happened to her sister and the baby. Frank said he'd take us in the wagon and watch the sheep while we were gone. So, my mother and I put together the food we had and got our blankets, sheepskins, and some other things ready. Then I gathered up the children and Frank took us and my mother over there. Beautiful Woman came later with her husband, Tom Scott, and the little ones they had at that time; Garnett was the oldest and I think there was another one by then, too, a boy.

We stayed over there until the four days passed and we all washed. Then it was decided Chubby Woman would be given to Son of Yucca Fruit Man, and that she'd take Ida and Betty. Those girls were her nieces already and that way, they also became her stepdaughters. Chubby Woman lived with that man almost ten years and had children for him; they were John Brown, not the policeman as you know, and Eva, Bobby, and Samuel Hashkaan. There were some others, too, who died either when they were babies or right after they started walking; there was at least one like that, but maybe there were others, too, even three. Bobby was the youngest of those who lived; he was still very small and Eva was about five when Chubby Woman herself passed away, probably in childbirth, too. But that was later.

Later that summer, when we were already harvesting some things, I had my next baby. It was a girl and Frank suggested she be named Augusta because she was born in the month of August. So we did that. Agnes was still home from Fort Apache when that happened and we were still living over by Mary no. 1's. There were still almost no fences anywhere; that hadn't started yet. It wasn't quite time for the children to return to school and Agnes wanted to come into the hogan to see what we do about childbirth. But my mother told her no, children are never allowed to see that. I thought maybe it'd be all right; Agnes was growing up and I knew she would soon reach her womanhood. She was starting to ask me questions about becoming a *kinaaldá* and I knew we needed to talk with her soon about those things. But at that time, I hadn't done it. Because of what my mother said, only she and the singer we hired to do the Blessingway Ceremony for me were in the hogan when I gave birth. Mary no. 1 wanted to come over and help, but my mother told her no, too. She was pregnant with another child then. That was her daughter, Louise, who was born about a month after Augusta. That's why my mother didn't want Mary no. 1 in there at that time; she said you're not supposed to do those kinds of things if you're pregnant.

Everything went all right with that birth, and the baby lived to grow up, as you know. So, when Agnes left for Fort Apache again, she had a new sister. I was here with Ruth, David, Howard, and the new baby, Augusta. Mary no. 1 was married and very pregnant with her second child. Mary no. 2 had already started high school; she didn't come home much in the summer after she started at Fort Apache. She told us she wanted to work at different jobs she was offered in the summer and we let her do that. Ruth and David were old enough to help in many ways then, and Howard was running around. Pauline, of course, had already passed away.

After Agnes went back to Fort Apache, Augusta's face started swelling up under her right eye beside her nose, just like your face does if there's an infection in your sinuses or you're suffering from *ch'iish*.[20] She was still a new baby on the cradleboard. I showed that to Frank and he said we should take her to Fort Defiance, so we did. By then, her whole face was swollen. The doctors there didn't know what it was and they acted like they were afraid of it. They wanted to quarantine her but instead, we checked her out and came back home. I started rubbing an herb on her face, one that makes you sneeze. After I did that several times, it started to clear up; the swelling started going down. But Frank also did something, too. One night when he was holding her, looking at her face, he saw a yellowish thing sticking out of her top gum, where her teeth would be later. She used to fall asleep with her mouth open and one time he saw that in there. So he took a pair of tweezers and pulled it out. It was like a skinny yellowish piece of bone. After he did that, the swelling went away so he said maybe that was causing it. But both of us were worried when he found that thing and removed it; we didn't know what that was or how it got in there.

Later that fall, something happened to me. I don't know what that was; maybe it was some kind of stroke or something. One morning when I got up, I felt like my face was paralyzed; it felt all twisted up and when I asked Frank to look at it for me, he said it was all twisted. Neither of us knew what had caused that; I had been in good health since we had that Navajo Windway done for me, after my second rattlesnake bite. So for a while, we didn't say anything about it. But it seemed to keep getting worse; my face got all lopsided and people starting asking me what was wrong with it. More parts of it were paralyzed, too. So finally Frank said we should get a hand-trembler to find out what was causing it. I forget who we got, but that man said I needed to have a Windway done for me. We have two kinds of those; the Chiricahua Apache Windway is a short ceremony and you're supposed to have that done sixteen times for it to cure you. The other one, the Navajo Windway, is a five-night ceremony. I had already had one of those done the second time I was bitten by a rattlesnake because it seemed like the Beautyway Fingerless Man had done had not made me immune from it like it is supposed to.

After we were told those things, Frank went and hired someone to start singing the Chiricahua Apache Windway for me. I had that done three times, one right after the other, and then because my face was a little better, we stopped. Augusta was just a tiny baby when I started having those ceremonies because my face was lopsided and twisted. But then after a short while, that paralysis started spreading again, twisting up my face in a different way. So Frank went and got another hand-trembler. He said we should try a Navajo Windway for it since it didn't seem like the Chiricahua Apache Windway was helping too much. Frank wasn't sure about that so he got another hand-trembler. That man said the same thing. So then I had another five-night Navajo Windway. The same thing happened; despite all the expense and work involved with that, and even though I followed all the singer's instructions about what to do after it was over, even with that my face didn't get any better. Frank got Ugly Bottom of the Mountain Man from Many Farms to sing that for me.

Frank was worried about me but I knew he was also worried about standing the expense of those things. I tried to tell him to let it go, maybe I'd get better if more time passed. But I kept getting worse and I started worrying about it. I talked with my mother, my sisters, and other relatives, whenever they came around, to see if any of them could help me figure out what I might have done to cause it. But none of us could think of anything. That's probably because my father and mother had brought us up to follow all the rules we have about avoiding dangerous things, respecting lightning, water, and all those things, even bears and snakes. I knew I hadn't broken any rules during my pregnancies or any rules we have about contact with dead people or places where they've died. With Frank, I knew he had broken lots of them; he even said so, but he also said that wouldn't affect me, just himself, and I believed him. So I went on, not knowing what was happening to me, while I kept getting worse.

Finally Frank got another hand-trembler. He told him about everything we'd already tried and that it hadn't helped. Finally that man said I should have a Shootingway Ceremony and we should also make plans to finish the rest of the Chiricahua Apache Windways I needed. He said those didn't help unless you did all of them, all sixteen. And then too, he found out the second Navajo Windway, the one we had after the Chiricahua Apache Windway had been done three times, had never been finished. He said that was affecting things, too. I knew it hadn't been finished. The singer who did that, Ugly Bottom of the Mountain Man, said he wasn't sure about some of the final night parts of the ceremony and he wanted his brother, Slim Bottom of the Mountain Man, to come and do it. So he only did the first four days, which are mainly Fire ceremonies, and went back home. Frank didn't understand why he said that because he had a good reputation for performing the whole ceremony. When he left, I was feeling better so I encouraged Frank not to worry about why that man had left like that. I knew he really didn't want to stand the expense of having another singer come to finish it. So we decided not to do it; we never sent word to that man's brother to come over and do the final night for me. And then, when I got worse again, it didn't seem like the Navajo Windway had helped, anyway.

After the hand-trembler had talked with us and left, Frank and I talked about it. Then he went and talked with some of our relatives, too. We had already used up some of our sheep having those other ceremonies for me, and Frank didn't have much income at the time, so we needed others to help us get ready for the Shootingway. Different ones said they'd help, and so after a while that ceremony was done for me. Frank went and got Bead Man's Son, who was also called Sand Man and Herbert Mitchell's stepfather, to do that for me. That man had already done a Shootingway for Frank, sometime after my father died, and we knew he had a good reputation.[21] I never had another Shootingway. That ceremony didn't cure me altogether, either; my face was still the same when it was over. But finally I got so I could move the parts that were paralyzed, and eventually, some of the places that were twisted up, lopsided, started going back where they belonged. So maybe the Shootingway did help; I don't know. We also went ahead and during the years from then on, I had the rest of the Chiricahua Apache Windways. Every now and then I'd have another one, until I finished all sixteen. Maybe those helped, too. Whatever it was that started affecting me right after Augusta was born and kept making my face lopsided and paralyzed like that while she was a small girl finally stopped. Once that happened, it never came back; I never got like that again.[22]

Frank as a Traveling Man 14

Frank as a headman . . . news of Chapters and the Depression . . .
locating Seya . . . Frank as a Blessingway singer . . . Frank works with
Father Berard and goes to the sacred mountains . . . we lose Mary no. 2 . . .
raising our children . . . marriage problems . . . Isabel's birth and end of
my childbearing . . . other ceremonies.

After Augusta was born and I had those ceremonies because my face got lopsided, it seemed to me that Frank started traveling more and more. Sometimes he was gone doing his Blessingway Ceremony. Other times he had to go places because he was a headman. Those leaders had lots of meetings; sometimes Frank would tell me what they talked about when he came back, before he went to gatherings and told those things to the People in our area. I think it was about this time he said the government was changing things; even though they were still going to be working with the headmen, they were rearranging the reservation and trying to set up places called Chapters. They were going to put up buildings so people would have a place to gather and listen to the leaders. And they were going to add in some new leaders, too, to work with the others. I think they got that started here in Chinle, but then it went downhill after Washington told us to get rid of our sheep. I know they didn't build the Chinle Chapter House until much later, after that started back up.[1] After that, Frank was a leader in that, too, but that was much later, after he got through being on the Council and being a judge.

Another thing Frank told us was that all around the country, things had gone down. There was no work for anybody; sands and dust were blowing the earth away from farms in different places, and even those trying to raise food were suffering. Seya said they were saying the same thing in Albuquerque, that everybody was out of work. He and Frank used to talk about it; I think they called it the Depression. But the new leader of the country eventually made plans for that. By the time Seya finished high school, they had programs whereby people who were willing to work could get some kind of income for their families.

One time when Frank had to be gone for a long time because of his job as a leader, it turned out to be a good thing. That's the time he discovered Seya had run away, taken off to Phoenix, without our knowledge. We thought he had gone to the Albuquerque Indian School after he finished at Fort Apache. He told us he was going to work there in the summer and then go to Albuquerque, where Mary no. 2 was already in school. So we thought he had. When those school boys were home for the summer, everybody knew it because they were all crazy for Squaw Dances.[2] Seya and his friends ran around to those all the time, whenever they were home. I used to worry about them; sometimes people would drink and gamble there, and then start fighting. But I tried to be quiet about it and just fix him food to take on his horse, whenever he said he was going to one of those. Of course, with the girls, we didn't let them go to things like that; we made them stay home instead of running around. Frank said boys were different; they could take care of themselves. But I still worried about them.

Frank and the other headmen were invited by the superintendent in Fort Defiance to go to Phoenix to see the state fair, to visit Navajo prisoners at the penitentiary somewhere around there, and to see some of the other schools where Navajos were enrolled. So Frank told me he was going; he went with other leaders, like Long Moustache from Black Mountain and Walker Norcross from here. When they got to the Phoenix Indian School, who did he find over there but Seya! I guess he'd gone there with some boys and had already started school. He was already enjoying the athletics and wanted to stay. But Frank wanted him in Albuquerque so the superintendent called him in and told him he had to go back with his father because he was supposed to be enrolled in Albuquerque. The officials scolded him and said, "Don't act like that; do what your parents tell you; don't be running off without their knowledge." Frank brought him back here first, and I scolded him too, for taking off like that and running off to Phoenix when he was supposed to be in school with Mary no. 2.[3] After about a week, Frank took him to Fort Defiance and from there, in a few weeks, they put him and some other students who were late going to Albuquerque on the train in Gallup.

At this time, Frank was also getting established as a Blessingway singer, and people were always coming around, asking him to do his ceremony. Sometimes he was asked to do it when people got married in the traditional way, or when a woman was about to have a baby, or a girl had reached womanhood. All those things are included in the Blessingway, of course. Other times, people wanted him to do it to make sure things would continue going along in the right way for them.

Around that time, Frank told me there was a priest at St. Michaels who was interested in recording different ceremonies. He knew how to write in Navajo and he was starting to bring different singers to the mission there to record their stories, songs, and prayers. Some singers, of course, didn't like that, but Frank thought it was a good idea. That would preserve these things for future generations so the People would always have them. Even though there were lots of singers at that time, Frank was worried that in the future, the young people wouldn't be interested in learning the sacred things. He said if that happened, then ceremonies couldn't be passed along and they'd disappear, and then, where would we be? He was starting to talk with other singers about how to encourage younger people to apprentice themselves to those who knew the different ceremonies, so they could follow them around, help them, and learn from them in the right way. That's the way we do it, and it takes a long time and lots of hard work. And then too, there are expenses involved in it. People don't teach those things without compensation. And, when you're finally qualified and ready to have your own medicine bundle, you have to acquire all the things you need for that, too. So, Frank was happy about the news that this priest was doing that at St. Michaels. His name was Father Berard, and the People used to call him "Little Priest Who Knows."[4]

I'm not sure how Frank got involved with that. Of course, he had worked at St. Michaels before we started living together, so he knew some of the Fathers over there. And because he was a headman, he went to meetings there to talk about problems in different parts of the reservation. He also used to stop there while traveling to Fort Defiance to meet with the agent. So maybe that's how he got to know Father Berard. I don't know. Of course, he heard things from our relatives, too; some of them, like Charlie Mitchell and Chic Sandoval, were helping the Fathers with things at St. Michaels.

Eventually Frank told me he was going to work with that priest. At that time, Father Berard was interested in recording the Blessingway from different ones trained in it, and Frank was asked to help. Slim Curly and Curly Hair Water Flows Together Man also helped with that; maybe it was Curly Hair who suggested Frank for that; he was a clan uncle and a close friend.[5] So Frank went over there and stayed for a while, working on that. They didn't get it all done at first, so he kept going back over there, whenever the priest sent word for him to come and do more work. That's how the things Frank had learned from his teachers, my father and his own father, ended up in the book on Blessingway.[6] I never went over there with him; I was here with the children, the farm, the sheep, and my mother. But he used to tell me about those things when he came back. I just listened. In the beginning I wasn't sure what my father would have said about doing something like that, but I understood how Frank felt about it. So, as I heard more about what he was doing with the priest who was working on Blessingway, I supported him in it. I always prepared food for him to take on the trips to St. Michaels; sometimes he went in the wagon and sometimes he went on horseback.

I think because Frank helped with that Father Berard invited him to go on the trips he had planned to the sacred mountains. I remember they already had a car at St. Michaels and they had asked Chic Sandoval, who was doing lots of interpreting for them and others in those days, too, to be the driver on those trips. Frank wasn't able to go on all of those, but he did go on most of them. As he explained it to me, it took all kinds of special preparations on the parts of everyone who went. They had to cleanse themselves and follow certain restrictions before they left, and then make special offerings and do very special prayers and other things when they approached the sacred mountains. Even the food they took had to be the kind we use in ceremonies, not just everyday mutton and fry bread. I, of course, knew how to fix those ceremonial foods because my mother had taught all of us that when we were growing up. So I prepared those things for him. I knew that was important to him. That was how he added the sacred earth, the Mountain Earth bundle, to his Blessingway *jish*. Lots of singers don't have those because of all the preparations, expenses, and hardships involved in acquiring those things in the correct way. You can't just do it any old way, grab dirt from any old place. And you can't just show up on those mountains and gather it without following all the rules. Those things were established by the Holy People way back. When you learn about the Blessingway, those are among the things you should learn. But some people don't finish their learning; they may learn the songs and prayers, but not the stories that go with those, that explain how those things started and how they go together. Or they may not learn the procedures for fixing up a new bundle, or a Mountain Earth bundle, or how to renew a bundle or themselves. There's a lot that goes with that and not everyone sees it through to the end. And then, too, teachers never pass on everything they know; we believe that weakens you and your knowledge so we don't do that. That's why if you're really serious about learning all those things, you need more than one teacher for different parts of it. Frank said that by adding together what he learned from my father and his own father, he had learned the complete ceremony. The only thing he was missing was a Mountain Earth bundle. That's why he was determined to go on those trips with the priest and others to the sacred mountains.[7]

Because I had been raised with my father's Blessingway and I believed in it, I supported Frank in all those things. The Blessingway was our main guide for life; that's how I was trying to live and raise our children. And so, each time Frank prepared for one of those trips, I abided by the rules surrounding it. He had to purify himself in the sweathouse and say certain prayers to get ready. We didn't sleep together either, during that time. Besides that, I prepared all the special foods they needed each time, and I also made sure his clothes, his moccasins, and his jewelry were in good condition. They wore their ceremonial clothes when they journeyed to those places and all those things have to be kept in proper order, too. After the priest found out I knew how to prepare the special foods they needed, he told Frank to ask me to do that each time, for everyone who went. I guess the other singers had wives who didn't know those things.*

When all those mountains had been visited in the proper way and Frank had assembled the sacred earth he needed for preparing the Mountain Earth bundle, he had a special ceremony. During it, that was put together. That's why he has it in his *jish*, and that's how he got it. It wasn't among the things my father owned and gave to him in the bundle before he passed away. It was Frank who added it. Once he had it, everybody knew about it. That made even more people ask him to do his ceremonies. It's special when you have that in your *jish*; lots of singers never go through the hardships to acquire it.

And then, too, once Frank got serious about his ceremony and living in the right way, people learned he respected his ceremony. Sometimes, when people would come around asking him to do something, he'd put them off because he hadn't had himself renewed yet. He was taught he should only do his Blessingway four times, and then stop and get himself renewed, reblessed with it. He always stuck to that; he respected it and was very, very careful about keeping track of how many times he had performed his ceremony so he never abused that. Of course some singers weren't that way; they did their ceremony over and over and over, never renewing themselves, getting their *jish*, their songs and other things reblessed, refreshened. Frank said that would bring harm to them and their *jish*, and whoever had hired them. That's what he was taught and he observed that very carefully. Sometimes, when he had to tell people he couldn't help them right then because of that, they got angry with him. But that's one thing he believed in strongly, and he stuck to it his whole life.

I don't remember exactly when Frank met Father Berard. But I know before he started recording his Blessingway for him and before they went to the sacred mountains to gather the sacred earth for the Mountain Earth bundle, we lost our second oldest daughter. I know that was in January 1931 because the priests made a record of it and that's one thing I remember very clearly. Even now, it saddens me.

Mary no. 2 had gone to the Albuquerque Indian School for high school. She'd been over there for about two years, and Seya had already followed her over there. Agnes was still at Fort Apache but Seya had finished there; even though those three followed each other around in their schooling, Agnes didn't get to Albuquerque until Seya was finished there.

Mary no. 2 didn't come home much after she started high school. She always found work in the summer and wanted to stay around Albuquerque or Santa Fe, doing whatever jobs she found so she had some income of her own. We weren't opposed to that; we wanted her to take whatever opportunities came her way because of her education. We believed those things were important. So, when this happened, we hadn't seen her for a while.

One day Frank had gone to the store, either Garcia's or the Thunderbird. When he came back, he said Mary no. 2 was coming home from school. He said, "I was told my daughter was coming home." We didn't know why she was coming because it wasn't time for vacation for school children. So we talked about it and wondered about it. The school, of course, had never notified us she was sick in any way.

The next day a car arrived in front of our hogan. We were still living over where Mary no. 1 lives now. The white lady who was driving the car just sat in there while some other white people got out and came in. They told us Mary no. 2 was in the back, and was very, very sick. So we rushed out. When we looked in there, we saw Mary no. 2 and we knew right then she was pretty far gone, nearly ready to die. When we saw her she was just swinging her head around and she was unconscious. When I saw her in that condition, I couldn't hold myself in. I started yelling at the top of my voice and crying. We got her out and tried to hold her but she was restless and started fighting us. She was not in her right mind. She was so very, very sick it was as if she was almost gone.

Right away, Frank got very angry at those white people. He started yelling and questioning them, asking when she got that way and why they hadn't notified us. I guess they said she had been like that for only a short time, and that they had tried various things, but nothing helped her. So then, they decided to bring her back to us. But we didn't believe them; we didn't think they were telling us the truth and we got very angry. We thought that must have happened a long time ago and that those school people waited until it was too late before they brought her back.

She lived only a few days, maybe three or four, after that. Right away we carried her into the hogan and laid her on sheepskins and covered her with blankets. She was thrashing around and had a high fever. She was mainly unconscious but whenever she tried to speak, she kept asking for smokes. Frank got on a fast horse and went and got a hand-trembler he knew. Even though that man suggested some ceremonies, he also said she was very near the end, that it was too late. He was right; she kept getting worse. Even though we started trying different ceremonies for her, shortly after that, she passed away. She never came back to her right mind. It all happened so fast we didn't even have time to notify our relatives who lived farther away.

We never really found out what made her get like that. Frank went up to the mission and asked the priest there, Father Remy, to bury her. So he came and got her and did that for us. She was buried in the cemetery behind the mission.[8] Later, Frank got a priest to help him send a letter to the superintendent about what had happened to Mary no. 2. He was very angry at the school and the way none of the officials ever communicated with the parents of children who were at various places, getting their educations. Of course, that had already happened to us and others around here, when we lost Pauline at the Chinle Boarding School. Lots of people were upset about those kinds of things, and they supported Frank when he said he was going to write the superintendent and demand he come out here to Chinle to talk with the parents and explain these things. I think that man finally sent someone out here, and Frank and others went to the meeting. I, of course, stayed home with our small children. But even with that, we never found out what happened to Mary no. 2.[9] When Frank came back from the meeting, he said he didn't get anything definite from it. He said those officials came and tried to explain, but he didn't believe what they told the People. I guess he got really angry over at that meeting, too. He told me, "Before they had explained that to my satisfaction, the superintendent tried to leave. I went after him and grabbed him and demanded he explain the whole truth. I pulled him back into the room. He just pleaded with me, saying they had tried all kinds of medicine but she just kept getting worse. They couldn't save her. He never said what the cause was. He pleaded with me saying they had done their best but they couldn't save her." We still don't know what caused her death.

That's why Ruth and Isabel never went to school. We were very upset about that and we were scared of the schools because of it, so we never enrolled any more of our children. Of course, Seya went and Howard and Augusta, too. Mary no. 1 didn't but that was because she was born in a crippled condition. Ruth and Isabel didn't get put into school because of our losing the other Mary, Mary no. 2. We were angry at the school for a very long time.[10]

Later, when the officials came here asking for Isabel to go to school when she was five or six, we told them no. They came here over and over for a whole year, repeating that Isabel needed to go to school. After a year, they were even sending police here to get her into school. When that started, Frank said we'd better do it so we both went over there with her in the wagon. But when we got there, the Chinle Boarding School was all filled up. We were told there were no vacant beds in the dormitory and that we'd have to wait another year to enroll her, after some of the local children finished and went away for more school. But when the next year came and we inquired again, again we were told there was no room. So we never took her back.

We never got a satisfactory answer from those people about what happened, what caused Mary no. 2's sickness. When they brought her home shortly before she died, she was all run down; even though she was already a grown woman, she looked like she was starved and hadn't had anything to eat for a long time; she had no flesh on her. Later we heard from somebody that Mary no. 2 had been working for a family in Santa Fe in the summer and that they had taken her to Mexico.[11] I guess she was taking care of their children or cooking and helping with the dishes, doing things like that. I think somehow she got hold of some kind of weed either there in Santa Fe or down in Mexico, and started smoking it. That made her go out of her mind. Frank said when people got like that and could only talk about smokes and ask for smokes, it was because they were addicted to something, some kind of harmful thing. The hand-trembler we got for her said the same thing. So maybe that's what happened to her.[12] Even though Seya was right there at the school, he was never told his older sister was sick. The officials didn't bother to tell him until after they came back from bringing Mary no. 2 home. And by then, of course, she had already died. Seya wasn't sure he wanted to remain at that school after that happened but Frank told him to stay; he was almost done at that time.

As Frank and I went along together, I tried to support him in his jobs as headman and Blessingway singer. Even before he started with the Council, lots of times he'd be gone for various reasons. I never complained about it. I remembered my mother telling me years ago I shouldn't worry about those things. My job was the children, our hogan, our sheep, our farm, and whatever else I needed to be taking care of around here, like cooking, hoeing, or weaving. So I tried to follow that. I never asked him where he'd been when he came back; sometimes I knew because he'd tell me ahead of time, before he left. Other times, I didn't. But even then, I didn't say anything about it. He had pretty much settled down; after my father died and Frank started performing the Blessingway as someone qualified to do that, he was more serious. Of course, every now and then he got the notion to gamble or do something like that with others, but he wasn't known for that anymore. A lot of people respected him for his talks to the People, his advice as a leader, and for his Blessingway Ceremony.

As the children were born, Frank always told me I was in charge of the hogan and the children. He expected them to listen to what I said and do what I told them to do every day. He said to scold them if they needed it because he wanted them raised right. But I always tried talking to them nicely, saying, "My Little One, My Little Daughter, My Little Son, My Children," something like that.[13] Sure, sometimes I got angry with them when they took off playing instead of watching the sheep carefully, or bringing back water or wood I had sent them to get, or things like that. Each morning when I got them up early to say their prayers to the Dawn and to run, I fixed them something to eat, whatever we had around for food. And while we ate, I told each of them what they needed to do that day, like hoe the fields before it got too hot, or clean around the place, or card and spin wool, herd, dye wool, or other things. Of course sometimes we needed to go pick pinyons, or gather berries or *dleesh* or other things I needed. Then I'd usually take one or two of them with me on horseback, or more in the wagon, if it was available, and we'd go do those things, too. Every day there was always plenty for them to be helping with, and I always made it clear what needed to be done, asking them in a nice way to do that. I don't think I ever cussed them out, or called them any bad names, like "Little Coyote," "Little Bear," or "Little Snake." And I never made fun of them when they made mistakes. You're not supposed to abuse your children or talk to them like that.

Frank used to ask in the evenings if they'd done what I'd asked. If they hadn't, he used to get angry and scold them. He had a way of talking to them all together in a scolding manner. He'd do it so it included everybody, whenever something was left undone or something wasn't done right and he found out and got upset about it. As they got older, it seemed to me he used a louder voice. Sometimes it was almost like he was preaching at them, like he was talking to the People at a gathering. I know later some of our children couldn't take that; some of them, like Ruth, Howard, and Isabel used to get up and leave, when he started doing that. But that was later.

I don't think either of us hit the children very often. Maybe once or twice somebody would get slapped or switched for not doing what they were told, or for not being careful enough about the sheep or things like that. I remember a few times switching the girls. Once that happened with Agnes. She was home from Fort Apache and was herding, using my mother's donkey like she did while my mother was still living. She didn't pay attention and the sheep got in the corn. I saw them so I went looking for her; I found her somewhere else, playing, not watching them. So I scolded her and she took off running toward the cornfield. She was by herself and some of the sheep started going back in there as soon as she got the others out. She started crying because she couldn't get them rounded up. So I went hurrying over there too, and I grabbed some sticks on the way from a greasewood bush I passed by. When I got over there I hit her a few times on her legs with those; she should have been watching the sheep instead of playing. You have to pay attention to keep them out of the corn, and she was old enough to be responsible about those things. But later that day, toward evening, I was sorry I had done that; I remembered how hard it is to herd without help when there are lots of animals to watch and when you're on foot. So I told her I was sorry I had gotten angry and switched her.

Another time I remember scolding Agnes was about Uncle John's sheep. Frank's brother, John, had lots of sheep and for a while, he kept them over here with ours because he had no help. Sometimes Seya or others herded for him or Uncle Jim, who also had lots of animals. But at that time, nobody was available so John brought them here so they got herded in with the others. It may have been that same summer; I don't remember, but I know Agnes was home from Fort Apache and was the person in charge of herding those sheep, too. None of my children liked John too much; he was stingy with everything and he never helped us out very much. No matter what anyone did for him, it seemed like he never gave anything back. Agnes needed new shoes that summer and I know Frank mentioned it to his brother because John was quite well-off. But he just turned him down on that. And even when those sheep lambed, he never gave us one. Often, if people herd for you, you give them a lamb or a kid or something like that. But he was a miser about that, too. Lots of people said that about him, even though we're not supposed to talk like that. That summer one of his goats was pregnant. One morning when I was out by the corral, I noticed it was missing. So I asked Agnes where it was; she thought it was in with the rest of them. When I questioned her some more, it turned out she hadn't seen it probably for two days; she hadn't even missed it! So I scolded her again about paying attention while she was herding and told her we needed to find it. I went with her and she finally remembered where she'd been when she knew she had seen it. Sure enough, it had gotten lost. We finally found it; it had fallen down in a hole in the Wash and died in there, upside down with its legs sticking up because it couldn't get out. Of course, even the baby inside it was dead. I scolded her again, right there, for a long time. I told her you always have to pay attention to the sheep and goats, and know how many you have and where they are. That's when she told me she didn't care about her uncle's goats and sheep and she wasn't going to herd for him any more; she said he was too stingy. Because it was almost time for her to go back to school, I didn't say any more about it. But I told Frank about what had happened and that he should tell his brother to find someone else to do his herding. I guess John did because soon after that, he came and took his sheep and goats some place else.

With Frank I tried to be the same as I was with the children. I know lots of married people fight with each other all the time, calling each other nasty names and using bad words against each other. When we started out together, we were told not to act like that, but instead, to try to work together, and make plans together for our future and whatever children we might have. So, we tried to live according to that. We always tried to speak to each other nicely, not in anger. I always called him, "The Man I'm Living With, The Man I am Making a Living With," and he did the same with me, calling me, "The Woman I'm Living With, The Woman I am Making a Living With." We both liked that way of talking; it was more respectful to say that, at least in those days, than "my old lady," "my old man," or even "my children's mother or father, or my daughter's father, or my son's mother." Some people who were married called each other that, but that shows no respect, no love, and we didn't ever say that to each other. We followed that all the years we were married; we always used those words to each other.

But, of course, every now and then as we went along, we had problems. I don't think any of those things happened because I stepped ahead of him in planning things, because I never did. I always let him do the planning, and just listened to what he said. That's the way my mother did with my father, too. When Frank asked for my opinion on something, I'd give it to him, if I had one. Sometimes, when it concerned the children, I'd really speak up when we were discussing things at night, after they were asleep in the hogan with us. That was because it was often me, not him, who knew what they needed, because he was gone so often. It was that way with their clothes, their shoes, or even things we needed from the store. I'd mention those things to him because I knew about them by being home all the time. Of course, the schools helped with some of those things, like coats and caps and shoes, once we enrolled some of our children. It was the same way with the animals; sometimes I'd tell Frank if a horse was acting lame, or a ewe was about ready to lamb, or if I thought we should butcher an animal up in its years. Of course the butchering was left up to whomever owned the animal; only that person decided it. And then, too, if I needed Frank's help, I'd always bring that up. If it was time to shear and there weren't enough adults around to help me, I'd ask him to help, or if I needed to use the wagon or we needed to go some place to help one of our relatives. The same was true with sicknesses; if someone needed help with illness, I'd always make sure he knew about it so he could get a hand-trembler, star-gazer, or someone else like that who knew how to diagnose things.

Most of the time we didn't argue or quarrel over things; we just went along smoothly. But there were a few times in the early years, while I was still having children, when we did have trouble. The two times I really remember were while my mother was still alive. The first was during the summer; Agnes was home from Fort Apache for vacation so she was the oldest one around here when this happened. Frank had been asked to do a Blessingway over in Black Mountain somewhere so he was gone and we were here by ourselves. All of us were sleeping in the hogan together, like we always did. During the night I thought I heard something moving around outside, up near the door of the hogan. But I didn't get up to check on it. The next morning I got up early and went out and found big footprints walking away from the hogan. That upset me so I followed those tracks until they just stopped, and disappeared a ways from here, in the sand. When I came back, I got the children up. After they said their morning prayers with the corn pollen and ran their race, I made breakfast for them. Then I told them what I'd heard and what I'd seen outside. I asked if they had heard anything, but none of them had.

When Frank came home later that afternoon from the ceremony, I told him about it. Right away he started acting jealous and suspicious, asking who had been here with me in his absence. He started accusing me of doing those kinds of things right in front of the children, and that really hurt me. After he got through saying those things, he stopped talking to me for the whole day. He went to sleep for a while, having just finished his ceremony, but even when he got back up, he didn't speak to me. That made me very, very sad because I knew I hadn't done anything. I never was with another man after I started living with Frank; all the years I lived with him, I *never* did anything like that, even though I know at times it was not the same on his part.

While he was acting like that toward me, Agnes and I went outside to do something. I asked her why she hadn't said something on my behalf when he started accusing me. She was the oldest one there, and she knew I had found those big shoe tracks by the door early in the morning because I'd shown those to her while I was worrying about it. I guess Agnes was still bashful at that time and she held back because of that.

I know she was upset about it, after she heard her father talking that way to me. She told me she wished she'd opened her mouth and spoken up on my behalf.

Frank acted like that for that whole day and evening. Agnes got up early the next morning and took the sheep out while he was still sleeping. When he got up, it was all over. For some reason, he was happy again. He went to the store and got us a sheep to butcher so we could all celebrate and have a big meal together. That was the end of it. He was like that; when he got mad, usually it didn't last too long, at least within the family.

The next summer I had another baby. Even though they had just opened a small hospital here in Chinle, I had this baby at home. I did that with all of my children. This baby was a girl, and we named her Isabel. After I had her, I never got pregnant again; she was my last one. I remember Frank was already working with Father Berard when Isabel was born; they were starting to talk about traveling to the sacred mountains. After Isabel came, I was here with my mother, who was up in her years. We were still living over where Mary no. 1 lives now, but sometimes we were closer this way, north of Ida's place, but on the same side of the dirt road. Some of the children were at home with me—Ruth, David, Howard, Augusta, and the new one, Isabel. Seya and Agnes were still away at school and Mary no. 1 was still having children for Woody. She had another baby, Walter, shortly before I had Isabel, so those two are almost like twins, too. Then she had another one, a girl, but it passed away. After that, she didn't have any more children, either.

Shortly after I had Isabel, Howard got sick. It rained a lot that summer and one day, it rained so hard I made the children stay inside. As soon as it stopped, Howard ran out. He was like that when he was little; he was always playing in water and getting all covered with mud. Even when he herded, he always found mud to play in.* That day he ran over to the field where the corn and the melons were. I guess he decided to eat a melon right there. It turned out the field had been struck by lightning during the heavy rain, but of course, he didn't know it. About a day later, he started getting sick and very quickly he couldn't even stand up or walk. We had to carry him outside in a blanket when he needed to go out. I got worried right away so Frank got a hand-trembler. That man said lightning had caused it so we got an old crippled singer to come and do some things from Lightningway for him right away. By the time the ceremony was over, Howard was able to get up; that cured him. After that, when different ones went to the field, they said you could see where the melons had been struck by lightning. The same thing happened to Mary no. 1, too. I don't remember if it was at that time, or a little later, but she used some corn struck by lightning without knowing it. So, she, too, had to have the effects of that removed. Woody went and got Bead Man's Son to do a Shootingway Ceremony for her. Sometimes we used that man, too, for those kinds of things.[14]

About the same time, right before Frank went on one of those trips to the sacred mountains with Father Berard and the others, Ida became a *kinaaldá*. She was being raised by Chubby Woman who had been married to her father, Son of Yucca Fruit Man, and they decided to have the Puberty Ceremony for her. They asked Curly Hair to be the main singer for that and Frank went there to help out with the songs during the night. You get part of the cake we bake in the ground if you help with the singing. So he told me that's why he was going over there. I stayed here with the children and our new baby, Isabel.

But when Frank came home the next morning, when I touched his hands and his arms, he was all cold. That made me think he hadn't gone to the singing, that he'd been somewhere else during the night. I didn't say anything to him right then because that same morning those people were coming to get him to go to one of the sacred mountains. When he came in, after we greeted each other he told me he wanted to get some sleep before they came. So he went and lay down.

I was suspicious about where he'd been and I started thinking about it, getting angry. So, after a while, I asked Ruth to watch the children and I started off, to see if I could track where he'd gone. I knew there was a woman nearby who had a bad reputation; it seemed like she was grabbing every man she could find and running around wild. That was one of Cecil's sisters; she wasn't married yet and she lived not far from here. Later she got married several times, finally to Philemon. I don't know if that settled her down or not. But when this happened, I suspected Frank was among the men who were visiting her, whenever they could get away from their wives and children. From what I'd heard, lots of men were doing that and she was encouraging it.

If you know about footprints, moccasin tracks, you know how to follow them. Frank's were always easy for me to locate; I knew what they looked like. Sure enough, when I went to where they had held Ida's *Kinaaldá*, I found his tracks coming out of the hogan and heading over toward where that woman lived. So I went over there, following his tracks. When I got close to her hogan, I broke off a big stick from one of the greasewoods growing in the area. Maybe I was going to hit her with it; I don't remember now why I did that.*

When I got there, here was Mary no. 1 sitting in there with her, eating a melon they'd broken. In those days, we didn't cut melons with knives; we just broke them open and ate them. My daughter was sure surprised to see me, but I don't think the other woman was. I came right out and said what I had to say, even though it was in front of Mary no. 1. I told that woman I knew she'd been with my husband during the night because he'd come home all cold. If he'd spent the night at the ceremony, he would have been inside by the fire and not felt that way. So I knew he'd been out doing something, and I'd tracked his footprints right to her place. I told her those things. I also told her if she didn't stop doing that with Frank, I was going to beat her and report her to the officials. She just sat there. At first she denied it. She said, "Sure, he came here, just like you said. But I scolded him and told him to go home because he was married, he already had a wife and children. After I got after him, he went home." But I didn't believe her so I said so. And I told her off, right there. I called her a whore; I told her she was living like a female dog, taking all the men in the Valley; I said she really was a whore. Mary no. 1 didn't say anything the whole time we were exchanging harsh words. I guess I waved the stick around too, probably just missing her a few times with it. She finally stopped saying anything and just sat there. She wasn't even eating the melon anymore while I went on, saying what I had to say about her acting like that.

When I finished my words, I came back over here. I was going to talk to Frank about it, too, and get it right out in the open. Even though I had never brought up things like that before, I decided I needed to tell him I was hearing things like that about him. I knew he shouldn't be doing those things; he was respected as a leader and as a singer, and he was supposed to be acting right, living according to all those teachings, and treating his wife and children in the right ways, too. I decided it was time to remind him of those things, even though I'd never said anything like that before. All the years we'd been married, I'd never brought those things up; I'd never asked him questions about his travels or why he was late sometimes coming back from wherever he had gone. But this time, I decided it was time. Maybe it was because I'd already heard from others he was among the men going to see this woman. And then too, I guess I was really upset because he was doing that during the time when he'd been helping with a Puberty Ceremony, singing his sacred songs. He went directly from that over to her place, instead of staying there to help during the whole night like he should have. And on top of that, he did this right when they were going to the sacred mountains. That was serious. I knew how important that was to him and I knew about all the rules he had to follow in order to prepare himself to make those trips because he had already been on one, or maybe two of those before he did this. Here, they were leaving in the morning and he did this during the night. I guess for all those reasons I was very upset.

But when I got back home, he'd already left; those people had already come and they'd left for another of the sacred mountains. It was several days before he returned from that trip and by then I'd had more time to think about it. Maybe I shouldn't have said anything, but I decided it was important. So I went ahead and brought it up, right out in the open, after he got back home from his trip. I really got after him, lit into him about all of that. I told him here he was supposed to be doing holy, sacred things instead of running around. I said nothing good would come from his trips to the mountains or from his ceremony if he was fooling around on the side at the same time. I told him he'd better settle down and behave in the future, stop doing disgusting things like that. I didn't leave anything unsaid about his running around wild. When I did that, he just sat there quietly, not saying anything. Maybe he was surprised by my words, I don't know. But then, there wasn't much to be said, because I told him I'd followed his tracks and I also told him what I'd said to that woman. After that, he never went over there again. Other men did, and finally, some of the other wives went there and told her the same things I had said. I don't know how many more years she acted like that; it was a while from what different ones told me.

I don't know if Frank did that with any more women after her or not. I never asked. I never had reason to suspect him again so I never went tracking his footprints again, either.* Years later, he brought that up one time we were talking. It wasn't until then that he told me he knew he had been foolish at that time, and that he shouldn't have been disrespecting his Blessingway by acting like that. He said even though he had done lots of foolish things in his younger days, by the time that happened, he should have been through with those things. Later, he was sorry he'd put me through that kind of suffering; he told me that, too. But I didn't say anything. It was years later when he finally said something, and it was over. My daughter who witnessed that never said anything about it to me at all. For a while after that, she didn't come over very much; we had very few words for a long time. It was probably a year she was like that with both me and her father. I didn't say anything to her, either. Maybe I embarrassed her. I don't know if she was friends with that woman, or not, or why she was there eating a melon with her. I never asked her. Even when she finally started coming around again, we never talked about those things.[15]

My Mother[1]

Living with my mother after Man Who Shouts dies . . . my mother's
interactions with our children and her teachings to them.

After my father died, my mother stayed close by us, especially Frank and me. Of course, they avoided each other because she observed the mother-in-law rule the People used to have. She always had her own hogan, a little apart from where we were, and even when Frank did a Blessingway for her, he always hung up a blanket to separate them, and sang from behind it.

Because my mother was with us from the time we put Seya into school, many of my children got to know her very well. Of course by then, she was in old age; before that, she was with my father; they did things together so it wasn't until later my children saw a lot of her. That was true for all of them except Isabel; she was still very small when my mother passed away. And it was mainly the girls my mother spent time with, teaching them things and talking to them. Sometimes when I'd hear what she was saying, it'd make me laugh to myself; I'd remember her saying the same things to me when I was small. Other times I'd wonder if she wasn't being too harsh with them. But she was like that; it seemed to me she scolded my children more than Frank or I did when they were small. Some days it seemed like all she did was scold one or another of them for something they'd done. Then she'd come over and tell me what had happened. When it got like that, at night I'd remind them she was an old age person and needed to be treated kindly and with respect.

One thing about my mother that seemed to cause trouble was the way she was always walking somewhere.[2] Almost every day I'd see her going down the road on foot, traveling somewhere, with her cane. My mother was very, very tall before old age shrank her, even taller than me. She never minded the hot weather; she wore heavy, lined skirts and in the summer, she'd put a white towel on her head so she didn't feel the heat. She liked to visit people. The old people were like that; they always visited each other and sometimes stayed for a day or two, before coming back. Clan relatives do that, too; your relatives always give you something to eat or a place to stay when you're visiting. My mother was always going to see my younger sister, Small Woman, over by the Hard Ground Place or my half sister, Slim Woman, down near Valley Store. She also visited Curly Hair and his family a lot; they were over near Nazlini then. Towering House Woman was another one; she was also known as the Woman Who Kicks Dirt because she walked sideways, kicking the dirt with one of her feet as she went along. She was a close relative and they visited back and forth, too. And there were others, like the Nelson Gormans in their big stone house down the road. Nelson was a close clan relative, too. Of course, lots of times when she got to where she was going, other relatives would be there. That's another reason she'd stay and talk and talk for a long time.

As my mother got up in her years, I worried about her walking by herself. So I started telling one of my girls to go with her, wherever she wanted to go. Agnes, Ruth, and Augusta all had to do that for me, and all three of them didn't like going with her. She always traveled great distances; sometimes when one of them was complaining to me about that, they'd say it was like she was walking to Gallup, even though they did-n't even know where that was.* She walked fast, ahead of them, and never let them stop to rest their small legs, or get a drink at the windmill or water holes. Then, when she'd get where she was going, she'd visit and visit. The whole time she talked she'd be spinning; she always took her spindle and some wool along on her travels. My girls got hot and tired, and they got bored listening to older people talking. They were all small and bashful then and didn't like visiting. They also got hungry. So, sometimes they'd take off and run back here, leaving her wherever she'd gone visiting. I always scolded them for that, telling them they were supposed to stay and watch her. And when she came back, she scolded them too, saying, "Why did you leave me over there? You were told to walk with me." As those things kept happening, my girls would run and hide themselves whenever they saw her coming so they didn't get told to walk with her. And after she had really scolded them, they'd tell me she was too mean and they weren't going to go with her anymore.

Sometimes she'd also scold them about something they did during those travels. Agnes seemed to be the one I heard the most about for that reason; when she was home during the summer from Fort Apache, she was often the one I sent with my mother. Later, I sent Ruth a lot, too, and then Augusta. One time at Curly Hair's place, Agnes hid behind a young woman when some dogs frightened her and some-how, she pulled the woman's skirt off by grabbing it.* I guess that embarrassed my mother; she scolded her there and all the way home. Another time they walked up to Garcia's; my mother took some sheepskins there to trade, like we do. That time, she got a box of sweet crackers, like vanilla wafer cookies today, and told Agnes to carry it.

Agnes thought those were for her; she really liked them so she ate them all up on the way home. When my mother asked for one, over by Uncle John's place, they were all gone. She was still scolding Agnes, saying, "There's no reason for you to be acting that hungry," when they got back. She never had her carry anything else when they walked to the store after that.*

Another time I remember it was already fall; we were harvesting and it was time for Agnes to go back to Fort Apache. We were living near our cornfield close to the Chinle Wash. I sent Agnes with my mother and she took her to see the Ye'iis for the first time, without telling her. Poor Agnes didn't know anything about that; my mother got a ride for them at Garcia's so they went in a wagon over toward Sawmill. Agnes was scared the whole time; she didn't know anyone in the crowd at that Nightway, she didn't know where they were, and she didn't know anything about getting initiated. You can't just go and watch those dancers without being initiated; if you do, you'll go blind. And if they don't put the mask on right so it's straight with your eyes, you get eye trouble from that, too. My mother kept reminding Agnes to make sure it was right by her eyes. In this way, my mother took care of that for her on one of those trips; she didn't do that for any of my other children.

But sometimes, funny things happened when one of my girls would be walking with her. I heard about those too, when they came back. I remember something that happened concerning the Old Owl Man.* Frank and I used to joke about him; I guess somewhere along the line we started using him to scare our children, probably like the bogeyman or something like that. I don't know why we ever started that; maybe all parents scare their children saying, "Some creature is going to grab you, kidnap you, or harm you in another way," to make the children listen.[3]

In those days, lots of people would pass by on the dirt road near our home, walking, riding, or traveling in their wagons to haul water, go to one of the stores, or somewhere else. I used to tell the children to stay away from the road but they liked to see who was going by. Sometimes they'd watch while they were hiding in the big ditch that used to be across from here, running to the north. Lots of people hauled water from it and sometimes brought animals there, too. Or they brought their sheep and horses to another water hole, behind where Augusta lives now. There used to be one there, too, and even though I said no, sometimes the children would swim in there after Seya taught them how.[4] Water was scarce lots of times in those days. When we settled in this area, there were a few windmills to help with that, and they'd already appointed Dick Dunaway to take care of them. He was another person who was always traveling along the road with his wagon and mules. The children used to be scared of him but he was really a nice, old man. He'd always yell to any children along the road, even if they were hiding in the corn when he went by.[5] Later, the government put in some deep wells and some dams and other things. But lots of those dried up after a while, too, just like the ditch we used. That was probably because of the droughts.

The man we called the Old Owl Man used to pass by a lot; he used two big, white horses on his wagon, and we used to tell our children he was looking for children who were bad. I don't know why we said that, but we did.* So, they were scared of him, too, and they'd hide whenever anyone saw him coming. One time when Agnes had gone with my mother to Garcia's, when they were coming back walking over by the Chinle Wash where all the trees are now,[6] they came across his wagon. Agnes got really scared, knowing the Old Owl Man was right there, but my mother went over and greeted a young woman who was fixing some food in the back, under the cover of the wagon. Then she told Agnes to come over, too; that really scared her. When she got over there, my mother told her to look in the back. So she climbed up a little. There she saw an old, old man, with long, white hair and whiskers, all crippled with arthritis, lying on a mattress. She had never seen anyone in that condition, so that scared her, too.

I guess she started thinking about it and about that one being the Old Owl Man, and so she came right out with it and asked my mother when they were walking back from there. My mother said she just started laughing.* She told her we had made that up; that man had been like that for a long time and he couldn't harm anyone in his condition. But she also told her not to tell her brothers and sisters what she had found out about the Old Owl Man. She made her promise, and Agnes did. My mother told me about it when they got home, and Agnes did too, later, when the others were not around. After that, we used to laugh about it together, whenever the others would run and hide because he was coming down the road.[7]*

While my mother was with us, she taught my children many things. Some of those were about ceremonies. She helped with the Puberty ceremonies we had; Ruth had both of hers before my mother passed away, and some of the others did, too. I remember her instructing the children about racing with the *kinaaldá*; we were living over by Mary no, 1's when Ruth did both of hers. The fields were plowed in sections then, but there were still no fences. Ruth also had a Blessingway about that time for something else. She had gone to bed with her necklace on but somehow it was off the next morning. When she told Frank about it, he said it wasn't good when something happens in your sleep and you don't know about it. So he went and got Old Curly Hair to say a one-night prayer for her and then do a Blessingway on top of that; Old Curly Hair put her beads back on her while he was singing, to correct that.

Woody's mother, *Nabah*, passed away, too, while my mother was living near us. That was the first time some of my children went through that, so she tried to teach them the rules we follow when someone dies. Because she was very strict about traditional things, she really got after them the whole time, about not looking in the direction the body was taken, not eating until it was out of sight, and not sleeping. *Nabah* died in a little shelter next to the hogan over where Louise lives. They'd carried her out there like we do when it looks like somebody isn't going to get well. Some of my children were sneaking around outside, peeking at what was going on. They saw the four men chosen to do the burial; they had let their hair down loose, and stripped to their moccasins and G strings, before they went to the burial place. Those men took her up near where the gravel pit is now, below the cemetery. When they came back, someone met them at a distance with a bucket of medicine, the lightning-struck plants we use for Evilway. They washed with that and then covered themselves with ashes before coming back. Then, for four days they stayed separate on the north side of the hogan, not touching anyone and eating from their own dishes. After the four days were over, we all washed and went on with what we always did. Because my children didn't know about those things, they kept watching and asking questions, and my mother kept scolding them after *Nabah* died and we went through that.

My mother also taught my daughters lots of other things. Whoever was around her got the benefit of that. The two Marys and Seya were the ones with me while my father was still alive. And then Mary no. 1 started having children for Woody, and the others went to school. Agnes was around my mother a lot but mostly in the summer, after she started at Fort Apache. Of the ones who survived, she learned things from my mother, and so did Ruth and Augusta. Isabel was still too little.

Some summers, I sent Ruth to live with my mother and help her with things, while I was over here with a new baby. As I remember it now, there were several summers where both Ruth and David stayed over by the Chinle Wash with my mother, at her place on a little hill near the center of our cornfields. My brother, Man with a Cane, was there, too, and the four of them took care of the corn while Frank and I were over here, near where Mary no. 1 lives now. My mother did things the same way we did, so whoever was with her had to get up early, say their prayers at dawn, and then run to strengthen themselves before she fixed their morning meal. Then they started helping with whatever work she had planned. Some days my mother would send Ruth over here to milk the goats and bring the milk back over there, or she'd come and do it herself. And then too, every day they'd carry water from the Chinle Wash, going there on foot with two buckets and the wooden kegs we carried on our backs. We all did that every day; that's how we got water. I know that's how we were living when I had Howard and then got bitten again by a rattlesnake, and also when I had Augusta and started having problems with my face getting twisted.

When Agnes came home from Fort Apache, I kept her over here with me because she was herding and helping me with the wool and other things. Sometimes she'd also help me hoe in the fields, early in the morning, before it was too hot. And Agnes was also the one I asked to gather corn pollen; she enjoyed that and always seemed to gather more than the rest, at least until she ran into two snakes. That scared her and then, for a while, she seemed to spend more time looking for snakes than collecting pollen.* Frank raised a lot of corn each year; we used that for our own food and also for the horses; and we used the pollen for ceremonies and for our prayers at dawn and in the evening. All those things were up to me and whatever children were here; Frank was busy with his work as a headman and with the priests and with his Blessingway.

During those times, my mother told me Ruth was old enough to learn to make traditional foods so she started showing her all the ways of fixing corn, from the time it gets barely ripe right on through until it's fully ripe. She also taught her the different ways to fix yellow and blue cornmeal, with and without juniper ash, and how to make big and little tamales; different dumplings, even the little marble ones; different kinds of mush; different breads—like tortillas, fry bread, kneeldown bread, lazy bread, and others, even the ones baked in the ground—and all the foods we fix only for ceremonies. My mother and I made paperbread a lot, too; Augusta and Garnett liked to help keep the fire going. Ruth tried to learn paperbread, too, but she always got burned. So that was the only one she didn't learn out of all the things my mother taught her about traditional foods. My mother showed her, saying, "This is how it's done." She'd make her do it over and over, until she got it right. Then she'd say Ruth knew that one. I remember how proud Ruth was when she made some of those foods for Frank and me for the first time, and they came out the right way.* I was happy my mother was teaching her those things; Ruth got a good schooling, even though we didn't send her to school.

My mother also taught Ruth and some of the others about the wild foods. Even in her old age, she'd take her on horseback to the places where certain foods, like yucca fruit, *haashch'é'édą́ą'* and other berries like *chiiłchin*, prickly pear fruit, Navajo and Mormon tea, *tł'ohdeeí*, *'ostse'*, the old Navajo peaches that grew in the Canyon, and even pinyons, were growing. They'd take her donkey along, too, so it could haul back whatever they gathered. Sometimes they'd roll up their sheepskins and go toward Round Rock, or Tsaile, or Red Rock near Black Mountain, to gather the different kinds of red berries. At the right time of year, if it rained, those berries were plentiful in those areas so they'd camp overnight while they gathered them. In those days, you could stay out in the open without worrying about drunks roaming around. We all did that when we went to gather those foods. Of course, that way Ruth learned where those things grew, how to gather them, and then how to fix them as food to be used soon or later, in the wintertime. With the berries, Ruth learned both ways of fixing them.[8] My mother told all my children those were the main foods she had to eat when she was little. They practically lived on wild things they found and they went out far, looking for them, even while they herded. She said sometimes it'd take them three or four days to gather them and bring them back. After they found lots of them, they'd prepare themselves and go and stay there however many days it took to pick all of them. They never wasted their time on the little, bitty ones or places where there were just a few in her younger days.

My mother also taught some of my children about the plants we use for different ailments, or to keep snakes, bugs, or other things away. Ruth learned many of those things from her, too; they'd go on horseback to gather juniper, cliffrose, sagebrush, pinyon, and other things, like plants from lightning-struck areas, and *nábįįh*. She'd show her how to fix those either by themselves, or together to make medicines used in Evilway, Shootingway, and some of the other ceremonies. My mother always kept those things on hand, and so did I.

Of course, my mother and I were always weaving when we weren't busy doing other things, and we'd tell the girls to sit and watch us. We'd show them how and let them try, too. My mother helped teach Ruth to weave and to respect the loom and all the weaving tools; she taught her to take care of those things properly because that was part of learning to weave, too.

While I was happy my children were learning all those things from my mother, there was something else she did that I felt differently about. Maybe I shouldn't talk about it, even now. It used to upset me and I guess when I remember it now, it still bothers me. That was the way she talked to my girls about men. Sometimes it embarrassed me to hear what she was saying; she was pretty harsh with them and with some of the things she said about being a woman. And sometimes the way she talked to the girls, especially in her old age, scared them. I don't think she meant to be like that; maybe it was just her way when she got into her old age. Whenever she'd talk about becoming a woman or being around men, she'd get harsh with her voice, almost like she was yelling at them because she thought they weren't listening or had no minds or something like that.

Sometimes she said they shouldn't even think about getting married, not to do that. Other times she'd suggest, by the way she said things, they were too dumb to know when they got their periods, or so stupid about their relatives they'd probably marry a close relation without knowing it. When she started saying those things, it bothered me. I didn't believe in talking to children that way. She even used to call them "crazy" or "stupid," like some people do now when they talk to their children. But that's not right.

When she'd be giving one of her talks about men, I think she scared them about things they were curious about and didn't know about yet. Instead of explaining things in a calm, quiet way, her voice got loud and she'd start saying things that confused them. She always made it sound like they could get pregnant if a man even walked beside them, or they would have babies if someone even kissed them.* Things like that. She also told them men only wanted their pleasure from women, and once they were satisfied, they'd leave you. She said you don't just go with a man because he wants you to go somewhere; all they wanted was to take advantage of you; that's all they had in mind. She also said it wasn't right to let a man do anything to you, or to get pregnant without having a husband. Some days it seemed to me all she talked about to whichever girls were around her was not doing the wrong things with men. I think she confused them and scared them about some things.

She probably did that because she didn't want them getting into trouble in any way, even with their relatives; that's why she was warning them, trying to tell them to understand who they're related to so they didn't start going with anyone who was a clan relative. You have to know those things so we always tried to explain who people were and how they were related to us whenever anyone came around, if those people were relatives. That's the only way children can learn those things. But the way my mother talked, she made it sound as if they didn't know any of those things. I didn't think that was true and I didn't want her making them scared of people. I know she frightened them and made them wary of Navajo men and I was afraid she'd scare them about their own relatives, too.

In the old days, it was mainly the men who told the generation stories, how people were related to each other and how that went way, way back. Women didn't do too much of that. I don't know why it was that way; maybe because men traveled around more, going hunting and trading, going to the stores or to meetings, meeting different people, here and there, they were the ones who knew more about those things. Maybe that's how they learned those things, and how to explain them. If you don't travel around and visit people, then you don't learn who's who, who's living where, or what relatives are still living. In those days, the women were always home with their children and the sheep. Of course they knew who their relatives were, too, but it was usually the men who explained who was who and how people were related way back. Of course, they didn't just start talking about it at any old time; you had to show you were interested, you had to ask.

When I was growing up, my father did that for us. Whenever we asked who somebody was, he'd explain it and then go way, way back with their other relatives, too. Around here, Frank knew those things, both for his own side and mine, too. So, when he was home and somebody needed to understand things like that, he usually explained it. But when he was gone and those things came up, I did it. Some of my children were interested in things like that, and some of them weren't. But both Frank and I wanted them to know who their relatives were. And even though I didn't go to far away places very much like he did because I was here raising our children and taking care of the sheep and the corn, and weaving, I still could explain those things, if anybody asked. Of course, you don't tell children those things when they're small; they need to be older. Then you explain it to them. I remember explaining about my half sister who married Old Red Bottom Man, and about other ones, too, like Man with a Cane, and Frank's brother, Jimmy, who lived in Fort Defiance and married Rachel, a Towering House woman. So, when my mother said my children didn't know those things, I knew it wasn't true.[9]

I know certain things are hard to explain to young girls. As mine got older, they started asking how they'd know they had become *kinaaldá*. I kept putting them off, just saying you'll know and that I'd talk with them later. When they were little, my mother did the same thing; she always tried to change the subject. But of course as they grew up, they saw different ones having their Puberty ceremonies and they heard us saying they'd have the same thing when it was time. So it wasn't strange they wanted to know about it. I think one of the problems was Mary no. 1 had hers when Agnes was very small so she didn't really learn anything from it, except that the *kinaaldá* runs races and gets molded [or shaped]. And then, because Agnes was at Fort Apache when she became a woman, she never had either of those ceremonies; she was the only one who didn't. Eventually, I explained that to each of them. I talked to them nicely about it and I didn't say any of the things my mother was saying.

I never told my mother I didn't want her saying those things to my daughters. She was in her old age and I didn't want to upset her or argue about things. I was happy with all the other things she was teaching them. And then, too, some of the things she said about being a woman I agreed with. Like my mother, Frank and I didn't want our children getting into trouble in any way, either. That's why we didn't let them run around or go places without an adult. I never asked them to go even to the trading post on horseback to get something for me by themselves because I didn't want them going around alone. That's when things happen. Even with the ones who went to school, I didn't ask them to go to the store by themselves until they got into their high school years. Even then, I worried about them until they came back.

The same was true with ceremonies. Although Frank was a Blessingway singer, we didn't let our children go into ceremonial hogans when they were little. Even though we were living according to the Blessingway and raising them with it, saying prayers at dawn and again toward evening, when they were small we didn't want them sitting in there, watching things they didn't understand. After they were maybe ten or twelve, old enough to help cook and feed the People, chop wood, wash dishes, and do other things, then we let them go in and out. And if Frank was doing a ceremony for someone in the family right here, then I did take them in and made sure they stayed awake and observed all the other rules, too. So gradually they started learning things about the Blessingway Ceremony from that. Sometimes now I wonder if maybe we should have handled that differently. Maybe if we had encouraged them earlier, one of them would have followed in Frank's footsteps and learned the Blessingway, as he hoped they would. I don't know.

With the other ceremonies, the girls were never exposed to those while they were growing up. Most of them never went back to a Nightway after they got initiated until they finished high school or got married and went to that or to an Enemyway with their husbands. Of course, the ones we kept home, the ones who didn't go to school, probably learned more about those things because they were around here helping all the time. But even with them, we never let them run around, going to whatever ceremonies were going on. With the boys, it was different; all of them got warrior names at Enemyways and all of them were allowed to go to those on horseback, or in wagons with others. Frank said that was all right; boys can protect themselves.

We Lose My Mother

16

*Seya finishes school, Agnes starts high school, and Howard gets enrolled in
Chinle . . . New Deal programs start . . . Stock Reduction . . . Beautiful
Woman dies . . . my mother gets sick and passes away.*

Seya finished his schooling in Albuquerque while my mother was still here, walking around visiting people all the time. Agnes was still at Fort Apache but they told her to skip the next grade and go to Albuquerque to start high school. So she went there right after her brother finished. At the same time, we decided to enroll Howard in school; he started here at the Chinle Boarding School when Agnes started high school.

Seya had already told us he was worried about finding a job; in Albuquerque they were telling the students that all over the country, people were out of work because everything had gone down. Here, it was the same way; there was no work, even for those with some education. Of course with us, with Frank being a headman and a Blessingway singer, he had jobs. Those brought in a little income, and along with the farm and my rugs, we were managing to feed our children. That's what my father had told Frank when he was learning the Blessingway; it would last his whole life and give him something to fall back on. The same was true with my weaving. Frank kept reminding our children to help with things so I could keep weaving for things we needed. He always encouraged me to do that.

One time when Frank came back from one of the meetings he was always going to, he told us the government was starting programs to try to get people working again. Those things were coming to the reservation, too, and men who had families to support could get jobs building dams and other things. Seya heard about it and when he finished his schooling, he got a job with one of those programs. Those things were called CCC, ECW, SCS, nicknames like that.[1] Woody and others did that, too; he and Seya were among those hired to make the dam by Moaning Lake.[2]

The same time those things were starting, Frank came back from another meeting, very upset. He said they were talking about how the land was going down, too. There was no rain and everything was drying up. There was very little grass for the sheep; all over the reservation, people were saying it was hard to find places where you could herd the livestock. He said the officials were talking about it and trying to make a plan. I knew those things were true; it was always very dry when I'd hoe weeds early in the morning, and the children who were herding told me there was hardly anything left for the sheep to eat. I used to think about those things and worry about them.[3]

When Frank came home, he told me the officials said there were too many animals roaming around the reservation, eating the little grass that was left, and that something was going to be done about it. Right away, he was worried; he knew that news would upset the People. I got worried, too; sheep and goats, and even horses and cows — we all raised those and depended on them.

The headmen were told to have meetings and tell the People these things. So Frank did. I guess the Council wanted to go around the reservation and check on the conditions first because in some places there was still enough grass while in others, there was almost none. Then they were going to decide how to cut back on the animals. The different leaders were already arguing about what plan should be made. Some people had lots of sheep, while others had only a few, barely enough to support themselves. By then, we were more like that; I don't remember how many sheep and goats we had, but it wasn't many. Frank really liked horses so he had a lot more of those. We had only enough sheep and goats to use for food and milk and wool. But others, like Woody, had lots of them from their mothers. Finally the officials announced the plan; we were told that Washington had ordered us to get rid of a certain number of our animals. I forget how they figured out how many sheep or goats, or horses or cows each family was allowed to keep. The rest had to be turned back. At first the People couldn't believe what they heard. They said they weren't going to cooperate and they started getting angry.[4]

I don't remember how many animals we lost at that time, but it wasn't too many compared to some of our relatives. From what Frank told us, at first it was mainly horses they cut back on. They started rounding up the horses roaming around on mesas or down in canyons, running wild, and putting them in corrals. If they didn't belong to anybody, they hauled them away in trucks. And around Tuba City and other places, they shot them. Sometimes they sent the meat somewhere to be made into food for dogs and cats, but sometimes it was left there in the sun, to rot. They did that with sheep and goats, too, and probably cows. That's what really hurt the People.

Here in our family those times were very difficult. We were affected by it in several ways, not just by losing some of our animals. Frank was one of the leaders at that time, and he and the other leaders really took the brunt of it. People were very, very angry and they started saying nasty words to all the leaders, blaming them. Even though Frank explained the order came from Washington, for some reason people blamed him. They even threatened to harm him and his children because of it. Those things worried me greatly. But he kept telling us he had to do his job; the People were going to have to listen and obey those instructions. He said if they didn't, the reservation would have no future; the land would never recover and everything would come to an end.

Finally they added range riders. Seya worked with them for a while, too; he had to go with an official, travel all over the Chinle District to wherever the range men were rounding up animals. Then they'd hold meetings in each area for people to identify which animals were theirs, and then get issued a permit. They started doing that, giving you a permit showing how many sheep, horses, goats, or cows you were allowed to have. For a while the government bought some of the extra animals, when people had to reduce their flocks. Seya had to interpret at those meetings, and do the paperwork about the brands and the permits. So, like Frank, he knew lots of things about what was happening, and he and Frank used to talk about it. They both were among those who were being blamed for causing this hardship to come on the People.[5]

Everybody suffered from that in some way or another. In some families, they just rearranged who had the animals. They gave sheep or horses to somebody else in the family who was living in another part of the reservation. That was done district by district and most people had relatives in more than one of those places. So sometimes they worked it out that way. When they gave their sheep away like that, they usually got something in return, like a blanket, basket, or some jewelry for one sheep. Of course, some of the People butchered their own and used the meat right then. Others had to turn their animals in, the ones they were told were "extra." It was hard to do that, even if you took them to the store and sold them. At that time, they weren't worth very much. And to make it worse, in lots of places like Salina, when they rounded up the animals, they killed them right there in the corrals they had made, right in front of people. That really hurt the People. If you didn't go along with it, then the police came and put you in jail, and took your livestock and slaughtered them, anyway. People still talk about the stock reduction and the suffering it caused. In our family, we don't talk about it very much because it brings back the hardships it caused for Frank and Seya, and others who had to enforce those orders. It wasn't right that people blamed them for causing it; the overgrazing did it. But some of the People couldn't understand that, so they blamed all the leaders, from Washington right on down through Fort Defiance, Fort Wingate, Window Rock, to the headmen in the local areas.[6]

While those hardships were going on, here in our family we suffered some others, too. About two years after Isabel was born, Beautiful Woman died and then the next year, my mother passed away, too. Beautiful Woman and Tom Scott were living across the Nazlini Wash, where Louise lives, and our hogan was near where Mary no. 1 lives now. Garnett was about ten at the time and her parents had already sent her to Fort Defiance for school. After she lost her mother, she tried living with her father's people for a while because Tom had taken the little ones over to his sister's, Big Water Man's wife. They were living at *Tóta*, the Island Place in the Chinle Wash.[7] But the little ones, three boys, all died soon after that. After spending a short time with her father and his sister, Garnett came over here and started living with us. Of course, she was already related to us on both sides. Her maternal grandmother was one of my older sisters, Little Woman;[8] she was one of the ones who had married Frank's older brother, Jim, so Jim Mitchell was her grandfather, her mother's father. From then on, Garnett was part of our family. She was around during the summers; sometimes she was right here with me and the other children; other times, she was with Adelle, helping her with her children, Don and Donna Mae.[9] When Garnett started high school at the Albuquerque Indian School, she worked around there in the summers and only came home for one- or two-week vacations. And then, like Agnes, she went to nurses' training and later started working as a nurse.

Garnett's mother, Beautiful Woman, had already had a number of children for Tom Scott, but most of them had died as babies. She was having another baby and they had already had the Blessingway done for her. When she went into labor, she started having trouble, and they asked me to come over and help her. I was still doing that for people, whenever they asked me to help. She and the baby boy she had survived that, but then she didn't recover like she should have. No matter what we did to build up her strength again, she got weaker and weaker. So they started doing other ceremonies for her. But even those didn't help; within a few days, she passed away, and so did the new baby. I stayed over there the whole time, trying to help with everything. My mother was there, too, even though she was way up in her years by then and not strong enough to do too much anymore. I asked Ruth to watch my small children who were here when I went over there; she was really helping around here with lots of things by then.

Seya helped bury Beautiful Woman. He was already finished with that Leader School[10] and was around here, working for somebody when that happened. It might have been the ECW or the CCC, or maybe he was already working at the boiler plant at the Chinle Boarding School by then. I don't remember. For a while he did that and also hauled coal for the school. But he also helped out at the mission with interpreting and other things, too.[11] I think that's why he said he'd help bury Beautiful Woman and her baby. I thought the priest was going to do it, after Seya took them up there, but later he told me only Brother Gotthard helped. When they buried her, they didn't use the cemetery behind the mission. I guess it was almost full by then so they were starting to put people over near the Canyon in a little cemetery at the foot of the hill where that Park Service ranger's station is now. That's where Seya said they buried Beautiful Woman and her baby.[12]

Besides Garnett, Beautiful Woman had three small boys who were still living at that time. After their mother died, the two older ones died, and then the other one, a boy who was about two, passed away, too. I don't remember who took care of burying the first two. Tom was with his sister at the Island Place in the Chinle Wash. But I know he got the priests to bury the last one, that little boy, so there's probably a record of him somewhere.[13] I don't know why Tom asked the priests to do that. He and Beautiful Woman used to be Presbyterians. They were really good friends with Mr. and Mrs. Bysegger, the preacher at the other church here in Chinle, the Presbyterian one.[14] Mr. Bysegger used to come around in his wagon and take the whole family to church. Even in the summertime, when Garnett first started living with us, she was going to Bible school up there with the Presbyterians. I didn't say much about it because some people around here, like Slim Woman and Old Red Bottom Man's family, Small Woman and her family, Ida Francis, Joseph Ganna, and a lot of the Gormans and Drapers were Presbyterians. But I guess sometimes I told Garnett that going to Bible school was probably a waste of time. When Tom, himself, passed away, I know the Presbyterians buried him somewhere. So his records are up there, if they keep records, too.[15]

After Garnett's mother passed away and Tom said he was going to take the children and go to his sister's, Frank asked him if he would switch land. Tom had the land where Isabel, Ruth, and Augusta live now. He agreed to switch that for some land of Frank's north of Mary no. 1's, more toward Valley Store but east of the Nazlini Wash. Tom's uncle, Long Moustache, his father's brother, had a big farm in that area; they raised lots of sweet corn, carrots, onions, and other things and hauled those in wagons to Garcia's to sell them. All the people there, and then down closer to Many Farms, really farmed. Like us, they all helped each other, too. Tom stayed with his own family for a number of years. When he remarried, he married another Towering House woman, *Dlinasbah*. I think that's when he told his brother, Joseph Ganna, he could use the land down there and have it. So that's where that land switch came in. But we didn't move over here where we are now until after my mother passed away.

After Beautiful Woman passed away, Frank was sent to the hospital they had started here in Chinle;[16] I don't remember what was troubling him, but he came back after a few days and told me something he had learned over there.[17] But I didn't think too much about it because I was busy, hoeing around the plants in the fields as they came up, trying to keep weeds out. A lot of the men Seya's age and even the younger boys were talking about the rodeo that had just started in Chinle; they were practicing and racing horses around so they could ride in it. Seya got kind of crazy about that for a while, and Howard did, too. But after they got hurt in one way or another, that settled down.[18]

After a while, it seemed like my mother was going downhill. At first, I thought it was mainly from old age. She stopped weaving and driving the buggy; she even stopped walking all over, visiting different relatives. She had more trouble getting around even with her cane, so she said she'd stay home. Sometimes we'd take her places in the wagon so she could see things. But more and more she said she didn't want to go anywhere; she just stayed home.

We were living where Mary no. 1 does now when I realized it was more than old age affecting her. She got some kind of sickness. At that time, her hogan was close to the Chinle Wash, near our cornfields. I used to go over there to take her food and check on her, and I used to send one of my children over there at other times, to be with her and to help with whatever she wanted done. It was clear she was really suffering; old age had shriveled her up, made her really small again; even though she was known as Tall Woman (and Beautiful Woman, and Tall, Beautiful Woman) and she was taller than me,[19] when she got in her last years, she shriveled up. When you touched her arms, sometimes it was like the skin was sloughing off. That happens when people get really, really old.

When she got worse, we made a little ramada for her closer this way, closer to the big ditch that used to be there. We made that right in the middle of the field, across from Ida's place, and we had to carry my mother over there in a blanket because she was sick. I stayed over there with her a lot, and told the older children to bring food to us. Mary no. 1 and David were helping me with that, and Seya did too, on weekends. He was working either at the boiler plant or the dairy at that time, and he used to walk or ride a horse over here on the weekends. We started doing small ceremonies for her at her ramada. Of course, we didn't allow the little children to go to them. My mother stayed in there, every day, going down. Somebody sent word to the priests and I think it was Father Anselm who came down to see her. Maybe he baptized her at that time; I don't know. When I couldn't go over there because of my small children, Mary no. 1 went to make sure my mother had food and that she ate it. Of course, we both had little children of our own when that happened.

When my mother got in that condition, all the small children were told to stay away from her ramada. But since the water hole was nearby, some of them played around there, hiding in the deep ditch that ran through there. After we did some small ceremonies for her, for a short time she seemed to be a little better. So Frank and I started talking about bringing her over to where we were living, and moving her into our hogan. But then, she got really bad again. It was late in the summer by then and even though we kept doing little ceremonies for her, when that happened, she didn't get any better.

One day I sent Agnes to get water from the water hole. That summer she was here for a short time, before going back to Albuquerque for another year in high school. She stopped to check on my mother, even though I had told her not to. Children are not supposed to be around people in that condition, and even though Agnes was in her teens, I still didn't want her exposed to things she didn't understand. Sure enough, when she came back, she was really upset.[20] She told me my mother was acting like she was out of her mind; she had dirtied the sheepskins we had spread in that shelter for her and was moving around, all dirty, herself. We were trying to keep her quiet on the sheepskins. I guess Agnes gave her some water; she drank some of it, but she kept talking to herself, making no sense. Agnes came running back over here to tell me those things and I scolded her for going over there. But soon after that, I went and got Mary no. 1, and together we went over there. My mother was just like Agnes had said. So we cleaned her up again, burned all those dirty sheepskins, and put down other ones for her to use. I stayed with her that night.

The next day I told Frank it was time to build a small shelter for her over here, close to our hogan by the Nazlini Wash. So he did that and we put her in a blanket and carried her there. We do that when a person is really sick; we move them out of the house, just a little ways from it. Her last little shelter was on the banks of the Nazlini Wash, between where we were living at that time, and where we live now. I stayed with her all the time after that and I was always telling Augusta and Isabel to go back home, to stop sneaking and peeking around like they were doing. Children aren't supposed to be around someone who is dying. They wanted to see her, but I kept telling them, "You can't do that; go back home and go inside." Frank had different ideas about that; he knew she was dying of old age and he said we shouldn't be afraid of a person like that. I knew that was true, because my father and mother had taught us the same thing. And she *was* dying of old age; her hair was really white and she was really in old age, even though she never lost her eyesight or her hearing. But I still didn't want my children exposed to it.

Shortly after we moved her, maybe the next day, she passed away during the night. We had made the children stay inside after we carried her to that little shelter. So, in the morning we told them she had died. We told them to stay inside and not even look toward her little shelter until the body was out of sight. Someone had already gone on horseback to notify Sam to come down in a vehicle to get her. He was back here, working for the little hospital they had built over there near the Chinle Boarding School, driving the vehicle they used as an ambulance. He had come to visit us the day before, knowing my mother was very near her end. When he came the next morning, he brought a big wooden box. The Nazlini Wash was full; it was running so he and Seya carried the box across, leaving the vehicle on the other side. Mary no. 1 and I had already fixed my mother up with new clothes and her jewelry. Sam and Seya helped wrap her in the new blankets we had for that purpose; then they put her in the box, carried her across the Wash, loaded that up, and drove away. She was buried behind the mission in the old cemetery; one of the priests helped with that on the day after she passed away at night.[21] I don't think any of the rest of us went up there while they did that. Maybe Frank did; I don't remember now.[22] That was the same place they told us they buried Pauline, and Mary no. 2. And that's where they put David, several years after my mother passed away. We were taught not to go to places like that, but I know Frank had to do that a lot. He was a headman and lots of times when they buried people, they asked him to talk to the People at that time.

After they took my mother away, we observed all the rules we have for when someone dies. We were careful about following those things for the next four days, and we made sure all the children did, too. We didn't go anywhere; even Frank stayed home during that time, instead of going somewhere to a meeting, or to perform his ceremony. After a while,[23] all the land my mother and father had, and what few animals were left from them were transferred to me; that included where Mary no. 1 was living so we gave her that part and some more, too. And, because Frank had switched land with Tom Scott, after Augusta started school he built us a new hogan and we moved away from where Mary no. 1 lives over to where we are now. That was the last time we moved.

four

Grandparent Years,
Late Adulthood

Going on Alone

Augusta starts school and I lose my teeth . . . Frank and the Constitutional
Assembly . . . Agnes starts nurses' training . . . Howard breaks his arm . . .
David suddenly gets sick . . . we lose David . . . Chubby Woman passes away
. . . Ruth marries Leo . . . Isabel gets TB . . . other changes.

When it was time for children to go back to school right after my mother passed away, we enrolled Augusta at the Chinle Boarding School; Howard was already there, ahead of her. When she started school, Ruth was already a young woman and was helping me with many things. David and Isabel were here, too; Isabel was still very small but David was already growing up, and helping Frank with the horses. He also helped me haul water, gather wood, hoe weeds, and do other things. He was already strong and in many ways, it seemed as if he was almost a man even though he was probably barely starting his teenage years. David never went to school; when the officials started questioning us about that, Frank said he wasn't going to do it because we needed him to stay home and help us with the farm and the animals. At that time, he was our only son at home and he was a good worker. He never was lazy about doing anything we asked him to do.

When Augusta started school, there were more buildings at the Chinle school and it went through six grades.[1] Other things had changed, too; if the children had transportation, sometimes the officials let them go home on the weekend. Of course, if it was cold or windy, or if it was snowing, we'd tell them to stay there where it was warm. If it was nice, Frank saddled a horse and went and brought them back. Sometimes only one could come; Frank would have that person sit behind him on the horse as they came back. He always sang whenever he was traveling like that. With our children, he made up a little song for each one; when they started growing up, whenever he was around them he'd sing their special song. The children really liked that, and it made me happy, too. Sometimes he'd still be singing to whomever was hanging on behind him when they got home; he'd come in with that child and finish singing while lying down on the sheepskins, rubbing that person's back or neck. He was like that with his children; he showed them affection in many ways. I was glad when I saw that. He was gone so many times they were always excited to see him, wanting to be with him whenever he was home. So, somebody was always hanging onto his hand, or his arm, or was curling up beside him on the sheepskins, asking for a neck rub, or their special song.

We were always glad to see the children when they came home, even if it was just for one or two days. Augusta's hair always needed to be brushed and fixed into a hair bun. At that time, it was down to her waist; it took lots of time to brush it and it seemed like I was the main one who did that for her. I think she gave up on it at school.*

I know when Augusta started school, she thought it'd be an easier life there, that there'd be no chopping wood, hauling water, or other work like she had to do at home. But when she got there, she found out those things had to be done even at school. The officials made the children work for part of the day and also on some weekends. Augusta was assigned to scrub floors at the Chinle school, and before she finished her schooling there, she was working in the kitchen at the Employees Club, and also helping clean at the Park Service offices and the priests' house. The school had different jobs for the children; Howard had to help haul water, chop wood, haul coal, and do other things, too. When they both got to St. Michaels for junior high, it was the same; all the children took turns working in the kitchen, dining room, scrubbing floors, washing clothes. They traded those things around, trying to teach the children different things. Augusta told me about all those things so I learned a lot about the school from that. Most of the time, the things she said didn't worry me. But one time, after some people killed a black bear that was roaming in the Canyon killing livestock, they hung it upside down on a swing the children were using, and butchered it right there. I don't know if they fed the children its meat, but they shouldn't have exposed them to a bear like that, because that can cause illness. That upset us, when we heard about it.[2]

Sometimes while Augusta was at the Chinle Boarding School, when she was helping clean at the mission she'd see Seya, who was working there, interpreting for the priest during religious instructions for the school children, and helping Brother Gotthard outside. Augusta used to like seeing all the chickens that Brother had; he was known for those, and for carrying the mail to Ganado. For a long time that was done in a small wagon with a mule on it.* But eventually, the priests got a vehicle, and Brother Gotthard started driving that mail truck. Frank and I never complained about the schools making our children work; we did that at home and we knew whatever they learned at school would prepare them for their future lives. Something might come along and they could get some income because of things they learned at school.[3]

After my mother passed away, for a long time I was sad. I tried not to think about it but somehow, things were different. Now it felt like I was by myself; both my mother and my father had passed away. They were gone from us now. That made me feel—I don't know—like they had left us behind somewhere. I tried to keep those things to myself, but sometimes I'd think about it. I'd even cry when I was out with the sheep or hoeing, doing something by myself. I never said anything to Frank about it. He didn't seem to be affected too much by my mother's death. He said it was to be expected, it was from old age, and she truly was an old age person. I knew he was right, but somehow, after that, things were different for me.

Maybe men aren't affected by those things in the same way. Maybe that's when I realized I was no longer a young girl, that I was in my middle age. I don't know. My sister and my half sister felt the same way, too. We used to talk about it when we'd visit with each other. All of us were sad; we missed my mother a lot, and sometimes we'd cry together, even though we're not supposed to think about those things after the four days are up. We couldn't help it. We did that just by ourselves; their husbands were the same way. They said it was from old age and not to think about it. But it really affected me and my younger sister, Small Woman, and my half sister, Slim Woman. Now we were the only ones left from our family and somehow, that made all of us feel strange.

But we had to go on so I kept these thoughts to myself and kept weaving, grinding corn, and doing other work around here. There was always something that needed to be done, even before Frank decided to start raising more food.[4] When Howard or Augusta was allowed to leave school for the weekend, they helped with chopping wood, hauling water, or herding sheep. At that time, after my mother passed away, I was here with Ruth and David, and also the youngest one, Isabel. All the other children who were still surviving were either in school somewhere or already grown up, like Seya and Mary no. 1. Augusta always helped me with the wool when she came home; because she was in school, she learned the loom part over there. I taught her all the other things that go with it. She also helped with the cooking. She was already interested in learning about fixing traditional foods so as she got older, I showed her those things. Ruth had learned them from my mother so she showed Augusta too, when she wasn't herding or weaving. She was already a young woman by then.

David helped in lots of ways, too. He was the one who took care of the horses for Frank and he also helped me with the children, especially Isabel, Howard, and Augusta. He always seemed to know what needed to be done without asking, and he'd go and do it. Even with the smaller children—he'd scold them if they needed it. Sometimes because of that, they'd tell me he was mean but I knew he wasn't. As he got older, he and Frank got very close, too. They were always going places together and David helped him with lots of jobs. He even traveled with him when Frank talked to the People and after a while, when David talked, it sounded like Frank. It's as if he was starting to pick up those things too, learning to talk to the People.

In the fall, one thing I always asked the children to help with was husking corn, even if they were just here for one or two days. And sometimes, Frank would go and get Augusta to help us grind corn on the weekend up at the Presbyterian mission, where they had that big grinder.[5] I'd husk corn during the days in between, whenever I wasn't weaving, and Ruth and David would help, too. We got it ready and put it into big sacks. Then we'd go up there in the wagon. We used the corn we ground there as feed for all the horses Frank had during those years, along with the alfalfa we raised. Sometimes Frank would take Augusta and me to the grinder on a weekend with an extra horse to work on that while he took Howard to help him haul wood down from the mountains. After they finished, they'd come back in the wagon and load up the sacks we had ready. Sometimes the wood was for our use; other times it was for the Chinle Boarding School. They burned wood over there when Howard and Augusta first started school, and Frank used to be hired to bring it in. He did that until they changed to coal. Then Seya was one of the people who delivered that for the schools.

Of course, sometimes Frank went to the school for other reasons. The officials always asked the headmen to come and talk to the children, whenever someone got out of line, didn't listen to the teachers or follow instructions from the officials. Frank did that while his children were enrolled there, so they had to listen to his talks at the school, too.* But they already knew what he'd say about education being important and staying in school to learn from it; he always said that at home.*

Old Curly Hair was another one who did that; I remember Augusta telling us all the children were afraid of him because of his big, loud, deep voice. One time she imitated it for me and made me laugh; she kept saying "*Yíí,*" just like he did when he was talking there, telling the boys not to act out of line at this early age, and all the children that education was important, and they should listen to their parents and their teachers, pay attention, and do what they were told. He also told them he never had a chance to go to school himself and he regretted it; they should try their best to get something out of it. He was known as a really good talker but whenever they asked him to come to the school, he really scared the children.

Sometimes the headmen, or even the whole community, were invited to things the school was doing for entertainment. Now and then they'd decorate the auditorium and have things they called square dancing, folk dancing, *not* Squaw Dances.* Other times they showed silent movies without charging. Frank did some of those things, too; I always stayed home with my other children, but he'd tell me about what he saw over there, like the long dresses girls wore for the dances with shiny black shoes with some kind of different heel on them, or the cornstalk decorations, or what different ones did in the movies.

I think it was the next year, when Augusta went there the second time, that she started having trouble with an eye infection. The school officials told Frank lots of children were suffering from it and she needed to be treated at the Fort Defiance Hospital.[6] So they transferred her to the school there while she got her treatments; Garnett was still there then and Frank would check on them when he was there for meetings or other reasons. That hospital cured Augusta's eyes; after that year, she transferred back to Chinle, where Howard was still enrolled.

A short time after she came back, I ended up in the hospital here at Chinle. For a long time my teeth had been troubling me but I didn't mention it. Finally the pain got worse and I told Frank something was wrong with them. When he started asking around about it, he heard they had a dentist who came from Fort Defiance to the Chinle Hospital about once a month. He thought I should go over there. So after a while, when the pain kept getting worse, I agreed, and he took me there in the wagon. They made me stay there and before I knew it, they had pulled out all my teeth, every single one.* I don't remember much about it now; Augusta used to come and visit me from school; Sam was still driving the ambulance they had, and Adelle was working there, too, cooking in the kitchen. After a few days, Frank came to take me home again. That was the end of the troubles I was having with my teeth.*

Soon after I lost all my teeth, Frank told me he'd been selected to serve in Window Rock. They had moved the Tribal Council to the new hogan building there and they were changing things again. He said Father Berard had been helping the agent and others go around the reservation, looking for more leaders to help with things because they were revising it again.[7] Frank was among those chosen and for a long time after that, he wasn't home very much at all. He was over in Window Rock, or in other places for meetings; they even went to Washington, to talk to the President about establishing Day Schools for our children and other things the People needed. They put Frank on lots of committees too, along with the Council, and those groups had meetings, too. So that was the beginning of a *very long time* when he was gone again. When I think back on it now, it seems that happened a lot while we were married; he was gone for one reason or another *many, many times*. But I just went ahead here, taking care of things that needed to be done. We managed like that and after a while, I got used to it.[8]

While Frank was involved with those things, Agnes finished at the Albuquerque Indian School. She wanted to be a nurse; after Frank and her teachers encouraged her, she started training in Albuquerque for that, too.[9] She was doing that when we suffered another hardship; the next summer we lost David and for a while, I was afraid Frank was not going to recover from it. David was already working by then; Seya had helped him get work with the SCS[10] so he was busy planting trees the government was adding to Chinle. David was the one who planted the Chinese elms and the cottonwoods[11] you see here around our place, too, the ones that are old and huge now. He did that for us and he also planted all the trees around the Chinle Boarding School. I think the Park Service was doing that too, planting tamarisks, Russian olives, peach leaf willows, cottonwoods, Chinese elms, and other things in the Canyon to stop erosion. David was working on that while Augusta was in school in Chinle; she used to see him outside, working. Of course at home here, he was always busy helping me with the children, with hauling wood or water, or whatever else I needed done. He never complained or tried to get out of things I asked him to do; lots of times, he saw them first, before I asked, and went and did them. He was always like that with me. With Frank it was the same; David was the one he depended on for help with the livestock. He took care of the horses Frank had, just like my big, heavyset brother did for my father years ago. We didn't have any cows, but Frank had lots of horses out on the mesa and David took care of them, and helped with the sheep and goats, too. And he traveled around a lot with Frank; they went places together. David was even starting to help Frank with his ceremony; he'd go with his father when he was performing over in the Black Mountain area and help with it. Frank thought David was interested in learning his ceremony; I've often wondered if maybe he would've been the one who carried it on if he had survived.

We had recently lost Towering House Woman and some others, too, when David got sick.[12] I remember it was summer and we were hoeing weeds and harvesting some things when that happened. Before that, Howard had gotten hurt, racing horses up and down across from here. A horse fell on him while he was racing it, breaking his right arm. First Frank took him over to the Chinle Hospital. Even though he was suspicious of those places in his younger days, after he started learning things as a leader, Frank began to change his mind, at least in some ways. I guess the government was trying to teach the leaders about other medicines available to cure illnesses faced by the Navajos.[13] Frank said they were building more hospitals and bringing more doctors to the reservation; he and some other leaders were involved in meetings about those things. His friend, Chee Dodge, was very much in favor of it and Frank told me they talked a lot about it. I remember one time when the leaders were invited to a ceremony they had a short time after the new hospital in Fort Defiance started up.[14] When Frank came home, he said a Blessingway singer, Pete Price, had helped with it. He was wondering about doing that; blessing other things besides hogans was new at that time and for a while, Frank and the other singers didn't know what to think about using their ceremony in that way.[15] After Howard had spent a day at the Chinle Hospital, they said he needed to go to Fort Defiance because of his broken arm and stay there for maybe one or two months. So Frank and others in the family were already going over there to visit him when David got sick.

That came on David suddenly; one day he told me he had a bad headache. I mixed up some herbs for him, but he didn't get any better. The next day he had a fever; I gave him some other herbs, but they did no good. I told Frank about it right away; after Jake Tom came to do the first hand-trembling, we started doing ceremonies for him, including those where you put the person-being-sung-over in a pit lined with hot charcoal ashes, while other things are done. But that seemed to make him worse. Frank got other hand-tremblers and also star-gazers, and we did whatever they suggested, but David kept getting worse. Frank and I got very worried.[16] Finally Frank decided to see if any of the white doctors could help, so we took him in the wagon to the Ganado Hospital. I stayed over there with him, and Agnes got leave from her nurses' training to come there to stay with us. We stayed there probably for one or two weeks, day after day. Others in the family went back and forth, coming when they could, but Agnes and I sat there with him all the time. But David just kept getting worse. Even though those doctors tried all kinds of medicines, his fever went up and he was unconscious lots of times. After maybe another week, he passed away over there.

When that happened, we were all stunned; we didn't know what had caused it, and the doctors didn't seem to know, either.[17] Agnes and I came back and she stayed here for the four days. Frank got the priests to bury him in the cemetery behind the mission. Seya, Woody, Son of Yucca Fruit Man, and Frank helped with that, and then stayed on the north side of our hogan, separate, observing all the rules about that for four days.[18] I tried not to cry about it in front of people, in front of my children, after Agnes and I came home from the hospital. We believe if you do that, you're asking for something bad to happen to someone else in the family. Frank and I believed that so we always tried not to cry after those who were gone. But when my sister and half sister came to visit me, I cried a lot with them after David died. I couldn't seem to get over it.

That happened so quickly Howard didn't even know his brother was in the hospital, like he was. It wasn't until several weeks later, after it was over, that Frank went to see Howard and tell him about it. Right then, Howard started crying and crying; it almost killed him, too. He told the doctor he wanted to go home and finally that man agreed. When Howard came back with his cast on, I remember I ran out and started crying as soon as I saw him, telling him his brother was dead. I guess I hung on to him for a while, too, saying those things. I was still crying, even though I knew I shouldn't do that. Later, Howard cut his cast off by himself. I told him to exercise his arm and to carry a little can of water around to restrengthen it. Eventually it got all right again.

It seemed to me that my mother had just died, and then we lost David. Even though I know two or three years passed between those things, it seemed like they happened together. Maybe that's because I took both of them so hard. They really affected me. With my mother, it hadn't really affected Frank. But with David, it was different.

David was really close to both of us; he didn't go to school so he was here with us all the time. Frank and he were very close, too; sometimes I used to think he favored him over the other children.

When David died, that was the one time I saw Frank really affected by someone's death. Before that, even when some of his own children passed away, sooner or later he got over it. Of course, some of them died in infancy, or when they were still little, like Pauline. And with Mary no. 2, he always blamed the school in Albuquerque. But David hadn't gone to school; he was here with us, and he and Frank were very close. He was older than Howard so he was the one doing things with Frank, working on the farm, hauling water and wood, and riding around on horseback together. After he died, Frank got very depressed. For a long, long time, he went down. He started drinking a lot and staying home, yelling and shouting about things. I tried consoling him, talking to him about losing our son because I, too, was suffering. But he didn't seem to hear me, no matter what I said. I tried to stay out of his way when he was drinking like that; even later, I always removed myself, went some place else, when-ever he'd start that. He wasn't too bad with it, like lots of other men were, but he did that, too. And when David died, he really started drinking.

Shortly after we lost David, Frank got into a fight with John Brown, the policeman, at some meeting in a public place. Different ones told me about it, and I worried about Frank acting like that when he was on the Council.[19] One day, after he fought with the policeman, he was in that same condition around here. He came outside and saddled his horse. Then he got on it and started yelling, saying he was going to kill someone, while the horse went round and round in circles. He got off, went inside, came back out with a gun, and got back on his horse. He was saying he felt like hurting someone because David had died, had left us, had been taken away. I knew what he was threat-ening to do was serious and that I needed to do something about it, even though he was drunk. So I went to where he was sitting on his horse, waving his gun around and shouting, and I started raising my voice. I think that's the first time I ever did that to him. I got really angry at him then for the very first time since we were together. I don't remember what all I yelled, but I kept yelling at him to get off his horse and put his gun away. I told him he was acting crazy, like he was out of his mind. I shouted that going off and hurting someone else wasn't going to fix anything, bring our son back. It would just bring more suffering on him. I reminded him he was a leader and a Bless-ingway singer, and shouldn't act like that. He shouldn't be drinking, or saying things about killing people. I guess because I started hollering right there, it surprised him. I *never*, *ever* did those things; I was always calm and quiet. But that time, I knew some-one needed to stop him from causing harm, so I decided I had to go out there and step into that.

Finally, I guess what I was saying quieted him down. I told him to go inside and sleep off his drinks. He sat on his horse, staring at me for a long time while those words kept coming out of my mouth. Finally, he got down. I put the horse back in the corral and he went back inside and lay down. I don't remember if he said anything about it when he woke up. After that, slowly we started recovering from losing David. He was the last of the children we lost. It's always more difficult when you lose a child; that's not from old age. David was just getting into his manhood when suddenly, he got sick like that and died. We were both very close to him and it was hard to understand he was no longer with us. We were sad for a *very long time*. Even now, I still miss him.[20]

I don't remember too much about what happened right after we lost David; both of us went down for a while because of that. I remember my sister, Small Woman, lost her husband shortly after David died; Elsie was small then, only about five, when her father died. My sister sent word to the Presbyterian preacher after he passed away, and Mr. Bysegger came and took him away. I think they buried him somewhere in the dunes.

Another one we lost around that time was Chubby Woman. She had already had a number of children for Son of Yucca Fruit Man: the ones named John Brown, and the Hashkaans — Samuel, Eva, and Bobby, and maybe one or two others; I don't remember. But I know Eva was about five and Bobby was very little when Chubby Woman died having another baby.[21] After she died and the four days were up, Eva came here to live with Frank and me. She did that for several years, I think, until her father put her in school some place else. Later, he took the rest of the children over to my half sister, Slim Woman. She helped him raise those children along with her others, and after a while, the two of them married each other. That's how she ended up with Son of Yucca Fruit Man. They never had any children together; they were both up in their years by then.

When we were going through those hardships, my other children, except for Ruth and Isabel, were gone elsewhere. Howard went to St. Michaels probably a year after he lost his brother, but Augusta was still here at Chinle. Right after we lost David, Garnett went to the Albuquerque Indian School for high school. That's where she learned about taking pictures, I think in her second year at that school. When she'd come home, she'd always bring her camera and take lots of pictures of us, and others, too.* Some of those are still around here mixed in with pictures others took, or had taken of themselves, at other times [see Figs. 21–30]. When Garnett finished in Albuquerque, she followed Agnes into nurses' training but she went through the program they had at the Ganado Hospital for that. Seya left Chinle, too; after Howard went to St. Michaels with Acey and some others, Seya got transferred there, to start coaching. So Howard saw him over there until he quit school.

Here at home, Ruth got married to Leo Shirley; first they had a traditional

FIG. 21. Mary no. 1 with her three children, ca. 1939–42. Left to right: Walter, Louise, Mary Davis, and George "Acey." Photographer, Garnett Scott Bernally. Courtesy of Garnett Bernally.

FIG. 22. Seya, in his Chinle baseball uniform, ca. 1939–42. Photographer, Garnett Scott Bernally. Courtesy of Garnett Bernally.

FIG. 23. Isabel, ca. 1939–42. Photographer, Garnett Scott Bernally. Courtesy of Garnett Bernally.

FIG. 24. Howard, in Wyoming, 1954. Photographer, Henry Haven, Nazlini. Courtesy, Garnett Scott Bernally.

FIG. 25. Ruth, with her first child, Alfred, 1942. Photographer, Garnett Scott Bernally. Courtesy of Garnett Bernally.

FIG. 26. Ruth (left) and Isabel (right), ca. 1940. Photographer, Garnett Scott Bernally. Courtesy of Garnett Bernally.

FIG. 27. Garnett, 1940.
Photographer, unknown.
Courtesy of Garnett Scott
Bernally.

FIG. 28. Agnes, in uniform. Copied
from a colored studio photograph, November 1942. Photographer, unknown.
Courtesy of Garnett Scott Bernally.

FIG. 29. Augusta, 1962–63. Photograph
from Chinle High School Yearbook, Employees section. Photographer, unknown.
Courtesy of Augusta Mitchell Sandoval.

FIG. 30. Tall Woman with two of her children, 1941. Left to right: Isabel, Tall Woman, and Ruth. Photographer, Garnett Scott Bernally. Courtesy of Garnett Bernally.

ceremony and then they got a tribal license. Leo and his father, Old Man John Shirley, raised lots of corn and alfalfa. But before she got married, Ruth got sick. The hand-trembler told us she needed a Shootingway and so we had Bead Man's Son come and do a five-night ceremony for her. That was because she was burning weeds by our alfalfa field one time, and somehow, some of the prayersticks deposited over there during Mary no. 1's Shootingway got burned up. That was an accident because Ruth didn't know they were there, but she got sick from it and needed that ceremony. Isabel was with her when that happened, and so after a while, when she got sick in the same way, she, too, had a Shootingway done for her. We used the same singer for hers.

But before Isabel got sick from that, she got sick from TB. When she was a little girl, it always seemed to us that she was sick. She was always very thin, no matter what food I fixed for her to eat, and she was always telling her sisters she felt sick. I know they thought she was trying to avoid helping with things I told them to do with the sheep, the fields, and other things; I heard them tell her that. Sometimes she said it was a headache, sometimes a leg ache. When she complained about her legs hurting, sometimes Frank would massage them for her while he was lying on the sheepskins with his children. Other times, I'd take old rags I had tied together, or a string, or somebody's old shoelace, and tie her leg up; I'd go back and forth, wrapping it like I was lacing a shoe, pulling it real tight to cut off the aching. I'd leave that on her leg until she fell asleep; then I'd remove it.

But it wasn't just those things making her sick so we started wondering what was wrong with her and talking about it. We knew that one time when she was playing, she climbed on some logs stacked here in the ramada, and those rolled down and hit her. So we thought maybe she had bruised herself inside in some way. Frank got a hand-trembler and we probably did some small ceremonies for her; I don't remember.

When she didn't get any better, Frank said maybe she should go to the Chinle Hospital and have them check on her. That's where they discovered she had TB, even though she wasn't coughing very much. They told us she needed to go to the Fort Defiance Hospital and stay there. Augusta was still here in school at Chinle when that happened. We knew something about that illness because Frank's brother, John, had already been sent to Fort Defiance because of it; they had a place in that hospital for people suffering from TB, and they were using a machine there to take pictures that showed that disease on your insides. John was kept over there for a long time, and Frank used to go and visit him. Lots of people suffered from that, even way, way back. Frank had sponsored a Navajo Windway for John after the hospital released him. We stood the expense of it for him, even though he was always stingy. That ceremony helped, too, because when they took another picture of his insides, his lungs, the disease was gone. So, when we were told Isabel was suffering from it, Frank remembered what he had done for John and wanted to do that for Isabel, too. But she went to the hospital first; even though she was still a small child, she was there a very long time, maybe a whole year. When Frank brought her back, we had Francis Slim Man do that same ceremony, a five-night Navajo Windway, for her. And the same thing happened; the next time they took a picture of her, that spot had disappeared. So Frank really believed in the effects of that ceremony.[22]

While Isabel was in the hospital, it was mainly Ruth and her husband who were here helping me with things whenever Frank was gone. Of course, we checked Augusta out of school when we could on weekends so she could help, too; we kept doing that until she finished over there and went to St. Michaels. Ruth helped me all she could and I was glad for her help. We were always busy with the livestock, the wool, the corn and the rest of the farm, or other things. Sometimes, Seya would come to see us when he was around on the weekends. He and Adelle were together by then, living upstairs at the Big House, and in the spring, they had a baby boy, the one called Butch.

Soon after he was born, one time when Seya was home he told me he'd been put in charge of taking some people on a trip. St. Michaels was part of a celebration the Catholic churches planned for Mother Drexel's jubilee, and Seya was going to take people on a month-long trip, first to where that Mother Superior was located and then on to Washington, D.C. He was the only one from our family who went on that. He asked me to prepare some food for him to take and so, I butchered and fixed lots of boiled mutton and other things. When he came back, he told us about it. I guess the school children made drawings to send over there, and they took people who could help with entertainment. He said they even did some Squaw Dancing and imitated Ye'iis, too, for those evening programs for people in different places. They also had a woman with them who demonstrated weaving. Of course they shouldn't have been imitating the Nightway dancers, but Seya just laughed and said they did that differently, changed a lot of things about it when they performed there, and none of those people watching them knew the difference. Even some Pueblo students there at St. Michaels were in the group he took, and some of them did a few of their dances, too. That's the first time he saw Washington, and he sure had lots of stories about everything when he got back.[23]

Of course, after a while Ruth had a baby for Leo; that was in the summer, after Butch was born, and I assisted her. I was still doing that for people, and that baby boy was her first. They named him Alfred. But soon after he was born, he got sick and the doctors at the hospital here told Ruth he needed to go to Ganado.[24] So Ruth and the little baby went over there for a long time. Agnes was working at the Fort Defiance Hospital by then; she'd finished her nurses' training. The doctors didn't think Alfred was going to live; he had pneumonia and they finally removed one of his little ribs so they could get the fluid out of his lungs. Finally, he pulled through. That's why Howard stopped going to school; when he came home from St. Michaels at Christmas vacation and found out about Alfred, he never went back; because of that, he quit in the eighth grade. He and Leo used to drive back and forth to Ganado in the wagon, taking Ruth clothes and food, and spending two or three days over there before coming back. Sometimes, they'd see Agnes, too. For a while after that, Howard stayed here, helping with everything that needed to be done, especially with the farm and the horses. But then, like Seya, he started working in different places; he left for jobs that gave him some kind of income. Because of all those things, the farming got left to the women when Frank decided to start raising more corn, alfalfa, and other things.

Daily Round and Expanding the Farm[1]

Things we did every day while our children were growing up . . .
Frank decides to enlarge the farm.

After my mother passed away and Frank moved us to where we live now, he started talking about trying to raise more food for our children, and more alfalfa for his horses. He wanted to increase those things but he was worried about who would help with it. He knew he was gone a lot and I was already busy with weaving, taking care of the children, the sheep, and other things. So for a while, we just talked about it. Sure, it was a lot of work, but I kept telling him his children and I could manage it for him; we were already taking care of the foods we were raising at that time so we knew how to do it. So, eventually he decided to go ahead. That's when we really started farming; once we did, we kept those things going for probably twenty years. Only just recently, right before you came here, we started cutting back on those things. But of course, by then, we were both up in our years; our old age time had begun.*

Once we started that, I just added those things on to what we were already doing. It didn't affect some things. I still made the children get up early in the morning[2] to say their prayers, offer pollen to the Dawn, and then run races. Frank and I had been raised with that, and we believed in it; that strengthens you. If you run that way, you can face anything that comes along in your life and you won't be lazy. If you're still lying on the sheepskins when the sun comes up, then you won't be worth anything. So I kept making the children do that; Mary no. 1 was the same with her children, so sometimes they all ran together. I know sometimes they just ran until they were out of my sight and then sat down and hid, until the rest came back, and then joined in again. If I saw them do that, I scolded them when they came back; otherwise, I didn't say anything.[3] And sometimes in the winter, I relaxed those things and told them they didn't have to run. The children, of course, were barefoot all the time; Frank made them each a pair of moccasins but we didn't use those on a daily basis. Most of them

236

didn't get any shoes until we sent them to school; then they got those black, high-top ones the schools made them wear.[4] And with their clothes, they were mainly second-hand; they were passed along to each one until they became rags.* But our children always had clothes and they always had food, so we didn't think we were suffering.

While they were running, I fixed them something to eat after I ground corn to use if I hadn't done that or had them help me with that during the night. Their morning meal was whatever we had around to eat, like cornmeal mush or pancakes from yellow or blue cornmeal. While they ate, I told them what my plan was for them for the day. That's the way Frank said to do it, so I followed that all the time. Even if he was home, he never interrupted me or argued about the plans I made for the children. That's probably because he told them the mother is the heart of the family and the hogan is our center of living. He told them all the things that go with it—the dishes, weaving, foods, everything connected with it—are the mother's. He told all his children the mother is the one who holds everything together in the hogan and because of that, they had to listen to what I said and do what I asked whenever they were here. Of course, if he needed somebody's help hauling wood or something else in the wagon, he'd tell me during the evening and I'd include that when I explained the plans to them in the morning.

Even before we started farming a lot, there was always something that needed to be done. All of them had to help haul water and gather wood, and the sheep always needed to be herded. And then too, someone needed to remember the horses. I always had someone help clean up the hogan when we finished eating—wash dishes, shake out the sheepskins and blankets, and straighten up other things. Then they went off to do whatever I asked them to do. Of course, sometimes I helped with that; I used to go with them to haul water. Sometimes we'd get it from the ditch across from here; other times, we'd walk over to the Chinle Wash. We hauled it mainly in metal buckets from the store and small, wooden kegs which we carried on our backs. They had some rings and straps on them for that purpose. I think Irene Nez was about the only one still using the water belly bags people used in my mother's time and earlier. We'd see her with those, over by the ditch or behind here, where people also brought their livestock to a water hole. Later, the government started digging wells; those were rock-lined and covered with boards and we got our water from them, too. Eventually, Frank got a big barrel from the store, and we'd haul enough each day to fill the barrel before we stopped. At first it was wooden, and then later, it was a metal one, like we have now.[5]

We also had to gather firewood every day. That was easiest after water came down from the Canyon; it hauled dead wood and even roots with it, and we'd go over and look for those along the Chinle Wash. We also hunted for wood along the Nazlini Wash. Wherever we found it, we'd gather all the wet ones and all the dry ones we could find; we'd even pull out dead roots and carry them back, often on our backs, tied up in old blankets or burlap sacks. Sometimes I'd go, but usually I sent some of the children to do that. All of them, all the way along, helped with that. Of course, sometimes there'd be no wood along the washes. Then we'd have to hitch up the wagon and go elsewhere. When Frank was around, he took care of that. Seya and Howard both used to help him, going north of Houses Standing in a Line, and also above Spider Rock to haul wood for our own use. And David used to do that, too; lots of times he took the wagon and went by himself, or with his father, to get wood from the mountains. Sometimes in the fall when lots of men were doing that, six or eight wagons would go together, especially if a ceremony was going on somewhere. They'd get wood in the mountains first, and then go to where that was happening, and camp there for the night. I know from what Seya told me, a lot of times they'd play cards and the Shoe Game all night,[6] after tying the horses up and feeding them alfalfa they hauled in the wagon. Of course, they were gambling when they did that. In the morning, they'd put feed bags on the horses while they ate corn, and then they'd start back here with the wood.

I guess our children didn't do too much playing along the way. A few times I'd see them playing in the wagon, or riding around on my mother's donkey for fun, or climbing up on a roof of some building around the place. Of course, I didn't want them climbing around like that, so I'd scold them. Sometimes they'd play right around the hogan, outside, sitting on the ground, imagining things; other times, they hid from each other over by the big ditch. But I think the only time they really got to play was while they were out herding; that was true for me, too, when I was a child. Children usually do the herding, after they're old enough, and they usually herd with others. So, of course, they start playing. From what different ones told me, I knew mine were that way, too. They were making mud toys and also playing with sticks, rocks, colored pebbles, and scraps of material they took with them. And if they got a doll from the school or the mission at Christmas time, they'd take that out with the sheep too, to play with it. If there was water around, well then, some of them played in that, even though I told them not to. Howard was always doing that, playing in the mud. I told him his feet would crack and get painful from it, and they did.[7]

My children herded with lots of others; over the years those changed according to who was sent to school and where people were living. But some of them who herded with my children were Chubby Woman; Mary no. 1's children; Small Woman's daughter, Esther, before she got killed by lightning; Charlie Davis's daughter, Esther Tso, and his son, Tully Davis; Nora and Tom Tsinijinnie; Irene Nez's younger sister, *Yiłtaazbah*; and then Elizabeth and Jack Begay Jones, her brother. Lots of times they all herded on foot, but sometimes they had a donkey to use. Agnes used my mother's donkey, and Garnett used to ride on it too, while she herded with Bah's daughter, Elsie. She used to whip the donkey around the ears and head; that made it go round and round in circles. Frank and I would laugh when we saw that, and we'd tease her about it, too. Most people kept at least one donkey around in those days. After Bah became known as Mrs. Joseph Ganna, Garnett used to ride her donkey, too, and Augusta and Acey used Paiute Woman's donkey sometimes, when they herded.

Of course, when you herd, you're supposed to be watching the sheep and the goats, paying attention to them. When they got busy playing, sometimes we ended up having trouble because they'd forget about the animals. Then I'd scold them. But most of the time, my children were good about herding. Whoever I sent to take care of that each day did it in the right way. Sometimes I'd tell them to gather tea, berries, or other things we needed, if they found them while they were herding. With the berries, I know sometimes they went ahead and ate them, forgetting to bring any back when they brought the animals home.* But I didn't scold them when that happened. Of course, if no children were around to do the herding because they were in school or gone other places, then I did it, as soon as I gathered wood and hauled water for the day. Someone always had to do that.

Another thing we did every day was work on the corn. At the right time of year, I'd send the children out really early to gather pollen before the sun was too hot. But every day, no matter what time of year it was, we had to grind corn. I would tell different ones to help with that in the morning, too, after we ate. Sometimes I'd make special things my children really liked to eat; if they knew I was going to fix *haashch'é'édą́ą́'* berries with *nomasi dleesh*, they always wanted to lick the grinding stones when I got done; they really liked how that *nomasi dleesh* tasted.* Another one I fixed in the wintertime, when it was cold enough to freeze things outside. I'd mix up *taa'niil* [one kind of cornmeal mush] but then I'd set it in a bowl some place out of the way, like up on the hogan roof. When it's frozen we have a different name for it, *dah 'astin*; the children used to love that and sometimes Howard couldn't wait until I told them it was ready to eat. He'd crawl up there and get it, and eat it all up. Once when he did that, I got angry and told him I was going to put some "shit" up there next time because of him.* After that, he stopped stealing it.*

Of course, whenever I made any of the breads baked in the ground, or anything out of blue cornmeal, or paperbread, the children loved those, too. If I were going to make paperbread, I always needed them to gather extra wood to keep the fire going all day, and someone to keep grinding as I went along with that. Mary no. 1 and I often made that together; we'd hang a blanket over the hogan door to keep the drafts out and then, it'd get all smoky and hot in there. The others would help by keeping the fire going and grinding corn. The same was true on days when I washed and dyed wool; I'd ask the children to haul extra wood and extra water then, too, because I needed to fill the big round washtubs I used and then build fires to heat the water to boiling before washing the wool, or later, adding the commercial dyes. And then too, sometimes I made my own dyes from plants and other things. That took extra water, too.

I'd always try to weave during the day, too. When Mary no. 1 got old enough, a lot of times she cooked the morning meal while I started weaving, and then she did that too, while the others did different work after they ate. Of course, whoever wasn't busy was encouraged to sit and watch whoever was weaving and learn that way. But even if they were watching, I'd ask them to work on the wool. Just like with grinding, we were always working on the wool, even at night. Of course, near the end of the day, when the sun was setting, I'd gather the children together and we'd make an evening offering with our corn pollen and say some more prayers, before it got dark. Then I'd fix the evening meal. After we ate, we'd go back to working on the wool. Sometimes, we'd have to remove burrs and sticks that got in there before carding it for spinning. Mary no. 1 helped teach some of the others those things because she was older, and of course my mother did, too, while she was living. There's a lot that goes into sheep; even after children are old enough to herd, they still need to learn about the wool and about weaving. Of course the adults do other things, like shearing and butchering; children just watch those things until they get older. But the rest of it they learn early. We'd weave and work on wool whenever we weren't busy doing something else; lots of nights, after the children went to sleep, I'd be spinning or weaving with light from our kerosene lanterns. Mary no. 1 was the same way too, after she started raising her own children.

So those kinds of things went on all the time, before we really started raising lots of food and after that, too. And then too, some days I had different things planned for the children. After they got the usual things done, I'd take them with me in the wagon to places where I gathered wild plants for food or for making medicines, or to where I dug the *dleesh* I used to whiten the wool, or to where I gathered the grasses we used in a bundle as hairbrushes or brushes for the grinding stones. Those broom grasses used to grow by the Nazlini Wash but south of here, closer to the Catholic Church. Sometimes I'd take only one of the children with me, and we'd go on horseback, maybe leading another one along, if we were going to use it to haul sacks of things back that we gathered. I think all of them went with me at one time or another to do those things. Of course where we went depended on what I wanted to gather; the *haashch'é'édą́ą́'*, yucca fruit, prickly pear cactus, *tł'ohdeeí*, the *nomasi dleesh* I used when fixing certain berries, wild potatoes, wild onions, wild carrots, wild spinach — all those grew in different places, just like other kinds of berries, the two kinds of teas we picked, *'ostse'*, and those "yellow eyes" we used for making cheese. Some of those grew right here, coming up wild in our cornfield, and others were over by the Chinle Wash. But for most of them you had to travel, like toward the Black Mountain area, over on the mesa, or more toward the Window Rocks and Seya's Rabbit Hunting Rock where we used to live, or toward Round Rock or Wheatfields, or other places, like Moaning Lake. Sometimes we'd camp overnight, just like my mother did, and spend two days gathering those things before we came back. I tried to teach my children where they grew, how to gather them, and how to prepare them for use. Frank and I both believed in using those things as foods; that's the way we were raised and we wanted our children to know that, too. So those were among the things I did with them. And then, when we came back, as they all got old enough, I tried to show them how to make different traditional foods, and even those we make just for ceremonies.

Sometimes we traveled to gather juniper, sagebrush, and other things I used as medicines. I guess I mainly did that by myself because I liked to keep big supplies of those things on hand for different ailments that came along with the children and myself and Frank, too. I knew where those things grew[8] and how to make medicines from them. There were different kinds that we used for earaches, eye problems, pimples, hives, chickenpox, stomachaches, diarrhea, toothaches, dizziness, laziness, colds, fevers, coughs, cuts, bites and stings from red ants, centipedes, or spiders, menstrual cramps, internal injuries, bruises, aching joints, snakebites, and other things.[9]

All the old people knew those things. I remember one time when Frank was suffering from something, probably an internal injury of some kind. I was fixing different medicines for him, but he had lost his appetite and was barely eating the different cornmeal mushes I was making for him. Sometimes he seemed like he was almost unconscious so I was worrying about him. One day, an old lady came to visit us; I forget now who that was, but when she saw him in that condition, she told us she had a medicine for that. The next day she brought me some kind of cactus, all dried up. She told me to boil it for him and make him drink it, so I did. After he drank that, he came out of it; he started eating again right away. I asked that woman which cactus it was, because I knew it wasn't the prickly pear we used. But she said she didn't know; someone had given it to her a long time ago and told her it worked for injured tissues, pulled muscles, and things like that. In those days, lots of people knew things like that. But now, nobody bothers with it; a lot of those plants have disappeared and even the ones still available for our use, younger people don't know anything about them, not even what yucca fruit looks like.*

Another thing we used to do at the right season was pick pinyons. Sometimes we'd go toward Lukachukai; other times we'd go past Spider Rock toward the mountain, or even to other places where people said there were lots of nuts. Some years there were lots, and other times, they were very scarce. I remember one time in particular; Frank took Mary no. 1, Howard, Isabel, and me in the wagon up past Spider Rock; we had decided to camp there while we picked pinyons, so we built a brush shelter. Frank was hauling wood for our wintertime use at that time, so he left us there and went on in the wagon. There was a juniper tree west of where we made our shelter. We were all around there, and Howard was lying on the ground, resting. The axe we had brought with us was behind his head. Just then, a bull came around. When Isabel saw it, she ran to the tree and climbed right up to the top of it; Mary no. 1 and I started to do that, too, but we only went a little ways up in that tree. Howard started yelling at us: "What are you women trying to do by climbing up there? That bull isn't going to climb way up there after you. If he starts toward us, I'll use the axe on his head." He also started teasing Mary no. 1, telling her she looked like a big owl in that tree! Mary no. 1 told Isabel to come down by where she was sitting and she threw a blanket over a branch in there. Here, that branch was rotten. When Isabel jumped down on it, even though she was skinny at that time, it broke and she fell down, landing right near the bull. That knocked her out.

I got worried so Mary no. 1 and I climbed down and started yelling at the bull. Howard just lay there laughing at us, saying, "Now what are you women going to do?" Finally we poured some water on Isabel and she came to. The next day, while Howard went with Frank to help load wood on the wagon, we moved to Charlie Claw's mother's place. I wanted to get a small ceremony done for Isabel because of that, so I went over there and we spent the night there. That's where they told us there were lots of bears roaming around in the Canyon again and fighting with the bulls. Because of that, the bulls in the area were acting mean. We didn't know about that until then. The next morning, we went back to where our brush shelter was and finished picking pinyons. We didn't see that mean bull again.*10

Another thing we used the wagon for was gathering peaches in the Canyon. Lots of times Frank went with us when we did that, after hitching up four horses. He had clan relatives in Canyon del Muerto; one of those groups, the Wilsons, lived on the top and farmed in the bottom, where they had a huge orchard like lots of people did. They were very close to us. Sometimes Frank would take Howard with him when he'd go to help them cut alfalfa or gather peaches. But other times, all of us went with him to get peaches they gave us. Of course, they asked Frank to do his ceremony for them many times, too. Eventually, William Wilson gave Frank an area in the bottom of Canyon del Muerto that was filled with peach trees; that was while Frank was on the Council. For many years we went back and forth in the summer, taking care of those trees. You have to prune them, clean up around them, irrigate them, and do other things, too, even before the fruit gets ripe and ready to be picked. Sometimes the children and I'd go there and work on those things, even if Frank was gone. When the peaches got ripe, we'd bring them out in wagon loads. Sometimes I'd go and other times, Frank would take Ruth, Augusta, or Howard with him to help with that. The people who lived in there dried the peaches right on the rocks, after brushing them off, splitting them open, and removing the pits. They hung up scarecrows and tin cans and other things that moved and made noise in the wind to keep the crows and chipmunks away, and whatever else came to eat the peaches. We'd see those things when we went in there by their orchards and also in their cornfields. When we brought the peaches back, we, too, split them open and took the pits out. We ate some of them right away, of course; they were really sticky. But we spread lots of them out in the sun to dry before putting them away for our wintertime use. Sometimes I even put them on the hogan roof to dry in the sun.*

Finally, taking care of those trees got to be too much. When it didn't rain, the sand was deep in the Chinle Wash and it'd take us a whole day to get there in the wagon. Then we'd spend two or three more days working around those trees, before starting back. We'd worry about how to get water to those trees back in there. And at the same time, I'd be worrying about whoever I left behind over here, with the sheep, the food we were raising, and other things at home. When Frank started traveling more and more, he couldn't help us with those things too much. Seya was already working in other places, and Howard was starting to do that, too. So I finally told Frank I thought it was too much to keep that going. We talked about it for a long time because we all liked the peaches and didn't want to give them up. But we finally had to. So he told William Wilson to take the land back, that he was too busy and his children needed to be home taking care of the fields, the sheep, his horses, and other things. We couldn't spend half our summer going back and forth because of those trees.* So that was the end of them.[11]

Whenever I was with my children by myself, without Frank, we always tried to enjoy ourselves even though we'd be working on something. When we'd be traveling, or even when we'd be here working on wool or grinding corn, I'd tell them about my own early days, and my mother's time, too. I'd even tell them some of the funny things that happened to me, like when my sister and I would be herding and we'd get thrown off the donkeys, or some of the things we did to play tricks on people. That way they learned how we used to move around with my parents, what we ate in those times, and what it was like before the stores came. I told them lots of things about my father, too—how he got his name, what he did as a headman, and how he finally passed away. Some of my own children never even knew him; that was true starting with David, so I wanted them all to know those things. I also told them whatever funny stories I remembered about things that happened earlier, at gatherings of the People, or the names we'd give certain ones. Some of those were really funny and they'd just laugh about it.[12]

Sometimes I took my children to visit relatives in other places. A lot of times, if I was planning to do that, I'd tell them ahead of time, while we ate our morning meal. I'd say after we washed the wool, ground so much corn, or finished something else, then I was going on a trip and I wanted them to come, too. I teased them, saying I was going to make them walk like my mother used to do, and then right away, they'd say they didn't want to go.* We laughed about that, after she was no longer with us. Sometimes some of them didn't want to go where I was going, so I only took one or two others and we went on horseback. But sometimes we went in the wagon. If we were going toward Black Mountain, I always made sure Frank knew about it because we'd stay overnight before coming back. Of course, sometimes he'd want to come with us, to visit Long Moustache around Fish Point, or Jim Mitchell's children, or the Lees over near Moaning Lake. In the summer, sometimes we'd haul trees to people living in other places, when they wanted to make ramadas, after we cut those near the Chinle Wash. Sometimes we'd take people mutton from here. And of course, sometimes when we went visiting like that, people would give us a sheep to bring back. We might butcher it first and bring it back that way on the horse. If we were going to add it to our flock, we tied it in the wagon and gave it a ride home.* Sometimes, of course, I went to visit my sister and my half sister; they were still living where they had when my mother walked there all the time, but I'd ride horseback. Of course, I walked too, if I was just going to see people who lived near the stores, over by the bridge, or somewhere else nearby. Then I'd take Howard or somebody else with me. I guess sometimes I did travel alone, mainly on horseback, but I didn't really like doing that. Now and then, Frank would give me money to get a sheep from somebody so I'd saddle a horse and go do that, butchering it right there so I could bring back the meat. Sometimes he'd tell me to pick up a sheep someone had given him for doing a ceremony, or even part of a cow that was already butchered. And then too, while I was still helping women with childbirth, sometimes I'd go back the next day either in the wagon or on a horse, to get whatever they wanted to give me for helping them.

Because we did those things now and then, we did go out from here, even though the children and I didn't travel around as much or as far away as Frank did. Of course, some of them did when they started going to school away from Chinle. Because of those things, the days around here always passed quickly and always seemed to be different. We worked hard, of course, but we also did other things, even after Frank started raising more food and we had more work to do in the fields every day. Sometimes, of course, I traveled with him, too. When he was home, we tried to spend time together; I guess we missed each other.* As Ruth got old enough to watch the others, from David on down, Frank and I would go places in the wagon, like to the stores, the Chapter House, or to Enemyways, Nightways, or other ceremonies different ones were having. Sometimes I also went with him when he had to talk to the People. When we went to ceremonies, I always worried because we might be gone for several days. So even as I was leaving with him, I'd turn around and call back to Ruth, to remind her to watch the children, watch the house, watch the sheep.[13] I'd always remind her not to scold the children, too; it's not good to do that. It hurts their feelings and sometimes makes their minds start thinking the wrong way and then maybe they even run away. But Ruth was careful about those things; she always took care of things in the right way whenever I was traveling like that.

There was one special thing the men did on Sundays; I don't know if that was true in other places, but once we settled here, after my father died and we stopped moving around, I noticed men got together to hunt rabbits and it was always Sunday when they did that. For other things, they hunted when they could, but with rabbits it was different. So, as the boys got old enough, they started doing that too, with the men. They kept doing that for a long time; I think it wasn't until Augusta finished high school that rabbit hunting in that way came to an end. Maybe they had killed them all off by then.*

All those men would get together on horseback across from here, along the highway that goes toward Many Farms; in those days, that area, on both sides of the road, was covered with greasewoods. Men would assemble there on horses with sticks and everybody would be saying, "Let's go chase." I remember some of my girls hearing that and asking me where they were going, what they were chasing?* Even small boys went over there; they'd run along on foot. Sometimes the men would ride along in a line, throwing their sticks at whatever rabbits they saw, driving them. Other times they'd get in a circle, and then close in on the rabbits. Everybody would be yelling, shouting, and laughing; it took a good aim to throw the stick at the rabbits and knock them down while your horse was running, and I guess lots of times they missed, or their horses would throw them off, or fall in a hole with them. They'd use those long sticks if the rabbit tried to hide in a hole, too; they'd jump off the horse and put that stick in the hole and twist it into the fur and drag the rabbit out that way. When Seya or David went with them, then sometimes we'd have rabbits to eat. Of course they hunted those at other times, just like Howard did. Seya did that with Sam, from the time he was little, when we were with my parents up around the Window Rocks, the Rock Bridge, and his Rabbit Hunting Rock.* And Howard used to hunt jackrabbits on the north rim of the Canyon in the winter, just below where they put the water tank. I was always glad to fix any rabbits anyone brought back.*

The boys hunted other things too, as they were growing up. Whenever it rained a lot, they went looking for prairie dogs because they always came out of their holes then. Sometimes, too, if we were hungry for prairie dogs, they'd take water with them, and pour it down the holes, just waiting for them to pop out. When deer were in season, they hunted them sometimes, too. And one time I remember Frank killed a porcupine; he saw its tracks when he was riding his horse around somewhere so he followed them and found it. When he brought it home, here my children didn't even know what it was.* So he cut off the tail with all the spines in it, split it open, gutted it, and then singed it. You fix prairie dogs and rabbits the same way; you singe the skin and the fur, take out the insides, put salt in the stomach part, and sew it back up. Then you bake it in the ground. Both Frank and I knew how to do that; we ate those when we were children, and we liked using them as food. A few times I fixed squirrels, too, when someone went to the mountains where they lived and brought them back. And once I almost had a badger to fix.* One time I told Howard and David to go look for Frank's horses. David was the one taking care of the horses for us; we didn't have any cows. And as soon as he was old enough and no longer afraid of them, Howard started helping with that, too. Even when he came home from the Chinle Boarding School he'd help with the horses, feeding them, rounding them up for our use, or taking them to the water pools in the Canyon. This one time, when Howard came back, he told me that he and David had found a badger hole. When the badger came out, David hit it with a stick and threw it in a sack, telling Howard to haul it home on his back. After they went on just a little ways, still looking for the horses, here that thing started growling. Howard told me he threw the sack down right there, yelling, "It's alive, it's alive," and then took off running. So that was the end of their badger meat.*

All the things I've been talking about were things we did the whole time all our children were growing up. So, when Frank decided to raise more alfalfa, corn, and other things, we just added those in with the things we were already doing.[14] Of course, before he decided that, we were growing things like watermelons and other melons, squash, beans, and corn. Those were for our own use as food; with the corn, we also used the pollen for our ceremonies and our prayers. And any ears that bugs had started eating or that got frozen, we set aside to grind up as food for the horses and the sheep in the winter. We were also growing some alfalfa for the horses. So we were already planting these things, and then hoeing weeds and harvesting different foods when they were ready. We were already trying to grow the foods we needed. And I knew how to fix them so we could use them in the winter; each fall, I'd do that as much as possible. Sometimes I'd sun-dry things before storing them for winter. With the meat, sometimes I'd use salt to preserve it for later, or cut it into strips and dry it, like jerky. We didn't have electricity then.

All of us already knew farming was a lot of work and that everybody needed to help with it; even before Frank started planting more things, we knew that. I always tried to do as much as possible. But each morning, I'd also tell the children who were home what I needed them to do in the fields. Of course, at different times of year, there was different work to do. The plowing was first and Frank always tried to be home for that. He'd go around, just like my father did, and tell different ones it was time to clean the irrigation ditches and start plowing. Because he was a leader, they'd listen to him; they'd make a plan and then all gather in one place, and start working. Like in earlier times, in the beginning when we were trying to raise more crops, the People were still helping each other. Some of our relatives would come down from the Black Mountain area and help us, bringing their teams. Even the ones who weren't farming in the Chinle Valley would help, and sometimes there'd be over twenty teams here, when people were cleaning the ditches.[15] Then they'd go back and get their plows; anyone who had any kind of scoop, troughlike pan, plow, or other equipment would bring it to where people were getting ready to plant in this area. And again, they'd all help each other with the plowing. Wherever they were working, the women there would butcher and prepare food to feed all the people working together.

Here in our family, the boys helped Frank with cleaning the ditches and then with the plowing; David always did that, and after he passed away, Howard helped sometimes, and Seya did too, if he was here. But when both of them left for jobs in other places, Frank asked some of his daughters to start helping with those things too, even though that was heavy work. Augusta learned how to harness the horses and run the plow.[16] I think she was still going to school in Chinle when she started doing that. She also became responsible for running the scraper to open up the irrigation ditch over there by our fields. She kind of took those things over after David died and she kept helping with the plowing whenever she was here during her junior high and high school days, right up until after she started having her own children. I used to worry about her doing that, thinking she'd hurt herself inside in some way. I know one time she almost broke her wrist when the scraper flipped while she was working on the irrigation ditch with Howard,[17] and I imagine there were other times she got hurt, too. But she was good with the horses. Frank always had lots of nice horses around; some were just for farming and others we used for riding or with the wagon. Augusta never was afraid of them, even when she was little.

All the children who were around learned to plant as the ground was being plowed. I told them we needed all of them to help plant so they did that, too, even though sometimes it was already hot by then. They seemed to have fun doing it, but sometimes they got mixed up and forgot which row to put the seeds in, or how far to walk before putting in the next ones. We always plowed in a circle, just like my father and other people had done. Everyone was doing it that way here in the Valley and down in Many Farms and other places, too. They'd start plowing from the center and work outwards, ending up about two feet from the irrigation ditch; that way the water from the ditch got to all the plants when they started coming up.[18]

The fields were irrigated first, once the ditches were cleaned and ready. They went all around the fields and were about a foot or so deep, after they were cleaned. After the water was let in, it soaked into the ground. Then, when the top part, maybe about three inches, was dry, the People with the plows would get ready. The teams pulling the plows, usually about six or eight of them, would follow each other, coming across the ditch with the plows turned over to the right, on their sides, until it was time to put them down and start plowing from the center. Then they'd all get behind each other and start plowing, making the rows bigger each time until they were wide and deep enough. The children walked along carrying whatever seeds were being planted in little sacks tied to their waists with a rope, or in small cans or buckets. We told them to mark where they put the seeds with a small stick, take three, great big steps from the stick before putting the next one in, and to do that *before* the teams pulling the plows came back again, following each other in a line, and covered up the row. That meant the children had to pay attention, and also hurry, to stay ahead of whoever was driving the team pulling the plow [see Fig. 31].

Sometimes the children got confused about which row to work on, or they forgot to take three big steps, or they threw lots of seeds in one place. They'd worry about the horses coming, breathing down their necks, or they'd say that watching the plows go in

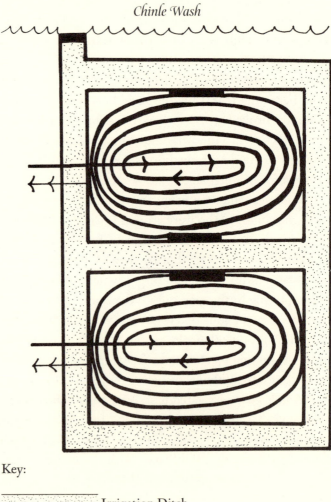

FIG. 31. Farming Our Fields, as sketched by Augusta Sandoval, March 1997. Professionally drawn by Jennifer A. Frisbie.

Chinle Wash

Key:

Irrigation Ditch

Irrigation Ditch Gate

circles made them dizzy, made them forget what row they were in.* You always knew if they got confused when the corn came up; here and there it'd be growing too far apart and in other places, there would be too much too close together. We'd always laugh about it and tell them that's where you threw all your seeds or over here you took sixteen big steps, too many.* If the people driving the teams saw the children getting mixed up, they'd start yelling at them, but they didn't stop moving with the plows. Once they started plowing, they didn't stop until all the fields were planted. I, of course, helped plant if we were short-handed. But if enough children were around, then lots of times, I was out herding sheep while they all helped Frank with the planting.

In the summer, as soon as the weeds started coming up, I'd get the children up very, very early. We'd hurry through everything we did first and as soon as we ate, we'd all go out to the fields to hoe weeds before it got too hot. I taught them how so they left no weeds around. Those drank up whatever rain came and that was needed by the corn, melons, and other things. We used hoes to chop out the weeds. Sometimes the children would get into arguments while they were hoeing; I remember hearing Augusta and Howard doing that several times, and also Agnes and Howard, one time when she was here helping us hoe. I guess he didn't always hoe it clean and she was reminding him about that. Sometimes they even threw pieces of dirt at each other, or almost hit each other with their hoes, by accident. When they got like that, I'd have to scold them.

Besides hoeing, I asked them to gather corn pollen when it was ready in the fields. We used a lot of that, and all the children gathered it, in pans. And sometimes when it didn't rain, we'd haul water out to the fields in the wagon to water the plants. That was a lot of work so we always hoped it would rain and water would come down from the Canyon and fill the irrigation ditches we made coming off the Chinle Wash.

During the summer, we also worked on the alfalfa, whenever it needed to be cut. We tried to get four or five cuttings from our fields and for a long time, I cut that by hand with a long scythe. Garnett and some of the others helped me cut alfalfa that way. Finally, Frank got some kind of cutter, a mower, and also a rake and a baler. Those were pulled by the team; someone sat on them or stood on a little step built on them off on the side, while managing the horses. Those farm machines are still setting over there on the little road that goes back toward the Chinle Wash. We stopped using them a few years ago, when we quit doing so much farming, but they're still over there. Augusta and Howard learned how to run those things too; once we had them, we started doing the alfalfa in a different way. When Howard ran the mower, in two days he'd have one cutting done. Then, after we raked and baled it, we'd load it on the wagon. Frank usually sold the first two or three cuttings at Garcia's; he and Howard would haul the bales up there.[19] The other cuttings we saved for our own use and stored them around here, in our barnlike place. But even after we started using those machines with the teams on the alfalfa, sometimes I'd still go out there with a sickle. If the team didn't go straight, the cutter and baler would miss alfalfa in places, here and there. So I'd go and cut those, collect the loose ones, and put them in a sack to use for the sheep in the winter when they were lambing. I didn't want any of that going to waste so I always checked for those things. I still went over there.

Later in the summer, some of the food was ready to be harvested. With the corn, I went by what my mother taught me about making food from its four stages, so we'd gather some of it when the kernels were tiny and just forming, and some more a little later, before it was fully ripe. In the fall, I asked the children to help harvest again, when the corn was fully ripe.[20] We'd always go out early, before the dew was off the cornstalks. As soon as the sun comes up, it starts drying the corn out and then it's harder to handle. That's when the corn plant leaves cut your hands, too, like knife blades. We didn't have gloves to wear while we harvested, but I always told them to wear long-sleeved shirts or jackets. We'd pile up whatever we picked at the edge of the field, and then someone would walk home and come back with the wagon, to load those things up and haul them home. With the corn, we'd bundle up the stalks, and try to husk the corn before bringing it back, if there was time. We always husked it early in the morning, when it was wet from the dew because that made that work easier. As we husked it, we made two piles inside the fence. In one, we put the good corn, the ears that had no marks from bugs chewing on them or no signs of frost on them. In the other, we put the ones that were too small or too buggy. We kept the two piles separate, even after we hauled the ears home in the wagon.

After the harvest was finished, I needed to prepare things for our wintertime use. Some of the things we grew we ate when they were ready; others I sun-dried or put away whole in storage places we had. With the corn, it had to be husked so I'd start working on that, even at night. And I'd ask the children to help with that too, early in the morning or at night, or on the weekends when they were home from school if they were here in Chinle. The good ears we used for making lots of different kinds of food, after the corn was dry. Sometimes I dried that on the ground; we'd gather lots of reeds and dry them in the sun, before spreading them out and putting the ears of corn on them, to dry. When it was ready, we'd put the corn in twenty-five pound sacks. For many of the foods I fixed, the dried corn had to be ground on the grinding stone; but you could also roast the fully ripe ears and eat them that way, without shelling off the kernels. We dried the bad ears, too, but we kept them separate.

I remember David and Ruth helping me a lot with husking the corn during the week, and putting it in sacks. We hauled the "bad" ears up to the Presbyterian Church, where they installed that big grinder for everyone's use.[21] I'd load eight or ten sacks into the wagon and go up there. Somebody else had to go with me, because one person had to hitch a horse to the grinder and lead it around and around, while the other one gathered up the ground corn as it came out. Sometimes David would go, but lots of times, after Augusta was in school in Chinle, Frank would check her out to help me do that on the weekend. You could grind up the cobs, too, in that machine because it had a place on the side where you could adjust it to whatever fineness you wanted. I'd take a big canvas with me to spread on the ground underneath where the corn came out. Whoever was gathering it tried to catch all of it in the empty sacks or even in buckets or washtubs. When we finished, we put all of it back into the sacks; then we resewed those, loaded them on the wagon, and came home. We used to feed that corn to the horses in the winter.

Of course one of the main reasons Frank decided to start growing more food and alfalfa was that he had lots of horses. He really liked those so he built those up. All his animals were good ones; some were big farm horses and others were saddle horses, for riding. Taking care of those animals, the livestock we had like that, also had to be done by someone else during that time because Frank was busy with the Council and his ceremony. He wasn't around enough to look after the horses himself. While David was with us, that was his main job. After he died, who would do that was a question. There was nobody here to do it every day, and Frank started worrying about it. He tried to do it for a while, but as he got busier working as a judge, he wasn't here at all for long periods of time. So we talked about what to do about his horses; by then he had about seventeen, not like the few we have now. Some summers they were out on the mesa, toward Black Mountain but often north of the Pinon Junction; other summers we'd chase them across the Chinle Wash to places below Houses Standing in a Line where many trees had started growing. But in the winter, we'd bring them home and put them in the corral where we could feed and watch them. Howard helped with those things when he was around, and Ruth and Isabel did, too. And whenever she was home from junior high at St. Michaels or St. Catherine's where she went to high school, Augusta also helped with the horses.

Augusta was the one watching them the summer that two got lost; I think she had just started St. Catherine's when that happened. One of those was a big chestnut stallion. Frank bought that from somebody in the Canyon and he was loaning it out to different ones for breeding purposes. That horse was beautiful; even though it was huge, it was very tame. It came when Augusta whistled, and she rode it bareback, without a bridle, all over the place. It was home here and we had been using it on the farm. One afternoon after she fed and watered the horses, Augusta turned them loose. Frank had told her to do that, that they'd stay around here because they were getting fed. The next morning, the others came back but the stallion didn't. We knew that Frank had promised to loan it to Zhealy Tso next; somebody had come asking to borrow it and he told them they'd have to wait because it was already promised. So, when it didn't come back, Augusta took another horse and rode over toward the west, on the hill where they made the community cemetery. She tracked it to where the other people who wanted to borrow it lived; even though it had sprinkled during the night, its big tracks were still showing, here and there.

But all she saw there was a shack with oats spread on the ground; the people said they hadn't seen it, even though its tracks went to their place. When she came back, she told me about it, and I told her to go back over there and ask some other people who were riding around in the area. And sure enough, one of the men she asked told her he had seen a dead horse in a ditch not too far from where she had turned around. It sounded like Frank's horse so she came back here. By the time Frank came in, late in the afternoon, she was crying. Right away she told him about it. Even though he got upset, he told her it wasn't her fault. He also told her to stop crying, that we shouldn't cry over horses. Those things couldn't be helped. The next morning he went to the BIA office to get the police and somebody else who could cut open the horse's stomach. When they did that, sure enough, they learned that horse had been poisoned with those oats. By then, those people were gone so nothing was ever done about it. Later that same summer, another of Frank's horses didn't come home. When Augusta went looking for it, she found it dead. But that one died from old age.

After he lost those two horses, Frank went and got a pair of mules from a man in Sanders to use with the farm work. Those were a perfectly matched set, and Frank and I thought they looked nice, pulling the plow and other things together. But Augusta was afraid of them; she said their ears were split and they scared her. Ruth and Isabel felt that same way. They said they were mean, even though they were pretty to look at because they were perfectly matched. Because they felt like that, Ruth, Isabel, and Augusta all said they wouldn't help with the farming if they had to use those things. Frank tried to change their minds by encouraging them to get used to the mules, to give them a try for about two or three months, but they wouldn't budge about it. I think if he'd been able to stay home and do the farming himself, he would have kept those mules for his own use. But because he was depending on us to do those things, when his daughters who were the ones helping me with the farming said those things, Frank finally decided he had to get rid of them. That was the only time he tried having mules around; after that, he just stuck with his horses.*

19

The War Years

World War II and its effects on our family . . . Augusta goes to St. Michaels
. . . Howard's eye injury . . . I decide to stop helping women in labor.

When Howard left to start working in other places, that's when the women here started doing all the farm work, like I've told you. But lots of other things seemed to change, too, at that time. From then on, there were no men around for a long time. Of course, sometimes Frank was here. But he was always busy with his ceremony and with being a leader, and even when he came back, soon he'd take off again. Even though he didn't get put back on the Tribal Council, Chee Dodge wanted him to be involved with those things so he kept going to meetings in Window Rock and other places. I think he'd already been named as a judge by then, but I'm not sure. When that started, he was gone because of that, too.[1]

With other families, the same thing was true. But in those cases, the men had joined the service. Another big war had started, this time with Japan. When that happened, lots of people here lost their jobs; the government shut down the CCC and other programs that were providing incomes for people. So, men decided to fight in the war. You probably know about the ones who did the code-talking; they're still famous for that. In our family, it was Agnes who enlisted. She did that without telling us; after her orders came, she caught a ride home from Fort Defiance to tell us she was leaving the next day for the war. Frank wanted to have a Blessingway Ceremony for her, for her safekeeping while she went far away to be a nurse in the Army. But there wasn't time. So we put that off until years later, after she came back.[2] I remember Garnett had already started nurses' training at Sage Memorial Hospital when Agnes did that and I wondered if she was going to go into the service, too, when she finished that. But she didn't; the war was over by then.

Except for Frank, the men in our family started working in different places, doing things for the war. Seya went to Barstow, California, for a while to work unloading freight trains and the ones carrying the mail; lots of Chinle people did that. Ruth's husband, Leo, went over there and so did Woody, Mary no. 1's husband, and his brother, Willie, and others. When those men came home on leave, if there were ceremonies going on, of course, they'd go. I remember Woody still had his Nightway dance teams; he organized those even when he worked in different places so they could do that wherever they found a ceremony going on. I remember one time when he and Leo came back, there was a Nightway Ceremony down by Valley Store. We had already decided to take Augusta there to see the Ye'iis, to get her initiated. You can't go to those dances, even to watch them, unless you get that done. Frank had decided we should do that for her. She was in her last year at the Chinle Boarding School then; that's when she became a *kinaaldá* and came home from school on the weekends when she had both of her ceremonies. By then, Frank had already made a plan with the priests for her to go to St. Michaels next, and had told her that was his plan about it. So in the winter, when they were having a Nightway, we checked Augusta out of school. Mary no. 1 and her children went with us, and Ruth and Leo did, too. We went in the wagon and Woody and his team danced over there. They put all the children getting initiated on one side of the hogan, and then one at a time, they did that. I told Augusta she needed to get that done four times before she could start going to those ceremonies. When you go for that reason, you don't stay very long; you come right back with your children after that part is over. Lots of people took their children to that ceremony, to get them initiated.

When the men came back from Barstow for good, Seya told us he'd found a job around Flagstaff at the Ordnance Depot they had located at Bellemont.[3] So, soon, he left again; this time he took his whole family—Adelle, their new baby, and the other children she already had. After a while Howard, David Gorman, and others joined him in Bellemont, and started working over there on war things. Seya stayed over there many years before he moved back. But Howard didn't stay too long because he got hurt. One time when they were playing baseball, somehow a bat injured his eye so he came home. We used herbs on that first, the ones we have for eye injuries. But they didn't help. Then Frank asked different ones what to do about it, and they said maybe a Lifeway Ceremony would help. So we asked Old Curly Hair to do that for Howard. But that didn't help, either. So finally Frank took him to the Chinle Hospital. Right away they sent him to Fort Defiance. But even over there, they couldn't help; they kept him for probably two months and then the doctors said he had a permanent injury. Lifeway isn't used for something like that, and the herbs we have for eye problems don't work for that, either.

When that happened to Howard, Augusta was already over at St. Michaels for junior high. She had to work there too, hauling water and coal, and helping in the kitchen and dining room. Sometimes, maybe because of that, when she came home she acted too tired to help around here, almost like she was having trouble from laziness. That worried me because I needed her help with the farm, the horses, and other things. Finally, I told her there was an herb that would help with that, remove the bilelike thing that was inside, slowing her down. I told her I could fix it for her; you make that from the cliffrose bush, the same one whose bark we used for cradleboard pads. Sometimes people call it buckbrush, too, but around here, we call it *Dilawo'ii*'s [Racing Man's] medicine. We used to get that herb from an old man named Racing Man who lived near Fluted Rock, so we named it after him; when he passed away, we called it Racing Man's Son's medicine because his son always kept that around, too, at his place on the rim of the Canyon, near White House.

I knew if Augusta took it, it would clean her out and bring her strength back. But first it would make her very sick, probably for a whole day. So I told her that, too. She said to go ahead and fix it for her. I told her not to eat anything in the morning, just drink that and then lots of water. So she followed my instructions. Around noon, she ran outside, and stayed by the ditch being sick to her stomach all afternoon. I fixed her some clear mutton broth; you drink that after that herb cleans you out. After she took that, from then on she never was lazy again. Later she thanked me for showing her how to take care of those things.[4]

I think it was while Augusta was at St. Michaels that we lost two more people in the family. One of those was Frank's youngest brother, Tom. He lived in Tsaile but he came to visit us a lot. He was tall and slim, and his hair was very long. Whenever he was around, Mary no. 1 would wash his hair and his clothes for him. The whole time he'd be teasing my children in lots of different ways. Tom had two boys; the one named Tom like his father married one of the girls my half sister had for Old Red Bottom Man. The other one, Ben, went to Fort Apache with Seya. Tom's hair was just starting to get gray when he passed away; I don't remember if he had some kind of sickness but I know he wasn't in his old age when that happened.

The other one we lost was my half sister's husband, Old Red Bottom Man. My younger sister's husband, the one called *Hastiin Łaashi*, had already passed away by then. When Old Red Bottom Man got sick, he suffered for a long time. Frank and I started helping them in every way we could; they tried lots of ceremonies for him, and I went over there many times to help with those things. Sometimes I took Isabel with me in the wagon; other times Ruth watched her and I went on horseback. She already had two more children by then, Timothy and Lynn, so she was here with them, and with her oldest one, Alfred. Sometimes we thought Old Red Bottom Man was not going to come back; he'd go unconscious and they'd move him to a separate little shelter, but then he'd come out of it for a while again. That's how bad he was! Things went along like that for a *long* time; he really suffered with whatever caused that. Finally he passed away. The Presbyterians probably buried him; I don't remember now but lots of people in that family were with the church on the hill at that time.[5] For quite a while after that, my half sister stayed by herself, raising all their children and some other ones, too, from those who had died. Then Son of Yucca Fruit Man went over there with most of his children, and after some more years passed, they got together.[6]

While that war was going on, during one of those winters, I, too, got sick. I think it was shortly after Ruth had her second baby, Timothy, maybe around the time the plane crashed in the Canyon.[7] The hand-trembler Frank got said I was suffering from bear sickness and I needed a Mountainway. Lots of people were having that ceremony then; maybe that's because there were always lots of pinyons for people to pick at that time. When you do that, of course it exposes you to places where bears have left their scent and their tracks, and that can harm you. So, Frank got a singer called Mule Man and his son, Wallace Staley, to do a five-night Mountainway for me, after we got everything ready. That was the first time I had that ceremony done; after it was over, that sickness left me.

I guess it was after Ruth had her third child, the girl called Lynn, that I decided to stop helping women with their labor.[8] Of course, whenever people had babies here in the family, I was still available, but most of the time, they didn't need assistance. I think the last baby born here at our place was Augusta's boy, Augustine. When he was born, it was like Louise's birth; Frank was singing and we were all laughing, not even ready, when each of those babies popped out.*[9]

As I got older, my joints were full of pain. I didn't say much about it; I kept on hoeing, harvesting, grinding, weaving, and doing other things. I just used different herbs I knew about when the pain was strong. But when those things started happening to me, I also started losing some of my hand strength and my arm strength. You need to have strong hands when you help a woman in labor, so you can knead her, turn the baby around if it's in the wrong position, and do other things. So, I began to think I should stop doing it.

I'd been doing that for a long time. My mother had taught me those things and people knew I could help women in labor in those ways. Of course, I had a lot of children myself so I knew about a woman's labor. And I also used those things on the sheep; sometimes, when the lambs were upside down inside, I'd put fat on my hands and reach in carefully, and turn them around so they could get born. So, I had all of those experiences along with the things my mother taught me. Over the years, I guess I became known for that; different ones would come and get me, even in the middle of the night, to go back with them to help a woman who was having trouble.[10] Sometimes, they wouldn't come until they had tried other women and gotten no results. So sometimes, when I got there, the woman in labor would be suffering because others had caused her more pain with their hands, trying to reach and grab for the baby any old way. You have to know how to do that right; your hands have to be strong but you have to be gentle so you don't cause pain for the woman. Childbirth can bring suffering. It's like our ancestor I've already mentioned, *Tanabah*, the one who had a baby by herself while trying to escape from her enemies;[11] and it's like what happened to my half sister when she was born. She was all bruised up from people trying to pull her out.[12] I don't think there was ever a time when I couldn't get a baby turned around so it was born. Of course, sometimes women didn't survive childbirth, even with someone there to help. They didn't regain their strength after they went through that and they passed away, like Beautiful Woman. A lot of times, the baby passed away too, if it had already lost its mother. And sometimes, a baby was born dead, strangled by the cord. That's why you shouldn't tie knots in things when you're pregnant. It's also why we don't get things ready for a baby until after it's born; too many things go wrong if you start assembling things beforehand.

There are lots of things that go into helping women go through childbirth. Some women act as the one who catches the baby; our word for that means "the one who takes them out." That's the woman who sits in front; she catches the baby, cleans it up, ties the cord, and then wraps it up in a new sheepskin or a blanket. She also takes care of the afterbirth; we catch that on a shaved sheepskin. You cut the wool off before you use it for that purpose. The woman who takes care of those things carries the afterbirth outside and disposes of it properly. All of those things are her job. She's also the one who saves the cord; the new parents decide where to bury it. If you hope for an excellent weaver, you might bury it by the loom; for someone to have lots of healthy livestock, you might put it near the corral. That's up to you, but you bury it somewhere around where you are living. It ties you to that place, your home, because that's where your cord is buried. We have believed that and gone according to that for a *very long time*. I did that with all my children.

What I did was different. I don't think we even have a word for it. We always just said I was "a woman who knew how to turn the baby around."[13] When I went somewhere to help, I made sure someone had hung up the sash belt or tied a rope to one of the crossbeams in the roof of the hogan. You do that in the west, behind the fireplace. If you don't want to use a crossbeam, you can use a pole or some kind of post; anyone can put up the pole and then tie the sash belt or rope to it, or to the beam. Some like to use both the belt and a rope; others say if you want a fast delivery, then you use a sash belt. After I made sure all the children had been chased out and everything had been made ready, I told the woman to remove her underskirts. Of course, she leaves the top one on. Then I checked the baby's position; if it needed to be turned around, then I turned the woman upside down, just like *Tanabah* did for herself way, way back, when she crawled headfirst between those rocks. Then I turned the baby with my hands on the outside of her stomach, very slowly and very gently, the way my mother taught me. I often had the woman put her head on a pillow or a blanket, if we were going to do that. You can also shake her a bit to help with it, when she's in that position. If the woman is skinny, it's easy to tell how the baby is lying; if she's fat, then it's difficult; the fat gets in the way when you're trying to feel the baby. Working on her stomach that way, manipulating it so the baby turned around, was one thing I did if it was necessary. I knew how to check for that.

When that's finished, the woman squats, and takes hold of the belt or the rope, however they've chosen to do it. I helped her get on the rope; that's how she supports herself during her labor, by hanging on to that. If her labor goes on a long time, or if the woman gets tired in that position, then I'd tell her to change to a kneeling position. You can do that in either position.

I always stayed behind the woman who was in labor; the one catching the baby stays in the front. Of course we'd be in the west side of the hogan near whoever was singing. We use Blessingway for that so someone would be there singing the songs from that; the songs help chase the baby out just like the feathers, the fan does. Sometimes the singer will use the fan we use in Evilway Blackening ceremonies for that, to speed up the birth for the mother. The Blessingway blesses the mother and the new baby as they start their lives together. From behind the woman, I directed her labor; I'd tell her to push down with her contractions while I'd be lifting her up from behind, and from underneath her ribs. We worked together like that until the baby was born. Sometimes I also used the fur hairstring, the same kind the *kinaaldá* wears; I'd tie that around her stomach and knead her, push down with that. That brings a fast delivery, too.

Once that happened, the other woman, the baby catcher, went to work. Her job was the baby; I never touched it. My job was the mother. I stayed behind her and started squeezing her stomach to help the afterbirth come out. Sometimes I used a small, flat, round stone for that, pressing down on her stomach with it. You can use the mano for that if no other small, flat stone is available. You have to make sure all the afterbirth comes out; that can kill you if it doesn't so whoever is doing that has to inspect it, check it, to make sure it's all there. Sometimes I used pepper to make the mother sneeze; sneezing expels the rest of it. There are some plants you can use for that, too.

When all that was finished, then I wrapped the mother's stomach up with a wide band. You can use an old sheet, heated up, or another sash belt to bind her with, real tightly. Sometimes the woman would have already gathered cedar [juniper] and have it ready. Then you heat that up, too, and put it under the belt or whatever you're binding her stomach with. Those things help reduce the pain. In earlier times, my mother said that after giving birth, women covered themselves with juniper they had warmed in the fire; they used the heat from that on both their back and their stomach to stop the pain. I always mixed up herbs, too; there were three kinds I usually mixed together for the woman to drink. Those removed blood clots and cleaned out any blood remaining from that. We used the same ones if a woman miscarried, to clean her out from that, too. Of course, we have other ones we can use for labor pains before birth, or for menstrual cramps, ovary problems, or other things women go through.[14] And then, if the People had blue cornmeal already ground, I'd instruct them to make a mush for her from that, so she could regain her strength quickly. After the woman changed into a clean skirt and the other one was discarded, my job was finished.

When I went to do those things for people, I usually traveled alone, on foot or on horseback. But sometimes I took the wagon and somebody with me. Garnett went several times and I think Agnes did too, once or twice when both my mother and I were doing that when Sam's sister was having some of her babies. Children aren't supposed to see childbirth or be exposed to those things, and the same is true if you're pregnant; you shouldn't be helping with that. So, if I took someone along, I always told them to stay outside.[15] If it was nighttime, I told them to go to sleep in the wagon or somewhere, in their blanket, until I got done in the hogan. They just went along for company; I never asked them to assist me in any way. And most of the time, I went alone; Ruth always watched Howard and Augusta and Isabel for me.

One or two times when I did that, Frank went with me. Those were the times he was asked to do the Blessingway when a woman was going to give birth. I know one time was when Chubby Woman was having one of her babies; I usually helped her just like I helped Mary no. 1 because they often had hard labors. When Frank was the singer, he'd be compensated with a sheep, or material, a few dollars, or even a trade slip for use at one of the stores. For a long time you could get a sheep for $5; you could do that with a trade slip if you wanted one to butcher or to rebuild your own flock. Frank never asked for any compensation and I didn't either, when I helped women in that way; I was glad to help them with what I knew. But people always gave me something, too, like a sheep, a blanket, a basket, some material, or food—like corn, melons, squash, or meat they had already butchered. Sometimes they gave me a few dollars or a trade slip. So, at times, I had extra income to use for my children because of that. I might bring back whatever they gave me when I came home, or I might go back later to get it in the wagon.

But even with that, when my joints started to cause trouble for me later in my life, when Augusta was almost finished with junior high, I decided it was time to stop assisting women with their labors.[16] During childbirth, both the one who catches the baby and the woman who stays behind like I did are exposed to blood, and it's hard not to get that on yourself. We believe contact with blood like that is damaging; it causes your bones to swell; it makes them all crooked and it blows up your joints. The only kind of blood that isn't dangerous in that way is the blood from the first two menstrual periods, when a girl becomes a *kinaaldá*. That's why we do the Puberty

Ceremony at those times; the blood isn't dangerous the first two times; it's sacred. But after that, you shouldn't have contact with blood; it's harmful to get it on your hands or other parts of yourself for any reason. It causes your joints to swell, your bones to get out of shape, and it harms you in other ways, too, as you get older. These are among the things we explain to girls when they grow up; we call menstruation *chooyin*; we explain why blood is sacred the first two times, during the first two *chooyin*s, but that after that, you need to keep yourself clean and not get it on yourself.[17]

By helping with childbirths like that, I was in contact with blood lots of times, even though I tried to be very careful about it. When my joints started hurting, I decided it was from that. I didn't ask Frank to get a hand-trembler to find out what was causing it; I just decided it was time to stop. So, even though that was giving me some kind of income, I started telling people I was too old to do it, that my hands were no longer strong enough to do it in the right way. Maybe old age was starting to catch me.* I never showed any of my own daughters how to do it; they never asked. Maybe that was because I was here to help them when they had babies at home. Or maybe it was because some of them had most of their babies at the hospital. Mary no. 1, of course, had all of hers at home, but both Augusta and Ruth only had one of theirs at home. Isabel had two of hers at home; the rest were born in the hospital. That's where Agnes had hers, too. The People were starting to do that; by the time Augusta finished high school, those things were really changing. By then, there were things called pregnancy checkups, before birth. Now people tell me they even have machines to take pictures showing where the baby is. I guess no one knows how to do that with their hands anymore.

Frank's Judge Job and Its Effects

Agnes returns from the war . . . Frank as a judge . . . Isabel gets bear
sickness . . . Howard leaves for a job on the railroad in Wyoming . . .
more weddings and other changes.

When Agnes came back from the war and went to Fort Defiance, she found Frank sleeping in the jail there. I think he was already a judge by then, so maybe he was there because that was a place to spend the night. But, maybe somebody put him there to sleep off something he'd been drinking.[1] Anyway, he and Agnes came back home in a government vehicle. I was very, very happy to see her, and we went ahead, right away, with the Blessingway Ceremony Frank had wanted to do for her earlier. Everyone who was home came to help and to visit with Agnes. Augusta had already started high school in Santa Fe, at St. Catherine's, so she wasn't here at that time. Agnes stayed with us for a while; some of the things she told me about her travels and the experiences she went through while she was a war nurse scared me, but I tried not to say too much about my worries. After some time, she left again; later she wrote to us that she was working in a veterans hospital in California. That's where she ended up; as you know, even now she lives over there with her family.

Because Chee Dodge was sorry to see Frank get left out of the Council when they had the election right after David died, he encouraged him to go on with those things. Maybe it was on account of him that Frank got appointed to be one of the judges when they set up the courts on the reservation; I don't remember how that happened. But when he started that, he was gone from here even more than before. The judges had to travel around, having court in different places on the reservation for weeks at a time. That's how Garnett used to see him in Crownpoint; he'd be over there for court while she was working in the hospital as a nurse. That's where she went when she finished her training. When he was here in Chinle for court, sometimes he'd come home. Then I'd see him, too, because he'd stay here at night and go

261

back in the morning to where they held court.[2] But most of the time, he'd be gone. For weeks and weeks, we wouldn't see him. So I started teasing him about it whenever he'd come back. Right in front of our children, I'd say, "Well, here you are again. I thought maybe you got married again somewhere else and that's why you didn't come back to see us."* That'd make him laugh. That also made the children laugh, when I talked like that with them while he'd be gone for a long, long time.

And even when he was here, there were always people coming to talk to him about their problems, the disputes they were having in the family, things like that. The hogan was always full of people. I tried to stay out of the way, after boiling some coffee for those people, but I stayed up with him.[3] Because of that, I'd hear some of those things and they started worrying me. The more I learned about the kinds of work he was doing as a judge, the more worried I got about him doing that. It's bad to be exposed to those kinds of things, to have to listen to them all the time and go where people are arguing and saying bad things about each other. That can bring harm to you and even to your family, your livestock, and other things. And with that, when you're a judge, you have to make decisions on things. You don't just listen and say nothing. You have to come up with a plan to settle disputes and arguments, and you have to tell it to everyone who is fighting with each other. Of course, when you do that, somebody is not going to be happy with what you've said. And then they get angry at you for that, too, and maybe wish bad thoughts on you, or decide to get back at you in some way, through skinwalkers or other kinds of witchcraft. Those things really frightened me.[4] So, I didn't like it that he was exposed to all those things as a judge. I worried about what that might cause and I hated the fact he was working as a judge. It's true some people were jealous of anyone who had some kind of income from working for the Council, or being qualified to perform ceremonies. And it's true that some of that judge work was like being a headman because those leaders had to hear disputes, too. But being a judge was worse because that's all you did, day after day after day.

Whenever Frank was home for a few days, whatever children were here would always ask him about the things he was doing as a judge. They'd want to hear about the meetings he went to, and that's when I found out that sometimes, when they knew he was having court near where they were going to school, they'd sneak over there, peek in, and listen to what was going on. They heard some things that way, too, and they were curious about them.[5] Right away, I scolded them for that, and told them not to bring it up. But they went ahead and asked him right out about different matters that came before him.

That kind of surprised him. But right away he said he didn't want to talk about it, that doing that was no good. He said those things were nothing good; they were ugly and awful, and not to be discussed with children or other family members. But late at night, after they'd gone to bed, we'd sit up and talk. He'd tell me about all those things because he worried about them, too. Sometimes we'd talk way into the night, almost until dawn. I tried to listen carefully and give him my opinion on things when he asked for it. When he didn't, I just listened.

In the beginning, when he first started that, I told him I was worrying about him doing that job. I came right out and expressed myself about it. But right away, he said he had to do it; he had been appointed to help the People in that way and he knew something about it. He said, "Sure, it's tiresome; people come by at all hours of the night wanting my advice on things. Sometimes I feel like saying the hell with it, especially when I know them and I know that no matter what I say, they aren't going to listen to my words or do anything to correct their troubles. But I can't do that. I was elected to do this; it's my job, and I need the little income that goes with it."

He also told me not to worry because he had his Blessingway to protect himself with, and he believed in it. He said that had already shown its power to him; by means of that he had learned to talk to the People in the right way, so his words made sense and they wanted to listen to them. He said the songs and prayers he used before he went to meetings cleared his mind, removed his fear, and prepared him for any crowds that might gather. Once again he told me he hoped some of his children would learn some of the Blessingway songs, especially the Mountain Songs and the Horse Songs, so they could have those for their own lives, too. He knew I knew many of those songs, even other ones; I always sang along when he was performing here, for someone in the family. But he was still wondering if any of his children were going to learn anything about his ceremony. He knew those songs would help. He reminded me again he hoped they'd do that, and told me to keep encouraging them about it. He used to try and do that by singing his Blessingway songs at night in the hogan when they'd be going to sleep on their sheepskins. He'd sing in a loud voice, probably hoping they were listening and following along in their minds, trying to learn those things. If someone asked him why he was doing that, he'd always say he knew lots of songs by heart, and was keeping them all fresh in his mind by singing them like that. But I knew he was also hoping the children were listening and following along.[6]

Frank also told me he had always respected his ceremony and he'd continue in that way, never abusing it or performing it to get money, instead of to help the People. He knew that by going on in that way he'd be strong. He reminded me of all these things. He also told me if we all kept saying our prayers at dawn and near evening while he was away, we'd be protected, too. Whenever he was home, we always did that together; that was the last thing we did before he left home; each time, I gathered the children together and we all prayed and made offerings. He told me once again to keep doing those things; they'd keep us strong and help him not worry too much about us because he'd know we were in good hands right here at home. He reminded me over and over we both had been raised with the Blessingway and we were using that to raise our own children, too. He had a very strong faith in his ceremony and his *jish*, and he knew the Blessingway would keep all of us strong.

So after that, I never brought up my worries again to him. I stepped aside about it and kept those things to myself. I also made up my mind right there that we'd keep things going in the right way at home for him while he was doing that work, that we'd handle whatever came along so he didn't have to be worrying about us, too. I knew he was counting on me to be strong about everything, so I went ahead that way. Sometimes he'd give me a little money he got from that work to buy things for our children. But it was never very much so I just kept working hard on the farm here, and weaving and taking my rugs over to the stores to sell them. We were counting on those, too.

Since he was rarely home all the years he was a judge, I told the children we needed to be very careful not to upset him with anything when he was here. So that whole time, whenever he was around, I tried very hard to be calm about everything and not even scold the children, no matter what came up. I also paid attention to my own words wherever I went. I made sure I never said anything bad about anybody, either in the family or on the outside, to someone else. I tried to be nice to everyone, never talk about people or make bad remarks about anything.[7] Even if I got upset, I kept it to myself. I didn't want to say or do anything out of line at home or some place else that would upset him, or bring harm to him while he was working in public places with ugly things. And I told the children the same thing, that all of us needed to be very careful not to add to his worries, his troubles through our own words or actions.

Another way I guess that changed me was that I paid more attention to bad dreams or other problems we had here while Frank was gone. Every day, when I called the children so we could make our offerings and say our prayers, I told them to pray for him and for *everybody* in the family, that things would go well for all of us, and that everything would be all right. I reminded them the Blessingway was our source of strength and if we followed it, we'd be protected. Besides that, from then on, if anything happened around here, I never let it go. I always did something about it. If an owl came near, or somebody saw a coyote running in front of them, or had a bad dream, I got worried and started thinking something bad was going to happen to us. One thing I did was use herbs to keep bad things away, like the *nábįįh* I've already mentioned that smells like mountain tobacco, and others, like herbs from lightning-struck places, sage, pinyon, juniper, and others we mix together to protect ourselves. I kept those around, and some of those I spread around the outside of the hogan and the ramada when bad things happened. And when the children had nightmares or other kinds of bad dreams, I'd mix herbs from lightning-struck places with water and have them drink it and wash themselves and their hair with it, too, before going back to sleep. When Frank came home again, I'd tell him about it right away. Then he'd do something; he usually knew the right prayers and songs to use to correct those things so we'd gather the children together and he'd do that for all of us.[8] But if I knew he wouldn't be back for a long time, then, when anything like that happened, I made the children do extra offerings and say extra prayers to remove the effects of that until he came home. I never stepped ahead of him and went and got a singer for our own use when he wasn't here. Of course, if it affected me, if I was the one who had a bad dream, then when he came home, he had to get somebody else to do a small ceremony; that's because he couldn't do his own ceremony for his wife.

I think working as a judge changed Frank, too, in some ways. He had to travel even more than earlier, when he was on the Council or working with the priests, or just doing his ceremony and talking to the People as a headman. He was more tired whenever he came home for a few days, and he was more worried. One thing that was different was our long talks, way into the night, about the troubles being brought before him. I guess he knew I wasn't going to mention those to anyone, not even the children, that he could count on me to not gossip about what he said. He also started adding some things into his own talks to our children; sometimes he'd tell them that when they became young adults, he didn't want them abusing people, beating anyone they were making a living with, arguing with their in-laws, squabbling over land, being jealous of others, or doing things like that. I guess in that way he was trying to tell them something about the disputes that came before him as a judge, without really talking about anything specific. I know some of the children asked me why he was saying those things to them. But the older ones never said a word; they probably figured it out.

There was one time Frank did tell the children something about a dispute. He really had to because he was brought back sick from listening to it. He came back with a policeman who said he was really worried about him because of the bad thing that had happened where they went. He told us we needed to do something for Frank right away. And after Frank talked with us about it, we ended up having a ceremony for him to correct the effects of that.

One time, in the summer, there was a big land dispute going on down in the Canyon. Frank and a policeman had to go down there on horseback to meet with the family, and they stayed overnight because they didn't get it straightened out the first day. When he came back, he was really in pain. When we asked him about why he was in that condition, he told us what happened. He said when they got there, they put their horses in the fence and started the meeting about the troubles. Because they made no progress the first day, he and the policeman agreed to stay overnight and talk some more with the family in the morning. They went to sleep outside in the ramada and the people were in the hogan. Sometime after midnight, Frank said he woke up because he heard the hogan door open. Then he saw someone covered with a blanket come out and start walking toward some bushes where there was an old road. He said to him, the figure looked like a woman with all her hair down. So he stayed awake for a long time, to see if it returned, and it never did. That worried him, why that person hadn't come back. But finally he went back to sleep.

When he woke up again, early in the morning, he had a real bad toothache. So right away, he got up, and asked the policeman if he had heard anything or seen anything. He said no, so while they were eating breakfast with those people, Frank asked them, "Did any of you go out during the night?" Everyone said, "No." Then he told them what he'd heard and seen; he told them about the figure going by, back into the bushes over there. The woman there said she didn't like it at all; she said there was a place up there where there was a pile of wood that might have been a grave or a place where a body was taken out of a hogan. So they all walked over to where Frank had seen the person going. But there were no tracks there, even though the ground around there was very sandy. That's when they knew it wasn't a live person he'd seen. So those people went and got a hand-trembler. Right away that man said there was a grave there. He told Frank what he'd seen wasn't good. Of course, Frank already knew that; that's why he'd stayed awake, waiting for that person to come back. He said he also listened for the dogs around there to bark at that figure, but they didn't. That, too, told him it wasn't good. And then, when he woke up with a bad toothache, he knew.

When he was telling us what had happened, he also told his children again that because of things like this, he didn't want to talk about any of those troubles with them. All the things he had to listen to and decide about concerned people arguing, saying bad things about each other. Sometimes they were even talking about dead people and their land, too. Frank told us, "Here, I'm just doing my job; I'm an innocent bystander, and now look how I've been harmed by this. It's not good. That's why I'm not going to talk with you children about any of these things. I don't want you to get harmed because of it; these are not good things."

After he finished talking with us, we hurried and got a singer to come and do an Evilway Blackening Ceremony for him and a prayer. After that, his toothache went away. From then on, the children didn't ask him about those things anymore.

As the years went on and Frank kept working as a judge, it seemed to me the troubles he had to listen to got worse. Sometimes, when he'd be here for a few days and he'd tell me about the most recent ones, I didn't even know what to say when he'd finish and ask for my ideas about it. Even though I knew he wanted me to answer, I didn't always know what to say. I continued to worry that he was exposed to things like that where people were always angry, no matter what he decided. He tried to work things out so they compromised, reached an agreement or consensus on things, before they left, but usually someone was still upset. That was especially true when it concerned land or livestock permits.

One time when Frank really needed my opinion on something, I didn't know what to suggest. Then he said maybe I didn't know about those things because I never got out and traveled around and learned about them. He said maybe I didn't have the kind of mind to figure those things out. He didn't mean to say I had no mind at all. He said I had a really good mind for remembering the weaving designs, how to fix traditional and ceremonial foods, plant medicines, and all those things, for remembering those without having them written down and without having gone to school. He said I was really good at keeping those things straight and remembering how to do all of them so they came out right. But he said I didn't travel around and talk to lots of different people. He said I'd never learned how to get up and make a speech at meetings or in front of all the People in crowds. He said that's the way you really had to educate yourself if you were going to understand the problems people had now, and the quarrels they were getting into with one another. He told me I'd get more education from that than from just being at home with the children, the farm, and the sheep all the time. And he also told me, right there, that I'd probably have a poor memory when I got into my old age because the things I knew best concerned right around here, my family, the weaving designs, the different ways to fix traditional foods, and things like that.

From then on, even though he still talked with me and asked for my opinions about disputes he had to resolve, whenever I couldn't give him some advice, he always teased me and said some of those things again. And now, I think maybe he was right. He always remembered things; right up until the end, his memory was sharp, as you know. But with me, it's different. I seem to be forgetting things now, and getting more and more confused. That never happened to him. Maybe that was the one good thing that came out of all those years he was a judge and got exposed to all those ugly things. I don't know.*

After Isabel got cured from TB and had her Shootingway Ceremony, for a while she felt better. Then one day, she told me she was going to have a baby. I got after her at first because I didn't know she'd been seeing anybody. I guess when she went with different ones to water Frank's horses over by the Island Place in the Chinle Wash, she learned who lived around there and met a boy she got together with and had a baby for. She was very young and I was upset about that. But Frank said the baby was her responsibility now, and there was no sense in scolding her anymore. So I never said anything more about it and I never asked her brothers or sisters what they knew about it, either.

A short time after Isabel had her baby, maybe a month or two later, she got sick again, and this time she started acting almost crazy. It was in the spring; Howard had come back from California, where he'd been working, to help us with the planting.[9] Isabel got like that while he was here so he never went back over there. He stayed here trying to help me with her because Ruth was busy with her family, Augusta was at St.

Catherine's, and Frank was gone, working as a judge. When Isabel started thrashing around, the two of us couldn't hold her down. So Howard went and got Acey to help him. Pretty soon they were doing that almost all the time. By then she was muttering things about bears. I was very worried about her so I sent word to Frank, with someone who was headed to wherever he was holding court at the time. He came back as soon as he could and right away, went and got a hand-trembler. But the first one didn't seem to know what was causing it, so he got some more. They were the same way. We started trying small ceremonies for her, following whatever they suggested, but she just kept getting worse. Right about then, I found something that later helped us know what to do for her.

I guess one time when Isabel was herding sheep she was looking around and she found a carved bear. Those are made from the root of a plant or a tree; if somebody is sick from bears, the singer makes that and tells the person to take it somewhere in the mountains, and make an offering with it. It was one of those that she had found and of course, she didn't know what it was. She never should have touched it but I guess she thought it was a toy. So she picked it up, even though it had been offered back for someone and put under a bush. It was all covered with turquoise when they made it and some of that was still on it. Here, she put it in her jacket pocket and kept it, hiding it from the rest of us. I didn't know she had that for a long time. The only thing I had already noticed was she was sleeping with her jacket rolled up as a pillow on her sheepskin.

As she kept getting worse, she said more and more things about bears bothering her. One night it was as if she was almost completely out of her mind. So even though it was late, Frank took a fast horse and went over and begged Philemon to come and do the hand-trembling for her. He had already quit doing that because he said it made him sick, it made his arm and his side so painful he didn't want to do it anymore. But she was so bad that Frank really begged him. We had already had almost everybody else come and do that, and we were ready to give up. None of the ceremonies we had done for her on the basis of what the others had said had helped at all and we were frightened. I guess losing David came back again to both of our minds, even though neither of us brought that up.

Philemon finally agreed so he came back with Frank. As soon as he started that, he saw that her condition was from the bears and he told us we needed to do a Mountainway Ceremony for her right away before we lost her. When he said that, I remembered what I'd found about two weeks before that. One time I told her to go do something and she left without her jacket. It was still on the sheepskin so when I was sweeping in the morning, and taking the sheepskins and blankets outside to clean the hogan after she had left, I picked up her jacket. That thing fell out of the pocket and when I saw it, I knew right away what it was. When she came back, I asked her where she'd gotten it and she told me she found it. When she looked at it again, it had split right in half. So, I took her back over to where she found it and we returned it, offered it back.

I thought that had taken care of it, but I guess it was already too late. I didn't even think about it anymore until Philemon said that, after he finished doing the hand-trembling that night. Right there, I remembered it. So I made her tell him she'd found a carving of a bear, and had kept it in her pocket all that time, taking it with her and playing with it. How long she had that before she got sick we don't know. That's why we went ahead and had that Mountainway for her. That's a big ceremony and it was a lot of expense to do it, but we went ahead and did it for her anyway, as soon as possible. We got Gray Water from near Spider Rock for that; he had a bear paw in his *jish*, and he knew how to make the right medicines and what to do with them and that paw while he was doing the ceremony for her. Very few people who sang that at that time had a bear paw in their *jish*, or even knew anything about using it in the right ways. So he was highly respected for those things; that's why we hired him to be the one to sing over Isabel. After that ceremony was over, her mind came back.[10]

A short time after Isabel had that ceremony, Frank lost his oldest brother, Jim, the one who was also called Tall Water Flows Together Man. By this time, Frank had already lost a younger brother, Tom. This one, Jim, was Chubby Woman's father but he passed away after she did. He was still living over in the Black Mountain area, near Red Rock Mesa, when he got sick from something. Frank heard about his sickness in the winter and went over there to help with things. It was in the late spring or early summer when Jim passed away. When that happened, Frank helped his children get the priests here in Chinle to bury him.[11]

The next spring Augusta finished high school in Santa Fe and came back to Chinle and started working. Isabel's baby was here with us, and was already walking around by then, and Howard had already left again for another job. I think that's when he went to Wyoming to work for the railroad and didn't come back for a long time.

After Augusta had been working for a while, she got married to Cecil Sandoval. They got a state license for that. And right about the same time, Mary no. 1 came over to tell Frank and me we had just become *great-grandparents*! Her daughter, Louise, had just had her first baby to survive, a girl they named Ramona. And around that time, too, Garnett told us she was getting married to Ned Bernally in Chicago, where they were both working. She had known him for quite some time and she said after a while, they were going to head back this way. I think it was several years later, after their first child was born there in Chicago, they came back. Eventually, they settled in Shiprock, as you know. With all these things happening, by then, out of our children it was only Agnes and Howard who weren't married or having babies for someone. Sure enough, pretty soon Agnes told us she'd met a man named Tony Sanchez there in

California and they were getting married by a priest out there. Here, I'd been teasing her about getting old without a husband, so that was the end of that.*12

Here at home, other things were changing, too. Leo left Ruth and the seven children she already had for him. When that happened, of course Ruth stayed right here. I started trying to help her all I could, so she could face the hardships that brought her. I really got busy helping raise all those grandchildren! Augusta and Cecil were the same way; even though they started having their own children, they tried to help her in different ways, too, during those years. Eventually Ruth got married again, to a man named Wilson Yazzie and had two children for him. But that was later. By the time I started helping with her children, those grandchildren of ours, I knew old age was here, at least for myself.

five

Old Age

Old Age Catches Us and We Lose Frank

Frank comes back and starts working with outsiders . . . ceremonies . . .
my wrist gets broken . . . starting to tell our stories . . . Frank gets sick . . .
his last wishes . . . we lose Frank . . . more ceremonies . . . I go back to
Houses Standing in a Line . . . changes . . . my thoughts about the rest
of my story.

When Frank finished being a judge, he came back home. But first, he tried to get back on the Tribal Council. That's when he had that picture taken for the ballots that we have around here;[1] they had started using pictures of the ones who wanted to be elected so the People could remember them when they went to vote.* But he didn't get selected, so that was the end of Window Rock for him.* That was when he really started living with us again, all the time. But by then, both of us were already up in our years. We knew we were in old age; that just creeps up on you when you're not looking.*

For my part, I was happy Frank was back for good. I think he felt that way, too; we missed each other a lot so it was nice to be here together every day again, talking, joking and teasing each other, doing things, and going places. Of course, we always shook hands and hugged each other whenever he'd come back from being gone for a long time. That's what the People do; we don't kiss and carry on in front of others like white people. After Frank came back, of course sometimes he'd still go places. But now, it was mainly to do his ceremony or to go to meetings here in Chinle. He started helping with the Chapter and got put in as President of that, too, for a while, after he came back.

Soon after he returned and we went back to making a living together, John, his older brother, got sick. Years before, we had gone through the Shootingway Frank sponsored for him because of his TB. But now, it was different. Of course, John was up in his years, like us. And at that time, it seemed like he was alone. Maybe because he had been so stingy for so long, nobody seemed to worry about him, or try to help him out. Frank was concerned about that so he started going down the road a lot to check on him. John was living in his log cabin that's still right there; later, that and his land went to one of his daughters who married Charlie Claw.

John started complaining about his stomach. When he finally went to the hospital, the doctors told him he had cancer and they wanted to operate on him. That scared all his children; they didn't want to stay with him at the Fort Defiance Hospital while he went through that. So Frank told Augusta to write to Howard and ask him to come back from Wyoming to help with his uncle. When Howard returned, John was already in the hospital. Isabel and Howard went over there to take turns staying with him at night, and Seya, who had come back from Bellemont for a short visit, went there, too. He and his brother went right into the operating room, too, while those doctors worked on John.* They sure made us laugh when they came back and told us how one of the nurses had fainted during the surgery.* Through that, they found it was just his intestine; that was all twisted and he didn't have cancer at all. So they fixed that, and he came home. Augusta was there at the hospital having her first baby while John was there. So she visited him, too, until they let her come back with her baby, Cecilia.[2] That's where she saw Howard for the first time in many years. She said he really surprised her; when he left, he looked like a skinny, bean pole to her and now, he was big and tall, not a bean pole at all; he looked like Frank. So we teased him about that.*

From there, we went along. Frank took over the farmwork but after a while, he said maybe we should cut back on it. So we did, after he got rid of some of his horses. I was still weaving all the time and trying to help with my grandchildren around here. Now it was mainly my grandchildren I was worrying about, instead of young children of my own.* Mary no. 1 was still living nearby, like before; Ruth was living right here with all her children, and Isabel and her baby were here, too. Eventually, both of them had more children; Ruth got together with Wilson Yazzie and had two children for him, and Isabel had some more children, too. Augusta and Cecil also had more children.[3] So that's how we were going along.

When Howard finally came back for good from working in Wyoming on the railroad, he was suffering from some kind of sickness. After we got a hand-trembler for him, it was discovered that contact with lightning-struck things was causing it and he needed a Shootingway. We got Mary no. 1's husband, Woody, to do that five-night ceremony for him. We did the same thing for Seya, too, several years later. He finally quit working over in Bellemont and moved back to Cottonwood with his family. He used to come and see us many times and bring his children, too. That's how we knew he needed to have that ceremony done; he had been exposed to lightning-struck wood like Howard, and was suffering from the effects of it. So we went ahead and stood the expense of that again. Those Shootingways cured whatever was ailing them, so we didn't mind doing that. They are our children.

On Frank's side, another relative passed away. A nephew of his, the son of his younger brother Tom, a man who was also named Tom, got killed in a vehicle accident.[4] That man was married to Bartine and they had lots of children, so she faced many hardships after that happened.

After Frank finished serving as a judge, you white people started coming around. Before you, yourself, came here, he was working with others, already doing things like that. But most of them came to ask him about other things, not his ceremony. I know he helped a woman, Mary Shepardson, who was trying to learn about politics, and the judges and courts on the reservation. And he worked with another Anglo I remember, Clifford Barnett; Chic [Sandoval] used to bring him here to talk about how Anglo doctors and medicine people could work together better. That probably happened because Frank helped with some of the things connected with the project some college ran in Many Farms for a while.[5] And then, there were other Anglos, too.[6] In those years, he met your teacher, and made the Blessingway film. Frank sang that for Isabel because she needed it done; that was right before she had her baby, Joseph.[7] I remember Frank was very happy his ceremony could be recorded in that way. For a while, at different times, one or two would come and talk to him about learning Blessingway. There was one in particular who started trying to do that in a serious way; he'd travel with Frank to help out and Frank said he was really starting to learn the songs and prayers. But eventually that came to an end; that man quit. I think he got converted by one of the revivalists who had started going around all over the reservation.*

After Frank had started working with white people and after Isabel had her baby, Joseph, Long Moustache passed away. I remember that happened in the winter; we had known Long Moustache and had been close friends with all of them for many, many years, even back when my father was alive and they moved around with us. He was very, very old when he passed away in Black Mountain.[8]

Shortly after he passed away, I started having other troubles. That's what happens when you get into your old age.* Even though I was eating and cooking lots of things for Frank and others, I started losing weight. And then too, when I'd get up from my loom or from the grinding stones, I'd feel like I was going to black out. I kept getting very dizzy. So, after those things had been going on for a while, I mentioned them to Frank and my children because they started to worry me. They could see I was losing weight and they were asking me about it, but they didn't know I felt like I was going to faint lots of times. Of course, I was always having troubles from my aching joints and from something in my stomach, maybe indigestion, but this was different. This just came upon me and I started getting like that. So Augusta, even though she was working, decided to take leave and take me to the Ganado Hospital. And there, they discovered it was thyroid. Those doctors said sometimes they did surgery for that, but because I was up in my years, they didn't think it was a good idea. So they wanted to try to fix it with medication. That's what they did; the medicine stabilized those things and finally, they settled down.[9] I had to go back and forth for them to check on the medicine. And because I was having other problems, they did some other tests on me while they were checking on my thyroid. Because of that, they discovered I had gallbladder trouble, too. But we didn't get that news until after you went back in the fall, after you'd been here for the first time.

Right after I came back from the hospital with my thyroid medicine, that same spring, Frank was asked to dedicate the new Chapter House when it was ready for use by the community. They built that when they were building the new Public School[10] and all the houses for the employees; there was lots of building going on in Chinle at that time. I know we went over to the new Chapter House in the wagon for that ceremony; I don't think Howard was here at the time; I think he had left again, to work for a different railroad. But after a while, he came back because his feet got broken over there.[11]

Of course, once Frank stopped being a judge, all the things he'd done for that began affecting him. He started suffering from different pains and wondering what was causing them; sometimes he'd say maybe his work for the Tribe or the films he'd been in, or jealousies were causing it.[12] I didn't know what to think because he'd done so many, many things, a lot of which might bring harm. So, he started getting hand-tremblers. On their advice, one of the ceremonies we did for him after he stopped working as a judge was a nine-night Male Shootingway. That's a big ceremony with lots of sandpaintings, but lots of people came to help us with food and other things. We had Gray Man from Valley Store do that for Frank. I remember it was in the fall, probably about a year before your teacher came here for the first time. Ruth's son, Frankie, was still a boy, maybe nine or ten at the time, and he sat behind the curtain, helping move the snakes around like they do when they perform that with the Sun's house screen. That ceremony also uses one Ye'ii, the Humpbacked one, and a little bear. I remember Charlie Davis was the little bear, but we had to let the Ye'ii part go. At that time, no one could locate the mask and other things needed for that part.

Frank got some results from that Shootingway; it helped cure his suffering for a while. But later, he started feeling sick again so he got some more hand-tremblers. Eventually, one of them said all the things he'd done in earlier years with burying dead people and working on Anasazi things were now affecting him, and he needed an Enemyway. So we did that, too; Augusta's daughter, "Tiny," wasn't quite a year old at the time, and Frank had just dedicated the new Chapter House here in Chinle right before we did that. On the second day of his ceremony, Rose Mitchell was added in as a co-patient because she was very sick at the time. She's married to David Mitchell, one of the sons of Bill and Rachel. *Lots* of people came to help us with Frank's Enemyway, and Frank said the ceremony helped; the things troubling him stopped, after it was over. Of course, right after you have one of those, people can ask you to receive the stick for other Enemyways. Frank was asked to do that, too, and so we went through three more of them because he received the stick three times.[13]

It wasn't too long after Frank's Enemyway that his older brother, John, got sick again. This time he died. There was a big dispute over his property, maybe because he'd always been stingy. Frank had to go to all the meetings about it and once again, the way people were arguing with each other upset him. For a while, he talked and talked about it with me at night, worrying about it. But finally, those squabbles came to an end.[14]

Around here, shortly after John passed away, Augusta had another baby. I remember that because she was pregnant in the summer, during Frank's Enemyway. Augusta had already had some other children for Cecil, but all of them were born in the hospital. The year before Frank's Enemyway, in the summer, she and Cecil had helped build a house for her, here with us. That's when Augusta had the baby we call "Tiny." But the next year, after John died, later that fall, she and Cecil and their children moved up by the mission to be closer to their jobs. They had a small place behind there where they were staying and for a while, Howard stayed over there with them, too.

When it was almost time for Augusta to have her next baby, of course we had a Blessingway for her. But with this one, she went into labor right after Frank had started doing the ceremony, so she ended up having a hogan baby.* That was her son Augustine, the one we call "Eesert." Even though I had stopped helping women with those things, I was there in the hogan to help her, as I've already mentioned.[15] I think he was the last baby born here, at least up to now.*

There were other ceremonies going on around here, too. I think that's when Isabel had a Shootingway, to correct the effects of burning up those prayersticks with Ruth by accident years earlier. That finally started troubling her and causing her to be sick so we had that done for her by Bead Man's Son, who had done it for Ruth. She also had an Evilway, Ghostway, to remove the effects of handling a miscarriage Mary no. 1's daughter, Louise, had around that time. That was before Frank was asked to do another public blessing, the dedication of the new Chinle Boarding School when it was ready for use.[16]

As for myself, I think about this time it was decided I needed a Mountainway to cure some things troubling me. Frank asked Tall Man's Son to sing it so he came and did that for me. That was a five-night ceremony and it was the second time I had a Mountainway. After we waited a week, Tall Man's Son came back and finished it with the one-night ceremony we use with that.[17] I don't think Howard was around during these things; he left again after Frank's Enemyway to work somewhere else.[18] Because he kept finding different ways to make an income, sometimes he'd be around and sometimes he'd be gone. And whenever he came back, he'd stay with Augusta and her family at the mission; Seya's son, Butch, was doing that, too, while he was going to high school. Sometimes, he and Howard went rabbit hunting to contribute to the food they were eating over there.

Last year, about a year before you came here the first time, I had an accident. Isabel and her baby, Joseph, the one we call "Mann," and I had gone to Garcia's in the wagon to fill the water barrels and get some things. She'd gone into the store and I was standing up in the back of the wagon, doing something. I don't know what happened but all of a sudden, there was a loud bang, like a shotgun noise, from the highway. That frightened our horses and they ran off with the wagon. I lost my balance because of that and got thrown out of the wagon. I guess when I hit the ground, I cut my head and landed on my right wrist, breaking it. Somebody outside the store saw that and right away got someone to take me to the clinic and some other person to catch our runaway team. Pretty soon Howard heard about it; maybe he was in the store then, getting supplies for where his crew was working on a dam in the Canyon.[19] Right away, he went over to the mission to tell Augusta I was at the clinic. They set my wrist there, but I guess they didn't do it right because in another week, it was all swollen. So Augusta took me to the Ganado Hospital; they kept me there for a week while they re-broke it and set it again.[20] When I got home from there, Frank had Jacob Azye come and do a Flintway Ceremony for me and also a one-night one. I still haven't had the other part I need to finish it up but now, my wrist is fine; all that's left is a scar. I remember when I came back from Ganado, Chic Sandoval was here with that Anglo, Clifford Barnett, working with Frank. That man sure wanted to know what had happened to my wrist.* And, I think that was about the time Dr. George from California came here for the first time, to visit around and take pictures [see Fig. 32].[21] I *know* that same year I got thrown from the wagon was when old man Garcia and his son, Abel, got killed in a plane crash. I remember that happened to them in the fall, after I broke my wrist in the spring.[22]

Right before you came, probably just a few weeks before, Seya came back from California. He had gone over there to help Agnes and Tony with some repairs on their rental properties, but instead, he got gallbladder trouble and ended up having surgery. He got discharged in time for the Chinle rodeo but right away, when he got back, he was thrown from a horse he was racing, and broke some ribs. That same day, Frank got thrown, too, by a horse he was riding over near the cornfields. Somebody saw that and brought him home in a wagon on the very same day that happened to Seya. But, after he rested from his injury, Frank said he wasn't troubled by it; nothing was broken.

Of course when you came the first time, your teacher, the same one who had made the film of Frank's Blessingway, came too, but only for a short visit. That's when you were working on *Kinaaldá*, trying to learn about that, and that's when those people from California were filming a Red Antway Ceremony at Valley Store. Of course, they heard we were going to have a *Kinaaldá* here for Ruth's daughter, Marie, so they

FIG. 32. Tall Woman, 1962. Photographer, Dr. George McClelland, Sr. Courtesy of Augusta Sandoval.

came here, too, to make a movie of Frank doing a *Kinaaldá* [see Figs. 33, 34]. I remember all those things; that Old Man with the Cane was with them, always saying this and that about things,* and they're the ones who brought electricity to us.[23] That's when you started working with us, just like the other, earlier white people. And that's when you and I started talking about my stories, too, after I thought about it for a while.

I knew Frank was doing that with you; sometimes, when you were recording with him, I'd come in where you were working and sit, listening to what he was saying, and watching how you were doing that. And then later, we'd sit outside and talk; sometimes I'd tease him about the things he was telling you and we'd joke and laugh

FIG. 33 *(top)*. Preparing *'alkaan* batter in the hogan during Marie Shirley's *Kinaaldá*, June 22, 1963. Left, Marie; right, Tall Woman. Photographer, Charlotte J. Frisbie.

FIG. 34 *(bottom)*. Tall Woman starting to dig the pit for Marie Shirley's *'alkaan*, June 22, 1963. Photographer, Charlotte J. Frisbie.

together about earlier times. Of course, sometimes I'd scold him too, for the things he'd done in his younger days. When I did that, he'd laugh, say I was always scolding him, and he'd tease me, calling me "Mitchell Girl" and saying I was his mother-in-law.* That's the way we were; we were always laughing and joking with each other, and teasing each other about something. We also used to talk about those things at night, when he started recording his story for you. Finally, I told him you'd asked me to do the same thing, if I was interested. Right away, he encouraged me on that; he said it'd be a good idea to leave those things for our grandchildren. That way, even the ones who were born later, who would never know us, could learn what we'd gone through, even way, way back. So, after he said that, I told you I'd do it; I remember that, too.*

Of course, here in the family, my children know some of these things already. But the grandchildren and others didn't. I decided to talk about what I could remember so people could learn how things were, and how things changed as we went along. And like Frank, I was in agreement with having my words printed in a book, so whoever wanted to read them could. Of course, my story is different than his; I never talked to the People or traveled to different places for the Council or as a judge or to perform a ceremony. And I don't have too many funny things to tell, nothing like his story about the St. Michaels Woman.*[24] But still, I decided to do it. I remember telling my sister and my half sister I was doing that with you; I tried to encourage them to do it, too, but they just laughed and said their minds were so confused they'd have nothing to say.* But that wasn't true; whenever we got together, they remembered things clearly, even from our childhoods; we used to laugh and joke about lots of things we remembered whenever we visited each other, even after Frank passed away.

In the fall, when you went away the first time, we moved the electricity. I didn't want it in the hogan where those California people left it after making that movie, so we changed it. Frank said it was time to get his *jish* renewed, so we sponsored that for him, after the electricity got moved. And Howard left again; usually he found work for part of the year in other places. I know he was a firefighter in some forests for a while, but maybe that was earlier. After the *Kinaaldá* movie was made here, he left again in the late fall. I think from then until Frank got really sick, in the wintertime, he worked around Yuma.[25]

Even though both Frank and I were getting up in our years, we kept on the way we always did. We were in old age, but it wasn't getting us down [see Fig. 35]. Even though we both had white hair, we still had our eyesight and our ears and noses worked, too.* We weren't in *really old age* yet.*[26] And even though my joints really hurt, I was still getting around by myself. Years before, the doctors told me that was some kind of arthritis; lots of people suffer from that and sometimes, they get so crippled they can't move. I didn't want that to happen to me; I told my children I didn't want my gears getting frozen in place,* so I was going to keep herding sheep, weaving,

FIG. 35. Tall Woman and Frank Mitchell, seated on a bench outside their hogan, June 1963. Photographer, Charlotte J. Frisbie.

and doing all those things. Frank was the same way, too; he was still riding his horse, going places, and doing his ceremony when people asked him to help them. We still were traveling places in the wagon and I was still weaving when I wasn't busy doing other things [see Figs. 36–40]. Of course, I spent more and more time with my grandchildren, helping raise them right around here where they were living. That's the way we do things; grandmothers always help with that. I think grandmothers end up worrying more about their grandchildren than mothers do about their children;* I certainly did and that was true with everyone else I knew, too. That's probably a grandmother's job.*

Frank was still respected as a leader; even though some people had criticized him at a Chapter meeting for letting those California people make the *Kinaaldá* film, he wasn't bothered by it. He said that was from jealousy and not to worry about it; they'd probably come begging for his ceremony in the future even though they had said those things.*[27] And sure enough, when the new high school was finished here in Chinle, the officials asked him to dedicate that and he agreed. His granddaughter, Geneva, helped him, and we all went over there.[28] Augusta was head cook at that school by then.

FIG. 36. Tall Woman reroofing the cookshack, July 1963. Hogan in background. Photographer, Charlotte J. Frisbie.

FIG. 37 Tall Woman taking care of her grandson, Jerry, outside Isabel's house, June 1964. Photographer, Charlotte J. Frisbie.

FIG. 38. Tall Woman cooking an evening meal outside, August 1964. Left to right: Tall Woman, Isabel, and Isabel's son, Joseph ("Mann"). Sheepskins and goatskins airing on pole rack. Hogan in background. Photographer, Charlotte J. Frisbie.

FIG. 39. Tall Woman and various family members hauling sheep and goats by horse and wagon in the mud, June 1964. Left to right: "Frankie," Isabel, Tall Woman, Ruth, Lena, Elta, and "Bunni." Photographer, Charlotte J. Frisbie.

FIG. 40. Tall Woman ready to go to Garcia's Trading Post, July 1964. Ruth's log cabin and the Mitchells' barn in background. Photographer, Charlotte J. Frisbie.

Before we went there, Frank gave me the beautiful, old, squash blossom necklace that I now have; I wore it there for the first time. That really touched me; he didn't do things like that very often because he was always giving whatever he got from performing his ceremony to his children, to use in raising their own children. He loved all his grandchildren, too, and was always concerned about them, and trying to help out with raising them. We were both that way. I guess he must have put some things aside so he could acquire that necklace for me. I was really surprised when he did that; it made me cry.

But that same year was probably when we both started slowing down; maybe *really old age* was catching up with us by then.* It seemed like that was starting to get to us; there were some things we didn't seem to have the strength to do anymore. That's the way old age is; all of a sudden, it catches you. Frank was having pains again so we started doing small ceremonies for him. Finally he went to the Ganado Hospital and they took a piece of tissue out of him and sent it away, so it could be studied.

And at that same time, my own stomach troubles increased. My pains from that got really bad and so I, too, went over to that hospital. They said I needed gallbladder surgery. At first, I said no; I didn't want to go through that. Of course, I had already heard about it; Augusta had that done while she was pregnant, probably with "Bunni," and Seya, too, had that done, over in California.* With me, the doctors said it was risky; because of my age, I might not survive the surgery. So I came back and we talked about it here at home. Finally, Frank said to go ahead with it since it would kill me anyway. We had a one-night prayer to protect me, so that everything would be all right, before somebody took me back over there.

Augusta stayed there with me and she ended up seeing the thing they took out of me. The doctor wanted to show it to me, too, but I refused. He brought that thing to my room and asked me if I wanted to see it. But right there, I said *No*, and I told him to throw that thing out and let me go home! But Augusta looked at it; she told me it was huge, like a lemon. That's what had been troubling me all those years. I guess it was growing and growing, and finally got so big I could hardly stand the pain from it. I guess I was over there for about a month recovering from that. When I came home, I felt better; those pains I'd been having all those years, the ones I thought were from indigestion, were probably from that thing in my gallbladder the whole time. I hope I don't have any more surgeries; even though someone from the family always tries to stay with me whenever I go to the hospital, I don't like those places.[29]

Frank slowed down with performing his ceremony as you know, several years after you started coming here. I remember he did a Blessingway for Geneva in the summer and then in the fall, the traditional wedding for Lynn, Ruth's daughter who married Franklin Tah, after they came back from the Catholic Church.[30] After that, he did a few more Blessingways, but then he said he didn't have the strength to do it much longer.[31] When that tissue came back, they told us he had prostate cancer and it was going to kill him in the future. At first, he wasn't convinced that was causing his troubles, so we started doing ceremonies for him. I know in the fall, he had a one-night Beautyway, to finish the one he had a long time ago for himself, and then later, he had a one-night Evilway, Ghostway. When Agnes came to visit around Christmas, she wanted Frank and me to get baptized by the priest. Frank said he'd probably had that done earlier, way back when he was a school boy at Fort Defiance and had to go to religious instructions. But he agreed to it and so I said I'd go along with it, too. Agnes sponsored that for us; a few days after Christmas, Father Cormac came down here and did that for us.[32]

After Agnes went back to California, Frank started going downhill. Until then, we were still continuing with things; he was riding his horse, going places, and doing his ceremonies. He was like that for probably another year, even though he was slowing down. But then, the pains started getting worse. He went to see the doctors more and more at the Ganado Hospital. Sometimes, even the medicines they were giving him made him sick. And when he came back, we'd get hand-tremblers and do whatever small ceremonies they recommended. Even the priests were trying to help us; Father Bryant would come down and say mass for us, putting a saddle blanket I'd made over a table to make an altar.

You were here in those days so I'm not going to say much about them; it still makes me sad and it's hard for me to think about it and talk about it. I know you put something about his last days in his book, so I'm not going to say too much about those things.[33]

Finally, Frank got so sick he called his children together to give them his last instructions about things. He told them he wasn't going to recover, and he wanted to talk about the future of our land, our livestock, and his medicine bundle. He wanted the *jish* to stay in the family, to be kept by the Towering House People in all its future days, and he told them that. He also talked to them about many other things, like staying together, taking care of me,[34] and helping each other without squabbling over things. And he also explained his wishes about how to fix him up, when the time came for him to pass away. That's when he told them he was giving me one of the two strings of turquoise he'd had for a long time. Those were his beads; they were old with lots of big chunks of turquoise and then two shorter *jaatł'óół*, the earring pieces, hanging from there.[35] He got them from a Santo Domingo Indian he traded with, years ago, and always wore them when he did his ceremony. He told his children he wanted to take one string with him; the other one he was giving to me, to use however I wanted.

I didn't sit in there with him when he did that; he was staying in the cabin we had built years before beside Isabel's house, near the hogan, and when he talked with his children like that, they went over there, where he was lying down. Of course, he and I talked, too. For a while, I didn't believe what he was saying about not recovering; I told him to be quiet about those things, not to talk like that because that would bring it on him, that would be wishing for it. But he said, "No, I'm near the end. We need to discuss it because I'm going downhill; I know I won't recover now." So we talked.

He told me he knew I'd be lonely without him but I should remember to be strong, and to go on. He even tried teasing me, saying because I'd always been a strong woman, here I was even going to outlive him. I guess he was trying to get me to laugh about things, but I didn't. He also said I was to have his *jish*; he reminded me to see that it got cleansed and renewed, and then transferred to me after he was gone and we had settled other things. He reminded me again that his ceremony would see me through, the Blessingway would be my support; it would continue to help me face whatever hardships came along, just like it had all the years we were together. He also told me our children had promised to take care of me in my old age. He said he knew they'd keep their word about it so I shouldn't worry about being lonely or hungry, or needing help with anything. He said all those things to me right there. And then too, he said lots of other things, apologizing for different sufferings he'd caused for me during our years together, especially by his gambling, drinking, and running around. He said he wished he'd never done things like that to increase my hardships.

For a while, while he talked about those things, I was crying. But then, he told me not to do that right then or after he passed away, either. He said he'd already told all the children not to cry after he was gone or people would think his spirit was lonely and was coming back after another of them. When he said that, I stopped crying and listened. When he finished, I told him not to be worrying about things from the past; I'd let those go; they were over a long time ago and I wasn't still suffering from them. I also said I'd try to be strong and go on, taking care of things here. Then I tried to console him about what he was facing, what he was going through. We'd been together a *very long time*.

You know he wanted to stay home, and pass away in his cabin.[36] He told the children those were his wishes, and he told me, too. But on that, I disagreed with him. I didn't want that place to become a house of death so it had to be burned up or torn down. I know he believed it'd be all right not to do that in his case; he said he was an old age person, that was an old age home, and that made it different. He always said you didn't have to be afraid of people dying from old age or of their things, and he taught our children that, too. But I didn't agree with him on that and he knew it. So I told him right there I didn't want it that way; I said when he felt his time was near, he should go back to the hospital. He didn't say too much about it after that. After a few more days, one of my children came over to where I was weaving and told me Frank said it was time for him to go back to Ganado. So I went back over to his cabin and helped him gather up his things. He tried to joke, tell me he'd be right back, but both of us knew it wasn't so. After we said a few more things to each other, somebody helped him get into a vehicle and they left for Ganado. That was the last time I saw him. He passed away in that hospital not too long after he went back there.

I didn't go to his funeral and I didn't go to the cemetery afterwards, when you all buried him. My beliefs about staying away from those things, not being in contact with them, are very, very strong, so I didn't do any of those things. You know about everything that happened because you were among the people who came from great distances to help us go through that. I stayed home, cooking and consoling the people who came here because he had passed away. Even though you all ate, I didn't; I observed all the rules we have for the four days, and I tried to get his children and grandchildren to do that, too. But of course, some of them felt differently about those things. That's why I've never been to the cemetery to see where he was buried. I really don't want my children doing that either, but some of them do. But they don't tell me about it until after they come back from cleaning up around the headstone Howard and Seya made for him, checking the little fence, or putting flowers up there, on Memorial Day. I don't believe in that so I stay away; what others do is up to them.[37]

It was very hard for me after Frank passed away. Even though he'd told me to be strong, I missed him *very, very much*. I was very lonely and I missed him terribly, even though my children and grandchildren were here, and even though I stayed busy with my weaving, cooking, hoeing, working on the wool, and taking care of the sheep and other things, too. I was very sad for a *long, long time*. I cried a lot, too; I couldn't seem to stop crying about things. I didn't feel like eating, no matter what people fixed for me. I guess I was like that most of the summer. My joints were really bothering me and my legs started swelling up, too.

After he passed away, some of my children started having bad dreams, so finally we had a Protection Rite done for ourselves. After that, I started getting my appetite back and some of the swelling in my legs started going down. For a while, people told me maybe I should have a Beautyway; maybe the snakes that had bitten me many years ago were causing my legs to swell up. We started planning for that, but things kept getting in the way and we never went ahead with it. In the fall, the Ten Days Project workers came and moved the hogan, like we do after someone dies. Even though Frank hadn't passed away in there, we did that. It'd been used for many, many ceremonies, so we needed to relocate it and refurbish it in other ways. When that was moved, I had a Blessingway; my children sponsored it, and we had Little Black Sheep from Black Mountain come and do that for me.

I told the children that by doing those things, we were still respecting Frank's ceremony. I kept reminding them the Blessingway was our guide and Frank had taught all of us many, many things about it. I told them never to forget any of those things, and to keep their faith strong by using that ceremony and upholding his teachings. Of course, they saw I was going on in that way; I was still respecting those things because I believed in them deeply.

After I had that Blessingway, I went back to trying to keep things going along in the right way here at home and in the family. My health was all right for someone in old age,* even though I did have to go back to Ganado to get another thing fixed. They called that hernia trouble.[38] I had that done right after we lost Mrs. Joseph Ganna; later that fall, we lost Garnett's father, too.[39]

The next year after Frank died, we made plans to take care of his *jish* like he'd told me to do. You can only renew those at certain times of year so that was one thing we had to plan for, and then you need a buckskin and some other things, too, in order to do it in the right way. But on top of that, since he had passed away, his medicine bundle needed to be cleansed. So we decided to have a five-night Evilway Ceremony for me and add a Blessingway to that, to take care of cleansing and renewing his medicine bundle. It took us a while to find a singer who knew how to cleanse and renew the *jish*; just like Frank had said, lots of people, even though they know Blessingway, don't know how to do those things. Finally, we found a singer, Bucking Horse's Son, from Smoke Signal; he came in the early fall to do the Evilway, and then, after we waited a while, around September, a singer from Round Rock, the one called The Cook, sang the Blessingway part. So, that's when Frank's bundle was washed and dried with corn pollen, and transferred. I was the one-sung-over for that but my daughter, Isabel, sat in for me, during the Blessingway part because I wasn't sure I could follow the singer and repeat the prayers without making any mistakes. By then, every now and then, I was having trouble with my memory. That had already started happening, but only once in a while. You have to be very careful about those things, and not confuse any words when you say the prayers right after the singer. Because of what had started happening with my memory, I was worried about it so I asked Isabel to do that in my place, and she agreed. So, by means of that, Frank's bundle was cleansed, renewed, and transferred to me.[40] Of course, that had happened to me before, too; after my father passed away, one of his *jish*, the one with the cranes, was transferred to me according to his wishes about it.

The next year, after the Evilway and Blessingway were done, about two years after Frank passed away, I went back to where we used to live, over there across the Chinle Wash, near Houses Standing in a Line. It was in the fall, right before the frost came. I went back across over there to get some corn. Charlie Mitchell's place is over near there now. They had a big field and had replanted more corn in June. That corn was just getting ripe when it started to freeze so Bertha, one of my granddaughters from there, came and told me to come and get some of it. She wanted me to help use it up; she didn't want to lose it by letting the frost ruin it before it ripened. Corn is like that; it gets ruined if it freezes before it ripens. So that's why Bertha came and told me to come and take all the corn that was left. Bertha is related to us on both my mother's side and my husband's side, as you know; she was there by herself, taking care of her mother, Bartine, who was very sick.[41]

When I went there, I wanted to do that by myself so I did; I probably already knew I was going to visit the place where we used to live after I finished harvesting the corn, but I didn't mention it. I hitched up the team and drove our wagon over to Bertha's near the place where we used to live with all those stone houses in a line and the big corral. I went there and brought back all the corn that was still growing there. The whole wagon was full and I used that to make kneeldown bread; you can only make that from that kind of corn [see Fig. 41]. There was another field of corn to the side of the one I picked that was just starting to get its silk. It was already late in the fall when I went there; I wonder if that other corn ever ripened or if it got frozen. I never heard what happened to it.*

FIG. 41. Tall Woman husking corn outside Ruth's house, after her return from Houses Standing in a Line, Fall 1969. Photographer, unknown. Courtesy of Evonne Shirley.

While I was over there, I decided to go around and visit the area up there where we used to live. At that time I found that not very much of it was left. Most of the rocks were all gone by then. I guess people had taken them to use as foundations and other things. While I was there visiting what was left of my father's house, the ruins of it, it was really touching to think about the ground and see nothing left but those little pieces of rock. Earlier I used to be able to stand right here and see the whole foundation still standing up. But when I went back over there the last time, the only things that remained were little pieces of rock, here and there, in the place where the foundation had been for Houses Standing in a Line, and the corral. There really was nothing left of that place anymore that you could see; the dunes had already covered up whatever might have been left. There was almost no trace of anything from my younger days.

It made me feel strange to go back there; it really affected me. I don't know why I did that, why I went back over there. Maybe I was thinking I'd see something that reminded me of my earlier days. It really was touching.[42]

Every now and then, when you get leave from your job you come back to stay with us.[43] Then we talk some more about Frank's book and mine, and the progress being made on them. Of course, you see the family at these times, too, like my grandson, Doogie, who is now at one of the schools in the east helping with the instruction on songs and things. When he sings, he reminds me of Frank. I hope he'll start learning the Blessingway in the future; he could get started with those tapes your teacher and you made of Frank's ceremony. I know his memory is good enough to learn those things, and I think he's interested, too.[44] He always comes to visit me when he's around in the summer. He likes to hear about the old days, even way back to *Tanabah*, the one who had to leave her baby behind. So we talk about those things, too, when he's here. He was here again last Christmas, visiting me when that school had vacation.

This time you've brought your firstborn child, your little Elizabeth with you, so she can learn something about the sheep and other things.* I like watching her around here; she follows me around, trying to help out the best she can, even though she's very small. And when she tries to speak Navajo, the way she says things makes me laugh. But I'm very happy she's trying to learn. Of course, sometimes I have to scold her, too, just like I do with the rest of my grandchildren. Sometimes children do things they shouldn't and you have to scold them. But I'm glad you brought her to stay with us; you should leave her here so she can herd for me and I can show her how to weave.*[45]

As you can see, now I'm suffering from old age. Just like Frank said, my memory is starting to fade, and I'm getting confused about things. But still, on some days, I'm fine, just like I used to be. Other days, I barely remember anything; I'm confused about where I am or what time of year it is. People tell me when I'm like that I start talking about things that happened long ago. And then too, they say I'm always worrying about the sheep and goats, and calling out about them. Of course I still worry about them. I need to know somebody is herding them and watching them carefully, not running off playing, forgetting them. Some of my grandchildren are too young to be doing that in the right way; if I could still get around and had my strength, I'd rather be out there, taking care of the sheep myself. But instead, I don't because now I'm unsteady lots of times, even with my cane. Last week, I fell off the porch steps here, as you know, when I was going to Ruth's so she could fix my hair in a *tsiiyééł* [hairknot], after I had washed it. It's like that now; even with my cane, sometimes I fall down. So all my children have said they don't want me out herding the sheep anymore; they say someone else will do it for me. So most of the time now I just stay here, sitting outside or inside, doing things like weaving or cooking. Of course, I still like to go places with people, even in cars.* We haven't used our wagon now for quite a few years because several people around here have vehicles. So I've learned how to ride in them; of course, that's different and I'll never drive those like I used to do with the wagon.*

A few days ago, while we were working together on my book again, you asked me what else I want to put in my story. I know I've now told you everything I can remember about what happened a long time ago, and what I remember about how we went along from there, through the years all the way up to here, right now. And I know we still have work to do because now you have questions to ask me about some of the things I've already talked about. You still need my help in explaining some of those things again, so you understand this or that about them. I've already told you I'll help you with that, too, and we'll work on that until we get finished with all your questions.* But the other one, the other question you asked me, about what else I want to say for my story, is different; that's why I told you a few days ago I'd have to think about it. So I've been doing that, thinking about what kind of an answer to give you on it.

How I feel about it now is that the rest of my story, whatever happens with me from here on, you can put in my book by yourself. I know you'll keep coming back in the future, to spend time with us when you can and help us out as we go along. So you can finish that part by yourself. But I do want to talk about something else, first. There are some things I want to say to my children and their children, and the children who come from them, too, all the way down the line. Maybe that's only because I'm still worrying about all my grandchildren, like grandmothers do.* But I still want to talk about those things. After I do that, say the things I want to say to our future generations, then probably I will have reached the end of my words for my story.*

Words to the Future Generations[1]

The other things I want to say to my children's children, their children,
and all the rest, all the way down the line.

The way things are now are very, very different from when I was a small girl, or even when I was a young woman. What Frank used to say about how things would change in the future is true; sometimes I don't know what to make of the new things that are coming along, or even what to think of them. Maybe that's because I never had a chance to go to school and because of that, now I've been left behind. But school is not all there is to it; you need to learn other things like your language, your ceremonies, how to be a good person, how to live according to the Blessingway. You need to understand that, use the Blessingway in your own life, and follow it as a guide to keep yourself and your family strong, and to face hardships as they come along. That we always did. Even now, I believe in that very, very strongly. Only with that will all of us right here and other Navajos, even those living in distant places off the reservation, have a future.

Today, some of the things I raised my children with the young people probably don't need to know anymore, like how to harness and drive the team and wagon, or grind corn with the grinding stones. Now the People have cars and pickups, and there are machines for grinding and chopping up different foods, washing clothes, plowing fields. Now some of the People have electricity, and running water right in their homes, and radios and TVs; and sometimes when people travel great distances, they use things called airplanes. Even our land here is changing; as it gets passed along to future generations, it'll be divided into smaller and smaller pieces; pretty soon, nobody will have enough to raise foods to support themselves and their children. Even the sheep may go that way unless women keep the weaving going, or the People keep getting hungry for mutton.* Those things are not up to me; future generations will have to decide about them.

What I want to talk about are not these kinds of things; instead, they're things Frank and I tried to teach our children as we were raising them. I want to encourage my children to pass those on to future generations so they know how we tried to do things, and what we believed in. Maybe that will give them something to use with their own children as they go along, too. I worry when I see the things the younger generations are getting into now, and the problems they have to face, even at an early age. In my days, it was mainly gambling and drinking and running around that caused trouble. But now, while those are still causing trouble, more and more young people are getting into other trouble, fighting, stealing, even shooting people! Sometimes, that's because they've had no guidance, no one to teach them anything at home, and they've started using drugs or running in gangs. Now, there's no respect for children or parents, or people in any kind of leadership position. Relatives squabble with each other and even go to court with their arguments. Even those up in their old age are getting abused; no one cares for them in the right way. Just like white people, Navajos are dumping their elders into nursing homes and leaving them there to die. But it's not just around here or just with white people; now, there's trouble all over the world in different places. Some days when I think about these things, it seems like everyone has gone crazy. For all these reasons, I worry about my grandchildren and their children, and then theirs, all the way down the line.

The hogan should be the center of the family, and the mother, the heart. That's where the mother should make a home for everyone and keep things moving along smoothly. Women need to set an example about those things so children can look at them, see they are living right and working hard, and learn how to be that way, too. If a woman is lazy, only thinks about herself, neglects her children, no good comes from it. That's where she should be teaching her children to work and do all the traditional things they need to know, like carding and spinning, weaving, herding, fixing different kinds of foods. Children need to be taught right from the beginning to listen when adults talk to them, to do what they're told right away, without talking back or needing things repeated. They need to be encouraged to sit and watch whatever the mother is doing, to learn from it in that way. And they also need to learn from whatever advice adults give to them, by listening and respecting the teachings of their parents and others older than themselves. Of course, it's up to the parents to talk with their children like that, teach them things; if they ignore their children or say they're too tired to do this or that with them, or think they'll get around to it later, how will children ever learn anything? They need to practice the things being done at home until they learn them. Only in that way do children learn to think, figure things out, and stand up, ready to be on their own. Otherwise, they'll be helpless, always saying, "I don't know how," or "What should I do about it?" Children have to be taught to use their heads right from the start; when they're small, they don't understand their parents aren't always going to be around to take care of them.

By the time children go to school, they should already have that foundation inside themselves. That's up to the parents, not the teachers; those people have their hands full with other kinds of instruction. They, too, need to be respected and listened to. It's an opportunity to go to school and learn other kinds of things; children need all of those now to make a living wherever they end up establishing their home, their center. So, when they go to school, they need to pay attention, do their work, and try to get everything possible out of it all the way through. And they should stick to it; even if it's hard, they should not get discouraged and quit, walk away from it. Going to school will give them new ideas and new skills; those help prepare them for the future. So encourage children to do that. Frank realized education was important even when it was just starting, and I supported him in that, telling our children to follow his advice about it and his plans for them about school. But now, it's even more important that children go as far as they can with that kind of learning, following it through, getting all they can out of it. When school things are added to the things they should learn at home, all the things that give them their foundation, then children are truly ready, fully prepared for their future life. Then they can take all the changes that keep coming along in stride. They'll know how to figure them out, think about whether those are good or bad, and what to do about them.

Just like school, marriage is a very serious business. Teach the future generations the clan rules we have; trouble comes from not respecting those. Also tell them to establish their own home, not to live with their in-laws. If you do, your children will always be crying for food from the other people and somebody will be bothering you or complaining about you. It's not up to your in-laws to take care of you, feed you, help you with your children. That's your responsibility. And along the same line, be very careful to always speak nicely to your in-laws, or talk kindly about them. Don't offend your husband, your wife, or your in-laws by saying anything out of line about them or their relatives. Too many young people have trouble now with their in-laws because everybody is forgetting these things which used to be very strong in the past.

And with the person they decide to make a living with, tell them to treat that one with respect and affection. Don't abuse each other with your words; never say anything you'll be sorry about later. Think before you open your mouth; words are powerful things. And don't argue and fight with each other, either. Teach the girls to never, ever stay with someone who abuses them, tries to beat them, knife them, or hurt and mistreat them in other ways. Anyone who acts like that is crazy; if a person gets like that, starts acting that way toward them or their children, they should leave. They should never let themselves be treated in that way, no matter what the cause is.

Another thing that's important when you live with someone is to avoid jealousy. That's very hard for both the man and the woman, but don't be jealous, don't follow your husband or wife around, tagging on their heels when they have to go off to different places to do other things. Stay home or at your place of work, and do whatever you're supposed to be doing; keep your mind on it, instead of getting jealous. That brings trouble, too. There'll probably be times when the woman or the man wonders about things, or even gets suspicious. Then I guess they'll do whatever they need to do about it; maybe they'll even act like I did, when I called that woman a female dog, a whore, back in our early married times.* But whatever they do, tell them not to stay angry; take care of it and then drop it, let it go.

Another thing that's important when you try and make a living with someone is to keep talking with each other. Of course, if they're gone all the time, that's hard to do;* then, you're pretty much left to raise the children and take care of other things on your own. But when they're around, talk about things and listen to each other. Only in that way can you work things out, make plans together for the future. And only then will you be saying and doing the same thing about raising the children. It's very important that you think ahead, make plans for the future. And, you need to discuss those with each other, share in that way, so you can support and help each other, rather than going in two different directions about things. If you don't work together, children get confused; they don't know who to follow and pretty soon, they wander off, not following anything either of you wants them to be doing or living by.

Sometimes now, especially with younger married women, I hear talk about who should be in charge, who should make the decisions about this and that in a marriage. In some places, all those things fall to the woman because she's raising the children alone. But if you're making a living with someone, you should share in that, too. Both the man and the woman have jobs to do about all of that; both of them are necessary to make things complete and to raise a family in the right way. That's how things were established by the Holy People at the beginning, and that's how we should be going along, even now. Frank and I tried to do that. He said I was in charge of the hogan and everything concerned with it; he always said that, and supported whatever daily plans I made for the children. With other things, like their schooling or what singers to get when someone needed a ceremony, he was in charge, and I was behind him. I never got in the way or argued about whatever he decided concerning those things; I never jumped in or stepped ahead of him on that. Of course, we talked about the future too, trying to look ahead together, to figure out how much corn to grow for our own use and for our livestock, and what other work to do in order to have a little income. But the jobs that brought in a little money, or a sheep, or something like that, were up to each of us; Frank decided if he wanted to haul wood or other things in the wagon for someone, if he was going to do his ceremony, or if he would serve in politics. And I decided how many rugs to weave for the traders, how to spend whatever little money he gave me to use for our children, and even when to stop helping women who were facing childbirth. In all those things, we supported and encouraged each other, but we didn't decide them for the other one. Those things are only up to the individual they concern, not somebody else. It's just like my father's *jish* with the craneheads; that was left to me and it was up to me to decide when people asked to borrow it to use with their ceremonies. So, in that way, we respected each other, went along together, supported each other; we didn't try and step ahead of each other, or speak for each other. Because there were two of us trying to raise our children, we tried to add in both parts, the woman's and the man's, according to the ways we were taught.

Sure, people have problems when they're married; no Earth Surface Person is perfect. Even with the Holy People, only Changing Woman is totally dependable and without a side that may bring harm. If you learn those things and have them as your foundation, you understand that. With Frank, most of my problems were early, when he was running around, gambling, drinking, and taking off for long periods of time, leaving his children and me here, with hardly any food or means of support other than my weaving. Most of that was before he finished learning the Blessingway; that settled him down and turned him into a responsible, mature person. Of course, even later, he drank; as I've already mentioned, sometimes that caused problems for him and others, even here in the family. But whenever that happened, whenever he put himself in that condition, I always tried to remove myself and whatever children or grandchildren were here. There's no point in staying around, putting yourself or your children in any kind of danger from someone who is acting crazy because of drinking. And there's no sense in yelling at drunks, either; it's no use. I learned those things, too, as I went along.

On Frank's part, I'm sure I did things to upset him, too, even though I never went around with another man for any reason once he and I started living together. Sometimes he'd say I was too quiet, that I should speak my mind about things more often, especially if I was worrying about something or somebody. I was always quiet, and I probably got quieter, keeping more things to myself, as the years went along and he started working in politics and as a judge. I know sometimes when I was quiet instead of answering him about something he asked, he'd say maybe I was backwards and my mind didn't have opinions in it.* He used to say that in a joking way, but maybe he wasn't joking. I don't know, now that I think about it. I do know we always tried to talk nicely to each other, speak with respect toward each other, instead of yelling and screaming, arguing and fighting like lots of married people do. We were never like that with each other, even way back in the beginning. And when we had problems, we tried to talk about them by ourselves, not in front of the children; we always tried to be careful about that, too.

The other thing I know we always tried to do is laugh with each other; we liked to tease each other and we both liked to joke; being that way toward each other helped, too. I think if men and women do those things, treat each other with respect, talk with each other, learn to plan together, help each other, work together, and if they show affection by holding hands, hugging, and acting in those ways at home, then it's possible to stay together for many, many years, just like we did. Now, it seems like people hardly ever do that anymore; even right here, my children and grandchildren are getting divorced for one reason or another. Of course, that's up to them; that's all I have to say to them about it. The way Frank and I looked at it, marriage was for life. My father and mother used to tell us that marriage was a very serious business and you needed to give it very careful thought before jumping into it.

It's the same way with raising your children. I worry that in the future, the People will forget how to raise their families in the right way. For Frank and me, that meant working hard to support our children and make a good home for them. It's important to set a good example for children; they're always watching what you're doing, and how you go about things. It's your job to talk to them so they can learn from your advice, and show them how to do the things you want them to know. If you're not doing those things, how can they sit and watch and learn? Who will do that for them?

Frank and I also believed children needed to be scolded when they misbehaved, and corrected when they started squabbling, mistreating each other, or acting out of line in any way. I guess we had different ways of correcting our children; I was always here with them so I did more scolding. And a few times, I had to spank someone, or switch or whip their legs. Even Frank had to spank one or two of them now and then. But that didn't happen very often because most of the time, our children listened to what I said and did what I asked. I always tried to talk to them in a nice, calm way. I tried not to excite myself too much over whatever they had done wrong or fly off the handle about things. We didn't believe in calling our children bad names, or yelling at them, or cussing them out. Those things have bad effects; you hurt children's feelings that way and once that happens, lots of times, their minds wander elsewhere and they may run away and never come back. So I always tried to speak to them nicely, calmly, calling them, "My little one" or something like that, showing them respect and affection, even while I was saying, "what you did here is not right." I scolded whoever needed it when something happened, and I tried to explain to them in a quiet, nice way why they needed to stop doing whatever it was that upset me. Some days it seemed like most of them were busy thinking up more tricks to play on me about whatever I had asked them to do, but even then, I tried to be calm, and to correct them nicely.

Frank, of course, only scolded them when he was home. Most of the time, he'd get them together in a group for that. And then, lots of times, it sounded to me like he was preaching. He'd use his big, deep, loud voice, not his regular one, and he'd sound like he was yelling, even though he always said, "I'm not scolding you" when he started talking to them that way. He was temperamental about things and sometimes he'd go on and on, even sounding real harsh, when he was getting after them. When they got older, sometimes different ones got restless and quit listening, fell asleep, or got up and went out. Some of them were afraid of him when he talked like that; maybe that's why he did it that way, or maybe he thought that was the only way they'd remember his words in the future. Or maybe his voice just got like that from talking to the People all those years.*

I stayed out of the way when he did that. I knew Frank could see ahead; he understood their lives would be very different from ours, and he worried they wouldn't learn from our advice and get prepared for their own futures. I agreed with what he was saying to the children; I said the same things when he wasn't here, but my ways of talking to them were different. So both of us corrected them, but differently; that's your job, too, as parents, to correct your children so they learn what is right. No matter who was doing it, both of us tried to be careful with our words when we were scolding them. Frank always told me not to chew somebody out over and over and over about one little thing. He believed human life was more important than hurting someone by chewing them out with harsh words. I agreed with him on that so we both tried to never say anything we'd be sorry about later.

And with the children, both of us tried to adjust our talks to whatever age they were as we all went along. There are some things that get explained right away to all children, and others that get left until they are old enough to understand. Sometimes, you can tell children are ready for certain explanations because of the questions they come out and ask. But then, too, sometimes they may hold back and be shy about things. I always tried to talk with the girls about things that concerned them when we were here by ourselves. That's when I'd instruct them on being modest, sitting right, and not doing things that didn't look right, like fooling around with their brothers, or teasing and joking in the wrong way with clan relatives or others, or being loud and noisy, running wild, or going to ceremonies or other places where there were crowds. I'd talk with them about all those things and about why they needed to take care of themselves in the right way, and stay away from dangerous places and things.

Frank did the same thing with the boys, too, about treating girls right, not getting themselves or others in trouble, things like that. And with all of them, as they got older we both started talking more about marriage and taking it seriously. And then, I spent more and more time telling all our children about earlier times, what I knew about different things the People faced, even before they were marched to Fort Sumner. Frank did that too, but he was gone a lot when they'd be here helping me with things. So I told them all those things, too. I also explained how they were related to different ones so they understood those things. That's important, too; if parents don't explain who the relatives are on both sides and how that goes way, way back, children won't know why people tease each other according to clan rules and practices, and they may end up like my mother said, marrying a clan relative because they're stupid about those things.*

Another thing about raising children that we both always tried to do was praise them when they got something right we were trying to show them, like hoeing all the weeds out of the corn or melons, when they did something without being asked or told it needed to be done, or when they accomplished something for the first time, like weaving a rug good enough to take to the traders, or harnessing the team. We also praised them when they did more than we asked, like carding lots of wool, grinding extra corn, hauling extra wood, things like that. It's easy to forget to praise children; Frank and I used to talk about that because sometimes, especially when my mother was in her old age and going on without my father, it seemed to us that all our children heard was someone scolding them about one thing or another. People need praise; you need to show them with your words that what they've done makes you happy. Praising them is another way of showing affection; it's like speaking to them in a nice way. Sometimes now when I hear people talking to their children, I worry about it; it seems like they never learned how to praise them, that they never say anything encouraging or kind to their children.

The other thing about having children that young people need to understand is that once you do that, it lasts your whole life. You can't run away from being a mother or a father; those responsibilities stay with you until the end of your days. Both Frank and I tried to impress that on our children as they got older; having your own children is a serious thing. That's where a lot of your own pleasure comes to an end. You're no longer free to run here and there and do what you might want to do, even to advance yourself. From then on, children are your main concern and you forget the rest. Your place is in the home with your children. There will always be babies to take care, children to worry about, especially if you're the mother. Your children become your first thought for both the mother and father; they're always there, from then on. You shouldn't neglect them, let them go hungry or without blankets or clothes. And you shouldn't let them cry. Even in the middle of the night, you have to get up, check on them, find out why they're crying, pay attention to them so you know what's wrong. When they're little, they can't tell you why they're hurting, or if they're having a bad dream, or they're wet. If you don't pay attention all the time, misfortunes can happen; you can even lose them.

Whenever I hear my grandchildren cry, I say all those things Frank and I used to say all over again. Hearing that brings back lots of memories for me; sometimes I even think of different children we lost along the way for one reason or another, and all the hardships we went through. So, even now, I remind my own children and my grandchildren to take care of their children all the time in the right way. After you have them, you no longer have time for yourself; even if you come home from work tired or sick yourself, it doesn't matter; your children have to come first. That's your job for the rest of your days so you need to make yourself strong so you can care for them even when you're tired or sick. And both the father and the mother need to plan their own work so they keep things going all the time, even when they have to sit up all night suffering from no sleep because of their children. Those things really change once you start having children, so you shouldn't be doing it just for the fun of it. People need to raise their children and grandchildren so they understand that. So those are among the things I'm trying to teach my grandchildren right now; I'm their grandmother and I'm still worrying about them and all these things.

Another thing they need to be taught is to be a good person, one who lives in the right way. There's lots of things that go into that. Maybe you can't teach all of it to your children; I don't know. Frank used to preach about it here at home and also at gatherings, when he was talking to the People. I think some of it you can talk about. But with other parts, you just have to use your own head, think about it as you get older, and figure out what you're going to do about different things that come along. Frank and I wanted our children to turn out right; we wanted them to be people who lived in a good way, not people who were known for causing trouble, fighting, running wild, or talking in harmful ways against others. We used to correct them if they said mean things to each other, or about someone who was here; we'd say, "Don't talk like that, don't say those things."

Part of it is your words, how you speak to others. But there's more to it. You need to be friendly to people; you need to try and help others. Even if you have only a little food or coffee, you need to share what you have, and try to help others whenever they need your help. You need to show you're like that not only with your relatives, but even with outsiders. Frank always said that; even if you don't have any money or any sheep you can butcher, there's always something you can share, something you can help with. Sometimes, just taking time to sit and listen to someone's troubles helps; it gives them encouragement; sometimes all a person needs is advice. We both tried to be that way and live like that, being nice to everybody, and sharing and helping in whatever ways we could. And we wanted our children to act like that, too.

The reason that's important is that it comes back to you. Everyone goes through sufferings as they go along; you never know what's going to come up, or what hardships you'll have to face. You don't know what's ahead; you have to be prepared for everything because you *will* have hard times, difficulties with your children, yourself, your spouse, your relatives. Whatever comes along, you have to be ready to face it and take it in stride. Even if things go smoothly for a long time, sooner or later, something will come up. When you're young you think you'll always be that way, strong and healthy. You forget that old age is waiting for you, if you're lucky enough to live that long and get up in your years. Then you'll have aches and pains, you'll start slowing down and need help with things; maybe you'll even get some serious illness. Right there, if not earlier, how you've been treating other people comes back on you.

If you've always tried to help and share what you have, then others will help you; they'll go out of their way to show their concern and do things to help ease your sufferings in one way or another. If you've been kind all the way along, people will have already learned to appreciate you for that, and they'll try and come to your rescue. But if you've mistreated others, said you didn't have time for them, were stingy with your possessions along the way and didn't help out, then who will be there for you? It always comes back and by the time those things hit you, you can't turn them around. It's too late to wish you had treated others with kindness and friendliness in earlier times. No one will take care of you, help you out, come to visit you, bring you food, or worry about your sicknesses; they'll just forget about you, or make sure you get dumped some place far away and left with nothing to look forward to, no news of anybody. When that happens to people, they just give up. They have no reason to try to keep going on because nothing good is coming back to them. But then, that's really their own fault.

We both used to tell our children that over and over and over. Even now, I say these things to my grandchildren. Both Frank and I knew those things were very, very true and that they were very important. And the way we felt about it, it wasn't just your relatives who should be helped; you should be that way with everyone who came along into your life for whatever reason, if they were good people, themselves. If you are known for your friendliness and kindness, your helpfulness and thoughtfulness, all of that will come back to you tenfold. When you get sick or face other hardships and sufferings, people will help you. But if you haven't helped your relatives, your neighbors and friends, visitors who come around, and others, if you've been stingy and haven't shared whatever you could, then that's what will happen to you, too.

I know my children are living up to the promises they made to Frank before he passed away about how they would take care of me in my old age. And I want to thank them for that. Until about a year ago, I was still strong enough to do most of the things I did earlier. But now, things are different. More and more, I'm unable to do things to take care of myself; now that my memory is fading it's even harder, because sometimes I don't even make sense. I'm just living back in earlier times some days. I know I'm getting like that and it upsets me. But I know it happens when you get into really old age; most people get like that. I know my children understand that; even though Frank didn't get that way, others did and they saw them as we tried to help different ones when they got up in their years.

I want my children to know I appreciate what they're doing to take care of me; because I can count on them for that, I'm not worrying about being hungry, having no blankets, catching cold, being served food I can't eat, falling down, or not having the medicines I need now for my diabetes. That crept up on me too, but so far, the doctors are keeping it stable with medicine and diet. Maybe later it will get worse; they say it often does. But right now, it seems stable and my children are making sure I get taken to Ganado or to the clinic here to get my medicines. There's nothing in our ceremonies that can be used for that, if diabetes is what's causing your sickness, so I haven't asked them to sponsor any ceremonies for me. I know seeing me in this condition is hard on all my children. Now they have to take care of me along with their own children, and some of them even have grandchildren too, or jobs they have to go to, to get income to support their families. But they aren't complaining about anything, and I'm not either. I'm trying to do what they ask, without fussing about it. They talk with me in a nice way and I still do that with them, too.

I hope in the future my children and grandchildren, and even their children will follow the teachings we raised them with. I hope they will stay right here and take care of the place where we made our home. The hogans and the other structures, the livestock, the land — all those things are here for their use. If they take care of them and treat them with respect as we taught them, those things will continue to support them and benefit them in the future.

We taught our children to stay together and help each other; I hope they and their children, and their children's children will remember that in the future. When Frank and I used to talk with them, we'd stress that; we told them many times there'd come a day when we'd be gone and they'd be left here by themselves, to go on without us. Maybe they didn't understand it when we said those things in earlier times. But now, Frank has already left us. That's what we were trying to explain a long time ago, that we weren't going to be here forever, and they'd need to look out for themselves.

When that happens to children, it's important they help each other and stay close together as a family without fighting with each other or having disputes over things. Those left behind should care about each other and follow the traditional ways we have taught. Even if they have hardships to face with their own children or grandchildren, they should never forget to do the best they can to help their own brothers and sisters. We taught them all those things, saying, "Stay together and help each other in the future, no matter what sufferings come along." If children don't do that, it's as if their parents taught them nothing. People look at them and say they learned nothing, they have no sense, that's why they're squabbling, using harsh words toward each other, saying and doing things that are out of line toward their own family, and taking off, leaving the land and their home, now that their parents have passed away. I hope our children remember our teachings and don't act that way toward each other, or the land, or the other things we left behind. If they don't follow our teachings on that, things will fall apart for them.

The other thing I want to stress to my grandchildren and their children concerns the Blessingway Ceremony. Teach the future generations to keep it sacred and live by it, to respect it always and use it in their own lives for their own well-being. Our children were raised with it; we went according to the Blessingway from the very beginning, all the way down the line, with each one of them, and we tried to teach them about it, too. Teach the future generations, the children and grandchildren, about our ceremonies; respect them and the ones who become qualified to perform them in the future, and use them whenever they can help alleviate sufferings. Also teach them to help each other with planning ahead for ceremonies, getting prepared for the expense and work that go with them. Remember the Blessingway can be used at anytime, unlike the healing ceremonies. Don't forget about it; uphold it and use it to keep things going along in the right way, or to protect the children or grandchildren when they're facing something like a long trip, or surgery, or childbirth, or going off to war in some distant place. Use it for celebrating, too; keep celebrating the arrival of womanhood with the *Kinaaldá* and pass it on to future generations. The same is true with weddings; even if the grandchildren or great-grandchildren use a church, add Blessingway to it so it brings more benefit to those who are starting out together.

Frank and I taught our children all these things. I hope they pass our teachings on to the future generations. The Blessingway carried us through all our sufferings. With it, by means of it, we were able to manage all the hardships that came to us as we went along. Tell them these things. Tell them the Blessingway will give them a guide to go by during their entire life, even into really old age, if they believe in it and use it in the right way. Maybe some of them will abandon it, start believing in other things, or add other things in with our own beliefs and practices. There are some churches that make fun of Navajo ceremonies; now revivalists are going around telling the People to destroy or burn up their medicine bundles, calling them "things from the Devil." I know the future generations will have to decide these things for themselves and maybe they'll change their minds once, or twice, or even more as they go along with their own lives. It's up to them what they do about it. But teach them, no matter what they decide, to never abuse the Blessingway or let anyone make fun of it. Treat the Mountain Earth bundle that was Frank's with respect; handle it carefully, get it renewed in the right way at the right times, and don't ever let anyone abuse it. If that happens, there will be bad effects and the harm that comes from it will come back on them. The things like that, Frank's bundle and the *jish* with the cranes that belonged to my father, Man Who Shouts, are sacred things; they're here in the family for the benefit of everyone, not just one person. So teach the new generations as they come along to treat those things in the right way, preserving and protecting them for the future, too. That's up to *all* our children and grandchildren together to continue on in the future, living according to the Blessingway, upholding our teachings. Keep those things here in the family, and use them in the right way for the benefit of all the children, their children's children, and their children, all the way down the line. Let the Blessingway be their guide; live by means of it. I believe in that very, very strongly and I know it will see all of them through whatever hardships they have to face, just as it did for Frank and me all the way along.[2]

Now, I'm finished; this is the end of everything I can remember and everything I want to say, the way I'm thinking about it. So, this brings it to an end; this is the end of my words for my story.

six

Epilogue:
1971–77
and Concluding
Reflections
of Tall Woman's
Family

Epilogue[1]

The 1971–76 years . . . Tall Woman's last year, death, and funeral
in 1977 . . . her family's concluding reflections.

The last extensive interactions and "work sessions" Tall Woman and I had were during the summer of 1971, a time when it was clear that her situation was changing. Some days she was like her old self, and was constantly busy; as she said, "If I don't keep working, I'll pass away." Her activities included cooking, weaving, sweeping, winnowing corn, chopping weeds, swatting bugs, trying to eradicate red anthills with boiling water, cleaning pans with sand, or sorting drawers and storage boxes, while baby-sitting lots of grandchildren. She also traveled to medical checkups and the homes of relatives to visit, after changing her clothes, getting her *tsiiyééł* retied, and donning her beads and other jewelry. By walking around with her cane or a stick, she also kept a careful eye on the construction of an addition to Isabel's place; the whereabouts of the sheep, goats, and horses; and general comings and goings of all. She always enjoyed talking, teasing, and joking with visitors or anyone who appeared alongside her to help with whatever she was doing [see Fig. 42].

Other days, however, she appeared disoriented; she'd have times when she didn't recognize family members, and would indicate she was in "another time" by telling whoever was around to pack up specific things and start loading the wagon, because "we're moving back home now" to be with people who had already died. On such days, she'd sit outside verbalizing concerns about her swollen legs and ankles, arthritic joints, diabetes, and the heat, wind, or blowing sand. Or she'd be found sitting inside crying about missing Frank, current conditions, peoples' behaviors, or other worries. Occasionally, she'd start rummaging through clothes, and bundling things together. Then she'd begin to walk off, saying she was going to visit someone already deceased. If anyone could convince her to take a nap on such days, it never lasted more than twenty or thirty minutes.

In 1971, Tall Woman remained in the hogan next to Isabel's. Jimmy Deschine, a

FIG. 42. Tall Woman and her daughters, outside Augusta's house, August 2, 1971. Left to right: front row — Mary Mitchell Davis (Mary no. 1), Tall Woman, Isabel Mitchell Deschine; back row — Ruth Mitchell Shirley Yazzie, Augusta Mitchell Sandoval, and Agnes Mitchell Sanchez. Photographer, Charlotte J. Frisbie.

Blessingway singer from Wheatfields, had joined the latter's household, and the addition under construction was to give Tall Woman her own room under their roof and to facilitate Isabel's caretaking of her mother. As Jimmy's presence in the area became known, requests for his ceremony started increasing, and Isabel began traveling with him. Then too, both of them were employed part-time through various Title programs in the schools to teach aspects of Navajo culture; Jimmy helped teach the "Navajo Shoe Game," and the construction of bows and arrows, looms, and weaving tools, and Isabel taught weaving and traditional foods. These activities also took them away from home, leaving Tall Woman increasingly unsupervised, and as her memory and orientation problems increased, it became clear that other caretakers were going to have to be identified. Late in the summer, another Chiricahua Apache Windway was held for Tall Woman because of the suggestions of a hand-trembler contacted on July 4.[2] In the fall, her children sponsored a Blessingway for her that was sung by Chee Carroll from Chinle.[3]

The following year, while family members continued wagework jobs, planting some crops, herding, and other activities, Tall Woman continued to decline, both physically and mentally. Mobility problems increased and she began to fall because of loss of balance. Occasional incontinence began. Other problems also arose about expenses and welfare-assistance income, and who should, would, or could be responsible for various matters. Agnes had already opened a savings account for her mother the previous summer, but a number of issues remained unresolved.

I returned, in December 1972, to attend the funeral of her grandson, Doogie, who had died unexpectedly while in Connecticut.[4] He had visited during the summer, bringing his friends the Luciers,[5] and his death was a great shock to everyone. After the funeral mass at St. Michaels, Agnes, other family members, the Luciers, and I returned to Chinle, amidst a severe winter storm and icy roads. By then, Tall Woman was having very few "good days" although she was cognizant of Doogie's death, grieving appropriately, and expressing worries about the effect of cemeteries on those of us who had gone to the funeral. While she was still weaving occasionally and staying in the front room at Isabel's since heat had yet to be installed in the addition, most of her time reportedly was spent watching her grandchildren play, or the television at Augusta's house. On some days, she still walked around, albeit slowly and with support from others and her cane. At night, she continued to prefer to sleep in the hogan with a grandson who many jokingly called her baby, namely, Isabel's youngest son, Jerry, for company.

In March 1973, another relative, Bartine, passed away.[6] In April, Tall Woman suffered her first stroke, which left her paralyzed on the right side and quite helpless. This changed home-care requirements significantly, and permanently ended her life as a weaver. After more family discussions, those who had agreed to help take care of her sought training from the Indian Health Service so as to be able to supervise and encourage her with the exercises designed to help her regain the use of her right hand and arm. Her diabetes continued to be monitored on a regular basis, with medicines and diet appropriately adjusted. "Heart medicines" and a catheter implant were added, and Augusta began the processes involved in acquiring both a wheelchair and a hospital bed for her mother's use. Both were obtained by August 1973, the time when, after another family meeting, it was decided to move Tall Woman to Augusta's house, where more grandchildren were available to help and there was a gas furnace. Earlier in the summer, Mary Lucier returned for a short visit, bringing another video-artist friend of Cecilia's and Doogie's, Shigeko Kubota.[7] An Enemyway was also held for one of Ruth's sons, Frankie, who had been injured in Vietnam in 1971. In December 1973, Adelle, Seya's wife and Doogie's mother, suffered a fatal heart attack.[8]

Tall Woman's blood-sugar levels shot up again in April 1974, resulting in a series of trips to the hospital to achieve stabilization. When the school year ended, Augusta taught a one-week class on traditional foods during a nutrition workshop held at the University of Arizona. Since she used her mother's recipes, "some people from Tucson" wanted to meet Tall Woman when the class was over and thus came back to Chinle with Augusta. As she said, "By then, my mother was totally senile, but she smiled and was very nice to the people who came back with me to meet her, and was glad for the company."

In April 1975, Tall Woman suffered another stroke and her first diabetic coma. After being quickly transported to the Chinle clinic, she was taken to Sage Memorial Hospital in Ganado, where the diagnosis for her April 30, 1975, admission was "Hyperosmolar Coma as well as Diabetes Mellitus and superficial decubitus ulcers." She remained hospitalized for two weeks until her blood sugar was stabilized and further tests were completed. By June, when I was able to arrange a short trip to Chinle, she had also had a colostomy, again changing the conditions of home care.[9] Agnes came to help during the summer; while she was there, attempts were made to settle problems about livestock and land permits that had remained unresolved after Frank's death, and to make decisions about Tall Woman's care. Requirements of the latter now included monitoring blood sugar and medications; blending her food; preventing bed sores and urine infections; trying to alleviate her suffering from swollen legs and feet and arthritic joints through heating pads, exercises, and massages; taking her to medical appointments; and trying to keep her both comfortable and involved with others. Since all were strongly opposed to nursing homes, after reviewing dwindling options it was decided that "Bunni" [Cynthia], Augusta's second daughter who had just graduated from high school, would assume primary responsibility for the care of her grandmother, Tall Woman, at the end of the summer.[10]

Although Tall Woman was mainly disoriented, there were at least two times around Christmas of 1975 when she was reportedly "very clear." The first was when the Nightway dancers, "the Ye'iis we call 'The Beggars, the Ye'iis who come around,' came to the house," during a local Nightway Ceremony. Bunni and her older sister, Cecilia, were there with their grandmother, but "weren't sure what to do." When they went into her bedroom and asked her, Tall Woman with great clarity told them exactly what was necessary and appropriate to give to the Ye'iis at the door, and they proceeded to do so. The other time was when her half sister, Slim Woman, visited. She had come to help with a *Kinaaldá* being held across the road, but undoubtedly, also to visit, since she was still mobile and had transportation. Those who witnessed this extended visit told me Tall Woman was "clear the whole time." The two spent hours sharing memories of earlier days, joking about things that had happened to them and tricks they had played on others, and they laughed a great deal. Reportedly, as Slim Woman got ready to leave, Tall Woman teased her about the visit, saying people would think she had started "hanging around here" if she didn't get back, and that she was out "looking for another man."

During a sabbatical in the spring of 1976, I was located in the Southwest[11] and thus was able to spend time in Chinle while working on several projects. Another of Seya's sons, Butch, died in March.[12] When I got to Chinle at the end of that month, Tall Woman was completely bedridden; posted on the walls in her bedroom were hourly, daily, and weekly schedules that showed medications, special diet, exercises, and other health-care plans. It was clear that everything possible was being done to keep her warm, dry, and comfortable. Most days she seemed fully entertained by the television and her various grandchildren, mainly Augusta's sons who were involved with school sports teams. Some of them would do their "barbell exercises" in her room so she could watch and comment on them, which she did.

Her mind, however, was constantly wandering; she frequently called to the sheep and the goats, and yelled her concerns about who was herding them and where they were and what they were doing about the animals. She also was very verbal while watching western movies, especially whenever lots of horses appeared on the screen. The same was true with football games, when players emerged from huddles. She also always dialogued with a disc jockey, Harry Billy, during his morning, bilingual radio show from Holbrook (a program many listened to and enjoyed), replying to him both appropriately and rapidly in Navajo. Other times she'd call out, sometimes thinking she saw a man hanging from the trees, or telling people to come and eat, or that they couldn't start to eat until their father got home. Among her other, frequent comments were: "Go get the sheep, herd the sheep." "Did you tie it up?" "Move that; I don't want the dogs getting into my dough; they're prowling around again." She also asked if her sister were there, "hanging around outside again," obviously referring to Slim Woman's December visit.

A few times during the spring, Tall Woman had clear periods while I was there; then we worked on some of my remaining questions. Those, of course, reactivated memories of "the old days," and she talked extensively about her tears when her parents refused to let her go to school, various "traditional beliefs" she expected people to follow, the rules for Nightway dancers, and other things. She also talked a great deal about the specifics of cooking and fixing traditional foods in different ways, and using plants as medicines.

When the weather was nice, "not too cold, not too windy, and not too hot," we'd move her, by means of a big sheepskin and two people's assistance, from her bed to her wheelchair, which we had taken outside, so she could sit and see what was happening, while we were cooking under the trees. Sometimes she'd ask to be "driven around" to visit the sheep in the corral, the hogan, or her other daughters' homes, and we'd comply. Marie, one of Ruth's daughters, was working at the Chinle Extended Care Facility at the time and came by, when possible, to offer assistance with some of the nursing duties. Augusta had purchased a washing machine to make it easier to do her mother's laundry, and whoever was around tried to relieve Bunni at meal times, since by then, Tall Woman needed to be hand fed. She continued to enjoy traditional foods and was eating well, although her diet was monitored closely because of blood sugar and other problems. At one point in April, Augusta said, "She knows she's home and that she's being well taken care of. I know she appreciates what we're trying to do for her. We promised Frank we'd take care of her, not stick her in a nursing home, so that's what we're trying to do. We keep her clean, bathe her carefully, and brush her hair every day, and we always talk with her. Of course her mind is wandering, but you learn just to go along with that. In return, she's being sweet. She's easy to take care of, maybe because of that. She always eats for us and lets us roll her over and change her catheter; she takes her medicine and her shots, and she never complains. She never, ever complains about her condition or what we're trying to do about things for her."

That spring, I took Tall Woman and others to several of her medical appointments in Ganado. Each time she traveled quietly, clearly enjoyed the scenery, and made appropriate comments on things she saw. Visits from relatives also stimulated periods of orientation. However, she also had "bad days" when she'd get upset by noise or noisy activities of her grandchildren. Among the things that agitated her were firecrackers; rough-house playing (especially with "Dino's" [Cecil, Jr.'s] rodeo clown barrel and other equipment); fighting over bikes, balls, and other toys; or if she saw or heard anyone imitating and denigrating her speech or mobility. Then she'd call out and express her dissatisfaction, sometimes even using the equivalent of cuss words such as "Coyote, Little Coyote." A few times, when a grandchild in close range didn't listen, I saw her reach out with her hand or cane, and slap or tap the person in question.

Sugar imbalances remained a problem, despite regular attention to diet and medications, and careful monitoring. On May 7, 1976, Tall Woman went into another diabetic coma and was rushed by ambulance to the Chinle clinic where she was stabilized and her insulin and other medications were readjusted. Agnes came again in early June to relieve Bunni. After my family arrived in Santa Fe on June 19, I brought them to Chinle for a brief visit. Tall Woman clearly remembered Ted and Elizabeth from earlier years and enjoyed two days of watching Jennifer, who would turn four years old in a few days and who she had never met.[13] On June 22, good-byes, tearful for all, had to be said. That was the last time I myself saw Tall Woman alive. On September 15, 1976, while Agnes was still there and Augusta was on sick leave from her new job as Food Service Supervisor because of knee problems, Tall Woman made her "First Communion," with Father Bryant Hausfeld, O.F.M., and three Sisters coming to the house for the occasion. When Agnes went back to California in late October, she and her husband located and purchased a used "green jeep" for Augusta to use in her new job, one which involved much traveling. That same month, Ruth and her family enjoyed a major pinyon picking trip and her daughter, Mildred, gave birth to Lorencita, giving Tall Woman yet another great-grandchild.

When 1977 began, things were going along as above, with Bunni caring for Tall Woman in Chinle while Augusta traveled around, supervising nine school kitchens. The month of February brought several more changes in the family; Marcus Yazzie, one of the sons of Man with a Cane, died,[14] and two more great-granddaughters for

Tall Woman were born when Ruth's daughter, Evonne, had Shellie and Isabel's daughter, Josephine, had Kimberly Marie. On April 14, a foster baby, Dennison Tsosie, joined Augusta's family; she'd been caring for foster children when possible for a number of years and decided to try to adopt this one. That month Agnes came for a few weeks to help again, and David and Susan McAllester visited, while working on their book on Navajo hogans.[15] It was then that Susan, at the family's request, took a variety of family photographs, including one that became the last picture ever taken of Tall Woman [see Fig. 43].

In May 1977, it became clear to everyone that Tall Woman's condition was deteriorating. From the twenty-third until the twenty-eighth, she was hospitalized at Sage

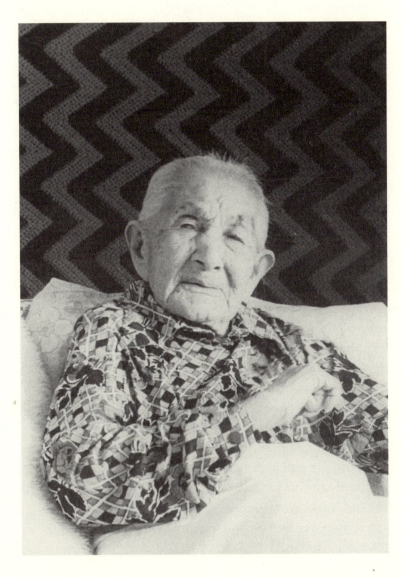

FIG. 43. The last picture of Tall Woman, in her bedroom at Augusta's house, April 24, 1977. Photographer, Susan W. McAllester. Courtesy of the late Susan McAllester.

Memorial in Ganado and put on an IV because of dehydration. After being stabilized, she was brought home and for a week, rallied and "started eating better." Then her condition worsened and after refusing to eat for two days, on June 11, she was taken to the Chinle clinic for IV feeding. Further urine complications resulted in a transfer to Ganado on June 13. Ruth stayed with her the first two nights, and Augusta brought Mary no. 1 to visit on the fourteenth. As Augusta said, "At that point, our mother had quit eating; her eyes were open but she didn't respond to us. We told her Isabel was coming to see her tomorrow and Agnes was on her way again. Sister Agnes had been here with us in April, helping out with our mother, but had gone back." By then, Tall Woman's bed sores refused to heal and a stomach tube was inserted because her arms were too swollen for further IV treatments.

Once Agnes arrived, the sisters met and decided to bring their mother home and "try to keep her on an IV. The doctors told us there was nothing more they could do. She didn't know anyone or anything at this point." Tall Woman was brought home on June 18 and Father Bryant Hausfeld, O.F.M., began visiting daily. On June 28, via ambulance, Augusta and Agnes took Tall Woman to the Chinle clinic to get help with her infected bed sores. There she was given "some penicillin, a pain numbing shot, and they disconnected her IV. The shot made her sleep all day and night. When it wore off early the next morning, it was clear she wasn't going to go on. So we notified Father Bryant and he came to administer the Last Rites. About two minutes after he finished, at 9:50 A.M., our mother passed away." The ambulance was called and her body was taken to the Chinle Extended Care Facility, accompanied by Agnes, Ruth, and Evonne. There she was officially pronounced dead at 10 A.M. and by earlier arrangement, her body, after being washed by the above family members, was placed in one of the two "coolers" at the facility until the family could make funeral arrangements. Agnes and Augusta then left for Ganado to return unused medical supplies to Sage Memorial Hospital and to inform the staff of her death; Ruth and her family went to notify Tall Woman's sister and half sister. By that evening, many people had assembled at the Mitchells' to grieve and plan the funeral. Cecilia said her mother, Augusta, was one of the main speakers at this meeting, emphasizing "respecting old age people and taking care of parents and grandparents at home, instead of putting them in nursing homes and forgetting about them."

Having been in touch by telephone with Agnes and Augusta during this entire period, I flew to Albuquerque on June 30, arriving in Chinle late in the afternoon with groceries and other things I was asked to pick up. Isabel, Mary no. 1, and Ruth were greeting people with the customary wailing, whereas Agnes and Augusta were focused on the fact their mother "[was] now in good hands, her suffering [had] ended." More of Tall Woman's grandchildren and great-grandchildren had arrived, and others did so the next day. People were stopping by, bringing plastic floral arrangements for use at the cemetery, food, and other things. The night of June 30 was spent sewing four new, figured cotton print skirts and a new, brown velveteen blouse for Tall Woman from materials provided by Agnes. We also shared news while making lists of people who had already donated food, money, and offers of assistance. Concerns were voiced over the size of the grave dug by Don Nelson from the Catholic Church, and the whereabouts of Tall Woman's string of "big pieces of turquoise" and her squash blossom necklace, both of which Frank had given her. Work needing to be done the next day was also itemized and while that was being discussed, I was asked to write the obituary notices for the *Navajo Times* and the *Gallup Independent*. I agreed to do so, if all would help.

July 1 was spent notifying more people, running errands in Gallup, cooking, and going to the Rosary. Via Tsaile, Agnes, Augusta, and I went to Gallup where the first stop was Cope's Mortuary. After extensive discussions, two hundred memorial cards and a "Guest book" were ordered, and print styles and information needed for the former, including Tall Woman's birthdate and the pallbearer list, were settled.[16] Then we went to the Blossom Shop where a variety of floral arrangements, all to be ready by late afternoon, were ordered.[17] Lunch was followed by a phone call to Chinle for an update from Cecilia on Isabel and Jimmy's plans to go to Gallup, and what Mary Alice Mitchell had already started cooking at the high school kitchen for the reception after the funeral.[18] Then we went to a variety of stores, searching for things still needed for Tall Woman, including socks, head scarves, and silver buttons for her new blouse. At Richardson's we met Isabel and Jimmy, who had already purchased the moccasins and the *jaatł'óół* as previously agreed. After the buttons were chosen and purchased, we went to Albertson's to get plates and other paper goods for the reception; the lumber yard to get the wood, cement, paint, and brushes needed for the construction of the cemetery cross; and the Gallup Cathedral to get a rosary and a crucifix. Agnes wanted the latter imbedded in her mother's concrete cross when it was made by Howard. Then we picked up the orders at Cope's and the Blossom Shop, and started back with a stop at Fed Mart for more groceries.[19] That stop was short since the Rosary had been scheduled for 7:30 P.M. at Our Lady of Fatima Church in Chinle.

After waiting for the entire family to arrive and then deciding to start rather than wait any longer, the Rosary, with Father Bryant Hausfeld, O.F.M., officiating, was held from 7:50 until 8:10 P.M. A photograph of Tall Woman, taken by Dr. George McClelland, Sr., and usually on a wall in Augusta's living room [see, above, Fig. 32], was displayed near the altar during the service. Participants included: Agnes, Augusta, Mary no. 1, Ruth, Seya, Howard, Cecilia, Sarah and Bahe Jones, David and Rose Mitchell with their children, Mary Tsosi from Black Mountain (Adelle's half sister), and me. After the service, we took the flowers to the cooler at the high school and then went home. When Isabel returned, we learned she and Jimmy had gone from Gallup to Wheatfields to check on the sheep that had been moved to his sister's place in the mountains for summer grazing the week before; there, they had discovered that Augusta's goat had died from an infected udder.

While this was discussed, I sewed the buttons on Tall Woman's new velveteen blouse while Cecilia ironed the skirts Marie had just finished hemming. About 10 P.M., while Agnes continued talking with Mary no. 1 and her granddaughter, Ramona, who had arrived, Cecilia went to the church hall to set up tables, and Augusta and I went to the high school kitchen. There we made tossed salads, punch, cut up meat and vegetables for stew, and baked two sheet cakes. Mary Alice had already made three, institutional-size, sheet cake pans full of fruited Jell-O, seven similar pans full of rolls, and cooked all the meat (which included hams and turkeys as well as mutton). Cecilia joined us eventually and we finished doing what we could; sometime after 1 A.M. we went home. After setting out all the clothes to be used in dressing Tall Woman in the morning and reviewing remaining jobs and making plans for them, we went to bed. Four sheep had been butchered during the day while we were gone.

For us, Saturday, July 2, 1977, the day of the funeral, began shortly after 6 A.M. with the further assembling of things to be used in dressing Tall Woman.[20] Cecilia and Augusta went to the high school kitchen shortly after 7 A.M., while Ruth, Agnes, and I headed for the Chinle Extended Care Facility. After finally locating someone with a key to the "cooler," we went in at 7:50 A.M., just as Leroy Mitchell came in his truck with Howard, Seya, Jimmy, and Timmy. They left the coffin and took the outer box to the cemetery where, with shovels, they enlarged the width of the 4' x 4' hole another six inches to accommodate the box. Meanwhile, Ruth, Agnes, and I removed Tall Woman's body from storage, unwrapped its outer plastic and inner bedsheet coverings, changed her bandages but not her diaper, and then started to dress her, beginning with her feet. While Agnes pinned the skirts in place, Ruth and I did her hair and then put on her jewelry, before placing remaining items in the coffin. The men returned and lifted Tall Woman's body into the coffin, just as Augusta arrived. After arranging her appropriately, Tall Woman was covered first with a new Pendleton blanket and then, her own. Howard was told to incinerate the wrappings and old dressings, and about 8:30 A.M., we all departed, after the coffin was loaded in the pickup and most of us had shed some more tears. By then, it was already very hot and the body was thawing rapidly.

Ruth and I went to the high school kitchen to pick up the rolls, jars of pickles, watermelons, and other things and take them to the church hall. Mary no. 1, her daughter, Louise, and Isabel were there helping set tables and making iced tea. After I made another trip for things at the high school, we all changed our clothes in the church hall and headed for the church. Leroy arrived with the coffin; the pallbearers helped unload it while the rest of us set up the guest book,[21] pinned white carnations on the pallbearers, and took care of remaining details before people began arriving at 9:45.

The funeral, scheduled for 10 A.M., started at 10:05 and was a Requiem Mass, in En-

glish, with over 120 people present. Father Bryant Hausfeld, O.F.M., officiated, assisted by Father Ivo Zirkelbach, O.F.M.; the former's eulogy stressed Tall Woman's
goodness and generosity, long and fruitful life, 1965 baptism with Frank, her communions, and Last Rites. Before communion, Augusta spoke for about five minutes in
Navajo, stressing proper care and respect for parents and grandparents, and the importance of family and "traditional values" before thanking people for their help, and
extending an invitation to the meal in the church hall after the cemetery burial. At the
end of the mass, the pallbearers escorted the coffin down the aisle to the vestibule and
opened it, enabling people to view the body and say their good-byes to Tall Woman,
if they wished to do so, before departure. Then, after the church doors were closed,
the family did the same.

Tall Woman's sister, Small Woman, who had remained in the vestibule without approaching the coffin, started talking to all of Tall Woman's children, reminding them
"not to cry after their mother." Chauncey Neboyia[22] had begun similar speeches with
an emphasis on "being strong" in the aisle a few minutes earlier; soon, both of them
went outside and started addressing the People waiting there, almost in litany fashion,
until their speeches were joined by words from Jimmy Deschine. Inside, we said our
good-byes.[23] After Agnes added a rosary to the coffin, the lid was closed and we followed it out of the church and watched while it was loaded into Leroy's truck. His
wife, Sally, and Ruth rode in silence with me in the procession of twenty-seven cars
that went, with police escort, to the Chinle Community Cemetery. There, after Father Bryant finished the graveside service, the coffin was lowered into the box already
in the ground. Don Nelson and Timmy nailed the box shut and at noon, the pallbearers, using shovels, began to fill the grave while others filed past, adding handfuls of
dirt and sometimes, prayers. While this was going on, Chauncey again spoke to the
crowd which consisted of about one hundred people, only two of whom (Father
Bryant and me) were "white."

Augusta, Agnes, Sally, and I returned to the high school kitchen to pick up more
food and transport it to the church hall. Then we began serving a line of 136 people;
20 others, who arrived later, served themselves after family members sat down to
eat.[24] Around 1:45, after people started leaving, we began cleaning up, finishing that
by 2:30 and then returning things to the high school kitchen. Agnes and I went back
to the cemetery to try to learn where some of the flowers had come from so their
donors could be thanked. But since no cards were attached to the five containers of
mums and two of daisies in question, we left. Agnes and Augusta then napped; Ruth
and some of her family went to Tsaile Lake while others tried to fix car troubles for a
relative. Cecilia and I returned more things to the church hall and then went out for
coffee before coming back to help Agnes and Augusta make supper. My evening was
spent getting a tour of the new hogan under construction for Isabel, and visiting with

family members. I again asked for input for Tall Woman's obituary, reminding everybody that my summer teaching job prevented me from remaining until the "four days were up" and that I had to depart the next afternoon. Some ideas about the obituary were forthcoming as were some more questions about when Frank's book might appear and when I'd be able to start working on hers. We all regretted that Frank's was still "in press" and that Tall Woman didn't live to see it emerge (which it did the following year, in November 1978).

The next morning, I drove Isabel, Jerry, and Cecilia to mass, while Ruth came with Stella, and Augusta, with Agnes. Seya appeared at the church hall during the subsequent coffee hour to say good-bye to me, since he was going back to Cottonwood to take care of other things. Agnes wanted to treat people to breakfast; after discovering the Thunderbird cafeteria was closed, we ended up at Fleming's Cafe. When we returned, Isabel discovered a sister-in-law waiting; Agnes and Augusta started making iced tea, while I packed. Mary no. 1 arrived with a clan relative who needed transportation. After much joking, she asked what jewelry had been buried with Tall Woman, and conversations turned to that and issues surrounding land and livestock permits. I went to Ruth's and Isabel's to say tearful good-byes to family members, and then loaded the rental car before saying good-bye at Augusta's, where Agnes, Augusta, and Mary no. 1 were making decisions about the transportation request, an afternoon picnic invitation, and the need to return to the high school to make sure the kitchen was ready for summer school use in the morning. During my night flight to St. Louis I finished writing the obituaries. After typing, they were mailed to the Mitchells for their review, corrections, or approval, with enclosed stamped, addressed envelopes to use in forwarding the results to the papers.[25]

Tall Woman was predeceased by her parents; her husband, Frank; and at least five children: two unnamed infants, Pauline, Mary no. 2, and David. Only two of her siblings, her "real sister," Small Woman, and her half sister, Slim Woman, survived her; they passed away, respectively, in September 1981 and on December 15, 1983. In addition to them, as shown in Appendix A, Tall Woman's survivors included seven children, six of whom (all except Howard) were married or divorced at the time of her death, and parenting anywhere from two to nine children apiece. Besides these grandchildren, Tall Woman's survivors also included a number of great-grandchildren since five of her own married/divorced children (all but Agnes) had already become grandparents by June 1977.

Family's Concluding Reflections

Although memories of Tall Woman will continue through all the generations who knew her personally,[26] in 1996, her family asked that the Epilogue portion of "her story" end with their thoughts on her "most outstanding qualities," the things by which they continue to remember her. The format they preferred was a composite list of their thoughts, "uncluttered by identifications of who said what, or other things" (from me, including rank orderings of comments and analyses of frequency). While many recalled specific incidents in the course of these discussions (which had taken place between July 1977 and August 1990), in 1996, when finally viewing them in assembled draft form, the family also decided to exclude these since Tall Woman herself mentioned them in her narrative. The composite list that follows is based on discussions with all of her children and also Garnett, Small Woman, and Slim Woman. I am presenting it below as requested in 1996, "uncluttered" by references to places in her narrative that illustrate the identified qualities, and without adding my own thoughts about why I too found Tall Woman to be "outstanding."

1. Her hard work throughout her entire life: "She had unending energy; she was always working from before dawn until after dark." "She worked circles around us, without ever getting tired." "She was always so full of energy, even in her old age; we still don't know how she did it." "Even in the heat, she'd be hoeing with a towel on her head, or reroofing the cookshack, or cooking, or doing something. In the fall, she'd be busy preserving things for our winter use. She just never stopped." "She was a real worker; she went right into old age and kept right on going; even that didn't slow her down, ever!"

2. Her kindness to all people, no matter where they came from: "She never said a harsh word about her children, her husband, family members, in-laws, clan relatives, visitors, strangers — anyone." "Even here at home, she never said harsh things about people, or used abusive words about anybody." "She never used bad words about anybody; she taught us to respect others and to be kind and friendly to everybody." "She was never a jealous person; she said there was no point in being that way, that it wasn't a good thing; we never saw her express jealousy toward anybody for any reason."

3. Her strength as a "traditional woman": "She really had very deep, very strong beliefs in Navajo traditions, all our traditional beliefs and practices, and our own ceremonies, especially the Blessingway. She lived according to that and raised us with that, too." "She was the most traditional woman I ever knew. She never once put any of those things aside." "She was very, very traditional. She respected all our traditions and lived by them, and she believed we should do that, too."

4. Her strength, both physical and moral: "She was the strongest person we ever knew, inside herself. It was as if there was no end, no limit to her abilities to endure and withstand all kinds of sufferings and hardships." "She was able to endure everything without falling apart, going to pieces; no matter what suffering came up, she always managed to make a plan and to survive." "She was a very, very strong woman; she reminds me of a Russian woman or of Rose Kennedy. She endured all kinds of

sufferings." "She was so strong; those hardships she went through seemed to harden her, make her even stronger, so she could endure even more suffering." "She challenged all her own pains and hardships; it was like she toughened herself up by going through those, learning to live with them; all those things made her very, very strong, instead of destroying her." "She was such a strong woman she even outlived Dad."

5. Her skills as a midwife: "She had special knowledge that allowed her to turn babies around and help women going through difficult labors. She was really famous for that." "She was very well known as a midwife in all the places they lived; people knew she had that knowledge. She was respected for it and people were always coming to get her to help in that way." "She was the preferred midwife wherever we lived, but she never advertised herself for that or anything else; she was very modest about all the things the People used to respect her for."

6. Her excellence as a weaver, first of Chief Blankets, and then of "Chinle-style rugs": "She was really well known in this area for her weaving; she knew how to do lots of different kinds of weaving and kept all those things in her mind." "She never had any trouble selling her rugs; people would ask for rugs she made. She was really respected for her weaving." "Without all the rugs she made for years and years, we wouldn't have survived; we wouldn't even be here. It's mainly on her account all us kids didn't starve to death." "I hope she's made it clear to you while telling you her story that without her weavings, our whole family, especially in the early years, wouldn't have been able to survive. My Dad sure doesn't talk about that in his story but all of us know she really deserves credit for raising us and for our very survival."

7. Her knowledge of traditional plants and how to use everything in the environment for food: "She was well known for her ways of cooking, fixing all the traditional foods, even the ones needed for ceremonies, or trips to the sacred mountains." "Even when we were growing up, people were starting to forget about how to fix those traditional foods, and they'd come to her to refresh their memories, or to ask her to teach them how to fix those different foods." "She really knew about all the traditional foods and we're lucky she fixed those for us, and showed us how they did that; now, hardly anybody knows those things."

8. Her care of and respect for her father's *"jish* with the craneheads": "She was well known because of one of the bundles her father had, the one with the cranes that he left to her for safekeeping. Those were very rare and she was well known for having it and being very careful about keeping it in the right way and loaning it only to those who were really qualified and knew how to use it."

9. Her quietness: "She was always quiet, always silent about her own physical problems. She never complained or bellyached about her teeth, infections, painful joints, stomach problems, broken bones, and other problems, even in the face of gallbladder troubles, arthritis, diabetes, her own surgeries." "She was a very, very quiet person;

she really kept things to herself. Sometimes, when people do that, those things build up and then start causing problems. But with her, they didn't. She had a way of being quiet, being calm and peaceful. She was really a lovely person, a very special woman for all those reasons."

10. Her patience and self-control: "She never flew off the handle about anything or with anybody, never cussed people out, never yelled, screamed, waved her arms all about." "She was always calm; she never let herself get overly excited about anything, no matter what happened." "She was always patient with everybody; it didn't matter if they were people way up in old age or little children, or what somebody did. She never went to pieces over anything; she never lost her cool."

11. Her love for her children: "We always knew she really loved us. That wasn't because she went around giving us lots of hugs or kisses, because she didn't. Instead, we knew she loved us because of the way she spoke to us. She always used the loving, respectful ways of addressing us, even when she needed to scold us." "She was a very loving person; she was always there, giving us attention, showing us things. And she always spoke to us with affection, showing us respect, even when we were very small. That way, we knew she loved us, even when we acted out or did foolish things. She always was concerned about us, trying to do things for us. She really lived her love by showing it in the ways she acted toward us every day. Even then, a lot of parents always seemed to be yelling at their kids, never praising them or showing them kindness or respect. She was very, very different." "She was always very, very concerned about her children and her grandchildren; they always came first. She didn't like to hear children crying because that meant something was wrong and somebody wasn't paying attention to them, like they should."

12. Her willingness to teach her children: "She was always trying to show us things so we'd learn the things she knew, no matter what it concerned." "She was so different about talking with her children; she made you know she really wanted you to learn things, that it really mattered and that she was willing to show you. She never belittled our efforts; she made you want to learn." "So often, even then, it seemed like parents didn't bother to talk with their children, spend time showing them things, teaching them about the traditions. She wasn't like that. She really talked with us, adjusting her words to however old we were and what we were going through." "I don't know where any of us would be without her teachings, all of her talks. She didn't preach to us but she sure took time to try and teach us everything she knew so we could be prepared. She really believed that was important. Even now, I remember her talks." "She really wanted us to be prepared for whatever came along in the future. Lots of times I think about her words now, and I am so thankful she bothered to talk to us about life. All those things she said about how things would change, how there would be hardships to face and go through, and what old age would bring, all those things came to be true

for us. By talking to us and teaching us, she helped prepare us for everything. Now I believe all the things she said and I'm grateful she bothered to talk to us about everything like she did."

13. Her ability to find a use for everything, never waste anything: "She knew all kinds of ways to preserve foods, and fix animals that were hunted or butchered. She never wasted one thing." "Lots of times she'd say, 'Don't throw that out,' because she knew how to make something from it, or how to use it in making or fixing something else. She said everything was put here for our use and that we should know how to do that with respect and in the right ways. Even with the different plants; a lot of those she knew could be used for food, medicines, dyes for the wool — even different parts from the same plant. I don't remember her wasting anything, ever! Even if it meant she had to stay up way late to keep working on something to turn it into something she could use, she'd do that."

14. Her generosity to all: "She was a caring, sharing, loving person and she tried to be like that toward everybody, not just her children or her relatives." "She always tried to help people with whatever little food, or material, or plant medicines, or other things she had around, or even just by fixing coffee and listening, offering suggestions or consoling words. She always said we should learn to be like that, to do whatever we could to help others at all times. That's the way she lived every single day. In so many, many ways, she was a wonderful model for all of us."

Appendixes

Introduction to Appendix A: Genealogy

The genealogical information presented in the following appendix is based on extensive work with Tall Woman, her sister and half sister, all of her children as well as others raised by her, other relatives, and mission and census records. It needs to be emphasized that, as in any family, the members of Tall Woman's have different understandings of and experiences with relatives and thus, sometimes, different opinions about portions of their genealogy. Among the factors influencing the diversity are birthdates, birth order, and age; linguistic skills and preferences; amount and location of Western schooling (if any); gender; personal life cycles and histories; experiences in earlier geographical locations; interest in kinship matters; and present locations and physical conditions. Some never asked Tall Woman about her siblings or other relatives, and some never paid much attention when these people were being discussed while they were home. During our discussions, it also became clear that Tall Woman herself did not talk about such matters with some of her children, thus creating differences in transmission. She was already well into "old age" when I started working with her and sometimes could only respond with "I don't remember anymore" when asked about specific genealogical matters. Later, when mental confusion set in and she had her first stroke, such questions became futile.

Besides the diverse understandings within the family, other factors contributed to the problems that arose during the genealogical work. Archival materials, both census- and mission-based, sometimes did not confirm family information and often showed internal inconsistencies, as well. The differences between Anglo and Navajo kinship terms were also problematic, especially when interpreters used gloss terms in either or both languages. Other problems stemmed from the habits some had of calling their mother their grandmother, or interchanging grandmother and great-grandmother terms, and/or "he" and "she" pronouns, when speaking in English.

The numbers, names, life spans, and birth orders of Tall Woman's siblings and earlier relatives were problematic for many, including her. Among the approaches used by her children and her sister and half sister when trying to reconstruct birth orders was that of "comparative dating." They considered whether or not they ever saw X "when they were old enough to realize things," a point the women often tied to their first Puberty Ceremony, since for them the ceremony was the time when they "began to remember and understand things." They also considered whether X was still living when someone else passed away; how old, tall, gray, "shriveled up," or whatever X was, or where that person was living when they themselves were doing something datable or significant in their own lives, such as starting or finishing at specific federal boarding schools, or when an event significant in Navajo history, such as the flu epidemic, was ongoing.

Multiple names and nicknames attributed to single individuals also caused confusion during our discussions, as did the transmission of these to later generations and the recurrent use of a single name, such as The One Who Returned from the Warpath in a Bad Mood, for a number of offspring in different generations and branches of the family. Likewise, some of the intermarriages between Frank's side and Tall Woman's relatives, as well as within Tall Woman's extended family itself led to confusion, so much so that some had "given up trying to straighten it out so we understand it." The same was true for some of the numerous cases where children were raised by people other than their parents, or renamed someone's son or daughter when they biologically were not. Cases where individuals had married a series of sisters in succession also caused confusion for some, as did second and subsequent marriages, especially those producing children. Then too, for some, being involved in genealogical discussions led to "family tree surprises," both in terms of the second wife of Man Who Shouts, and children produced for someone "other than the person one was thought to be with."

Diverse opinions about genealogical matters sometimes led to arguments during discussions, as well as after-the-fact evaluative comments about why X didn't really understand the matters at hand, and why I shouldn't be wasting my (and others') time consulting X further. As my own understanding of the chronology of Tall Woman's life deepened, other inconsistencies in information became apparent, especially ones concerned with when and where individuals had died, and who had been involved in the burials. Further discussions usually brought resolution by group consensus. Deference to Seya's [SM's] opinion was often shown, since he was the oldest son and the family member with the "best understanding" of Navajo history and family genealogy. However, there were a number of things that he too wasn't sure about or had never heard about, because of his years away at federal boarding schools. He and Mary no. 1 [MD], the oldest daughter, were the main sources for identifications of relatives and others who moved around with Tall Woman's parents "in early times," when Tall Woman herself could no longer help with these questions.

Without the willingness to persevere and try to unravel genealogical connections displayed by Tall Woman, all of her biological children and Garnett [GB] and Ida [IF], as well as her sister and half sister, some of their children, and a number of Tall Woman's grandchildren, it would have been impossible to reconstruct much of her genealogy. We all realize that despite our efforts, many questions remain. We also now fully understand that these questions should have been asked much earlier in time, when those who knew the answers were still alive and in full possession of their mental faculties. Thus, it is acknowledged by *all* who have worked on Tall Woman's genealogy that the diagrams that follow as A-1, A-2, and A-3 represent "the best we can do." As per our agreement, the diagrams reflect Tall Woman's explanations of kin connections, rather than the diversity of opinions extant within the family about particular parts of the "family tree."

Of the four components in Appendix A, the three diagrams show a reconstruction of Tall Woman's forebears, natal family, and the conjugal family she and Frank produced. They are inconsistent in that they pursue subsequent generations to variable depths, according to both family knowledge and relevance to Tall Woman's narrative. Needless to say, more energies were devoted to clarifying and tracing Tall Woman's nuclear family, both natal and conjugal, than her extended one. But even here, the results are incomplete.

Since the Mitchells wanted their genealogy followed through time into the present, the last component in this appendix (A-4) lists what information we were able to collect concerning the descendants of each of the surviving children born to Tall Woman and Frank, and of Garnett Scott (later, GB) within the parameters of an agreed on *cutoff date of 6/1/1997*. List format was chosen over a diagrammatic approach in view of the numbers of individuals to be accommodated. Individuals who survived into adulthood are arranged according to birthdate, with the oldest, MD, appearing first. Some information is missing, and what appears is variable; given the size of the family and their diverse locations at present, not all relatives could be visited and asked to provide accurate information about themselves. Additionally, the manner in which individuals are shown reflects the choices each made in 1996–97 about whom should appear, and how much and what information should be included. The only exception to the cutoff date of 6/1/1997 was the decision to include the death dates of Seya Mitchell, Jimmy Deschine, and Louise Woody Davis, events that transpired while manuscript preparation was still in process.

Appendix A consists of:

Appendix A-1: Tall Woman's Forebears

Appendix A-2: Tall Woman's Natal Family

Appendix A-3: Conjugal Family of Tall Woman and Frank Mitchell

Appendix A-4: Descendants, as of June 1, 1997, of the Children of Tall Woman and Frank Mitchell who survived into adulthood, and of Garnett Scott who, for years, was raised by them.

Appendix A-1: Tall Woman's Forebears

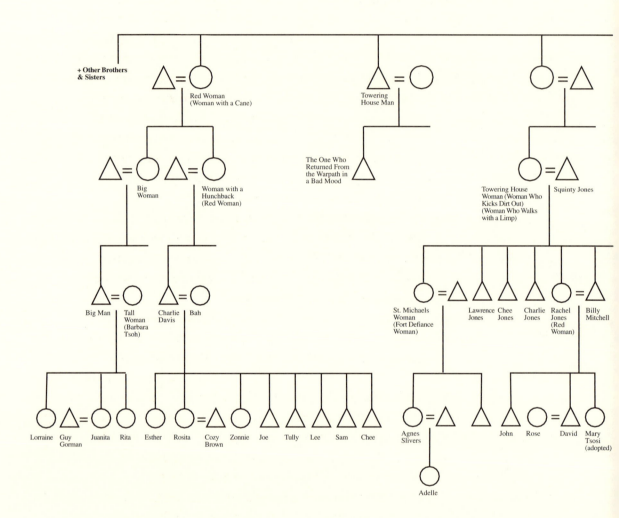

+ Other Brothers & Sisters

Red Woman (Woman with a Cane)

Towering House Man

Big Woman

Woman with a Hunchback (Red Woman)

The One Who Returned From the Warpath in a Bad Mood

Towering House Woman (Woman Who Kicks Dirt Out) (Woman Who Walks with a Limp)

Squinty Jones

Big Man

Tall Woman (Barbara Tsoh)

Charlie Davis

Bah

St. Michaels Woman (Fort Defiance Woman)

Lawrence Jones

Chee Jones

Charlie Jones

Rachel Jones (Red Woman)

Billy Mitchell

Lorraine

Guy Gorman

Juanita

Rita

Esther

Rosita

Cozy Brown

Zonnie

Joe

Tully

Lee

Sam

Chee

Agnes Slivers

John

Rose

David

Mary Tsosi (adopted)

Adelle

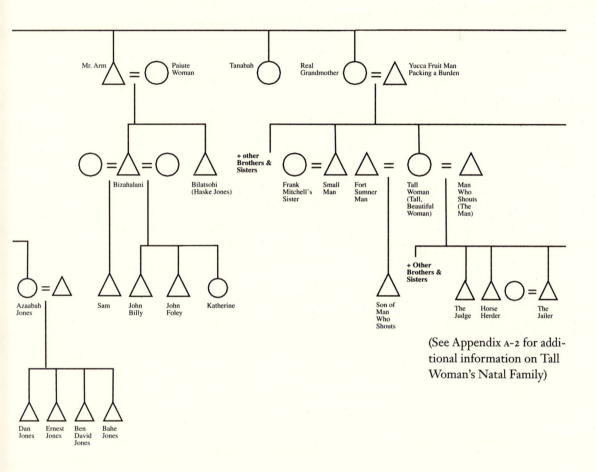

Mr. Arm — Paiute Woman

Tanabah

Real Grandmother — Yucca Fruit Man Packing a Burden

Bizahalani

Bilatsohi (Haske Jones)

+ other Brothers & Sisters

Frank Mitchell's Sister — Small Man

Fort Sumner Man — Tall Woman (Tall, Beautiful Woman) — Man Who Shouts (The Man)

Azaabah Jones

Sam

John Billy

John Foley

Katherine

Son of Man Who Shouts

+ Other Brothers & Sisters

The Judge

Horse Herder — The Jailer

Dan Jones

Ernest Jones

Ben David Jones

Bahe Jones

(See Appendix A-2 for additional information on Tall Woman's Natal Family)

331

Appendix A-1: Tall Woman's Forebears *cont'd*

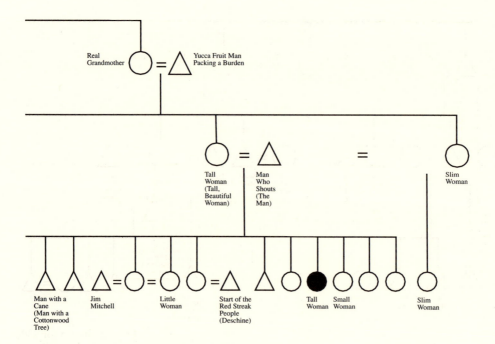

Real Grandmother

Yucca Fruit Man Packing a Burden

Tall Woman (Tall, Beautiful Woman)

Man Who Shouts (The Man)

Slim Woman

Man with a Cane (Man with a Cottonwood Tree)

Jim Mitchell

Little Woman

Start of the Red Streak People (Deschine)

Tall Woman

Small Woman

Slim Woman

Appendix A-2: Tall Woman's Natal Family

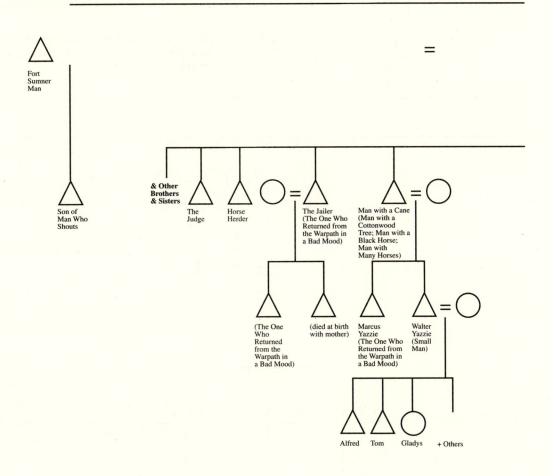

Fort
Sumner
Man

Son of
Man Who
Shouts

**& Other
Brothers
& Sisters**

The
Judge

Horse
Herder

The Jailer
(The One Who
Returned from
the Warpath in
a Bad Mood)

Man with a Cane
(Man with a
Cottonwood
Tree; Man with a
Black Horse;
Man with
Many Horses)

(The One
Who
Returned
from the
Warpath in
a Bad Mood)

(died at birth
with mother)

Marcus
Yazzie
(The One Who
Returned from
the Warpath in
a Bad Mood)

Walter
Yazzie
(Small
Man)

Alfred   Tom   Gladys   + Others

Appendix A-2: Tall Woman's Natal Family *cont'd*

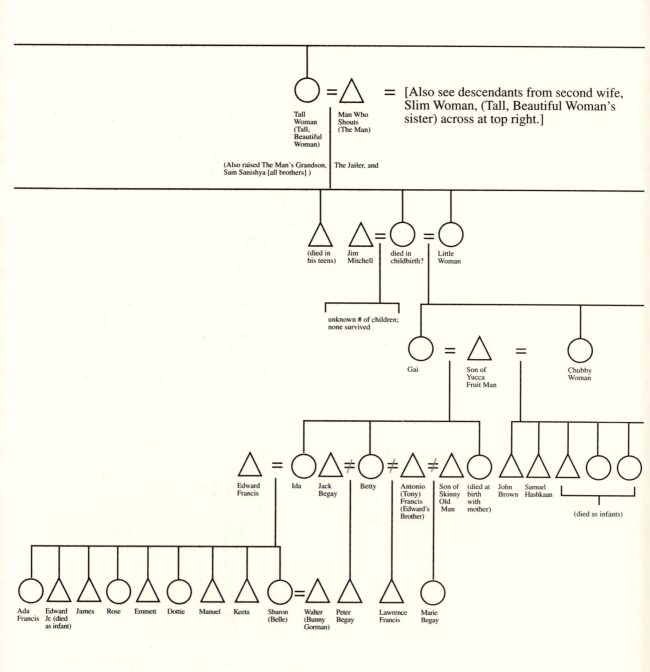

334

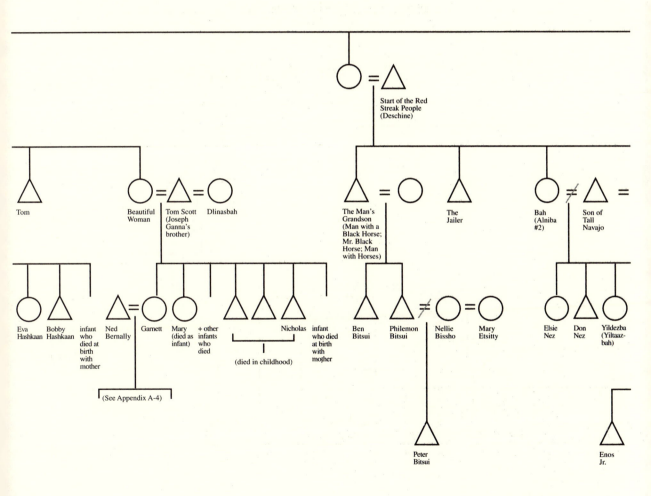

Start of the Red
Streak People
(Deschine)

Tom

Beautiful
Woman

Tom Scott
(Joseph
Ganna's
brother)

Dlinasbah

The Man's
Grandson
(Man with a
Black Horse;
Mr. Black
Horse; Man
with Horses)

The
Jailer

Bah
(Alniba
#2)

Son of
Tall
Navajo

Eva
Hashkaan

Bobby
Hashkaan

infant
who
died at
birth
with
mother

Ned
Bernally

Garnett

Mary
(died as
infant)

+ other
infants
who
died

Nicholas

infant
who died
at birth
with
mother

Ben
Bitsui

Philemon
Bitsui

Nellie
Bissho

Mary
Etsitty

Elsie
Nez

Don
Nez

Yildezba
(Yiltaaz-
bah)

(died in childhood)

(See Appendix A-4)

Peter
Bitsui

Enos
Jr.

335

Appendix A-2: Tall Woman's Natal Family *cont'd*

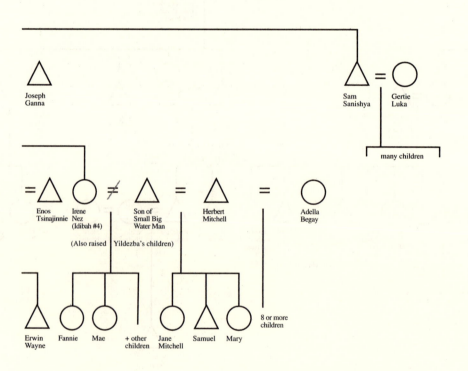

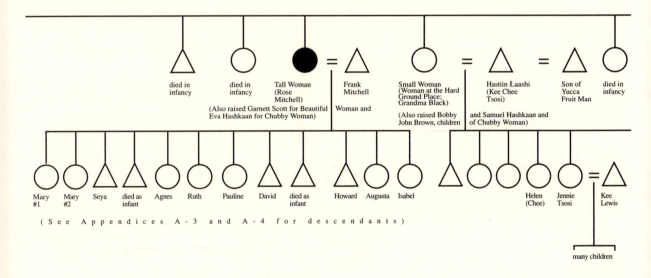

died in
infancy

died in
infancy

Tall Woman
(Rose
Mitchell)

(Also raised Garnett Scott for Beautiful
Eva Hashkaan for Chubby Woman)

Frank
Mitchell

Woman and

Small Woman
(Woman at the Hard
Ground Place;
Grandma Black)

(Also raised Bobby
John Brown, children

Hastiin Łaashi
(Kee Chee
Tsosi)

and Samuel Hashkaan and
of Chubby Woman)

Son of
Yucca
Fruit Man

died in
infancy

Mary
#1

Mary
#2

Seya

died as
infant

Agnes

Ruth

Pauline

David

died as
infant

Howard

Augusta

Isabel

Helen
(Chee)

Jennie
Tsosi

Kee
Lewis

(See Appendices A-3 and A-4 for descendants)

many children

337

Appendix A-2: Tall Woman's Natal Family *cont'd*

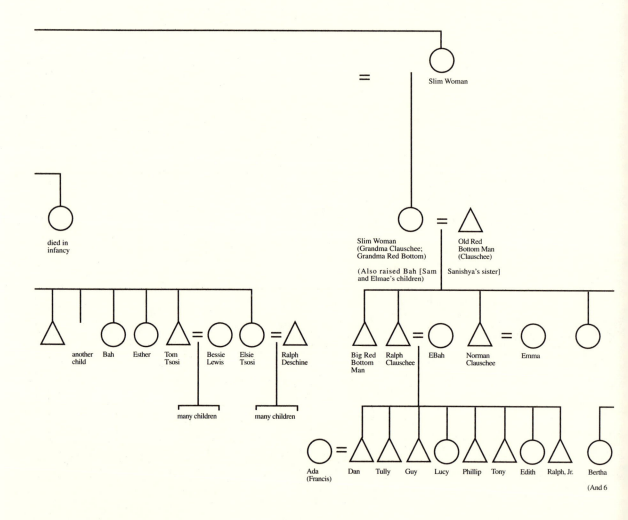

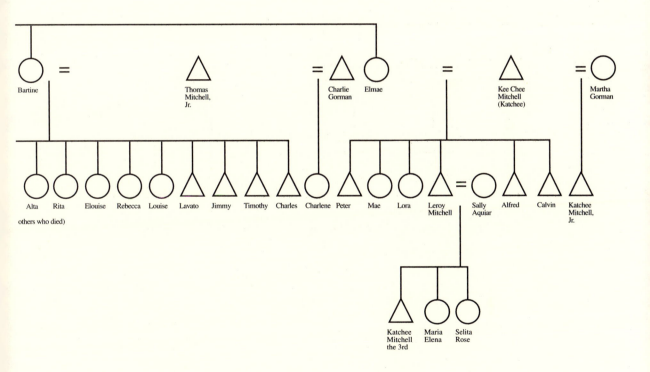

Bartine =   Thomas Mitchell, Jr.   = Charlie Gorman   Elmae   =   Kee Chee Mitchell (Katchee)   = Martha Gorman

Alta   Rita   Elouise   Rebecca   Louise   Lavato   Jimmy   Timothy   Charles   Charlene   Peter   Mae   Lora   Leroy Mitchell = Sally Aquiar   Alfred   Calvin   Katchee Mitchell, Jr.

others who died)

Katchee Mitchell the 3rd   Maria Elena   Selita Rose

339

Appendix A-3: Conjugal Family of Tall Woman and Frank Mitchell*

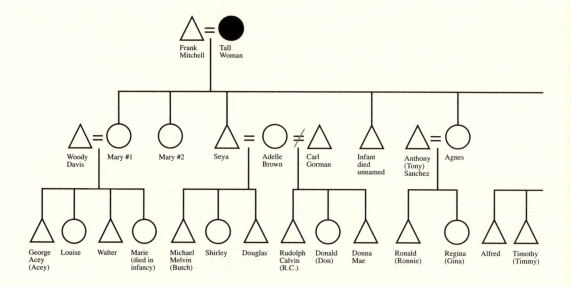

★ Appendix A-3 illustrates all of the grandchildren born to Tall Woman's and Frank Mitchell's children. For later generations, see Appendix A-4.

Tall Woman and Frank Mitchell also raised:

1. Garnett Scott, daughter of Beautiful Woman and Tom Scott, from 1934 on (see text and Appendix A-4).
2. Eva Hashkaan, daughter of Chubby Woman and Son of Yucca Fruit Man, for several years beginning in 1939 (see text).

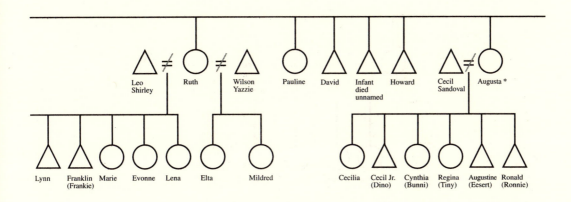

*Augusta also raised Dennison Tsosie
(Burger), ward, beginning in 1977.

Appendix A-3: Conjugal Family *cont'd*

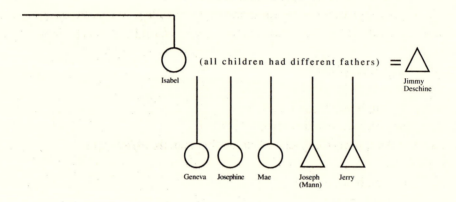

Appendix A-4

Descendants, as of 6/1/1997, of the Children of Tall Woman and Frank Mitchell who survived into adulthood, and of Garnett Scott who, for years, was raised by them.

1. Mary Mitchell Davis, b. ca. 1908 (see Chap. 7, n. 1); m. (pre-church wedding, 2/2/1927), Woody Davis (b. ca. 1900; d. 9/5/1980)
   A. *Children:*
      1. George Acey Davis ("Acey"), b. 9/8/1926; d. 4/30/1986
      2. Louise Davis, b. 9/25/1928; d. 7/8/1991; first m. Dennis Begay; then divorced; had children for Edward Francis; then m., 5/30/1970, Harold Tso; no children with Harold
         a. *Children (Louise and Dennis):*
            1. girl, died at birth
            2. Ramona Ann, b. 10/8/1949 (unmarried)
            3. Dennison Michael, b. 8/27/1950; m. Priscilla
            4. Caroline Ann, b. 11/10/1952; m. Daniel Hickman (b. 10/9/1949)
               a. *Children:*
                  1. Jennifer, b. 8/26/1981
                  2. Denise, b. 12/4/1985
            5. Margaret Ann, b. 3/4/1954; m.
               a. *Child:*
                  1. Myron, b. 5/7/1983
            6. Dennis, Jr., b. 6/8/1955 (unmarried)
            7. Boyd John, b. 6/8/1956; d. 2/14/1977
         b. *Children (Louise and Edward):*
            1. Marshall Francis, b. 10/23/1957; m. Martha Begay (b. 2/21/1960)
               a. *Children:*
                  1. Murphy, b. 9/21/1976; m. Bernadine Tso (b. 10/23/1975)
                     a. *Children:*
                        1. Meshia, b. 8/30/1993
                        2. Melcolm, b. 8/23/1995
                  2. Marsha, b. 2/9/1978; m. Freddie Jumbo (b. 2/15/1975)
                     a. *Children:*
                        1. Irvin, b. 8/15/1995
                        2. Marisha

3. Marcie, b. 7/4/1980 (unmarried)
4. Monique, b. 5/21/1987 (unmarried)
5. Marli, b. 8/25/1989 (unmarried)
2. Darlene Francis, b. 1/22/1959; m. Rex Ray Begay (b. 7/23/1958)
   a. *Children:*
      1. Reginald Roscoe, b. 11/8/1979
      2. Ronnie Roscoe, b. 12/10/1980; m. to Jolene
3. James Francis, b. 2/13/1960
   a. *Children:*
      1. Jeremy, b. 12/6/1981
      2. Ivan, b. 8/14/1983
      3. Tyler
4. Carol Francis, b. 10/4/1961; had daughter, Cleora, b. 12/26/1977; m. Edison Begay
   a. *Children with Edison:*
      1. Tamara Jean, b. 10/10/1986
      2. Kyle Edward, b. 12/12/1987
      3. Corey Edward, b. 10/1/1989
      4. Charmayne Jean, b. 5/21/1993
5. Gary Francis, b. 10/29/1962; m. Marion Nelson (b. 11/15/1964)
   a. *Children:*
      1. Garrick, b. 7/12/1981
      2. Eric Cody, b. 3/11/1983
      3. Errica, b. 3/1/1986
      4. Damion Gary, b. 1/27/1988
      5. Caleb Tyler, b. 1/27/1988
6. Michael Francis, b. 11/4/1964; m. Clara Tsosie
   a. *Children:*
      1. Michaelina
      2. Cordell
      3. Savanna
3. Walter Davis ("Junior"), b. 5/8/1930; d. 5/20/1997; m., 4/6/1953, Louise Woody (b. 3/29/1939; d. 6/10/1999)
   a. *Children:*
      1. Glenn, b. 7/3/1956; m. Doris B. (b. 4/6/1956)
         a. *Children:*
            1. Glendalyn T. Davis, b. 3/7/1974; m. Shawn D. Yazzie, (b. 5/10/1971)
               a. *Children:*
                  1. DeShawn Davis Yazzie, b. 6/1/1991
                  2. Shawneil Sean Yazzie, b. 1/19/1994
            2. Gwendolyn Tara Davis, b. 6/16/1975; m. Julius Smith (b. 3/21/1974)

3. Gaylyn Tamara Davis, b. 10/28/1978
4. Phillander Begay, b. 5/25/1980
5. Gerilyn Dawn Davis, b. 11/18/1986
2. Julie Ann Stevens, b. 2/11/1959
   a. *Children:*
      1. Natasha Davis, b. 9/11/1975; m. Calvin James
      2. Elissa Stevens, b. 11/24/1981
      3. Bo Channon Clark, b. 9/24/1986
      4. Simalcolm Davis, b. 4/17/1989
3. Lorenzo Davis, b. 5/1961; d. 8/10/1985; formerly m. to Caroline D.
   a. *Children:*
      1. Dory Davis, b. 4/29/1978
      2. Shawn Davis, b. 3/5/1982
4. Daniel Davis, b. 5/30/1963; formerly m. to Loretta Begay (b. 5/15/1963)
   a. *Child:*
      1. Danelle Davis, b. 10/25/1982
5. Walter Davis, Jr., b. 12/31/1964; first m. Darlene Skenadore no. 1
   a. *Child:*
      1. Savanna Davis
   Then m. Rita Begay no. 2;
   a. *Children:*
      1. Shennie Davis
      2. Chetman Davis
      3. Shwayne Davis
6. Emmanuel Davis, b. 8/11/1967
7. Emmalene Davis, b. 1/21/1969; m. Herbert Tsosie (now deceased)
   a. *Child*
      1. Emery Davis, b. 8/27/1982
8. Ricky Davis, b. 9/7/1972; m. Tieva Hoostwood
   a. *Child:*
      1. Eligah Davis, b. 2/16/1994

2. Seya Mitchell, b. 6/30/1913 (see Chap. 7, n. 9); d. 7/10/1998; m. Adelle Catherine Brown (b. 6/14/1907; d. 12/13/1973) [Adelle's parents, "Zonnie Marie" (also known as *'Asdzáán Tseyanichíí* [Red Rocks Woman, Woman from the Red Rock Canyon]) and John Brown no. 1 ("The Policeman") both had children with others, as well; for example, Zonnie Marie also had Mary Tsosi, Dolly Chee Begay, and John Day; John Brown no. 1 also had Bessie Martin, Zonnie Lewis, Anna Lewis, Helen Heyde, Virgil Brown, Sr., Louise Badoni, and Calvin Brown. Adelle Brown first m., 12/19/1930, Carl Gorman; divorced, 1944.
   A. *Adelle and Carl's Children* [R. C. kept Gorman surname; Don and Donna Mae changed theirs to Mitchell]:
   1. Rudolph Calvin ("R. C."), b. 7/26/1932

2. Donald Francis [Mitchell], b. 1/21/1938; first m., 7/31/1963, Shirley Anne Wagner who already had a son, Darin Begay, now m. with children; divorced; then Don m., 7/31/1982, Elouise A. (b. 1/1/1951); she already had two daughters from earlier marriage, both of whom have children now: Jennifer Brown, Jeanette Brown

    a. *Children (Don and Shirley):*
       1. Dallas Mitchell, b. 1/21/1964
       2. Daryll Mitchell, b. 10/23/1966; m. with children
       3. Ladonna Mitchell, b. 1/20/1974

    b. *Children (Don and Elouise A.):*
       1. Karen Mitchell, b. 3/16/1981
       2. Jeffery Mitchell, b. 3/6/1988

3. Donna Mae [Mitchell], b. 10/31/1939; m., 1/19/1961, Leo Dennis Scott (b. 5/2/1939) who had son from previous marriage, now deceased

    a. *Children:*
       1. Jeanette, b. 8/27/1963
          a. *Child:*
             1. Garett, b. 7/17/1991
       2. Maria, b. 8/17/1964; m. to Aaron Barker

B. *Seya and Adelle's Children:*

1. Michael Melvin ("Butch"), b. 3/18/1941; d. 3/10/1976; m. "Minnie"
    a. *Child:*
       1. Boyd

2. Shirley Yvonne, b. 3/20/1944; m., 1964, later divorced; then m., 9/21/1972, Roderick Robert Beecher ("Bobby")
    a. *Children from first marriage:*

3. Douglas Franklin ("Doogie"), b. 10/21/1946; d. 12/4/1972
       1. Martina ("Tina"), b. 10/30/1964
          a. *Children:*
             1. Monike Damran
             2. Mickey Damran
       2. Monique ("Woody"), b. 12/18/1965; m. Daron Curley
          a. *Children:*
             1. Monty Curley
             2. Ty Curley
       3. Maynard ("Jim"), b. 8/14/1967
    b. *Children with "Bobby":*
       1. Vonda Rae, b. 7/7/1973
       2. Michele, b. 1/25/1979

3. Agnes Mitchell Sanchez, b. 8/20/1918; m., 6/24/1950, Anthony Sanchez ("Tony") (b. 7/5/1919)

A. *Children:*
  1. Ronald Anthony, b. 3/6/1952 (unmarried)
  2. Regina Maria, b. 11/15/1954; m. to Alfredo Elizondo (b. 10/1/1958) but keeping maiden name
     a. *Children:*
        1. Antonio Elizondo, b. 8/11/1986
        2. Armando Elizondo, b. 3/12/1991
4. Ruth Mitchell Shirley Yazzie, b. 6/20/1920; d. 9/17/1994; m. first, 1940, Leo Shirley; later divorced; then m. Wilson Yazzie; later divorced
   A. *Children (Ruth and Leo):*
     1. Alfred Shirley, b. 8/6/1941; m. Ella (b. 4/28/1948)
        a. *Children:*
           1. Delphine, b. 9/20/1964
           2. Murray, b. 9/18/1965; m. to Brenda Donna Holian (b. 4/11/1966)
              a. *Children:*
                 1. Melanie Brenda, b. 1/22/1991
                 2. Tayo Gyles, b. 9/2/1992
                 3. Trevor Lyle, b. 9/15/1994
           3. Alfonso, b. 8/26/1967
           4. Davina, b. 9/9/1970; m. Kurt Jolma
              a. *Children:*
                 1. Jeremy
                 2. Douglas
           5. Rebecca, b. 8/17/1973; m. Lyle Jackson
              a. *Children:*
                 1. Alicia
                 2. Ashley
           6. Art Arlando, b. 7/4/1977
           7. Jessica, b. 7/1/1980
     2. Timothy Shirley ("Timmy"), b. 12/24/1942; m. Wilmina Begay
        a. *Children:*
           1. Mina, b. 1/4/1960
           2. Derrick, b. 8/13/1989
           3. Garrick, b. 5/23/1997
     3. Lynn Shirley, b. 8/26/1944; m. first, 9/25/1965, Franklin Dennis Tah; then divorced
        a. *Child:*
           1. Trevious Tah, died at birth, 12/16/1966
        b. *Lynn's Later Children:*
           1. Vsue, b. 6/30/1974; m.
              a. *Child:*
                 1. Vtora Ann Qumayousie, b. 6/25/1995

2. Vina S., b. 2/7/1979
3. Velma S., b. 2/26/1981
4. Sonny Stone Cody, b. 9/2/1982
5. Victoria S., b. 10/7/1986; d. 1/1/1987
6. Victoria Sioux, b. 1/28/1988

4. Franklin Shirley ("Frankie"), b. 2/19/1946; m. Stella Louise (b. 2/1/1948)
   a. *Children:*
      1. Shannon Ruth, b. 6/28/1976
      2. Heather Maria, b. 3/26/1985

5. Marie Alice Shirley, b. 2/2/1948; m. first, Frank Tully Begay; then divorced; then m. Ben Lee, Sr. (b. 2/13/1945)
   a. *Children (Marie and Frank):*
      1. Calvin T., b. 1/24/1967; m. first to Cory who already had two boys; later divorced; then m. to Matilda
         a. *Child:*
            1. Calvina
      2. Janice B., b. 2/16/1968; m. Robert Thinn, Sr.
         a. *Children:*
            1. Doriscita, b. 10/21/1986
            2. Jancelita Crystal, b. 5/4/1988
            3. Robert, Jr., b. 4/30/1989
            4. Rodney J., b. 4/29/1990
            5. Yolanda, b. 8/21/1991
            6. Jeanita Marie, b. 7/4/1994
            7. Rodrego Joe, b. 1/31/1995
            8. Rodrick Joe, b. 8/29/1996
      3. Victor T., b. 1/21/1969; m. to Manny
   b. *Children (Marie and Ben):*
      1. Jancita A. Lee, b. 9/30/1977
      2. Lucinda L., b. 4/19/1979
      3. Ben C., Jr., b. 11/19/1982
      4. Nathaniel C., b. 4/15/1984

6. Evonne Shirley, b. 3/18/1949
   a. *Children:*
      1. Brian, b. 5/15/1974; d. 2/23/1996
      2. Shellie, b. 2/1/1977; now with Gary Kayonnie
         1. *Child:*
            a. Justice Ruth, b. 1/12/1996
      3. Terin, b. 9/21/1979

7. Lena Lou Shirley, b. 9/18/1950
   a. *Children:*
      1. Drena Lynn Laughlin, b. 11/15/1971; m., then divorced;

a. *Child:*

    1. Timera Begay, b. 12/10/1993

  2. Terri Lynn Laughlin, b. 12/29/1975

    a. *Children:*

      1. Kimiko Sonja Laughlin, b. 4/30/1989

      2. Taime Vaughn Tso, b. 5/2/1997

  3. Marlynda Tina Shirley, b. 3/7/1979

  4. Latasha Teller, b. 6/7/1985

B. *Children (Ruth and Wilson):*

  1. Elta, b. 3/13/1957

    a. *Children:*

      1. Gilbert Etsitty, died at birth, 2/8/1974

      2. Lamar Desidero, b. 3/13/1975

      3. Juanita Desidero, b. 10/20/1976

      4. Lisa Begay, b. 3/3/1981

        a. *Child:*

          1. Robin Ruth Hudson, b. 5/21/1997

  2. Mildred Yazzie, b. 6/9/1960; m. Benson Kee (b. 8/3/1958)

    a. *Children:*

      1. Lorencita, b. 10/30/1976

      2. Benson, Jr., b. 10/31/1981

5. Howard Mitchell, b. 5/20/1926 (unmarried)

6. Augusta Mitchell Sandoval, b. 8/14/1928; m., 10/1949, Cecil Sandoval (b. 1921 or 1923; d. 10/13/1992); later divorced

A. *Children:*

  1. Cecilia, b. 5/9/1951

  2. Cecil, Jr. ("Dino"), b. 9/9/1952; m. Shirley Anne Ross

    a. *Children:*

      1. Rachelle Lee, b. 4/5/1975

      2. Crystal Rae, b. 9/27/1979

      3. Kimberly Ann, b. 12/30/1986

  3. Cynthia ("Bunni"), b. 7/20/1954; m., 6/30/1971, Lacey Fredenberg

    a. *Child:*

      1. Karri ("Oishie"), b. 11/13/1977

        a. *Child (with Josh McCoy):*

          1. Jasmine James McCoy, b. 4/3/1997

  4. Regina ("Tiny"), b. 8/13/1958; m. August Simmons; later divorced

    a. *Children:*

      1. Piet Simmons ("Boo"), b. 9/8/1981

      2. Ian Simmons ("Bird"), b. 2/17/1984

  5. Augustine ("Eesert"), b. 11/17/1959; m. Louise Tsosie (b. 8/5/1960) who already had son, Ronnie

      a. *Children:*
        1. Aneka Louise, b. 10/26/1985
        2. Odessa Renee, b. 9/26/1987
        3. Lewis Parker, b. 7/1/1990
    6. Ronald ("Ronnie"), b. 5/21/1965 (unmarried)
    Also: Dennison Tsosie (ward), b. 12/18/1976

7. Isabel Mitchell Deschine, b. 8/6/1932; m., 1970–71, Jimmy Deschine (b. 6/14/1922; d. 5/8/1999)
    A. *Isabel's Children:*
      1. Geneva Mae, b. 2/9/1947; m., 6/14/1968, Clifford Toledo (b. 12/28/1945)
        a. *Children:*
          1. Christopher, Jr., b. 9/10/1969
            a. *Children:*
              1. DeVonti Dre Toledo, b. 5/28/1994
              2. McKayla Mae Toledo, b. 6/2/1995
          2. Profilia Mae Toledo, b. 11/20/1973
            a. *Child:*
              1. Anaclicia Mae Martinez, b. 9/9/1996
      2. Josephine Marie Mitchell, b. 12/6/1953
        a. *Children:*
          1. Danalle Regina, b. 3/25/1974; m., surname, Williams
          2. Kimberly Maria, b. 2/10/1977
      3. Mae Christine, b. 5/11/1956; m. John F. Stensgar (b. 6/24/1960)
        a. *Children:*
          1. John F., Jr., b. 1/5/1980
          2. Eric Swan, b. 4/6/1983
      4. Joseph Klade ("Mann"), b. 4/26/1958; m. Agnes
        a. *Children:*
          1. Jackie Lynn Klade, b. 4/3/1983
          2. Rebecca Ann, b. 10/15/1985
          3. Tyson Damont, b. 10/8/1988
          4. Alexander Joseph, b. 5/12/1996
      5. Jerry, b. 10/21/1963; now with Freida Holtsoi
        a. *Jerry's Children:*
          1. Jerry, Jr., b. 7/25/1990
          2. Frank, b. 9/23/1992

8. Garnett Scott Bernally, b. 10/2/1923 (Raised by Mitchells by mother's request; parents were Beautiful Woman [d. 1934], and Tom Scott [d. 9/27/1968]. Garnett's other siblings died; Tom remarried; next wife, *Dlinasbah*, also a Towering House woman.) Garnett m., 11/5/1948, Ned Bernally (b. 8/23/1915) in Chicago.
    A. *Children:*
      1. Elroy, b. 5/2/1949

2. Gary, b. 3/4/1951
    a. *Children:*
        1. Kevin Bernally, b. 12/10/1971
        2. Tisa Begay, b. 9/28/1973
        3. Maylin Bernally, b. 2/23/1979
        4. Shebe Bernally, b. 3/12/1980
3. Bernadette, b. 8/7/1953
4. Lauren, b. 11/25/1955
    a. *Child:*
        1. Loni Bernally, b. 4/28/1982
5. Lonnie, b. 11/10/1956
6. Karen, b. 12/08/1958
    a. *Child:*
        1. Aaron Uentillie, b. 12/14/1980
7. Karla, b. 3/19/1961; m. Evan Craig (b. 7/28/1956)
    a. *Children:*
        1. Siobhan Kristen Craig, b. 7/24/1986
        2. Evan Lowell Craig, b. 8/27/1987

Appendix B: Chronology

Attempts at establishing chronologies are, at best, fraught with difficulties, given variable and incomplete documents, diversity in published opinions, and the frailties of human memories. This appendix has been designed to add a chronological sense to Tall Woman's narrative for "Western" readers, and to document a few of the events that happened in the family and community after her funeral on July 3, 1977, until the completion of work on the manuscript. It features events important in her narrative, with only occasional reference to tribal or national/international events, or the field-work done in conjunction with this project. The latter is documented in the Introduction; those interested in more detailed information on political developments, the community history of Chinle, or the diversity of opinions in the Franciscan, trading post, boarding school, and other more specific literature, should consult both the chapter endnotes and the more specialized resources cited therein. Entries listed below are arranged chronologically within years, where possible. Events marked "ca." indicate those where no documentation was available to support more precise dating; those marked with a question mark (?) indicate that the sequential order of the event could not be reconstructed. Events spanning multiple years are positioned before those attributable to individual years within a given period.

Ca. 1850
    Tall Woman's mother, Tall, Beautiful Woman, is born
1863–68
    The Long Walk and incarceration at Fort Sumner
1868
    6/1: Treaty signed, ending captivity, and exodus begins, 6/15
    Trading with non-Indian outsiders begins after captivity ends
1869
    Presbyterians establish themselves in Ganado
1871
    Episcopalians establish mission in Fort Defiance
Ca. 1874
    Tall Woman reportedly born, around Steamboat
1876 (or 1878)
    J. Lorenzo Hubbell builds trading post in Ganado

1879–81

Construction of Fort Defiance Boarding School

1880–87

Atlantic and Pacific Railroad built through the Southwest

1880

Eleven Navajos issued wagons, but results not successful

1881

Manuelito and Ganado Mucho given wagons;
Frank Mitchell born at Wheatfields;
Fort Defiance Boarding School opens

1882–83

Trading begins in Chinle from a tent store run by Little Mexican; 1883:
     Agent shuts down because of no license

1886

First license to trade in Chinle issued to C. N. Cotton and J. L. Hubbell; first
     permanent store opens in an abandoned stone hogan; remains later incor-
     porated into Garcia's Trading Post

1887

C. N. Cotton and J. L. Hubbell fail to get their Chinle license renewed; store
     starts having a succession of owners

1889

Fort Wingate Hospital opens

1890

Man Who Shouts begins job as headman; eventually gets wagon and buggy;
Man Who Shouts definitely trading at Hubbell's in Ganado

1891

Mother Katharine Drexel founds Sisters of the Blessed Sacrament

1892

7/13: Appropriations Act makes Indian education compulsory;
October: Trouble at Round Rock

1893

Small Woman (Tall Woman's real younger sister) is born

1894

Sisters of the Blessed Sacrament open St. Catherine's (Santa Fe)

1896

Mother Katharine Drexel purchases land and interests Franciscan Fathers of
     St. John the Baptist Province in establishing a mission center on it (St.
     Michaels, Ariz.)

1898

October: St. Michaels Mission established in St. Michaels;
10/9: St. Michaels chapel dedicated

1900

First baptisms at St. Michaels;

4/16: Man Who Shouts and both wives definitely trading at Hubbell's in Ganado

1901

Sage Memorial Hospital (Presbyterian) opens in Ganado

1902

9/1: St. Michaels recognized as settlement; post office established with John G. Walker as postmaster;

Sisters of Blessed Sacrament build elementary boarding school in St. Michaels, after another land purchase;

Sam E. Day builds/opens Chinle Trading Post later known as the Thunderbird;

Father Leopold Ostermann, O.F.M., begins to visit Chinle;

10/25–10/30: Father Anselm Weber, O.F.M., Miss Josephine Drexel, Frank Walker, and Sister Agatha visit Canyon de Chelly, staying with the Days while in Chinle;

12/3: St. Michaels School opens with forty-seven students gathered by Father Anselm Weber

1903

Mail delivery to Chinle starts (once a week); Charles Day, postmaster, also appointed (late May) custodian of Canyon de Chelly archaeological sites;

Chinle has agency farmer and two field matrons who taught school on an informal basis—one was Mrs. Henrietta Cole, also a Methodist missioner;

Rumors about future federal boarding school in Chinle;

Father Leopold Ostermann, O.F.M., assigned to Chinle and starts visiting for several weeks at a time, staying with the Days;

4/16: Franciscans select mission site in Chinle and local Navajos approve it four days later;

Franciscans request land from Washington, D.C., which was granted, 6/20;

July: Navajo Agency divided, with two superintendents now in charge;

9/23: Father Leopold Ostermann, O.F.M., holds first public service in Chinle;

10/25: Franciscan mission dedicated at St. Michaels

1904

8/15: Father Leopold Ostermann, O.F.M., and Brother Placidus Buerger (or Gervase Thuemmel) settle part-time in Chinle, renting an old, two-room, stone building (later incorporated into Garcia's Trading Post)

1905

Spring: Sam E. Day sells Chinle post to Charles Weidemeyer, who asks Charles Cousins to manage it; agency farmer reportedly living in old Hubbell-Cotton post (1886) not being used as store at the moment;

8/15: Specific site selected for Franciscan mission in Chinle and ground broken next day for combined residence/chapel;

Late October/early November: Trouble in Chinle between Navajos and Superintendent Reuben Perry;

November: Brother Placidus becomes ill and leaves Chinle

1906

January: Franciscan residence habitable but not finished; Father Leopold moves in;

2/19: Brother Placidus dies;

Summer: Frank Mitchell works for Father Leopold until Brother Gervase Thuemmel assumes full-time duties in August;

Son of the Late Little Blacksmith assigned to Chinle area as peacemaker;

Ca. late summer: Tall Woman and Frank Mitchell start living together

1907–9

Frank works at sawmill; eventually earns wagon and works on bridge construction;

Frank's mother dies

1907

January: Father Marcellus Troester, O.F.M., arrives as Father Leopold's assistant; stays until 1915;

7/24: With ceremony, Franciscan building raised to a residence

Ca. 1908–9

Man Who Shouts builds spring/summer homes at Houses Standing in a Line

1908

Peter Paquette becomes superintendent of Navajo Agency (1908–25);

Ca. 1908: Mary no. 1 born in winter, in Black Mountain area

1909

7/8: School ordered built in Chinle by federal government;

9/21: School site inspected;

Fall: First annual Shiprock Fair;

Fall: Construction of Chinle Boarding School begins, as does construction of Franciscan stone chapel; school is within half-mile of mission; Frank works on school construction and, with Tall Woman, lives in small house he builds near site

1910

Ca. 1910: Mary no. 2 born;

Nelson Gorman builds and opens trading post in Chinle;

First automobiles in Chinle;

4/1: Chinle Boarding School opens with forty-nine pupils;

8/15: Annual report of Fort Defiance Agency notes one hundred students at Chinle Boarding School;

Fall: Eighty students at the school; Franciscan chapel finished ?;

12/12: Priests start performing marriage ceremonies for Navajos in Chinle; headmen also begin witnessing marriages

1911

Construction of Franciscan chapel completed, if not earlier; chapel used from 1911 (or 1912) until 1960;

Father Leopold begins serving as postmaster; Chinle Post Office now in stone building next to chapel;

Fall: Sam Sanishya enrolled at Chinle Boarding School

1912

2/22: Frank Mitchell on Fort Defiance agent's list of employees at Chinle school, as laborer;

Ca. 1912: Frank starts working as freighter (until ca. 1919);

Fort Defiance Hospital built;

3/25: Chinle Franciscan chapel, second oldest Franciscan mission on reservation, named and dedicated as the Annunciation Mission, as per request of Marquette League;

Sometime shortly thereafter, Protestant missionaries (both Episcopalian and Presbyterian, including Rev. Fred Mitchell), start coming to Chinle from Fort Defiance and Ganado, respectively, with converts meeting in believers' hogans;

6/30/1912 (or 6/30/1913): Seya born;

John Kirk and/or other members of Kirk family operating store on site of original Hubbell-Cotton post; expand it (again) and add trader's residence;

Nelson Gorman builds/opens trading post at Black Mountain;

Ca. 1912 (late summer): Trouble at Houses Standing in a Line; Tall Woman loses three older sisters and one older brother; family finally permanently abandons site

1913

J. L. Hubbell's stationery changed to indicate start of horse-drawn stage and freight service from Gallup to Ganado, Chinle, and elsewhere (some say 1915);

J. L. Hubbell doing business in Chinle; Sam Day II works for him, on and off, as clerk and driver of Hubbell's high-wheeled, open automobile;

Seventy-five students enrolled at Chinle Boarding School; construction of addition to dormitory building to accommodate 150;

Man Who Shouts builds spring/summer homes at Place of the Reeds;

Man Who Shouts has Flintway *jish* assembled;

Tall Woman loses baby in spring; starts having ceremonies;

Beautiful Mountain uprising;

11/24: Man Who Shouts witnesses marriage of Gai to Son of Yucca Fruit Man

1914

First World War starts;

5/3: First group to complete Catholic religious instructions baptized and makes First Communions at Annunciation Mission;

Nelson Gorman sells Black Mountain store to J. L. Hubbell;

Fall: 100–150 students at Chinle Boarding School

1915

At least six Navajos in Fort Defiance Agency own cars; two hundred students reportedly enrolled at Chinle Boarding School;

J. L. Hubbell's Chinle employees include Cozy McSparron (1915) and Mike Kirk (1915, 1916);

Letter from Kirk, 12/15, indicates Hubbell considering building Big House

1916

J. L. Hubbell builds Big House, two-story trading post/hotel in Chinle, across from Franciscan mission;

Spring: George and Jean Kennedy buy old Sam Day Trading Post;

9/19: First annual Crownpoint Fair

1917

Enrollment at Chinle Boarding School still increasing; those receiving Catholic instructions do so three times a week, twice at school and once at the chapel, and attend mass each Sunday;

John K. Andrich and J. B. McCoy identified as Hubbell's Chinle employees

1918

8/20: Agnes born;

Fall: 165 students at Chinle Boarding School;

October: Influenza epidemic strikes, many die;

Man Who Shouts and family leave Place of the Reeds and spend winter near Nazlini Wash;

December?: J. L. Hubbell sells two-story post in Chinle (Big House) to C. N. Cotton

1919

Spring: Influenza epidemic briefly returns in some areas;

Kennedys sell trading post to Cozy McSparron, who soon names it the Thunderbird Ranch;

Nelson and Alice Gorman decide to give their Chinle post, home, and barns to Presbyterians;

Construction of more buildings at Chinle Boarding School reportedly bringing physical plant to that present in 1940; Franciscans report enrollment ca. two hundred, shortage of teachers, and Mr. Fred Lobdell as new principal;

Frank ends job as freighter and returns to Chinle; has Beautyway; starts learning Blessingway from Man Who Shouts;

May: Presbytery grants permission for mission in Chinle;

7/30: Fort Defiance agent notes formal protest by some Chinle Navajos over Protestant activity in community;

Fall: Mary no. 2 starts Chinle Boarding School

Late fall 1919 or early 1920

C. N. Cotton hires Camillo Garcia to manage Big House when he has a vacancy; Garcias come to Chinle

Ca. 1920–21

The Jailer dies; Man Who Shouts sells his cattle

1920

National Prohibition (1920–33);

5/30: Mary no. 2 baptized Catholic;

6/20: Ruth born;

Fall: Mary Cabot Wheelwright visits McSparron's Trading Post;

Man Who Shouts gets injured when thrown from horse, starts having many major ceremonies after return to Black Mountain area

1921

Spring: Frank builds hogan near Chinle Wash for Tall Woman and family;

April: Indian Presbyterian Church of Chinle formed with twenty-four members by Northern Arizona Presbytery; first pastor, Reverend A. K. Locker and his wife arrive and live at former Gorman Trading Post; construction of Presbyterian church and the manse begins;

Summer: Pauline born;

Fall: After return to Black Mountain area, Frank finishes learning Blessingway from Man Who Shouts and Water Edge Man, and both sponsor Blessingway for him to announce his qualifications;

Chinle Navajo Catholics file petition protesting approval of Presbyterian mission site;

Man Who Shouts starts to decline; part of family moves with him to Whippoorwill for short time for more ceremonies, but then returns to Window Rocks area in Black Mountain

1922

Winter: Man Who Shouts dies; family relocates to The Flats on Red Mesa;

Eventually, Frank becomes a headman in Man Who Shouts' place;

Three-person Business Council negotiates oil leases;

April: Seya enrolled at Chinle Boarding School;

Summer: Many Puberty ceremonies in family;

   Beautiful Woman marries Tom Scott;

   David born;

Fall: Frank's father, Water Edge Man, dies;

Family stops returning to Black Mountain area for winters

1923

Cozy McSparron, Camillo Garcia, and Hartley Seymour (C. N. Cotton's son-in-law) reportedly purchase all three (?) trading posts in Chinle; Cozy focuses on combining trading and tourism at the Thunderbird; Camillo acquires store developed on the 1886 Hubbell-Cotton site by subsequent owners, including John Kirk, and later, this store becomes Canyon de Chelly Trading Post or Garcia's; three reportedly decide to close the store at the Big House, leaving Chinle with two trading posts; Garcias move to Canyon de Chelly Trading Post;

7/7: Meeting of first elected Tribal Council (twelve delegates, twelve alternates, and chairman, Henry Chee Dodge);

10/2: Garnett Scott born

1924

U.S. citizenship extended to all American Indians;

Reverend and Mrs. Locker depart; Chinle Presbyterian Church completed, but manse not quite finished;

Frank has Evilway, Ghostway;

Ca. June: Tall Woman loses one-week-old son;

July: Reverend Charles Bysegger and wife, Rose, arrive to serve Chinle Presbyterians, stay until 1952;

Tall Woman bitten by rattlesnake, has Beautyway

1925

7/8: Tribal Council meeting at Fort Wingate approves idea of National Monument at Canyon de Chelly;

Father Leopold begins to suffer health problems;

Fall: Seya and Agnes go to Fort Apache Indian School;

Jean Jackson starts public school upstairs at Big House

1925–ca. 1930

Big House upstairs space used two to three years for Chinle Public School classes; also site of new bakery and providing available living space in community

1926

According to Greyeyes, Chinle Chapter starts; others say 1934;

5/20: Howard born;

Late summer: Filming of "Redskin";

9/8: Tall Woman and Frank become grandparents with birth of George Acey Davis to Mary no. 1 and Woody Davis;

Fall: Pauline enrolled at Chinle Boarding School;

Tall Woman bitten by another rattlesnake; hospitalized for infection at Fort Defiance Hospital, and has Navajo Windway upon return home

1927

    1/1: Navajo Agency divided into Northern, Eastern, and Southern agencies
       (organization used 1/1/1927 to 7/1/1935);

    2/2: Mary no. 1 and Woody married by Father Emanuel Trockur, O.F.M.;

    Ca. March: Pauline dies at Chinle Boarding School;

    Chapters started in Leupp;

    Presbyterians start instructions at Chinle Boarding School

Late 1927 or early 1928

    Father Leopold leaves Chinle permanently for health reasons; sometime
       thereafter, post office moved to first of two sites at Chinle Boarding
       School and Franciscans stop serving as postmasters, evidently until 1934

Late 1920s

    Regional styles in weaving emerge; Chinle style established by the 1930s

1928

    Spring: Man with a Cane dies;

    Summer: Gai dies;

    Chubby Woman married to Son of Yucca Fruit Man;

    8/14: Augusta born;

    Fall: Tall Woman starts having trouble with facial paralysis; has several
       Chiricahua Apache Windways, another Navajo Windway, and a Shooting-
       way Ceremony

1929

    Movie "Redskin" released in the United States;

    Addition to Fort Defiance Hospital;

    Fall: Seya starts Albuquerque Indian School, after first running off to
       Phoenix Indian School

1929–39

    Great national Depression

1930s

    Concerns over range conditions on reservation apparent, eventually leading
       to stock reduction;

    Frank starts working with Father Berard Haile, O.F.M.;

    Conditions in Chinle described as including minimal social life beyond that
       offered by events at boarding school and churches, and recreational hunt-
       ing of coyotes and bears; road from Ganado still not surfaced or drained,
       but graded in mid-1930s by CCC; no bridge across Nazlini Wash

1930

    First erosion control efforts in Canyon de Chelly;

    Bootlegging apparent on reservation;

    4/10: Father Leopold Ostermann, O.F.M., dies;

    Presbyterians finish stone addition to original Chinle church;

9/8: Local Navajo petition against Canyon de Chelly National Monument;

10/2: Monument rediscussed on Chinle Court Day, leading to new petition supporting idea

Early 1930s

Construction of one/two-room building for Chinle Public School (one of the "Accommodation Schools") on hill behind (east of) boarding school; used until 1959 when construction of new public school is finished; then converted to apartments and rented out;

Garnett enrolled at Fort Defiance Boarding School (possibly 1930, but unclear)

1931

1/15: Mary no. 2 dies; buried next day by Father Remigius Austing, O.F.M.;

2/9: Frank writes Superintendent Reuben Perry;

3/9: Perry meets with Chinle Navajos;

4/1: Presidential proclamation creates Canyon de Chelly National Monument

1932

Chinle gets a health center including a fifteen-bed hospital; this is converted to a clinic in 1950;

Chinle Mine No. 1 near Blue Gap opens and runs until ca. 1955;

8/6: Isabel born;

9/18: Father Berard Haile, O.F.M., and others make first trip to one of sacred mountains on reservation; others visited shortly thereafter with Frank in attendance;

October: Cozy McSparron buys out Hartley T. Seymour and becomes sole owner of Thunderbird again

1933–35

Study of range conditions on reservation

1933

Start of Franklin D. Roosevelt's presidency, which brings John Collier as Indian commissioner, the New Deal era, and numerous programs, such as WPA, CCC, SEC, SCS;

Spring: Seya graduates from Albuquerque Indian School;

Summer: Chinle reportedly has earthquakes;

Frank arranges for Seya to get warrior name at an Enemyway;

Summer/fall: Dam built at Moaning Lake;

Fall: Agnes starts Albuquerque Indian School;

Howard enrolled at Chinle Boarding School;

December: Seya chosen for "Leader School"

Winter of 1933–34

Voluntary stock reduction started

1934

Indian Reorganization Act (IRA);

Canyon de Chelly/Canyon del Muerto Chapter organized (if not earlier, in 1926);

January-May: Seya attends "Leader School";

4/21: Father Anselm Sippel, O.F.M., and Brother Gotthard Schmidt come to Chinle; Father becomes postmaster; Brother stays until 1952 (is also poultry farmer and mail carrier);

4/28: Canyon de Chelly Chapter resolution approving National Park Service presence in area;

May-October: Seya sent to teach at Lukachukai Boarding School;

6/11: John Foley resigns as interpreter for Chinle Franciscans to take SCS job at Frazier's (Valley Store); Joe Carroll hired on 6/21 as church's interpreter;

Summer?: Beautiful Woman dies in childbirth;

Seya starts working in Chinle at numerous jobs (until fall 1939);

Frank switches land with Tom Scott;

8/18: Robert Budlong starts duties as first custodian of Canyon de Chelly National Monument; no residence or headquarters buildings yet

1935

Ca. 1935: Chinle Chapter acquires corn-grinding machine and locates it on hill by Presbyterian Church;

Chinle rodeo starts;

mid-June: Frank briefly hospitalized at Chinle Health Center;

7/1: Agencies (Western, Eastern, Northern, Southern, Leupp, Charles H. Burke School, and part of Hopi Agency) consolidated; Navajo Central Agency established with Chester E. Faris, superintendent (7/1/1935–4/15/1936); John Collier chooses Window Rock for the capital;

Documentation available for fees for accommodations, meals, and trips into the Canyon from McSparron's Thunderbird;

7/5: Two-year-old Nicholas Scott dies, is buried next day;

8/3: Tall Woman's mother is baptized Catholic;

8/7: Tall Woman's mother dies;

8/8: Tall Woman's mother is buried by Father Anselm Sippel, O.F.M., in mission cemetery;

8/28: Construction of custodian's residence starts at Canyon de Chelly National Monument;

Fall: Augusta enrolled at Chinle Boarding School;

Frank and Tall Woman move to what became their permanent residence site;

11/11: Catholic priests start using cemetery "across the wash" for most burials (until 3/30/1946)

1936

Voluntary stock reduction ended; enforced stock reduction begins;

Land Management Units and Grazing Districts established;

SES introduces tamarisks, cottonwoods, willows in Canyon de Chelly;

National Park Service headquarters at Canyon de Chelly and superintendent's residence completed; work on White House Trail;

Fall: Augusta spends school year at Fort Defiance Boarding School because
of trachoma treatments

December 1936–March 1937

Tribal Council reorganized

1937–41

Time of systematic, enforced stock reduction

Ca. 1937

Wilsons give Frank land with peach trees in Canyon del Muerto;

Frank decides to expand the farm (spring 1937 or 1938)

1937

Spring: Tall Woman's teeth extracted at Chinle Health Center;

3/10: Frank selected for Constitutional Assembly service;

Range Riders established;

Livestock surveys on reservation;

Another addition to Fort Defiance Hospital, this time one hundred-bed TB
unit;

4/5: First meeting of Constitutional Assembly; Frank appointed to Constitution and other committees;

May: Agnes graduates from Albuquerque Indian School and goes to St.
Joseph's School of Nursing (later called Regina School of Nursing),
Albuquerque;

5/31: Son of the Late Little Blacksmith dies;

6/17: Frank's trip to Washington, D.C., begins

1938

4/3: Towering House Woman dies;

5/4: Garnett graduates from Fort Defiance Boarding School;

5/10: Dedication of newly expanded Fort Defiance Hospital;

Summer: Howard breaks his arm, is hospitalized at Fort Defiance;

August: David suddenly gets sick; hospitalized at Sage Memorial in Ganado;
dies 8/21, is buried same day in Annunciation Mission Cemetery;

Shortly thereafter, Small Woman loses husband;

Fall: Garnett starts high school at Albuquerque Indian School;

9/27: Frank loses reelection bid;

11/8: New members of Constitutional Assembly take office;

Frank possibly starts job as Tribal Judge at this time

1939

Spring: Seya and Adelle get together;

Fall: Seya goes to St. Michaels Elementary School as Boys' Advisor and
coach, replacing Murray Lincoln (who later returns), and remains in this
position until October 1941;

Howard goes to St. Michaels for junior high;
Chubby Woman dies

1940

Livestock permit system implemented;
Ruth marries Leo Shirley;
Isabel diagnosed with TB, is hospitalized at Fort Defiance

1941

Early in year: Federal government action settles the spelling of Chinle by
    choosing "Chinle" over former "Chin Lee" or "ChinLee";
Spring: Agnes graduates from nursing school and starts working at Fort
    Defiance Hospital;
4/18–4/20: Mother Katharine Drexel's Golden Jubilee at Motherhouse in
    Cornwells Heights, Pennsylvania;
9/20: Old Curly Hair dies;
October: Seya leaves St. Michaels for work in Barstow, California;
12/7: United States enters World War II; Navajos join military service and
    get war-related jobs at munitions depots and elsewhere; New Deal pro-
    grams stopped;
Christmas: Howard quits eighth grade because Alfred has been hospitalized

1942

Spring: Garnett graduates from Albuquerque Indian School and starts
    nurses' training at Sage Memorial, Ganado;
May: Seya returns from Barstow, and again works around Chinle;
Summer: Frank arranges for Howard to get warrior name at an Enemyway;
Fall: Agnes enlists in military;
10/31: Agnes sworn in for service in Army Nurses Corps;
Film "Desert Song," filmed earlier in Canyon de Chelly in which Frank and
    his brother John had parts, is released

Winter 1942 or 1943

Tall Woman diagnosed with bear sickness and has Mountainway

Ca. 1943–45

Frank's brother Tom dies;
Slim Woman loses husband, Old Red Bottom Man

1943

Seya gets job at Bellemont Ordnance Depot and moves family there (stays
    until 1958);
Spring: Howard leaves for farmwork job in California; returns to Chinle ca.
    November;
Fall: Augusta goes to St. Michaels for junior high

1944

1/24: Bomber crashes in Canyon de Chelly;

Howard starts job at Ordnance Depot in Bellemont; leaves after left eye gets injured, and comes home, where he is hospitalized for two months at Fort Defiance Hospital;

Frank serving as a Chinle Chapter officer with John Gorman;

6/10: Wife of Old Curly Hair dies

Ca. 1945

Tall Woman stops "midwife" work

1945

Spring: Garnett graduates from nursing school and starts working at Crownpoint Hospital;

Fall: Augusta goes to St. Catherine's in Santa Fe;

Howard starts job at ice plant in Needles, California

1946

Frank serving as Tribal Judge as of now (if not earlier);

2/1: Agnes officially discharged from service;

3/30: Catholic priests do their first burial in new Chinle Community Cemetery;

5/1: Chinle Franciscans stop serving as postmasters again; Ambrose Howard appointed acting postmaster;

St. Michaels (Mission) High School opened;

Agnes begins job at Ft. Miley VA Hospital, San Francisco;

Fall: First annual Window Rock Fair

1947

May: Howard returns on leave from California to help with farm, then stays and works around Chinle until 1950;

Isabel diagnosed with bear sickness, has Mountainway

1948

Irene Stewart begins fifteen years as secretary of Chinle Chapter; Joe Carroll begins sixteen years as Tribal Council delegate;

6/20: Jim Mitchell dies;

11/5: Garnett marries Ned Bernally in Chicago

1949

May: Augusta graduates from St. Catherine's, returns, and starts working in Chinle;

October: Augusta marries Cecil Sandoval;

10/8: Tall Woman and Frank become great-grandparents with birth of Ramona to Louise Davis and Dennis Begay

1950

Howard leaves for job with Union Pacific Railroad in Wyoming;

Balakai Mine, Chinle No.2, started by Notah Tayah;

Chinle Health Center, opened in 1932, converted to a clinic;

Agnes sent to Fresno to establish new VA hospital;

4/9: Slim Woman baptized Presbyterian;

6/24: Agnes marries Tony Sanchez;

Fall: Agnes moves to Stockton, California;

October: Agnes starts job at Stockton Blood Bank;

First tribal election using pictorial paper ballot; Sam Ahkeah reelected Tribal Chairman (1951–54 term)

Early 1950s

Successful trading posts start changing to combination department stores and supermarkets;

Chinle's Big House, no longer being used for any purpose, starts to fall into ruin after roof collapses;

Frank starts working with outside researchers; returns land with peach trees in the Canyon to the Wilsons;

Leo leaves Ruth and children

1951–61

Decade of progress, growth, and change in Chinle

1951

End of Frank's years as a judge;

Construction of formal campground at Canyon de Chelly National Monument starts;

Spring: John Mitchell gets sick; Howard comes back from Wyoming on two-week leave

1951 and 1952

Frank serves as Chinle Chapter president

1952

Garnett and Ned Bernally move to Shiprock;

5/18: Ida Francis baptized Presbyterian;

June: Reverend and Mrs. Charles Bysegger leave Chinle's Presbyterian Church

1953

6/15: Reverend and Mrs. Joseph Gray arrive at Chinle's Presbyterian Church;

Paving of the road from Window Rock to Ganado finished

1954

March: Thunderbird Ranch sold by Cozy McSparron to J. Nelson, A. B. Nelson, and Ida Borum;

4/19: Mike Hedrick, manager, arrives;

4/20: McSparron leaves, after forty-one years in Chinle;

August: Construction (completed 1/1/1955) of new Presbyterian church and manse; interpreter's house enlarged; old church (except for stone addition) torn down;

November: Annunciation Mission gets dial telephone service;

Shortly after dial service installed at boarding school, Chinle Post Office moved to another building at the school (which formerly housed switchboard)

Ca. mid-1950s

Ruth marries Wilson Yazzie

1955

Federal government transfers responsibility of medical care for American Indians from Bureau of Indian Affairs to Public Health Service;

Frank again serves as officer in Chinle Chapter;

Mid-January: dedication of new Presbyterian Church;

5/6: Tom Mitchell, Jr., killed in accident;

June: Canyon visitors camping near "cemetery across the wash," although NPS campground not yet established;

7/1: Navajo Agency reorganized; five subagencies established (Chinle, Crownpoint, Fort Defiance, Shiprock, Tuba City), each with its own superintendent

Ca. 1956–57

Frank has Male Shootingway

1956–62

Navajo-Cornell University Health Research Project, Many Farms, Arizona

1956

Annunciation Mission renamed Our Lady of Fatima Church of Chinle

1957

Frank's Blessingway Ceremony is filmed by David P. McAllester

Late 1950s

Frank reduces amount of land the family is farming;

Howard leaves Union Pacific Railroad job because of sickness

1958–62

Population increase, much construction, expansion of businesses, and upgrading of services in Chinle

1958

Howard works for Santa Fe Railroad for six months, then goes to Kingman, Arizona, to work in furniture store;

Seya and family move back from Bellemont/Flagstaff, settle in Cottonwood;

Seya begins many years of service to Cottonwood Chapter;

New Chinle Chapter House built;

Construction of new Chinle Public School and housing for personnel started;

Summer: Augusta's house built at the Mitchells';

Catholics start building larger, cinder-block church; sanctuary use of original stone chapel at Annunciation Mission stopped as soon as new church finished;

9/21: Efforts to pave road from Ganado Junction to Chinle, and road from Chinle to Many Farms, begun by Richey Construction Co.;

11/10: Richey Construction Co. goes bankrupt; roads not done, but Ganado-Chinle stretch completed in 1959

1959

Indian Presbyterian Church of Chinle renamed Trinity Presbyterian Church;

2/14: Long Moustache dies;

5/14: Tall Woman admitted to Sage Memorial Hospital for hyperthyroidism;

June: New Public Health Service Health Center opened in Chinle;

6/20: New Chinle Chapter House dedicated by Frank Mitchell;

Summer: Frank has Enemyway Ceremony; Howard home on two-week leave from Kingman job;

Fall: Augusta starts job as cook at Chinle Public School (built in 1958, with 450-student capacity) when school opens;

Construction of new Chinle Boarding School started as well as "subdivision" for personnel housing;

9/22: John Mitchell dies;

October: Augusta and family move to Catholic mission, living in renovated building (former chicken house) until 1962;

11/17: Augusta has "hogan baby" at Mitchells';

Winter: Howard leaves job in Kingman and returns to Chinle, then begins working as supervisor/foreman for many tribal/community irrigation, water, and construction projects for next two decades (when not otherwise employed)

1960s

Civil Rights Movement; Red Power

1960

3/27: New Chinle Catholic Church dedicated;

5/30: Thunderbird Ranch sold to Justin La Font;

10/3: New Chinle Boarding School opened with ca. one thousand students;

Late 1960?: Remaining ruins of Big House demolished before construction of new jail begins nearby

1961

5/19: Frank dedicates new Chinle Boarding School;

New Chinle police substation under construction as part of Law and Order complex with court and jail, too;

Arizona Presbytery organizes forty members from Del Muerto into Del Muerto Presbyterian Church;

Summer: new jail completed;

Fall: Tall Woman has second Mountainway Ceremony

1962

Healing *v.* Jones creates the JUA;

Fundamental evangelism noticeably growing on reservation;

Howard supervises crew working on Black Rock Canyon dam;

5/11: Tall Woman admitted to Sage Memorial Hospital with broken wrist;
later, has Flintway Ceremony;

Summer: Augusta and family leave house at mission and move back home;

10/1: Camillo Garcia and son, Abel Garcia, killed in private plane crash on
Chinle airstrip at night; are buried from Gallup Cathedral on 10/5 by Father Pius Winter, O.F.M.;

Construction of new Chinle High School begins

1963

Paved road extended north from Chinle to Many Farms;

June: Editor meets the Mitchells;

6/19–23: American Indian Films, Inc., films a Puberty Ceremony at the
Mitchells'; family gets electricity;

Annie Dodge Wauneka receives Presidential Medal of Freedom;

Howard supervises reforestation around Durango, Colorado;

December: New Chinle High School opens upon completion; Augusta starts
head-cook job there

1964–66

Each winter for four-five months, Howard and Cozy Brown supervise farm-
workers in Yuma, California

1964

2/29: Frank dedicates new Chinle High School;

Frank starts having "small ceremonies";

4/20: Tall Woman has gallbladder surgery at Sage Memorial Hospital; diabetes mellitus also diagnosed at this time;

June: Completion of new NPS Visitor Center at Canyon de Chelly
National Monument; summer brings enormous increase in numbers
of visitors

1965

5/21: Last grandchild of Tall Woman and Frank Mitchell born;

Summer: Frank does several Blessingways, including one for granddaughter,
Geneva;

8/28: Hubbell's Trading Post in Ganado becomes a National Historic Site;

9/25: Traditional wedding at the Mitchells';

Fall: Frank begins to slow down; has more ceremonies, and tests later reveal
terminal prostate cancer;

12/27: Frank and Tall Woman baptized by Father Cormac Antram, O.F.M.

1966
New legal services, DNA, established in Window Rock;
February: Frank decides to stop performing Blessingway;
Bridge built over Chinle Wash, increasing access to Canyon del Muerto;
Presbyterian Church at del Muerto enlarged and cemetery established there;
Frank has more ceremonies as illness increases;
Summer: large increase again in numbers of visitors to Canyon de Chelly National Monument

1967–69
ONEO Navajo Culture Project

1967
4/15: Frank dies at Sage Memorial Hospital, Ganado;
4/20: Frank Mitchell's funeral at Our Lady of Fatima Church, Chinle, with burial in Chinle Community Cemetery;
Summer: Family has Protection Rite, and later, Tall Woman has Blessingway;
Howard works fighting forest fires near Canadian border;
October: Declaration of Basic Navajo Human Rights; Tribal Council Resolution removes 1940 ban on peyote

1968
4/11: Indian Civil Rights Act;
4/28: Mrs. Joseph Ganna dies;
5/13: Tall Woman has umbilical hernia surgery, Sage Memorial Hospital, Ganado;
Start of Rough Rock Mental Health Training Program;
Late summer/fall: Evilway and Blessingway for Frank's *jish* and transfer of *jish* to Tall Woman;
9/27: Tom Scott dies

Ca. 1969
Chinle Post Office moves to new building on site of former Big House; land withdrawn from Tribal Law and Order use in 1967

1969
7/31: La Font ends trading post function of the Thunderbird and sells stock to Garcia's Trading Post; old post converted into new restaurant;
Fall: Tall Woman returns to Houses Standing in a Line

1970s
Increased nationalism; growing concerns over repatriation and ethics of collecting; arts and crafts market craze

1970
Christmas: "Doogie" Mitchell visits Tall Woman

Late 1970–early 1971
Jimmy Deschine joins Isabel's household

1971
>5/1: Fiftieth anniversary celebration at Trinity Presbyterian Church, Chinle;
>Summer: Tall Woman and the editor have last extensive work sessions;
>Seya starts job as secretary/treasurer of Cottonwood Chapter; serves until 1979;
>Tall Woman has another Chiricahua Apache Windway;
>Fall: Tall Woman has another Blessingway

1972–74
>Howard works night-watchman job at Chinle Extended Care Facility

1972
>First class graduates from Rough Rock Training Program;
>Increased tribal concerns over preserving antiquities;
>June: Tribe establishes Navajo Health Authority and its Office of Native Healing Sciences;
>Summer: "Doogie" Mitchell visits again, bringing the Luciers;
>8/31: Reverend Joseph Gray and his wife, Mildred, retire and leave Trinity Presbyterian Church, Chinle;
>12/4: Doogie dies;
>12/9: Doogie's funeral at St. Michaels

1973
>3/18: Bartine Mitchell dies;
>April: Tall Woman has first stroke, marking the end of her weaving days;
>Summer: Franklin Shirley has Enemyway; Mary Lucier visits and brings Shigeko Kubota; Adelle and Augusta make trip to Connecticut;
>August: Tall Woman moves to Augusta's house;
>12/13: Adelle Mitchell dies

1974
>Navajo-Hopi Land Settlement Act;
>Summer: Augusta teaches one-week class on traditional foods at University of Arizona

Ca. 1975–76
>Howard works maintenance job at Chinle Valley School for Special Children

1975
>1/4: Indian Self-Determination and Education Assistance Act;
>April: Tall Woman suffers second stroke and first diabetic coma, admitted to Sage Memorial on 4/30;
>June: Editor makes short trip to Chinle, for meetings about Frank's book;
>July: Three-member Navajo-Hopi Relocation Commission established;
>Late August: "Bunni" assumes responsibilities as primary caregiver for Tall Woman;
>Christmas: Ye'iis visit Tall Woman's house; Slim Woman also visits

1976

January: Indian Health Care Improvement Act; new Trader Laws take effect
on reservation;

3/10: "Butch" Mitchell dies;

Late March: Editor starts one-quarter residency at SAR and returns to Chinle
as frequently as possible to spend time with Tall Woman and her family;

5/7: Tall Woman suffers second diabetic coma;

6/20–6/22: Editor's family visits Chinle briefly; then, all say good-bye;

Fall: Augusta starts job as Food Service Supervisor on ten-month contract;

9/15: Tall Woman makes "First Communion"

1977–82

Planning and development of Chinle Comprehensive Health Care Facility
with interior native healing sciences room

1977

Start of Relocation;

Tribal Zoo moves to Tse Bonito Park;

Tribe creates Navajo Nation Archaeology Department;

2/3: Marcus Yazzie dies from cancer at Fort Defiance Hospital;

4/14: Dennison Tsosie joins Augusta's family as an infant;

April: Navajo Community College Museum opens; McAllesters visit the
Mitchells;

May: Tall Woman's health starts to deteriorate further;

5/23–5/28: Tall Woman hospitalized at Sage Memorial Hospital, Ganado;

6/11: Tall Woman taken to Chinle Health Care Center; transferred to Sage
Memorial Hospital on 6/13;

6/18: Tall Woman brought home; Father Bryant Hausfeld, O.F.M., starts
daily visits;

6/28: Tall Woman taken to Chinle Health Care Center, is given pain-
numbing shot, and sleeps all day and night;

6/29: Tall Woman receives Last Rites shortly after 9 A.M.; pronounced dead
at Chinle Extended Care Facility at 10 A.M.; body washed and placed in
"cooler" while funeral arrangements made; notifications begin; funeral
meeting at night;

6/30: Editor flies to Albuquerque and goes to Chinle;

7/1: Errands done, food and supplies purchased; Rosary at Our Lady of Fatima Church at 7:30 P.M.;

7/2: Tall Woman's Requiem Mass at Our Lady of Fatima Church, 10 A.M.,
with reception at church hall after her burial in Chinle Community
Cemetery;

7/3: Editor prepares obituaries while flying home;

Fall: Augusta starts job as head cook at Tsaile Elementary School; commutes
until moving to vacant trailer there in January 1978

1978

August: American Indian Religious Freedom Act (AIRFA);
November: Frank Mitchell's book is published

1979

Planning starts for *Tseyi'* Mall in Chinle;
September: Archaeological Resources Protection Act (ARPA)

1980

Old NPS custodian's residence transferred to the Thunderbird concessionaire; twenty-year remodeling and expansion program at the Thunderbird;
9/5: Woody Davis dies

1981

Seya suffers first heart attack;
Chinle/Canyon del Muerto get new Chapter House in Chinle;
3/14: Bashas' Supermarket in *Tseyi'* Mall dedicated;
Late May/early June: Post office moves to new building in *Tseyi'* Mall;
September: Small Woman dies

1982

Howard works for Navajo Communications;
8/28: New Chinle Comprehensive Health Care Facility dedicated;
September: Isabel has Enemyway

1983

Garnett retires from nursing;
July: Frank's *jish* reblessed;
12/15: Slim Woman dies

1984

Mary Jones, White Dove Inc., becomes concessionaire of Thunderbird
Ranch via twenty-year contract with National Park Service; continual re-
modeling and expansion program converts Thunderbird Ranch into motel
and dining facility;
Howard serves as foreman for demolition of old Chinle Chapter House and
old preschool;
September: Agnes retires from Stockton Blood Bank job;
Howard retires

1985

Summer: Ruth has one of many Enemyways

Late 1985–early 1986

Garcia's Trading Post is closed, evidently then becoming tribal property;
consideration for National Historic Site status initially proposed but
Tribe decides (1990 or 1991) to sell property to Ocean Properties Ltd. for
economic-development purposes

1986

Ned Bernally retires from El Paso Natural Gas Company;

2/20–2/22: First Annual Navajo Studies Conference, Albuquerque, co-founded by editor and David M. Brugge;

4/30: George Acey Davis dies; funeral, 5/3, at Our Lady of Fatima Church

1988

Plans begin for new Our Lady of Fatima Church

1989

June: Our Lady of Fatima Church (the cinder-block one) torn down;

August–December: New hogan-style church built; first used on Christmas Eve;

August: Agnes has Enemyway;

September: Seya has Enemyway

1990

6/3: New Our Lady of Fatima Church dedicated

1991

7/8: Louise Davis dies; funeral, 7/10

1992

6/7: Construction begins for new Holiday Inn on site of former Garcia Trading Post;

10/13: Cecil Sandoval, Sr., dies;

10/15: Grand opening of Chinle Holiday Inn;

Late October: Mrs. Camillo Garcia (Pauline Corez Garcia) dies at age ninety-five;

10/30: Augusta retires, but all in group rehired to work through end of school year, May 1993

1993

6/11: Augusta moves back to Chinle from Tsaile

1994

9/17: Ruth Mitchell Shirley Yazzie dies; funeral, 9/22, at Our Lady of Fatima Church; burial in Chinle Community Cemetery

1995

5/16: Jimmy Deschine suffers paralyzing stroke that ends his days as a ceremonial practitioner;

12/12: Helen "Chee" Tsosi dies

1996

2/23: Brian Shirley is killed; funeral, 2/29, at Our Lady of Fatima Church; burial in Chinle Community Cemetery;

4/13: Memorial mass for Frank at Our Lady of Fatima Church;

6/26: Editor starts sabbatical year in Albuquerque to finalize work on Tall Woman's book;

7/21–7/23: Alfred Shirley has Enemyway;

8/3–8/11: Seventy-fifth Annual Gallup Inter-tribal Indian Ceremonial;

8/31–9/8: Golden Anniversary, Navajo Nation Fair, Window Rock;

12/15: Seya falls and breaks "good hip"; extended hospitalization begins, with other complications and surgeries, first in Albuquerque and then Flagstaff (February 1997)

1997

Late March: Seya finally discharged to his daughter Shirley's home in Chinle;

3/30: Anthropologist Mary T. Shepardson, b. 5/26/1906, dies in San Francisco;

4/18: Augusta helps editor present paper on "Final Stages of a Life History Project," in session on "Doing Life History Work" at Tenth Annual Navajo Studies Conference, Albuquerque, 4/16–20;

5/20: Walter Davis dies; funeral, 5/23, at Our Lady of Fatima Church; private land burial;

5/25: Shirley, family, and Seya move back to Cottonwood;

6/12: Editor moves back to Illinois to spend summer revising manuscript for resubmission to Tall Woman's family; work with the Mitchells continues by phone and letters;

7/17: Rachel Jones Mitchell dies at age ninety-five;

8/6: Family returns revised manuscript with additional comments and requests for revisions, and signed family approval letter;

8/11: Dedication of new Navajo Nation Museum and Library in Window Rock, and opening of inaugural exhibit, "Woven by the Grandmothers," on loan from the National Museum of the American Indian, Washington, D.C., until 10/17;

8/18: Editor returns to full-time teaching; work on revisions and "loose ends" continues when possible;

9/8: Navajo Nation Historic Preservation Office agrees to review manuscript in present "nearly finished" form;

9/15: Manuscript and family approval letter mailed to Window Rock with cover letter identifying and discussing loose ends; Confidential Appendix (finished) also submitted;

9/19: Historic Preservation Office review begins; art work and genealogy charts, now finished, submitted to family for review; discussions continue by phone;

10/18: First of Franciscan Centennial celebrations marking the east, in Crownpoint, New Mexico;

11/10: Grand opening and dedication of Chinle Veterans Center, north of Chapter House; Annie Dodge Wauneka, b. 4/10/1910, dies; funeral, 11/13, at St. Michaels with burial on family land;

11/13: Kay "Kaibah" C. Bennett, b. 6/5/1920, dies; funeral, 11/15, at Gallup Cathedral;

12/14: Anthropologist John Adair, b. 4/27/1913, dies in San Francisco

1998

1/16–2/22: Agnes Sanchez is featured, with other women, in Marilyn Cohen's
exhibit "Teach Me the Songs My Mothers Sang," at Thomas Walsh Art
Gallery, Fairfield University, Fairfield, Connecticut;

1/21: Navajo Nation Historic Preservation Office approves Tall Woman's
book pending remaining revisions;

1/29: Carl N. Gorman, b. 10/5/1907, dies; funeral, 2/2, at Gallup
Cathedral;

2/9: Irene Stewart, b. 7/1/1905, dies; funeral at Trinity Presbyterian Church,
Chinle, with burial on family land;

2/21: Franciscan Centennial celebration in the south, at Ganado;

Spring: Photography and maps completed for the book;

4/21: Franciscan Centennial celebration in the west, at Tuba City;

6/13: Franciscan Centennial celebration in the north, at Shiprock; Mary
Davis hospitalized in Albuquerque;

6/17: Father Simon Conrad, O.F.M., dies; funeral, 6/22, at St. Michaels;

6/24: Father Blane Grein, O.F.M., celebrates twentieth anniversary at Our
Lady of Fatima Church, Chinle;

7/10: Seya Mitchell dies; editor goes to Chinle to help, 7/13; Agnes Sanchez
arrives; Rosary, 7/14; Requiem Mass, 7/15, at Our Lady of Fatima Church;
burial in Chinle Community Cemetery;

7/21: Editor returns home from Chinle;

7/23: Navajo Nation approves budget for new Ceremonial Apprenticeship
Training Project;

10/1–10/4: Seventy-fifth anniversary of Northern Navajo Fair, Shiprock (although first documented one was 1909);

10/3: Final Franciscan Centennial celebration at St. Michaels;

10/7: Navajo Nation Day of Recognition and Appreciation for Franciscans,
by Navajo Nation proclamation;

10/17–10/31: Editor goes to Chinle; presents paper with David M. Brugge at
Eleventh Annual Navajo Studies Conference in Window Rock, to which
Augusta also goes; old Chinle clinic is being demolished; work is starting
on future home of Central Navajo Youth Corrections Center; another
sign announces future home of *Tseyi'* Cultural Center near rodeo grounds;
additional buildings at the old boarding school boarded up and awaiting
demolition;

12/15: Tall Woman's book submitted for publication consideration

1999

Throughout the year, communications between editor and family members,
mainly by phone and letters;

1/10: Sam Sanishya, b. 12/28/1901, dies; funeral, 1/14, at Our Lady of Fatima
Church, and burial in Chinle Community Cemetery;

February: Discussions start with University of New Mexico Press about publishing Tall Woman's book;

April: Joint paper, Frisbie with Sandoval, is published;

5/7: Editor signs contract with University of New Mexico Press for publication of *Tall Woman*;

5/8: Jimmy Deschine, b. 1/14/1922, dies; funeral, 5/13, at Our Lady of Fatima Church, and burial in Chinle Community Cemetery;

June: Work begins on drafts of catalog promotional copy for *Tall Woman*;

6/10: Louise Woody Davis, b. 3/29/1937 (according to her obituary), dies; funeral, 6/14, at the Chinle Church of Jesus Christ of Latter-Day Saints, and burial on family land in Chinle;

10/19–28: Editor returns to Chinle to visit Mitchells and others, and to help with the "traditional wedding" of Josephine Mitchell to Manny Lopez on 10/23. Construction of Central Navajo Youth Corrections Center still in process in Chinle;

11/20: Garnett and Ned Bernally celebrate fiftieth wedding anniversary

2000

January: Editor works with copyeditor on the book; manuscript returned to Press on 1/31;

7/28–9/21: Editor proofreads and indexes page proofs of *Tall Woman*

Appendix C: Schooling

As explained in the narrative, some, but not all, of the children born to and/or raised by Tall Woman and Frank Mitchell (or Man Who Shouts and his first wife) went to on-reservation and off-reservation schools. The following list identifies the schools involved and the dates individuals gave for experiences at different institutions. Although mission census cards included information on schooling at least in some cases, this was often incomplete and at variance with that provided by individuals. Question marks (?) indicate uncertain dates.

Individual	Elementary/Jr. High (grades 1–8)	High School	Other
1. Sam Sanishya	Chinle Boarding School first four years (1911–15); Fort Apache Indian School for next four (1915–19?).	Sherman Institute, Riverside, Calif.; dates ?; graduated.	
2. Mary no. 2	Chinle Boarding School first four years (1919–23?); Fort Apache Indian School for next four (1923–27?).	Haskell Institute, Lawrence, Kans.; dates ?; transferred to Albuquerque Indian School (1929); died before finishing (1/15/1931).	
3. Seya	Chinle Boarding School first four years but finished in three (1922–25); Fort Apache Indian School for next four (1925–29).	Albuquerque Indian School (1929–33); graduated.	
4. Agnes	Fort Apache Indian School for first eight but skipped eighth (1925–33).	Albuquerque Indian School (1933–37); graduated.	St. Joseph's School of Nursing, Albuquerque (1937–41); graduated.
5. Pauline	Chinle Boarding School first year but died before the end of the year (1926–27).	——	
6. Garnett Scott	Fort Defiance Boarding School for first eight (?–5/4/1938).	Albuquerque Indian School (1938–42); graduated.	Sage Memorial Hospital, Ganado, School of Nursing (1942–45); graduated.
7. Howard	Chinle Boarding School first six (1933–39); then St. Michaels for Jr. High but stopped at Christmas in final year (1939-41).	——	
8. Augusta	Chinle Boarding School first six (1935–43, with 1936–37 year at Fort Defiance Boarding School; then St. Michaels for Jr. High (1943–45).	St. Catherine's, Santa Fe (1945–49, with 1946–47 year at Anadarko, Okla.; graduated, St. Catherine's).	

Notes

CHAPTER 1

1. The Navajos refer to themselves as the *Diné*, the People, a practice followed through-out this work. For a classic work on the Navajos, see Kluckhohn and Leighton (1946); al-though outdated in places (despite later, revised editions), it remains ethnographically sound and is an appropriate place to start learning about the People for those interested.

2. See later chapters and Appendix A for Tall Woman's genealogy. As Chap. 2 indicates, her "real grandmother" or maternal grandmother chose to stay behind instead of following government orders to go to Fort Sumner.

3. Being matrilineal, Navajos belong to the clan of their mother and are "born for" that of their father. Tall Woman's clan was *Kiyaa'áanii* (or *Kin yaa'áanii*), the Towering House People (or Standing House People, as her husband preferred [Mitchell (1978)]); she was born for *Tó dích'ii'nii*, the Bitter Water People. See Young and Morgan (1980:351–52) for a list of the Navajo clans. In Navajo kinship, mother's sisters are all called "mother" and mother's mother's sisters are all called "grandmother." In addition to the introduction provided in Kluckhohn and Leighton (1946), see Witherspoon (1983) for an overall picture of Navajo social organization. His bibliography indicates the extensive, more specialized literature on Navajo kinship and related practices, and includes other well-known sources, such as Reichard (1928), Aberle (1961), and Witherspoon (1975).

4. As later chapters show, in Tall Woman's girlhood days, the moving around was related to the family's subsistence pattern, which combined pastoralism, foraging, and later, horti-culture and eventually agriculture, rather than the need to run and hide from enemies.

5. As noted in the Introduction, no attempt has been made in this work to compare Tall Woman's ethnohistorical narratives with those published elsewhere, although to do so would undoubtedly be instructive. The "Pre-American," pre-1846 period of Navajo history was a time when numerous outsiders continued to push into the Southwest in search of land and, perhaps, precious metals and adventure. Skirmishes and raids, retaliation and conflicts were frequent, as were the efforts to capture prisoners in order to support the extensive slave trade also characteristic of these times. Conflicts were numerous both among specific Na-tive American groups, and between them and outsiders. Politically the Southwest was first under Spanish (1598–1821), and then Mexican (1821–46) control, until the United States gained possession of the region from Mexico. Among the scholarly references available for those interested in accounts of Navajo history before the Long Walk and incarceration at Fort Sumner (1863 or 1864 to 1868) are: Acrey (1988, 1994), Bailey (1964a), Bailey and Bailey (1986), Correll (1976), Hendricks and Wilson (1996), Iverson (1981, 1990), Lyon (1996), Mc-Nitt (1964, 1972), Mitchell (1978), Sundberg (1995), Van Valkenburgh (1938), and Young (1968, 1978). Navajo narratives covering this period can be found in some of the classic life histories cited in the Introduction, as well as in other places, including Johnson (1973).

6. In 1989, SM suggested that here his mother was probably referring to other stories in the family concerned with "Apaches or Mexicans." He then shared stories about conflicts with White River Apaches at Apache Canyon and Where the Apaches Came Up, and with Mexicans at Smoke Signal.

7. Tall Woman laughed many times while relating her narrative. For those interested in the emotional dynamics of narration and storytelling, ethnopoetics, Navajo humor, and other issues, in this work the times when she (or identified others) laughed are marked with an asterisk. When she or others were visibly affected by sadness or other emotions during her narrations, the place is marked with an endnote. Tooth Woman's story was still being told and still causing laughter in the family in 1996–97.

Hearing this story on tape again in 1989 triggered the recall of yet another humorous one by SM, one of Tall Woman's sons; although it was among the narratives transmitted by the old people, it was not included in the text because I heard it from SM, rather than from her.

"There's another story in our family that made everybody around here laugh, too, even though it happened far from here, around Albuquerque. Sometime before the Navajos were sent to Fort Sumner, I guess people from lots of different places were trying to settle the place that became Albuquerque. That is near the Sandia Mountains in the east, and the old people said that way, way back, a long time ago, there used to be volcanoes to the west, on a mesa. I think they even call that the West Mesa now. At that time, there were some Navajos in that area, and they used to go up on the mesa to get wood for their fires. The old people said that one time an old man took some trash up there and threw it in one of those old volcanoes and set it on fire. When the people down below saw smoke coming from there, they thought the mountains were going to erupt again. They started rushing around, collecting all their belongings; some of them even started moving away from there that night. I guess those early settlers who had wagons were running around, trying to harness their horses, hitch up their teams, and load their belongings on to those wagons. They were watching that smoke and worrying about those volcanoes. When that old man came back down, the old people said he sure started laughing about what those others were doing, running around like that. He knew he had just been burning trash, weeds, and other things up there. The way the old people told that story, it was April Fool's Day when he did that. I guess that really fooled all those people at that time.*"

8. Navajos believe in various kinds of witches and thus in the practice of witchcraft. For further information, see Kluckhohn's (1944) classic study, as well as Brugge (1977); Toulouse (1982); Brady (1984); Levy, Neutra, and Parker (1987); and Blue (1988), among others. The recent, coauthored volume by Teller and Blackwater (1997), both from Chinle, Arizona, has added Navajo authors' voices to published discussions.

9. See Map 2; this is *not Tó 'ádin* [No Water Mesa] found in Van Valkenburgh (1941:154) and on maps to the north of Sweetwater, Arizona.

10. Hand-trembling is among the forms of divination used by Navajo diagnosticians to ascertain the causes of illness, bad dreams, misfortunes, and other indications of imbalance with all of the world's forces. For further information, see Morgan (1931) and Levy, Neutra, and Parker (1987), among others.

11. The implication here is that they "talked on top" from the bottom by using ventriloquism. A family member, upon hearing this story again in 1996, added, "Nowadays, I guess

they wear animal skins over themselves when they do those kinds of things." This is a reference to skinwalkers. See n. 8 above and Morgan (1936).

12. As shown in later chapters, sometimes the family's pastoral cycle included living around the old Black Mountain Trading Post, which burned down sometime between 1963 and 1970. See later chapters for information on other trading posts significant in Tall Woman's life. Van Valkenburgh (1941:11), McNitt (1963), Allen (1963), and Faunce (1981) are among the sources on "the original Black Mountain Store" or Trading Post; also see Hegemann (1963:210, pl. 206) for a photograph of the store in 1928.

13. This account is a composite of the multiple versions I recorded from Tall Woman, as well as ID's retelling of it. The latter was done in a group situation, with other sisters present; they occasionally added details that Tall Woman had included when telling them individually, thus creating a group version. In the various versions, *Tanabah* had nine other names, all available from the editor and all female war names conveying the sense of being on the way back, returning, or one who has returned from raiding, with or without mingling with others of the raiding party. The family chose *Tanabah*, their pronunciation of *Tanáábah* [Woman Who Is Returning from Raiding, Mingling (?) with Other Members of a War Party] as the variant preferred for publication. Concerning the translation, two preferred "Returning Back from the Warpath," and one, "Returning from Captivity"; again, the translation used in the text was a group decision. It is well known that nineteenth- and early twentieth-century Navajos often had war-related names; for examples, see the Franciscan Fathers (1910:118–29; 1912:207–12), and Young and Morgan (1980:417–18).

SM, who knew much of the family history, had never heard this story; as he said, "My mother never told me that, she never mentioned anything about that. But then, I wasn't even around here all those years, you know, because of school." After learning about it, he asked his sisters a number of questions and then formed his own opinions on specific aspects of the story, as shown below. Given the fact that SM was very well versed in many of his mother's other stories from her own mother and grandmother, his unfamiliarity with this one is interesting. Possible explanations for this situation, besides the one he offered, should perhaps include the narrative's heavy emphasis on "women's issues and concerns." However, work with the family indicated quite quickly that among the factors underneath their differential experiences and differential understandings were differences in transmission. Tall Woman did *not* share all of her narratives "from the old people" or all of her own life experiences with all of her children.

Tall Woman's children have diverse opinions about *Tanabah*'s identity and genealogical connection with them and by 1963 the issues involved could no longer be explored, given the deaths of others who would have known. Tall Woman herself usually told the story with *Tanabah* being "my mother's mother's sister," that is, "a sister of my real grandmother." However, a few of her children maintain that they heard the story with *Tanabah* having other identities, including those of being Tall Woman's real grandmother, the real grandmother's sister who became the grandmother to Charlie Davis, or Tall Woman's mother's mother's sister's daughter. SM, while reviewing ID's account of this story, said: "She said my mother told her that this woman was our great-grandmother, and that she's also the grandmother or great-grandmother to Big Man and Charlie Davis. But I know that they don't know anything about this. I went to ask each of them about this, after I heard you talking about it with my sisters. Those men have different mothers but the same grandmother. They don't know if that woman [*Tanabah*] was their grandmother and they don't know how they're related to us. They've never been clear on that. I guess it's through this, however it really was, that we're somehow real close together with them, real close relatives of theirs." All but one said *Tanabah* was a clan relative, a Towering House woman who was in the group that moved around with Man Who Shouts (Tall Woman's father). AS said, "All those old women died before I started going to the Chinle Boarding School. All of them were relatives of ours on my mother's side; they were our *nihichóí*, our distant great-grandmothers on our mother's side." The one who disagreed said, "*Tanabah* belonged to the *Mą'ii deeshgiizhniis*, the Coyote Pass People" [or Jemez clan], "just like our brother-in-law over there, Woody Davis [WD]. All of his people were roaming around in the Chinle Valley, down the road from here and across the highway. That was true even way, way back."

14. While ceremonies mentioned by Tall Woman are briefly explicated in endnotes, introductions to what outsiders call "Navajo religion" are provided in Wyman and Kluckhohn (1938), Kluckhohn and Wyman (1940), Reichard (1963), Wyman (1983), Frisbie (1987:1–10), and Levy (1998:110–52), among other sources. The Yeibichei Dance refers to part of the Nightway Ceremony, which is held to cure eye, ear, and other head ailments; arthritis; rheumatism; body paralysis, and other illnesses. Performances of either its five- or nine-night versions are restricted to after the first frost. While most events occur inside the ceremonial hogan in private, the final night may include a public exhibition by masked dancers, called *Yé'iis* (Supernatural beings, Giants [Young and Morgan 1980:756]), in an outdoor brush enclosure. The dancers, who perform in teams, sing and dance according to the rules of the Holy People or Navajo deities. Yeibichei dancers may also perform during the Mountainway, Featherway, and Coyoteway ceremonials. Nowadays, competitive team performances also characterize some of the Navajo Nation's regional fairs.

In the Navajo studies literature, numerous English spellings can be found for the *Yé'ii Bicheii* (translated as "God Impersonators" by Young and Morgan [1980: 421]), and for the term *Yei Bichei* when used as a gloss for the Nightway ceremonial, or *Tł'éé'jí*. The same is also true of signs posted along reservation roads to assist people in locating ceremonial sites. Since practices are not yet standardized, in this work I will use the anglicizations "Yeibichei" as the gloss term for the ceremony, when Tall Woman uses the gloss, and "Ye'iis" when she uses that term. For further information on the Nightway, with or without the optional Yeibichei Dance, see Matthews (1902/1995), Faris (1990), and selected essays in Halpern and McGreevy (1997). Some of its music and dance elements are discussed in McAllester (1971, 1979), Frisbie (1975c, 1980b), McAllester and Mitchell (1983), and Frisbie and McAllester (1992); Francis (1996) focuses specifically on Nightway dances.

The Fire Dance or Corral Dance refers to another kind of public exhibition that is optional and may occur during the final night of a Mountainway, Shootingway, and several other ceremonies. See Matthews (1887/1997), Haile (1946), Wyman (1975), and Haile (*in* Bodo 1998:41–47).

15. AS said when her mother told *her* this story, the container was "a metal can, like the canteens the People saw the Army using later, when the soldiers took them to Fort Sumner."

16. Tall Woman, in response to a question about the direction in which the woman was traveling, said, "My mother never told us which direction that woman was going or what mountain that was." Family members proposed three return routes for *Tanabah*, the first being through the Black Mountain area to the Chinle Valley. Another was that she crossed

the Chuska Mountains "through where the trees change, where the tree line is," to *Kin Naaztíʼí* [Houses Standing in a Line] (a place on the rim of Canyon del Muerto where Tall Woman's parents lived with the extended family before the 1918–19 influenza epidemic, as shown in later chapters). "In the days before Fort Sumner, some of our mother's relatives were living there, at least at times; some of them were taken to Fort Sumner from that area." "Those Utes were all over the place, even right near here in Canyon de Chelly and del Muerto." The other route suggested by family members was that *Tanabah* "returned to the place across the Chinle Wash that we call *Tó łizhini*" [Black Water].

17. See later chapters for information on childbirth practices.

18. Sashes (often termed *sis łichíʼí*, woven sash) are now part of the "traditional/ceremonial dress" for Navajo women. They are woven on a belt loom and may be worn by themselves, or underneath a concho belt. The role of wide belts, and others, including sash belts, in traditional childbirth practices becomes clear in later chapters. See Matthews (1884); the Franciscan Fathers (1910:248–49); Amsden (1934/1964); Kluckhohn, Hill, and Kluckhohn (1971), and others for information on sash belts and their production.

19. No matter who was narrating, this particular part was always told with great sadness; low, soft, quiet voice tones, and asides about how awful this event was, were common for both narrators and listeners.

20. Some narrators said the birds were buzzards, not crows.

21. Tall Woman said the herbs were not identified by the original narrator. She laughed when I asked, said the above, and then added, "I, myself, asked the same thing. I wanted to know if they're the same ones we use now. But nobody knew."

CHAPTER 2

1. The baptismal records at Our Lady of Fatima Church in Chinle, Ariz. (*Liber Baptismorum*, Vol. 1 [1907–40]) list her (p. 72 no. 11), as "'Asdzan Rose Nizhuni" [Rose, Beautiful Woman], born ca. 1850 and baptized on 8/3/1935, with granddaughter, Agnes Mitchell, as sponsor, in "ChinLee," by Father Anselm Sippel, O.F.M. Tall Woman's own baptismal records list her mother's name as "'aszán ncasí" [Big Woman]. The burial records at the same church (*Liber Defunctorum*), list her mother (p. 9 no. 8) as "'Asdzan (Rose) Nizhuni," [Rose, Beautiful Woman] born ca. 1850; they also show her passing away in "ChinLee" on 8/7/1935, and being buried in the original Catholic church cemetery on 8/8/1935 by Father Anselm Sippel, O.F.M.

2. As explained in the Introduction, unless plants are common their Navajo names are being used in the text. Later chapters include more information about those utilized for food. Tall Woman's mother continued to use them while raising her children, thus transmitting her ethnobotanical knowledge.

3. See Kluckhohn, Hill, and Kluckhohn (1971:239–42) for information and illustrations of the various kinds of woolen dresses, or "traditional, Pueblo-style dresses" worn by Navajo women. The two-piece, woven dress called *biil*, Hill's Type B, has been documented to at least the middle of the eighteenth century and is usually viewed as deriving from the Pueblos.

4. Tall Woman's mother is referring to the site of the Fort Defiance Boarding School, which was constructed after the Treaty of 1868, between 1879 and 1881. Mitchell (1978: 49–76, 116 n. 23) describes this school. See Mitchell (1978) and Frisbie (1996) for introductions to Navajo

experiences in federal boarding schools (after Indian education became mandatory in 1892), the impact of coercive police roundups of Navajo children, and relevant literature. Also see later chapters.

5. At this point, the interpreter, Albert G. "Chic" Sandoval [CS], added that his own family had very similar stories about the detrimental consequences of these rations. Navajos received no instructions about how to use any of the unfamiliar foods issued to them, either here or slightly later, at Fort Sumner.

6. Many narratives about the Long Walk and incarceration at Fort Sumner are now available. In 1963, when I began working with Tall Woman, it was not uncommon for people in her generation to share these memories when visiting one another. Now, in the late 1990s, with the passing of this generation, the vivid details and strong emotions associated with these recollections are fading. However, generalized narratives remain as part of the understanding of Navajo history in specific families, and contemporary Navajo educators, interested in perpetuating Navajo culture, values, and language, are calling for a revival of oral traditions, including the transmission of stories of the Long Walk. Among the resources available on the Long Walk experience, in addition to some of the life histories mentioned in the Introduction, are Bailey (1964b), Shinkle (1965), Frink (1968), Link (1968, 1971), Young (1968), Kelly (1970), Johnson (1973), M. Mitchell (1973), Correll (1976), Thompson (1976), F. Mitchell (1978), Roessel (1980), Trafzer (1982), Acrey (1994), and Sundberg (1995).

7. This refers to her first menses, and to the Puberty Ceremony Navajos hold to celebrate a girl's achievement of womanhood. The Puberty Ceremony is one of the subceremonies within Blessingway (see Chap. 3 endnotes). For studies of the *Kinaaldá*, see Frisbie (1967/1993), Begay (1983), R(uth) Roessel (1981), M. Roessel (1993), and Page and Page (1995: 152–56, 160–69), among others, as well as later chapters. Lena Carr, Navajo filmmaker (see Chap. 19 endnotes) produced a one-hour 16mm. color documentary on *Kinaaldá* in her home community of Steamboat, Arizona, during the summer of 1998. The film, entitled "*Kinaaldá*: Navajo Rite of Passage," was made with funding from the Corporation of Public Broadcasting and Native American Telecommunications, and will be aired on PBS television in the future (*Albuquerque Tribune* 11/15/99: A-2).

8. See later chapters for explanations of how Tall Woman's father got his name. *Delawoshí* is derived from *dilwosh*, "he/she's shouting."

9. This was true in many places. In addition to information provided in reservation histories on post-Fort Sumner enemies, see more specialized works, such as Moore (1994); for witchcraft problems, see Brugge (1972a:107), Blue (1988), and other sources cited in Chap. 1 endnotes.

10. In earlier times, it was common for people related by clan to move around together under the direction of a single headman. In Tall Woman's family, many Towering House People traveled as a group under the leadership of her father, Man Who Shouts. As becomes clear in later chapters, when she was small, the group was large. Besides her parents, her sisters, and her brothers (until marriage), the group included many of those shown in Appendix A, as well as others. The group continued moving together during her father's lifetime, expanding as individual women started living with men and having children, and contracting with deaths, and/or other postmarital residence practices. Tall Woman herself stayed in this group with her parents, sisters and their families, other grandmothers, and other clan relatives after her marriage to Frank Mitchell. In addition to the practice of matrilocal post-

marital residence rules among the Navajos (wherein women continue to live at home after marriage, with husbands moving in), as shown in later chapters, during the early years of her own marriage, Frank was rarely around.

11. See Mitchell (1978:113–14 n. 17) and Frisbie (1987:257–59 ff.) for introductions to the advent of Western health-care services on the Navajo reservation. The first hospital accessible to some Navajos but off the reservation opened in Fort Wingate in 1889.

12. It is acknowledged that Mr. Arm disregarded clan rules by marrying into his mother's clan. His older son's name derived from the fact that "he talked all the time, almost without stopping." AS said, "His name, *Bizahalani*, is like that bird's, *zahalánii* [mockingbird], the one that repeats what people say."

13. See later chapters for this family's pastoral cycle and the transhumance, or movement patterns associated with it.

14. While Tall Woman mentioned her father frequently, she never said whether or not he had gone to Fort Sumner, as did her own mother. When I realized I didn't know, it was too late to ask her. Her oldest surviving children, MD and SM, don't remember Man Who Shouts ever talking about the Long Walk as part of his own life experiences, at least with them. Thus, the question is among those that remain unanswered.

15. According to Mitchell (1978:303–4 n. 3), Man Who Shouts served as a headman from 1890 until his death in 1922.

16. Tall Woman didn't know if her parents had followed the customs of the time when they got married, whereby Man Who Shouts or one of his relatives would have arranged the marriage with her parents or other relatives. She also didn't know whether or not they had followed Blessingway practices and had a Wedding Ceremony when they "got together." Some of the other marriages in the family are described in later chapters.

17. This is SM's translation; Young and Morgan (1980:418) give it as Warrior on the Way Returning, noting that the addition of *Yił* before the last word is necessary for a name that translates as He is Returning in Anger. The term *Haské* [Warrior], however, implies He who is Angry or Mean (Young and Morgan 1980:417).

18. See later chapters for the impact of the 1918–19 influenza epidemic on Tall Woman and her family.

19. AgS and RY, two of Tall Woman's daughters, said they had heard Man with a Cane was crippled because he had been "shot in the back with an arrow." Another, MD, said he had fallen off a wagon and broken his hip in early adulthood when he was over in the Black Mountain area. All knew he had an *'Iináájí* [Lifeway Ceremony] after he was hurt; unlike other curing ceremonies, Lifeways address injuries caused by accidents and are usually continued for as long as needed.

20. Alfred W. Yazzie, a respected Nightway singer (or chanter, as he prefers) and author, is one of Walter's children. While speaking during the Eleventh Annual Navajo Studies Conference in Window Rock in October 1998, Yazzie said that after more than two decades of professional service as a policeman, including the job of Chief of Police at Navajo Community College, Tsaile (renamed Diné College in 1997), in 1993 he became the Senior Cultural Advisor for the Navajo Nation's Historic Preservation Department. For further information, see Faris (1990) and Yazzie (1984a, b, c). One of Alfred's siblings, a brother, Tom, is a well-known wood carver.

21. SM confirmed this, telling many stories about their interactions which included lots

of joking and teasing. Among SM's memories of Man with a Cane were those of him as an artist: "He used to keep track of the days on a sheet of paper so he wouldn't go to the store on Sunday when it was closed. He really liked going there; he'd put his cane in the stirrup, swing himself up that way, and take off. When he wasn't busy marking off the days, he'd be drawing. He was a real artist; he used to draw horses and cows on paper bags, cardboard boxes, anything he could find. He really was good at that."

22. Others who may have been real brothers to Tall Woman include two men known as Horse Herder and The Judge. After I first found them in census records, I asked family members what they knew about them, if anything. One challenge was to ascertain whether these were different individuals from those in Tall Woman's narrative or more multiple names for those already mentioned. This was especially true for Horse Herder, given The Jailer's involvement with his own and his father's livestock. The results of our discussions were inconclusive for *Łįį́ na'niłkaadí* [Horse Herder], but more certain for The Judge, who appears in census records as both *'Anaawe'aii* [The Judge] and *Bit'ahí* [The Attorney, according to SM]. SM also called the latter *'Anuhui'ahi* and *Nuhui'ahi*, which he again translated as The Judge [*'Ánihwii'aahii*]. SM, MD, and GB remembered him and said he was another son of Man Who Shouts, another older brother of Tall Woman. They also said that like others, The Judge was "very famous as a Yeibichei dancer; people knew him for that."

23. According to Small Woman, Tall Woman's real younger sister (with whom I worked in 1976), these three older sisters "passed away when they were up in their age, but not too far up, maybe in their thirties or forties." (Tall Woman said they were in their late twenties or early thirties.) Like Tall Woman, Small Woman also said that lots of other sisters and brothers died in infancy or childhood; she didn't know how many there had been because "our mother didn't remember."

24. Despite numerous attempts, I have not been able to learn how to translate this word, which is viewed as "one of those old Navajo words" by those I've asked. To date, Robert W. Young, who has also been "asking around" on my behalf, has had the same results. The only suggestions I've been given are those saying the term might have implied being a virgin and/or unmarried.

25. Mitchell (1978) preferred the translation, "Two Streams Meet Clan" for his mother's (and thus his brothers', sisters', and own) clan; therefore, that translation was used in his story.

26. Here, Tall Woman is referring to the Chinle area. As is well known (Hodge, Hammond, and Rey 1945:85–89, 306), Catholics initiated the first missionary efforts among the Navajos in the 1620s, although these were not formalized until St. Michaels Mission was established in October 1898 (see Wilken 1955; Butler 1991, 1993; Chap. 6 endnotes, and later chapters herein). In the interim, Presbyterians established themselves, at least temporarily, in Fort Defiance in 1869, and by the end of the century had been joined on the reservation by Episcopalians (see Liebler 1969), Methodists, and missionaries from the Christian Reformed movement and the Church of Jesus Christ of Latter-day Saints (see Warner 1970; Frisbie 1992, for an overview and bibliography; and Lyon 1998).

As shown in later chapters, endnotes, and Appendix B (Chronology), the Franciscans were first to reach Chinle, in 1903; they raised their combined residence/church to a residence in July 1907 and dedicated their newly built Annunciation Mission (renamed, in 1956, Our Lady of Fatima Church) in March 1912. Itinerant Protestant missionaries came shortly thereafter, leading to the April 1921 formation of the Indian Presbyterian Church of Chinle (renamed in 1959, Trinity Presbyterian Church) and the construction of the church and manse shortly thereafter.

27. According to some of Tall Woman's children, it seemed to them that "all of her sisters and nieces were marrying Mitchells at that time. At least two older sisters of hers were married to that *Tó'aheedlíinii Nééz*. Then, too, one of that man's sisters married *Hastiin Yázhí* [Small Man] from Black Mountain. That man, Small Man, was one of our mother's mother's brothers." This sister, however, is *not* included in the genealogy Mitchell gave for his own natal family (Mitchell 1978:346–47).

28. Tall Woman didn't remember if this was the older sister she mentions frequently as her herding companion during childhood days. In Mitchell (1978:346), according to what Frank reported, Jim's wife is shown as having produced five sons for him.

29. As shown in Appendix A, Gai [no translation or English name given] married Son of Yucca Fruit Man; she had Ida and Betty for him, but then died in childbirth. Her younger sister, a girl called *Jool* or *Dijool* [Chubby Woman] "because she was small and chubby," "really short like a Hopi woman," then married Son of Yucca Fruit Man. This woman raised Ida and Betty and also had children for Son of Yucca Fruit Man, including Bobby, Eva, and Samuel Hashkaan, John Brown, and a baby boy and two girls who did not survive. When Chubby Woman passed away in childbirth (reportedly when Eva was about five years old), Son of Yucca Fruit Man "took Bobby, Samuel, and John Brown over to my real sister's, Small Woman's place; she was already a widow by then and eventually, they married each other." For several years after Chubby Woman died, Eva was raised by Tall Woman and Frank; see later chapters.

The other daughter, *Nizhóní* [Beautiful Woman] married Tom Scott, and had Garnett, another girl, Mary, and other children, including three boys. Mary died before she was ten days old and some of the others died "as babies." Beautiful Woman died in childbirth while Garnett was in school at Fort Defiance; the three boys died shortly after their mother, leaving Garnett as the sole survivor. After staying with her father and his sister, *Tótsohnii's* wife [Big Water Man's wife] for a while, Garnett started living with the Mitchells. Henceforth, she was raised by Tall Woman and Frank, according to her mother's wishes, and today, continues to be an integral member of the family.

30. The Mitchells pointed out here that the Peter Paquette census of 1915, which lists these four as children of Man Who Shouts, is wrong. MD knew The Jailer, and SM was very close with Sam Sanishya while growing up, as is apparent in later chapters. None of Tall Woman's children, however, ever saw or knew the names of either of the parents of these four children. Despite Tall Woman's account here, in actuality, when the parents died, the four children were separated. The boys stayed with Man Who Shouts and his family, and the girl, Bah, was raised by Tall Woman's half sister, Slim Woman, who called her "my daughter." Before marrying Joseph Ganna, this girl was married to WD's older brother, *Diné Nééz biye'* [Son of Tall Navajo], and had children for him (see Appendix A).

Among Sam's own childhood memories were those of being "really close" with Tall Woman's own mother, Man Who Shouts' first wife. He reportedly had a photograph of her, a copy of which Ethnobah Sandoval, wife of the late Albert G. "Chic" Sandoval, also had; however, both pictures had been lost by 1989. Both SS and SM confirmed their close friendship, and in 1989, enjoyed recalling numerous childhood experiences, which included playing baseball together, and frequently accompanying Man Who Shouts to Yeibichei dances in his buggy and on other trips. Everyone in the family said these two were his "favorites."

SS said that The Man's Grandson, one of his older brothers, was also called Man with a Black Horse, Mr. Black Horse, and Man with Horses. He "lived at the bottom" of Waterless Mesa during much of his life and became the father of Philemon and Ben Bitsui. SS also said he was a "great Yeibichei dancer; he took after my other older brother, The Jailer, in that." He used to dance a lot with WD, MD's husband. The Man's Grandson got Man Who Shouts' summer farm site upon the latter's death, and eventually gave it to James Francis, Ida's son, before he died (in 1989).

31. The 1915 Peter Paquette census gives two names, "*Benai yosani*," and "*Beniyilani*," for Man Who Shouts' wives; neither meant anything to Tall Woman or her family. Both MD and GB learned about this second wife and her daughter from Tall Woman's mother, who was "the first wife"; for SM, their close kinship connection was one of the "family tree surprises" associated with this project.

32. Slim Woman said, "I was old enough to be chased around by the sheep when [Tall Woman] was born, probably about five." LM confirmed that Slim Woman, his grandmother, talked about their age differences this way many times.

33. This was *not* the usual pattern followed by other Navajos of the time; the multiple wives usually lived in close proximity and moved around in the same group. In 1976, Slim Woman said, "We lived apart from my father's other wife and her children so I never really knew how many children the other wife had. I do know a lot of them died when they were small and some more died when they were grown up. I have two younger sisters left now: the one you're asking about, and Small Woman. I never learned too much about my father's other family; he used to tell me about them, but I never knew how to ask him questions about those things. I'm about the same age as *Hashké Náádááł* [The One Who Returned from the Warpath in a Bad Mood]; he's the son of one of my own mother's older brothers." (The brother's identity remains unknown, unless Small Man was also among those who had a son bearing this name, which was clearly popular in the family.)

34. Slim Woman confirmed this during my work with her in May 1976. She was certain this omission was the cause of her own problems, which then included failing eyesight and increasing deafness, and she wished someone would sponsor a Nightway Ceremony for her to correct those things. In 1976, Slim Woman was a tiny woman, slightly over four feet tall, blind, and deaf, but her mind was sharp. She related the story of her own birth as follows: "My mother told me I almost killed her when I was born.* She was in hard labor for four days and her husband, my father, Man Who Shouts, got a hand-trembler to see what was wrong, why I was not getting born. They said he had broken some rules we have about fixing up those Yeibichei masks; he had sewn some of those shut while his wife was pregnant. That is why they said I was refusing to come out. So they just started doing small ceremonies from the Nightway for my mother while she was in labor, and when I finally was born, they kept doing those things for a while for her and for me, too. So, my first ceremony was when I was being born and it was in the Yeibichei way.* When I was born, I was all bruised up, even my head and my forehead. My mother said there were lots of people there trying to help with that. Later, I was added in as a co-patient when my father, Man Who Shouts, had a Nightway done for himself. They said that should be done for me, by myself, but I never had one. During my life I've always had eye trouble and it's probably because I never had that ceremony. I had cataract surgery a while ago,

but it didn't help too much. I've always had pinkish colored eyes and I've had trouble seeing because of what happened when I was born. Not too long ago, I fell and broke my hip so now I'm going around on a walker."

35. AS, AgS, and others who accompanied their maternal grandmother on her walks in her old age said that many of their maternal relatives congregated at Grandma Red Bottom's place; it seemed to them that others "were *always* there, visiting and visiting."

36. AS said this was in the early 1940s, when she herself was in junior high at St. Michaels. The death records at the Chinle Trinity Presbyterian Church do not date back to this period, nor is there any information on Slim Woman's husband in Gray (1986).

37. Slim Woman reportedly was a Presbyterian all her life, "like all the *Tł'ááshchí'ís*." This is confirmed in Gray (1986) and in the Register of the Chinle Trinity Presbyterian Church wherein her name is written "Ason Tsossie ClausChee," and she is listed as communicant no. 191, baptized on 4/9/1950. According to AS and HM, Slim Woman's daughter, Elmae, who was Leroy's mother, was very young when she had children for Kee Chee (called Katchee) Mitchell. She died "from some disease" right after Calvin, the youngest, was born, and Slim Woman, their grandmother, raised all of the children (Leroy, Pete, Lora, Alfred, Mae, and Calvin) in the beginning; "then Good Shepherd Mission took over and all of them were put in school there."

LM said his father, Kee Chee [Katchee] Mitchell, had been raised by his mother's sister, the wife of Mr. Sand, also known as Bead Man's Son, because his own mother died when all of them were small. After LM's mother died, Kee Chee, a World War II veteran, remarried, "this time to Martha Gorman. They had one child together, Katchee Jr., before Katchee passed away." LM married Sally Aquiar on 11/3/1969 (according to Trinity Presbyterian Church records); their first child, a boy, was named Katchee after his grandfather; as LM said, "he's Katchee, K. C. the 3rd." (See Appendix A.)

Slim Woman died on 12/15/1983 (according to a handwritten note in the Presbyterian Church's Chronological Roll of Communicants). Family members said that "a granddaughter who was caring for her insisted that she be buried from Potter's House. So they used that church for her funeral instead of the Presbyterians, and then buried her on family land, next to [LM's] older brother." This independent church started, according to Father Blane Grein, O.F.M. (p.c. 10/10/1990), in 1982 when it was known as Potter's House. Since then, it has undergone several name changes with the arrival of new pastors. Subsequently, it became known as The Door, Victory Chapel, and then ?, and in 1990, Grace Fellowship Full Gospel (still its name in 1998). (For information on independent churches on the reservation, see Dolaghan and Scates 1978, Scates 1981, and Frisbie 1987, 1992, among others.)

Genealogical work shows that the ties between Slim Woman's family and the Mitchells continued through time in a number of ways. One example is that a grandson, Dan (one of Ralph's children) married Ida's daughter, Ada. Ada is communicant no. 173 in the Trinity Presbyterian Church Register, having been baptized on 4/6/1947. Her own mother, IF, was baptized as communicant no. 218, on 5/18/1952. Another tie came through Slim Woman's other daughter, Bartine, who married Thomas Mitchell, Jr., the son of Frank's brother, Thomas. As shown in Appendix A, Bartine and Thomas Jr. had a large family before he was killed in a car accident in the 1950s; the children included Bertha, Alta, Rita, Elouise, Rebecca, Louise, Lavato, Timothy, Charles, and Jimmy, as well as six others they lost, including their oldest daughter who died as a teenager, and two babies. After Thomas Jr. was killed, Bartine married Charlie Gorman; they had one child, Charlene, before Bartine died in 1973 from cancer. In 1976, her daughter, Bertha, was taking care of the house, fields, sheep, and horses, with the other sisters and brothers coming in on the weekends to help. She never went to school, but instead stayed home, caring for her parents. It was Bertha who, in 1969, told Tall Woman to come and get corn at their place; as shown near the end of her narrative, this trip was highly emotional for Tall Woman, since the field was near one of her family's earlier homesites, namely Houses Standing in a Line.

38. Tall Woman's grandchildren, especially RY and ID's children, named this woman Grandma *Zhinii* [Grandma Black] "because she always wore a long black coat when she drove over here in the wagon to visit [Tall Woman] when we were very small." This woman's tombstone in the Chinle Community Cemetery shows her name as Asdzaan Yazzie Tsosi Begay and her lifespan dates as 1893 to September 1981. The Presbyterians reportedly buried her, after she died in the Gallup IHS hospital. She suffered from gallbladder trouble; during surgery, cancer was discovered, which spread rapidly and was fatal. None of the records I was able to locate at Trinity Presbyterian Church pertained to her; the Register of Deaths covered from 10/8/1953 to 4/8/1971 and the file folder on funerals started in October 1983.

I worked with Small Woman, Tall Woman's "only real sister," in May 1976, after meeting her in the 1960s and getting to know her in the 1970s, when she frequently visited. She looked very much like Tall Woman, a fact noted by many every time she appeared. While Frank was still alive, she used to come to his ceremonies whenever possible, because she knew many Sheep, Horse, and Mountain Songs from the Blessingway and contributed them with a "good, strong voice."

39. No one in the family knows the meaning of this name, but it continues to evoke laughter whenever recalled. When again discussing it in October 1996, MD and AS said it "probably came from one of his favorite, or frequent expressions, which probably was *łah*, 'at one time' or *łą́*, 'many' or 'much.' He probably kept saying that every time he talked, and so People just started calling him *Hastiin Łaashi*."*

40. Helen (3/15/1909–12/12/1995), called "Chee" by the family, was buried in the Chinle Community Cemetery next to her mother. During her life, she suffered from an unnamed condition, which over the years gave her periods of hair loss and severe mobility problems because of crippling. She had numerous ceremonies and, at times, "looked and felt good"; then she was "busy herding sheep, cooking, and taking care of the place." Elsie, the youngest, married Ralph Deschine from Rock Point, and works at the BIA school there. She, her sister, Jennie (who married Kee Lewis), and brother, Tom (who married Bessie Lewis), all have a number of children (see Appendix A). The family sponsored an Enemyway for brother Tom in the summer of 1990 and in 1996–98, remained actively involved in ceremonial and other kinship obligations. Elsie (born in 1933) said she thinks she was "about five" when her father died.

41. Tall Woman's birthdate will never be known for certain. I used 1874 when preparing her obituary (Frisbie 1977a, b) because of post-funeral discussions with her children. Most insisted she was *older* than Frank (who was born in 1881) when the two started living together. Both AS and SM said they had discussed this matter at length with relatives in Black Mountain who were in the group that moved around with Tall Woman's mother and father in the early days. These relatives knew she was older than so and so, and so and so, and they

had tracked down the dates on some of those people, especially in the genealogical lines leading to both Charlie Davis and Big Man. Because of these discussions, which began in the early 1970s, they were certain that at the time of her death, Tall Woman was "well over 100 years old." Collectively, her children settled on December 1874 as her birthdate, which made her "102 plus" at the time of her death, June 29, 1977. The same date appeared on her memorial cards and the concrete cross later erected above her grave in the Chinle Community Cemetery. While such a lifespan equates with the cultural ideal of 102 (see Frisbie n.d.), the 1874 birthdate is at odds with data in all five of the early census records. As shown in Mitchell (1978:350), four of the latter give 1890, and one, 1888 as her birthdate. Some readers may also find 1874 inconsistent in at least two other respects: her childbearing years, which ended in 1932 with the birth of ID, and the number of siblings she had who were reportedly born before her but after their mother's return from Fort Sumner and marriage to Man Who Shouts. Frank himself said he didn't know when Tall Woman was born, although he always talked as if she were younger than he was. As he said (Mitchell 1978:97, 120), when he first became interested in her (after noticing her while visiting his older brother, Jim, who was then married to one of her older sisters), "she was just a young girl." The only other possible comparisons are to her older half sister, Slim Woman, and younger real sister, Small Woman; the former was buried on private land without a tombstone; the latter's 1981 tombstone shows an 1893 birthdate.

42. This belief about shrinking because of old age was common and shared, at least in this particular extended family.

CHAPTER 3

1. Blessingway is a prophylactic rather than a curing ceremony. Viewed by many as "the backbone of Navajo religion," it emphasizes and reinforces the ideal, desired state known as *hózhǫ́* (which signifies harmony, peace, good fortune, balance, good health, happiness, and other positive events), and prevents misfortune before it occurs. Blessingway, according to the Kluckhohn and Wyman (1940:184–85) classification, includes five variants distinguishable by differences in songs and sacred narratives. The subceremonies derived from it are the Girls' Puberty Ceremony, the House Blessing Ceremony, the traditional wedding, the Rain Ceremony, and the Seed Blessing. In addition to the uses implied by these names, Blessingways are also performed to bless traveling and travelers; pregnant women before delivery; new leaders, medicine people, and medicine bundles; members of the armed services; and livestock and other things. Besides these and other uses, Blessingway, in whole or part, is added to all curing ceremonies to compensate for omissions or errors that might otherwise render these ceremonies ineffective. For further information on Blessingway, see Wyman (1970a), Mitchell (1978), Farella (1984), Hadley (1986), and Levy (1998:117–52), as well as sources cited elsewhere for both the Puberty and House Blessing ceremonies.

2. This name was explained as follows: "*nat'oh* means tobacco, *ná'ásht'oh* means to smoke tobacco, so he was called for that, *Diné T'ohi*, Man with Tobacco, Tobacco Man."

3. This pattern was followed later, too, since the family lived with Small Man many winters after Man Who Shouts became a Blessingway singer. Tall Woman said that at least several times in later years, her half sister, Slim Woman, and her children would go up there for the winter with them. Remember that when Slim Woman's mother (Man Who Shouts' second wife) was alive, she and her only child moved around separately, not with the first wife,

Tall Woman's mother, and all her children. See Robert Roessel (1983) and Witherspoon (1983) for introductions to Navajo history from 1850 to 1923, and the basics of Navajo social organization.

4. Among the sources for Navajo architecture, its history, different house styles, and changes through time are Mindeleff (1898), the Franciscan Fathers (1910), Ostermann (1917), Haile (1937, 1942), Kluckhohn, Hill, and Kluckhohn (1971:143–62), McAllester and Mc-Allester (1980), and Jett and Spencer (1981). For the ceremonies associated with both Navajo dwellings and more recently, public buildings, see Frisbie (1968, 1970, 1980c) as well as some of the above.

5. McNitt (1963) is one of the basic sources in the extensive literature on trading posts, trading practices, and specific traders in different time periods and locations. Left-Handed Mexican Clansman et al.(1952), Underhill (1953), Adams (1963), Link (1968), and Mitchell (1978) also contain useful information. For specific traders and/or memories of their families, see Gillmor and Wetherill (1934), Hegemann (1963), Kennedy (1965), Richardson (1986/1991), Roberts (1987), Williams (1989), Moon (1992), Gibson (1994), Cousins and Cousins (1996), Valette and Valette (1997), Wagner (1997), Batkin (1998), Graves (1998), Haile (*in* Bodo 1998), and Blue (2000), among others. For a specific focus on historic posts, see the papers in Vol. 57 (3) of *Plateau* (1986). For examples of journal and newspaper articles, see McPherson (1992) and Donovan (1997c, d), among others. Research on traders and trading practices continues; for example, see Blue (2000), M'Closkey (1993, 1994, 1996, 1997), McPherson (1998), and Reinhart (1997, 1998). Information is also available in the literature on Navajo economics and in many of the studies of weaving and weavers. Citations specific to Hubbell's Trading Post, which was established in its present location in Ganado in either 1876 or 1878, and to the history of trading in Chinle are given in later endnotes.

Navajos began trading with Anglos in 1868, shortly after the return from Fort Sumner, exchanging wool and blankets for staples. Lorenzo Hubbell was clerking in Stover and Coddington's store in Fort Wingate by 1869, the same year that Damon bought Neale's store in Fort Defiance. Navajo interactions with traders were in part determined by the areas encompassed in their pastoral movement cycles; however, word of mouth about traders' personalities and the fairness of business transactions also affected choices Navajo families made about where to trade.

6. See Hill's (1938) classic study of Navajo hunting practices, among other sources, for further information on deer, rabbits, and the other animals Tall Woman mentions.

7. See Kluckhohn, Hill, and Kluckhohn (1971:282–90 ff.) for moccasin-making styles, techniques, and history. At least some Navajos, including young people, continue to make moccasins today (1998), learning techniques from elders or in school courses.

8. Tall Woman was well known for a variety of things, including her specialized knowledge about midwifery, rug designs, and traditional foods. Her narratives emphasize the latter, but not to the exclusion of her other areas of expertise.

9. Also see Mitchell (1978:32) for descriptions of the two ways of making cheese. Among the sources for Navajo ethnobotany are Matthews (1886), the Franciscan Fathers (1910), S. Young (1938), Wyman and Harris (1941, 1951), Elmore (1943), Vestal (1952), Mayes and Lacy (1989), and Mayes and Rominger (1994).

10. This refers to the fourth or rennet stomach of ruminants, specifically to the mucous membrane lining of that stomach in a sheep or goat, which acts as a substitute for rennin.

11. Here, Chic Sandoval [CS] added: "You can also use the real bellies of goats for water bags, too. All you have to do is turn the smooth side in; in other words, just turn that stomach inside out, and then fill it with water. That kind is easy to make, but it's smaller than the one she's talking about. We used both kinds in my family." See Mitchell (1978:31) and Kluckhohn, Hill, and Kluckhohn (1971:105–6 ff.) for other descriptions of "cased goatskin or sheepskin water bags." SM (born 1912 or 1913) reported that when he was young, Tall Woman was still making water belly bags and she and Frank were still using them. He also said that was before water tanks, reservoirs, and windmills were built on the reservation. Both MD (born ca. 1908) and RY (born 1920) confirmed the family's use of these bags before metal barrels, wooden kegs, or other things were available. They also knew that Tall Woman had learned how to do this from her own mother, and provided other descriptions of the manufacturing process, which Tall Woman had taught all her children. While both accounts echoed Tall Woman's, RY added that after cutting off the hooves, the skin is pulled off from the bottom to the head, with attention being given to keeping the neck all in one piece. The bag is sewn in the neck area and the legs are tied together; then it is filled from the neck. She also said that some people added a shoulder strap out of rope or rawhide to the water bag to make it easier to haul on your back. Finally, RY said that when she herself was old enough to help carry water, the family had switched to using buckets and hauling barrels in their wagon to water tanks.

12. Tall Woman chose not to elaborate on her knowledge of pottery making, stating that she had never done it by herself, but only helped her mother while growing up. She also said after her mother died, she never again participated in it and thus, had not passed it on to her children. MD, in Mitchell (1978:158 n. 9) makes it clear that *both* Tall Woman's mother and father knew how to make pottery, and did so in a separate hogan, with Tall Woman's help. MD and other children used to gather the sheep dung needed for firing, and then sit and watch. When discussing this further, Tall Woman said she guessed she had never done it herself because she was always busy taking care of small children and weaving rugs. She also said there were so many rules that had to be followed when you made pottery that it was hard to remember and obey all the restrictions. She knew from experience that if you ignored them, even if you forgot only one, the pot would crack, break, crumble, or be ruined in some other way (a point made by Tschopik [1938] and others while studying both Navajo pottery and basketry). Among the sources on Navajo pottery are the Franciscan Fathers (1910), Hill (1937), Tschopik (1938, 1941), Brugge (1963, 1964, 1983, 1987), and Kluckhohn, Hill, and Kluckhohn (1971:140–41). For discussions of contemporary developments in Navajo pottery, see Hartman and Musial (1987), Wright (1987a), the papers in Vol. 58 (2) of *Plateau* (1987) (which include Bell [1987], Wright [1987b], and Wright and Bell [1987]), Bernstein and McGreevy (1988), Schiffer (1991), and Rosenak and Rosenak (1994), among others. Various Indian Art magazines also frequently feature Navajo potters and their work; see, for example, the article on Lorraine Williams (*Indian Artist* Fall 1997:70). Among the new ideas in evidence in Albuquerque shops in October 1998 was "cera pottery" by a Navajo couple, Gail and Skeeter Vail.

13. Here, CS interrupted to add his own account to this: "My mother made those jugs too, and she wove them from sumac. Lots of women did that when I was little. After they got them done, they got pinyon pitch and set it in the fire to make it boil, to turn it into a liquid. Then they smeared it all over the woven surface, but not by hand. While it was still

warm, they used those rocks to smooth it over; they went over the surface of that jug on the outside with those pebbles, just like you use a rolling pin on dough. After they had smoothed the whole surface like that, they let the jug settle until the pitch hardened. When it was thoroughly dry, they'd always test it by pouring water into it and making sure that it didn't leak."

Other descriptions of *tóshjeeh* [pitched water basket bottles or jugs] can be found in Kluckhohn, Hill, and Kluckhohn (1971:107–9) and Mitchell (1978:31). When Tall Woman finished describing these woven jugs, she was silent for a while and then added: "The last water jug my late mother made was a small one. We had that around here for a very long time after she passed away, because I wanted to keep it. But now it's gone; I can't remember just who we decided to give that to."

14. In 1963, sheepskins and goatskins were still the preferred bedding in the Mitchells' hogan. Over the years, this practice gave way to the use of beds, mattresses, and the like. Toward the end of his days as a practicing Blessingway singer, even Frank used to take a mattress roll with him when going to do Blessingways for others. Earlier, when discussing options and decisions open to singers, he identified the potential problem of lice-ridden sheepskins in hogans of patients as among those many considered when deciding how to respond to requests for their ceremonies (see Mitchell 1978; Frisbie 1980a).

15. A number of elderly Navajo women emphasize the amount of time they spent herding, when discussing their memories of hard but essentially happy childhoods. Another context wherein herding is emphasized is in very old age; when confusion sets in, it is not uncommon for people to spend waking moments talking to the sheep, calling them, or worrying about their whereabouts and condition. Apparently, it is also not uncommon for elderly women to dream about sheep herding. On 5/20/1976, Slim Woman, Tall Woman's half sister, expressed it this way: "When I go to sleep I dream about herding the sheep. I know as I get older I'll do what others have done. I'll start imagining all of that in my mind even during the day. People do that when they get real old. They talk about the sheep day and night, all the time. It's like they forget everything else except the sheep. That's because that's all we were raised with, that's all we did—take care of the sheep."

16. Three family members, while listening to this story on tape, all had the same reaction: "Navajos have great respect for bears; just like she says, we never say that word right out like that. Instead, we just call them 'the thing that roams in the mountains.'" Among the sources that discuss the sacred nature of bears as well as the respect and avoidance Navajos show toward them are Reichard (1963) and Hill (1938:157–61). Matthews's (1887/1997) and Wyman's (1975) studies of the Mountainway provide introductions to one of the main curing ceremonies associated with afflictions caused by bears. Newcomb (1940) and Bulow (1991) are among sources documenting Navajo taboos.

CHAPTER 4

1. Manuelito and Ganado Mucho were reportedly the first Navajos who successfully learned, in 1881, to harness horses and drive wagons (Mitchell 1978:161 n. 13; Underhill 1953:207; Haile [*in* Bodo 1998:65–67]). As far as can be determined, Man Who Shouts did not get his wagon and buggy until sometime after 1890, when he became recognized as a headman.

2. See Appendix B for a chronology. As shown there, Hubbell's Trading Post in Ganado

was built in either 1876 or 1878. While at least four trading posts can be documented for Chinle at different time periods, with the conversion of the original Sam Day post to a motel and restaurant, and Garcia's to a Holiday Inn, the community's trading posts per se went out of existence. An introduction to each of the community's posts follows; for further information, see: McNitt (1963), Kennedy (1965), Stewart (1980), Greenberg and Greenberg (1984), Gray (1986), Kelley (1987b), Harrison and Spears (1989), McKenna (1989), Rosenlieb and Smillie (1990), Cousins and Cousins (1996), and Frisbie (1998), among other sources cited below.

The first trader in Chinle, reportedly a Mexican, was Little Mexican, who from 1882 to 1883 operated a store from a tent located in a spot that later was both across the road from the Garcia post and on the site of the later Dick and Cordelia Jackson Dunaway residence (who lived in a stone house there from 1928 until the early 1940s) (Van Valkenburgh 1941:39, among others). Being unlicensed, Little Mexican was shut down within the year by Agent Denis Riordan. Three years later, he was followed by the first licensed traders in Chinle, J. Lorenzo Hubbell and C. N. Cotton (an influential Gallup merchant/wholesaler and later, prominent banker; see Williams 1989) who, early in 1886, opened the first permanent Chinle store in an abandoned stone hogan (later incorporated into Garcia's Trading Post) to which they added several rooms (McNitt 1963:214). After failing to get their license renewed because of the complex politics surrounding the licensing of traders among the Navajos (see McNitt 1963 and Williams 1989), the store passed through a variety of nonconsecutive owners including Michael Donovan, Washington and Thomas Lingle, Bernard Mooney and James Boyle, and John Boehm in the 1886–89 period (McNitt 1963:214 n.). Then, at least for a time, it seems to have been abandoned until Father Leopold Ostermann and a Brother (first Gervase, then Placidus, then Gervase again) rented it for use as a residence/chapel from August 1904 until January 1906, while the Franciscan residence in Chinle was being built (see Ostermann 1913, 1914; Wilken 1955; Chap. 6 endnotes).

Later in time, ca. 1912, either one or more of the Kirks (perhaps brothers John and Mike, Gallup mercantilists), began running the store. Like earlier owners/operators, they added more structures, including the trader's residence (Kelley 1987b). Mr. and Mrs. Skagg were reportedly at the store, either as owners or operators, at least during the 1918–19 influenza epidemic (Gray 1986:7). Eventually, the store was purchased by Camillo and Pauline Corez Garcia, both of whom were from old Santa Fe families. Camillo had previous trading experience working for C. N. Cotton, first at Cornfields for over a year and then at the Big House in Chinle (see below) for three years before he bought the store (Delaney p.c. 7/26/1997; Frisbie 1998). Kelley (1987b) suggests a 1920 purchase date, based on Spears's (1987) interview with Margaret Garcia Delaney; McNitt (1963:215) says it was 1923. In 1997, Delaney (p.c. 7/26/1997, 7/27/1997) said it was 1923, but couldn't remember from whom her father bought the store; she didn't think it was either John Kirk or "Mr. Staggs" although she "was so small, [she] didn't really know much about the business end of things at that time." Whether the Mr. and Mrs. *Skagg* mentioned by Gray (1986:7) and SM were really the W. M. *Staggs* who Kelley (p.c. 7/19/1998) found documented as running a store in Crownpoint in 1924, and Van Valkenburgh (1941:57) mentioned as being among the Fort Defiance traders in the late 1930s, is presently unclear. However, that William M. Staggs is probably the same individual Kelley (p.c. 8/30/1998) found documented as an Industrial Teacher at the Chinle Boarding School in Peter Paquette's 2/22/1912 letter to Rev. F. G. Mitchell of

Tolchaco, Arizona, in response to the latter's request for information about employees at the schools in the Fort Defiance Agency (Correll n.d., 1912 Chronological File).

Upon seeing some 1920s photographs of Chinle taken by Leo Mark Studer and loaned to the editor for duplication by AS, Delaney (p.c. 7/20/1998) recalled that her father bought their store in Chinle in 1923 from Studer. Documentation Studer included in the photograph album noted that he was appointed Power House Engineer at the Chinle Boarding School and arrived in November 1921 after a two-day trip from Gallup to "Chin Lee" via mail buckboard and an overnight stay at Hubbell's in Ganado. Reed Winney, a local Navajo, was Acting Engineer before Studer's appointment, and during Studer's two-year tenure, Sam Gorman, another Chinle Navajo, served as Assistant Engineer. Documentation on the back of the photographs stated that "in 1923, [Studer] bought and ran the store later owned by the Garcias from William Stags who then bought a store in Crownpoint, New Mexico." Studer's ownership of the store was evidently short-lived since Delaney also reported 1923 as the date of her parents' purchase. Additional documentation suggested that Studer stayed in the area until 1924. The only other data currently available on Studer (also known as "Sam") is that in the 1940s he was living in Bootjack, Michigan, but still maintaining friendships with earlier traders, especially Ray Dunn, identified as the Indian Service Farmer in Chinle (at least from 1921 until 1922 or 1923) and later, the owner of stores in Chilchinbito, Navajo Mountain, and Fort Defiance. Sometime in the 1980s Studer, with a nephew, K. B. Gibson, returned to Chinle for a visit before the Garcia post was closed and Mrs. Camillo Garcia and Margaret Garcia Delaney left the community; he evidently died about 1992.

After the Garcias purchased the store, the original stone hogan and the Kirk structures were incorporated into renovations; the trading post became known as Garcia's, the Canyon de Chelly Trading Post, and locally to some Navajos as the "lower store" in reference to its location relative to the Sam Day post, later the Thunderbird. Garcia's was periodically remodeled and expanded (Kelley 1987b); while the photograph in James (1977:65) is actually of the Thunderbird *despite* its identification as Garcia's, Hegemann (1963:210) provides a photograph of the store in 1926, and another, from the 1960s, is included here (see Chap. 12, Fig. 15). Garcia's flourished for over six decades; after Camillo and his son, Abel, were killed in a private plane crash near the Chinle airstrip in 1962, Pauline and their oldest daughter, Margaret, continued to run the trading post until it was closed either in December 1985 (Kelley 1987b, based on Spears 1987) or 1986 (Delaney, p.c. 6/10/1997), then becoming tribal property (Kelley 1987b). While there was initial interest in using it as a National Park Service Visitor Center and placing it on the National Historic Site Register (Kelley 1987b), the 6.4-acre property, located about a mile west of the Canyon de Chelly National Monument's Visitor Center, was eventually sold to Ocean Properties Ltd. for economic development purposes. A photographic exhibit in the restaurant in 1996, the historic component of which was prepared by Margaret Garcia Delaney (p.c. 6/10/1997), included an aerial shot of the property on 4/12/1992, and various stages of construction, which began on 6/7/1992 and ended with the resulting Holiday Inn's grand opening on 10/15/1992 (*Navajo Times* 1992a: A-1, 2). Delaney (p.c. 7/20/1998) continues to hope to document the Garcia years at the post in the future. Present sources include Mitchell (1978), Stewart (1980), Gray (1986), Kelley (1987b), Harrison and Spears (1989), Rosenlieb and Smillie (1990), and Tall Woman's narrative.

The second trading post to open in Chinle was Sam Day's, built in 1902 at the mouth of

Canyon de Chelly and run by the Days until 1905 when it was sold to Charles Weidemeyer, who asked Charles Cousins to operate it. Like Garcia's, this post then saw a series of owners/managers; those associated with the Day post are well documented in Harrison and Spears (1989) and McKenna and Travis (1989), as well as in McNitt (1963:215 ff.). Other information is available in Kennedy (1965), since George and Jean Kennedy owned the store from 1916 until 1919, when they sold it to Cozy McSparron (although McNitt [1963:215] again says 1923). While Sam Day established the cafeteria in 1902 (according to information displayed in 1996 on the wall by the old vault there), it was McSparron who named it the Thunderbird and maximized its tourist potential by establishing the Lodge. The history of this post is tied to the National Park Service National Monument at Canyon de Chelly, tourism, and Hollywood films, and can be best understood by reading Brugge and Wilson (1976), in addition to the sources mentioned above. In addition to Figs. 2 and 16 herein, James (1977:63–65) provides three photographs, although one is mislabeled (as noted above).

The third post, established in 1910 at the north foot of Presbyterian Hill, was built, owned, and operated by Navajos, Nelson Gorman and his wife, Alice. It flourished from 1910 until 1918–19; sometime evidently in 1919, the complex was given to the Presbyterians so the structures could be used by "the believers" while they built their church and manse on top of the hill, east of the Chinle Boarding School. While McNitt (1963), Kennedy (1965), and others fail to mention the Gorman post, it is well documented by Tall Woman as well as Gray (1986), Greenberg and Greenberg (1984), and Stewart (1980). Gray (1986) tracks the usage of and changes in the trading post's buildings through time. Photographs pertinent to the Gorman Chinle post are available in Greenberg and Greenberg (1984:12, 14, 15) as well as later in Tall Woman's narrative (see Chap. 7, Fig. 9).

The fourth post in Chinle, first singularly owned by Lorenzo Hubbell, is documented by McNitt (1963:214–15), Kennedy (1965), Brugge and Wilson (1976), Cousins and Cousins (1996), and Frisbie (1998), in addition to Tall Woman and others. Known as the Big House, it was a massive, two-story trading post/hotel located on a small hill directly east of the Annunciation Mission (now Our Lady of Fatima Church). The upstairs consisted of rooms for tourists and the manager's living area. Although McNitt (1963:214–15) and others following him say it was built in 1900, it is now clear that it was probably 1916 (Frisbie 1998). Sam Day II, Cozy McSparron, Mike Kirk, John K. Andrich, and J. B. McCoy worked at this post for Hubbell (Frisbie 1998:71) until he sold it to C. N. Cotton, probably late in 1918 and possibly to settle accumulating debts. As shown in Frisbie (1998), Cotton eventually hired Camillo Garcia to run the Big House, beginning either in late 1919 or early 1920. Photographs of the Big House, provided by Margaret Garcia Delaney, were first published in Frisbie (1998, figs. 1–5); also see Fig. 14 (Chap. 12) here.

McNitt (1963:215) suggests that in 1923, when Cozy McSparron, Camillo Garcia, and Hartley T. Seymour (Cotton's son-in-law) bought all three stores then extant in Chinle, the Big House was closed. However, other data suggest a later closing date (Frisbie 1998:75–77). After serving multiple purposes in the next few decades (Frisbie 1998:77, 79), the Big House was abandoned in the late 1940s and left to "fall into ruins" in the 1950s; eventually, probably 1960, the remains were demolished to facilitate construction of a new jail in an adjacent area in 1961 (Young 1961:282). As shown in n. 6 of Chap. 6, below, the site, after standing empty for a long time, eventually served as the fifth location of the Chinle Post Office, starting in 1968–69. When the Post Office moved to the mall late in May 1981 and its building was torn down, the site was reclaimed for use by the Law and Order Division. At least in the 1996–98 period, an empty concrete slab next to a blue trailer housing a portion of Chinle's Police Department's operations stood on the site of the former Big House.

3. Tall Woman and all interpreters followed the local practice of using "the Canyon" as a gloss for the combined areas known as Canyon de Chelly and Canyon del Muerto. Well known for their history, archaeological sites, peach orchards, rock art, and picturesque rock formations and scenery, these canyons continue to be "home" for many Navajos, either full time or in the summer, when bottomlands are utilized for farming and sheep herding (see Kelley 1986a and Andrews 1991). A portion of the area was proclaimed the Canyon de Chelly (pronounced "de Shay") National Monument in 1931, thus eventually bringing both the National Park Service and many tourists to "the Canyon." The community at the mouth of Canyon de Chelly is called *Ch'íníłį* [to flow out horizontally], or Chinle in English. The initial post office spelling, Chin Lee (which some wrote as ChinLee), was officially changed early in 1941 to "Chinle," the spelling in use by the U. S. Indian Service, after appropriate government actions (some of which are recorded in documents on file at Our Lady of Fatima Church in Chinle).

In addition to sources cited elsewhere in this work for Chinle, those specifically focused on "the Canyon" include: Bradley (1973), Brugge and Wilson (1976), Grant (1978), Anonymous (1981), Houk (1995), Hagerty (1996), Simonelli (1997), Jett (1997a), and Jett, with Neboyia, Morgan, and Young (2000). Grant's (1978) bibliography provides an introduction to the extensive archaeological literature pertinent to the area, where excavations began in the nineteenth century; the study by Fall, McDonald, and Magers (1981) is among the more recent reports.

4. SM said it's common to call a person or thing *ch'į́įdii* [ghost] when swearing, and that here, Man Who Shouts was implying that those who lived at the bottom of the Canyon were thieves. For information on the historical significance of Canyon de Chelly peach orchards, see Jett (1974, 1979) among other sources.

5. For some sources on Navajo farming practices, see the Franciscan Fathers (1910: 259–70), Hill's (1938) classic study, and Bingham and Bingham (1979).

6. Hill (1938:42–45), Kluckhohn, Hill, and Kluckhohn (1971:111–14), and Jett and Spencer (1981:187–91) are among those who provide further information on Navajo storage pits.

7. This term, which is derived from the Spanish *americano*, continues to be used at present (1998) with specific reference to non-Navajos who are "Anglos," rather than of other ethnic heritage. Haranguing against Anglos may occur in public settings if someone disapproves of their presence or actions. While there seems to be less "anti-*Bilagáana* talk" now than was true in some places on the reservation during the early 1960s (the early days of the Red Power movement), some individuals continue to be suspicious of outsiders, especially "Anglos." In such cases, the latter are often viewed as potential sources of desecration, use and abuse, appropriation of intellectual property, and destruction of cultural heritage; thus, associations with them are discouraged. In families more receptive to outsiders, the term *Bilagáana* may actually be used as a joke. However, to call a Navajo an Anglo is usually considered to be offensive, derogatory behavior since it implies that the person has become "too white," "too much like whites," or "whiter than whites" in his/her actions, values, or thoughts, especially those concerned with kinship obligations.

8. Tall Woman laughed here because her parents were monolingual and thus, attempts at

conversations with Man Who Shouts by whites went nowhere, unless the latter spoke Navajo.

9. This refers to the corn cake baked all night in a pit dug in the ground during the Girl's Puberty Ceremony. On this occasion, pieces of it are given as compensation to the singer in charge of the ceremony and others who helped in various ways. The cake, which has a variety of recipes, can also be made on other, nonceremonial occasions. Today, it is sometimes baked indoors in electric or gas stove ovens. See Bailey (1940), Frisbie (1967/1993), and others for further information. Young and Morgan (1980:838) give *'alkąąd* as the name for this puberty cake.

10. Sources on Navajo foods include the Franciscan Fathers (1910), Hill (1938), Carpenter and Steggerda (1939), Bailey (1940), Steggerda and Eckardt (1941), Johnson (1977a), some of the ethnobotanical and Puberty Ceremony literature cited earlier, and the various "cookbooks" that have been published over the years. Included in the latter are Lynch (1986), Keegan (1987), and Niethammer (1999), as well as two undated ones (which are very similar) published in spiral-bound, Xeroxed format by the Office of Navajo Economic Opportunity (n.d. 1, n.d. 2). Occasionally, recipes also appear in the *Navajo Times*, especially for fry bread; see, for example, the *"Ch'iyáán"* article in Section D of the August 29, 1996 issue [the special Fair edition], which consisted of eight pages of Native Food recipes, interspersed with advertisements and other information (*Navajo Times* 1996a).

11. The literature on Navajo weaving is extensive and in a variety of places and formats. It is now easy to learn about its historical development, changing styles, regional specializations, and contemporary innovations; it is also possible to locate "how-to" books on plants for dyes, dyeing as a process, preparing looms and wool, and weaving itself. Some of the sources are actually catalogs of various museum shows, and some are essentially consumer guidebooks. Many non-weavers become interested through Reichard's (1934/1997, 1936, 1939a) novels, and then begin learning through magazines (such as Vol. 52[4], 1981 of *Plateau*), personal vacation travels, guidebooks (such as that by the Southwest Parks and Monuments Association [1992]), and museum exhibits. The following is a list of some, but by no means all, of the resources available: Matthews (1884), Amsden (1934/1964), Maxwell (1963), Moore (1911), Kahlenberg and Berlant (1972), Blomberg (1988), Hollister (1903/1972), James (1927/1970), James (1977), Mera (1948), Wheat (1974, 1975, 1976a, 1976b, 1981), Brody (1976), Kent (1961, 1981, 1985), Bennett (1974), Bennett and Bighorse (1971, 1997), Bryan and Young (1940), Hoffman (1969), Dedera (1975), Dutton (1961), Dockstader (1987), Rodee (1977, 1981, 1987, 1995), Bonar (1996), Willink and Zolbrod (1996), Hedlund (1997), and Valette (1998). Some of the recent literature shows increased interest in the weavers, themselves; for examples, see Hedlund's (1990, 1992) ongoing work, Zolbrod (1997), Valette and Valette (1997), and Wilkins (1998). Weaving is also discussed in many overview, summary works on "arts and crafts" (see, for example, Ruth Roessel [1983]) as well as in the basic sources on Navajo art such as Mills (1959), Hatcher (1967), and Witherspoon (1977). Page and Page (1995:189–207) provide information on weaving and weavers in Ramah, New Mexico, and Heil (1998) adds to the literature concerned with Two Grey Hills textiles. The annual Navajo Studies conferences also provide another forum for weavers and discussions about their textiles, contemporary cooperatives, and other marketing strategies. For example, the Oct. 21–24, 1998, meeting included three presentation sessions devoted to the subject in addition to a demonstration of spinning and carding, exhibits of textiles from both

the Durango Collection and Toadlena/Two Grey Hills organized by Mark Winter, and a textile auction.

When I first met Tall Woman, she and the two daughters who were weaving [ID and MD] were producing "Chinle-style" rugs, as well as numerous single and double saddle blankets. According to her daughters, earlier in time Tall Woman was well known for her Chief Blankets, which they identified as "Phase Two" in style, after reviewing some pictures from Rodee (1981, 1995) and the Southwest Parks and Monuments Association (1992).

Given her mother's and her own reported birthdates, it seems safe to assume that the "rugs" Tall Woman learned to weave in her childhood were really "blankets," as the term is used in the literature on the history of Navajo weaving. It is clear from the text and family memories that the early weaving in her family (before her marriage) focused on saddle blankets (both kinds), Chief Blankets, and at least two others—those known as "*diyugis*" [soft, fluffy, utilitarian blankets, from *diyogí*, "shaggy, bushy, coarse blankets"], and the shoulder blankets worn by women in the mid-and late–nineteenth century. By 1900, the latter had been replaced by Pendletons, which became available after the railroad came across the southern edge of the reservation, and in demand after enough time had elapsed since the initial exposure to traders following the release from Fort Sumner (see Kent 1981, Wheat 1981, and Kapoun with Lohrmann 1992, among others). Although none of Tall Woman's mother's, sisters', or own early weavings are extant (at least in the family), it is clear later in the text that her specialty was Chief Blankets of the Phase Two variety. What their "value in trade" may have been is unknown; however, a letter from Supt. Reuben Perry to Charles L. Day in Chin Lee, 1/31/1905, requests that the latter find a weaver to make an all-wool Chief's Blanket for Mr. Frank Mead (General Supt. of Indian Reservations, Phoenix Office). The blanket was to be "like the one Mrs. Cole [then the Chinle Field Matron] has," and the purchase price Mead/Perry suggested was $12 to $15 (Correll n.d.). Like other Navajo women, Tall Woman shifted to the production of rugs, rather than blankets, for the traders. Once regional styles started emerging, she added "Chinle" designs to her repertoire, finally dropping Chief Blankets from her own production. See Chap. 12, and Figs. 17–19.

12. In addition to the information on the Hubbell family, the variety of posts owned by Lorenzo, and his business partnership with Gallup banker/wholesaler C. N. Cotton available in McNitt (1963) and other trading literature, some works focus specifically on Hubbell's in Ganado. See, for example, Boles (1981), Blue (1986, 2000), Brugge (1972a, 1972b, 1993), Levy (1968), Peterson (1986, 1989), and Bahe (1998). Manchester and Manchester (1993) provide an administrative history developed after Hubbell's Trading Post was declared a National Historic Site by congressional act on Aug. 28, 1965. Work with the Hubbell Papers and trading records is ongoing among contemporary scholars (including Blue, M'Closkey, Reinhart, and Wilkins). One current research question is, of course, the assessment of Hubbell's roles in affecting the production, design, and quality of southwestern arts and crafts, especially Navajo weaving. At present the roles are of interest both in themselves and within a larger frame of postmodern critical assessment of colonialism, paternalism, and appropriation as practiced by traders among Native Americans.

Tall Woman's comments about "Old Man Hubbell's" personality and treatment of Navajos echo others', despite the diversity of the "Hubbell literature." While Man Who Shouts and his family continued to prefer trading at Hubbell's throughout the former's life, the proximity of the Chinle trading posts started to prevail around 1910. After her father died in 1922, the family stopped moving to the Black Mountain area in the winter, and the trips to Hubbell's gradually ended. Tall Woman herself, as well as her mother and Chubby Woman, started exchanging their rugs for staples at the Chinle posts, especially "Garcia's." Tall Woman also developed a special relationship with Mrs. Cozy McSparron and sold some large Phase Two Chief Blankets to her. These reportedly were displayed in the McSparrons' living room at the Thunderbird Ranch for years. When family members viewed the rugs illustrated in Harrison and Spears (1989:17, 18), rugs in use about 1935 in both the main and dining rooms at the Thunderbird, none were recognized as those Tall Woman sold to Mrs. McSparron. Their current location, if they are still extant, is unknown.

13. In an attempt to document Tall Woman's reports of the importance of Hubbell's Trading Post in their lives, especially during her childhood, I decided to examine relevant portions of the Hubbell Papers (n.d.). These papers comprise a huge and rich collection which researchers interested in numerous and diverse issues are just beginning to study; they undoubtedly will prove to be a goldmine for several generations of future scholars. The Hubbell Papers were deposited at the Special Collections Library at the University of Arizona, Tucson, on July 1, 1971, and organized during the next seven years. Microfiche copies of the day books, ledger books, correspondence, trading records, advertisements and catalogs, and other materials in the collection are maintained at the Hubbell Trading Post National Historic Site at Ganado, Arizona. There, the records are grouped according to categories such as Correspondence, Vendor Files, and Business Books and Records, with subgroups within each. These correspond to box and volume numbers.

During the summer of 1990, I examined the records at Ganado for the stores there and in Black Mountain and Chinle. At that time, 525 of the 573 boxes that comprise the Hubbell Collection were at Ganado. Although I found many, many things in the Hubbell Papers that were of professional interest to me, the documentation of the visits of Man Who Shouts, his wives, daughters and/or other relatives, and the blanket/rug production within the family was more sparse than I had expected; such documentation appears in 1890, 1900, 1905, and 1910, although it did not always cross-check in other records kept of transactions of the same period. The notations of most interest to Tall Woman's family were those showing that both wives went there together on 4/16/1900; Man Who Shouts never appears in the records by himself, even though other men do. What I found appears below, complete with the spelling used in the records; all information is from the Ganado store, unless otherwise indicated:

Box 328—Journal for 1890
p. 33 shows "Hastin Delguos-uoi"
      Aug. 2   Blanket   4.00
                  Sell Sheep   4.00
                  Flour   .25
      Oct. 12   1 Bk. Bolts?   4
                  Corn   1.75
[Journal cards run through p. 91; cash book starts on p. 150 and runs through p. 161; covers 7/16/1890 through 7/28/1890.]

Box 331—Indian Accounts, 1900–05
p. 38- and continued to new ledger on p. 49, "Hastiin Del-go-shi Bitsoi" has accounts on

Jan. 15, June 15, July 2, 7, 12, 20, 28, Aug. 2, Aug. 15 [1900]. Bill marked "settled" in many places during the records from the summer.

Box 344, Indian Accounts, 1905–08

p. 49, microfiche card no. 12, shows that on 1/1/1905, "Hastiin Dilyoshi niBitzoi" paid $16.00 to balance account listed on p. 38 in Box 331. It also says "see p. 1," but there is no p. 1 in this Indian Accounts series, since those start on p. 33. [There is no relevant entry there, either.] By 1904, recorders switched back to writing out items involved in transactions rather than using code numbers. The only evidence in the Indian Accounts for 1906–12 [Box 344] is found on p. 68, where a $5.00 ticket was voided for "H. Dilayoshi Bitzoin" in 1910. No account numbers were being used for individuals at this time.

Box 344, Card no. 2, Indian Accounts, 1900–02

p. 93 — 1900 "Hastiin Dilgoshi Ba-ad no. 1"

　　　　　April 16　　$15.70 mds.　　"Settled"

p. 94 — 1900 "Hastiin Dilgoshi Ba-ad no. 2"

　　　　　April 16

　　　　　June 12

　　Both women have two columns:

	13–2–	1.50	
P. 93	15–15–5–10	4.50	
	mds.		6.00
	14–14–2	3.00	
	5–5	1.00	
			10.00
			16.00
			.30
			15.70

P. 94	13–2	1.50	
	15–15–5–10	4.50	
	mds.		6.00
	14–14–2	3.00	
	3–2–2	.70	

	13–	1.00	
	10–25–25–8	6.50	
	mds.		6.00
	6–6–2	1.45	
	6	.60	
	3–3–2–3	.96	
			10.11

3. "Hastiin Diyoshi Bitzi" no. 96

1900 May 15

```
13–2        1.50
15–15–8–5   4.30
10–10–5–3   2.82
  mds.              6.00        "Settled"
6-          .06
                    9.20
                   15.00
```

Examination of the Journal in Box 331 which covers from 9/1/1892 through 9/30/1900 did not elucidate the above, nor did examination of Box 333, the Day Book from 1/1/1900 through 12/31/1900.

Box 345 — Indian Accounts 1908–11
p. 190 shows John Mitchell's wife, Many Horses Niece, making purchases in 1909 and 1910, including some turquoise "for daughter."

Box 381 — Indian Accounts 1911–12:
p. 1 – "Hastin Dilgoshini Bitzoi" transfers 1908 balance of $16.00 to new O.P. [1911]. Charlie Mitchell and John Mitchell show up on pp. 190, 349, and in new ledger on p. 137. Page 336 shows John Mitchell's wife has a big account due in 1912, the record of which continues in new ledger, p. 177.

Box 383 — Indian Accounts, ledger sheets 1913–30 cards 8–13: John Mitchell's wife, "Badoni," no. 116 – 1920 account; card no. 15, John Mitchell (Acct. no. 65) records for 1919, 1926, 1930, as well as debts of his wife, and records from Black Mountain store, too.

Box 384 — Indian Accounts, ledger sheets 1913–23; many destroyed by mildew. John Mitchell and wife, Many Horses' Niece, and daughter, and son = Acct. 21.

No further documentation of any family members was located in Box 355 (Indian Accounts 5/1920–6/1921); Box 382 (Indian Accounts, 1913–16); Box 385 (Day Book, Indian Accounts 8/13/1914–12/14/1915; Box 386 (Indian Accounts 1917–18); Box 391 (Item 4: Accounts, Indian accounts, various other items from 1897–98, 1907–8, 1913–17, and scattered pages; Item 5, Indian accounts 1929); Box 394 (Indian Accounts 1921–24). I also searched Group III: Business Books and Records. In Series 1, there is a record of a man called Black Horse (written "Biłi lizhin") trading at the Black Mountain store and selling cows and cowhides in 1916. I am quite certain this was Tall Woman's older brother, selling some of their father's cows, after their troubles at Houses Standing in a Line. There is also evidence of George Mitchell, a relative of Tall Woman's after marriage, trading at that store in 1923.

The Ganado store is documented in the Business Books and Records in Boxes 327 through 390; these contain cash records from 1883 through 1935, although sheep and cattle records end at earlier times in this series of boxes. On Frank's side of the family, Box 524 of the Ganado store records shows his older brother John's wife, "Badoni," selling thirty lambs at $4.50 each and three old ewes for $3.75, but still having a balance owed of $225.00 on 10/13/1922. That particular day she was there with Mark Ramon, recorded as her son-in-law.

The quality of the microfiche of Box 528, which reportedly contains "Payment chits to Indians for merchandise redemption at Trading Posts, 1900–1927" does not allow reading of names on most of the tickets. In Series 2, Summary Records, Box 496, Ganado portion, Indian accounts and Miscellaneous records from 1889, 1903, 1906, 1908, 1911–12, 1914–26, and 1930–34: John Mitchell is shown in 1930 with an account of $14.00 and his wife, with one of $371.03. Box 523 which reportedly contained some Indian accounts contained no such documents. Boxes 556–562 were missing (Group VIII Sales Books).

The records in Group IX: Advertisements, Price Lists and Catalogs, Boxes 563–573 are an excellent source for understanding wagons, farm and garden tools, sheep shearing and wool carding equipment, and other things available at the time.

In terms of Chinle, in Group I: Correspondence, Series I-Incoming, Box 43, cards 9, 10 show Supt. Reuben Perry attempting on 10/19/1903 to straighten out a buggy purchase by "Mrs. Cole, field matron at Chin Lee," since her buggy arrived without its ordered top; with double harness, the total was $125.00. Another letter, 6/9/1904, states she has reported she is still waiting, and on 6/14/1904, Perry suggests that Hubbell order it by freight if he has to, since $25 cannot be subtracted from the Dept. of Interior account. Another letter, 11/18/1905, from Perry, refers to headmen Charlie Mitchell, Peshlakai, and Many Horses. A 1908 letter shows that Tom Morgan has earned a wagon which needs to be picked up before 6/10/1908, since it was authorized by a W. H. Harrison, "Supt. under Perry" and Harrison will no longer have such authority by that date.

After examining the Hubbell Papers at Ganado, I discussed my findings with Martha Blue, Dorothy Hubbell, and Kathy M'Closkey in an attempt to decipher the code clearly being used to record what the wives, daughter, and grandchild of Man Who Shouts who appear in the records were bringing to the store, especially since Tall Woman's text implies these were rugs. However, to date, the problem remains unsolved. In a reply to my letter, Dorothy Hubbell (p.c. 7/25/1990) said she was not familiar with the kind of record keeping I found for April and May 1900, but thought that maybe if she saw the original she would recognize the handwriting and then know what the figures in the left-hand columns meant. "If those figures represent weights, it could be skins. Sheep skins, cow hides and goat skins were brought in." M'Closkey's work has uncovered several "codes," but I don't think they apply to the records I am trying to decipher. I continue to suspect the numbers represent weights of rugs, or perhaps some combination indicating type of rug, size, quality, and weight.

14. AS said that here Tall Woman is referring to *beeldléí*, "the regular thin blankets people use, *not* the Pendleton robes or shawls worn for dress occasions." However, given the role of traders in introducing Pendleton blankets to the Navajos, the attraction these had, and the fact that by 1900 they had displaced the earlier handwoven shoulder blankets worn by women, I remain uncertain about Tall Woman's intended meaning. For further information on Pendleton and other trade blankets, see Kapoun with Lohrmann (1992), among others.

15. Van Valkenburgh (1941:64), Blue (1986:11), and Brugge (1993:26) give two names for Don Lorenzo Hubbell, the "old man," which are slightly different. They say Navajos called him either a name related to his eyeglasses, that is, *Nák'ee sinilí*—Eyeglasses, or *Nák'eznilih*—Man Wearing Glasses, Wearing Spectacles, Double Glasses, or *Naakaii Sání*—Old Mexican. Bodo (1998:242 n. 6) gives only the latter. When asked about these other names, Tall Woman maintained she had never heard them used by anyone she knew. Man

Who Shouts' name for Old Man Hubbell may be a family-specific (?) variant of the one recorded as *Nák'eznilih* by others, including Blue (2000: xxvi–xxvii, 41, 99–100).

16. Tall Woman is referring to the federally mandated stock reduction of "New Deal" times, which began to be implemented in October 1933 when John Collier was the Commissioner of Indian Affairs. Memories of this remain bitter, as the extensive literature demonstrates. Examples include Roessel and Johnson (1974) and Parman (1976), as well as appropriate sections in Bailey and Bailey (1986) and Acrey (1994). Tall Woman's family, however, has different attitudes about the stock reduction, in part because her husband, Frank Mitchell, was a political leader during its implementation and thus, was viewed with hostility by many who thought *he* "was responsible for it." Then too, one of their sons, SM, worked with government inspectors and Range Riders, enforcing the stock reduction order in Black Mountain, Cottonwood, Nazlini, Chinle, and surrounding areas of the reservation.

17. The places used by Navajos staying overnight are not among the various structures on the grounds of the complex at the Hubbell Trading Post Historic Site documented in Levy (1968), Brugge (1972b:107–8), Manchester and Manchester (1993), and other works. The "Stone Residence," reportedly constructed between 1913 and 1920, was built too late to be the site used during the time period Tall Woman is discussing here, although it did serve as a bunkhouse for freighters and other employees (Peterson 1989; Manchester and Manchester 1993:73). Evidently, the places used by Man Who Shouts and others were no longer extant when the archaeological and ethnographic surveys were implemented in conjunction with the change to "national historic site" status. Brugge (p.c. 4/27/1997) noted that in earlier times, one or more hogans were located toward the wash and that they, as well as the old Leonard Buildings, may have been used to accommodate Navajos.

18. As others have noted, traders were supportive of Navajo leaders, and provided important links for them with federal government officials, such as agents and others, while simultaneously offering gathering places where discussions could be conducted among the leaders and other Navajos themselves. In the case of Man Who Shouts, the Franciscan Annunciation Mission in Chinle also served the second purpose.

CHAPTER 5

1. Variable dates are reported for the construction of this and many other federal boarding schools. For Chinle, they range from 1909 to 1911; see Frisbie (1996) and Mitchell (1978:116 n. 23), among others. However, Agent Peter Paquette's Annual Report for the Fort Defiance Navajo Indian Agency, dated 7/8/1909, suggests 1909; "The Chin Lee Boarding School has been ordered built and a day school in the vicinity of Ganado is also about realized so that with these added facilities a much greater work can be done for this worthy thing." On 9/21/1909, Paquette noted that, "Mr. Smith and Mr. Hildebrand [went] to Chin Lee today to look over the school site . . ." (Correll n.d., 1909 Chronological File).

2. Here, AS added some comments on how smart her grandfather, Man Who Shouts, was. She pointed out that even before Tall Woman became a woman, her father had good ideas. "He was a smart man; he started lots of things like that. Others would see it was a good idea and then ask if they could help with the work so they could use it, benefit from it, too. That's probably why he became a leader in this area. The People already looked up to him for his ideas."

3. There were, however, early irrigation projects in several places on the reservation. Mitchell (1978:91) mentions that his brother John worked with C. C. Manning on such projects, before the latter became a trader and John went to work for him at his store in Fort Defiance. Those projects would have been ongoing around 1886, using Mitchell's timeline for his brother John's various jobs and other experiences. The ones John worked on were in Wheatfields, Tsaile, Lukachukai, Shiprock, Red Lake, and Fort Defiance, and around the San Juan River.

4. According to several of Tall Woman's children, at one time Man Who Shouts "owned" most of the Chinle Valley; what they meant was that his fields and those of his relatives covered much of the area from the boundaries of the federal boarding school in Chinle to where the community of Valley Store (Frazier's, earlier) began.

5. Depending on the speaker, the big tamales were called *ɫeeh yilzhoozh* ["laid side by side in the earth" (Young and Morgan 1980:516)] or *ɫee'hilzhoozh*, while the small ones were called *taajilehíí* or *taahilehíí* (*taah jiléhí* [the thing that people put into the water]). The larger ones are made with two corn husks tied in three places; they are cooked in the ground. The "little ones" are tied in two places and boiled in water.

6. See Mitchell (1978:158–59 n. 9), Kluckhohn, Hill, and Kluckhohn (1971:127–28 ff.), and the Franciscan Fathers (1910:207, 219) for some variations in the process of preparing these grillstones. MD said that both Tall Woman's mother *and* father knew where to find these stones, which were white, and how to prepare them. When the latter went, he hauled lots of these white rocks back, in all sizes. The surface was ground down with stones that had been made smooth by rolling over and over in water for a long time. After the surface was smooth, it was coated with *jeeh* [gum or pitch] which was applied to the rock while it was in the fire. That was burned into the surface, and then burned off. Then Man Who Shouts brushed off the surface with a pine branch. MD also said that both he and his wife added one more step by melting sheep fat on the surface, after it had been brushed. Only then, when it was removed from the fire and cooled, would it be as smooth as ice. According to MD, this was another thing her grandfather taught her and her sister, Mary no. 2, to do, while they were growing up and living with Tall Woman's parents (ca. 1910–20).

7. Here, CS added that his mother also made this bread when he was little, and his wife still made it. However, he was fully convinced that the art of making paperbread without getting seriously burned was being lost among the Navajos and that very few in the next generation even knew how to make it, or how to prepare the grillstone. In Tall Woman's family, only RY learned the process from her although others watched many, many times. GB recalled grinding corn often for her when she was making it with MD; "the hogan would get all smoky and they'd both get very sweaty working over the hot grillstone.*" GB and RY said that Tall Woman's grillstone had cracked and been discarded (by 1970); ID recalled that during her own childhood in the 1930s, her mother was using a grillstone from Horse Woman, the wife of one of Frank's clan relatives, *Tó'aheedlíinii Chischilly* [Curly Hair Water Flows Together Man, who all called Old Curly Hair]. She also said Tall Woman set the grillstone on rocks to raise it four to six inches above the fire she built under it; the fire had to be kept going the whole time and many helped chop wood when she was making paperbread because the fire had to be "very, very hot." Tall Woman made the paperbread sticks out of skinny pieces of cedar with flat ends about one-half inch wide. Kluckhohn, Hill, and Kluckhohn (1971:441) say that by the 1930s, these grillstones had been almost en-

tirely replaced by metal or cast-iron griddles. Tall Woman, however, used grillstones until the early 1960s, although she and others acknowledged that cast-iron griddles could be used for making paperbread, tortillas, blue bread, and other kinds of cornmeal breads. GB said, "If you try to make paperbread that way, you have to put the batter on with a paintbrush." Paperbread, also a favorite among the Pueblos, is sold at regional fairs, Pueblo Feast Days, and sometimes at other places. Prices (1985–96) ranged between $1 and $2 for one piece, which, of course, is rolled up on itself.

8. The People I know always call this "Fry Bread," rather than "Fried Bread," the term given in Young and Morgan (1980:895).

9. 'Anaa'jís [Enemyway ceremonies] are used to cure sicknesses attributed through diagnosis to actions of alien ghosts, those of enemies, and/or non-Navajos. The ceremony is performed in three- or five-night versions; while its use is most often said to be restricted to the late spring and summer, before the first frost, I have also been told otherwise: "That's not true at all. We use that ceremony whenever it's needed, even in the winter." Popular in earlier raiding and warfare times as a means of exorcising the effects of ghosts of slain enemies, it serves similar functions today for those who have served in the military or had other kinds of harmful contact with non-Navajos. In addition to the sacred, decorated rattlestick carried by a young girl and other private components held in ceremonial hogans at several locations, Enemyways include public parts such as the evening dancing known as Ndáá' [War Dance or "Squaw Dance"]. During the latter, women choose partners and women and men dance together to a variety of songs sung to the accompaniment of a pottery drum. For further information on the Enemyway, see Haile (1938), McAllester (1954), Harman (1964), Jacobson (1964), Witherspoon (1975), and Mitchell (1978), among others. According to Tall Woman, the Navajo use of the anglicized name for the ceremony, "Squaw Dance," as a gloss for Enemyway dates at least from her girlhood; Frank (Mitchell 1978:295) is among those who consider the origin of the anglicized term, one he viewed as distasteful and nonsensical.

10. CS added that these instructions to girls were very common. "Parents always said that if you did not talk, a man might rape you because you would not talk about it later with anyone. But if you answered, they knew you would tell if they tried to cause you any harm." Materials in the 1890–1924 Chronological Files (Correll n.d.) confirm the need for such instructions; rapes of women/girls who were herding sheep were often among the problems reported by local leaders to government officials at Fort Defiance.

11. The history of Navajo leadership, government, and politics both before and after Fort Sumner is covered in a variety of sources. Chief among them for the time period covered by the life of Man Who Shouts, and thus Tall Woman's childhood and young adulthood, are Shepardson (1963), Van Valkenburgh (1936, 1945), Hill (1936, 1940), Williams (1970), and Young (1978). Additional information can be found in the literature dealing with treaties and pre- and post-Fort Sumner events, life histories of individuals with the same lifespan, as well as in Mitchell (1978), Henderson (1982), Frisbie (1986), and Navajo Nation, Office of Navajo Government Development publications (Navajo Nation 1997, 1998), among others.

Naat'áaniís were, in fact, a continuation of the earlier Peace Chiefs, one of two kinds of leaders in pre-Fort Sumner days (the others were War Chiefs). They were, as Williams (1970:16) states, local leaders selected by the People; those who had a modest amount of wealth, were mature and male, and who had "the knowledge and ability to perform one or more Sings" were preferred. After 1868, government agents, with final approval from the

Secretary of the Interior, appointed a head chief and other chiefs, thus imposing an alien superstructure on top of the continuing traditional pattern of Navajo leadership. Sometimes agents appointed former peace leaders and/or recently reformed war leaders to these "chief jobs," but not always. In any case, the appointed chiefs were called to Fort Defiance by the agent when it was necessary to relay information about government policies, rations, law enforcement, compulsory education, or the like. In Navajo history, the first such head chief was Barboncito from the Canyon de Chelly area. As Shepardson (1963:14) and others indicate, he was supported by the efforts of Manuelito as chief of the east (east of Chuska Mountains), Ganado Mucho as chief of the west (Chinle Valley-Kinlichee), and Mariano as chief of the Fort Wingate-Dutton Plateau areas, as well as Haskeneinii of Kayenta-Oljeto Valley, Largo, Delgadito, Francisco Capitan, Becente of the east, and many others. When Barboncito died, Manuelito was appointed head chief, and many suggest that Ganado Mucho, who was both wise and wealthy, was second in command. Manuelito was reportedly deposed by the agent in 1884, at which time Henry Chee Dodge was appointed head chief by the Secretary of the Interior. Simultaneously, other American institutions such as scouts, policemen, courts, and interpreters were being added, all sanctioned, of course, by the presence of the army stationed at Fort Wingate and elsewhere. By 1900, some thirty regional *naat'áanii*s were recognized with titles and cards "in place of canes and medals" (Shepardson 1963:78; Van Valkenburgh 1945:71, 72); the chain of command went from the agent (who had army support) to the head chief to the regional leaders and then the local ones. Thus, underneath the alien superstructure, the local leadership patterns remained intact.

Man Who Shouts functioned as a regional level leader. Frank Mitchell's letter to Supt. Reuben Perry on 2/9/1931 (Mitchell 1978:239 n. 13, 303 n. 3) documents the term of Man Who Shouts (therein called "old man Hosteen Del Woshy") as a recognized headman in the Chinle area from 1890 until his death in 1922. At that time he was succeeded by his son-in-law, Frank Mitchell, who served in this role until becoming a member of the Navajo Constitutional Assembly in 1937. McNitt's (1963:289) list of headmen involved in rounding up the Navajos who caused the "Perry incident," or Trouble in Chinle during late October or early November 1905, included "Hosteen Dilawishe," that is, Man Who Shouts.

12. For other accounts of the Trouble at Round Rock, which occurred in October 1892, see Mitchell (1978:50–54, 57, 69 n. 2, 69–73 n. 4, 74 n. 9), Chic Sandoval's account therein [69–73 n. 4], as well as Van Valkenburgh (1938), Lipps (1909), Left-Handed Mexican Clansman et al. (1952), and Haile (*in* Bodo 1998:95–100, 184–89), among others. The headmen at the time, according to Mitchell (1978:50), included a clan relative, Charlie Mitchell, Old Man Silversmith, Henry Chee Dodge, Weela, and Man Who Shouts, as well as others.

13. Here, Tall Woman is referring to the 1892 federal law that made education mandatory for Indian children; the school at Fort Defiance, the first built on the reservation, was constructed between 1879 and 1881, and opened during 1881. Frank Mitchell was among those who were enrolled, at least briefly (see Mitchell 1978: 49–76 ff.). Lockard (1995) provides a summary of early attempts at providing Western education on the reservation, as well as tracing the history of the development of Navajo language literacy. For discussions of kidnapping of children for school, see Frisbie (1996) and Haile (*in* Bodo 1998:95–100, 179–89). Frisbie (1996) also provides references to more recent literature on Indian boarding school experiences and the aftermath thereof, a topic of much interest to many, at present. (See, for example, Tohe [1999].) It was not uncommon at the turn of the century for Navajo families

to send only one child to school; however, by 1963 the identity of the one sent from Man Who Shouts' family was beyond recall.

14. These memories triggered pauses, a slower, softer voice tone, and sadness for Tall Woman.

15. Mitchell (1978:27, 90–91 ff.) includes more information about this man who was the oldest child in Frank's natal family. From Frank's narrative, one learns that Jim was born in 1871, and had lots of clothes and other property when he became a man whose main occupation was caring for stock and breaking horses. It is clear that Frank's father and his mother's brothers were the people who made plans for Jim's marriage. When the arrangements were made to have him marry Tall Woman's older sister, he had already been married "in the Navajo way" to a woman from the Salt clan, and had fathered one child with her who died in infancy. After that, he "just went wild with women and started acting like a billy goat." This reputation had been established by the time his brother, John, and others (not including Frank) came to discuss their proposal with Man Who Shouts and his wife. Perhaps that's why it took a "long time" and they had to "plead and plead."

16. Jim's younger brother, Frank, who later became Tall Woman's husband, was not among them. He didn't see her until he returned from his job with the Franciscan Fathers at St. Michaels and began visiting Jim, who was then living with the family of Man Who Shouts (see Mitchell 1978: 90, 96). Frank's mother was already very sick at the time of the wedding, and had left her second husband, Star Gazer's Son, after giving him another wife, a girl who was her daughter from her first marriage. Frank's father had returned, after leaving another of his own wives, and the family had settled in Chinle near where Jim was living with Tall Woman's sister. The pastoral cycle in Frank's family during his childhood included movements from the Wheatfields and Tsaile areas into the Canyon and back, before they moved to Chinle (after Frank's mother became ill with a "chronic ailment," probably tuberculosis; see Mitchell 1978: chap. 4).

17. This is a reference to the so-called Navajo wedding baskets, described in a variety of sources including Matthews (1894), the Franciscan Fathers (1910), Tschopik (1938, 1940), Stewart (1938), Fishler (1954), Kluckhohn, Hill, and Kluckhohn (1971), and others. As is well established, in the nineteenth century, Navajos made three types of baskets; two were utilitarian, with one being a burden basket (not mentioned by Tall Woman) and the other, a pitched water jug (see text). The third type, ts'aa', a coiled basket made from sumac, is called "the wedding basket" because of its ritual functions in Navajo weddings, as well as serving as containers or drums in others, and in general, as an appropriate gift with which to compensate singers for performing ceremonies.

The source of the basket used during this wedding is unknown. It possibly was made by Tall Woman's mother or father, since both knew how to make baskets, and passed the skills on to their children (but not their grandchildren, according to MD [in Mitchell 1978:159 n. 9]). Thus, Tall Woman herself is also among those who may have made it for her sister since she did not stop making baskets until her own marriage.

For a while, Navajo basketry declined, in part because of the low economic value assigned to it by the traders, and the amount and kind of work and number of restrictions involved in its production. Thus, it was not uncommon for wedding baskets to be acquired through trade, especially with Utes and Paiutes. Now (1998) basket-making has been revived, and Navajo-made wedding baskets bring prices ranging from $75 to over $450, depending on source, size, quality, and design. Pitched baskets in a variety of sizes, styles, and shapes (including water jugs and wedding baskets) are also being marketed. Among the sources on contemporary Navajo basket-making are McGreevy (1985), Bernstein and McGreevy (1988), Schiffer (1991), and Edison (1996).

18. The Navajo mother-in-law/son-in-law avoidance rule is discussed in numerous places, including the Franciscan Fathers (1910:447, 449). While it was still being observed in the early and mid 1960s in Navajo families I knew, by the early 1980s, at least in those families it had been dropped.

19. At this point, CS (7/11/1963) added his own account of traditional wedding practices: "I want to add something here because she didn't tell you all of it. The bride brings the basket and puts it in front of the bridegroom. The host, or the toastmaster, brings in the jug of water; he can be the father or the uncle of the bride. He sets that down. The jug has a gourd ladle in it. He gives that to the girl and then he pours the water into the ladle. After the host pours that water in there, the girl pours the water on the groom's hands and he washes them. Then that is repeated, but this time the boy pours the water on the girl's hands. Then the host takes out corn pollen and sprinkles it to the east, to the west, and back again to the east over the mush. Then he sprinkles it to the south, then to the north, and then back to the south. Not everybody follows the same custom about that. Some people just sprinkle that pollen east to west and then south to north. Some do it east to west and then back to east. There are two ways to do that; which one is used depends on the host's instructions.

"After that, the host puts the corn pollen all around in a circle. Here again there is variation; some make one clockwise circle; others make this circle and then reverse it and come back, so it's double. Some turn the basket so that the opening is facing the couple as they are sitting. Some leave the opening facing the east.

"The groom then takes a pinch of that mush from the east and gobbles it down; the bride follows suit and with the groom in the lead, pinches are eaten from the east, south, west, and north, and then the center, according to the host's instructions. Then the couple eats the mush. Usually, they do not finish it. The remaining part is given to the groom's party. They clean out the basket with their fingers and then lick their hands. No spoons are used for that; they are not allowed. Then the basket is kept by one of the womenfolk of the visiting party; usually she is the aunt or the mother of the groom.

"All of my three sons had this ceremony when they got married, even though they also had church weddings. The church affairs were in the morning and then the wedding feast was at night, on the same day. My wife has the three baskets from their weddings. I will show you those the next time we are at my house."

For further information on traditional wedding practices, see the Franciscan Fathers (1910:446–49), Stewart (1980:24–25), Roessel (1981), and many of the sources cited for life histories, Navajo social organization, and the Blessingway. For an illustrated account of contemporary practices, see Page and Page (1995:149–51, 170–75), among others.

CHAPTER 6

1. CS disagreed, in part, with Tall Woman here, saying that in the beginning and for the first ten years after the release from Fort Sumner, the government issued wagons, seeds, hoes, plows, rakes and different agricultural implements, and other things to anyone who wanted them, as per the agreement in the 1868 Fort Sumner Treaty (see Article VIII of the

Treaty). The construction of the Atlantic and Pacific Railroad through the Southwest between 1880 and 1887 facilitated the delivery of such government supplies. As Underhill (1953:207) notes, while the wagons issued to eleven Navajos in 1880 were ill-fated, in 1881 Manuelito and Ganado Mucho, two early leaders, were given wagons and after learning to harness and drive, Manuelito became a highly successful freighter hauling supplies for traders in the railroad's early days. Of course, some Navajos who were working on the railroad or at other jobs preferred to buy their own wagons and harnesses, especially if they thought they were of higher quality than those available through government issue or after completing work stipulated by government agents. Early catalogs from mail-order companies illustrate the range of vehicles available, as well as the costs of these, harnesses, covers, and the like. Haile (*in* Bodo 1998:67) says many of the early Navajo wagons were Studebaker wagons made by the Studebaker Co., South Bend, Indiana, although some were made at the Haskell Institute in Lawrence, Kansas.

The boarding-school literature shows that in addition to government issue or work, sometimes Navajos acquired wagons by enrolling their children in school in the early days. Promises of wagons, carriages, buckboards, buggies, farm tools, cooking implements, and other things were major motivating factors at least for some by 1899 (see Mitchell 1978: 161 n. 13). These practices in themselves inspired the accusation levied at some Navajos by others that they were "selling their children" to the school recruiters in order to acquire these things. See Frisbie (1996) for an introduction to these rumors and accusations, and the extensive literature now available.

2. For further information on Father Leopold Ostermann, O.F.M. (1863–1930), see Trockur (1976), *Padres' Trail* (1976a), Wilken (1955), the Franciscan Fathers (1949), and Haile (*in* Bodo 1998:1, 7, 19 ff.), among others. As Trockur (1976: n.p.) notes, Father Leopold, who was known as *E'nishodi Tso*, "Big Long Gown" spent ca. twenty-five years in Chinle, rarely leaving for any reason. Bodo (1998:7–8) gives his name as *Endishodi Tsho*, "the Chunky (or Big) Priest." In Chinle, Father Leopold was well known for his horse "Frank," the buggy Tall Woman mentions, his service as postmaster (see this chapter's later endnotes), his piano playing for dances at the Chinle Boarding School, and other community involvement. (Regretfully, no photographs of Father Leopold's buggy could be located in the Franciscan archives, either at St. Michaels or Cincinnati, during research for this project.) Also a prolific author (see later endnotes and References), Father Leopold Ostermann, O.F.M., assisted Fathers Berard Haile and Marcellus Troester, O.F.M.(s) with the preparation of the 1910 *Ethnologic Dictionary* credited to "the Franciscan Fathers" (see Haile *in* Bodo 1998: 23–27). Occasionally, especially during group baptisms and first communions, Father Leopold was assisted in Chinle by other priests sent out from St. Michaels. See, for example, Father Emanuel's (Trockur 1922) description of his 5/29/1920 automobile trip to Chinle for such purposes. Taken sick at age sixty-two in February 1925 (Trockur 1976: n.p.), for brief periods during the next several years, Father Leopold was replaced in Chinle by others, including at first, Father Emanuel Trockur, O.F.M. Eventually ordered to a lower altitude, Father Leopold left his beloved Chinle permanently in 1928, although a 1907 record book at the church gives his tenure in Chinle as 1904–27. Bodo (1998:238) defines it as 1907–23, saying it was followed by a period at St. Michaels, from 1924 to 1930.

3. The early Franciscan roles in Chinle are best documented in Wilken (1955: 109–19), Ostermann (1913, 1914, 1927a–r, 1928a–e), and Haile (*in* Bodo 1998). Ostermann (1927i:

634) was sent at some time in 1902 to "look the place over as a prospective point for a branch mission of St. Michaels." Inspired by his report (described in Ostermann 1927i:634) and one from a round trip that Father Anselm Weber, O.F.M., Frank Walker, Miss Josephine Whorton Drexel, and Sister Agatha made (10/25–30/1902) from St. Michaels to Chinle via Ganado to see Canyon de Chelly (Wilken 1955:97; Frisbie 1998:70–71), as well as by increasing competition from Ganado Presbyterian Reverend Bierkemper for a Chinle site (Wilken 1955:109–11), the Franciscans, with assistance from Sam Day, Sr. and his two older sons, Sam II and Charlie, secured approval from local Navajos for a mission site on Apr. 20, 1903. Additional approval was secured from Washington, D.C., on June 20, 1903 (Wilken 1955:111). As Ostermann (1927i:634–35) makes clear, Father Anselm Weber, O.F.M., chose the Chinle location for four reasons: the possibility of a future government boarding school; the centrality of Chinle; the fact that Navajos from Black Mountain traveled through Chinle on their way to Fort Defiance, Gallup, and other points; and the fact that Navajos from many different places came to Canyon de Chelly to harvest ripe peaches each fall.

Shortly after the 1903 federal approval, Father Leopold Ostermann, O.F.M. (1863–1930), started visiting Chinle on and off, for two or three weeks at a time, always staying with the Day family at their trading post while visiting Navajos in and around the Canyon. His first public service was held in Chinle on Sept. 23, 1903 (Wilken 1955:112). On Aug. 15, 1904, he and Brother Placidus Buerger took up part-time residence in Chinle and moved there in a covered wagon. In describing the trip, Ostermann (1927j:635) notes that upon arrival, they began renting an "old, much dilapidated stone house from a Navajo for this purpose" (see Fig. 3).

Variable descriptions exist for this stone house (illustrated in Ostermann 1914:28 and Long 1992:95, although misidentified in the latter source as located at Rough Rock) which was about one mile east of the future, permanent Franciscan residence/mission and definitely incorporated later into the Garcia Trading Post (see Wilken 1955:112 n. 16; Kelley 1987b; Frisbie 1998). Wilken (1955:111–12) says Father Leopold Ostermann, O.F.M., and Brother Gervase Thuemmel took up part-time residence "in an abandoned stone and log building originally intended as a trading post." In one place, Ostermann (1914:26) says that this old stone building, "which originally had been built for a trading post, and which is still used by one of the traders as a store room," was fixed up as a temporary residence through considerable expense, and hard work by the Day boys. In another article, Ostermann (1927j:635) says, "this old stone house was originally built for a store or trading post, but had been abandoned years ago and left to go to ruin." Of the three rooms in the building, on one the roof was entirely gone, and on the others "part of the original dirt roof was still on, but doors and windows gone." The repairs gave the Father and Brother two serviceable rooms; the smaller served as a kitchen, pantry, and dining room, while the larger, longer room became a combined "dormitory, parlor, and chapel" with a "rude altar" set up at one end (Ostermann 1927j:635). Ostermann (1927k:22–23) describes some of the church services held here, and elsewhere (1914:26–27; 1927j:635–36) discusses life in this "home sweet home" that included a dirt floor and leaky dirt roof, occasional snakes, and scorpions.

The identity of the Brother who accompanied Father Leopold in 1904 varies according to source; while in some places Ostermann (1913, 1914, 1927i) does not name the Brother, when he does (Ostermann 1927j:635), he specifies Brother Placidus Buerger as his companion on his Aug. 15, 1904 move to the rented stone house in Chinle. Brother Placidus is also named in a handwritten list inside one of Father Leopold's 1907 record books still at the church today; there, the early Chinle staff members and their dates of service are documented as follows: Brother Placidus 1904–6; Brother Gervase 1906–12; Father Leopold Ostermann, O.F.M., 1904–27; and Father Marcellus Troester, O.F.M., 1907–12. However, Trockur (1976: n.p.), Wilken (1955:112), and Haile (*in* Bodo 1998:71–73) say it was Brother Gervase Thuemmel, O.F.M., who shared the 1904–5 times with Father Leopold in Chinle.

On Aug. 15, 1905, the mission site was chosen by Fathers William Ketcham, Anselm Weber, and Leopold Ostermann, O.F.M.(s), with work on the combined residence/chapel building beginning the next day (Wilken 1955:113). Brother Placidus Buerger returned the same month and with Father Leopold Ostermann, was able to supervise the construction. However, in November 1905, he became sick and on 2/19/1906, died from stomach cancer after being hospitalized in Albuquerque. Thus, Brother Placidus was *not* in Chinle when Father Leopold moved out of the rented stone building into the permanent Franciscan residence in January 1906, before the rectangular adobe structure designed by Father Anselm Weber, O.F.M., was completely finished (Wilken 1955:114). Brother Gervase returned to Chinle evidently in August 1906, and assumed full-time duties with Father Leopold. At first, as shown in Ostermann (1914:30) and Fig. 4 here, the residence lacked a porch; it included six 12′ x 12′ rooms, and a larger, 12′ x 24′ one, used as the first chapel (1906–11 or –12) (Ostermann 1914:29). Father Marcellus Troester, O.F.M. (1878–1936), who eventually became known as "The Census Taker" because of his Navajo census efforts, joined the Chinle staff as Father Leopold's assistant in January 1907 and stayed until 1915, according to Rademaker (1976a). When Father Berard Haile, O.F.M., was sent from St. Michaels to Lukachukai to become the first resident priest at St. Isabel's Mission in August 1915, Brother Gervase was sent with Father Berard (Haile *in* Bodo 1998:73–79, 154–59).

The Franciscans were instrumental in promoting the establishment of a government boarding school in Chinle (Wilken 1955:115–16; and here Chap. 7, and that chapter's n. 9). Once construction of the school was started (fall 1909), the Friars began work on the stone chapel and the stone building directly to its south, which was first used as Chinle's post office with Father Leopold as postmaster (see n. 6, below). Brother Gervase's carpentry, masonry, and other skills were fully utilized, under the supervision of W. E. Hildebrand, contractor for the school which was built less than half a mile from the mission (Ostermann 1913: n.p.; Wilken 1955:116). Father Marcellus designed the altar in the chapel (illustrated in Ostermann 1914:34), and he and Brother Gervase built it (Hetteberg p.c. 5/12/1997). Although "long finished" before the fall of 1911, the chapel was not named until the Marquette League of New York donated $1,000 in answer to an appeal from Father Anselm Weber, O.F.M., and requested it be named The Chapel of the Annunciation (Ostermann 1913:n.p.; 1914:34–35; Wilken 1955:116). While possibly put into use upon its 1911 completion (Hetteberg p.c. 8/15/1997), the stone church (or third chapel, if one counts the one in the rented store building as first and the living room one as second) was officially dedicated on Mar. 25, 1912, an event described by Tall Woman (see Chap. 7) since her parents were among the Navajos in attendance. Ostermann (1914:31–35) describes and provides illustrations of the early phase of construction of the Chinle Boarding School, the initial years of Catholic instructions to school pupils, and the 1912 dedication ceremony. Articles written for *St. Anthony Messenger* (Ostermann 1927a–r, 1928a–e) provide additional information on priests' roles in the Chinle area in the early years; for example, see Ostermann (1927a–e) for competition with Protestants, and Ostermann

(1927g, h, r) for instructions to school children. Other accounts of the early period at the Annunciation Mission can be found in Sandford (1949), the *New Mexico Register* (1955a), and Trockur (1922, 1976).

Various sources document the Annunciation Mission through time, including Sandford (1949), Winter (1961), Rademaker (1973), Grein (1978), and Wintz (1994). The Franciscan complex remains extant today, albeit with many significant changes. The mission's name was changed in 1956 to Our Lady of Fatima Church. The early stone church, which served community needs from its 1911 completion until 1960, is still standing but no longer serving its original function. In 1935, when it was discovered that the landmark structure was "slowly sinking into the ground from its own weight," four support cables were added to help stabilize its walls (Grein 1978:63). The stone building to the south of the stone chapel (which was first utilized as Chinle's post office during Father Leopold's time, as shown in n. 6, below) has been structurally modified over time, and other additions and changes have been made to the overall physical plant. In 1958, construction started on a new, larger, cinder-block church positioned in front of the Fathers' residence, but slightly to the north. This church was dedicated in honor of Our Lady of Fatima on Mar. 27, 1960 (see Winter 1961:33). More recently, a large, hogan-shaped church (described and illustrated in Wintz 1994) was constructed on the same site between August and December 1989, after parishioners had torn down the cinder-block church in a week's time in June. The hogan church was first used on Christmas Eve 1989, but not formally dedicated until June 3, 1990. In June 1998, Father Blane Grein, O.F.M., celebrated twenty years of service in Chinle. At that time, the staff at Our Lady of Fatima Parish also included Father Pio O'Connor, O.F.M. (who edited the 1998 *Padres' Trail Centennial Celebration Issue*); Sr. Margaret Bohn, O.P., Pastoral Ministry; Sr. Adelaide Link, S.F.P., Social Outreach (see Stevens 1998); and Shirley Jean Britt.

4. Tall Woman spoke these last two sentences in a low voice, full of pauses and sadness, and then paused several minutes before continuing.

5. Some of the numerous reactions of visitors to the display of the 1868 Treaty during the 1998–99 year at Northern Arizona University's Cline Library, through arrangements with the National Archives, Washington, D. C., can be found in Becenti (1998). At the October 1998 Eleventh Annual Navajo Studies Conference, faculty (mostly from NAU's Navajo Language Program) explained the process of obtaining and displaying the Treaty, Navajo reactions to the exhibit, and the educational benefits of the university's year-long Navajo Treaty Project.

6. The dates available in a variety of ethnohistorical sources (including Van Valkenburgh 1941, McNitt 1963, *New Mexico Register* 1955a, Brugge and Wilson 1976, Mitchell 1978, Link 1968, Wilken 1955, Ostermann 1913 and 1914, Trockur 1976, Greenberg and Greenberg 1984, Gray 1986, and others) support Tall Woman's recollections. See Appendix B, Chronology, for the numerous changes that took place during the period covered in her narrative.

In the early years, post office functions in Chinle were among the services provided by the Franciscan Fathers. After a U.S. Post Office was established on 9/1/1902 at St. Michaels, John Walker was appointed postmaster (Wilken 1955:88). Service from Gallup to Chin Lee via Ganado reportedly was inaugurated on 5/25/1903; while Wilken (1955:88 n. 107) says this was "daily," others disagree. Charles Day was appointed as Chinle's first postmaster in January 1903 (Cousins and Cousins 1996:15), suggesting that the community's first post office operated from inside Sam Day's trading post (built in 1902 near the mouth of Canyon de

Chelly, as described above). Exactly when Father Leopold Ostermann, O.F.M., began serving as Chinle's (then Chin Lee) second postmaster is unknown, but it seems to have been in 1911, after the 1909–11 construction of the Annunciation Mission and the stone building south of it was finished. Father Berard Haile, O.F.M. (*in* Bodo 1998:69) says that Charlie Day (still) had the mail contract in 1910, when, for the first time, he drove the car Lorenzo Hubbell had given to Father Anselm Weber, O.F.M., at St. Michaels. Ostermann's 1914 article (which from the text appears to have been written late in 1911), and the photographs in Ostermann (1913, 1914) make it clear that Father Leopold was established as the postmaster in the "Chin Lee Post Office," the stone building south of the chapel, by the time the Annunciation Mission was dedicated on 3/25/1912. (As of 1998, the building was still extant, but being utilized by the church for other purposes.)

The early mail deliveries to Chinle were done by various types of buckboards drawn by horses or mules, and according to Gray (1986:3, 26) and others, were once a week into the 1920s. Father Leopold's service as Chinle's good-natured postmaster is well documented (see Wilken 1955 and Kennedy 1965, among others) and apparently continued until he took sick in February 1925 and eventually was forced to relocate. The young trees initially planted by the stone building at the mission where the post office was located grew quickly, as shown in later photographs of the site; cf. Fig. 10 with Figs. 5 and 6 here.

According to Father Mark Sandford, O.F.M. (p.c. 2/18/1997, 5/16/1997, 8/8/1997) who was at the Annunciation Mission in Chinle from 8/1/1945 until 6/30/1950, the Franciscans who served in Chinle *after* Father Leopold's tenure *until* Father Anselm Sippel, O.F.M., came in 1934 did *not* have responsibilities as postmasters. These Fathers, all O.F.M., included Emanuel Trockur, Clementine Wottle, Remigius Austing, Frederic Hartung, and Odwin Hudiburg.

Father Anselm Sippel, O.F.M., who was accompanied by Brother Gotthard Schmidt, O.F.M., in 1934, resumed the postmaster duties but *not* from the stone building south of the Annunciation Mission. After Father Leopold left Chinle, postal services were relocated, at an unknown date, to a third site, a stone building in the easternmost row of buildings at the Chinle Boarding School, north of the warehouse and garage/icehouse, and south of the Employees Club and principal's house. By August 1996, this structure had been demolished; the site was directly west of the white, frame, dormer-windowed house (which had served as Chinle's one- or two-room public school earlier in time, as shown below, before being converted to rental apartments used at least into the 1970s. In 1996, while still extant, the white frame structure was boarded up and reportedly awaiting demolition). When shown a copy of St. Michaels Photograph c539.9–3 R450 (a picture of the boarding-school building eventually used as Chinle's third post office), AS, SM, Delaney (p.c. 6/10/1997), and Father Mark Sandford, O.F.M. (p.c. 2/18/1997) remembered it well as the location of the community's post office during the 1930s and 1940s.

Once the Franciscans again became involved in postal services in the community in the mid-1930s, it was Brother Gotthard who earned the reputation as mail carrier, now with a truck that made three trips a week, Monday, Wednesday, and Friday. According to Father Mark Sandford (p.c. 5/16/1997), Camillo Garcia had the contract to haul the mail between Chinle and Ganado at that time, and Brother Gotthard drove for him, with the mission supplying the truck and covering all its costs, and Garcia "turning over the check each month." (For further information on Brother Gotthard, see Chap. 16 and later endnotes.

This Brother's name, while often spelled Gotthardt in print [cf. Antram 1998:107–9], is correctly spelled Gotthard, as shown on his official appointment cards in the Franciscan Archives, Cincinnati [Hetteberg p.c. 6/30/1998].)

The Annunciation Mission House Chronicle for 1945 shows that Brother Florence Mayrand, O.F.M., was appointed acting postmaster on 10/9/1945, when Father Mark Sandford, O.F.M., was appointed postal clerk; Brother Gotthard was still driving the mail truck, although other Franciscans substituted for him when necessary. On 5/1/1946, when Father Mark decided to get rid of the post office duties because of other pressing work, Ambrose Howard was appointed acting postmaster, thus bringing the 1936–46 Franciscan involvement in postal services to an end. Father Mark also said "shortly after" he left Chinle, in June 1950, the post office was moved to its fourth site, another building at the Chinle Boarding School.

In August 1996, this building, although extant, was boarded up and awaiting demolition. Local Navajos who had gone to the boarding school said that before the building became the next post office, it had been used for home economics classes, the superintendent's office, and the switchboard until the dial telephone system was installed in the 1950s. "After the switchboard was moved out, the Post Office was moved in." A date of 1954 for the post office's move to this building seems possible, since the House Chronicle shows dial service was installed at Annunciation Mission in November 1954. The House Chronicle also suggests that for another period of time, the Franciscans again helped with postal service; the actual dates and kinds of involvement are unknown since the only reference in the Chronicle (after Father Mark's 1946 decision, noted above) is one showing that on 7/1/1954, "the mail was carried for the last time" because the Fathers lost their bid, submitted in May, for the Ganado, Chinle, Lukachukai route.

The Chinle Post Office was still in this building, historically its fourth site, in 1963, when I began working in the community. From there, it moved, in the late 1960s, to its fifth location, a new building and the first one to be constructed as a post office in Chinle, erected directly east of Our Lady of Fatima Church on the former site of the two-story trading post/hotel known as the Big House (see Chap. 4 endnotes; Chap. 12 ff.; Frisbie 1998:79). The Tribal Council's Advisory Committee (Resolution ACMA-34–65) authorized an agreement between the Navajo Tribe and the United States Post Office for construction of a post office on a 0.413-acre section of land situated within the Chinle Police and Court tract, according to the Plat map. The area was surveyed in August 1965, and then withdrawn for such usage by the Chinle Chapter and the tribe's Advisory Committee Resolution ACJY-153–67 on 7/26/1967. Lease arrangements for the site suggest that the post office moved there in 1969 with a ten-year lease, although the exact date is not clear.

In 1979, negotiations were begun for a new post office building at the proposed *Tseyi'* Mall, being developed in three phases by Dineh Cooperatives, Inc., also known as DCI Shopping Center (with Jon D. Colvin, president), a nonprofit, Navajo-run group in charge of planning Chinle development. However, when the Bashas' Supermarket in the mall opened on 3/14/1981 (*Navajo Times* 3/19/1981: 1, 14), the post office building was not yet ready for occupancy. Numerous 1997 discussions with SMB (postmistress since 4/1/1997), and documents provided by her show that the relocation to the mall site was compounded by problems at *both* the new and old sites.

When the ten-year lease (3/1/1981–2/28/1991, and subsequently renewed) started with

DCI, necessary electrical and plumbing work was not completed in the post office building, thus making the move impossible. The problems were evidently corrected between March and May 1981. The lease between the U.S. Postal Service and the DCI Shopping Center (drawn up on 3/27/1981, with a 3/1/1981 starting date) was notarized on 5/15/1981 by Glenn Stoner, Justice of the Peace and Notary Public in Chinle. Six days later, on 5/21/1981, the San Francisco Postal Service Field Office released the back rent due to DCI (for 3/1–5/31/1981). Evidently the post office's move to the mall took place directly thereafter, on a weekend. Although it was not publicized in the *Navajo Times* and its exact date is not apparent in available records, it definitely was in late May 1981, thus invalidating the 1988–89 date suggested in both Harrison and Spears (1989) and McKenna and Travis (1989) for this move. When SMB started working at the Chinle Post Office in January 1982, other employees said the new building had been in use for "five or six months." The end-of-year advertisement that DCI ran in the *Navajo Times* (12/19/1981:19) for Phase II occupants of the *Tseyi'* Mall showed Phase I space finished and completely occupied by Bashas' Supermarket, Yellow Front/Checker Auto, Elite Laundry and Dry Cleaning, Rainbow Ice Cream, First American Optical, and the U.S. Postal Service.

The other problem connected with the Chinle Post Office's move to its sixth and present (1998) location in the *Tseyi'* Mall stemmed from the fact that the Tribal Police moved into the recently vacated post office building on 6/10/1981, before the post office's five-year lease (which started on 11/1/1980) expired on 10/31/1985. Legal entanglements with the Tribe ensued that apparently were never resolved. The result was that after withholding rent, the San Francisco Postal Service Field Office's Real Estate Department halted efforts to sublease the site to another occupant, and terminated its lease/rent agreement, effective at the close of business on 6/30/1981, with official notice to the Tribe on 7/27/1981. In June 1996, an empty concrete slab next to a light blue trailer, which housed a portion of Chinle's Police Department and Law and Order operations, stood on the post office's fifth site; the earlier building had been demolished, as had the Big House, before it (see Frisbie 1998). Thus, as of 1998, the Chinle Post Office was in its sixth location; since the start of postal services to the community in 1903, the functions had been provided from within other buildings, including a trading post, a building at the Annunciation Mission, and two buildings at the Chinle Boarding School. By 1996, one of the two latter structures had been demolished as had the first building actually erected as a post office in the late 1960s.

7. Many internal troubles stemmed from quarrels over land use and livestock as the population expanded and people settled closer to each other (see Mitchell 1978). However, there were also others; earlier accusations of witchcraft continued as did a variety of troubles at trading posts. As Brugge and Wilson (1976:284) note, Hastiin Biwosi of Canyon del Muerto, who was among the signers of the 1868 Treaty, was killed as an alleged witch near Ganado in 1878. Another Navajo known as Klah, accused of killing an Aneth, Utah, trader, was tracked down and arrested in Canyon de Chelly by Agent Riordan and Henry Chee Dodge in 1883. Troubles at trading posts continued into the twentieth century, sometimes resulting in the murders of traders (among whom were Richard Wetherill, Charles Hubbell, Charles Fritz, and the trader at Cross Canyon [Correll n.d.]). Wilken (1955), Gray (1986), Greenberg and Greenberg (1984), Butler (1991), and materials in the Correll Collection (Correll n.d.) document conflicts in Chinle among missionaries and believers of various faiths during the first two decades of the twentieth century.

8. Here, CS added his own version of this event:

"Black Man and his brothers and cousins all got together near where they were living in the Canyon. They had gotten into trouble over a woman and an agent from Fort Defiance sent the police out here to bring them in for questioning, to see if the accusations about that were true. They refused to go into Fort Defiance. So the agent sent another policeman and the same thing happened. And then he sent another one, and again, they refused. So the agent finally had to come to Chinle on a certain day on some other business. That was Reuben Perry, and this happened in 1905.

"When the men heard that Agent Perry was coming, they decided they would go into Chinle and get the matter settled while he was there. They met him over the hill from the Thunderbird Lodge, while he was driving in his buggy with a mule team. There were policemen riding behind him on horseback during that trip. Those men, I guess there was a gang of about seven of them, stopped the Agent on the road right there and said, 'Let's settle this business.' The Agent said, 'No, we have to go to Fort Defiance where the court is.' The gang said, 'No, you are here now; we'll do it now.' They pushed the policemen away and started to pull the Agent out of the buggy. Outsiders who were around there rushed in and stopped the fight. The Agent went on and took care of his business in Chinle and then he went back to Fort Defiance. That gang went back into the Canyon. They were staying in there, in a protected cave. Finally, an old man, John Brown, and another old man went in there, into that protected cave. They talked them out of what they were doing and got them to agree that they would come out. I guess when they did, they just took off. They were finally grabbed at a ceremony that was going on somewhere around here; the police who were there spotted them and just grabbed them and took them back to Fort Defiance. After that, they were sent to California to a prison there on an island for eighteen months."

Frank Mitchell (1978:97–102) gives a different account of this event which is known as "Trouble at Chinle" and "The Perry Incident" (after Superintendent Reuben Perry, who was put in charge of the southern half of the reservation, when responsibilities were divided, and served in this capacity from 10/1/1903 until 10/16/1906). In Frank's version, the incident was caused by a gang of roaming troublemakers who had tried to rape a woman while she was out herding sheep. Other accounts of this incident, which most authors date to late October or early November 1905, can be found in McNitt (1963), Van Valkenburgh (1941), Wilken (1955), Brugge and Wilson (1976:285), Cousins and Cousins (1996:16–19, 49, 100–101), and in the November-December portion of the Correll Chronological File (Correll n.d.). Comparisons of the enormous variability in the published sources are shown in Mitchell (1978:117–18 nn. 26–27, 29, 31–33). Interestingly, in none of the sources is any of the participants called Black Man, as happens in both the accounts of Tall Woman and CS. Perhaps "Black Man" was the name used locally for the ringleader who was then recorded historically under one of his other names. In any case, as shown in Mitchell (1978:118–19 nn. 34, 35), Man Who Shouts was one of the headmen involved in rounding up the troublemakers and defusing other troubles expected in the area in the same week. As documented in McNitt (1963) and Cousins and Cousins (1996:16–19, 49, 100–101), the latter troubles included break-ins and robberies at two trading posts, one of them Cousins's place in Chinle (originally the Sam Day post, which had recently been sold to Charles Weidemeyer who hired Charles Cousins to operate it). Cousins and Cousins (1996:101) provide a 1938 photograph of their three-year-old son, Edward, showing Blackman (Black Man) in the background. Bill

Cousins's father, Charles (Edward's grandfather), identified this man as one of the Navajos involved in the robbery at his post in 1905. Whether or not this is the same individual as the Black Man in Tall Woman's and CS's accounts remains unknown.

9. It seems safe to assume that the summer of 1906 was when Frank and Tall Woman started living together. Frank (Mitchell 1978) suggested 1904, but since Tall Woman said they had not met when the late October 1905 Trouble in Chinle happened, I suspect it was the following summer. There are no other ways to anchor this milestone now, especially given the uncertainties surrounding the recorded birthdates of their first three children.

10. Tall Woman shared these memories very slowly and quietly, and paused for a very long time at this point, before continuing.

CHAPTER 7

1. Mary no. 1's birthdate is uncertain; as shown in Mitchell (1978:350), reported dates range from 1903 through 1911 according to various census records and other sources. The problem continues today despite the Tribe's shift to "official birthdates." Her Medicare records report 1/1/1903, while Social Security and the Tribal Census Office, at least in August 1996, said 7/02/1911 was her birthdate. Given what I know about Tall Woman, her marriage, and her narrative, what seems appropriate is a wintertime date in 1908, the year given in the Peter Paquette census of 1915. According to Tall Woman's story, she did not even meet Frank until the summer of 1906. 1911 is suspect because Mary no. 2 was born *between* Mary no. 1 [MD] and Seya [SM], who had two birthdates in the "official Tribal records," 1912 and 1913. MD herself, in the fall of 1996, said there were "about four years" between herself and SM, thus confirming what both Tall Woman and Frank said when computing unrecorded birthdates, that is, that their children were born "about once every two years."

2. Tall Woman describes home births and her own work as a midwife later in her narrative.

3. While Frank gave 1906 as her birthdate, various census reports used 1910 or 1911 (see Mitchell 1978:350). Since her name was also Mary, it is possible that the current, "official" Tribal census date of 7/02/1911 belongs to her, rather than to MD. However, if one accepts 1908 as MD's birth year and follows the "every two years" model reported by both Tall Woman and her husband, 1910 would be the year, as reported in the St. Michaels Census and the Peter Paquette one from 1915. But there are at least two problems with the latter assumption. First, *unlike* the next child, SM, at *no time* during my years in Chinle and discussions about family birthdates and their relationships to other community developments did I ever hear Mary no. 2's birth discussed in reference to any phase of the construction of the Chinle Boarding School. Second, Tall Woman's narrative (later in this chapter) indicates that when she went to live in the house Frank built close to where he was working on the construction of the first few school buildings, she took the children they then had with her, namely, both Marys. *If* Frank was hired at the beginning of the project, Tall Woman's statement implies that Mary no. 2 had already been born by the fall of 1909.

4. The bark of the common cliffrose is very soft, and easily shredded, thus explaining why this part of this evergreen shrub was used as a cradleboard lining, and why both the plant and the cradleboard share the same Navajo name, *'awééts'áál*. Shredded cliffrose-bark linings were used for generations, at least as far back as Tall Woman's grandmother's time,

as a way to absorb and remove urine; Tall Woman explained later that the linings were always dried in the sun and reused a number of times. She viewed the bark as superior to cotton cloth diapers and later "Pampers," reporting that it never caused "diaper rash" and some of the other problems experienced by babies today. (See Mayes and Lacy 1989:27–28) for an introduction to the cliffrose and supportive botanical literature.) The cradleboard, which is grounded in Navajo sacred narratives and is still in use today by some Navajos, is documented in a number of sources. The Franciscan Fathers (1910:467–74) and Kluckhohn, Hill, and Kluckhohn (1971:191–201) provide discussions and illustrations of the varieties of both the board and its canopy. The type used by Tall Woman's own mother for all her children is termed "the whole cradle" by the Franciscan Fathers (1910:469) and the "solid-back cradle" (reportedly rare) by Kluckhohn, Hill, and Kluckhohn (1971:197). Tall Woman's text shows that while her mother used that kind, when Mary no. 1 was born, at least in the regions where Man Who Shouts and his family lived, the preference was for the split-back cradle, which does *not* have the "drainage hole" which some now call a "butt hole."

5. According to MD, she suffered from congenital hip disease. Barnett and Rabin (1970: 128–39) and Chisholm (1983:75, 81–84) are among the sources examining this affliction among Navajos.

6. Frank worked at the sawmill between 1907 and 1909, and got his wagon apparently some time in 1909 (Mitchell 1978:359). Given his description of his job (Mitchell 1978: 120–34), it appears that the sawmill at which he worked was the second one established by the federal government, to provide materials for agency buildings in Chinle; see Underhill (1953:225), Young (1961:178–84), and Mitchell (1978:157–58 n. 7).

7. Lorenzo Hubbell was among those who had a high-wheeled, open car in the early 1900s; when Sam Day II clerked for him at Hubbell's second post in Chinle, the two-story Big House, he also served as his driver (McNitt 1963:215). Using the Fort Defiance Agency census of 1915, Link (1968:25) lists five Navajos who owned cars at that time: Chee Dodge, Tom and Willie Damon, Hosteen Yazza, and Clitsoi Dedman (see Valette and Valette 2000). Nelson Gorman should be added to this list since he bought an old Model T described as "one of the first on the reservation" in 1915 (Greenberg and Greenberg 1984:15). When discussing the first car, a Ford, that she and her husband bought in 1916, Kennedy (1965:28, and figure on p. 19) says that "since it was the first one in Chinle, it was in great demand." Studer's photographs illustrate a variety of automobiles in Chinle in the 1921–23 years, including a Dodge originally owned by Dick Dunaway, which was later purchased by Camillo Garcia, only to be lost to the quicksand in Canyon del Muerto. Father Berard Haile, O.F.M. (*in* Bodo 1998:69–70) notes that in about 1910, after some of the first cars came to Gallup, they were immediately purchased by some of the traders. Lorenzo Hubbell, having bought several, gave one of his to Father Anselm Weber, O.F.M. at St. Michaels; Father Berard's first experience with driving a car was in this vehicle. He also documents buying a Ford touring car from an unnamed but disgusted trader in Lukachukai (who had several posts on the reservation) in 1914, after being sent to that community with Brother Gervase Thuemmel; he and Brother Gervase converted this car to a pickup truck (Haile *in* Bodo 1998:74, 76–77).

8. MD, who remembered living here, said the structure was a temporary one, "like a little shack out of lumber, not a hogan. That's the only time my father built something like that for us to live in."

9. Supt. Peter Paquette's Annual Report of the Fort Defiance Indian Agency, dated 7/8/1909, is the first indication that I have found that "The Chin Lee Boarding School has been ordered built" (Correll n.d.). At that time, in the Fort Defiance Agency, Paquette reported two government boarding schools (Fort Defiance with 232 students, and Tohatchi, with 128) and two mission schools, St. Michaels, with 130 pupils, and Rehoboth (Dutch Reformed), with 22. The Chinle site was inspected by a Mr. Smith and Mr. Hildebrand from Fort Defiance, on 9/21/1909; construction started that fall and continued, intermittently, at least through the 1930s, even though Van Valkenburgh (1941:39) says that by 1919, "the present school plant was established." Wilken (1955:115–16 ff.) documents the Franciscans' role in the building of this school, which was within a mile of the Franciscan mission, and which opened on 4/1/1910 with 49 students. Ostermann (1914:31) says that in the fall of 1910, this number increased to 80, which Wilken (1955:116) says was the capacity of the early buildings. Enrollment figures provided later by religious and government personnel, and others, vary according to source and time of census. Examples include: 1910–49 growing to 80 in the fall, although Paquette, in his 8/15/1910 annual report, gives the Chinle enrollment as 100 (Correll n.d.); 1911–80; 1913–75 (Ostermann 1913). Records at Our Lady of Fatima Church and Ostermann (1914:32) indicate that 1913–14 brought an addition to the dormitory, enabling the accommodation of 150 students. Link (1968:25) gives the 1915 census as 200 students; 1918 found 165 students at the school (Wilken 1955:165). Father Anselm Weber's editorial (in *The Franciscan Missions of the Southwest* 8) notes 200 pupils in 1920, although the school shut down from mid October to early November 1918 because of the flu epidemic. (See Fig. 13 here for one view of the school's physical plant ca. 1920). Among the sources for further enrollment data are Ostermann 1913 and 1914; Wilken 1955; and editorials in *The Franciscan Missions of the Southwest* through the last volume in 1922. The data in the latter were submitted a year prior to publication and written by Father Anselm Weber from 1913 until 1921, and in the final year of publication, by Father Marcellus Troester, O.F.M. (Hetteberg p.c. 8/15/1997; Bodo 1998:242–43). The early records at Our Lady of Fatima Church are also helpful in identifying some of the first students at the school, namely those whose parents agreed to their children receiving religious instructions from the priests and who, upon successful completion of these, were confirmed.

Other information about the early days in the community and at the school can be derived from documents in the Correll collection (Correll n.d.). For example, Mr. J. E. Wetenhall was Government Farmer, and a Miss Judge, Field Matron in Chin Lee at least in May–June 1909, a time when Government Farmers were designated by the federal government to serve as custodians of prehistoric ruins, including those in Canyon de Chelly. On 9/29/1911, Mrs. Mary Kennedy, Field Matron in Chin Lee, was ordered by Fort Defiance Agency Supt. Peter Paquette, along with a woman only identified as Ethnobah, to report to the Chin Lee school where they were "short of employees and unable to deal with 30 cases of measels [*sic*]" (9/29/1911, Letter from Paquette to Kennedy, *in* Correll n.d.). In his annual report for 1911, Paquette reports that the Chin Lee school, where no farming is done, "is in need of a small hospital, one span of horses, a spring wagon and harness." He also notes that the Arizona State Course of Study is being followed as much as possible in the Fort Defiance Agency federal schools. Industrial training for boys is concerned with farming, gardening, irrigating, blacksmithing, care of stock, carpentry, and engineering; girls focus on general housekeeping, sewing, laundering, nursing, weaving, and cooking. A letter to

Rev. F. G. Mitchell at Tolchaco, Arizona, from Paquette, dated *2/22/1912*, provides a list of "employees at the Chin Lee School" at that time: "Roger W. Bishoff, Principal; Lucy A. Case, Teacher; Ollie (?) Leach, Kindergartner; William M. Staggs, Industrial Teacher; Tillie Slane, Matron; Ruth Gorman, Assistant Matron; Laura Alverson, Seamstress; Belle McCue, Laundress; Lila A. C. Burr, Cook; Jas. J. Devine, Engineer; George Devine, Assistant, and *Frank Mitchell, Laborer*" (emphasis added). At least two changes were made in the school staff in 1913, when a Miss John went to Chin Lee as Matron on 6/14/1913, and a Mr. Cox, as Industrial Teacher, on 10/13/1913 (Correll n.d.).

Initially, the Chinle Boarding School provided an elementary education and after four years, students went to a variety of off-reservation government schools or on- and off-reservation church-affiliated schools for junior high and high school (see Frisbie 1996 for a summary of the locations of these options and the pertinent literature). Despite the size of the Chinle school's physical plant by the late 1920s and early 1930s, in the beginning it only consisted of a few buildings, as did the community itself. Mitchell (1978:97) says that when he was working for Father Leopold (1906, *before* school construction had started), the only buildings in or near Chinle were the Franciscan Father's residence, the Sam Day trading post that later became known as the Thunderbird Lodge, and a government warehouse (where he had worked earlier) known as the Place Where the Mule Burned, or Burnt Mule.

Although my understanding of the sequence of construction of additions to the school's physical plant is incomplete at present, it is clear that the addition to an earlier dorm, or actual construction of larger dorms occurred in 1913–14, allowing the school's capacity to reach 150 (Ostermann 1914:32), although Kennedy (1965:24) says "several hundred" were enrolled at the school in 1916. Gray's (1986:3) assessment of the community of Chinle in 1920, based on records kept by the Byseggers, reports "less than 25 buildings from the junction to the Thunderbird." They included "the small school," offices of BIA employees and homes for teachers and workers, all of which were in a small valley between the well-known clay butte and "Presbyterian Hill," and three trading posts and the Catholic mission.

The Employees Club, which is not shown in the 1912–13 photographs of the school in Ostermann (1914:31), can be documented at least by 1921 through an unpublished photograph by Leo Mark Studer. The hospital on the grounds had definitely been constructed by 1932. As usual, over time, some school buildings served other purposes (some of which become apparent in Tall Woman's narrative and in supporting endnotes) while others were torn down, apparently without documentation. In 1960, the Chinle Boarding School, then among the oldest on the reservation, was closed, when a new facility with a capacity of 1,024 students was completed (Young 1961:21, 29). Construction of this new school started in December 1959; it opened with 720 students on 10/31/1960, and was formally dedicated on 5/19/1961, as shown later in Tall Woman's narrative and the Dedication Program on file at Our Lady of Fatima Church.

Unlike others, Mitchell (1978:97) says that construction of the Chinle Boarding School did not start until 1910; his son, SM, agreed, adding that the school did not open until 1913. Without having a dated sequence for the construction of individual buildings at the school or a clear understanding of what stage of early construction Frank assisted with or Tall Woman is recalling when thinking about her first son's birth, SM's birthdate remains uncertain. As shown in Mitchell (1978:351), various census records and family members gave dates that ranged from 1908 until 1916. In August 1996, SM's "official" Tribal Census Office records listed a birthdate of 6/30/1912, while his medical records showed 6/30/1913. Given Tall Woman's comments about childbirth spacing and other events at the time, in 1996, the 1912 birthdate seemed to be the best choice. However, when SM died on 7/10/1998, the family chose the 6/30/1913 date for his eulogy and obituary.

Like his birthdate, SM's first name had various explanations. While some said Tall Woman and Frank named him "Seya," others credited either Sam Sanishya [SS] or Chic Sandoval [CS]. The latter and his wife, Ethnobah, were working at the Chinle Boarding School when SM was enrolled there in 1922. Since no one could recall any childhood nickname SM was known by, the consensus was he never had one; as one family member said, "Sometimes, kids don't have a funny name or some other kind of name when they're small; nobody gives them one."

10. For information on the early Presbyterian days in Chinle, the Gormans and their Chinle store, and the Gorman-Presbyterian connection, see Stewart (1980), Greenberg and Greenberg (1984), and Gray (1986). The store, built in 1910 from stone and wood with an earthen roof, was erected "in a clearing near the Chinle Wash" and "only a few hundred yards away from the entrance to the beautiful Canyon de Chelly" (Greenberg and Greenberg 1984:12). The Gorman home was attached behind it; time brought additions of bedrooms, two barns, and a small separate stone house for the man who baked the store's bread (see Fig. 9 here). Gorman, a successful trader and stockman, had large herds of cattle roaming on Black Mesa; he opened another store, his fourth, in that area in 1912, but sold it in 1914 to Lorenzo Hubbell, who evidently then hired Winslow (Win) Wetherill to run it for four years. For some information on the Black Mountain store, where some of the Mitchells traded (as shown in the Hubbell Papers), see Chap. 1 endnotes, McNitt (1963), Allen (1963), and Faunce (1981, despite the use of pseudonyms therein).

According to Greenberg and Greenberg (1984) and Gray (1986), Nelson Gorman had six children with Alice before her death in 1924; later, he had five others with his second wife, Elouise. In 1916, a year after he acquired an "old battered Model T Ford," Nelson built a large stone house for his family several miles west of the post, on land from Alice's father. Alice, herself a well-known weaver, was a staunch Protestant, first as an Episcopalian, and then as a Presbyterian; she contributed her musical talents to the latter group, opened her home for church services and other meetings of like-minded Presbyterians, and was one of the people who spearheaded the development of the Chinle congregation. After losing some family members to tuberculosis and later, the 1918–19 flu epidemic, and losing their life savings when the McKinley First State Bank in Gallup closed, the Gormans decided to give their post and the home and buildings attached to it to the Presbyterians. While converts had been meeting in individuals' homes before this time, this was the group's first permanent building and meeting place. Rev. A. K. Locker, the first Presbyterian missionary pastor assigned to Chinle, arrived in 1921, after the Northern Arizona Presbytery organized the Chinle group into a congregation and formed the Indian Presbyterian Church of Chinle with twenty-four members (Gray 1986:11; see also Gray's observations on the politics that Protestants faced in getting land-leases for church sites, both from the agent and from Washington, D.C., at the time). Roger Davis, who served as interpreter, arrived shortly thereafter. The next several years were focused on building the church and manse on land near the Gormans' Chinle post; the latter was not quite finished in July 1924, when Rev. Charles and Rose Bysegger arrived, but the congregation had a home and the Byseggers were able to concentrate on their ministry. The early days were difficult because of Roman Catholic opposition (Gray 1986:15). Superintendent Peter Paquette of the Fort Defiance Agency notes a 7/30/1919 visit from a Chinle headman, "Halta Nezne Begay," to report continuing trouble with Protestant missionaries who some "want to run off" and to request that the agent "come to the school to talk to older Indians and those in good standing reputation" (Correll n.d.). Butler (1991:42–43) documents a petition from Chinle Navajo Catholics protesting the granting of a mission site to the Presbyterians in the fall of 1921, forwarded by Father Leopold to Father Marcellus at St. Michaels, as well as the latter's response. Ostermann (1927a–e) documents Catholic-Presbyterian competition over parental signatures for instruction of school children, which the Presbyterians began at the Chinle Boarding School in 1927. In addition to discussing this (Gray 1986:17), Gray (1986) also documents the use of the various buildings on "Presbyterian Hill" and changes through time at this church, Chinle's second.

11. It is clear that the same construction company, W. D. Lovell of Minneapolis (Ostermann 1914:31), built the Franciscan church after completing the school, and that Brother Gervase Thuemmel, who had developed stonemason skills, helped considerably with the process (see Chap. 6 endnotes). The Annunciation Mission Church was dedicated on Mar. 25, 1912 (Mitchell 1978:115 n. 21; *New Mexico Register* 1955a:26; Ostermann 1913, 1914:33, unnumbered figure; Trockur 1976). The eighteen boys and twenty-four girls who constituted the first group to complete religious instructions from the priests (probably mainly in conjunction with attending the Chinle Boarding School) were baptized and received First Communions on May 3, 1914. Gray (1986:6) makes it clear that itinerant Protestant missionaries, including Rev. Fred Mitchell who spoke Navajo, arrived in the Chinle area shortly after the Franciscans opened their church, traveling out from the Episcopalian mission at Fort Defiance and the Presbyterian mission at Ganado to preach in the scattered Navajo camps typical of the area at the time. For additional information on Protestant efforts, see Salsbury (1941), Means (1955), Salsbury, with Hughes (1969), and Lockard (1995), among others.

12. Frank's freighting years began ca. 1912 and ended ca. 1919 when he settled in Chinle (see Mitchell 1978:136–55, 157–59 n. 9–10, ff.).

CHAPTER 8

1. *Kin Naaztí'í* essentially means a row of houses standing in a line. The term is similar but not identical to one given by others for several of the Hopi villages on Second Mesa. Reichard (n.d.:211) recorded *Kin naazti'í,* "houses strung about" as the name for Shungopavi, Arizona. The Franciscan Fathers (1912:203) give *Kinazt'i',* "a line of houses," as the name for "Shipauolovi Pueblo," Arizona, and Haile (n.d.:11) gives *Kinaazt'i',* "Circle of Houses," as the name for Shimopovi, Arizona. Haile (1951:261) gives *Kinázt'i'* as the name for Shimopovi, Shipaulovi, and Young and Morgan (1980:1008) provide the term *Kin Názt'i'* for Shungopavi, and *Tsétsohk'id* for Shipaulovi (Toreva, Mishognovi) (Young and Morgan 1980:1007). MD remembered living there in "stone houses in a line that all had roofs slanting down only one way, not like the two-sided roofs houses have today." SM only remembered going to his first Enemyway at the site, when he was *very small;* the earliest summer location he recalled is the Place of the Reeds, where Man Who Shouts located his family the next summer, after the one that brought all of the troubles at Houses Standing in a Line.

2. AS said the way her mother always talked about the size of their herd when they lived there suggested they had "lots more than several hundred sheep, probably closer to a thousand."

3. When discussing this part of her life, Tall Woman always chose to identify these siblings only as "three of my older sisters" and "one of my older brothers," rather than by name. Thus, it remains unclear which of the older siblings shown in her genealogy (Appendix A) died at this time. However, on the basis of discussions with the family and SS, I suspect that among the sisters were the one who was married to Jim Mitchell as his *second* wife (Little Woman, the mother of Gai and others), and the one who married Deschine and then gave birth to Sam and his siblings. Records at Our Lady of Fatima Church indicate that when Gai married in 1913, her mother was already deceased, and the Peter Paquette census indicates that by 1915 Man Who Shouts was raising Sam and his siblings because their parents had died. From SM's early childhood on, he and Sam were inseparable. Later in Tall Woman's narrative, it becomes clear that the older brother who died at Houses Standing in a Line was *not* the one called The Jailer and *not* the one called Man with a Cane.

4. The literature on Navajo mortuary beliefs and practices is extensive. An introduction to the topic and its basic bibliography can be found in a special symposium issue of *American Indian Quarterly* devoted to these matters (see Frisbie 1978). Griffen (1980), Ward (1980), and Jett (1996) are among the more recent resources. The Enemyway (see Chap. 5 n. 9) can be and is used to cure illnesses attributed to contact with things associated with Anasazis, ancient Puebloan Peoples.

CHAPTER 9

1. When I worked with Sam, during the summer of 1989, he gave his birthdate as 12/18/1901 and the birth order of his siblings as The Jailer, The Man's Grandson, Bah, and himself as the youngest. Sam had a few dim memories of his father, Deschine, but none of his mother. He wanted to make sure I knew The Jailer was an excellent Nightway dancer. His dance team included "two men from the Canyon, two from the foot of Black Mountain, and others." The Man's Grandson also was a Nightway dancer and had a team whose members were all from Black Mountain. Eventually he became the father of Philemon and Ben. Sam said he himself was enrolled in the Chinle Boarding School in 1913 and was immediately put in a group receiving religious instructions from the priests. Records at Our Lady of Fatima Church list his date of birth as 1905. They also show him enrolled in the school in 1911 and in the group of eighteen boys baptized on 5/3/1914 by Father Marcellus; others included Joe Carroll, Stephen Bizadi, Henry Draper, Benjamin Gorman, and Ben Mitchell. The same day twenty-four girls, including Rachel Jones and Adela [Adelle] Brown, were baptized; most in both groups, including Sam, were confirmed on 11/23/1915. After the Chinle Boarding School, Sam went to Fort Apache Indian School and then to Riverside, California, for high school (the Sherman Institute). He said he was already at Riverside when SM started school in Chinle (in 1922). Sam died on 1/10/1999 and was buried in the Chinle Community Cemetery on 1/14/1999.

2. Flintway or *Béshee* is one of the major curing ceremonies in the group known as Lifeway. Usually performed as a five-night ceremony, it is used to cure accidental injuries, external or internal, as well as to restore consciousness. The ceremony has both male and female branches and its use is not restricted to any particular season. The Flintway *jish*, which includes equipment specific to the ceremony such as a hoof rattle with attached flints, and the

craneheads mentioned by Tall Woman, can also be used for Shootingway, as long as appropriate adjustments are made in some of the equipment. For further information on Flintway, see Haile (1943) and Gill (1981), among others; for information on the medicine bundle, see Frisbie (1987).

3. Tall Woman was silent for a long time after this, before continuing with what follows. As shown later in the text, she never did announce plans for this *jish*. After her death, in 1979 one of her daughters sold it reportedly without discussion and for "lots of cash and cattle" to the mother-in-law of one of her nieces. The niece, this woman's brother's daughter, made the request because someone on her mother-in-law's side was reportedly qualified to use the *jish* and needed it (cf. Frisbie 1987:141, 142 ff.).

4. While there are many infants noted in the *Liber Defunctorum* records (which were started on 7/7/1912 by Father Leopold) at Our Lady of Fatima Church, none of them is identified as a son of Tall Woman and Frank during the 1913–18 period. If a birthdate of 6/30/1912 is accepted for SM, this infant brother would have been born at the Place of the Reeds in the late spring of 1913.

5. Although prayersticks, made from reeds and other materials, are prepared for use during many curing ceremonies, Tall Woman never identified the ceremonial affiliation of this *jish*. She only said this particular medicine bundle passed to her crippled older brother, Man with a Cane (Man with a Cottonwood Tree), upon the death of Man Who Shouts because he had started to learn how to use it. See Haile (1947) for a study of the prayerstick cutting associated with the male branch of Shootingway.

6. Because Tall Woman did not elaborate on this remark, I asked her about it later. She said she remembered losing two of her children as babies; one of them was the baby boy mentioned here who was born after SM. In 1970, all that she remembered about the other was that it lived only a week; she couldn't remember when it was born or whether it had been a boy or a girl. AgS said her mother told her she had lost two as little babies before she herself was born in 1918. However, Frank (Mitchell 1978:145, 146 ff.) said the second one, also a boy, was born between RY and Pauline [PM] and died as an infant; he also said he buried it, despite having just had a Ghostway Ceremony and being forbidden to have further contact with the dead in any way. But, if the birthdates for RY (1920) and PM (1921) are correct, this second baby boy had to have been born either earlier or later than Frank suggested. In later chapters, Tall Woman's narrative suggests it may have been between David [DM] (1922) and HM (1926).

7. At a later time, when Tall Woman was again talking about her father with me, she said: "The agents appointed other ones as time passed and so we had men like Manuelito, Chee Dodge who was headman for Fort Defiance, and Charlie Mitchell, for the Lukachukai area. I think my father was being considered to be over the whole western part of the reservation, but then, for some reason they didn't pick anyone, from what we heard from Fort Defiance. Or maybe it was because he died before they could appoint him to that, before they could make him head of the western part of the reservation. I don't remember now."

CHAPTER 10

1. AgS's "official birthdate," according to the Tribal Census Office, is 8/20/1918, a date she also uses, despite the disparity shown in Mitchell (1978:351).

2. The Spanish influenza pandemic of 1918 was worldwide and killed at least 21 million

people, including 500,000 Americans (Wallechinsky and Wallace 1975:547–48). As Russell (1985:380) and others note, American Indians were among the most severely affected in the United States. Among the studies of the effect of the disease on the Navajos, where the epidemic devastated the population between the fall of 1918 and spring of 1919, are the works by Reagan (1919, 1922) and Russell (1985). The latter, in particular, includes useful references to studies of the social and psychological effects of the event, which were as devastating to the Navajo population as the high mortality rates, if not more so. Other information can be found in a variety of places, including Bailey and Bailey (1986:119–20), Brugge (1980:306–9 ff.), and Gillmor and Wetherill (1934:222–29). Native explanations of the event varied; for example, Reichard (1928:147) mentions that some Navajos attributed the catastrophe to a solar eclipse on June 8, 1918, and Greenberg and Greenberg (1984:35) note that some blamed it on the fact that some Hopis joined a Nightway Ceremony at Antelope Springs. Kennedy (1965:36–37) provides some remarks about the situation in Chinle; George and Mary Jeannette Kennedy owned the Thunderbird from 1916 until the spring of 1919, when they sold it to Leon H. Cozy McSparron (Kennedy 1965:38).

At present, scientific attempts to understand the deadly virus continue; for example, an international team, with researchers from Norway, Canada, Britain, and the United States, in August 1998 exhumed remains of six eighteen- to twenty-five-year-old coal miners on an Arctic island north of Norway. The goal was to obtain data that would lead to an understanding of the genetic structure of the deadly virus that killed these victims in October 1918. The Spanish flu, which globally resulted in more deaths than those caused by the fighting in World War I, was characterized by sudden fever, chills, headaches, muscle pain, malaise, pneumonia, and rapid death (*St. Louis Post Dispatch* 1998).

3. The first records of baptisms and burials at Our Lady of Fatima Church (in a combined volume, *Baptismal Record and Burials*, dating from 9/12/1907 through 2/17/1925) document (pp. 21–22) seven deaths from the flu, with six of them from 10/23/1918 through 11/3/1918, and one on 3/13/1919. Those recorded show death two to three days after baptism, with baptisms beginning of "those very sick with Spanish influenza" on 10/21/1918; five males are recorded, with ages identified as one, seventeen or eighteen, twenty-five (2), and no age (1); both girls were seven years old. The only school child identified was the girl baptized on 3/11/1919 and removed from the Chinle Boarding School by her parents; after being taken home, she died. Father Anselm Weber, O.F.M. (1919:39) indicates that the school was closed because of the epidemic by mid-October 1918, and was still closed on November 1. At that time, "about 26 persons [had] died around and about Chin Lee, in consequence of the epidemic." No deaths had been reported at the Chinle Boarding School, although at one time, about fifteen school children were suffering from mild cases of the disease.

4. Ghostway, *Hóchx̨ǫ'įjí* is also known as Evilway and Uglyway. The curing ceremonials in the Evilway group address afflictions attributed to native ghosts, contact with the dead or their possessions, or witchcraft by focusing on the exorcism of a variety of evil influences. A Blackening Ceremony is one of the features of Evilway ceremonials, although it may also be performed separately, as shown in Chap. 8. For further information on Ghostway or Evilway, see Haile (1950b), among others.

5. Baptismal records (*Liber Baptismorum*, Vol. 1 [1907–40]) at Our Lady of Fatima Church show that Mary no. 2, listed as Mary Rose Mitchell (p. 16 no. 9) was baptized by Father Leopold and given the baptismal name Clara on 5/30/1920. According to Tall Woman, she

received religious instructions from the priests while at the Chinle Boarding School. Although the priests sometimes did private baptisms at the school, Mary no. 2 was baptized in a group of ten Navajo girls; Father Emanuel baptized a group of fifteen Navajo boys on the same day.

6. Upon request, on 8/15/1989 SM prepared various drawings of the brand Tall Woman had sketched for me in 1964. The one used here as Fig. 12 is based on SM's work, as redrawn by Jennifer A. Frisbie in 1997.

7. Exactly when Man Who Shouts started raising cattle or where the first ones came from remain unclear. AS said he may have traded some sheep or a horse or two for the first few cattle he got. It is also possible, of course, that the first ones came as compensation for his work as a ceremonial practitioner. Payment with a cow was not unheard of, even in 1963. SM said while he was growing up, before he went to school in 1922, Man Who Shouts' cattle frequently roamed all the way down to Fish Point. Some years the branding was done in corrals there.

CHAPTER 11

1. SM said that in the 1920s school boys *did* gamble, at least at times, even though it was against school rules. One person shot an arrow and others tried to hit it or get within two fingers of it. If you did either, you didn't have to pay the wager. He said in his childhood they made self bows from oak, juniper, alder, or sumac; arrows were made from reeds or hardwoods, if the bark was removed and one end sharpened to a point. After nails became available, SM said they flattened them, inserted them into reeds, and secured them with sinew bindings. Kluckhohn, Hill, and Kluckhohn (1971:23–43) are among others providing information on bows and arrows.

2. Matthews (1889) provides information on the Moccasin Game in his detailed study of its associated songs. Other information about the songs can be found in Frisbie (1977c, 1980b, 1987, 1989), the Diné Bi 'Ólta Association (1973), and elsewhere. Cliff (1990) and Levy (1998: 225–29) provide more generalized discussions of Navajo games, including this one.

3. See Mitchell (1978:78, 80, 109 n. 3, ff.) for information on Frank's gambling days, which were clearly remembered by MD, SM, and RY even in the 1990s. AgS recalled only a few instances, since "I was always away in school when that was going on." Among those she remembers is one day when two men appeared on horseback, right after Frank had returned from doing a Blessingway somewhere. They said, "Come on, Frank, let's go," and so all three took off, even though the wind was very, very strong at the time, and Frank had already been gone for several days. Shortly thereafter, Jake Tom came and asked Tall Woman if Frank had already left. AgS was wondering where they had gone by this point and hoped to find out. But Tall Woman only said they had already gone. "It was clear she was very, very upset but she didn't say anything to us about it. That went on for a long time; Frank would take off, leaving us alone while he ran around doing those things. That's probably why later, when he was preaching to us, he said so many of his younger days, when he was running wild, were no good." It is clear, from both his children and Tall Woman, that although Frank settled down later, he still gambled every now and then. Information on card games such as Monte and Coon Can can be found in Mitchell (1978:109 n. 3), the Franciscan Fathers (1910:473–74), and Culin (1898, 1907). Family members reported that Casino also dated to "before Frank's time." It was still popular in 1996–98, as was another card

game, often played during Enemyways by both women and men, called Navajo Ten. Another time I saw Navajo Ten played (outside, in the bed of a pickup truck) was on 6/30/1977, in the evening; then, men not directly involved in the planning of Tall Woman's funeral played it "to pass the time."

4. Beautyway, *Hoozhónee*, is a curing ceremony belonging to the Holyway group. It is firmly associated with snakes (and sometimes with lizards and certain water creatures), and deals with illnesses attributed to snake infection, such as rheumatism, sore throats, skin rashes or sores, and other problems. Beautyway is also among the curing ceremonies that may be recommended for problems attributed to the abuse of snakes, and after actual snake bites have been treated in other ways (as shown later in Tall Woman's narrative). For further information, see Mitchell (1978) and Wyman (1957), among others.

5. RY used 6/20/1920 as her "official birthdate," despite the disparity shown in Mitchell (1978:351).

6. As shown in later endnotes, a fifteen-bed hospital, located in the outermost row of buildings on the east side of the Chinle Boarding School grounds, opened in 1932.

7. The ceremonies held for Man Who Shouts during his last two years were major curing ceremonies; most belong to the Holyway group, although Big Starway is now most common in an Evilway form, and Flintway belongs to the Lifeway group. Holyway ceremonials address appropriate Holy People and are aimed at exorcising evil, attracting good, and restoring the one who is suffering. Nightways and Flintways have been briefly described in earlier endnotes. The Big Starway, *Sǫ'tsohjí*, in its Ghostway or Evilway form is used to treat sicknesses attributed to witches or native ghosts. The wide-ranging symptoms include fainting, insomnia, bad dreams, and weight loss, among others; see Wheelwright and McAllester (1956). The Mountainway, *Dziłk'ijí*, has several branches and may include the Fire or Corral Dance, explained earlier. Mountainway deals primarily with illnesses attributed to mountain-dwelling animals, especially bears, but also porcupines, squirrels, skunks, and others. Bear disease is often suspected in cases of mental disturbance, arthritis, or other symptoms; see Matthews (1887/1997), Haile (1946), Wyman (1975), selected essays in Halpern and McGreevy (1997), Levy (1998), and Zolbrod (1998). Shootingway, *Na'at'oyee*, always popular, has numerous branches, rituals, sandpaintings, and other elements, and has been studied by a number of outsiders; for examples, see Newcomb and Reichard (1937), Reichard (1939b, 1963), Kluckhohn and Wyman (1940:155–68), Wyman (1970b), McAllester (1980), and Levy (1998). The ceremony is recommended to treat sicknesses attributed to thunder and lightning, or snakes and arrows, with troubles manifesting themselves in a variety of symptoms including gastrointestinal, chest, and lung diseases.

8. In contrast to Frank's (Mitchell 1978:351) account, Tall Woman's implies that PM was born in the summer of 1921. No "vital statistics records" of PM's life could be located.

9. See Mitchell (1978) for Frank's own account of learning to become a Blessingway singer.

10. Both MD and SM remembered the numerous ceremonies and the crowded hogans. The small children often fell asleep and would awaken to find themselves positioned between people they didn't know. SM said he and Philemon Bitsui were often frightened by this, especially when they'd wake up next to "a woman with no chin"* or someone comparable.

11. The *Baptismal Record and Burials* volume (1907–25) at Our Lady of Fatima Church shows (p. 28) that on 3/18/1922, "a very old Navajo lady, said to be over 100 years old, was

baptized privately by her granddaughter, Rachel Jones, before death"; a "Christian burial" by Father Leopold followed on 3/19/1922. This may have been the mother of Towering House Woman and thus, a real sister of Tall Woman's own maternal grandmother, as shown in Appendix A. Whether this woman died before or after Man Who Shouts is unknown, since the date of his death is only documentable as the winter of 1922.

12. This conflicts with Frank's (Mitchell 1978:197) statement that Man Who Shouts was buried by Man with a Yellow Face, his son-in-law, and Frank himself. However, two of Tall Woman's children who remember "peeking" when the men departed and later, when they came back, concur with their mother's account, not Frank's.

CHAPTER 12

1. While the semiannual pastoral movements stopped after Man Who Shouts died, herders continued to take the sheep to different grassy areas in the summer, including The Flats and closer to Valley Store after the family settled in Chinle. "The Flats" refers to an area north and west of where the Chinle community dump was located before it closed as a landfill area. In 1996, a number of trailers and a gravel pit were located in part of the area. Family horses remained up on the ridge and on Red Mesa until the early 1960s. Later, Tall Woman explains how Frank switched land with Tom Scott, thus enabling the family to move to their present location (around 1936). According to her children, only thereafter did Frank really start emphasizing farming.

2. Tall Woman called rocks with concretions "bubbly rocks"; the shiny ones were pieces of obsidian; eventually she showed me a piece she had found and kept.

3. *Liber Matrimoniorum* records at Our Lady of Fatima Church, Vol. 1 (12/12/1910–8/9/1924) show Gai marrying Son of Yucca Fruit Man on 11/24/1913, with Man Who Shouts as the witness (marriage no. 30). The latter's residence is listed as Chinle; Son of Yucca Fruit Man is listed as twenty years old with Yucca Fruit Man and Yucca Fruit Man's Wife as his parents. Gai is listed as "18?" with unnamed parents listed as deceased. Gai's mother clearly was dead by 1913; her father, Jim Mitchell, however, wasn't; instead, he was with another wife by then. Census records at Our Lady of Fatima Church list Ida's birthdate as 1920 and Betty's as 1923.

4. RY's earliest memory was of living in her parents' "small hogan right by the fields" at this site. According to her, they also had a ramada there. Man with a Cane lived nearby, by the cottonwood tree he had planted, and some summers Tall Woman's mother's place was also here, next to Tall Woman and her children. RY remembered spending the summers here after DM was born (1922) and after AgS was sent to Fort Apache with SM (1925). They were also living here when Tall Woman and her mother started teaching RY about fixing different traditional foods. Sometimes when the family lived here, RY was in the group responsible for herding; other times, she was among those sent to wherever the flocks were, to milk the animals and bring back the milk to those living by the fields.

5. SM remembered this incident vividly. In July 1989, he said he didn't know why he was so afraid since "they didn't hurt you when they did that." He thought this old cure for stuttering ended with his grandparents' generation. He never saw his parents or any of their peers practice it or heard it suggested for cases similar to his.

6. See Chap. 7 and its endnotes for discussions of the construction of various buildings at the Chinle Boarding School. The Employees Club, for example, is not extant in Franciscan

archival photographs of the 1913–14 dormitory addition construction or completion shown in Ostermann (1914:31) but is apparent in Fig. 13 here, where it is the building on the left in the back row. This figure is a reproduction of a picture dated "c. 1920" and on file in the St. Michaels Archive, C539.9-3, R450; it is also available on an undated, colored, penny postcard produced by Feicke-Desch Printing Company, Cincinnati, Ohio, with caption, "Navaho Indian School, Chin Lee, Ariz." Another photograph in the St. Michaels Archives, C539.9-1, R112, includes an additional building in the left foreground, but could not be reproduced with publishable quality. The Employees Club is also shown in Leo Mark Studer's unpublished photographs of "Chin Lee" in a picture dated "1922 or 1923," showing "L. M. Studer, Bob Fraser and his sister, Freda Cassidy, and Helen Brown on the building's porch." The "Frasers" were identified as children of "the Frasers [Fraziers] who ran the Valley Store Trading Post at the time; Brown, from Gallup, was visiting them. Cassidy was the daughter of the Cassidys who owned and ran the Lukachukai Trading Post at that time. Cousins and Cousins (1996:23) confirm that the Employees Club was functioning and in service for government employees and other community members by August 1925. Perhaps it was among those structures in existence when Van Valkenburgh (1941:39) said that the "present [Chinle Boarding] school plant [was established] in 1919."

7. SM said he gave this brother his English name, David [DM], in the 1930s when DM went to get working papers so he could join SM on an ECW or SCS project (see Chap. 16, n. 1). No one could recall DM's Navajo name.

8. Records at the Our Lady of Fatima Church in Chinle show Frank was witnessing marriages in his capacity as a headman by 1924.

9. SM said other headmen in the area at the time included Eli Smith (Nazlini), Old Curly Hair (Frazier's, later called Valley Store), Big Legs (Rough Rock), Gray Horse (Salina), and Long Moustache (Black Mountain). The latter was the same Long Moustache who used to move around with Man Who Shouts, and who stayed with the family for a while after he passed away. He had a wagon and was known to "take really good care of his wife and his children" (after he remarried, having lost his first wife and child in the flu). He continued to live near Fish Point and both Tall Woman and Frank exchanged visits with him and his family through the years. Old Curly Hair, one of Frank's clan uncles, was a singer, headman, and another close friend who is mentioned frequently in Tall Woman's narrative.

10. See Mitchell (1978: 210–39 ff.) for Frank's accounts of these matters.

11. A three-person Business group, consisting of Chee Dodge, Charlie Mitchell, and Dugal Chee Bekiss, negotiated the oil leases in 1922. The first elected Tribal Council consisted of twelve delegates and twelve alternates plus the "Chairman;" it met for the first time on 7/7/1923 and elected Henry Chee Dodge as the first Tribal Chairman (1923–28). The Council was reorganized between December 1936 and March 1937 and members of the new Constitutional Assembly were chosen on 3/10/1937. Frank was part of that group, as clarified later. See Shepardson (1963) and Iverson (1981), among others, for Navajo political developments through time.

12. As shown in Mitchell (1978:148–51, 163–66 nn. 23, 24), when assembling Frank's narrative, it was impossible to identify the archaeological site on which he worked.

13. There are no records of this infant who was apparently born in May or early June 1924. SM said those herding were out on The Flats again when this baby was born and then died.

14. *Liber Defunctorum* records (p. 3 no. 11) at Our Lady of Fatima Church indicate Tom Scott and his wife lost a ten-day old baby girl, Mary, on 5/10/1924, and that she received a cemetery burial the same day by Father Leopold Ostermann, O.F.M.

15. Hartley Seymour, C. N. Cotton's son-in-law, was the other person who joined Cozy McSparron and Camillo Garcia in purchasing the three extant stores in Chinle in 1923, although some sources question this date (see Frisbie 1998:75, 77; Chap. 4, n. 2). McSparron was called "Cozy," and Garcia was known as "The Mexican," "Winking Mexican," and later, "Old Mexican," at least to some Chinle Navajos. Additional information on both of these men can be found in McNitt (1963), Stewart (1980), Cousins and Cousins (1996), Wagner (1997), Frisbie (1998), and elsewhere, including the literature on trading posts, and early churches in Chinle since the McSparrons were Presbyterian and the Garcias, Catholic. Photographs of Cozy are available in Cousins and Cousins (1996:70), and, with his wife, Inja, in Wagner (1997:2). The use of *Kin Ntsaaí* as the name for the Big House appeared to be a common practice among Chinle Navajos. See Chap. 4, n. 2, for a brief history of Chinle's trading posts, and Appendix B for chronological developments.

16. SM had the most numerous memories of walking to the Big House with his mother when she needed something. He said she went there because it was a "little closer than Garcia's," and that he'd always wait outside while she went in. He said one time he found some baby chickens in a pen at the Big House. He took one while his mother was inside, and put it in a burlap sack she'd given him to hold. "It never made a sound while we walked back home, so it sure surprised her when it popped out while she was unloading the few things she had traded for. She got after me for doing that but we kept the baby chick, letting it run loose around our place." (Frisbie [1998] provides further information about the Big House, as well as photographs, including Fig. 14 here, on pp. 74, 76.)

17. The weaving literature cited earlier documents changes in different parts of the reservation, and the influence of specific traders, such as J. L. Hubbell and J. B. Moore, on various parts of the weaving process and markets. Kent (1981:18–19; 1985) provides documentation of Mrs. Cozy McSparron's (Inja's) involvement with weavers in Chinle, after a visit from Mary Wheelwright in the fall of 1920 at their trading post (also see Amsden 1934: 223–25). McKenna and Travis (1989:109 n. 4) also emphasize the importance of Wheelwright and McSparron in the rug revival in Chinle, a point de-emphasized by Garcia during his 1958 interview with McNitt. For a while, Inja dyed yarn for Chinle weavers and tried to encourage better work from more women. Regional styles emerged in the late 1920s, a time when earlier, more classic patterns based on stripes organized in wide bands were also "revived" to give rugs another designator, "Revival Style." The "Chinle style," established by the 1930s, was "revival" and was based on vegetal and chemical dyes. Designs in a "Chinle style" rug were based on "serrate patterns" (to use technical terms) woven into stripes or bands. Additionally, the rugs were borderless. Numerous sources (cited earlier) illustrate the "Chinle style" and also show its connections to weaving developments in Wide Ruins (cf. Wagner 1997), Pine Springs, Nazlini, and Crystal.

18. In the fall of 1996, MD (born ca. 1908) said she was in her teens when Tall Woman started shifting away from Phase II Chief Blankets and emphasizing designs. She said her mother's early designs featured a figure comparable to that shown in two narrow bands on a Wide Ruins rug illustrated in one of the books I showed her (Southwest Parks and Monuments Association 1992:19). She also said her mother taught her about plant dyes, including

how to process *k'ish* [speckled alder, hoary alder] bark "to get the reddish-purple color sometimes used on moccasins," as well as double weaving, and the "Chinle design." MD also sketched the latter and the saddle blanket designs for me (see Figs. 18 and 19 here), and confirmed the local name for the Chinle design, which made her and others present laugh. She also remembered asking Man Who Shouts about designs during the last year of his life; she reports he told her "to just watch others to learn how they did that, how they put the designs into the weaving. He told me I should be able to figure that out on my own because I knew enough about weaving by then." MD reported learning double diamond pattern weaving from "Mama Catron" (Olive Catron), "one of Frank's relatives who worked in Chinle as a BIA school dorm parent and weaving instructor," *not* from her mother or grandparents. AS (born in 1928) remembers her mother weaving Chief Blankets throughout the 1930s; red, black, and white were the predominant colors, although at times she used browns and grays. AS, who sketched one of her mother's Chief Blanket designs for me in 1996 (see Fig. 17 here), also remembers seeing some of her mother's rugs in the McSparrons' living room in the 1940s; none of those illustrated in Harrison and Spears (1989:17, 18), however, were attributed to Tall Woman by any family members (but both photographs were taken in 1935). AS recalled Cozy telling her that her grandmother, Man Who Shouts' first wife, was the first woman he ever knew in Chinle who made Chief Blankets (Phase II style). She also said by the time she finished junior high at St. Michaels (1945), her mother was only making Chinle-style vegetal dye rugs; this led her to conclude that the transition in her mother's repertoire occurred in the early 1940s. AS confirmed Tall Woman's statement that her own knowledge of weaving came from school, not from her mother. She also said MD and ID "are the two who have really carried on our mother's weaving," and that they "both have all her designs." When I first met Tall Woman in 1963, she was always weaving Chinle vegetal dye rugs (see cover illustration here); the same was true of two of her daughters, MD and ID. At times, Tall Woman also wove single and double saddle blankets. Except for a few months off while recovering from a broken wrist in 1964, Tall Woman continued producing and marketing rugs until a stroke (her first, in March 1973) ended her days as a weaver.

19. In 1997, ID said the *dleesh* available in the hills west of the highway through Valley Store "isn't really very good to use on wool." The kinds of *dleesh* are not interchangeable in usage. The wool-whitening clay is soft; the white clay used during *Kinaaldás* (to paint the pubescent girl) is hard and must be shaved off or scraped from the lumps that have been dug from the ground. One of the places at which Tall Woman gathered the latter kind was *Naasilá*, which Haile (1950a:143) gives as the name for two hills between Thoreau and Crownpoint, New Mexico. Another kind, *nímasii dleesh* (also called *nomasi dleesh* in Tall Woman's family) [wild potato white clay], is used in preparing certain wild foods, especially berries, to remove their bitterness.

CHAPTER 13

1. At another time Tall Woman said WD had his own team in Chinle later. "He always put teams together wherever he'd go, working on odd jobs for the ECW [see Chap. 16, n. 1] when that started, over in Bellemont at the Ordnance Depot, or elsewhere. Those dance teams always practiced a lot; they got together at night somewhere out in the open, away from any hogans, built a fire, and then practiced their songs and dances." According to her, WD was a Yeibichei dancer by the time he was enrolled at the Fort Defiance Boarding

School. "He was there when the flu came and killed so many of the People. His family lost lots of people to that and he wanted to come home, but the school said no. So, the next time they dismissed the children for vacation, he never went back."

2. In 1970 Tall Woman, when discussing WD's family, added: "He had lots of brothers, like Tall Navajo's Son, Willie, and Tom. I don't think Willie ever married. The oldest one, Tall Navajo's Son, married Sam's sister, Bah. They had some children together [see Appendix A] and then some others who passed away. And then I think he passed away. Later that woman married Joseph Ganna; they never had any children together. She died recently, just a few years back." The *Liber Defunctorum* records at Our Lady of Fatima Church show that after she moved from Winslow back to Chinle, this woman, whose baptismal name was Mary, died on 4/20/1968 and was buried, with a funeral mass, on 4/24/1968, by Father Adam Wethington, O.F.M. In those records, she is listed as Mrs. Joseph (Mary) Gona, C no. 66707, age seventy years, and the cause of death is listed as old age.

3. SM recalled an initial bad experience at the Chinle school, which involved getting an infected tooth extracted shortly after he was enrolled over there with Philemon Bitsui. The boys' advisor sent him over to one of the buildings; "When I walked in there, all the children were crying. Pretty soon I was crying too, from having my tooth pulled. But I got over it."* Lockard (1995) is among the sources that include other information from SM about this school.

4. SM said at that time the racetrack was where the Kentucky Fried Chicken place was in 1995. He also said in the 1930s, Chinle had a half-mile racetrack in the area where the airport was built later. People "used to race horses over there, turning around to make it a mile-long course." When the airport was built, according to SM the track was torn down. "It used to be right beneath where the water tank is currently located." In the fall of 1996, several people in the family said, "Chinle should have been keeping records about these things, instead of always tearing things down, leaving no trace of them. Even today, nobody is keeping track of these things; they still just knock them down. The old clinic building is going to be next." (It was demolished in mid-October 1998; see Chap. 16, n. 16.)

5. Howard Wilson [HW], who is also mentioned in other sources, including Stewart (1980:49, 81) and Cousins and Cousins (1996:27), although *not* in McNitt (1963), was one of Cozy McSparron's nephews. SM said at this time HW was dating various teachers and eventually married one named Sybil. Margaret Garcia Delaney (p.c. 6/10/1997) added that this woman, Sybil Fry, first taught at the public school (originally located upstairs in one room of the Big House) before becoming a teacher at the boarding school. Among the other teachers at the latter school at the time were Lucy Jobin, the girls' supervisor; Lottie Glenn (shown in a 1918 photograph in Kennedy 1965:33); and Cordelia Jackson Dunaway, who later taught at the Chinle Public School. Sybil Fry Wilson and HW left Chinle when their one child, a daughter, was small; first, they went to Gallup and then, to the Chilchinbito Trading Post. Later, they had a store north of Gallup. Both Jean Cousins (Cousins and Cousins 1996:27) and Margaret Garcia Delaney (p.c. 6/10/1997) have fond memories of visits to the Wilsons at their Chilchinbito store during their own childhoods. When Mary Shepardson worked with HW in 1958, he was serving as the sheriff of Gallup (Stewart 1980:81).

Tall Woman said HW used to call Seya "Boy Who Shouts," after his grandfather, her father. He knew her father, too, "probably from dancing at Nightways." SM, AS, and HM noted that HW was the father of Cecil, who later married AS. All said Cecil was known as Charles Lee, brother of the singer, Ed Lee Natay, "until he changed his name in the service." Cecil's census card lists HW (white) as his father, Son of the Late Little Blacksmith as his stepfather, and Charles Etsitty as another of his own names; no one is named on the card as his mother. AS said Cecil "never saw his mother but everybody knew she was light-complected"; Delaney (p.c. 6/10/1997), who remembers this woman, said she was beautiful, had many admirers, and a number of children before settling down with a doctor in Keams Canyon. Cecil (who was born in either 1921 or 1923) was raised by Mary Etsitty (born 1912) who also raised her sister, Alice Lee Etsitty. After a series of marriages (including one to Chee Carroll), Mary became the wife of Philemon Bitsui. The census records at Our Lady of Fatima Church show that Mary, Edward Lee Etsitty (born 1914), and Charley Lee Etsitty (born 1921) were the children of a woman recorded as *K'ééłxábaa'* no. 1 (or *K'ełhabaa'* no. 1) and the Son of the Late Little Blacksmith. Alice Lee Etsitty was born in 1927 to this woman and Harry James no. 1, also known as Frank Lee Etsitty, according to census records. The Son of the Late Little Blacksmith mentioned here was the *same* individual who was assigned as a peacemaker in Chinle, and with whom Frank spent much time in the early days of his marriage to Tall Woman. AS remembers seeing this man when she was very small; she said he was from the Crownpoint area, was "dark-complected," and "very outspoken."

6. Navajo footracing is among the games considered in Levy (1998:225–29); Maxwell and Nash (1993) examine it within the Navajo symbolic universe.

7. This still caused laughter for MD and AS during 1996 discussions. Both said piercing ears when births were difficult was an old practice. AS said when a boy is born now, some people say, "Here's another wino."* Tall Woman provides additional information on midwife practices later in the text.

8. According to SM, after coming back the first two summers he was at Fort Apache to help herd at home and for Uncles John and Jim, he started getting wagework jobs the school told students about. SM worked in fields in Colorado and in beet fields outside Kansas City the last two summers. He reported he earned $79 each paycheck and "sent half of the money home to Daddy each time, to help the family." His jobs, and the domestic ones Mary no. 2 held during the summers and AS had on weekends while in elementary school, are examples of the "outing principle" used in government schools at this time. See Frisbie (1996:157–59, 178 n. 15) for an introduction to this concept and appropriate literature.

9. Frank was not in "Redskin" but did appear in other films, including "Desert Song," wherein his brother, John, also participated (Mitchell 1978:306–7 n. 9, ff.). McKenna and Travis (1989:109) list ten movie or TV productions filmed between 1917 and 1987 at Canyon de Chelly that include footage of the Canyon and the Thunderbird; also see Kennedy (1965:34). Although *ciné* materials are not among those examined in Faris (1996), he, McPherson (1996), and Donovan (1997b) are among those interested in Navajos and the movie industry.

10. I finally saw "Redskin" during the Native Americas International Film Exposition in Santa Fe, New Mexico, 8/8–8/15/96. Information made available in the exposition program said that "Redskin," featuring Paramount star Richard Dix, was released in the United States in 1929. Victor Shertzinger directed the eighty-minute film, which was a "late silent movie," but one that used an optional Movietone music soundtrack. Its major novelty was that it was the first big film to be shot mainly on location in and around Canyon de Chelly, and to use Technicolor (but not entirely, despite the original plans). Like the 1926 Richard Dix film,

"The Vanishing American" (which was based on a Zane Grey novel), "Redskin" again portrayed the story of a Navajo man "caught between two cultures" but in a way Dix found closer to the realities of the plights of Native Americans. The film does include footage of the Thunderbird and Navajos riding in groups in the Canyon and around the store. For a number of years, the whereabouts of prints of "Redskin" were unknown; thus, it was only after its rediscovery in the early 1980s that it again became accessible at least to some viewers. The copy included in the 1996 exposition was a 35 mm. print preserved and made available by the Library of Congress, Washington, D.C.

11. Tall Woman said, "You use the root of this which usually is finger size, unless there's been a lot of rain; then it's larger. After digging it, you dry it out and grind it on the grinding stone. Then you mix it with water and sprinkle it around the hogan, ramada, corral, or other places to keep snakes away. It has a very strong smell, like mountain tobacco." Some family members continue to follow this practice in the present (1998). While no translation was provided for this plant's name, further information is available in Wyman and Harris (1941: 30, 43, 66) and Elmore (1943:92).

12. During the summer of 1963, electricity was brought to the Mitchells, at least temporarily, by the American Indian Films, Inc. group headed by Dr. Samuel Barrett, after Frank agreed to the filming of a *Kinaaldá* he was going to perform for his granddaughter, MS (see Frisbie 1967/1993). It was installed when the company finished filming a Red Antway in Valley Store and moved to the Mitchells' to film the Puberty Ceremony. Tall Woman remained opposed to its presence for quite some time; after the film company departed, the electric company announced its plan to remove the service. At that point, McAllester paid to make the installation permanent, and Tall Woman prevailed upon Frank to have it removed from the hogan and, instead, put into another structure on the premises. Later, others in the family, including RY, AS, and ID, arranged to have electricity brought into their dwellings. Thus, Tall Woman was exposed to it during her final days, after she was incapacitated by a stroke and started to live first with ID, and then AS. Until then, however, she continued to prefer to live by the sun, without electricity, and repeatedly said so.

13. When recording his own story, Frank (Mitchell 1978:286) wondered if his discussions with John about some sacred things at the wrong time of year the night before in the hogan had precipitated the snake's aberrant behavior. Frank (Mitchell 1978:290–92) also had a Navajo Windway and some other ceremonies because of killing this snake. As a curing ceremony, the Windway, *Nítch'ijí*, belongs to the Holyway group. As Tall Woman explains later in this chapter, there are two kinds, both of which she eventually had. The Navajo Windway, *Diné Binítch'ijí*, which has male and female branches, is usually done in a five-night version whereas the Chiricahua Apache Windway, *Chíshí Binítch'ijí*, is a brief, two-night ceremony perhaps originating during Fort Sumner days, if not earlier. Both kinds of Windways address illnesses attributed to all kinds of winds, snakes, lightning, and other factors which manifest themselves through stomach, eye, skin, heart, lung, and other troubles. See Wyman (1962), Kluckhohn and Wyman (1940:111–54), and Frisbie (1992), among others.

14. AS said when she came back she had a big scar on her left side by her waistband. AS has always wondered if maybe one of the "old style brass safety pins that were worn with sash belts might have opened up and caused a sore there which then didn't heal, and got infected." "Mary no. I took care of all the children and Frank helped with that, too, during this time."

15. In Chinle, priests began performing wedding cermonies for Navajos and recording

them on 12/12/1910. Records also show that headmen were witnessing marriages there in the 1910 decade. Those witnessed by Man Who Shouts begin in 1911 and end in 1919; in these records, his residence is listed variably as Chinle or Wheatfields (but the family says the latter location is an error). Among them are the marriages of his granddaughter, Gai, to Son of Yucca Fruit Man, on 11/24/1913, and perhaps another grandson, One Who Returns in Anger, at age eighteen, to Gray Girl, age sixteen and a half, on 12/11/1913. Given the lack of further identifying information in the records (see the church's *Liber Matrimoniorum*, marriages no. 30 and no. 31) and the fact that Man Who Shouts had one son and at least two grandsons who were called One Who Returns from the Warpath in Anger as one of their names, it is impossible to identify the man involved in the latter marriage with certainty. According to Father Blane Grein, O.F.M. (p.c. 5/30/1997), among the jobs of priests was that of Justice of the Peace for civil marriages; this function "stopped in the 1960s when the Tribe established JPs."

16. The *Liber Matrimoniorum* records (p. 3 no. 7) at Our Lady of Fatima Church in Chinle show Father Emanuel Trockur, O.F.M., married Mary Mitchell ("Asdzą́ Go Mitchell") and Woody Davis on 2/2/1927, with Frank serving as the sponsor. George Acey Davis's birthdate is recorded as 8/8/1926, and his baptismal date as 4/28/1928 (in the *Liber Defunctorum* book, p. 88 no. 7, when he died on 5/3/1986).

17. While illness and death from a variety of diseases were among the problems faced by children in the early government schools on the reservation (see Frisbie 1996), exactly what happened at the Chinle Boarding School at this time continues to be unknown to me. Perhaps answers could be found in the Fort Defiance Agency Letterbooks. (Formerly maintained in Window Rock, but then moved. On 11/13/1998, after a long search, I learned that some of these volumes were acquired by the University of California, Berkeley, Bancroft Library, while others were moved in 1972 to the National Archives and Records Administration-Pacific Region, Laguna Niguel, California. Thus, examining these records remains to be done.) There is no sign of any burials of Chinle Boarding School children in the *Liber Defunctorum* book maintained at Our Lady of Fatima Church, although the records for baptisms upon the completion of religious instruction (given at the school with the agent's approval) are clear. There were also some private baptisms, both at the school and at home, and in the first record book, *Baptismal Record and Burials* (9/12/1907–2/17/25), there are notations of baptisms of four Navajo school children (two girls, two boys, all eight to ten years old) "dangerously sick at the school" on 3/16, 3/17, and 4/5 in 1924, all of whom then died within a few days. However, the time period here, based on its relation to Mary no. 1 and Woody's church marriage and the described attempts of both Howard and Acey to "start sitting up" appears to be around March 1927. While other burials are recorded in the next volume for 1927, none are identifiable as school children either by age or name, and there are no Paulines among them. There is also nothing in the records to indicate a sudden rise in the numbers of burials handled by the priests. Given the cordial relationships among the Franciscans, the school, and the agent, documented and challenged by the Protestants associated with the "other church," the Presbyterian one "on the hill" established in Chinle in 1921 (Gray 1986), it seems likely that the priests would have been involved, had the school requested their services. The possibility of tractor-dug, mass graves comparable to those used during the flu epidemic, must be considered, especially given the lack of documentation at the Catholic Church and the fact that parents were not notified so they could claim the deceased and then follow their own cultural bur-

ial practices.

18. At a later time, Tall Woman said this statement referred to an incident involving SM. When he came home the first summer after starting at Fort Apache (1926), his parents hadn't even been told the school year was up and students were being dismissed. SM said the trader who had given him a ride dropped him off at Salina Springs because that's where he thought the family would be with the sheep. After "walking along a lot of washes," he finally met someone on horseback who said his family was down near Valley Store, at the place used later for sheep dipping. SM said, "When I finally got there, I really surprised people. I guess Mama and Daddy hadn't been informed by the school we were being let out. They didn't know I was coming. After they greeted me, Mama got very angry about how the school handled that." He added he heard his parents talking about it later, at night, and Tall Woman encouraging Frank to do something about those kinds of things at the schools since he was a headman. SM had first stopped at his Uncle Jim's place in Salina; some summers he or others herded sheep for Jim, and also Uncle John, since both had large flocks at the time. After learning where the family was and getting no offer of transportation, he walked on.

19. Tall Woman admonished me because of this belief in both 1967, when Frank died, and again, when I was working with her in 1971 and said I planned to visit the cemetery with some others in the family. In 1967, when she knew I was pregnant, she kept reminding me to stay away from cemeteries physically, and not even look out a window in the direction of the Chinle Community Cemetery. She also told me not to knit or crochet because that would make the umbilical cord wrap itself around the baby's neck, thereby strangling it.

20. While ch'iish actually means worms or maggots (Young and Morgan 1980:295), at least in Tall Woman's family, the term was used to refer to some kind of head cold that produces a runny nose, other signs of nasal infection, and facial swelling. In 1964, CS said that when the term was applied to a person's condition, it was commonly understood to imply a sinus infection.

21. See Mitchell (1978:143) for Frank's account of his own Shootingway, and Frisbie (1980a, 1980c, 1987) for discussions of how Navajo medicine people are evaluated, and how and why their reputations wax and wane.

22. No one in the family really knows what happened to Tall Woman at this point. Some of the medically trained people suggested "Bell's palsy," emphasizing that her symptoms matched, and noting that at least three of her grandchildren and one of her children had suffered from that and needed it surgically corrected. One of those holding this opinion suggested that Tall Woman might have had surgery to fix it and chosen not to mention it. As one of them said, "That Bell's palsy with its droopy eyelids seems to run in the family." Regardless of the cause, MD and RY clearly remembered their mother having this problem, its enduring nature, and its timing. The same was true for AS, who said the appearance of her mother's face and overhearing various discussions about it are among her earliest memories. MD's, RY's, and AS's accounts matched Tall Woman's description of symptoms, and the timing and sequence of ceremonies done for her. Unlike theirs, however, Frank's account (Mitchell 1978:129) places this problem and the resulting ceremonies much earlier in their marriage. The same is also true of the snakebite incidents; while Frank connected the first to an alfalfa-field accident as did Tall Woman, he said the second happened while she was nursing Mary no. 2, again putting the resulting ceremony much earlier in time (Mitchell 1978:285–87).

CHAPTER 14

1. The idea of starting Chapters, local community organizations established to enhance communication among Navajos, local and tribal leaders, officials from Washington, and others, is usually credited to John Hunter, superintendent of the Leupp Agency (7/1/1927–8/31/1928) and then the Southern Navajo Agency (1/1/1929–9/30/1934). Although begun in Leupp in 1927, many Chapters were disbanded before they became effective; during the 1932–50 period they became associated with stock reduction and range-management programs. After being revived in the late 1940s and early 1950s, they did start to reach their potential.

In the Chinle area, according to Greyeyes, Stewart's husband, a group known as the Chinle Chapter was organized in *1926* (Stewart 1980:69; Stewart 1988). The many people in attendance included Frank and John Mitchell and Old Curly Hair, all of whom spoke. Cactus Brown ran the meeting, which resulted in the following officers being elected to four-year terms: Hastiin Tah Tlishman, chairman; Jake Brown, vice chairman; and Phillip Draper, secretary. From 1926 until 1934, little is known about the Chapter, which was also known as the Canyon de Chelly Chapter and the Canyon del Muerto Chapter in its early days since both the sites and frequencies of meetings varied (Stewart 1980:69).

Among the issues this Chapter addressed in the 1930s were the ongoing discussions with the National Park Service about the National Monument created by Presidential Proclamation at Canyon de Chelly on 4/1/1931. Although the idea was initially approved by the members of the early Tribal Council (at a meeting at Fort Wingate on July 8, 1925), later some fifty to sixty local Navajos expressed concerns about boundaries and grazing rights and organized a petition to oppose it. CS, delegate for the Southern Navajo district, and Old Curly Hair, who was an alternate for the same district, spoke in opposition to the monument at the Council meeting on July 7–8, 1930. Both Frank and Old Curly Hair were among those who signed the 9/8/1930 petition, originally incorrectly attributed to two traders in Chinle at the time, Cozy McSparron and Hartley Seymour. After further explanation of the specifics at the Chinle Court Day on 10/2/1930, the petition was withdrawn and one in favor of the monument was substituted, after being signed by over 150 Navajos, including Frank. See Mitchell (1978:167 n. 33) and Brugge and Wilson (1976:8, 13–16, 22 ff.) for specifics. On Apr. 28, 1934, when the Chapter passed a resolution approving the presence of the National Park Service, the officers were: Hosteen Tonah, president; Jake Brown, vice president; and Dannie Bia, secretary. Tom Allen is listed as Chapter adviser (Brugge and Wilson 1976:22).

In the 1940s, records show that Frank Mitchell and John Gorman were Chapter officers in Chinle in 1944, and that at a 1948 meeting, where Joe Carroll was elected as the new Tribal Council delegate because of the resignation of the previous one, the following Chapter officers were elected: Thomas Attison, president; Harry Price, vice president; and Irene Stewart, secretary (Stewart 1980:55–57). Although the identities of the "top two" officers changed frequently, in part because of the criticism and lack of remuneration as noted by Shepardson (1963:94), Stewart held her post for fifteen years (1948–63), and Carroll was the Council delegate for sixteen. Frank Mitchell was president of the Chinle Chapter in 1951 and 1952, and also served as an officer (undesignated in available records) in 1955 (see Mitchell 1978:305–6 n. 5).

Stewart (1980:61, 83), Shepardson (1963:83–84, 93–97), and conversations with AS provide further information about Chapter meeting sites. According to Stewart (1980:61, 83), the "little house" built for the Chapter in the 1920s was taken back by the BIA and was being used as a schoolroom (in the late 1940s). Because of this, meeting places for the Chapter, before 1959, varied, and included a classroom and the old auditorium building at the Chinle Boarding School, Garcia's Trading Post, and, when the weather permitted, out in the open under the cottonwood trees at both Garcia's and the boarding school. AS confirmed these sites, adding that eventually, once a stage, basketball court, and other recreational facilities were created in the old auditorium, that space was in frequent demand and thus not often available for Chapter meetings. "At that point, meetings began to be held in a long, wooden building [originally surrounded by a barbed-wire fence with wooden posts] located west of the Chinle Boarding School auditorium, across the dirt road from the Post Office [the latter's fourth site], and underneath the [clay butte] hill." While this government building's original purpose was unknown to AS, she said that around 1942, the Chinle court started meeting there regularly. Perhaps this is the site Shepardson (1963:94) was referring to when noting that in 1954, the Chinle "Chapter House" was being used as "a schoolroom, a circuit court, and on Sundays, for the Mormon Church."

Much in need of space, Stewart (1980:61) says that in the 1950s, individuals were "in the process of completing one large room" of a permanent meeting place for the Chapter from old adobe bricks and logs obtained from "an old abandoned trading post which belonged to one of the traders" when the Tribal Council (in 1958) finally approved funds for new Chapter Houses on the reservation (see Young 1961:336–40). AS says this interim Chapter House, built in the early 1950s, was constructed close to, but south of the location of the new one built with tribal funds in 1958. In 1997, a warehouse and "garbage bins" occupied this site. As shown later in the text, the new Chinle Chapter House was dedicated on 6/20/1959, with Frank doing the House Blessing Ceremony (Mitchell 1978:239 n. 11) during other festivities described by Stewart (1980:83–84) and Shepardson (1963:96). This structure was replaced by another Chapter House in 1981 (still in use in 1998) and then demolished (see Chap. 20, n. 9).

Further information on the Chinle Chapter can be found in Shepardson (1963), Gray (1986), and Stewart (1980). Iverson (1981), Shepardson (1963), Williams (1970), Young (1961), and Mitchell (1978) are among the numerous sources for Navajo political developments. Bingham and Bingham (1976) and *Chapter Images* (Rodgers 1997) focus on Chapters. The latter, a study compiled and edited by Rodgers, and published "every four years or so" by the Navajo Nation's Division of Community Development, provides contemporary, statistical information on the 110 Chapters. Previous editions (Rodgers 1990, 1993) provide data from the late 1980s and early 1990s. As Donovan (1997a) and others indicate, to date the Navajo Nation continues to struggle with the thorny issue of correlating census data with comprehensive and accurate data on Chapter affiliations.

2. At a later time, Tall Woman elaborated on SM's love for Squaw Dances, saying that of course Frank had seen to it that both SM and HM received their warrior names at Enemyways when they were young. According to her, he also made the arrangements for both to participate in the *jashjini* portion (which was already becoming rare by 1965) and to have special friends with whom they would exchange gifts during their lives. Both SM and HM confirmed their mother's words and then shared still vivid recollections of their first Enemyways, as well as escapades at later ones. SM said his first was during the summer of 1933, right after he graduated

from high school; HM's was in the summer of 1942, after he had quit eighth grade in December 1941. MD, AgS, RY, and AS all confirmed that they were never allowed to go to Enemyways while growing up. RY frequently baby-sat for her mother's other children while Frank and Tall Woman went to them in their middle years, and MD, RY, and AS saw their first ones after they got married and went with their husbands. AS remembers being the only one in her high school Indian Club who "couldn't sing Squaw Dance Songs because [they] weren't allowed to do those things growing up."

3. Mitchell (1978:303 n. 3) indicates that Mary no. 2, after finishing at Fort Apache, went first to the Haskell Institute, Lawrence, Kansas [at an unknown date], and then transferred, upon the suggestion of Superintendent Reuben Perry, to the Albuquerque Indian School in 1929. SM clearly recalled the scolding he got at Phoenix (when the leaders stopped to see that school on their return trip), and from his mother for running away without notifying his parents. In 1989, he wished he "hadn't done things like that to worry my Mama and add to all her sufferings."

4. Father Berard Haile, O.F.M., (6/1/1874–9/30/1961), was a well-known scholar of Navajo language and ceremonialism during his work as a Franciscan missionary on the Navajo reservation from 1900 until he suffered a stroke in 1954. Before 1998, the sources providing brief accounts of his life and/or lists of his publications included *Padres' Trail* (1961), the *New Mexico Register* (1955b:50–51), the *Provincial Chronicle* (1962), Powell (1961), and the Franciscan Fathers (1949). While Tall Woman's manuscript was being prepared for publication, I learned of another work nearing completion that concerned Father Berard (Grantner p.c. 2/8/1997; Bodo p.c. 3/3/1997). In 1998, Father Murray Bodo, O.F.M., of Cincinnati published the results of his four-year project, editing and annotating the tapes Father Berard made while hospitalized during his final seven years (Bodo 1998). Therein, Father Berard gives *'Endishodi Yazzie* [The Little Priest] as his Navajo name (Bodo 1998:7). Antram (1998:57–59) gives other information on Father Berard, while citing *ee'niishoodii* (p. 39), *edneeshoodee* (p. 9), and *Ednishodi* (p. 121) [He Who Drags the Garment, One Who Wears a Long Gown or Garment] as the Navajo names for Franciscans. The spelling *Ee'neishoodi* was used in the pamphlet produced at St. Michaels in 1997 in conjunction with the Franciscan Centennial Celebration which culminated in October 1998. Therein, the names for the early "Big Four" priests were given as: *Ee'neishoodi Yazhi*, Little Priest—Father Berard Haile, O.F.M.; *Ee'neishoodi Nez*, Tall Priest—Father Marcellus Troester, O.F.M.; *Ee'neishoodi Tsoh*, Chubby Priest—Father Leopold Ostermann, O.F.M.; and *Ee'neishoodi Chischili*, Curly Hair Priest—Father Anselm Weber, O.F.M.

5. As a close friend, clan uncle of Frank's, headman for Frazier's/Valley Store, and as a Blessingway singer, Curly Hair appears frequently in Tall Woman's narrative as well as in Frank's. Within the family he was known by a variety of other names including Curly Hair Water Flows Together Man, Old Curly Hair, Old Curly, and Water Flows Together Man Curly Hair; in Mitchell (1978), Frank preferred Two Streams Meet Curly as the translation for the clan name. As noted earlier, the families visited each other frequently, despite changing locations during the years. As shown in subsequent chapters, Tall Woman's mother also visited them frequently in her old age, traveling to Nazlini with one of her granddaughters along for company. Curly Hair's wife, Horse Woman, another Towering House woman, gave Tall Woman one of her grillstones for making paperbread when she "got up in her years." She and her husband were the parents of Sherman, Joe, and Chee Carroll as well as

others, such as Carmelita; Sherman and Chee learned the Blessingway from their father, and Chee was at one time married to Cecil S.'s half sisters, first Mary and then Alice. As a "Chapter officer," Frank was involved in settling the land dispute resulting from Horse Woman's death. The dispute was heard at the Salina Springs Chapter and settled on 7/1/1944 (see Mitchell 1978:305 n. 5). Records at the Our Lady of Fatima Church show that Curly Hair died on 9/20/1941 at the age of seventy-one and was buried by Father Francis Borgman, O.F.M., in the cemetery at the foot of the hill near the present National Park Service headquarters at the entrance to Canyon de Chelly. His wife, C no. 67537, died on 6/10/1944 and was buried in the same cemetery, again in an unmarked grave, but "by the family instead of priests because her children preferred to do it that way."

Frank (Mitchell 1978:68) says Curly Hair named him "Big School Boy" after Charlie Mitchell, another headman and clan relative, who died on 7/15/1932 and whose death was investigated by both of them and others (Mitchell 1978:245–56, 274–75 n. 5). Although Tall Woman's children called Curly Hair "Grandpa" because of his clan relationship to Frank, as noted earlier, SM was afraid of him during his childhood. AS also remembers being afraid of him when he came to the Chinle Boarding School to lecture children on correct behavior during her elementary school days. Numerous people remembered his deep, big, very loud voice, his "white hair that was really curly," and his long moustache that "curled up." Mitchell (1978: 245–56, 274–75 n. 5) himself documents this man's temper, how he yelled and minced no words, and how his eyes "popped out of his head" when he got angry. Called River Junction Curly by Father Berard, Old Curly Hair was one of the three who recorded Blessingway accounts for the priest, which were eventually published (Wyman 1970a). He was also among those opposed to excavations in the Canyon, and as a leader from the "lower Chinle Valley," among those proposed (unsuccessfully) for the Constitutional Assembly (Mitchell 1978:151, 276 n. 8). For further information, see Mitchell (1978) and literature on Father Berard Haile, O.F.M., Navajo headmen, and St. Michaels Mission.

6. Tall Woman is referring to Wyman (1970a) wherein the Blessingway materials collected by Haile were finally published. As shown in Mitchell (1978: 245 ff.), Frank worked with Father Berard in the early 1930s. Two of the holograph notebooks give 1930 as the date, but Haile gave 1932 as the date in his Introduction to Version II of Blessingway (Wyman 1970a:xxiii). The process of securing support for the publication, first through Tribal Council approval (given on 3/4/1954) and then, funding, is documented in Wyman (1970a), Mitchell (1978), and Bodo (1998:126, 211–15). To this day, the family remains proud of Frank's contribution to this publication; his version appears in Wyman (1970a:343–492) as Version II; Mitchell (1978) includes a condensation of parts of the same materials. Comparisons of the three versions are available in a variety of sources, including Levy (1998).

7. Frank (Mitchell 1978:201–6, 209 n. 3), when discussing these trips, says he went on all but the first one, and that CS was the driver only for that trip. While Frank says the trips started around 1925, other sources (Haile 1938:66; and Wyman 1970a:18–20) give 9/18/1932 as the date of the first trip.

8. The *Liber Defunctorum* records at Our Lady of Fatima Church (Vol. 1 [1907–1940], p. 16 no. 9), show that Mary Rose Mitchell (born 1910, who was baptized "Clara" on 5/30/1920 and made her first communion on 6/13/1920) died on 1/15/1931 and was buried in the cemetery at the mission on 1/16/1931. Another set of records with the same title (p. 6 no. 3) list her as Mary Mitchell, daughter of Frank Mitchell and the "daughter of Hosteen

Dilawushy," and indicate she was born ca. 1911, died two miles north of the mission on 1/15/1931, and was buried on the following day by Father "Remy" [Remigius] Austing, O.F.M.

9. In the 1960s, a copy of Frank's letter to Reuben Perry, superintendent of the Albuquerque Indian School, written on 2/9/1931 with a priest's help, was among the "Old Chronicles—Daily" records at Our Lady of Fatima Church in Chinle. It is reproduced in Mitchell (1978:303–4) along with a letter that John Hunter, superintendent of the Southern Navajo Agency, sent to Perry on 2/24/1931, in response to Perry's notice to Hunter about the event. A meeting apparently was scheduled in Chinle for 3/9/1931 by Hunter and Perry, although I have found no further documentation thereof. CS interpreted for the meeting and according to Frank, Perry apologized (Mitchell 1978:283).

10. See Frisbie (1996) for an overview of trends in Western education on the reservation, and an introduction to the extensive literature. As shown therein, even though more Navajos were in favor of such education by the 1930s, attitudes were still mixed. Schools were overcrowded and even when the federal government started building day schools, for decades there still weren't enough places. Appendix C summarizes what could be learned about the Western education experiences of eight individuals in Tall Woman's narrative: Sam Sanishya, Mary no. 2, Seya, Agnes, Pauline, Garnett Scott, Howard, and Augusta.

11. AS, AgS, HM, and MD also provided accounts of this event based on what they saw and heard at home, and what they eventually heard from people who knew Mary no. 2 at the Albuquerque Indian School. The latter group reportedly said Mary no. 2 was "a very, very smart woman. She was always outstanding and always was given the best choices on things. I guess that's the reason she was hired by a Mexican family. She worked for them and traveled with them to Mexico and all over; they traveled to lots of places and Mary went with them all the time. That's probably how she got into this dope business. Maybe that family was using it too, before they even went there."

Being at home, they knew Mary no. 2 was moved outside near the end, according to custom. "Her little shelter was built on the other side of [MD's], where the ditch goes; they carried her over there, across the ditch, and that's where she passed away. She was still unconscious and thrashing around, out of her mind, when they took her over there." They also remembered how angry Frank was over the event, and that he had "really thrown that superintendent around during the meeting they had about that." They added that Tall Woman told them when the school brought Mary no. 2 back, "all she wanted, all she could imagine, was cigarettes, the kind with the dope smoke. She didn't know where she was or what was going on. All she would say was 'Give me that smoke that's right there; I can see it. Give me that smoke.'" MD said Frank told them when people smoke marijuana or things like that, it affects them that way. He also said if the school had notified them earlier, there *was* something they could have done for her. "Even now [1997], we have a ceremony that was used way back to help with that. Even now that can be performed for people on dope." ID said, "They combine that with a Sweathouse Ceremony for two days and smoke mountain tobacco both days. It's called *Mą'ii ná'ooljil*; it's used when people go crazy like coyotes or dogs with rabies." MD said this was the ceremony they started trying to do for Mary no. 2 but it didn't work. "It was already too late. That only helps patients if they've just started smoking those things; then it can cure them." Another family member said, "I don't know if anyone still performs that now, but I hope so; dope certainly is on the increase."

12. CS insisted that Mary no. 2 died from spinal meningitis, having lost a child the same way (Mitchell 1978:303 n. 3). Records at Our Lady of Fatima Church indicate that this disease was not rare, at least in the Chinle area from 1910 to 1945.

13. These ways of speaking were viewed as very respectful, friendly, loving, and special. They were preferred and highly admired. For another example, see Ashie Tsosie's comments in Johnson (1977a:119).

14. Some people use Lightningway and Shootingway as synonyms when referring to the Shootingway curing ceremony described earlier.

15. Both this story and the earlier one, wherein Frank accused Tall Woman of infidelity, were well known in the family where they're viewed as examples of Frank's foolishness and running around in his younger days. Later in life, when he was preaching about marriage and how to live as a couple to his children, he himself made sure they knew what he had done in both instances, using his behaviors here as examples of how *not* to act.

CHAPTER 15

1. As noted in the Introduction, this is one of the places where Tall Woman talked in a topical "chunk," or extensively about a single topic. This chapter, which covers activities ongoing from 1922 through 1934, is simultaneous with Chaps. 12–14 as well as the first part of Chap. 16.

2. Frank (Mitchell 1978:283–84) also mentioned this habit of his mother-in-law's, as well as her love for tomatoes; the latter was characteristic of many of the People before World War II, according to Wagner (1997:13, 24–25).

3. Another example Tall Woman gave me later was Spider Woman. She said sometimes the People tell children Spider Woman eats naughty children, after catching and hauling them to the top of her rock (Spider Rock) in the Canyon. While I never heard her do this, within the family over the years I did hear threats involving Wolf Man, skunks, mountain lions, and the bogeyman.

4. Tall Woman was afraid of swimming, even when I took her grandchildren swimming and on picnics at Many Farms Lake in the 1960s. Seya learned at Fort Apache and taught his brothers and sisters; they swam at the place mentioned here, and also at a swimming hole in the Chinle Wash behind the Presbyterian Church, which was created when the tailgate and irrigation system were put there to channel water from the Canyon to farms farther north.

5. While only briefly mentioned in Van Valkenburgh (1941:39, where his last name is given as Dunnaway), more information about Dick Dunaway is now available. One source is Cousins and Cousins (1996:2, 25, 26 ff.) for reasons clarified below. Dick, whose real name is given as Nobel, is described (Cousins and Cousins 1996: 25, 26) as a middle-aged bachelor (in 1925) who was employed in the government reclamation department, and was also the windmill tender. Documentation accompanying Leo Mark Studer's unpublished photographs (which include some of the Dunaway home across from Garcia's in 1922 or 1923) notes that Dunaway, who owned a Dodge auto later owned by Camillo Garcia, "had charge of the windmills for a certain area, and had a Navajo helper. Dunaway worked under Mr. Womack, Indian Service Bureau of Reclamation, who lived at Polacca on the Hopi Reservation."

According to SM, Dunaway "was a small, hunchbacked, old man with long whiskers who worked for the Indian Service checking windmills. His area of responsibility started by the Catholic Church and then came down the road [mentioned here] and went all the way to

Kayenta." He carried a tent, windmill parts, food, and a bedroll in his wagon; that was pulled by four mules. "It took him a month to check the windmills between Chinle and Kayenta, and then he'd come back the same way." SM added that Dunaway always teased any children near the road, and was always singing a song he made up as he traveled. SM recorded it; its words were "Dicky, Dicky, Dicky, D I C K." "The grownups really liked him and used to fool around with him, teasing and joking, at Garcia's. But kids always ran and hid when they heard or saw him coming, when I was small.*"

According to Margaret Garcia Delaney (p.c. 6/10/1997), Cordelia Jackson was a teacher first at the Chinle Boarding School (1925–28) and then at the public school there (1928–30), working in a one-room school (shown in the left foreground of St. Michaels Archive Negative C539.9–1, R112) before the public school was moved to a separate building east of the boarding school on the hill. (In 1997, that building, while still extant, was boarded up and condemned.) After "Cordie" married Dick in 1928, he became the stepfather of Jean, who married Bill Cousins in 1934 and then set up housekeeping for a short time upstairs in the Big House, which the Cousins (Cousins and Cousins 1996:77) say was then owned by Cozy McSparron (see Frisbie 1998). Dick and Cordie lived across the road from Garcia's Trading Post, in Dick's stone house which he soon enlarged. The government gave him a truck to use in his job in 1930 (Cousins and Cousins 1996:26). SM said that at that point, Dick also got two boys as helpers, Raymond Walker and Billy Bia. Dick and Cordie, who never had any children together, were still in Chinle in August 1938 when, for one month, Bill Cousins worked at Garcia's before moving to Wide Ruins with the Lippincotts (Cousins and Cousins 1996: 104–7). However, they eventually moved to California early in the 1940s (Cousins and Cousins 1996:147).

6. When people went to the store, they walked close to the Chinle Wash where there were a few trees, rather than on the dirt road. That "trail" came out by the "Presbyterian Hill" above Garcia's. It still does, although in 1992 a Holiday Inn was erected on the earlier site of Garcia's Trading Post, which closed in December 1985 or early 1986 (see Frisbie 1998:81).

7. Memories of the Old Owl Man still brought laughter in 1996–97. As one of Tall Woman's children said when learning about this during the project, "We should've paid attention to who was driving the wagon, instead of running away every time we saw it coming from the north. Obviously that man must have been riding in the back for a long time, and just having his daughter and her husband take him to the store or wherever he wanted to go because he was so crippled." Census information at Our Lady of Fatima Church shows there was a community member with the name Owl Man who was married to a Salt clanswoman and lived in the Chinle Valley. Family members also said GB's father was another person who scared them, especially HM, who'd always run and hide, most often in the ditch, when he was known to be approaching. No one knew why.

8. Her mother boiled them first, drained off the juice, and then sun-dried them. Tall Woman herself just washed them off to remove the stickiness before sun-drying them. Both made mush from them in the winter by boiling them with water and adding a white clay called *nomasi dleesh* (*nímasii dleesh*) to remove the bitter, tart taste of some of the berries they picked. The result was eaten in a variety of ways, both by itself and with other foods.

9. Many times during my work with Tall Woman, I heard her explaining such things to grandchildren who asked. She also told them many things about earlier times and events important in both tribal and local history.

CHAPTER 16

1. These public works programs characterized Franklin D. Roosevelt's presidency, which started in 1933, and the New Deal era, and were implemented on the reservation after John Collier became the Indian commissioner. Among the programs were those associated with the Civilian Conservation Corps (CCC), the Emergency Conservation Works (ECW), the Soil Conservation Service (Erosion Control) (SCS), and after 1935, the Agricultural Adjustment Administration, the BIA Extension Service, and the Works Progress Administration (WPA). Although the Indian Service had made earlier efforts to install wells and windmills in the 1920s, which in some areas were preceded by individual or group irrigation efforts, the New Deal programs focused on construction of dams, windmills, irrigation ditches, water reservoirs and storage tanks, deep wells with pumps, road grading (including the WPA project of grading the road west of Chinle) and later, on range management, prairie-dog poisoning, improvement of livestock breeding, and so on. Brugge and Wilson (1976: 286) note that the first major erosion-control efforts in the Canyon de Chelly area were made in 1930. A total of twenty-five CCC camps were located on the reservation, and at least one of them was in Chinle. The programs helped alleviate the disastrous socioeconomic impact of the national Depression while also starting the trend toward wage economics on the reservation. Other employment opportunities of the period included summer farmwork in Utah, Arizona, California, and elsewhere, and work on the railroads. By the late 1930s, however, half of the workers on the New Deal programs had been laid off, and when the United States entered World War II on 12/7/1941, the programs came to an end. After that, in addition to military service (1941–45), Chinle Navajos also worked in defense plants and munitions depots, especially those at Fort Wingate and Bellemont, near Flagstaff, but also in Barstow, California. Other sources of employment in Chinle included jobs at the clinic, the school, the National Park Service, the BIA offices, and a few positions at the trading posts and missions. Among the sources for this time period and these programs are Iverson (1981), Bailey and Bailey (1986), Parman (1976), Young (1961, 1968), and Underhill (1953, 1956). More personal information can be found in both Mitchell (1978) and Greenberg and Greenberg (1984).

2. This place also appears later in Tall Woman's narrative. There are numerous stories associated with Moaning Lake, also called Roaring or Groaning Lake, and among the appropriate framing references are those concerned with sacred places and identified earlier (see Introduction). USGS Maps give the name as *Toh di Niihe*, and the same has been adopted by the Navajo Nation's Historic Preservation Department, along with the translation, Moaning Lake. In Van Valkenburgh (1941:8–9; 1974:164) and Young and Morgan (1980:827), the name assigned to this place is *Be'ak'id Hatsoh* [Big Lake].

The Mitchells translate the name as "something that makes a sound, a noise," and "water that roars, water that has that roaring thing in it." Both Frank and Tall Woman talked about this place a lot, wondering what was making the sounds people long ago always heard coming from the lake. Tall Woman told her children a long time ago the lake was where some kind of monster was seen. For a long time, people heard moaning noises coming from the water, but couldn't see anything in there. And then finally someone reported seeing something coming out, some kind of big, long monster never seen before. When she and Frank were small, they were always told something huge lived over there, maybe even in the rocks, and that some people thought maybe it was some kind of four-legged reptile, or maybe a snake, or maybe even a "hippopotamus" [*tééhoołtsódii*—mythological monster (Young and Morgan 1980:916)] that was moaning in that lake. She and Frank referred to the place as "Something that catches you from underneath the Water." To this day, the area is associated with some version of this narrative. Some narratives or references therein can be found in the NNHPD confidential file in Window Rock, Cultural Resources Compliance and Traditional Culture Sections; others are known in families who have had contact with this area for one or more reasons.

The lake was huge while AS was in elementary school in Chinle. According to her, Father Anselm (Sippel, O.F.M.) used to take children and interested others over there with him in the winter in the mission truck to go ice skating, since he was a *good* skater. The Mitchells said the lake started drying up in the 1940s; after that, tamarisks planted by the SCS in the late 1930s took over; the lake was reportedly all gone by the early 1960s, leaving just a green place. Among the other meanings the area has for the Mitchells is that of it being a place with "little water, a little pond" in the 1940s, when ID, RY, and AS would individually go there with their mother on horseback to visit relatives and sometimes, to get a sheep given to Frank for a Blessingway he had finished. They also frequently went on horseback or in the wagon to different places in the area where they gathered berries and *tł'ohdeeí* seeds.

SM and WD worked on the dam built there by the ECW; SM said this was his first job after finishing high school, that Reid Winney was his foreman, and that occasionally Mr. Young (possiblyLyle) came out from Fort Defiance to check on their progress and update crew orders. SM also said when he and WD started working there, it had really been raining a lot; water was running down the Cottonwood Wash and all over the flats. So they told the men to stop and unharness their teams. Once the flats were flooded, "all the prairie dogs living there started popping out of their holes, just like they do when you pour water down there." They started grabbing them, and in no time had twenty-eight. They cooked those right in the tents where they were staying while they worked there, and ate them all up. When he told his mother about this when he came home for the weekend, she laughed and said, "Where are the prairie dogs you caught for us?" Later they also worked on SCS programs that "poisoned the prairie dogs that were taking over the reservation," and improved sheep and cattle breeding by setting up testing places at Frazier's (Valley Store), Nazlini, Sagebrush Flat, and other areas. They even tried to improve farms in Chinle and Valley Store, but that failed. There were also programs for building roads, irrigation ditches and windmills, and other things, too, like the dam at Many Farms Lake. SM and WD were among the workers for the latter project. According to SM, "The government decided to build a dam across the two hills and make a lake where the water came through there into the wash. It took us five or six months and we used lots of dump trucks for hauling rock and sand, and tractors, too. It was dusty all the time down there.*"

3. SM said Chinle had several earthquakes during the summer of 1933, right after he finished high school.

4. In the early 1930s, range-management efforts were focused on new ways to dip sheep to remove scabies and new ways of shearing. The first efforts at stock reduction were voluntary; Brugge and Wilson (1976) report that during the winter of 1933–34, the emphasis was on reducing sheep, and in the summer and fall of 1934, on sheep and goats. Studies of conditions on the reservation were done between 1933 and 1935, leading to the plan of establishing

land-management districts, also known as land-management units and grazing districts. Chinle became District 10 when these were established in 1936, the same year that saw the end of voluntary stock reduction. Between 1937 and 1941, reduction was systematic and enforced, in part by range riders who were established in 1937. The livestock surveys done in 1937 became the basis for establishing the "sheep permits" that went into effect in 1940. One sheep equaled one goat; four sheep equaled one cow, and five sheep equaled one horse.

The literature on the stock reduction is extensive; Aberle (1966) gives an excellent, detailed account of its different phases. Additional information is available in Bailey and Bailey (1986) and Boyce (1974), among others. Roessel and Johnson (1974) provide a poignant collection of the deeply painful Navajo memories of this time, which many viewed as a disgrace and disaster second only to the Long Walk and the days of incarceration at Fort Sumner. For people in Tall Woman's generation, the memories of the stock reduction were still fresh and painful in the 1970s. In Mitchell (1978), Frank's account of this time period is interwoven with information about the Constitutional Assembly since while he served with that group (4/5/1937–11/8/1938) he was put on the Grazing Committee, the Executive Committee, and the Constitution Committee. According to him, attempts at developing a Navajo Constitution (in accordance with the 1934 Indian Reorganization Act, or IRA), planning a trip to Washington, D.C. (which began on June 17, 1937, and in which he participated), and constant discussions of the traumas of enforcing the required stock reduction consumed most of their meetings (Mitchell 1978:257–60, 275–77 n. 8, ff.). Greenberg and Greenberg (1984) also include information on the Chinle area at this time since Carl Gorman [CG] worked for the SCS and as an interpreter, trying to explain the government's stock reduction plans to the People, until 1941. Brugge and Wilson (1976) provide other information for the Chinle-Canyon de Chelly area at the time, showing that a survey of vegetation in Canyon de Chelly was done in 1934. In 1936, the Soil Erosion Service introduced "exotic" plants, including Australian tamarisks, willows, and cottonwoods. The Indian Service was selling apple, plum, and peach trees to the Navajos in the area, and also planting grapevines, Chinese elms, and mulberry trees; the same source also documents the CCC projects in the Canyon through 1941. A letter from Reuben Perry to the Commissioner of Indian Affairs in Washington, D.C., dated *2/24/1905*, indicates that much earlier in time, and when Perry was buying fruit trees for planting at the Fort Defiance School, he suggested furnishing both apple and peach trees to the Canyon de Chelly and Nazlini areas, both of which he found suitable for such endeavors (Correll n.d.).

5. SM was the one who had to inform his parents about the number of animals they would be allowed with the permit system, that is, ten sheep. Frank (Mitchell 1978:259) confirms this and also says that the restriction to so few sheep was one of the reasons he could never be a stockman (1978:259–60). Other significant reasons, of course, were his preference for horses and the fact that he was so rarely home during this period.

6. Here, Tall Woman is mentioning various places important in the early days of tribal government and the locations of early Tribal Council meetings, before Window Rock became the "capital" under Chee Dodge. In 1996, MD, when remembering the stock reduction times, said, "Many women really had no idea what was going on then; they were just told they had to cut back. All they were told was that it had to do with Washington and John Collier. But, in our family, we knew more about those things because our father was one of the leaders at that time and used to talk to us about it."

7. At least in the 1930s and 1940s, there was a place in the Chinle Wash, north of where it passed by the Presbyterian Church and north of Black Water, where the Wash divided and waters flowed around a piece of land covered with reeds. This place was called "Land in Between the Waters" and "The Island Place" by Tall Woman and her family. Frank irrigated his fields from the western most branch of this Wash. Later, this branch dried up and its bed filled with sand, leaving no sign of any island by 1997.

8. As noted earlier, Little Woman, Garnett's maternal grandmother, may have died at Houses Standing in a Line; she was deceased by the time of Gai's marriage in 1913. Garnett never saw her.

9. As shown in Appendix A, Adelle Brown was first married to Carl Gorman [CG] on 12/19/1930 (*Liber Matrimoniorum*, p. 2 no. 1, Our Lady of Fatima Church). CG (Greenberg and Greenberg 1984:45–46, 54) mentions troubles with this marriage, which officially ended when he requested a divorce from one of the tribal judges. GB said that during summers at this time, "Don [born in 1938] and Donna Mae [born in 1939] were very small; R. C., the first born, was mostly with his Dad or his maternal grandmother." Tall Woman said Adelle was the daughter of Woman from the Red Rock Canyon (Red Rocks Woman) and John Brown, the policeman. According to Tall Woman, "Shortly after R. C. was born [7/26/1931], his father got busy working, furthering himself with education, and other things, and he and his wife drifted apart. Seya told us Carl had left Adelle and asked him to take care of R. C. After that, I guess the two of them got together." Tall Woman viewed R. C. and ID as "twins," since they were born within a year of each other. Other information is also available in (R. C.) Gorman (1992) and Mitchell (1978). While R. C. (Gorman 1992) never mentions SM, he notes (p. 23) that he stayed with his mother when his parents divorced when he "was about 12." His own close ties with Adelle are apparent in his text, which includes (p. 46) a colored photograph he took of her. In Mitchell (1978), the biological parentage of Don and Donna Mae was mistakenly attributed to SM, and Michael Melvin was thought to be two children, the first of whom was attributed to SM and the second to CG, because the editors did not fully understand the situation at the time. Apologies were made to all concerned upon discovery of the error, which is corrected here in Appendix A (and also clarified in CG's story [Greenberg and Greenberg 1984] and R. C.'s text [Gorman 1992:13]). SM said his first experience with childbirth was when Adelle [AM] gave birth to her first daughter. They were living upstairs at the Big House at the time, and SM tried to assist (see Frisbie 1998).

10. According to SM, the Mr. Young who was supervising the work on the dam at Moaning Lake notified him, at the end of December 1933, that he had been chosen to go to "Leader School." (My search for documentation of the "Leader School," to which SM assigned two different locations in 1989 and 1996 discussions, was futile; it remains unclear whether or not it was another of the SCS or CCC projects.) SM got WD to fill in on his other job since he was given almost no notice and had to leave the next morning. Mr. Garcia helped him assemble clothes and other things that night and Frank took him in the wagon up to the mission the next morning, as required. With Young's direction, four truckloads of men then traveled through Sawmill to Cameron (or Leupp). SM said the "Leader School" lasted until May and then graduates were required to go to other communities to teach what they had learned. In Cameron (or Leupp), participants lived in tents behind the trading post; subjects changed every two weeks and white instructors from Fort Defiance

taught numerous things, including: erosion control, range management, farm and orchard planting, well drilling, trail building, road surveying, welding, making telephone lines, castrating animals, and other skills. Upon "graduation," SM said he taught in Lukachukai from May until October (1934). Then he was hired to work in the dairy in Chinle that Mr. Maxwell was operating on the site where the Chapter House was built in 1958; by then, the dairy had been demolished. At the dairy, SM employed skills learned at Fort Apache, feeding cows and milking by hand.

11. In the 1930s, SM worked for three years as a fireman at the boiler plant at the Chinle Boarding School (while living upstairs at the Big House), and evidently simultaneously driving one of Notah Tayah's two coal trucks, after Notah took over the coal-hauling business and trucks from Wallace Gorman. The latter had a partnership with his older brother, CG, and both hauled coal on contract for government schools in the area (Greenberg and Greenberg 1984:46; Cousins and Cousins 1996:71). SM did the same, delivering coal to schools in a wide area around Chinle until he started working as a coach and boys' advisor at St. Michaels school in 1939. After that, SM continued to help Notah when he was available, both before and after his job in Barstow, California (10/1941–5/1942), until he and his family left for Bellemont in 1943.

SM said, "Coal was first hauled in wagons from a small mine called Salina Coal Mine, the other side of Salina store, in those mountains. Later the miners moved to Blue Gap, but that mine wasn't open too long. The next mine they opened was on the left side of the road toward Pinon; that was the Black Mountain Coal Mine. That was the big one and that's where I worked. Notah Tayah and I hauled to power houses at schools in Lukachukai, Chinle, Rough Rock, Nazlini, Round Rock, and Dennehotsoh." Discussions with Kelley (p.c.2/9/1997) indicated that SM's accounts of these mines provided somewhat earlier data than those in available archaeological reports. Chinle No. 2 or Balakai Mine (NNCRMP-86–300), six miles south of Salina, and started in 1950 by Notah Tayah (Kelley 1986b), is probably a later use of SM's Salina Coal Mine; Chinle No. 1 Mine (NNCRMP-86–301, AZ-I-64–3), in operation near Blue Gap from 1932 until 1955, is probably SM's Black Mountain Coal Mine (Kelley 1987a). SM also said when he was a student at Chinle, the school was burning wood; everybody helped haul it from the mountains around Tsaile using a wagon trail that went across the Chinle Wash. SM helped Frank haul wood for the school when he got older; they brought in wet wood and sold it for $5 a cord. Then the cost went up. According to SM, the Chinle Boarding School converted to coal sometime between 1925 and 1935; HM and AS said it was probably either in 1936 or 1937.

During this time, SM was also working at the Annunciation Mission in Chinle, as his mother said, with Brother Gotthard Schmidt, O.F.M., who arrived there on 4/21/1934, with Father Anselm Sippel, O.F.M., to replace Father Odwin Hudiburg, O.F.M., who was there between 1932 and 1934. SM helped Brother Gotthard, a lay Brother whom Navajos called "The Happy One" (Antram 1998:107–9), with the chickens. This Brother served as a cook and maintenance man, but was best known for other jobs as the mail carrier and as a poultry farmer. The mail duties included driving the mail truck three times a week in round trips between Chinle and Ganado (*Padres' Trail* 1959:5–6). Brother Schmidt, O.F.M., remained at the Annunciation Mission until 7/27/1952, when he was transferred to St. Michaels (Hetteberg p.c. 6/30/1998; House Chronicle for 1952, Annunciation Mission; *New Mexico Register* 1955a:26). SM also helped "Father Silver" (Father Silverius Meyer, O.F.M.;

see Antram 1998: 87–88, 104–7) by interpreting during religious instructions. However, he said the official interpreter for the mission, and the one who lived in the interpreter's house (at least in the 1939–41 period) was a man by the name of Tsohi Mitchell, a relative of Frank's from Tohatchi. SM said sometimes he, too, stayed with Tsohi. The latter evidently succeeded Joe Carroll; the church's House Chronicle only shows that Carroll was hired on 6/21/1934 to succeed John Foley who had interpreted for the church for a long time, finally resigning on 6/11/1934 to take a job with the SCS in "Frazers" (Frazier's, later called Valley Store).

12. Records at Our Lady of Fatima Church in Chinle show that the cemetery located at a distance west and behind the Annunciation Mission (designated with "Chin Lee" in the records) was used regularly until 11//11/1935, when Father Anselm Sippel, O.F.M., officiated at a burial in ground "across the wash" (*Liber Defunctorum* p. 10 no. 4). Discussions with Father Blane Grein, O.F.M. (p.c. 11/3/1996) suggested this was the name the priests gave to the cemetery at the foot of the hill where the National Park Service Headquarters was built. Beautiful Woman's burial, however, predates the official Catholic Church use of this area and is also not recorded in church records, possibly because Brother Gotthard, rather than a priest, assisted. The records suggest that from 11/11/1935 until 3/30/1946, most Catholic Church burials used the area "across the wash," most likely because the earlier cemetery was full, as Tall Woman suggests. However, exceptions were evidently possible since DM was buried in the cemetery behind the Annunciation Mission on 8/21/1938.

Brugge and Wilson (1976:106, 157, 159, 180, 181) provide some data on this "across the wash" cemetery, a cemetery not included in Jett (1996). Its location was among the concerns of local Navajos during the establishment of the National Monument, its offices, and campground. Although offices were built in 1936, camping facilities were not immediately installed. Visitors to Canyon de Chelly started camping there in June 1955, even though the NPS campground was still under preparation (Brugge and Wilson 1976:77, 131). The cemetery was fenced for protection; in 1996, only two markers were visible from the highway. At the end of March 1946, the Chinle Community Cemetery, which is still in use now (1998) was evidently opened; records at Our Lady of Fatima Church (*Liber Defunctorum* p. 32 no. 8) indicate that Fathers Mark (Sandford, O.F.M.) and Silver (Silverius Meyer, O.F.M.) used it for the first time for a Catholic burial on 3/30/1946, henceforth ending the church's use of the area across the Chinle Wash.

13. As noted earlier, the death of ten-day-old Mary, GB's first sister, in 1924 is recorded in Catholic Church records. There are no other notations concerning the Scott family until that indicating the death of the two-year-old son of Tom and Beautiful Woman, Nicholas Scott, on 7/5/1935 (the same day he was baptized [*Liber Baptismorum* Vol. 1, p. 72 no. 8]). He was buried the next day by Father Anselm Sippel, O.F.M., in the cemetery behind the Annunciation Mission. Church records (*Liber Defunctorum* p. 9 no. 5) show this boy's mother, Beautiful Woman (Zonnie Scott) was already deceased when Nicholas died, although there are no Catholic Church records of her death and burial.

14. See Gray (1986) for a history of the Presbyterians in Chinle. When GB was living with Tall Woman and Frank, Rev. and Mrs. Charles Bysegger were at the church; a year after they left in 1952 (having served since 1924), they were followed, on 6/15/1953, by Rev. and Mrs. Joseph Gray.

15. Indeed they do. The *Register of Deaths* at Trinity Presbyterian Church in Chinle shows

that Tom Scott died on 9/27/1968 and was buried in the Chinle Community Cemetery. All that was known about Tom's ancestry by Tall Woman's children was that his father was Long Moustache's real brother, and his mother's clan was Water Edge. He had at least two real siblings: a sister who married *Tótsoni* and lived at the Island Place in the Chinle Wash, and a brother, Joseph Ganna. When Tom remarried, he and *Dlinasbah* (perhaps from *Dlį Naazbaa* [Warrior Woman who Went Raiding and Came Back]) had a hogan at the Island Place.

16. The Chinle Health Center, which Tall Woman and others called the hospital, opened in 1932 and initially included a small fifteen-bed hospital. It was converted to a clinic in 1950 (Young 1961:69, 70, 89). After medical care was transferred from the BIA to the Public Health Service (IHS) in 1955, a new PHS Health Center as well as additional personnel housing were completed in June 1959 in Chinle. The 1959 facility was not replaced until 1982, when a new IHS hospital, the Chinle Comprehensive Health Care Facility, was dedicated on 8/28/1982. Among the latter's noteworthy characteristics was that it was the first facility on the reservation to include a native healing room within its interior, a place which was still being utilized, including by Tall Woman's family, in 1998. Before the new hospital, more serious cases by necessity went to Ganado's Sage Memorial Hospital or the Fort Defiance Hospital. See Frisbie (1987:302–4 ff.) for further information. The "old clinic" building, after housing the Twin Trails Treatment Center for a while after 1982, was demolished in mid-October 1998.

17. SM had evidently fathered a baby boy who was born at the hospital while Frank was there. The baby's mother met SM while she was in school at Fort Wingate and went to a Squaw Dance. The baby died the day it was born, 6/17/1935, after being baptized Edward Francis. After I noticed him in the "wall file" census records at St. Michaels in 1989 and inquired, SM confirmed the event and laughed, saying it was another example of his own foolishness at that time. "I was running wild then, just like Daddy had done in his day." He said, "I never saw that woman again after the Squaw Dance, but my Daddy told me about the baby and that it had not lived. He also lectured me some more about not acting like a billy goat.*"

18. The whole family, including Frank and Tall Woman, maintained an interest in attending rodeos in the 1960s, and the men followed rodeo competition news. SM said he suffered broken ribs when a race horse he was riding on the muddy Chinle track fell on him, but that he didn't stop racing until later, after getting hurt while hazing for David Gorman who was bulldogging. That was when he "got off the rodeo circuit; that was the end of my jockey days." The latter occurred in the 1940s while he worked at the Navajo Ordnance Depot. HM broke his arm while racing horses closer to home shortly before his brother, DM, got sick; he was in the hospital because of his arm when DM died in 1938. According to Tall Woman, HM's horse racing was a change since he was scared of horses when he was small. Frank used to put him up behind AS and then whip the horse, to teach him to get over his fears. After a while he did, becoming intensely interested in them. While he never lost his love for horses, his broken arm plus an eye injury from baseball several years later ended racing for him.

19. In 1970, Tall Woman said, "There used to be some pictures of my mother around here; I know Sam had a nice one for many years, but I don't know what happened to it. And I don't think those other ones are here anymore, either." None could be located.

20. AgS was still upset when remembering this in 1990. She viewed these practices as "superstitious" and "cruel." In particular, she objected to the fact that her "grandmother was left all alone over by the cornfield in her little shelter first, with people only coming once in a while to feed her." She also objected to children being excluded from seeing people near death, and to isolating the person near death in "a death lean-to." She said when she first found her grandmother in that condition, she was very frightened and scared because she didn't understand what was going on; nobody had told her. "They just kept scolding me for intruding or seeing any of it. Later, when I started using my head a little more, I thought it was very cruel. Even if my mother did go there all the time and was always with her, I still think that was very cruel. The way they treated people who were dying in those days was very, very cruel."

21. As noted in Chap. 2, n. 1, records at Our Lady of Fatima Church confirm her mother's baptism on 8/3/1935 by Father Anselm Sippel, O.F.M., as well as her burial in the cemetery behind the Annunciation Mission on 8/8/1935, the day after she died.

22. At a later time, Tall Woman started talking about this cemetery. She said, "I know how that looks from what some of my children, Howard and Augusta, told me later. When they went to the Chinle Government School they used to walk by that cemetery when they were out, going somewhere on weekends. That's how I know the priests put a fence around it and there were some crosses in there, here and there, where different ones were buried. But then they stopped using that cemetery; I guess there was no more room in there." Her mother's grave was originally marked with a white painted wooden cross to which was nailed a Navajo basket; both disintegrated over time (see Mitchell [1978:304–5 n. 4] for documentation of the condition of this cemetery in the 1940s and in 1970). By 1996, a few of the fence posts were still in place as were some pieces of barbed wire used on the original fence. The area, however, had seriously eroded because of floods from the Nazlini Wash. One of the floods that damaged the cemetery occurred on 7/31/1964, when the bridge washed out and seven Navajos traveling across it lost their lives (see Antram 1998:124–26, among others).

23. At a later date, Tall Woman mentioned that when they went over to her mother's hogan to get rid of her possessions after she had died, she discovered among them her father's big clay jug. "It was the old kind, the one called 'gray water' and 'half-and-half'" by some Navajos because it usually served as a container for corn whiskey (see the Franciscan Fathers 1910:217–18). Although Man Who Shouts' wife had kept it after his death, Tall Woman threw it and everything else out, when cleaning her mother's hogan.

CHAPTER 17

1. Gray (1986:85) includes an illustration of part of the physical plant of the Chinle Boarding School in 1928, taken from the clay butte looking northeast and thus showing the Presbyterian mission on the hill (in the background, on right).

2. See Mitchell (1978:300) for a similar remark while discussing ID's Mountainway, which was needed later in time because she had walked on a bear hide at the Presbyterian Church where the skin had been taken by Phillip Draper, after he shot the bear in the Canyon. Black bears were frequently reported on the reservation, in the Canyon, around Sawmill and St. Michaels, and also near other places. See Haile (*in* Bodo 1998:33–38) for Haile's description of his first bear hunt in the St. Michaels area in the early 1900s. Link (1968:36–37) includes a Ben Wittick photograph (archived at the Museum of New Mexico, Santa Fe) entitled, "Re-

turn of the Bear Hunters," taken "in front of the Thunderbird Trading Post in Chinle," and provides comments on some of the clothing and equipment portrayed therein. This posed group picture also appears in McNitt (1963:307) with the label "Navajos at Chinle" and date of ca. 1902. In the latter source, some individuals in the group posed outside the Sam Day, Sr., Trading Post are identified according to data from Sam Day II. The same photograph is reprinted as D6 in the Historic West Series Postcards (produced by Beautyway, Flagstaff, Arizona). Entitled, "Return of the Bear Hunters," its caption states that it depicts a group of Navajo hunters outside Sam Day's Chinle Trading Post, Chinle, Arizona, ca. 1890. For later reports of bears in the Canyon, see Kennedy (1965:36, and photographs of hunters on pp. 37, 38) for 1918, Gray (1986) for the 1930s, and Brugge and Wilson (1976:78) for 1941. SM added that in the late 1930s, he was asked to help a group searching for a five year old who had been stolen by a bear roaming around Sawmill. He said they "first got a Mountainway singer to talk to the bear, pray to it, like you have to do when that happens. We located the child four days later, unharmed. But almost right after that, a bear in the Chuska Mountains took a baby girl. Some white people organized a hunting party with guns. They didn't do that in the Navajo way. So the bear slammed that baby girl into some rock walls and killed her. She was dead when they found her. They should have prayed to it; the bear knew they were planning to shoot it and so it did that."

3. Tall Woman illustrated this with an aside about AS that essentially summarized her employment history: "Just look at Augusta; that proved to be true with her . . ." AS's early experiences in the kitchen and dining rooms at the Chinle Boarding School continued throughout her school years. When she finished high school at St. Catherine's in 1949, she first worked for the Chinle Agency as a switchboard operator at the government boarding school. Then she substituted as a dorm worker at the school "for about a year" before working "for two or three years" cooking and cleaning for the priests and coaching the girls' basketball team. When the Chinle Public School was built in 1958, she applied for a full-time cooking position, was hired, and went to work there in 1959. Although her own house at the Mitchells' was built in 1958, to be closer to their jobs, she, her husband, and their children moved and started living, in the late fall of 1959, in one of the buildings behind the Catholic Church, specifically the former chicken house that had been remodeled after Brother Gotthard's time. AS said she first helped Father Conall Lynch, O.F.M. (who was in Chinle from 7/5/1956 to 8/8/1957) clean out the building. When it was remodeled, running water was added, and it had a living room, dining room, kitchen, bathroom, and two bedrooms. Gradually AS worked her way up to head cook at the public school until she was hired in December 1963 as head cook at the new Chinle High School. In 1976 she "was drafted" to work as Food Service Supervisor for nine school kitchens on a ten-month contract. Instead of returning to the high school as promised in the fall of 1977, due to bureaucratic errors she was sent to the Tsaile Elementary School. She commuted to Tsaile until a teacher's trailer became vacant, enabling her to move (1/1978). She stayed there as head cook through the addition of the seventh and eighth grades to the school in 1982 until officially retiring in 10/1992. However, those retiring then were rehired to work through 5/1993. On 6/11/1993, AS moved back to her home in Chinle.

4. In the next chapter, Tall Woman, after elaborating on the usual "Daily Round" she followed while raising the children in Frank's absence, discusses Frank's decision and the resulting increase in the farmwork, which eventually fell mainly on her and three of her

daughters, namely RY, AS, and ID.

5. See Chap. 18.

6. AS said she was diagnosed with trachoma, an infectious eye disease that was among the serious health problems faced by Navajos, both adults and boarding-school children, during this time (see Adair and Deuschle 1970:18; Trennert 1998:100–102 ff.). A cure was discovered in 1938 and many Navajos received treatment at the Fort Defiance Hospital. Given the date the cure was discovered, this event may have occurred several years later than the way Tall Woman told it, since AS started school at Chinle in 1935 and spent the 1936–37 year at the Fort Defiance Boarding School.

7. When the agencies were consolidated and the Navajo Central Agency established in 1935, John Collier chose Window Rock as the site for the new Tribal, BIA, and PHS buildings. For illustrations of the architecture at the new location and the members of the Tribal Council at different time periods, see Link (1968:60–71).

8. Frank was selected for service on the Constitutional Assembly on 3/10/1937, after a reservation-wide survey that is documented in Mitchell (1978:275–77 n. 8, 278 nn. 13, 14). The group's first meeting was held on 4/5/1937. The committees he identified during his own life history work included the Executive Committee, Grazing Committee, and the Constitution Committee (in conjunction with the 1934 IRA). See Mitchell (1978:240–81) for this period and his memories of the Washington, D.C., trip, which started on 6/17/1937. Although Frank ran for reelection after a year, he lost during balloting on 9/27/1938 and finished his service with this group when the new members of the Constitutional Assembly took office on 11/8/1938.

9. After her spring 1937 graduation from the Albuquerque Indian School, AgS trained at St. Joseph's School of Nursing, which changed its name to Regina School of Nursing before her graduation in 1941. Then she worked at the Fort Defiance Hospital for a year before enlisting for military service as an army nurse in World War II. She got her orders and was sworn in "Halloween night, 1942."

10. SM said he, too, was working for the SCS at this time (1938), while also continuing to help Brother Gotthard, O.F.M., around the Annunciation Mission, and the priests with interpreting during religious instructions. SM said it was at this time the government tried to start Farmers Associations in Chinle and Valley Store. He was involved with those, too, making sure the government's share of the crops was stored downstairs at the Big House, where he continued to live, upstairs (see Frisbie 1998). He said this experiment failed in Chinle and was discontinued after a year or two. He also reported working as "a rod man for several months with a geological survey crew above Black Rock in the Canyon," finishing that job in October. SM left Chinle in the fall of 1939 to work at the St. Michaels Boarding School (elementary school) as the coach, replacing Murray Lincoln, and as a boys' advisor; he stayed there until 1941. AS noted that Murray Lincoln later returned to his coaching job at that school.

11. At a later time, Tall Woman said when AS was a baby, the seeds from the cottonwoods the Park Service had planted in the Canyon floated down the Chinle Wash, starting to spread trees in the area near this Wash. She also reiterated the fact that for a long time her brother, Man with a Cane, lived by the only cottonwood in the area, the one he had planted by this Wash.

12. Tall Woman didn't specify who she was thinking about; records at Our Lady of Fa-

tima Church (*Liber Defunctorum*, p. 14 no. 3, and p. 15 no. 11, respectively), show that within the family, Ida (the daughter of Gai and Son of Yucca Fruit Man), who had married Edward Francis, lost a three-month-old son, Edward, on 7/23/1937. Additionally, one of the women who had moved around with Man Who Shouts and his family for many years, and who was known by numerous names, including Towering House Woman (and Woman Who Kicks Dirt Out), died on 4/3/1938 and was buried the next day. In the records, she is shown as the wife of Squinty Jones and the mother of Rachel Jones (Mitchell), Chee Jones, and others, and her birthdate is given as 1868. As shown in Appendix A, Towering House Woman was the daughter of one of Tall Woman's real maternal grandmother's sisters. Her daughter, Rachel, married Billy Mitchell, one of the sons of Frank Mitchell's sister, Woman at War (Mitchell 1978:346). After Rachel died on 7/17/1997, in a Fort Defiance nursing home at age ninety-five, the memorial card at her 7/21/1997 funeral gave her birthdate as 6/15/1902. She was survived by a large number of great-grandchildren through her sons, David and John Mitchell.

13. The literature on the history and development of bicultural or holistic approaches to health care on the reservation is extensive. Between 1900 and the 1950s, progress was slow, and hospitals continued to be viewed as places to die, houses of death. Trennert's (1998) comprehensive work, which examines government health-care practices on the reservation from 1863 until 1955, expands the overviews and literature introductions provided by Bergman (1983) and Frisbie (1987:257–72). Adair and Deuschle (1970) document the Navajo-Cornell Field Health Research Project at Many Farms, Arizona, from 1956 to 1962.

14. According to Underhill (1953:278), the Fort Defiance Hospital was originally constructed in 1912, and was expanded in 1929 and 1939 (1937 is the correct date for the latter). Thus, the ceremony in 1938 was for a "newly expanded" rather than a "new" hospital.

15. See Frisbie (1968, 1970, 1980c) for further information on the Navajo House Blessing Ceremony and its private and public versions. As shown there, the earliest use of Blessingway for dedicating or blessing off-reservation public buildings seems to have been on May 25, 1923, with the Fred Harvey El Navajo Hotel in Gallup. (Photographs of this event were again made accessible to the public during the 1996 annual film festival in Gallup. In 1996, the festival was entitled "Silver Rails and the Silver Screen: An Era Revisited." In her coverage of the Oct. 18–22 festival for the *Navajo Times* (10/17/1996: A-1, 2), Shebala (1996), after interviewing Zonnie Gorman (the festival's program director), provided a detailed description of the 1923 dedication, the hotel's history, and the role of the Harvey Girls at southwestern Harvey Houses (see also Poling-Kempes 1991; Howard and Pardue 1996). Two photographs of the dedication accompanied Shebala's article. The El Navajo dedication was followed on the reservation with the Kinlichee Chapter House in 1930 (Frisbie 1980c:168), and perhaps other dedications such as those Pete Price may have done for the old Tribal Council headquarters in Fort Defiance (which would have been earlier) and the new 1935 location in Window Rock (Jett 1991:98, 100 n. 13). The May 10, 1938, dedication of the "new" PHS Hospital in Fort Defiance, which had "opened" in July 1937, was highly publicized and did include, upon the request of Henry Chee Dodge, a public blessing by Pete Price, a well-known Navajo singer (see Jett 1991 for information on Price; Frisbie 1968: 31–33; 1970:186–201, 218–21; 1987:257–58). Other early public dedications that were planned to involve the services of a "Navajo medicine man" are also documented, such as the blessing of the Museum of Navajo Ceremonial Art (later the Wheelwright Museum) in 1937, the

Gallup stadium in 1940, and the new hospital at Crownpoint in 1940; at the latter, Jeff King was the main singer, but numerous other medicine men were also involved (Bergman 1983:673 fig. 1).

Although the Franciscans provided models by "dedicating" the chapel at St. Michaels on 10/9/1898, the mission itself at the same location on 10/25/1903, and the Annunciation Mission in Chinle on 3/25/1912 (see Wilken 1955:36, 90, 116–17), as shown in the above sources, not all singers were in favor of using the Blessingway for public dedications. Frank *did* change his mind and later, like others who were willing to bless public buildings, did several such dedications (Chinle Chapter House — 6/20/1959; Chinle Boarding School [new plant] — 5/19/1961; and the new Chinle High School — 2/29/1964). For his later thoughts on this development, see Mitchell (1978:221–23).

16. One of DM's sisters said she has always wondered if he might have been saved if Frank and Tall Woman had taken him to the hospital immediately. She said that Frank was still opposed to the hospitals at this time. However, the family, including Frank, had already started using the Chinle Hospital, which opened in 1932, and Frank had already attended, with other headmen, the public dedication of the refurbished Fort Defiance Hospital in 1938. Another family member with medical training said the same, and added that some of the "traditional ceremonies" they did for DM clearly heightened his fever and made matters worse much more quickly.

17. AgS and SM requested an autopsy and attended it, without telling their parents. AgS was in her first year of nurses' training and this was her first autopsy experience. The results indicated "spinal meningitis" caused DM's death. Both said "that disease was killing lots of the People around here at that time."

18. See Mitchell (1978:284, 304–5 n. 4) for Frank's account, where he states that SM, WD, HM, and he himself helped with the cemetery burial. HM clearly did not participate since he was still in the Fort Defiance Hospital, with his broken arm. The fourth person was probably Son of Yucca Fruit Man, IF's father, as Tall Woman states. Traditional Navajo approaches were combined with the Catholic Church burial. The church's *Liber Defunctorum* records (p. 17 no. 2) show that DM, born in 1922, died on 8/21/1938 and was buried the same day by Father Anselm Sippel, O.F.M., in the mission cemetery. Both Frank and several of DM's siblings stated with certainty that he was buried right next to the wife of Man Who Shouts, whose 1935 grave was still marked with both a cross and a basket. Once again, Tall Woman did *not* go to the funeral or to the cemetery, a practice she followed throughout her life, including at the time of Frank's death.

19. See Mitchell (1978:284–85) for documentation of DM's death and this fight. It seems possible that Frank's behaviors after DM's death (his anger, deep depression, and public brawling) at least contributed to the reasons he lost his bid for reelection to the Constitutional Assembly. Data in Mitchell (1978:246 n. 8) indicate that at least by 1936, there was no love lost between the policeman and Frank.

20. Tall Woman shared her memories of DM's sickness and resulting death slowly, in a soft, low voice, pausing frequently while clearly remembering him. It was obvious that even in 1965, losing him was still painful for her. There was a long silence before she continued narrating subsequent events. Both SM and GB were home when the incident of "Frank and his gun" happened; they remembered it clearly and independently verified the details of her account.

21. I was unable to locate any relevant records at Trinity Presbyterian Church or Our Lady of Fatima Church concerning Chubby Woman's death, although she does appear in the latter's census files (no. 70058) as the stepmother of Ida and Betty Hashkaan (her sister's, Gai's, daughters with Son of Yucca Fruit Man). The census records at Our Lady of Fatima Church for both Eva and Bobby list Eva's birthdate as 12/9/1934 and Bobby's as 1938, and both cards are marked "Protestant." These dates suggest that Chubby Woman died in childbirth in 1939. No one in the family was able to recall any details beyond those in Tall Woman's narrative; SM said he had already gone to work at St. Michaels and, thus, was not in Chinle when she died.

22. See Mitchell (1978:300) for Frank's comments on this. According to Underhill (1953: 278), the expansion of the Fort Defiance Hospital (in 1937) included a small unit with one hundred beds for tuberculosis patients; this made it the only place on the reservation where sanatorium-type care was available at the time (see Young 1961:67–71). Greenberg and Greenberg (1984:22) note the disease was widespread in 1916; numerous other sources indicate that the Navajo TB rate before 1952 was between ten and sixty times the national average (Adair and Deuschle 1970:18–19), that the disease was a major cause of death on the reservation, and that before 1952, the People were in the "throes of a TB epidemic." Between 1955 and 1967, the rate was reduced by 70 percent (Bergman 1983:672). Among those honored for their health-education work among the People, work that was extremely important in lowering the spread of infectious diseases, was Annie Dodge Wauneka, who received the 1963 Presidential Medal of Freedom for her efforts. See Frisbie (1987:257–59), Bergman (1983), Adair and Deuschle (1970), Underhill (1953, 1956), Young (1961), Iverson (1981), Kunitz (1983), and others, especially Trennert (1998), for further information on diseases affecting the People during Tall Woman's time, and the efforts to improve Western health-care services, their delivery, and understanding and cooperation between Navajo medicine people and Western health-care providers.

23. This is a reference to the Golden Jubilee Celebration for Mother Katharine Drexel (1858–1955), who founded the "Blessed Sacrament Sisters for Indians and Colored People" in 1891, after completing her novitiate with the Sisters of Mercy in Pittsburgh, Pennsylvania, and taking her vows on 2/12/1891. Katharine was the second daughter born to Francis Anthony Drexel, a staunch Roman Catholic Philadelphia banker and philanthropist, and Hannah Langstroth, who died when Katharine was five weeks old. Two years later, her father married Emma Bouvier and together they had a daughter, Louise. Katharine's father was one of the sons of Francis Martin Drexel, the founder of one of Philadelphia's most influential banking houses in the nineteenth century, Drexel and Company. When Francis A. Drexel died in 1885, his daughters became beneficiaries of his estate's income while most of the estate was willed to the Catholic Church. Two of his younger brothers became Episcopalians and one of them, Anthony, founded the Drexel Institute of Art, Science, and Technology in Philadelphia.

When Katharine established the Sisters of the Blessed Sacrament, the Motherhouse was first located at the Francis A. Drexel family's summer residence, a country home in Torresdale, Pennsylvania, on the Delaware. Known then as "St. Michel," the earlier country estate is now the location of St. Michael's Shrine of the True Cross. In 1892, the Motherhouse was moved to Saint Elizabeth's Convent in Cornwells Heights, Pennsylvania, where the Sisters opened a school and then began their missionary work. Their southwestern endeavors started with the opening of

St. Catherine's "mission among the Pueblo Indians in Santa Fe" in 1894. Reverend M. M. Katharine became interested in working among the Navajos because of the efforts of Msgr. Joseph Stephan, the director of the Catholic Bureau of Indian Missions at the end of the century. After purchasing land in 1896 from Sam Day (see Wilken 1955), she interested the Franciscan Fathers of St. John the Baptist Province, Cincinnati, Ohio, in establishing a mission center on it in 1898 (known as St. Michaels) (see Haile *in* Bodo 1998:41–57 ff.; Antram 1998:175–95). After another land purchase, the Sisters of the Blessed Sacrament built and opened the elementary boarding school at St. Michaels in 1902; the high school followed in 1946, after Mother Drexel had suffered a severe heart attack in the fall of 1935, which greatly restricted her own activities until her death, twenty years later, on 3/3/1955 (Hanley n.d.:30; Sisters of the Blessed Sacrament 1992). She was buried in the crypt of the Motherhouse Chapel, The Blessed Katharine Drexel Shrine, located at 1663 Bristol Pike, Bensalem, Pennsylvania 19020. Katharine was beatified on Nov. 20, 1988 by Pope John Paul II. After passing both tests required for sainthood in Jan. 2000, on 3/10/2000, Pope John Paul II approved sainthood for Mother Drexel; canonization will occur on Oct. 1, 2000 at the Vatican. For further information, see Hanley (n.d.), Burton (1957, 1967), Wilken (1955), Duffy (1966), Butler (1991), Haile (*in* Bodo 1998), Antram (1998), and the Sisters of the Blessed Sacrament (1941, 1992). The latter's 1941 publication is the Golden Jubilee Program. It includes a brief history of the Sisters (pp. 19–22), which mentions the three-day celebration at the Motherhouse to mark Mother Katharine's Golden Jubilee on April 18–20, 1941 (p. 21). The description of the country-wide participation by mission schools in the event through greetings and handicrafts to be displayed in a "unique mission exhibit" echoes some of what SM told Tall Woman about the experience. The program also includes an article, "The Catholic Leaven among the Navajos" (pp. 60–63), which summarizes early work among the Navajos, and another, "Navajo Health Clinic and Day School at Houck, Arizona" (pp. 106–14), which discusses developments in Houck. All are well illustrated.

Additional information emerged in conjunction with the Franciscans' Centennial in 1998, for which planning was under way in 1996. One example can be found in the winter 1996 issue of *Padres' Trail*, which provides a brief history of Franciscan missionization work and notes the role of "a modern day saint, Blessed Katherine [*sic*] Drexel." Additionally, Father Murray Bodo, O.F.M. (1998) and Father Cormac Antram, O.F.M (1998) both saw the books they were preparing (Bodo p.c. 3/3/1997; Antram p.c. 5/30/1997) published during 1998. Centennial celebrations at Catholic churches in each of the four directions on the reservation began on 10/18/1997 in the East, at Crownpoint. These proceeded to Ganado in the South on 2/21/1998, Tuba City in the West on 4/21/1998, and Shiprock in the North on 6/13/1998. The final celebration was at St. Michaels Mission on 10/3/1998. Coverage, including photographs, appeared in a variety of places, including *Padres' Trail* (Centennial Celebration Issue 1998); Dotson (1998); *St. Anthony Messenger* (October 1998:5, 34); and Wicoff (1998a, b). Sheehan (1998) provides a few other comments, but is mainly focused on celebrating four hundred years of Catholic activities in New Mexico. In Window Rock, in honor of the Franciscan Centennial, and bearing the signatures of the president, speaker, and chief justice of the Navajo Nation, the Nation issued a proclamation declaring October 7, 1998, as, "The Day of Recognition and Appreciation of the Franciscan Friars Presence, Evangelization among the Navajo People, and Their Ethnological and Anthropological Contribution to the Navajo Nation."

24. RY said she rejected her parents' suggestions about having ceremonies for her first-born child, in part because she was still upset about DM's death and wanted to get her baby to the doctor immediately. The rest of her children were born at Sage Memorial Hospital in Ganado.

CHAPTER 18

1. As noted in the Introduction, this chapter is another place where Tall Woman spoke in a "topical chunk"; as such, it is simultaneous with at least all of the chapters in Part IV and the initial part of the first chapter in Part V, and covers from ca. 1935 until 1959. However, it should be noted that many of the daily activities were true much earlier in time, and date back to when she began raising children (with the birth of MD ca. 1908). The expansion of the family's farm efforts appears to have happened in 1937 or 1938, as discussed below.

2. The various children described this as "at the crack of dawn," "way before dawn even came up," and "around 4 in the morning." Some also explained they tried to get up before others, since among siblings squabbles occurred in the early morning when whoever got up first would get a piece of charcoal from the fire and draw moustaches on the faces of those still sleeping, making them cry when they woke up. Some of the children were known for having "terrible tempers," which were expressed verbally and physically toward others, but most often while out of Tall Woman's sight, such as while hoeing in the cornfields or hauling water back from the Chinle Wash.

3. AS, RY, HM, GB, and ID all confirmed this as well as running with DM during his childhood and MD's three children. AgS said in her day she only remembered running during girls' Puberty ceremonies. SM said he didn't have to run very often, either, so it seems to have been enforced beginning with RY's childhood, rather than earlier. All who had to run said no excuses were honored; "she told us to do that and so we did; we had to do what we were told all the time." They confirmed that racing was done barefoot, and even in the hot weather; however, they said it was often forgotten in the winter, if the snow was deep or the weather was very cold.

4. Government boarding schools had required uniforms for both boys and girls. See Chap. 5, n. 13, for references to the boarding-school literature.

5. In 1963, the family was hauling water with their wagon from nearby wells and filling several metal barrels. Frank had cut the tops off and covered them with canvas secured with ropes or pieces of rubber tires. Running water was not available in any of their homes until the 1970s. Going to get water was always a daily, time-consuming, group project, and the lines at the wells and windmills were long; however, it was also a time for lots of joking and laughter. When I went along on these trips (1963–67), usually either Frank or Tall Woman drove the wagon; after Frank got sick in the fall of 1966, it was more apt to be Tall Woman who drove.

6. See Chap. 11, n. 2 and n. 3, and Chap 13, n. 6, on the Moccasin Game, card games, footraces, and horse racing. SM's accounts of his childhood and young adulthood (before World War II) were full of examples of going, sometimes great distances, to ceremonies with others, mainly to enjoy the gambling done during the Moccasin Game.

7. Many of the stories his sisters told about herding with HM concerned not only the beautiful mud toys he made, but also his playing in water and the condition of his feet, which were cracked and "always in need of being cleaned." Sometimes his cracked feet bled

and were painful. One time, "when a sheep peed on them," it made them sting and burn. RY tried soaking and cleaning them when they got home, and poured what turned out to be motor oil on them, reportedly causing him to cry and faint.

8. Tall Woman's children said it was usually the adults who gathered the medicinal plants. While they talked about this in front of the children, no effort was made to take them along. MD learned what she knew about such plants from her husband, who was a singer; "I learned the ones that went with his ceremonies [Shootingway and Evilway] and also lots of the Lifeway medicines, too, from him." SM, RY, AS, ID, and GB however, attributed their own knowledge of medicinal plants to Tall Woman and requested that what follows be included in an endnote. They also assisted with the process of summarizing my very specific data so as to respect guidelines set about handling ethnobotanical information in this book (as explained in the Introduction). SM said Tall Woman taught him how to use Rocky Mountain Beeweed to combat body and foot odor, how to prepare "pimple medicine," and also how to prepare one from small, bitter, red berries to make chickenpox sores turn black and dry up. He used the latter, while he was in Fort Apache going to school, to cure his own chickenpox "because Mama had already taught me about that before I went over there." She also taught him how to make teas from the leaves and stems of sagebrush, an emetic from cliffrose (which he called buckbrush), and how to mix three specific plants together (the ones used in some ceremonial Blackenings) to use as a blood purifier.

In the cases of some plants, which could also be used for food, the children who gathered them with Tall Woman for food purposes also knew how she fixed them for use as medicines. *Haashch'é'édą́ą́'* provides one example; besides producing edible berries, Tall Woman dug the plant's fresh roots, which she then pounded up and boiled. After the mixture cooled, she gave it to her children to drink and to use in washing themselves whenever they suffered from hives that were caused by "spider's pee," among other things. It made them disappear. Another one they all mentioned was *kétłoh*, her name for "headache medicine." When making this, she gathered some local plants that were plentiful when her children were small; using either fresh or dried ones, she chopped them up and mixed them in water, and then told her children to rub the mixture on their heads and/or in their hair. The infusion reportedly had a "very nice smell; right away, we always went to sleep after we used that *kétłoh*. We got lots of headaches from working in the sun all the time." They all knew she kept lots of medicinal plant supplies on hand and that she usually boiled them alone or combined them with other plants to make teas, emetics, or liquids with which to wash the body and/or the hair.

GB also remembered another kind of treatment: "If you were aching, suffering from joint problems or leg or arm aches, she'd dig a small hole in the ground. Then she made a fire, heated up some rocks, and after those were hot, she sprinkled an herb on them. Then she'd tell us to sit right there and put our knee, or whatever was aching, over that hole, and let that herb work on it. That always stopped the aching."

Tall Woman used her medicines on herself, Frank, and also all of her children, as needed. In the latter cases, she reportedly always said, "My little one," "My little daughter," "My son, I have this herb that would help you with that." The processing usually involved drying, grinding or pounding, and boiling, and then using the result either warm or cold. For things made from juniper or sagebrush, she often added salt from Frank's supply from the Zuni Salt Lake. He brought back some big chunks of salt from one of his trips with Father Berard to the sacred mountains, and the salt lasted this family for years, being used sparingly and mainly for medicinal mixtures.

9. SM and HM said she *frequently* made the two of them drink an emetic tea made from sagebrush, when they returned from their early morning races "so we wouldn't be lazy." In 1964, Tall Woman showed me how she dried out the sheep's bladder, by hanging it in a tree after butchering. She used that as a medicine, too, saying, "When you rub that on rashes, sores, cold sores, it dries them right up." Undoubtedly there were other medicines that were derived from other sources, too, besides all of the medicinal plants.

10. This was one of the favorite stories in the family. RY and AS "died laughing" when they first heard it, and GB "laughed so hard she was in tears" when she heard about it. All said HM told the story for a *long* time, adding to it with each retelling and always making his mother "really mad" at him when he did so.

11. Frank definitely had the peach trees during the years he was serving as a judge. I suspect they were given up in the early 1950s, although this remains unclear.

12. Tall Woman's children gave me *lots* of examples of this, including lots of jokes about "first" events — seeing the first white person, the first car, hearing the first airplane — and lots of jokes about peoples' names that were frequently based on their physical appearance, their ways of walking or standing or sitting, or something they did which was funny, stupid, outrageous, or totally inappropriate (especially when they were Anglos). They also credited her with many of their own understandings of family and clan ties, and family history. In terms of tribal history, both parents talked about certain significant events from the past with their children.

13. RY told me this was quite true and added that she used to get angry with her mother for repeating her instructions over and over as they were leaving. She said she'd always think to herself, "Now, just who is going to come and drag the house away, harm the children while she's gone?" However, she also said when she became a mother herself and started leaving her own children in care of an older one, she had the same concerns. At that point, she said she understood why her "mother worried about those things every time she left for a day or more, or even only when she was going to the store in the wagon, and asked me to take care of things for her."

14. This expansion of the farm seems to have happened about 1937 or 1938, and lasted into the late 1950s. DM was involved in the expanded work, suggesting the 1937 date, but AS's information suggests the expansion took place the following spring. (However, that may have been when her parents considered her old enough to get involved with heavier work.) AS said she was probably in the fourth grade when they "really started farming" and the entire time she was in junior high and high school (1943–49), even though she wanted to earn money by working some place else in the summer, when she asked her parents told her no. "They wouldn't let me go; they told me they needed me to work on the farm at home, so I didn't ask again. From the fourth grade on, I worked like a horse on the farm. Even when I was having my own babies, we were still doing that." She and her other sisters who were home, namely RY and ID, also made it clear that the expanded farming operation activities fell mainly upon Tall Woman and the three of them, although HM did help when he was around. "The men were gone most of the time so we were the ones who did most of the work for all those things all those years." In 1989, when we were discussing this, SM agreed and also voiced regrets about it. "Daddy and I, and the other men around here should have helped them with all that heavy farm

work. It was the women who were the farmers in our family, not David, Howard, Daddy, or me; we were off working somewhere else or we were running around. I wish now I had helped my mother and my sisters with those things in those years." Some of RY's children had similar observations, clearly remembering in the late 1950s when Frank would "be lying under a tree in white long johns, supervising the hoeing instead of helping." They said his "supervising" was interrupted only when he'd start calling to Tall Woman that he was hungry; then she'd quit hoeing, come in out of the sun, cook something, and then call everybody to eat, including whoever else was helping her in the fields. "Even then, it was mainly the women doing all that kind of work around here."

15. In later years, HM was the foreman for the ditch-cleaning crews and was responsible for keeping the gates (used to divert water into different fields) and the sections of concrete at junction points in the irrigation system repaired and in working condition.

16. AS confirmed this, saying she really enjoyed learning to walk behind the plow and help plow the fields. Although earlier she helped with lots of planting, often with HM, once she learned to plow, "I never wanted to plant seeds again. I always wanted to show the men I could get behind the plow and do that, too. That was lots of fun. But then one year I was plowing and I got so dizzy I almost fell over. I was pregnant with somebody, probably 'Tiny' [Regina, RS], and I got dizzy, probably from that. We were still planting lots of fields the whole time I was having my children. But after that happened to me, I decided I shouldn't get behind the plow like that any more. So others took that back over, and I went back to helping plant seeds." She also said, "It was lots of fun to work in the alfalfa field" and that she also learned how to run the horse-drawn mower and rake they used there after Frank acquired them. As shown in Appendix A, RS was born on 8/13/1958. AS said, "She came early and was really small. That's probably because I was doing farm work. But then, that was also the time we were building the house where I live now; somebody went after logs for us, and I helped chop those, too. I chopped seven of those all by myself, and all of a sudden, I knew the baby was going to come. So we left for the hospital right away." Although AS's last child was born in 1965, Frank had already "cut back on" the amount of land being farmed by the family by the time I first met them in June 1963.

17. AS confirmed this, saying she and HM were trying to make their ditch deeper and she was driving the horses pulling the scraper in a muddy place. When it was almost time to turn the scraper over she whipped the horses, and somehow the whip, the end of which was around her wrist, got caught on the long wooden handle of the scraper. The horses took off, dragging her along before she could get the whip strap untied from her wrist. Although her brother was yelling at her, she freed up her arm, calmed the horses down, and then walked home without a word.

18. Several family members vouched for the effectiveness of this method, saying they used it in their adult lives when farming in other areas because it really worked. See Chap. 4, n. 5, for references to other information on Navajo farming techniques, such as that included in Hill's (1938) classic study, and Bingham and Bingham's (1979) more recent one.

19. HM said eventually, when they finished loading the wagon late in the afternoon, someone had to start sleeping by it, if they weren't taking it to Garcia's until the next day. That was because people had started stealing hay by then, right off of loaded wagons.

20. Tall Woman explained the four stages of corn as follows: (1) "In the first one, the corn is really little and the kernels are tiny. [AS said, "It's like the tiny pickled corn sold in

restaurants now."] You boil it and eat it right then. We call that, *'ayaazh*. Instead of saying, *naadą́ą́' yázhí* [little corn], we say *'ayaazh* [I'm putting you into last year's little bag.] That means your stomach; you say that when you eat corn in the first stage. We believe if you bring it in and fix it when the kernels are tiny, that brings you more ears as the corn keeps growing. That's why we do that, so we have lots of corn." (2) "The next stage is when the kernels are fully formed but still small. We gather some of that and cut it off the cob. Then we grind the kernels and make that into *nanoyeshi*, a mush, one that's not real doughy. You dig a hole in the ground, not too deep, and get the fire going until there's only charcoal left. On top of that, you layer the corn plant leaves, putting the edges of one on top of the next one. After you make one layer like that on the bottom, you pour in your mush, in the center of the corn plant leaves you've fixed. It spreads out like lava flowing on rocks. Then you cover that up with another layer of leaves, overlapping them just like you did on the bottom. When that gets baked, it's called *diitł'ogi 'alkaan*. Both of those stages of the corn come before it's ready to make kneeldown bread, *ntsidigo'í*; that's the third kind." (3) "Here the corn is fully ripe but the kernels are still milky. You grind those up and wrap them inside corn husks, not the plant leaves like the second one. Again you bake it in the ground. You can eat that right then, cutting it with a knife, or sun-dry it without the husks. If you dry it like that, then you store it. Later, you can use it as a dry cereal or cook it with something else and eat it that way." (4) "The last one is the fully ripe corn; that's the fourth. With that the kernels are fully ripe and they're hard. You roast them right on the cob, putting the ears in a pit in the ground or you can singe it in the charcoal. You either eat it that way, or dry it out after it's roasted. You can put away the dry corn just like that, leaving it on the cob after it's roasted, or you can shell it right then and put the shelled corn away for use in the winter. Then later, you can fix those dried ears by cooking them in boiling water. Or you grind up some of the kernels to use in making some of the mushes we eat, or as a sweetener to add to your coffee or tea. Or you can soak those kernels overnight and use them in making things like hominy and stew. That's the four of them; that's what my mother taught me about those; she was also called Tall Woman, as you know."

21. This grinder evidently was acquired by the Chinle Chapter, which then made arrangements to locate it on the hill near the Presbyterian Church. As noted in Chap. 14, n. 1, the Canyon de Chelly Chapter (or Chinle, or Canyon del Muerto Chapter) was established in 1934, if not earlier, in 1926. Tall Woman's account suggests the family started using the grinder shortly after 1935, and AS believes they were among the first to do so when it became available while she was at the Chinle Boarding School, going through her elementary school years (1935–43). DM clearly was among those who helped haul corn to the grinder *before* he got sick and died in August 1938. While family information suggests the grinder became available shortly after the Chapter was established, I have been unable to locate any early Chapter records which might have recorded the date and circumstances of the grinder's acquisition. It is not mentioned in the earliest "Diary and Chronicle of Chin Lee" housed at Our Lady of Fatima Church and covering 4/21/1934 through 2/20/1935, or in the next Chronicle, which covers 8/1/1945 through 1/31/1960. However, Gray (1986:21), in a chapter documenting Chinle Trinity Presbyterian Church activities for the 1924–52 period (when Reverend and Mrs. Bysegger were at the church), notes that as a service to the Chinle community, the Presbyterian Church "allowed the Chinle Chapter to set up a horse-powered grinder on the hill for anyone who wanted to grind corn."

CHAPTER 19

1. See Chap. 20. While Frank may have served as a judge from 1938 to 1951, the only dates I could confirm during work on his book were from 1946 to 1951 (see Mitchell 1978:279–80 n. 17, ff.).

2. AgS enlisted in the Army Nurses Corps, left the day after her orders arrived, and served in a variety of places, including New Guinea, before returning to the United States at the end of 1945. She was officially discharged on 2/1/1946.

3. Ordnance depots were located at a variety of places, including Fort Wingate and Bellemont, outside of Flagstaff. Underhill (1953:252–59) is one of many sources for information on Navajos during World War II and the ordnance depots at which many worked. The collection edited by Johnson (1977b) includes personal accounts of eleven Navajos (three women, eight men) who participated in this war. For specific information on the Navajo Code Talkers, see Paul (1973), Greenberg and Greenberg (1984), Kawano (1990), and Bixler (1993) among others, as well as several videos now available. Among the latter are the 55 min. color/black and white one produced by Brendan Tully and Francine Rzeznik in 1994, "Navajo Code Talkers: The Epic Story," and the 1996 video, "War Code: Navajo," coproduced and directed by Navajo filmmaker Lena Carr with Amy Wray for National Geographic. Carr, who runs "Indian Summer," an Albuquerque-based filmmaking company, was awarded an Emmy for an "Outstanding Historical Program" because of her work on this film about the four hundred Navajo Code Talkers. Her home community of Steamboat, Arizona, recognized her achievement with a celebration at the Chapter House; that and the Emmy were covered for the *Navajo Times* by Gilles (1996) in an article that included further information on the Code Talkers. Additional data appear in Greenberg and Greenberg (1984), since CG (10/5/1907–1/29/1998) was among them. CG was interviewed many times about his experiences as a Code Talker with the U.S. Marines, and he also wrote the foreword for Kawano (1990). When CG died on Jan. 29, 1998, at the age of ninety, he was the oldest surviving Code Talker (cf. *Albuquerque Journal* 1998a, b; *Albuquerque Tribune* 1998; *Gallup Independent* 1998; *Navajo Times* 1998). By the end of 1999, two movies about the Navajo Code Talkers were in production: "Windtalkers" (MGM/Lion Rock Studio) and "Whisper the Wind" (Pacific Western Productions/Red-Horse Native Productions, Inc.) (Shebala 1999:5).

4. AS remembered this vividly, having been sick "out of both ends" all afternoon, while lying by the irrigation ditch. "By about 5 o'clock, I looked like a wrung out mop; that stuff was greenish or yellowish and it tasted bitter. Later it turned dark red. It came out my nose, too, and made my throat very, very sore. It drained me out; I had no strength left. My mother kept coming out, checking on me. She brought me a blanket because you get chilled from that, too; that's why you never take it when it's cold outside; even lying in the sun, you get chilled from it. She told me to drink lots of water after I stopped vomiting. Later she dragged me back in the hogan and made me swallow the clear mutton broth she had fixed. By late that night, I could swallow again. By the next morning, I felt about six feet above the ground; I felt so good, so different, so clean." "We use that when we need to clean ourselves out; that stuff accumulates in you, and if you don't clean yourself out, it slows you down and it can kill you. When people suffer from simple dizziness, with or without a headache, you use this herb. Sometimes with that kind of dizziness, you may even see spots in front of your eyes, the way germs look under a microscope. The other kind of dizziness, severe dizziness,

is different; that's when you're very tired, weak, short of breath, and it's related to some kind of ceremony that needs to be done, like Mountainway, Chiricahua Windway, or another one. With that kind, you need to get a star-gazer, hand-trembler, one of those to diagnose what ceremony you need. You don't treat that with this medicine." AS reported she and others in the family also used this medicine later in life, whenever they felt the need to rid themselves "of all the stuff that slows you down."

When discussing this medicine, SM said his mother had given him some too, earlier in time, to clean him out. "She fixed that buckbrush up for me and I drank it early in the morning. That nearly killed me.* I kept vomiting all day, over by the ditch. It almost killed me. But late in the afternoon Mama hauled me inside and fed me some mutton stew, and then I started coming back from that." He also said that he, WD, and other men used it in the sweathouse, especially when preparing to dance as a team at a Nightway Ceremony. It was among some very specific things they did to "clean everything out" and "get [their] voices way up there" (in the falsetto range that characterizes some Nightway singing; see Chap. 1, n. 14). He, too, clearly remembered the unending vomiting, the bile ("which can choke you") coming out his nose, and the very sore throat that resulted. And like his sisters, he said it was used for certain kinds of headaches, seeing spots, and feeling generally lazy. All agreed that you don't do that very often; "once you drink that, the effects of it last a very, very long time."

5. SM said John Gorman, Robert's father, was the one who came in the car he owned in the 1940s from the Presbyterian Church to get Old Red Bottom Man; "he took him back to the church and buried him around there." He also said John "was one of the first Navajos to work as a missionary for the Presbyterians." Information on John can be found in Kennedy (1965), Mitchell (1978), and Gray (1986); both he and Frank worked hauling freight from Gallup in their early days, and both were serving as Chapter officers in 1944, when Old Curly Hair's wife died and there was a dispute about her land. John and his wife, Ruth Cleveland Gorman, had government boarding school educations and Ruth, like Alice Peshlakai Gorman (Mrs. Nelson Gorman), was among the earliest Navajos to respond to Presbyterian missionary teachings in the 1920s, and to encourage meetings in hogans before the Chinle church was organized (Gray 1986:5, 6). Gray (1986:8,9) documents John's conversion, and notes that while Ruth and John had no children together, they raised Robert, John's brother Arthur's child. They were among the charter members of the Chinle Presbyterian Church in 1921; John became an elder (church leader) in 1928, and was among those giving speeches at the retirement party for Rev. and Mrs. Charles Bysegger when they left Chinle in June 1952 (Gray 1986:11, 13, 28). While there is no mention of specific funerals in Gray (1986), burials were among the identified services provided by the church, and other "Claus Chees" appear on membership lists of the period.

To date, where Old Red Bottom Man was buried remains unclear. While it may have been in the cemetery some were using at the foot of the hill by the National Park Service Headquarters, it may have been elsewhere. According to Father Blane Grein, O.F.M. (p.c. 3/9/1997, 5/31/1997), a parishioner told him that before 1946, the Presbyterians used to bury members in a fenced area on the hill facing the Chinle Wash behind the church/manse complex. The man also reported that a few stone markers remained in the area. While a 1997 visit to this area revealed the fence, there were no visible indications of cemetery usage on the hillside. Additionally, the current pastor of Trinity Presbyterian Church,

Reverend Norma McCabe (p.c. 3/4/1997) knew nothing about it. There are also no references in Gray (1986:21) to a Presbyterian cemetery during the Bysegger years, although funerals are discussed as among the community services provided by the church (Gray 1986:21). Gray himself (p.c. 3/19/1997) said he never heard where burials of early believers were done before the Chinle Community Cemetery was opened (March 1946). Both he and Father Blane Grein, O.F.M. (p.c. 3/7/1997) said that in the beginning years of the latter, sections were assigned to both churches for burials of members.

I also asked GB, who was Presbyterian in earlier days and had lost all of her siblings, as indicated in the text. She said she never went to their burials and was only told they were "taken across the wash, over by Garcia's someplace, behind there, and buried. That place was *not* the cemetery at the foot of the hill by the Park Service where my mother [Beautiful Woman] was buried. They put them someplace else, but I never was told where." She, too, knew of no early Presbyterian cemetery and added that sometimes in the 1930s, people from "both churches" as well as others used the one near the Park Service Headquarters.

On Gray's suggestion, I also contacted Grace Davis, widow of Roger Davis who interpreted for both the Lockers and the Byseggers and later served as an elder and then lay preacher for the Presbyterians (see Gray 1986). Roger had begun interpreting for the Lockers in 1921, while the latter were living in the former Nelson Gorman Trading Post. After Roger's own marriage in 1925, he and Grace resided in the old Nelson Gorman house at the foot of the hill until the interpreter's house was erected on the hill, apparently in the late 1920s after the Presbyterian Church and manse were completed (Gray 1986:12, 15–16, 22). Davis (p.c. 3/6/1997) replied that at least until 1936, when she and Roger moved to Indian Wells to assume duties at the church there (which Grace continued after Roger's 1965 death [Gray 1986:16]), "Rev. Bysegger buried the deceased where they passed on." According to her, "The Presbyterians did not have a cemetery while [she and Roger] were in Chinle."

While following up on the leads discussed above, I also learned of another possible early Presbyterian cemetery from AS and HM. Both reported passing one while on trips from the Chinle Boarding School with a matron to "roll around and play" in the sand dunes south of the Thunderbird Lodge. According to them, on the hills south of the Thunderbird and east of the present dunes, there was a big cemetery with a big gate and heavy fence, a place that was well maintained and in active use when they traveled past it during the 1935–43 years. AS said she had been told in the 1930s it was "The Presbyterian Cemetery." Although she and I traveled to the general area in 1997, no traces of this cemetery were found. Additionally, none of the older individuals AS then contacted (two older men, who lived in the area, and one of her own school matrons), remembered it. While the latter was having memory problems by 1997, according to AS, the others probably claimed no memories of the place because "many traditional Navajos don't like to discuss cemeteries and things like that."

6. This happened *after* Chubby Woman died; also see Chap. 17.

7. Tall Woman suggested I ask HM about this event. In summary, he said during the early years of the war, in the winter of either 1942 or 1943, a bomber crashed in Canyon de Chelly near where Jake Brown then lived. Planes were always flying over and people wondered if they were enemy planes. Jake had come to see Frank two nights before, in the heavy snow, to get a Blessingway Protection Prayer done for himself because of a bad dream about some pending misfortune. Before the plane went down, people could hear it circling and circling, perhaps because the only visible lights were those from the BIA Boarding School. After

news of the crash spread, HM and (George) Acey Davis [AD] joined the search crew on horseback to look for survivors; of the eleven crew members, only one died ("from hanging"); his parachute caught in a pinyon tree on the rim of the Canyon and although he was alive when found by the search party he died shortly thereafter at the Chinle Hospital. Two others reportedly bailed out before the crash and were found to the north. HM said the winds were very strong at the time and they blew the plane south. Two weeks later he and AD, while still searching, found the plane's wing. The BIA school reportedly hauled school children in trucks to help pick up the pieces of metal scattered all over. After those were put into huge piles, government trucks came and hauled them away. (The National Park Service seems not to have been involved in the event; no mention of it was found in documents reviewed by Brugge and Wilson [Brugge p.c. 3/1/1997], nor is it documented in their account of the "lean years" [World War II years] at the Canyon de Chelly National Monument [Brugge and Wilson 1976:81–88]. HM's account, however, *is* verified in Salsbury, with Hughes (1969:198–99), where the bomber crash is discussed and dated at 1/24/1944.)

8. As shown in the text, according to Tall Woman, what she did to assist women during labor was different from what was done by the woman who takes the baby out. Young and Morgan (1980:123, 137, 945) provide the following Navajo terms for "midwife," "she [the woman who] causes her to start to give birth," or "she [the woman who] takes/pulls them out one after another": *'awéé' hayiidzísí; 'asdzání 'i'iiłchíhí; 'awéé' hayiiníłí.* Navajo childbirth practices are grounded in sacred narratives accounting for the births of Changing Woman and her sister, White Shell Woman, and later, the Twin Warriors born to Changing Woman. In addition to these narratives, information is available in a variety of other sources, especially those focused on Navajo children; Navajo women, their life cycles, and the beliefs and practices associated with different stages; cross-cultural studies of childbirth and the human body; woven sash belts; medicinal herbs; and so forth. Some of the many resources available include: Lockett (1939, viewed by some as "the classic work" on the topic), Leighton and Leighton (1944), Kluckhohn and Leighton (1946), Leighton and Kluckhohn (1947), Bailey (1948, 1950), Loughlin (1965), Anonymous (1977), Stewart (1980), Kunitz (1983), Milligan (1984a, b), Waxman (1990, a particularly useful overview), Begay (1985, a dissertation on Navajo childbirth practices), and Schwarz (1997). Other kinds of sources, such as Allen (1963:148–50, 179–86), provide information on both "traditional" and "hospital" approaches to Navajo childbirth. Hardeen (1994) and *Indian Country Today*'s special issue on "The Navajo Nation" (June 1995:30) focus on the approach used at the Chinle Comprehensive Health Care Facility, where "traditional woven sash belts" are available "as aids" to women in labor. Kluckhohn, Hill, and Kluckhohn (1971:313–14) describe sash belts as "belly binders."

In *Weaving a World*, the catalog accompanying their 1996–97 exhibit, as well as in the exhibit itself, Willink and Zolbrod (1996) present and discuss two textiles identified as "midwife blankets" by the weavers who assisted them. The first (Willink and Zolbrod 1996: 64–65, and pl. 13) is a "Late Classic Serape," dating from the 1860s. Their consultants said the yellow therein recalled pollen and cornmeal that facilitate births, and "Horny Toad's" role in childbirth. According to them, a midwife in preparation for childbirth would catch such a toad [*sic*, although Horned Toads are lizards] and "deposit pollen or yellow cornmeal on the creature's head, tail and torso and force some into its mouth before letting it hop [*sic*] away. Collecting any cornmeal and pollen the creature spit out and gathering that which fell from its back, head, and tail, she would place the mixture in her medicine bundle. The midwife would then administer the compound at birthing time to assure the easy delivery of a child who would grow up healthy and able. If a medicine man were not available, the midwife might sing the appropriate Blessingway songs herself." The second textile, a "Wearing Blanket" (pp. 66–67, pl. 14), dating from 1860, contains parallel zigzags which some weavers said represented women's sash belts. These belts, which serve as "drag ropes" during childbirth, have designs that were said to represent the sunbeam and rainbow strands utilized by Changing Woman while giving birth to the Warrior Twins, according to the sacred narratives. Thus, according to the weavers, the use of these belts identifies the woman in labor with childbirth as it was experienced at the beginning of time by the Holy People, and with all the subsequent births, that is, "with many things." To the best of my knowledge, this is the first time any Navajo weavers have labeled any nineteenth-century textiles "midwife blankets." When I showed plates 13 and 14 (*in* Willink and Zolbrod 1996) to five elderly weavers in the Chinle area in 1997, they were first mystified and then annoyed by the label. All emphatically stated during the ensuing discussions that as far as they knew, woven textiles had *never* been used by anyone during childbirth for any reason, "not even way back!" As one said, "To call them that [midwife blankets] gives others the wrong idea about how we go about that, what midwives use when helping women in labor." Their reactions raised a number of questions that would be interesting to pursue with future research.

9. See Mitchell (1978:300) for Frank's account of this birth, which occurred on 11/17/1959. AS had changed into her traditional clothes before the Blessingway Ceremony started, and her mother was getting things ready in the hogan. Frank had already started the ceremony and had bathed AS when her labor began. When she told her parents and expressed concerns over a home birth (since her previous children had been born in the hospital), Frank talked to her. AS summarized his words as follows: "He said the Blessingway cannot be stopped once the patient is bathed, so going to the hospital was out of the question, not an option. Furthermore, he told me I had gone to Catholic schools where the Sisters had taught me that Christ had been born out in the open, not in a hospital. He was still a Holy One; nothing went wrong for Him, so if I had faith, I wouldn't need to go to the hospital, either." AS said that comforted her; "it relieved my worries; my fear was gone." Frank and her mother were there, as well as AD who was helping Frank sing, MD who was the "baby catcher," and RY who was also helping. ID stayed outside cooking, with all the other children. AD had already dug the hole in the floor for one end of the pole and placed the other into the roof, after tying one end of the sash belt to it; AS used her mother's old belt, the one that was "really long because in those days, my mother was really big and heavy."

After saying these things to her, Frank started singing again with AD, and AS's son's head appeared; when nothing else happened for a while, Frank "panicked and got out the feather fan he used for Evilway Blackenings; he used to do those, too." Then he "drew a blank; he couldn't remember what to sing with that. So after waving the fan around, he threw it to [AD], yelling, 'Help me out; sing!' [AD] started laughing; he tried going around the fire with it, and started raising too much dust, so my mother started yelling about that.* She was also yelling at both of them, 'Start Singing!' Then [MD] and [RY] tried to go out the door at the same time and got stuck; my mother yelled again, this time at everybody for being too excited.* We all were laughing because of those things. And right then, the rest of the baby emerged; he started crying, and [MD] grabbed him."* [RY] was there, ready with the water, blankets, and other things. Tall Woman stayed behind AS the whole time, got the afterbirth expelled, and bound her stomach (as described in the text). AS also recalled that her mother "was really angry at Frank afterwards about what had happened. Then [RY] had to retie my son's cord because [MD] had left it too long. So she started teasing him about cutting his fish off."*

MD, when recounting her own experience, said after she told her parents she was in labor (with Louise), her mother "was getting things ready" and her father "was putting up the post for the string. Right then, the baby came out. I grabbed on to Frank's neck; he started scolding me, saying, 'Why aren't you screaming, crying like a goat if you're in labor?' He threw down the string. I just hung on to him until the afterbirth came out. He was sure surprised. He said usually women scream and he asked me why I wasn't doing that. But my daughter came out with no pain."

Both accounts convey the relaxed nature of hogan births (when all is going well) which take place with others present. In both of these cases, the others included the women's parents; in AS's experience, two sisters and a brother-in-law who was the other singer were also present.

10. All of Tall Women's children knew she did this. For all of her daughters, her knowledge and skills in this area were one of the special things they "remembered her by" after her death. They all said she did this *a lot* while they were growing up. GB reported accompanying her several times; AgS went once or twice, and AS, once. The rest never went; RY, especially, took care of her younger siblings while her mother was gone, helping other women with childbirth.

11. See Chap. 1, for *Tanabah*'s story.

12. See Chap. 2, for the account of Slim Woman's birth.

13. I have not been able to learn the Navajo term for this, if there is one. In the 1960s, none of those in Tall Woman's and Frank's generation knew a word for this, nor did Chic or Ethnobah Sandoval. Tall Woman laughed about this, saying what the word was didn't matter. "People didn't worry about that when they came to get me to do it. They all knew I wasn't the one who catches the baby" (which she variously expressed with the terms given in Young and Morgan [1980] and included in n. 8, this chapter).

14. As explained in the Introduction, the general ethnobotanical knowledge Tall Woman shared with me during our life history work sessions per se has been left in the text. However, the detailed, specific ethnobotanical data provided by both her and her children during extra, focused interviews have been excluded.

15. AgS told me about peeking anyway, and starting to worry about the suffering she saw the woman in labor going through. Since this was during the time her grandmother was preaching against men, she viewed what she saw as another example of the suffering men caused for women. As she said, "Of course, this was before I was old enough to understand the birds and the bees; I was still too young to get answers to my questions."

16. This would be ca. 1945.

17. Tall Woman's daughters all confirmed that while she avoided their direct questions about "the birds and the bees" when they were small, as they got older, when they were alone with her she did answer them directly and explain things clearly. "Before she decided we were old enough, she'd pass the buck on that; all she'd say was, 'Don't jump around in your teens or you'll become *kinaaldá*, or your *chooyin* will fall out.' Of course we'd wonder

what those things were, and we'd ask each other, when she wouldn't answer us. But later, she was really good at explaining those things to us, how you get your period and that you're able to have children from then on."

CHAPTER 20

1. Frank told me they did; Judge Shirley put him in overnight after rounding up him and others, including CS, for drinking at a Nightway being held near Fort Defiance at the time. According to Frank, the judge "really gave me a scolding because I, too, was a judge and shouldn't have been doing that."* He also said when he told Tall Woman about it, she, too, scolded him for the same reason. Bootlegging on the reservation was hardly a new phenomenon even in 1946. Carl Gorman refers to making extra money during Prohibition days (1920–33) by doing such work between 1930 and 1933 (Greenberg and Greenberg 1984:46; also see Cousins and Cousins 1996:71), and SM told me he did plenty of the same, in the late 1930s and during the 1940s. Despite the repeal of Prohibition, alcohol remained illegal on the reservation, as it is today; thus, customers continued to turn to those who would buy it in bordertowns and defy the laws by transporting it to others living on the reservation. According to SM, in the early 1940s, whiskey was selling for $5 a half-pint; when some individuals' preferences changed to wine in the late 1940s, that was selling for 80¢ a bottle.

2. Tall Woman, upon further thought, said it seemed like Frank came to hold court in Chinle about once a month, and then was allowed to come home only on weekends. It is clear that at least in Frank's case, when he worked as a judge, he stayed in various locations, perhaps because the matter of lodging was left up to individual judges. Mitchell (1978:302 n. 1) indicates that when court was in session in Fort Defiance, Frank stayed at St. Michaels and when the location was Crownpoint, he stayed with GB who worked at the Crownpoint Hospital from 1945 until 1947. AS said in Chinle, in those days, court was first held on certain days in the Chinle Boarding School auditorium. Later, when recreational use of that space increased, and she was in her last year at the school (1942–43), court proceedings were moved to a "long, wooden building across the road, under the clay butte hill that sticks up, west of the auditorium and the post office" (the latter's fourth site). At that time, this government building (whose previous function was unclear to AS and others) was surrounded by a barbed-wire fence with wooden posts. The court did not move again until ca. 1961–62, a time when the community of Chinle saw many changes. Among them was the opening of the new Law and Order building (constructed across the road from Our Lady of Fatima Church, and still in use in 1998) that included a police department, jail, and courtroom for the Chinle District (Young 1961:282; Gray 1986:65). By 1996, there were no traces of the Chinle court's earlier sites. As AS said, "Now they're all gone; they tore those down, too, just like they did with lots of the buildings at the old Chinle Boarding School and other places."

Mitchell (1978:270–73, 278–79 n. 15, 279–80 n. 17, 288–90 ff.) documents Frank's work (from 1946 to 1951) as a judge in the Courts of Indian Offenses, which were established in the 1930s. Initially the six judges were appointed by the Commissioner of Indian Affairs and confirmed by a two-thirds vote of the Tribal Council; terms were for four years and were renewable if specified conditions were met. Over the years, the number of judges and the ways in which they were chosen changed; by 1954, tribal courts were located in Shiprock, Fort Defiance, Chinle, Tuba City, and Kayenta. The Navajo Nation's judicial branch was not created by the Tribal Council until 1959.

As noted earlier, Frank may have started working as a judge in 1938 (Mitchell 1978:279–80 n. 17). He and John Brown (the policeman) definitely heard a dispute in 1944 over Old Curly Hair's wife's land after her death, but perhaps more as leaders or Chapter officers from the Chinle area. When his term as a judge expired in 1951, Frank ran for a seat on the Tribal Council, but again, lost the election. After that, he became active in the Chinle Chapter, serving as president in 1951 and 1952, and as an unidentified officer in 1955; later (6/20/1959), he performed a House Blessing Ceremony at the public dedication of the new Chapter House that was built during 1958 (see Mitchell 1978:274 n. 2, 305–6 n. 5). (That was replaced by a new building in 1981.)

In addition to Mitchell (1978), for information on the Navajo Nation's judicial system see Shepardson (1963, 1965), Young (1961), Iverson (1981), Frisbie (1987:160–75 ff.), and numerous other works, including *Navajo Nation Government* (Navajo Nation 1998:28–32). In October 1998, Chief Justice Robert Yazzie (1998) provided a cogent review of the history of Navajo Nation courts in his invited keynote address to participants at the Eleventh Annual Navajo Studies Conference. Then, after discussing the growing, international interest in Navajo peacemaking and peacemakers, he explained the current Navajo Law Project. Through this, he and others are seeking to define and incorporate Navajo Common Law and Navajo thought into the Nation's court policies and opinions. He closed by enumerating some of the challenges ahead for the Nation's courts as federal policymakers continue to try to limit their sovereignty.

3. For descriptions of this by AgS and AS, see Mitchell (1978:302 n. 1).

4. Tall Woman remained very afraid of witchcraft in all of its forms during her entire life. She never hesitated to voice her concerns about it; between 1963 and 1967, I heard and saw her do so often, especially with Frank. In response, he often, but not always, would joke about the possibility that someone was witching either him or someone else in the family, if not the whole group, their animals, or endeavors. He did, however, have his own concerns about it; see Mitchell (1978:288–90 ff.). Many of Tall Woman's children saw her beliefs about witchcraft as another example of "how very strong she was in all the traditional beliefs," and "how very traditional she was until the end of her days."

5. Several of his children said they did this in Fort Defiance, Chinle, and Crownpoint. Among the things they remembered hearing about were cases dealing with peyote, abusive marriages, divorce, and land and inheritance disputes. They also confirmed that while Frank was never aware of their presence, when he found out, he told them "in very strong words" to stay out of the courtroom because "only bad things go on in there."

6. Several of the children said they did try to learn a particular song they happened to like by listening to him at night, but never were any good at it. They also said sometimes when he'd bring them home from the Chinle Boarding School on horseback, he'd sing Horse Songs from the Blessingway and tell them that knowing some of those would make it possible to raise livestock in their future lives without having any problems. Another kind he'd sing was Blessingway Mountain Songs; both of these were in addition to the special songs he made up for each of his children and sang while transporting them or relaxing in the hogan with them, as mentioned earlier.

7. As shown in the Epilogue, among the things people remembered Tall Woman for after her death were her quiet, calm ways and her ability to be consistently nice to everyone, without exception. Thus, her personal resolves and decisions at this point in her life appear both permanent and noteworthy, when Navajos compared her with other peers.

8. Among the ceremonies Frank performed was the Protection Rite; this is among the ceremonial options when a person is diagnosed as needing the effects of bad dreams removed. See Mitchell (1978:300) for one he performed for ID (in 1957) for this reason; that particular one preceded a Blessingway she had before the birth of a son in 1958.

9. ID's daughter, Geneva, was born on 2/9/1947. HM said ID got sick in the spring of 1947, during the time when he had taken a leave from a "really good job" at an ice plant in Needles, California, to come back and help Frank plant the fields. HM never returned to this job where he had worked for two years; after staying around Chinle and doing different kinds of work for the government, in 1950, he and a friend, Henry Haven from Nazlini, left for jobs with the Union Pacific Railroad in Wyoming. Although he came home on a two-week leave in 1951, as Frank requested because HM's Uncle John was sick and was hospitalized, HM worked with the Union Pacific Railroad until 1957, when he left because he "was getting sick all the time." After that, he stayed in Chinle for about a year. Then he worked for the Santa Fe Railroad for six months, and next, for a furniture store in Kingman, Arizona (1958–winter 1959). After that, as shown in nn. 18 and 25 in Chap. 21, HM held a variety of jobs, both in and around Chinle and off the reservation, until retiring in September 1984. His last job was as foreman of the crew that tore down the old Chinle Chapter House (built in 1958, and replaced in 1981) and old Chinle preschool in 1984. When the demolition was complete, the windows, lumber, and other things that could be reused were auctioned off to members of the community.

10. Frank (Mitchell 1978:300) describes ID's symptoms slightly differently, and attributes her need for this ceremony to earlier contact with a bearskin rug at the Presbyterian Church, as mentioned in Chap. 17, n. 2.

11. The *Liber Defunctorum* records (p. 37 no. 6) at Our Lady of Fatima Church show that Jim Mitchell from Black Mountain died on 6/20/1948 and was buried in "Row 1 of the new Chinle Community Cemetery" by Father Mark Sandford, O.F.M., the same day. His age is recorded as seventy-five in ink, and seventy-two in pencil. Jim was remembered as "very tall, over six feet," as the owner of lots of sheep (which caused him to hire herders, including SM during some of the summers while the latter was a student at Fort Apache), and as a resident of the Black Mountain area, including locations around the old Black Mountain Trading Post. Jim appears frequently in the earlier part of Tall Woman's narrative since he was married in a traditional ceremony to one of her older sisters, and then another one (Little Woman) before he started "acting like a billy goat with other women." According to the family, among the women he was "maybe married to" later was Adelle's mother, after she reportedly ended her marriage to John Brown. This older brother was also one of the "Three Musketeers" Frank used to run around with in his gambling days.

12. AgS worked as a nurse at the Ft. Miley Veterans Administration Hospital in San Francisco from 1946 until 1950, when she was sent, with six other nurses, to set up a new VA hospital in Fresno. After her marriage to Tony Sanchez on 6/24/1950, in September the couple relocated to Stockton, California, where AgS began a new job as a nurse at the Stockton Blood Bank in October. She retired from that job in September 1984. AgS was among the women whose lives were celebrated in 1998 by the New York-based artist Marilyn Cohen, in a multi-textural exhibit entitled, "Teach Me the Songs My Mother Sang: A Celebration of American Women," on display at the Thomas J. Walsh Art Gallery, Fairfield University, Fairfield, Connecticut, from 1/16/1998 through 2/22/1998. The 41″ x 29″ collage featuring

AgS (created in 1997 and displayed as Number 3 in the 1998 exhibition) and its accompanying text panel were entitled "Agnes Who Remembers the Songs of the People" (Cohen 1998: 15, 21, and portfolio insert). Although AgS and her family were unable to attend the exhibition, Cohen provided her, and others who were featured or who had assisted, with copies of the exhibition catalog.

CHAPTER 21

1. This was the election that returned Sam Ahkeah to another term (1951–54) as Tribal Chairman, and the first one to use pictorial ballots. Frank ran against Joe Carroll and Walker Norcross, losing to Carroll as Council delegate from District 10, Province 2. His ballot picture is reproduced as fig. 10 in Mitchell (1978:273).

2. As shown in Appendix A, AS's daughter, Cecilia [CeS], was born on 5/9/1951. SM said he really didn't start to get to know his Uncle John until the latter moved back to the Chinle area, after he'd been with women from Fort Defiance, Deer Springs, one of Old Red Bottom Man's daughters, and a woman from Round Rock for a long time. He said John was living alone at this time, and that he was "really skinny. He always dressed up like a pirate; his long moustache was all twisted up, he wore big copper hoop earrings, and a bandanna, just like pirates."

3. See Appendix A for genealogies. All of Tall Woman's and Frank's grandchildren were born during both of their lifetimes; the last one, Ronald Sandoval, was born on 5/21/1965.

4. The *Liber Defunctorum* records (p. 46 no. 3) show that Tom, Jr., son of Frank's younger brother, Thomas, husband of Bartine, and father of Jim, Charles, Bertha, and others, died on 5/6/1955 at age forty-seven, after being crushed by a pickup on the Sawmill-Chinle Road near Fluted Rock. He was buried on 5/9/1955 as "no. 55 in Row 2 in the new Chinle Community Cemetery" by Father Daniel Wefer, O.F.M.

5. Tall Woman is referring to the Navajo-Cornell Field Health Research Project at Many Farms (1956–62), documented in Adair and Deuschle (1970). The later 1950s brought many changes on the reservation documented in numerous sources (see Young 1961, Gray 1986, and others), including attention to paving roads for use by school buses. Young (1961:139) documents the status of roads to and from Chinle as of June 1960.

6. See Mitchell (1978:369–70, Appendix C) for a list of anthropologists and others with whom Frank worked; also see References here.

7. See Mitchell (1978:300) for Frank's recollections about the ceremonies his children had. The Blessingway film, entitled "Blessingway," was made in 1957 by David P. McAllester with support from Wesleyan University and the Museum of Navajo Ceremonial Art (now the Wheelwright Museum). The original, unedited footage and an edited first copy, now on videotape, are archived at Wesleyan University's Audio Visual Department (McAllester p.c. 7/5/1998; also see McAllester [1984]). In accordance with Frank's and, later, the family's wishes, the film is not available for public viewing. Mitchell (1978:301, fig. 10) includes a still photograph of Frank and Isabel doing one of the litany prayers during the filming of the ceremony. Although Frank (Mitchell 1978:300) said this was held "about a month before Isabel gave birth to Jerry," the Blessingway was actually performed before an earlier son, Joseph ("Mann") was born, and clearly, several months before his birth on 4/26/1958.

8. The *Liber Defunctorum* records at Our Lady of Fatima Church (p. 48 no. 11) show that Long Moustache died from pneumonia at the Fort Defiance Hospital at the age of ninety on

2/14/1959. He was buried two days later in the Chinle Community Cemetery by Father Pius Winter, O.F.M.

9. Tall Woman's medical records at Sage Memorial Hospital show an admission and diagnosis for hyperthyroidism on 5/14/1959, a condition which did not disappear from her record until 4/1964.

10. The educational needs of non-Indian children on the reservation were met through public-school classes. Early in the twentieth century, having enough children to warrant the hiring of teachers, finding and keeping teachers, and then, finding space were all problematic (see Young 1961; Thompson 1975; Gray 1986). In Chinle for at least two years in the mid-1920s, space upstairs in the Big House was used for this purpose (see Frisbie 1998). By the late 1920s, public-school students were being taught in one of the buildings at the Chinle Boarding School (see Chap. 13, n. 5 and Chap. 15, n. 5, about Chinle teachers Sybil Fry Wilson and Cordelia Jackson Dunaway; also see St. Michaels Archive Photo c539.9–1, R112, building on left). Finally, in the early 1930s, when state-run "Accommodation Schools" began to be developed on the reservation, Chinle was chosen as one of the communities in which such a school was to be located (Thompson 1975:141). At that point, a one- or two-room public school was built on the hill east of the Chinle Boarding School. This building served public-school students until the fall of 1959, when the 1958–59 construction of a much larger public school had been completed and the new building, with a capacity of 450 students, opened. Thereafter, the Accommodation School building was converted to apartments and rented out until some time in the late 1970s. By 1996, this white frame building with dormer windows had been boarded up and was awaiting demolition. The physical plant of the public school, new in 1959, was being used as the site of Chinle's kindergarten, since another public school had been built in the interim.

11. Frank performed a House Blessing for the new Chinle Chapter House when it was publicly dedicated on 6/20/1959. HM confirmed Tall Woman's words here by recounting a series of mishaps during his jobs in 1959 with the Santa Fe Railroad in a variety of states, including Oklahoma, Texas, Colorado, and New Mexico. The mishaps were followed by an accident wherein a motor car rolled over his feet, breaking them, when they were working south of Belen.

12. See Mitchell (1978:289, 306–7 n. 9, ff.) for Frank's thoughts about the possible causes of these pains.

13. Frank's Enemyway was held during the summer of 1959; for his own account of this ceremony, see Mitchell (1978:292–95, 388 n. 12, ff.). AS said that part of this ceremony was held near Small Woman's hogan; she herself had to stay home because her daughter, "Tiny" (Regina, RS) was not yet a year old, and she "was designated to baby-sit all the kids." HM had a two-week leave from his job in Kingman, Arizona, which enabled him to participate in the ceremony. By June 1963, Frank had received the sacred, decorated rattlestick three times. Chap. 5, n. 9, provides information and sources on the Enemyway, wherein two groups participate, one as sponsors and the other, as the stick receivers. The latter role involves heavy expenses, much work, and a series of ritual obligations toward the sponsors; however, to be asked to receive the stick continues to be viewed as a great honor.

14. John Mitchell died on 9/22/1959, "in bed from natural causes" (according to Catholic Church records) at the age of eighty-eight. He was buried two days later by Father Pius Winter, O.F.M., as "no. 22, Row 3, in the Chinle Community Cemetery" (*Liber Defunctorum*

[p. 49 no. 3], Our Lady of Fatima Church). See Mitchell (1978:295–98) for an account of the squabbles over his estate, which included cash, land, and a Blessingway *jish*, among other things. AS, who had a second job working for Father Pius at the church at the time, added further details: "An old man came to our hogan before dawn, to tell Frank something was wrong with John. That man had been there visiting the night before, and he said they'd fallen asleep. John had rolled off the bed and wasn't waking up. Tall Woman came over to my new house early in the morning; we'd only been living in that about a year when this happened. She tapped on my windows, trying to wake me up so I could go wake up [HM]. At that time, he was living in the log cabin by [RY]'s. Tall Woman made coffee before Frank and HM left on horseback for Uncle John's. As soon as they saw him like that, Frank sent [HM] to get Father Pius to come on his horse, and also to get the police. Father Pius found a big baking powder can in Uncle John's house full of lots of money, probably about $2,000; he also had *lots* of jewelry, things people had pawned to him, as well as lots of his own. When the police came, they blocked off the whole area for two or three days while they investigated that. Poor Father Pius ended up having to help settle the estate; Uncle John had made a will and left it with Father Pius. I think when they buried him, they only spent about $250 on his coffin; [HM] helped bury him and also shot his beautiful horse, like we do. For a long time, Father Pius advertised that pawned jewelry, hoping the owners would come and claim it. I don't know if all of them ever did or not." Documents on file at Our Lady of Fatima Church show Father Pius's duties as administrator of John's estate were legally discharged on 11/22/1960 by Judge Paul Tso.

15. See Chap. 19, n. 9; Augustine was born on 11/17/1959.

16. Construction of the new federal boarding school in Chinle started in 1960; with its capacity of one thousand and associated subdivision of homes for personnel, the new school was among the reasons that Chinle saw an enormous expansion in population, buildings, and upgraded services in the 1958–62 period. See Gray (1986:63–65) for further information on growth in the community at this time. As noted earlier, the dedication ceremony for the new boarding school was held on 5/19/1961.

17. Tall Woman didn't elaborate on why she needed this second Mountainway; Frank (Mitchell 1978:286–87) dated it in 1959–60 and attributed it to her continued suffering from attacks of "indigestion," while also noting it provided significant, immediate relief.

18. HM said he worked in a furniture store in Kingman, Arizona, during this period. When he left that one-year job in the winter of 1959, he came back to Chinle to head up various Ten Days Projects focused on shallow wells, irrigation systems, and, later, construction of homes for the People. He said he stayed with AS on and off, in the place she and her family were using behind the mission, through the summer of 1962.

19. Later, HM explained that he was borrowed from Ten Days Projects to be foreman for this project. "My government job at this time was with the BLO, heading up the crew that was trying to put a dam back in Canyon del Muerto, around the place we call Black Creek, Black Canyon, or Black Rock Canyon. People used to live in there. We put a dam in there first and I guess the lightning cracked it. When it broke, the hogans and corrals and other places there got flooded when the water came down and went rushing through there. So, the crew got sent back to fix the dam and add a spillway. I think we worked over there for about three weeks. But then, the same thing happened; it started raining and the water in the Canyon started coming up. The lightning hit the dam again, and the spillway, too, breaking

those things. After that, the BLO gave up on that. Some of the People said they should have left the whole area alone in the first place; I guess the Anasazis used to live back there, around in that part of the Canyon, too." During a 9/1996 visit to the site, HM showed me where he had put a 1962 date in the concrete at the spillway; he also said he was the foreman for both jobs and showed me a picture that Charlie Mitchell of the BLO had taken of the crew, which included his nephew, Alfred Shirley.

20. Records at Sage Memorial Hospital showed Tall Woman was admitted with a malunion fracture of the right wrist on 5/11/1962. She clearly was still suffering from hyperthyroidism at this time. Frank (Mitchell 1978:287) also comments on this accident.

21. Dr. George McClelland, Sr. (1/1/1900–5/5/1985), an optometrist from Fullerton, California, was a friend of the Mitchells as well as many other Navajos, especially in the Valley Store, Chinle, and Canyon de Chelly areas. The Mitchells first met "Dr. George" through AS's school classmate and friend, the late Fanny John Price. In the 1960s and 1970s, "Dr. George" reportedly visited annually to enjoy Enemyways, other Navajo occasions, and life in the bottom of the Canyon near White House with the family of Harry and Sophie Price. Although not mentioned in Faris (1996), McClelland is remembered by many in Chinle for his "professional photographs" of Navajos (including the Mitchells) in northeast Arizona during this time period. As described by his son, Dr. George L. McClelland, Jr. (p.c. 8/15/1997), also an optometrist in Fullerton, McClelland, Sr., "was always interested in photography but had no professional training. An avid reader of *Arizona Highways* and an admirer of the work of Joseph Muench, [McClelland, Sr.], after buying his first 35mm. camera in the late 1930s, began his annual trips to the reservation in the mid-1940s. There, his interest in photography was soon joined by an interest in the People themselves, especially the family of Harry and Sophie Price."

22. See Appendix B, Chronology. *Liber Defunctorum* records (p. 50 no. 8) at Our Lady of Fatima Church show that Camillo Garcia (age seventy, and husband of Pauline Corez Garcia) and his son, Abel (age forty-four, and husband of Shirley Wallace Garcia) were both killed when their private plane crashed at 10:15 P.M. on 10/1/1962, one and one-fourth miles from the southwestern end of the Chinle airstrip. As Gray (1986:65) notes, the airstrip, positioned near the Catholic Church, had been enlarged in 1959 and had begun accommodating educational, medical, and construction personnel, in addition to the earlier traffic of traders and BIA employees. (See Map 4.) The Garcia men were buried in Gallup on 10/5/1962, after Father Pius Winter, O.F.M., officiated at their Solemn High Mass at the Gallup Cathedral.

23. In 1963, a group, American Indian Films, Inc., from the University of California at Berkeley, directed by Dr. Samuel Barrett, with William R. Heick serving as cinematographer, was on the reservation. With financial assistance from the National Science Foundation, and logistical assistance from Dr. Kenneth Foster, then director of the Museum of Navajo Ceremonial Art in Santa Fe (later renamed the Wheelwright Museum), the group made plans to film and make sound recordings of three nine-day Navajo ceremonies. One was a nine-day Red Antway Holyway Ceremonial conducted by the Son of the Late Tall Deschine at Valley Store from June 13 through June 21, 1963 (see Wyman 1965:10–11, 24, 35 ff.). For a variety of reasons, I was included in the group allowed to witness, photograph, record, and otherwise document segments of the ceremony; because of this, Barrett learned about the impending Puberty Ceremony and decided to come to the Mitchells during a lull to negotiate the filming and recording of MS's *Kinaaldá*. After successful negotiations, the

timing of the Puberty Ceremony was set for June 19–23, with the camera crew dropping in and out to capture corn grinding, molding, early morning races, and so forth, before the final afternoon and night's activities, all of which were scheduled to happen at their convenience after they were finished in Valley Store (see Frisbie 1967/1993). The film company did not stay for another Puberty Ceremony held from July 12 to July 16 for another of Ruth's daughters, LS, and also sung by Frank. The Old Man with the Cane (who was also called Old White Man with the White Beard) was Dr. Samuel Barrett, who was busy arranging and rearranging the hogan, sometimes at totally inappropriate times, wanting a pristine, "pre-contact environment" for the film. For example, any store-bought items he spotted were ordered out and thus removed instantly, at least from the cameras' eyes. Needless to say, he became the brunt of many Navajo jokes, from both women and men in attendance. However, Frank's willingness to have the ceremony filmed decreased the numbers who would have helped with the event, and brought about criticism of Frank at a Chapter meeting, as becomes clear later in this chapter.

The films and tapes made by this group were transferred to the Lowie Museum (now the Phoebe Hearst Museum, University of California, Berkeley) during the 1960s, but without editing or anything more than minimal documentation, and before any efforts were made to synchronize the audiotapes with the films. For that reason, both Ken Foster (who was in attendance during the Red Antway) and I helped Wyman assemble some data and "still photographs" when he was preparing a volume on the Red Antway (Wyman 1965), and William R. Heick joined us in contributing these and other "stills" as illustrations for Wyman (1983). Additional comments on the American Indian Films Inc. group can be found in Wyman (1965), Frisbie (1967/1993), Faris (1990, 1996), and Francis (1996), among others. Faris (1990: 22, 111, 133 ff.) documents the problems surrounding their filming of a Nightway in December 1963, in Lukachukai, Arizona. His later work (1996:221 ff.) places this group within the context of photography of Navajos in the mid-twentieth century while identifying and discussing additional problems with their Navajo projects. Francis (1996:118, 182–83 nn. 38–40, ff.) bases her remarks on her work with the group's films of the 1963 Nightway, a few stills from which are included in Wyman (1983) and Gill (1979).

24. This refers to a funny story Frank told repeatedly when discussing his early days; it was already well known in the family before he began recording "his story" and can be found in Mitchell (1978:94–96 ff.).

25. HM reported doing forest work (reseeding) near Durango for a week in the summer of 1963, and forest fire fighting "somewhere near the Canadian border for two weeks," probably in 1967. He also said he worked for the Pete Peskanalo Company in the Yuma area for four or five months each winter from 1964 through 1966, until Frank got very sick. There, he and Code Talker Cozy Brown supervised people, "mainly Mexicans and Navajos," who were hired to pick lettuce and cabbage.

26. One of the goals of Navajo life is to live to "a really old age" and "die from old age." The chronological age often cited for such a goal is 102. See Frisbie (n.d.) for further comments on some Navajo ideas about aging and an introduction to the literature.

27. See Frisbie (1967/1993:63–65) for documentation of this criticism at a Sunday afternoon Chapter meeting that both ID and AS attended for other reasons on June 23, 1963, after MS's Puberty Ceremony had reached its conclusion that morning. They spoke in their father's defense and also reported what was said to him, when they returned home.

28. The dedication of the new Chinle High School was held on 2/29/1964. Mitchell (1978:322, fig. 15) provides an illustration of the dignitaries involved.

29. Tall Woman's medical records from Sage Memorial Hospital indicate she was admitted for this reason on 4/20/1964. They also show that her diabetes mellitus was diagnosed at this time. The hyperthyroidism, which was part of her chart from 1959 through 1962, was no longer a problem.

30. Both of these were 1965 events, respectively in the summer and fall. Having just returned to the Southwest from my own wedding in Connecticut on 8/28/1965, Ted and I were able to participate in Lynn's wedding festivities both at the church and at home. My field journal and the *Liber Matrimoniorum* records (p. 22 no. 9) at Our Lady of Fatima Church show Lynn's wedding occurred on 9/25/1965.

31. Frank had made this decision by February 1966; see Mitchell (1978:330 n.).

32. Frank and Tall Woman were baptized on 12/27/1965, according to records at Our Lady of Fatima Church. The article about the event by Father Cormac Antram, O.F.M. (1989) shows that on his first visit at the appointed time, Frank refused. The following day, disappointed family members told Father Cormac such behavior was typical of cancer patients and not to give up. A few days later, he heard that Frank was ready again, and walked over in a deep snow to the Mitchells' "camp, about a mile back in the woods along the Chinle Wash." After appropriate instructions to Frank "and his aged wife," the baptisms were completed. (Also see Antram 1998:92–94.)

33. See the Epilogue in Mitchell (1978:330–41). There was a *long, long pause* here. After about four minutes, I broke it by confirming what Tall Woman had said, and also adding that she didn't need to say anything about it, if she didn't want to. From numerous nonverbal clues it was clear her memories were connected with deep sadness and sorrow. After my brief remarks (which she acknowledged), she remained silent for quite a while (about five more minutes), before choosing to continue as follows.

34. In 1971, AS, when recalling her father's words to his children, said that besides stressing caring for the livestock and the farm, and living happily in one household caring for each other as siblings, he "really emphasized looking after our mother. He was mainly concerned about that when he talked with us. He told us to take good care of her. He said, 'She will be hurt the worse by my going. Be very nice to her and be with her at all times. Treat her right so she doesn't miss me so much. That way she'll know I talked with you and that all of you listened to me. That way she won't be so lonesome.'"

35. This refers to short strings of turquoise beads of various lengths used as earrings or attached so as to hang at the bottom of turquoise necklaces.

36. On 7/17/1971, Tall Woman recalled Frank's words about this as follows: "Let me die in the house and don't do anything to it; it's an old age home. That's what I'm dying from and you shouldn't be scared of that. I'm not dying of anything to be scared of; we've been taught not to fear those who die of old age. So I don't want you putting me outside or sending me back to the hospital. And I don't want anyone burning my cabin down, tearing it up, or doing anything else to it after I pass away."

37. See Mitchell (1978: 330–41) for an epilogue that covers 1966–69, the time of Frank's increasing illness, death on 4/15/1967 and funeral on 4/20/1967, and ceremonies in the family thereafter, including both the Protection Rite and *jish* renewal and transfer described below in the narrative by Tall Woman. In 1996, HM pointed out an error in the description

of his father's funeral; in Mitchell (1978:334), the last word on the page, that is, the name of the person who led Frank's horse, should have been Walter, *not* Acey [AD]. Tall Woman *did* clean out and destroy most of Frank's papers and other possessions, but his cabin was not dismantled or destroyed. Later, HM started living in it.

According to a number of the children, Frank, during his last words to them, said it'd be all right to visit his grave, even though he knew Tall Woman was opposed to it. "He said he was dying from old age and because of that, no harm would come to us if we felt like going to the cemetery to visit his grave." When they started doing this, Tall Woman reiterated her opposition; eventually, those visiting the cemetery either didn't mention it at all, or only after the fact. As one of them said in 1971, "That's one thing that my poor Mom just never understood; she still doesn't like it when we go up there to check on things at the cemetery. She still doesn't want us visiting his grave. But then, she even says that about school trips to museums where you might see Anasazi things. She doesn't think her grandchildren should even go to those places, either." Over the years from then through 1998, the identities of who did and did not visit the cemetery kept changing. For some, this was because aging brought mobility problems; for others, some of their own illnesses were diagnosed as deriving from contact with deceased people, cemeteries, and the like. When they sought to rectify matters ceremonially, medicine people told them to stay away from cemeteries in the future, if they expected their recently completed ceremonies to be and remain effective.

38. Hospital records show a diagnosis of an umbilical hernia on 4/29/1968 and its repair on 5/13/1968. This was Tall Woman's last surgery, although not her last admission to Sage Memorial Hospital.

39. The *Liber Defunctorum* records (p. 56 no. 11) at Our Lady of Fatima Church show that Mrs. Joseph Ganna (Mary) C no. 66707 died on 4/20/1968, of "old age." A notation suggests her age was "70?" and that she had recently moved back from Winslow to Chinle. She was buried on 4/24/1968, with a funeral mass by Father Adam Wethington, O.F.M. GB's father, Tom Scott, died on 9/27/1968, according to records at Trinity Presbyterian Church. Both individuals were buried in the Chinle Community Cemetery.

40. See Mitchell (1978:338–39, 341 n. 11) for another description of the Evilway and Blessingway used for the cleansing, renewal, and transfer of Frank's *jish* to Tall Woman.

41. See Appendix A. Bartine was one of the children Tall Woman's half sister, Slim Woman, had with Old Red Bottom Man. Bartine married Thomas "Jr.," son of Frank's younger brother, Thomas, who was called *Diné Yázhí Bizhé'é*. Together they had many children (including Charles and Bertha) before Thomas was killed in a car accident documented above, in n. 4 (this chapter). Bertha cared for her mother during Bartine's last years, which were spent battling cancer to which she succumbed on 3/18/1973, at the age of sixty-four. She was buried from the Catholic Church on 3/22/1973 by Father Davin von Hagel, O.F.M. (See the *Liber Defunctorum* records [p. 62 no. 1] for "Bartine Bah Mitchell," also recorded as *Axaajibaa'* no. 3, wife of Tom.)

42. In 1971, Tall Woman became very sad while recounting her 1969 visit to Houses Standing in a Line. She stopped talking for several minutes after this sentence, and began again only after wiping her eyes. Although I knew from her voice tones, speech patterns, and words that recalling this visit brought back painful memories of many significant losses (the most recent of which was Frank's), her tears had been silent. She never again returned to Houses Standing in a Line.

43. As noted above, a *very long pause* occurred between the end of the previous sentence (and paragraph) and the start of this one. Unbeknownst to either of us, the summer of 1971 was the last time Tall Woman and I had any extended opportunity to work on her book. As explained in the Introduction, until 1976, I was able to be in Chinle only for five days in 1972, and a week in June 1975. For me, 1972 brought the birth of our second daughter, Jennifer, in June. Then my own father was diagnosed with terminal cancer and died in March 1973. A month later I began a twenty-six-month term as department chairperson, not becoming eligible for sabbatical leave until the fall of 1975. Since the leave was "split" and on the quarter system, except for a week-long visit to Chinle in June 1975, I did not have the opportunity to return to the Southwest until the spring of 1976. By the time I was again able to spend any significant amounts of time in Chinle, Tall Woman's own circumstances had changed drastically because she had suffered several strokes. When Elizabeth and I left at the end of the summer of 1971, her memory problems were already apparent, but not severe. As shown in the Epilogue, two years later, in April, she suffered her first stroke and became paralyzed. In August 1973, when her home health-care needs increased, she was moved to AS's house, where she remained until she passed away.

44. As shown in the Epilogue, this did not happen because Doogie died unexpectedly, in 1972.

45. At the time I was preparing to take a child "into the field" for the first time, I discovered that professional literature on the subject was minimal. Thus, after this first experience, I decided to address some of the issues involved in print (see Frisbie 1975a, b). Since then, the literature cited in those articles has been expanded by Cassell (1987), Butler and Turner (1987), and works of others, as well as by reflexive dialogues at professional meetings on the impact of fieldwork experiences on the children of anthropologists. One example of the latter was the invited session, "In the Field and at Home: Families and Anthropology," organized and chaired for the Society for Humanistic Anthropology by David Sutton at the Ninety-fourth annual American Anthropological Association meetings (11/15–19/1995), and including presentations by Gertrude Huntington, Alma Gottlieb, Philip Graham, and others.

CHAPTER 22

1. As shown at the end of Chap. 21, during the summer of 1971, Tall Woman decided what else she wanted to say in her story. Her words to her grandchildren and future generations were taped in a series of short sessions during that summer, with many being rescheduled because of her concerns about her memory, which she labeled "faulty," "failing," and "slipping" on given days. As she herself said, after she recorded her words to the future generations, there was still plenty of work left to be done on her book. But all of it was of a different kind, namely, directed interviewing with questions really being requests for expansions on and/or re-explanations of things she had mentioned earlier. Some of the remaining, directed work was completed during Tall Woman's "clear times" in December 1972, June 1975, and the spring of 1976. As shown in the Introduction and Frisbie (1997), her children, in a variety of ways, assisted with the rest during the years that passed between Tall Woman's 1977 death and the preparation of the manuscript.

2. Here, there was another *long* pause, obviously while Tall Woman decided if she had anything further she wanted to say.

1. As explained in the Introduction, the last part of Tall Woman's book has been authored by the editor, according to her wishes. Like the rest of the text, the Epilogue was reviewed by and discussed with her family. In this instance, the "polished draft" version was then revised extensively and expanded to incorporate the level of detail the family wanted. As an Epilogue, it is based on my fieldwork notes, journals, and experiences; communications with various family members by letter and telephone; and their comments during 1996–97 discussions of the manuscript drafts. As explained in the text, the final section, her "family's concluding reflections," was constructed according to family suggestions, both in format and content; for them, ending "her story" with their thoughts on why Tall Woman was outstanding, while preserving their anonymity by reducing our discussions to a constructed, composite list format, was "the best way to finish her book."

2. Having taken some of the family on another errand, I did not participate in this diagnostic event. The result, as reported to me that night, included three suggestions: "Navajo Windway for snakes, Shootingway which is for snakes, lightning, and bears, and maybe Evilway, too." The family decided to start with the "small, other kind of Windway," in part to complete the sixteen Tall Woman had been having performed over the years (or make sure they were completed, since "Frank had been keeping track of that" and no one was sure if sixteen had been done), as well as to see "if it did any good." I was told, "If that seems to help her at all, then we'll go ahead and have a big, five-night Mountainway or Shootingway done for her as soon as we can get prepared for it."

3. Chee Carroll was one of Old Curly Hair's children; he fell to his death in the Canyon on the night of 11/5/1971, while on his way to a Nightway being held at a hogan on the rim.

4. Douglas Franklin Mitchell, "Doogie," [DoM] died on 12/4/1972, in Connecticut, at age twenty-six from causes never understood by most of his relatives, although his stepbrother, R. C. Gorman, attributed it to heart failure (Gorman 1992:13, 46). He was buried in the Veterans Cemetery in Fort Defiance on 12/9/1972, after a funeral mass at St. Michaels, with Father Davin von Hagel, O.F.M., officiating (*Liber Defunctorum* records, p. 61 no. 6, Our Lady of Fatima Church). His mother, Adelle [AM] (also spelled Adele and Adela in documents), and AS flew to Connecticut the following summer, seeking additional information about and clarification of the circumstances of his death, but reportedly were unsuccessful. Musically talented since the age of three, DoM was well known both in Navajoland and in the Wesleyan and New York art communities. At the time of his death, a year when McAllester was on sabbatical from Wesleyan University and out of the country, DoM was a visiting artist in American Indian music and dance, in the World Music Program at Wesleyan. He and McAllester had already coauthored and submitted an essay on Navajo music for the *Handbook of North American Indians*; due to production delays, the volume in which it appeared was not published for eleven more years; see McAllester and Mitchell (1983).

5. Alvin and Mary Lucier were among DoM's friends at Wesleyan University. After completing a year as a visiting professor, Alvin, a composer, joined the faculty of the World Music Program in the fall of 1970. At that time, DoM was in his first year of residency as a visiting artist in the program, and Mary had already begun her career in video art. The Luciers accompanied DoM and Cecilia [CeS] to Chinle during the summer of 1972 for the first time. In 1973, Mary, in collaboration with CeS, produced "The Occasion of Her First Dance and How She Looked," a multimedia performance work first presented on April

20–21 at The Kitchen in New York during performances by the multicultural group known as "Red, White, Yellow, and Black" (consisting of Cecilia Sandoval, Mary Lucier, Shigeko Kubota, and Charlotte Warren); see Barlow (1993).

6. See Chap. 21, n. 41; Bartine Bah Mitchell died on 3/18/1973 at Sage Memorial Hospital in Ganado, after a long battle at home with cancer.

7. At the time, video artist Shigeko Kubota was continuing work on "Broken Diaries," begun in 1969, as well as other projects. While in Chinle, she made a videoscape that later became "An American Family" (Kubota 1981:42). In 1997, when CeS visited her family in Chinle (3/29–4/1), accompanied by Melinda Barlow, I learned more about Kubota's 1973 activities and was able to see the Chinle portion of the project on Easter Sunday night with other family members. The video had been brought by Barlow (who is on the Film Studies faculty at University of Colorado, Boulder, and continues her own interests in video installation artists and the "Red, White, Yellow, and Black" performance group mentioned above). The thirty-two-minute video art tape entitled "Video Girls and Video Songs for Navajo Sky," with Shigeko Kubota as the sole artist, is available from her distributor, Electronic Arts Intermix, New York (Barlow p.c. 4/20/1997), and Barlow had just used it in one of her classes. It includes 1973 daily life scenes (mainly of RY and her family's activities, since Kubota stayed with RY) as well as some of Chinle, and CeS as a participant in the 1973 Miss Chinle contest. There is also some footage of Tall Woman eating food from dishes on a tray, while seated in her wheelchair at ID's house. Later, Kubota (1981:48, 49) also published a number of the segments showing Tall Woman and sent a copy of the publication to the family.

8. The *Liber Defunctorum* records (p. 63 no. 6) at Our Lady of Fatima Church in Chinle show that AM died on 12/13/1973, at age sixty-eight, and was buried in the Chinle Community Cemetery by Father Davin on 12/18/1973. R. C. Gorman (1992:46) and the rest of the family, as well as others who knew her, said that although AM had been suffering from heart problems for years, when she lost her youngest child, DoM, in December 1972, "she never recovered from the blow," "she never got over it." For further information on AM, also see Chap. 16; Chap. 16, n. 9; and Appendix A.

9. This trip was planned to coordinate with AgS's and McAllester's schedules since it was the first in a series of meetings with the family about the manuscript of Frank's book.

10. HM and SM were not considered in these discussions; home health care was not viewed as a male responsibility and neither was available anyway. During his mother's final years, HM worked for two years as a night watchman at the Chinle Extended Care Facility, and then as a maintenance man at the Chinle Valley School for Special Children. SM, who was living in Cottonwood, was actively involved as secretary/treasurer of the Cottonwood Chapter, a job he held from 1971 until 1979. Among his activities at this time was assisting Lockard with her research (see Lockard 1995). CyS ["B"] had hoped to go to college after graduation or get a job; her willingness to take care of Tall Woman made it possible for others, especially AS, to continue with their wagework jobs. AS was then head cook at the Chinle High School and had begun to make retirement plans, having accumulated sixteen years of seniority toward that end. "B," who was interested in nursing, was reportedly able to start some college courses in relevant subjects through a correspondence program during this time.

11. As shown in the Introduction, I was then based at the School of American Research in

Santa Fe as a Weatherhead Scholar for one quarter. When asked to make a presentation on March 26, 1976, during the Annual Banquet for Trustees and the Weatherhead Foundation at SAR, I spoke on "Life History Research among the Navajos," with a focus on my work with Tall Woman (Frisbie 1976).

12. The *Liber Defunctorum* records (p. 66 no. 7) at Our Lady of Fatima Church show that Michael Melvin ("Butch") died at age thirty-five on 3/10/1976, from double pneumonia compounded by other problems. He was buried in the Chinle Community Cemetery by Father Davin on 3/17/1976. For SM, this was an incredible blow, following DoM's death in 1972, and AM's, in 1973.

13. It was during this visit that Jennifer was named *Bazhníbah* by ID, after Tall Woman's daughters observed her for a day. Years earlier, Ted had been named "Man Who Chops Wood," and in 1971, Elizabeth was christened, *Bíjíbah*. In 1976, family members told our daughters that their names were women's/girls' names, paired, and reminiscent of earlier warfare times as was customary (see the Franciscan Fathers 1910:119–29). When asked for translations, they said *Bíjíbah* "is something like, 'The Girl/Woman Who Goes Up, Upward to Something,' and *Bazhníbah*, 'The Girl/Woman Who Came to Something.'"

14. Marcus Yazzie died on 2/3/1977, at the Fort Defiance Hospital, from cancer at the age of seventy-six.

15. See McAllester and McAllester (1980); a few of the images included in this work were taken at the Mitchells', as documented in their List of Photographs (pp. 112–13). Susan W. McAllester, born 7/9/1919, died from pancreatic cancer on 8/31/1994, one day before the McAllesters' fifty-fourth wedding anniversary. Her interest in photography is now commemorated by the Susan W. McAllester Memorial Photography Contest sponsored by *The Monterey News*, a monthly publication in Monterey, Massachusetts, with which many members of the McAllester family have been involved for years.

16. The interactions here were not smooth because the woman "on duty" started asking prying questions about which funeral home was being used, and the cost and range of services it provided, while suggesting the memorial cards and guest book could not be purchased at Cope's since the family was not using that funeral home's "package deal." The family opted to get the "coffin and box" from Allen Hill, a Navajo who was an ordained Presbyterian minister (Gray 1986:60), World War II veteran, director of GAP (the Ganado Alcoholism Program), and who ran a mortuary business in Ganado until his death in the early 1980s. AgS told the woman the coffin and box cost $560, that the coffin *was* metal, and that Hill *didn't embalm*. The woman also said there could only be six pallbearers, but finally agreed to list the eight AgS and AS named. They had settled on that number to cover possible "no-shows," but since all came, there *were* eight pallbearers at the funeral on July 2. They included: Tall Woman's sons, Howard and Seya, and six of her grandsons: Alfred, Timothy, and Frankie Shirley; Cecil, Jr. ("Dino"), and Augustine ("Eesert") Sandoval; and George Acey Davis (Acey).

The memorial cards used Tall Woman's English name, Rose Mitchell, and gave her dates of birth and death, respectively, as December 1874 and June 29, 1977. When we picked them up, we discovered that the last name of the officiating priest, Father Bryant Hausfeld, O.F.M., had been misspelled, although all information had been submitted in hand-printed format. The two hundred cards cost $30, and the guest registry book $5.

17. The $140.40 bill here included a $50.00 coffin spray of mixed colored flowers, two bas-

kets of red gladiolas and white mums at $27.50 each, one arrangement of plastic flowers for $8.95, and two plastic crosses, "pink for Tall Woman and blue for Frank." Plastic arrangements were preferred for the cemetery, and by this time MD had already brought a bag of five such arrangements to AS's for later delivery to the cemetery.

18. ID and JD had already left for Gallup, as had ES and FS's wife, Stella, the latter to notify other friends and relatives and run errands for RY and others. The food preparations were on everyone's minds; as AgS explained to me, shortly after I arrived: "Nowadays at Navajo funerals, things are different. A lot of people just show up for the eats. They don't even know the deceased or the family; they just come in and sit down and eat and eat! People like that are disgusting, but you've got to have lots of food on hand because of that." Mary Alice, the wife of John Wayne Mitchell, was helping because AS had cooked all the food for the June 1976 funeral of a son of theirs, and because she was related by marriage. As shown in Appendix A, her husband, John Wayne, was one of the five children Mae Yazzie had for George Mitchell before he died and she married Herman Attson. George and his brother, Billy (the husband of Rachel [Jones]), were the children of Frank Mitchell's sister, Woman at War and Tall Bitter Water Man (Mitchell 1978:346). George's wife, Mae Yazzie, was one of the many children of Irene Nez and the Son of Small Big Water Man. Other links between the families were established when John Wayne's brother, Charlie, married Bertha, Bartine's daughter, and one of his sisters, Rose, married Dan Jones, brother of Sarah's husband, Bahe (see Appendix A). As becomes clear in the text, in addition to the results of all of Mary Alice's efforts, more food was prepared for Tall Woman's funeral reception both Friday night and early Saturday morning.

19. Certain expenses were covered from the savings account AgS had started for her mother several years earlier, including the coffin and box, the memorial cards and guest book, and the materials for the concrete cemetery cross. AgS told me that whatever money was left after settling all the funeral expenses from a $2,000 total would be spent on a wrought-iron fence that would be installed to surround the graves of both Tall Woman and Frank in the cemetery, after HM finished her cross. Other expenses that came up during the day, such as meals; the buttons, headscarves, and socks for Tall Woman; the paper plates and other disposable goods; and the groceries, were split by all three of us, or two of us, as they were incurred. HM had made Frank's concrete cross (painted white) and had saved the blueprint; Frank's included black hand-painted lettering that read "Our Beloved Frank Mitchell" on the horizontal arm underneath a medallion on the vertical arm; below those words and following another medallion, on the vertical arm (on separate lines) were "1881 *H* 15 April 1967." Tall Woman's cross was made to match from concrete and then painted white. The crucifix was positioned at the top of the vertical arm, followed by hand-painted black letters reading "Our Beloved Mother [first line] Rose Mitchell" [second line] on the horizontal arm. Below, on the vertical piece (again on separate lines), were "1874 *H* 1977."

20. RY brought over a new, striped Pendleton MD had given her to donate to Tall Woman, and a new headscarf. AS assembled all the jewelry Tall Woman had brought with her when she moved to AS's house in 1973; it consisted of one turquoise bracelet with three stones, and three turquoise rings, one square and two oval. AS also added a necklace of turquoise and white shell beads of her own, asking me to scrub them first with a brush and then dry them. This was because the whereabouts of Tall Woman's two necklaces, her string of big turquoise beads and her squash blossom (both from Frank), were still unknown; the

latter was located several years later and, in 1998, remained in the family. After RY left, AgS went to ID's and came back with a shoebox containing the following new items: a pair of moccasins, a string of turquoise and shell beads to which the "earring loops" had been added, a white woolen hairstring, a headscarf, two turquoise bracelets, and one turquoise ring. We also had Tall Woman's own Pendleton (which AS had had dry-cleaned); the four, new, gathered skirts; the new, brown velveteen blouse with its six silver and turquoise buttons; two pairs of white bobby socks; gauze and adhesive tape; and a few safety pins. As it turned out, we didn't have enough of the latter, so only two of the four skirts were actually put on Tall Woman. The others, as well as the extra pair of socks, the headscarves, and her dentures were placed in the coffin.

21. The original plan was for Augusta's daughter, "T" [RS], to take care of the guest book and encourage people to sign it as they left the church, which sixty-nine did. However, "T" was unable to go to her grandmother's funeral since she ended up being designated as the person who would stay home and baby-sit AS's foster son, LM's son, and EY's two children during the service, burial, and reception.

22. Chauncey Neboyia is a clan relative of Frank's from the Canyon. A rancher and long-term employee of the National Park Service (from which he retired in 1994), Chauncey, who was born in 1909 (Jett 1997a:484) or 1910 (census records at Our Lady of Fatima Church), is also known for his participation in the video "Seasons of a Navajo," and for his collaborative work with Stephen C. Jett during the latter's research on Navajo architecture, rock art, place-names, and the cultural geography of Canyon de Chelly and Canyon del Muerto (Brugge p.c. 6/3/1997; Jett p.c. 6/5/1997; see also Fisher [1989]; Jett [1997a:484]; Jett, with Neboyia, Morgan, and Young [2000]; and Mitchell [1978:165–66 n. 25]).

23. A variety of behaviors were displayed during this emotional time. MD, ID, and RY started wailing, and ES, JM, and CyS ["B"] (all granddaughters) "broke down." MYK told me that it is "customary for a daughter to be appointed to escort a mother away from a parent's coffin"; both RD and Tall Woman's sister, Small Woman, did this for MD, who "said good-bye" first. EY helped RY, and MM did this for ID. AS, AgS, and I had no escorts; AS went first, followed by AgS and me, together. When discussing things later, ES and MYK expressed real worries about the effect of their grandmother's death on their mother, RY, and RS ["T"] voiced similar concerns about her mother, AS. While I suspect *all* of us had our "more than difficult moments" during the funeral, those who chose to verbalize their feelings later (without any questions from me) said their "worst times" were when they first saw Tall Woman's sister (who looked a lot like her) and JeM, Isabel's youngest son who was viewed as "Grandma's baby" because "she raised him." My own "hard times" were different, but I did verbalize them to family members who asked.

24. The quantity of food received many compliments during the reception. The menu included: canned corn, hominy, baked potatoes, fruited Jell-O, tossed salad with three dressings, rolls, Navajo fry bread, tacos, stew, ribs and other cuts of mutton, three sliced hams, two turkeys, watermelon, cake, punch, and iced tea.

25. By 1977, there were several grandchildren in Chinle who had typewriters. We had all agreed before I left that they would make any changes the family might find necessary before submitting the obituaries to the newspapers. No changes were forthcoming, but the version appearing in the *Gallup Independent* contained a printing error, that is, the statement that Tall Woman was buried at the Chinle Community Center! See Frisbie (1977a and b).

26. During the years, it has become clear to me that Tall Woman's grandchildren also have a variety of diverse memories of her. For some, she was a "real Grandmother"; for others, she was "a real Mom." For those in the latter group, Tall Woman was the one who made sure they were washed and fed, had clean clothes to wear, were dressed appropriately, and had hair that was brushed. She also was a major source of hugs, love, and verbal support, and a significant source of protection against antics of older children toward younger ones. Although I certainly knew she "baby-sat" and "watched out for and helped raise" many of her grandchildren, for many years I wasn't aware of some of her grandchildren's perceptions of her. Nor am I sure, even now, that the depth and importance of the "motherly" aspect of her relationships with some of them is apparent in her narrative. I continue to encourage them to speak up and write their own stories, while fully understanding that what they choose to do about their own memories of and experiences with her is totally up to them.

References

Aberle, David F.

1961 Navaho. *In* Matrilineal Kinship. David M. Schneider and Kathleen Gough, eds. Pp. 96–201. Berkeley: University of California Press.

1966 The Peyote Religion among the Navaho. Chicago: Aldine Publishing Company.

Acrey, Bill

1988 Navajo History to 1846: The Land and the People. Shiprock, N.M.: Department of Curriculum Materials Development, Central Consolidated School District No. 22.

1994 Navajo History: The Land and the People. Shiprock, N.M.: Department of Curriculum Materials Development, Central Consolidated School District No. 22.

Adair, John, and Kurt W. Deuschle, eds.

1970 The People's Health: Medicine and Anthropology in a Navajo Community. New York: Appleton-Century-Crofts.

Adams, William Y.

1963 Shonto: A Study of the Role of the Trader in a Modern Navaho Community. Bureau of American Ethnology Bulletin 188. Washington, D.C.: Government Printing Office.

Albuquerque Journal

1998a Jan. 30: B-3. [Article on Carl Gorman.]

1998b Jan. 31: A-12. [Article on Carl Gorman.]

Albuquerque Tribune

1998 Jan. 29: B-8. [Article on Carl Gorman.]

1999 Nov. 15: A-2. [Article on Lena Carr's Puberty Ceremony film.]

Allen, T. D. [combined publishing name for Don and Terry Allen]

1963 Navahos Have Five Fingers. Norman: University of Oklahoma Press.

Amsden, Charles Avery

1934 Navaho Weaving: Its Technic and Its History. Santa Ana, Calif.: Fine Arts Press in cooperation with the Southwest Museum, Los Angeles. Repr. ed., Chicago: Rio Grande Press, 1964.

Andrews, Tracy

1991 Ecological and Historical Perspectives on Navajo Land Use and Settlement Patterns in Canyons de Chelly and del Muerto. Journal of Anthropological Research 47(1):39–67.

Anonymous

1977 Childbirth. Tsá'ászi' 3(1):25–28. [Spring; illus.]

Anonymous

1981 Chinle: Site of Ancestral Stronghold. Navajo Times Tourist Guide, May 28:B-4.

Anonymous

1991 The People of God in Chinle-Living Stones in the Desert. Friarworks 28(7):1–4. [July.]

Antram, Father Cormac, O.F.M.

1989 Laborers of the Harvest. The Voice of the Southwest, Diocese of Gallup 20(12):1–2. [July 16.]

1997 Personal communication, May 30.

1998 Laborers of the Harvest. Gallup, N.M.: The Indian Trader.

Bahe, Geno

1998 The J. L. Hubbell Trading Post. Indian Artist:70–72. [Winter.]

Bailey, Flora

1940 Navaho Foods and Cooking Methods. American Anthropologist n.s.42(2), Pt. 1:270–90.

1948 Suggested Techniques for Inducing Navajo Women to Accept Hospitalization during Childbirth and for Implementing Health Education. American Journal of Public Health 38:1418–23.

1950 Some Sex Beliefs and Practices in a Navajo Commmunity. Papers of the Peabody Museum of American Archaeology and Ethnology 40. Cambridge: Peabody Museum of American Archaeology and Ethnology, Harvard University.

Bailey, Garrick, and Roberta G. Bailey

1986 A History of the Navajos: The Reservation Years. Santa Fe: School of American Research.

Bailey, L. R.

1964a The Navajo Reconnaissance: A Military Exploration of the Navajo Country in 1859 by Captain J. G. Walker and Major O. L. Shepherd. Los Angeles: Westernlore Press.

1964b The Long Walk. Los Angeles: Westernlore Press.

Barlow, Melinda

1993 Mary Lucier: Biographical Notes. From Noah's Raven: A Video Installation by Mary Lucier. Toledo: The Toledo Museum of Art.

1997 Personal communication, Apr. 20.

Barnett, Clifford, and David Rabin

1970 Collaborative Study by Physicians and Anthropologists: Congenital Hip Disease. In The People's Health. John Adair and Kurt W. Deuschle, eds. Pp. 128–39. New York: Appleton-Century-Crofts.

Batkin, Jonathan

1998 Some Early Curio Dealers of New Mexico. American Indian Art Magazine 23(3): 68–81.

Becenti, Deenise

1998 Sacred Document of the Dine. Navajo Times, June 4:A-1, 2.

Beecher, Shirley

1997 Personal communications, June 12, July 2, 3, 14, 23.

Begay, R. W.

1985 Navajo Childbirth. Ph.D. diss., University of California, Berkeley. Ann Arbor: University Microfilms International.

Begay, Shirley M.

1983 Kinaaldá: A Navajo Puberty Ceremony. 2d rev. ed. Bilingual. Rough Rock, Ariz.: Rough Rock Demonstration School, Navajo Curriculum Center.

Bell, Jan

1987 Techniques in Navajo Pottery Making. Plateau 58(2):16–23.

Bennett, Noel

1974 The Weaver's Pathway. Flagstaff: Northland Press.

Bennett, Noel, and Tiana Bighorse

1971 Working with the Wool: How to Weave a Navajo Rug. Flagstaff: Northland Press.

1997 Navajo Weaving Way: The Path from Fleece to Rug. Loveland, Colo.: Interweave Press.

Bergman, Robert L.

1983 Navajo Health Services and Projects. In Handbook of North American Indians, Vol. 10, Southwest. Alfonso Ortiz, ed. Pp. 672–78. Washington, D.C.: Smithsonian Institution.

Bernstein, Bruce, and Susan Brown McGreevy

1988 Anii Anáádaalyaa'ígíí (Recent Ones That Are Made): Continuity and Innovation in Recent Navajo Art. Santa Fe: Wheelwright Museum of the American Indian.

Bingham, Sam, and Janet Bingham

1976 Navajo Chapter Government Handbook. Chinle, Ariz.: Rock Point Community School.

1979 Navajo Farming. Chinle, Ariz.: Rock Point Community School.

Bixler, Margaret T.

1993 Winds of Freedom: The Story of the Navajo Code Talkers of World War II. Darien, Conn.: Two Bytes Publishing Company.

Blomberg, Nancy J.

1988 Navajo Textiles: The William Randolph Hearst Collection. Tucson: University of Arizona Press.

Blue, Martha

1986 A View from the Bullpen: A Navajo Ken of Traders and Trading Posts. Plateau 57(3):10–17.

1988 The Witch Purge of 1878: Oral and Documentary History in the Early Navajo Reservation Years. Navajo Oral History Monograph Series No. 1. Tsaile, Ariz.: Navajo Community College Press.

2000 Indian Trader: The Life and Times of J. L. Hubbell. Walnut, Calif.: Kiva Publishing Company.

Bodo, Father Murray, O.F.M.

1997 Personal communication, Mar. 3.

Bodo, Father Murray, O.F.M., ed. and transcriber

1998 Tales of an Endishodi: Father Berard Haile and the Navajos, 1900–1961. Albuquerque: University of New Mexico Press.

Boles, Joann

1981 The Navaho Rug at the Hubbell Trading Post, 1880–1920. American Indian Culture and Research Journal 5(1):47–63.

Bonar, Eulalie H., ed.

1996 Woven by the Grandmothers: Nineteenth-Century Navajo Textiles from the National Museum of the American Indian. Washington, D.C.: Smithsonian Institution Press in association with the National Museum of the American Indian, Smithsonian Institution.

Boyce, George A.

1974 When Navajos Had Too Many Sheep: The 1940s. San Francisco: Indian Historian Press.

Bradley, Zorro A.

1973 Canyon de Chelly: The Story of Its Ruins and People. Washington, D.C.: National Park Service, U.S. Department of the Interior.

Brady, Margaret K.

1984 Some Kind of Power: Navajo Children's Skinwalker Narratives. Salt Lake City: University of Utah Press.

Brody, J. J.

1976 Between Tradition: Navajo Weaving toward the End of the Nineteenth Century. Iowa City: University of Iowa Art Museum.

Brugge, David M.

1963 Navajo Pottery and Ethnohistory. Navajoland Publications, Series 2. Window Rock, Ariz.: Navajo Tribal Museum.

1964 Navajo Ceramic Practices. Southwestern Lore 30(3):37–46.

1972a Navajo and Western Pueblo History. The Smoke Signal 25:90–112 (Spring). Tucson: Tucson Corral of Westerners.

1972b Hubbell Trading Post National Historic Site, Furnishings Study: The Hubbell House. Historic Preservation Team, Denver Service Center, National Park Service. MS. Copies on file at Hubbell Trading Post National Historic Site, Ganado, Ariz.; Southwest Cultural Resource Center, National Park Service, Santa Fe, N.M.; Harpers Ferry Center, National Park Service, Harpers Ferry, W.Va.

1977 The Navajo Witch Purge of 1878. Awanyu 5(4):12–13.

1980 A History of the Chaco Navajos. Reports of the Chaco Center 4. Albuquerque: National Park Service, Division of Chaco Research, U.S. Department of the Interior.

1983 Navajo History and Prehistory to 1850. *In* Handbook of North American Indians, Vol. 10, Southwest. Alfonso Ortiz, ed. Pp. 489–501. Washington, D.C.: Smithsonian Institution.

1987 Navajo Pottery in the Eighteenth and Nineteenth Centuries. Plateau 58(2):3–7.

1993 Hubbell Trading Post: National Historic Site. Tucson: Southwest Parks and Monument Association.

1997 Personal communications, Mar. 1, Apr. 27, June 3.

Brugge, David M., and Raymond Wilson

1976 Administrative History: Canyon de Chelly National Monument, Arizona. Washington, D.C.: U.S. Department of the Interior, National Park Service, NPS 577. [Spiral bound, 309 pp.]

Bryan, Nonabah G., and Stella Young

1940 Navajo Native Dyes: Their Preparation and Use. Washington, D.C.: U.S. Department of the Interior, Bureau of Indian Affairs, Department of Education.

Bulow, Ernie

1991 Navajo Taboos. Gallup, N.M.: Buffalo Medicine Books. [Originally published in 1972 under same title, by Ernest L. Bulow, as Navajo Historical Publications Cultural Series l. Research Section, Museum and Research Department, Navajo Tribe. Window Rock, Ariz.: Navajo Times Publishing Company.]

Burton, Katherine

1957 The Golden Door: The Life of Katharine Drexel. New York: P. J. Kenedy and Sons.

1967 Entry on 'Drexel, Mother Katharine.' New Catholic Encyclopedia IV:1059–60. New York: McGraw Hill Book Company.

Butler, Barbara, and Diane Michalski Turner, eds.

1987 Children and Anthropological Research. New York: Plenum Press.

Butler, Kristie Lee

1991 Along the Padres' Trail: St. Michael's [sic] Mission to the Navajo, 1898–1939. St. Michaels, Ariz.: St. Michael's [sic] Museum.

1993 'Éé'dneishoodii Bahane': The Story of the Long Robes of St. Michael's [sic] Mission. *In* Papers from the Third, Fourth, and Sixth Navajo Studies Conferences. June-el Piper, ed.; Alexandra Roberts and Jenevieve Smith, comps. Pp. 285–303. Window Rock, Ariz.: Navajo Nation Historic Preservation Department.

Carpenter, Thorne M., and Morris Steggerda

1939 The Food of the Present-day Navajo Indians of New Mexico and Arizona. The Journal of Nutrition 18:297–306. [July–December.]

Cassell, Joan, ed.

1987 Children in the Field: Anthropological Experiences. Philadelphia: Temple University Press.

Chisholm, James S.

1983 Navajo Infancy: An Ethnological Study of Child Development. Hawthorne, N.Y.: Aldine Publishing Company.

Cliff, Janet M.

1990 Navajo Games. American Indian Culture and Research Journal 14(3):1–81.

Cohen, Marilyn

1998 Teach Me the Songs My Mothers Sang: A Celebration of American Women. [Exhibit catalog accompanying exhibit of same name on display at Fairfield University's Thomas J. Walsh Art Gallery, Jan. 16–Feb. 22, 1998.] Fairfield, Conn.: Thomas J. Walsh Art Gallery, Regina A. Quick Center for the Arts, Fairfield University.

Correll, J. Lee

1976 Through White Men's Eyes: A Contribution to Navajo History. Vol. 1 [Earliest Times to June 1, 1868]. Navajo Heritage Center Publication No. 1. Window Rock, Ariz.: Navajo Times Publishing Company.

n.d. Collected Papers, including chronological files, copies of documents, interviews, maps, and other data amassed during employment with the Tribal Research Section. Now housed, with restricted access, in the Navajo Nation Library, Window Rock.

Cousins, Jean, and Bill Cousins

1996 Tales from Wide Ruins: Jean and Bill Cousins, Traders. Mary Tate Engels, ed. Lubbock: Texas Tech University Press.

Culin, Stewart

1898 Chess and Playing Cards. United States National Museum Annual Report for Year ending June 30, 1896:665–942.

1907 Games of the North American Indians. Bureau of American Ethnology Annual Report 24. Washington, D.C.: Government Printing Office.

Davis, Grace

1997 Personal communication, Mar. 6.

Dedera, Don

1975 Navajo Rugs: How to Find, Evaluate, Buy and Care for Them. Flagstaff: Northland Press.

Delaney, Margaret Garcia

1997 Personal communications, June 10, July 18, 23, 26, 27.

1998 Personal communication, July 20.

Diné Bi 'Ólta' Association

1973 Winter Workshop. Charlie Toledo, Navajo Music Instructor. Tape of Navajo Shoe Game Songs.

Dockstader, Frederick J.

1987 The Song of the Loom: New Traditions in Navajo Weaving. New York: Hudson Hills Press in association with the Montclair Art Museum.

Dolaghan, Thomas, and David Scates

1978 The Navajos Are Coming to Jesus. Pasadena: William Carey Library.

Donovan, Bill

1997a Redistricting Plans Up in the Air. Navajo Times 36(4): A-1, 2. [Jan. 30.]

1997b 'No Way John Wayne' Returns to Navajoland. Navajo Times 36 (5): A-1, 5. [Feb. 6.]

1997c Twenty-five Years of Trading Post Blues. Navajo Times 36(32): A-1, 2. [Aug. 21.]

1997d Two Traders Still Do Business the Old Fashioned Way with Respect for the Community People. Navajo Times 36(32): A-2. [Aug. 21.]

Dotson, Beth

1998 One Hundred Years with the Navajo. Extension [Magazine of American Catholic Missions]:6–9. [September.]

Duffy, Sister Consuela Marie, S.B.S.

1966 Katharine Drexel: A Biography. Bensalem, Pa.: Mother Katharine Drexel Guild, Sisters of the Blessed Sacrament.

Dutton, Bertha

1961 Navajo Weaving Today. Santa Fe: Museum of New Mexico Press.

Edison, Carol A., ed.

1996 Willow Stories: Utah Navajo Baskets. Salt Lake City: Utah Arts Council.

Elmore, Francis H.

1943 Ethnobotany of the Navajo. University of New Mexico Bulletin with the School of American Research. Albuquerque: University of New Mexico Press.

Fall, Patricia L., James A. McDonald, and Pamela C. Magers

1981 The Canyon del Muerto Survey Project: Anasazi and Navajo Archeology in Northeastern Arizona. Tucson: National Park Service Western Archeological Center Publications in Anthropology 15.

Farella, John R.

1984 The Main Stalk: A Synthesis of Navajo Philosophy. Tucson: University of Arizona Press.

Faris, James C.

1990 The Nightway: A History and a History of Documentation of a Navajo Ceremonial. Albuquerque: University of New Mexico Press.

1996 Navajo and Photography: A Critical History of the Representation of an American People. Albuquerque: University of New Mexico Press.

Faunce, Hilda

1981 Desert Wife. First Bison ed. Lincoln: University of Nebraska Press. Originally published, New York: Little, Brown, and Company, 1928, under Hilda Faunce Wetherill.

Fisher, Eugene
1989 I Could Walk These Canyons Forever — Chauncey Neboyia. The Walker's Magazine 4(5):24–27.

Fishler, Stanley
1954 Symbolism of a Navajo 'Wedding' Basket. Masterkey 28(6):205–15.

Francis, Sandra Toni
1996 The Yé'ii Bicheii Dancing of Nightway: An Examination of the Role of Dance in a Navajo Healing Ceremonial. Ph.D. diss., University of Ohio.

Franciscan Fathers
1910 An Ethnologic Dictionary of the Navaho Language. Saint Michaels, Ariz.: The Franciscan Fathers.

1912 A Vocabulary of the Navaho Language. Vol. 1: English-Navaho. Vol. 2: Navaho-English. Saint Michaels, Ariz.: The Franciscan Fathers.

1949 Navaho Saga. Franciscan Golden Jubilee publication. St. Michaels, Ariz.: St. Michaels Mission.

Frink, Maurice
1968 Fort Defiance and the Navajos. Boulder: Pruett Press.

Frisbie, Charlotte J.
1967 Kinaaldá: A Study of the Navaho Girl's Puberty Ceremony. Middletown, Conn.: Wesleyan University Press. 1993 paperback ed. with new preface. Salt Lake City: University of Utah Press.

1968 The Navajo House Blessing Ceremonial. El Palacio 75(3):26–35.

1970 Navajo House Blessing Ceremonial: A Study of Cultural Change. Ph.D. diss., University of New Mexico. Ann Arbor: University Microfilms.

1975a Fieldwork as a 'Single Parent': To be or not to be Accompanied by a Child. In Collected Papers in Honor of Florence Hawley Ellis. Theodore R. Frisbie, ed. Pp. 98–119. Papers of the Archaeological Society of New Mexico 2. Norman: Hooper Publishing Company.

1975b Observations on a Preschooler's First Experience with Cross-Cultural Living. Journal of Man [Lambda Alpha] 7(1):91–112.

1975c Review of Diné ba'aliil of Navajoland, U.S.A. Ethnomusicology 19(3):503–6.

1976 Life History Research among the Navajos. Invited Lecture presented at Annual Banquet for Trustees and Weatherhead Foundation, Mar. 26, School of American Research, Santa Fe.

1977a Death Notice-Rose Mitchell. Gallup Independent, July 19:6.

1977b Obituary-Rose Mitchell. Navajo Times 10(31):8–10. [Aug. 4.]

1977c Review of Navajo Corn Grinding and Shoe Game Songs. Ethnomusicology 21(2):355–56.

1978 Navajo Mortuary Practices and Beliefs. Special Symposium Issue. American Indian Quarterly 4(4):303–411. Guest ed. [Includes introduction, essay, and discussion by ed. and five other essays, by Brugge, Ward, Griffen, Shepardson, and Levy.]

1980a An Approach to the Ethnography of Navajo Ceremonial Performance. In Ethnography of Musical Performance. Norma McLeod and Marcia Herndon, eds. Pp.75–104. Norwood, Pa.: Norwood Editions.

1980b Vocables in Navajo Ceremonial Music. Ethnomusicology 24 (3):347–92.

1980c Ritual Drama in the Navajo House Blessing Ceremony. In Southwestern Indian Ritual Drama. Charlotte J. Frisbie, ed. Pp. 161–98. Albuquerque: University of New Mexico Press and School of American Research Advanced Seminar Series.

1986 Navajo Ceremonialists in the Pre-1970 Political World. *In* Explorations in Ethnomusicology: Essays in Honor of David P. McAllester. Charlotte J. Frisbie, ed. Detroit Monographs in Musicology 9:79–96. Detroit: Information Coordinators.

1987 Navajo Medicine Bundles or *Jish:* Acquisition, Transmission, and Disposition in the Past and Present. Albuquerque: University of New Mexico Press.

1989 Gender and Navajo Music: Unanswered Questions. *In* Women in North American Indian Music: Six Essays. Richard Keeling, ed. Pp. 22–38. Society for Ethnomusicology Special Series 6.

1992 Temporal Change in Navajo Religion: 1868–1990. Journal of the Southwest 34(4): 457–514.

1996 Gender Issues in Navajo Boarding School Experiences. *In* The Construction of Gender and the Experience of Women in American Indian Societies. Newberry Library D'Arcy McNickle Center for the History of the American Indian Occasional Papers in Curriculum Series 20:138–79.

1997 The Final Stages of a Life History Project [with additional comments by Augusta Sandoval]. Paper presented in organized session, Doing Life History Work: Joys and Challenges, at the Tenth Annual Navajo Studies Conference, University of New Mexico, Albuquerque, Apr. 16–19.

1998 On the Trail of Chinle's "Big House." *In* Diné Bíkéyah: Papers in Honor of David M. Brugge. Meliha S. Duran and David T. Kirkpatrick, eds. Archaeological Society of New Mexico Papers 24:69–85. Albuquerque: Archaeological Society of New Mexico.

n.d. Older is Better and REALLY OLD is Wonderful: Some Navajo Attitudes toward Aging and Aging Ceremonialists. In press in volume from the Third International Biology of Music Making Conference: Music, Growth, and Aging. [Conference held in Rochester, N.Y., July 14–20, 1991.]

Frisbie, Charlotte J., and David M. Brugge

1999 The First Navajo Studies Conference: Reflections by the Cofounders. *In* Diné Baa Hané Bi Naaltsoos: Collected Papers from the Seventh through Tenth Navajo Studies Conferences. June-el Piper, ed. Pp. 1–9. Window Rock, Ariz.: Navajo Nation Historic Preservation Department.

Frisbie, Charlotte J., and David P. McAllester

1992 Liner notes for Navajo Songs of the 1930s and 1940s, recorded by Laura Boulton. Smithsonian Folkways C-SF 40403. CD and cassette formats. Smithsonian Folkways Recordings.

Frisbie, Charlotte J., with Augusta Sandoval

1999 The Final Stages of a Life History Project. *In* Diné Baa Hané Bi Naaltsoos: Collected Papers from the Seventh through Tenth Navajo Studies Conferences. June-el Piper, ed. Pp. 63–67. Window Rocks, Ariz.: Navajo Nation Historic Preservation Department.

Gallup Independent

1998 Feb. 3: 1, 2. [Article on Carl Gorman.]

Gibson, Walter

1994 Nakai Toh: My Days with the Finest People on God's Green Earth. Bountiful, Utah: Family History Publishers.

Gill, Sam D.

1979 Songs of Life: An Introduction to Navajo Religious Culture. Iconography of Religions 10(3). Institute of Religious Iconography, State University Groningen. Leiden: E. J. Brill.

1981 Sacred Words: A Study of Navajo Religion and Prayer. Westport, Conn.: Greenwood Press.

Gilles, Cate

1996 Carr Earns Emmy for Film. Navajo Times 35(41):A-1, 2. [Oct. 10.]

Gillmor, Frances, and Louisa Wade Wetherill

1934 Traders to the Navajos: The Story of the Wetherills of Kayenta. Boston: Houghton Mifflin Company.

Gorman, R. C.

1992 The Radiance of My People. Albuquerque: Santa Fe Fine Arts.

Grant, Campbell

1978 Canyon de Chelly: Its People and Rock Art. Tucson: University of Arizona Press.

Grantner, Brother Gerald, O.F.M.

1997 Personal communication, Feb. 8.

Graves, Laura

1998 Thomas Varker Keam, Indian Trader. Norman: University of Oklahoma Press.

Gray, Reverend Joseph W.

1986 Light on the Hill: A History of the Presbyterian Church, Chinle, Arizona, 1919–1972. San Jose, Calif.: Paul Nelson. Chinle Edition. Copies available from Joseph W. Gray.

1997 Personal communication, Mar. 19.

Greenberg, Henry, and Georgia Greenberg

1984 Carl Gorman's World. Albuquerque: University of New Mexico Press. Reissued 1996, as Power of a Navajo: Carl Gorman — The Man and His Life, by same authors and press [with slight differences in size, cover, a few extra photographs, and additional pages of text].

Grein, Father Blane, O.F.M.

1978 Chinle Community Renewal. Provincial Chronicle n.s. 1(2):61–67. [Fall.]

1990 Personal communication, Oct. 10.

1996 Personal communication, Nov. 3.

1997 Personal communications, Mar. 7, 9, May 5, 31.

Griffen, Joyce

1980 Navajo Funerals, Anglo-Style. Museum of Northern Arizona Research Paper 18. Flagstaff: Museum of Northern Arizona.

Hadley, Linda

1986 Hózhǫ́ǫ́jí Hane': Blessingway. Lectures of Mr. Roger Hathale for Rough Rock Medicinemen Training Program. Rough Rock, Ariz.: Rough Rock Demonstration School.

Hagerty, Donald J.

1996 Canyon de Chelly: One Hundred Years of Painting and Photography. Places of Spirit Series. Salt Lake City: Gibbs-Smith Publisher.

Haile, Father Berard, O.F.M.

n.d. Place Names. Berard Haile Papers, Special Collections, Box 5, Folder 12. University of Arizona, Tucson.

1937 Some Cultural Aspects of the Navajo Hogan (mimeographed). Fort Wingate: Fort Wingate Summer School.

1938 Origin Legend of the Navaho Enemy Way. Yale University Publications in Anthropology 17.

1942 Why the Navaho Hogan? Primitive Man 15(3–4):39–56.

1943 Origin Legend of the Navaho Flintway. University of Chicago Publications in Anthropology. Linguistic Series. Chicago: University of Chicago Press.

1946 The Navaho Fire Dance or the Corral Dance. Saint Michaels, Ariz.: St. Michaels Press.

1947 Prayer Stick Cutting in a Five Night Navaho Ceremonial of the Male Branch of Shootingway. Chicago: University of Chicago Press.

1950a A Stem Vocabulary of the Navaho Language. Navaho-English. St. Michaels, Ariz.: St. Michaels Press.

1950b Legend of the Ghostway Ritual in the Male Branch of Shootingway (Pt. 1) and Suckingway, Its Legend and Practice (Pt. 2). Saint Michaels, Ariz.: St. Michaels Press.

1951 A Stem Vocabulary of the Navaho Language. English-Navaho. St. Michaels, Ariz.: St. Michaels Press.

[see also Bodo 1998]

Halpern, Katherine Spencer, and Susan Brown McGreevy, eds.

1997 Washington Matthews: Studies of Navajo Culture, 1880–1894. Albuquerque: University of New Mexico Press.

Hanley, Boniface, O.F.M.

n.d. A Philadelphia Story [Mother Katharine Drexel's story]. Reprinted from The Anthonian, 1984 first quarter issue by the Sisters of the Blessed Sacrament. 32 pp. booklet available from Sisters of the Blessed Sacrament.

Hardeen, George

1994 Hogans in Hospitals: Navajo Patients Want the Best of Both Worlds. Tribal College [Journal of American Indian Higher Education] 6:20–24. [Winter.]

Harman, Robert

1964 Change in a Navaho Ceremonial. El Palacio 71(1):20–26.

Harrison, Laura S., and Beverley B. Spears

1989 Historic Structure Report: Chinle Trading Post, Thunderbird Ranch, and Custodian's Residence, Canyon de Chelly National Monument. Southwest Cultural Resources Center Professional Papers 17. Santa Fe: National Park Service, Southwest Regional Office, Division of History.

Hartman, Russell P., and Jan Musial

1987 Navajo Pottery: Traditions and Innovations. Flagstaff: Northland Press.

Hatcher, Evelyn Payne

1967 Visual Metaphors: A Formal Analysis of Navajo Art. New York: West Publishing Company.

Hedlund, Ann Lane

1990 Beyond the Loom: Keys to Understanding Early Southwestern Weaving. Boulder: Johnson Books.

1992 Reflections of the Weaver's World: The Gloria F. Ross Collection of Contemporary Navajo Weaving. Denver: Denver Art Museum.

1997 Navajo Weavings from the Andy Williams Collection. St. Louis: St. Louis Art Museum. [Volume published in conjunction with exhibit at the museum, Oct. 16, 1997– Jan. 4, 1998.]

Hegemann, Elizabeth C.

1963 Navaho Trading Days. Albuquerque: University of New Mexico Press.

Heil, Diana

1998 Two Grey Hills Unravels Its Mystery Weave. New Mexico Magazine 76(8):78–82.

Henderson, Eric

1982 Kaibeto Plateau Ceremonialists: 1860–1980. *In* Navajo Religion and Culture: Selected Views. Papers in Honor of Leland C. Wyman. David M. Brugge and Charlotte J. Frisbie, eds. Museum of New Mexico Papers in Anthropology 17:164–75.

Hendricks, Rick, and John P. Wilson, eds.

1996 The Navajos in 1705: Roque Madrid's Campaign Journal. Albuquerque: University of New Mexico Press.

Hetteberg, Father Marcan, O.F.M.

1997 Personal communications, May 12, Aug. 5, 15.

1998 Personal communication, June 30.

Hill, W. W.

1936 Navajo Warfare. Yale University Publications in Anthropology 5. New Haven: Yale University Press.

1937 Navajo Pottery Manufacture. University of New Mexico Bulletin, Anthropological Series 2(3):1–23.

1938 The Agricultural and Hunting Methods of the Navaho Indians. Yale University Publications in Anthropology 18. New Haven: Yale University Press.

1940 Some Aspects of Navajo Political Structure. Plateau 13:23–28.

Hodge, Frederick W., George P. Hammond, and Agapito Rey, eds.

1945 Fray Alonzo de Benavides' Revised Memorial of 1634, with Numerous Supplementary Documents Elaborately Annotated. Albuquerque: University of New Mexico Press.

Hoffman, Virginia

1969 Lucy Learns to Weave: Gathering Plants. Rough Rock, Ariz.: Navajo Curriculum Center, Rough Rock Demonstration School.

Hollister, U.S.

1903 The Navajo and His Blanket. Denver: United States Colortype Company. Repr., Glorieta, N.M.: Rio Grande Press, 1972.

Houk, Rose

1995 Navajo of Canyon de Chelly: In Home God's Fields. [Includes primary research by Tracy J. Andrews.] Tucson: Southwest Parks and Monuments Association.

Howard, Kathleen L., and Diana F. Pardue

1996 Inventing the Southwest: The Fred Harvey Company and Native American Art. Flagstaff: Northland Publishing Company.

Hubbell, Dorothy

1990 Personal communication, July 25.

Hubbell Papers

n.d. Documents, personal correspondence, ledgers, journals, day books, advertisements, and catalogs of Lorenzo Hubbell. Archived in Special Collections Library, University of Arizona, Tucson. Microfiche copies available at Hubbell Trading Post National Historic Site, Ganado, Ariz.

Indian Artist

1997 Lorraine Williams. Fall:70.

Indian Country Today

1995 Visiting the Nations. Special Edition on The Navajo Nation. [June.]

Iverson, Peter

1981 The Navajo Nation. Albuquerque: University of New Mexico Press.

1990 The Navajos. Indians of North America Series. Frank W. Porter, III, Gen. ed. New York: Chelsea House Publishers.

Jacobson, Doranne

1964 Navajo Enemy Way Exchanges. El Palacio 71(1):7–19.

James, George W.

1927 Indian Blankets and Their Makers. Chicago: A. C. McClurg and Company. Repr., Glorieta, N.M.: Rio Grande Press, 1970.

James, H. L.

1977 Posts and Rugs: The Story of Navajo Rugs and their Homes. Globe: Southwest Parks and Monuments Association. 2d printing. Originally published, 1976.

Jett, Stephen C.

1974 The Destruction of Navajo Orchards in 1864: Captain John Thompson's Report. Arizona and the West 16(4). [Winter.]

1979 Peach Cultivation and Use among the Canyon de Chelly Navajo. Economic Botany 33(3):298–310.

1991 Pete Price: Navajo Medicineman (1868–1951): A Brief Biography. American Indian Quarterly 15(1):91–103. [Winter.]

1996 Modern Navajo Cemeteries. Material Culture 28(2):1–23.

1997a Place-Naming, Environment, and Perception among the Canyon de Chelly Navajo of Arizona. Professional Geographer 49(4):481–93.

1997b Personal communication, June 5.

Jett, Stephen C., and Virginia E. Spencer

1981 Navajo Architecture: Forms, History, Distributions. Tucson: University of Arizona Press.

Jett, Stephen C., with the assistance of Chauncey M. Neboyia, William Morgan, Sr., and Robert W. Young

2000 Navajo Placenames and Trails of the Canyon de Chelly System, Arizona. New York: Peter Lang Publishing.

Johnson, Broderick H., ed.

1973 Navajo Stories of the Long Walk Period. Tsaile, Ariz.: Navajo Community College Press.

1977a Stories of Traditional Navajo Life and Culture by Twenty-two Navajo Men and Women. Tsaile, Ariz.: Navajo Community College Press.

1977b Navajos and World War II. [Accounts from eleven participants, three women and eight men.] Tsaile, Ariz.: Navajo Community College Press.

Kahlenberg, Mary Hunt, and Anthony Berlant

1972 The Navajo Blanket. Los Angeles: Praeger Publishers, in association with the Los Angeles County Museum of Art.

Kapoun, Robert W., with Charles J. Lohrmann

1992 Language of the Robe: American Indian Trade Blankets. Layton, Utah: Gibbs Smith Publishers. [Peregrine Smith Books.]

Kawano, Kenji

1990 Warriors: Navajo Code Talkers. Flagstaff: Northland Publishing Company.

[Photographs by Kenji Kawano, official photographer for the Navajo Code Talkers Association.]

Keegan, Marcia

1987 Southwest Indian Cookbook: Pueblo and Navajo. Santa Fe: Clear Light Publishers.

Kelley, Klara B.

1986a Navajo Land Use: An Ethnoarchaeological Study. Orlando: Academic Press.

1986b An Archaeological Survey for the Balakai Mine Reclamation Project, Tselani, Ariz. NNCRMP-86–300. Report dated Dec. 10, 1986, on file, Navajo Nation Historic Preservation Department, Window Rock, Ariz.

1987a An Archaeological Survey for the Chinle No. 1 Mine Reclamation Project near Blue Gap, Ariz. NNCRMP-86–301. Report dated Feb. 6, 1987, on file, Navajo Nation Historic Preservation Department, Window Rock, Ariz.

1987b The Garcia Trading Post in Chinle, Arizona: Determination of Eligiblity for the National Register of Historic Places. Report prepared on Nov. 25, 1987, by the Navajo Nation Archaeology Department for the National Park Service, Santa Fe, N.M.

1997 Personal communication, Feb. 9.

1998 Personal communications, July 19, Aug. 30.

Kelly, Lawrence

1970 Navajo Roundup. Boulder: Pruett Publishing Company.

Kennedy, Mary Jeanette

1965 Tales of a Trader's Wife: Life on the Navajo Indian Reservation 1913–1938. Albuquerque: Valliant Company.

Kent, Kate Peck

1961 The Story of Navaho Weaving. Phoenix: Heard Museum of Anthropology and Primitive Art.

1981 From Blanket to Rug: The Evolution of Navajo Weaving after 1880. Plateau 52(4):10–21.

1985 Navajo Weaving: Three Centuries of Change. Santa Fe: School of American Research Press.

Kluckhohn, Clyde

1944 Navaho Witchcraft. Papers of the Peabody Museum of American Archaeology and Ethnology, Harvard University 22(2). Repr., Boston: Beacon Press, 1967.

Kluckhohn, Clyde, and Dorothea C. Leighton

1946 The Navaho. Cambridge: Harvard University Press. [Numerous reprints, and revised, updated editions available.]

Kluckhohn, Clyde, and Leland C. Wyman

1940 An Introduction to Navaho Chant Practice. American Anthropological Association Memoirs 53.

Kluckhohn, Clyde, W. W. Hill, and Lucy Wales Kluckhohn

1971 Navaho Material Culture. Cambridge, Mass.: Belknap Press of Harvard University Press.

Kubota, Shigeko

1981 Video Sculptures. Berlin: Museum Folkwang Essen.

Kunitz, Stephen J.

1983 Disease Change and the Role of Medicine: The Navajo Experience. Berkeley: University of California Press.

Left-Handed Mexican Clansman, et al.

1952 The Trouble at Round Rock. United States Indian Service, Navajo Historical Series 2. Phoenix: Phoenix Indian School.

Leighton, Alexander H., and Dorothea C. Leighton

1944 The Navaho Door. Cambridge: Harvard University Press.

Leighton, Dorothea, and Clyde Kluckhohn

1947 Children of the People: The Navaho Individual and His Development. Cambridge: Harvard University Press.

Levy, Benjamin

1968 Historic Structures Report, Hubbell Trading Post Historic Site. MS. Copies on file at Hubbell Trading Post Historic Site, Ganado, Ariz.; Southwest Cultural Resources Center, National Park Service, Santa Fe.

Levy, Jerrold E.

1998 In the Beginning: The Navajo Genesis. Berkeley: University of California Press.

Levy, Jerrold E., Raymond Neutra, and Dennis Parker

1987 Hand Trembling, Frenzy Witchcraft, and Moth Madness. Tucson: University of Arizona Press.

Liebler, H. Baxter

1969 Boil My Heart for Me. New York: Exposition Press.

Link, Martin A., ed.

1968 Navajo: A Century of Progress — 1868–1968. Window Rock, Ariz.: The Navajo Tribe.

1971 Hwelte (Fort Sumner). Navajoland Publications, Series 7. Window Rock, Ariz.: Navajo Tribal Museum.

Lipps, Oscar H.

1909 The Navajos. Cedar Rapids: Torch Press.

Lockard, Louise

1995 New Paper Words: Historical Images of Navajo Language Literacy. American Indian Quarterly 19(1):17–30.

Lockett, Clay

1939 Midwives and Childbirth among the Navajo. Plateau 12(1):15–17.

Long, Paul V.

1992 Big Eyes: The Southwestern Photographs of Simeon Schwemberger, 1902–1908. Albuquerque: University of New Mexico Press.

Loughlin, B. W.

1965 Pregnancy in Navajo Culture. Nursing Outlook 13:55–58.

Lynch, Regina H.

1986 Cookbook: Ch'iyáán 'íłʼíní binaaltsoos. Rough Rock, Ariz.: Navajo Curriculum Center, Rough Rock Demonstration School.

Lyon, William H.

1996 The Navajos in the American Historical Imagination, 1807–1870. Ethnohistory 43(2):188–233.

1998 The Navajos in the American Historical Imagination, 1868–1900. Ethnohistory 45(2):237–75.

McAllester, David P.

1954 Enemy Way Music. Papers of the Peabody Museum of Archaeology and Ethnology, Harvard University 41(3).

1971 Review of Night and Daylight Yeibichei. Ethnomusicology 15 (2):296–97.

1979 A Paradigm of Navajo Dance. Parabola 4(2):29–35.

1980 Shootingway, An Epic Drama of the Navajos. *In* Southwestern Indian Ritual Drama. Charlotte J. Frisbie, ed. Pp. 199–238. School of American Research Advanced Seminar Series. Albuquerque: University of New Mexico Press.

1984 A Problem in Ethics. *In* Problems and Solutions: Occasional Essays in Musicology Presented to Alice M. Moyle. Jamie C. Kassler and Jill Stubington, eds. Pp. 279–89. Sydney: Hale and Iremonger.

1998 Personal communication, July 5.

McAllester, David P., and Susan W. McAllester

1980 Hogans: Navajo Houses and House Songs. Middletown, Conn.: Wesleyan University Press.

McAllester, David P., and Douglas F. Mitchell

1983 Navajo Music. *In* Handbook of North American Indians, Vol. 10, Southwest. Alfonso Ortiz, ed. Pp. 605–23. Washington, D.C.: Smithsonian Institution.

McCabe, Reverend Norma

1997 Personal communication, Mar. 4.

McClelland, George L., Jr.

1997 Personal communication, Aug. 15.

M'Closkey, Kathy

1993 Mark-Ups and Middlemen: How Navajo Textiles Greased the Wheels of Commerce. Paper presented at the Seventh Annual Navajo Studies Conference, Navajo Community College, Tsaile, Ariz., Oct. 6–8.

1994 Marketing Multiple Myths: The Hidden History of Navajo Weaving. Journal of the Southwest 36(3):185–220.

1996 Myths, Markets and Metaphors: Navajo Weaving as Commodity and Communicative Form. Ph.D. diss. York University, Toronto, Ontario.

1997 The Silent Crisis: Economic Consequences of Multiple Appropriations of Navajo Weavers' Patterns and Production. Paper presented at the Tenth Annual Navajo Studies Conference, University of New Mexico, Albuquerque, Apr. 16–19.

McGreevy, Susan

1985 The Other Weavers: Navajo Basket Makers. Phoebus [A Journal of Art History] 4:54–61. Tempe: Arizona State University.

McKenna, Peter J., and Scott E. Travis

1989 Archaeological Investigations at Thunderbird Lodge, Canyon de Chelly, Arizona. Southwest Cultural Resources Center Professional Papers 20. Santa Fe: National Park Service Branch of Cultural Resources Management, Division of Anthropology.

McNitt, Frank

1963 The Indian Traders. Norman: University of Oklahoma Press. 2d printing. Originally published, 1962.

1964 Navaho Expedition: Journal of a Military Reconnaissance from Santa Fe, New Mexico, to the Navaho Country, by Lieutenant James H. Simpson. Norman: University of Oklahoma Press.

1972 Navajo Wars: Military Campaigns, Slave Raids, and Reprisals. Albuquerque: University of New Mexico Press.

McPherson, Robert S.

1992 Naalyéhé Bá Hooghan – 'House of Merchandise': The Navajo Trading Post as an Institution of Cultural Change, 1900 to 1930. American Indian Culture and Research Journal 16(1):23–43.

1996 Indians Playing Indians: Navajos and the Film Industry in Monument Valley, 1938–1964. Paper presented at the Ninth Annual Navajo Studies Conference, Fort Lewis College, Durango, Colo., Apr. 10–13.

1998 Seeing as Believing: Navajos, Tourists, and Rainbow Bridge, 1910–1950. Paper presented at the Eleventh Annual Navajo Studies Conference, Navajo Nation Museum, Window Rock, Ariz., Oct. 21–24.

Manchester, Albert, and Ann Manchester

1993 Hubbell Trading Post National Historic Site. Southwest Cultural Resources Center Professional Papers 46. Santa Fe: Southwest Regional Office, Division of History, National Park Service, Department of the Interior.

Matthews, Washington

1884 Navajo Weavers. Bureau of Ethnology Annual Report 3:371–91. Washington, D.C.: U.S. Government Printing Office.

1886 Navajo Names for Plants. The American Naturalist 20(9):767–77.

1887 The Mountain Chant: A Navajo Ceremony. Bureau of American Ethnology Annual Report 5. Washington, D.C.: U.S. Government Printing Office. Repr., Salt Lake City: University of Utah Press, 1997 [with Foreword by Paul Zolbrod and Orthographic Note by Robert W. Young].

1889 Navaho Gambling Songs. American Anthropologist 2:1–19.

1894 The Basket Drum. American Anthropologist 7(2):202–8.

1902 The Night Chant, A Navaho Ceremony. American Museum of Natural History Memoirs 6 (Anthropology Series 5). New York. Repr., Salt Lake City: University of Utah Press, 1995 [with Foreword by John Farella].

[see also Halpern and McGreevy 1997]

Maxwell, Gilbert

1963 Navajo Rugs-Past, Present, and Future. Palm Desert, Calif.: Best-West Publications.

Maxwell, Judith M., and Jesse W. Nash

1993 Navajo Foot Races. In Papers from the Third, Fourth, and Sixth Navajo Studies Conferences. June-el Piper, ed.; Alexandra Roberts and Jenevieve Smith, comps. Pp. 159–65. Window Rock, Ariz.: Navajo Nation Historic Preservation Department.

Mayes, Vernon O., and Barbara Bayless Lacy

1989 Nanise', A Navajo Herbal: One Hundred Plants from the Navajo Reservation. Tsaile, Ariz.: Navajo Community College Press.

Mayes, Vernon, and James M. Rominger

1994 Navajoland Plant Catalog. Lake Ann, Mich.: National Woodlands Publishing Company.

Means, Florence Crannell

1955 Sagebrush Surgeon. New York: Friendship Press.

Mera, H. P.

1948 Navajo Textile Arts. Santa Fe: Laboratory of Anthropology.

Milligan, B. Carol

1984a Nursing Care and Beliefs of Expectant Navajo Women. Pt. 1. American Indian Quarterly 8(2):83–101. [Spring.]

1984b Nursing Care and Beliefs of Expectant Navajo Women. Pt. 2. American Indian Quarterly 8(3):199–210. [Summer.]

Mills, George

1959 Navaho Art and Culture. Colorado Springs: Taylor Museum of the Colorado Fine Arts Center.

Mindeleff, Cosmos

1898 Navaho Houses. Bureau of American Ethnology Annual Report 16:78–198. Washington, D.C.: U.S. Government Printing Office.

Mitchell, Frank

1978 Navajo Blessingway Singer: The Autobiography of Frank Mitchell, 1881–1967. Charlotte J. Frisbie and David P. McAllester, eds. Tucson: University of Arizona Press.

Mitchell, Marie

1973 The Navajo Peace Treaty 1868. New York: Mason and Lipscomb Publishers.

Moon, Samuel

1992 Tall Sheep: Harry Goulding, Monument Valley Trader. Norman: University of Oklahoma Press.

Moore, J. B.

1911 The Navajo. Denver: Williamson-Haffner Company. [32-pp. catalog as a licensed trader at Crystal, N.M.]

Moore, William Haas

1994 Chiefs, Agents, and Soldiers: Conflict on the Navajo Frontier, 1868–1882. Albuquerque: University of New Mexico Press.

Morgan, William, Sr.

1931 Navaho Treatment of Sickness: Diagnosticians. American Anthropologist 33:390–402.

1936 Human-Wolves among the Navaho. Yale University Publications in Anthropology 11:1–43.

Navajo Nation

1997 Navajo Nation Government. [40-pp. booklet.] Window Rock, Ariz.: Navajo Nation, Office of Navajo Government Development. [First announced as available for sale in Navajo Times, Feb. 27, 1997:A-9.]

1998 Navajo Nation Government. 4th ed. [62-pp. booklet.] Window Rock, Ariz.: Navajo Nation, Office of Navajo Government Development.

[see also Rodgers, comp. and ed.]

Navajo Times

1973 Nov. 29 issue.

1981 Mar. 19, May 28 [see Anonymous 1981], and Dec. 19 issues.

1992a Oct. 15 issue [Pp. 1, 2: Grand Opening Chinle's Holiday Inn].

1992b Oct. 22 issue.

1996a Aug. 29 issue [Fair Edition].

1996b Oct. 10 issue [see Gilles].

1996c Oct. 17 issue [see Shebala].

1997a Jan. 30 issue [see Donovan 1997a].

1997b Feb. 6 issue [see Donovan 1997b].

1998 Feb. 5 issue [P. 5: Article on Carl Gorman].

Newcomb, Franc Johnson

1940 Navajo Omens and Taboos. Santa Fe: Rydal Press.

Newcomb, Franc Johnson, and Gladys A. Reichard

1937 Sandpaintings of the Navajo Shooting Chant. New York: J. J. Augustin.

New Mexico Register

1955a Second Oldest Navajo Mission is at Chinle. Friday, June 17:26.

1955b Fr. Berard, 'Priest Who Knows.' Friday, June 17:50–51.

Niethammer, Carolyn

1999 American Indian Cooking: Recipes from the Southwest. Lincoln: University of Nebraska Press.

Office of Navajo Economic Opportunity

n.d.1 Cookbook: The Navajo Homemaker EFMS. Window Rock: Office of Navajo Economic Opportunity, Emergency Food-Navajo Homemaker Program. [Spiral-bound, Xerox format; copy purchased 1963.]

n.d.2 Navajo Cookbook. Window Rock: Office of Navajo Economic Opportunity, Emergency Food-Navajo Homemaker Program. [Spiral-bound, Xerox format; copy purchased 1963.]

Ostermann, Father Leopold, O.F.M.

n.d. Mission at Chinle. 6 pp., typed MS. On file at Our Lady of Fatima Church, Chinle, Ariz., Historical Folder.

1913 From a Franciscan Missionary among the Navaho. The Calumet: A Quarterly published by the Marquette League for the Welfare of the Catholic Indian Missions in the United States. New York. Spring issue, April; inside 2 pp. of 4-pp. unpaginated issue.

1914 Navaho Indian Mission at Chin Lee, Arizona. The Franciscan Missions of the Southwest [Annual]:25–35.

1917 Navajo Houses. The Franciscan Missions of the Southwest 5:20–29.

1927a Signatures. In series, Little Mission Stories from Our Own Southwest. St. Anthony Messenger 34(9):466–67. [February.]

1927b Rip Van Winkle, The Father of His Children. In series, Little Mission Stories from Our Own Southwest. St. Anthony Messenger 34(10):524. [March.]

1927c Dine Naez Has a Child at School. In series, Little Mission Stories from Our Own Southwest. St. Anthony Messenger 34(10):524.

1927d More Shortcoat Ruse. In series, Little Mission Stories from Our Own Southwest. St. Anthony Messenger 34(10):524–25.

1927e A Right Bower. In series, Little Mission Stories from Our Own Southwest. St. Anthony Messenger 34(10):525.

1927f Many Goats and the Horse Herder. In series, Little Mission Stories from Our Own Southwest. St. Anthony Messenger 34(11):578. [April.]

1927g The Blessed Trinity. In series, Little Mission Stories from Our Own Southwest. St. Anthony Messenger 34(11):578–79.

1927h The Broken Window. In series, Little Mission Stories from Our Own Southwest. St. Anthony Messenger 34(11):579.

1927i First Beginnings at Chin Lee, Arizona. In series, Little Mission Stories from Our Own Southwest. St. Anthony Messenger 34(12):634–35. [May.]

1927j The First Mission House at Chin Lee, Arizona. In series, Little Mission Stories from Our Own Southwest. St. Anthony Messenger 34(12):635–36.

1927k The Old Wind Doctor. In series, Little Mission Stories from Our Own Southwest. St. Anthony Messenger 35(1):22–23. [June.]

1927l The Dying Child. In series, Little Mission Stories from Our Own Southwest. St. Anthony Messenger 35(1):23.

1927m Pete's Confession. In series, Little Mission Stories from Our Own Southwest. St. Anthony Messenger 35(1):23–24.

1927n A Double Sickcall. In series, Little Mission Stories from Our Own Southwest. St. Anthony Messenger 35(2):75. [July.]

1927o Catholic Children in Non-Reservation Schools. In series, Little Mission Stories from Our Own Southwest. St. Anthony Messenger 35(2):75–76.

1927p A Sick Call to the Peach Orchard. In series, Little Mission Stories from Our Own Southwest. St. Anthony Messenger 35(2): 76–77.

1927q Some Sick Children. In series, Little Mission Stories from Our Own Southwest. St. Anthony Messenger 35(6):301. [November.]

1927r 'I Always Say Truth.' In series, Little Mission Stories from Our Own Southwest. St. Anthony Messenger 35(6):301–3.

1928a A Thanksgiving Lesson. In series, Little Mission Stories from Our Own Southwest. St. Anthony Messenger 35(10):526. [March.]

1928b On a Runaway Horse. In series, Little Mission Stories from Our Own Southwest. St. Anthony Messenger 35(10):526–27.

1928c A Lost Trail. In series, Little Mission Stories from Our Own Southwest. St. Anthony Messenger 35(11):585–86. [April.]

1928d Horse Sense. In series, Little Mission Stories from Our Own Southwest. St. Anthony Messenger 35(11):586–87.

1928e Prove It. In series, Little Mission Stories from Our Own Southwest. St. Anthony Messenger 35(12):638–39. [May.]

Our Lady of Fatima Church [Chinle, Ariz.]. [Before 1956, called Annunciation Mission]
Baptismal Record and Burials, Sept. 12, 1907–Feb. 17, 1925
Census records
Diaries and House Chronicles, including Diary and Chronicle of Chin Lee Apr. 21, 1934–Feb. 20, 1935; Chronicle Aug. 1, 1945–Jan. 21, 1960; and later Chronicles
Liber Baptismorum, Vol. 1 (1907–40)
Liber Defunctorum Ecclesiae Records, Vol. 1 (1907–40) and Vol. 2
Liber Matrimoniorum in Ecclesia Records, Vol. 1 (Dec. 12, 1910–Aug. 9, 1924) and Vol. 2

Padres' Trail
1959 Brother Gotthard to Have Birthday [his 77th]. January:5–6.
1961 Father Berard Haile, O.F.M., Scholar of the Navajo, Dies. November:5–9, 16.
1973a June–July issue.
1973b October–November issue [Diamond Jubilee Issue].
1975 January–February issue.
1976a June–July issue.
1976b October–November issue.
1977 January issue.
1977–78 December–January issue.
1978 June–July issue.
1996 Winter issue.
1998 Centennial Celebration Issue:1898–1998. [Father Pio O'Connor, O.F.M., ed. 64 pp.]
[see also Rademaker and Trockur]

Page, Susanne, and Jake Page
1995 Navajo. New York: Harry N. Abrams.

Parman, Donald L.

1976 The Navajos and the New Deal. New Haven: Yale University Press.

Paul, Doris A.

1973 The Navajo Code Talkers. Bryn Mawr, Pa.: Dorrance and Company.

Peterson, Charles S.

1986 Homestead and Farm: A History of Farming at the Hubbell Trading Post National Historic Site. Prepared for Southwest Parks and Monuments Association, Tucson. MS. Mar. 1. Copies on file at Hubbell Trading Post National Historic Site, Ganado, Ariz.; Southwest Cultural Resources Center, National Park Service, Santa Fe; Southwest Parks and Monuments Association, Tucson; Utah State University, Logan, Utah.

1989 Big House at Ganado: New Mexican Influence in Northern Arizona. Journal of Arizona History 30(1):51–72.

Plateau [Magazine of the Museum of Northern Arizona]

1981 Vol. 52(4). Tension and Harmony: The Navajo Rug.

1986 Vol. 57(3). Issue on Historic Trading Posts.

1987 Vol. 58(2). Issue on Navajo Pottery.

Poling-Kempes, Lesley

1991 The Harvey Girls: Women Who Opened the West. New York: Marlowe and Company. Paperback ed.; first printed, Paragon House, 1989.

Powell, Donald M.

1961 A Preliminary Bibliography of the Published Writings of Berard Haile, O.F.M. Kiva 26(4):44–47. [April.]

Provincial Chronicle

1962 Father Berard. [Repr. of Editorial Comment in The New Mexico Register, Friday, Oct. 6, 1961.] Vol. 43(3): 356–57. [Spring.]

Rademaker, Father Martan, ed.

1973 Chinle Mission. Padres' Trail (June–July):2–11 (but n.p.).

1976a Father Marcellus Troester. Padres' Trail:2–13 (but n.p.). [December 1975–January 1976.]

1976b Father Emanuel Trockur, O.F.M. Padres' Trail:2–17 (but n.p.). [June–July.]

Reagan, Albert B.

1919 The Influenza and the Navajo. Proceedings of the Indiana Academy of Science 1919:243–47.

1922 The 'Flu' among the Navajos. Kansas Academy of Science Transactions 33(2):131–38.

Reichard, Gladys A.

n.d. A Dictionary of Nouns. English-Navajo. Gladys A. Reichard Collection, MS 29–52. Museum of Northern Arizona Archives, Museum of Northern Arizona, Flagstaff. Partial notes thereon, and some Xeroxes of pages of MS provided by D. Brugge, July 1996. [MS probably dates after 1945, the latest entry in the bibliography.]

1928 Social Life of the Navajo Indians. Columbia University Contributions to Anthropology 7. New York: Columbia University Press.

1934 Spider Woman. New York: Macmillan. Repr., Albuquerque: University of New Mexico Press, 1997 [with Foreword by Louise Lamphere].

1936 Navajo Shepherd and Weaver. New York: J. J. Augustin.

1939a Dezba, Woman of the Desert. New York: J. J. Augustin.

1939b Navajo Medicine Man: Sandpaintings and Legends of Miguelito. New York: J. J. Augustin.

1963 Navaho Religion. New York: Bollingen Foundation. 2d ed., 1 vol. Originally published, 1950.

Reinhart, Theodore R.

1997 The Trader and Navajo Culture Change. Paper presented at the Tenth Annual Navajo Studies Conference, University of New Mexico, Albuquerque, Apr. 16–19.

1998 Lorenzo Hubbell, Jr., Indian Trader. Paper presented at the Eleventh Annual Navajo Studies Conference, Navajo Nation Museum, Window Rock, Oct. 21–24.

Richardson, Gladwell

1991 Navajo Trader. Tucson: University of Arizona Press. 2d printing. Originally published, 1986.

Roberts, Willow

1987 Stokes Carson: Twentieth-Century Trading on the Navajo Reservation. Albuquerque: University of New Mexico Press.

Rodee, Marian E.

1977 Southwestern Weaving. Albuqerque: University of New Mexico Press.

1981 Old Navajo Rugs: Their Development from 1900 to 1940. Albuquerque: University of New Mexico Press.

1987 Weaving of the Southwest. West Chester, Pa.: Schiffer Publishing Company.

1995 One Hundred Years of Navajo Rugs. Albuquerque: University of New Mexico Press.

Rodgers, Larry, comp. and ed.

1990 Chapter Images: 1989. Window Rock: The Navajo Tribe, Division of Community Development.

1993 Chapter Images: 1992 Edition. Window Rock: The Navajo Nation, Division of Community Development.

1997 Chapter Images: 1996 Edition. Window Rock: The Navajo Nation, Division of Community Development.

Roessel, Monty

1993 Kinaaldá: A Navajo Girl Grows Up. Minneapolis: Lerner Publications Company.

Roessel, Robert A., Jr.

1980 Pictorial History of the Navajo from 1860–1910. Rough Rock, Ariz.: Rough Rock Demonstration School, Navajo Curriculum Center.

1983 Navajo History 1850–1923. *In* Handbook of North American Indians, Vol. 10, Southwest. Alfonso Ortiz, ed. Pp. 506–23. Washington, D.C.: Smithsonian Institution.

Roessel, Ruth

1981 Women in Navajo Society. Chinle, Ariz.: Rough Rock Demonstration School.

1983 Navajo Arts and Crafts. *In* Handbook of North American Indians, Vol. 10, Southwest. Alfonso Ortiz, ed. Pp. 592–604. Washington, D.C.: Smithsonian Institution.

Roessel, Ruth, and Broderick H. Johnson, comps.

1974 Navajo Livestock Reduction: A National Disgrace. Chinle: Navajo Community College Press.

Rosenak, Chuck, and Jan Rosenak

1994 The People Speak: Navajo Folk Art. Flagstaff: Northland Publishing Company.

Rosenlieb, Gary W., and Gary M. Smillie

1990 Floodplain Analysis for the Garcia Trading Post Area, Canyon de Chelly National

Monument, Chinle, Arizona. Technical Report NPS/NRWRD/NRTR-90/05. October. U.S. Department of the Interior, National Park Service. Copy on file at National Park Service Regional Office, Santa Fe.

Russell, Scott C.

1985 The Navajo and the 1918 Influenza Pandemic. *In* Health and Disease in the Prehistoric Southwest. Charles F. Merbs and Robert J. Miller, eds. Arizona State University Anthropological Research Papers 34:380–90.

St. Anthony Messenger

1998 October issue. [Two articles concerning the Franciscan Centennial: Walking Gently with the Navajos, by Father John Mittelstadt, O.F.M., p. 5; and One Hundred Years of Franciscan Presence among the Navajos, by Father Murray Bodo, O.F.M., p. 34.]

St. Louis Post Dispatch

1998 Researchers Pursue Spanish Influenza Virus. Aug. 17:A-7.

Salsbury, Clarence, M.D., with Paul Hughes

1969 The Salsbury Story. Tucson: University of Arizona Press.

Salsbury, Cora

1941 Forty Years in the Desert: History of Ganado Mission, 1901–1940. Chicago: Press of Physicians' Record Company.

Sandford, Father Mark, O.F.M.

1949 Chinle – A Place of Enchantment and Possibility. St. Anthony Messenger:26–29. [April.]

1997 Personal communications, Feb. 18, May 16, Aug. 8.

Scates, David R.

1981 Why Navajo Churches Are Growing: The Cultural Dynamics of Navajo Religious Change. Cortez: Navajo Christian Churches.

Schiffer, Nancy N.

1991 Navajo Arts and Crafts. West Chester, Pa.: Schiffer Publishing Company.

Schwarz, Maureen Trudelle

1997 Molded in the Image of Changing Woman: Navajo Views on the Human Body and Personhood. Tucson: University of Arizona Press.

Shebala, Marley

1996 Festival Brings Navajo History to Silverscreen [*sic*]. Navajo Times 35(42):A-1, 2. [Oct. 17.]

1999 Top Ten Stories. Navajo Times 38(52): A-1, 3, 5. [Dec. 30.]

Sheehan, Most Reverend Michael J., Archbishop of Santa Fe, ed.

1998 Four Hundred Years of Faith: Seeds of Struggle – Harvest of Faith; A History of the Catholic Church in New Mexico. Albuquerque: Starline Printing (for Archdiocese of Santa Fe).

Shepardson, Mary

1963 Navajo Ways in Government. American Anthropological Association 65(3), Pt. 2, Memoir 96. [June.]

1965 Problems of the Navajo Tribal Courts in Transition. Human Organization 24(3):250–53.

Shinkle, James D.

1965 Fort Sumner and the Bosque Redondo Indian Reservation. Roswell, N.M.: Hall-Poorbaugh Press.

Simonelli, Jeanne M.

1997 Crossing Between Worlds: The Navajos of Canyon de Chelly [with Photographs by Charles D. Winters]. Santa Fe: School of American Research Press.

Sisters of the Blessed Sacrament

1941 Souvenir Volume of the Golden Jubilee (1891–1941). Cornwells Heights, Pa.: Sisters of the Blessed Sacrament.

1992 Blessed Katharine Drexel: A Life Summary. Pamphlet available from the Sisters of the Blessed Sacrament.

Southwest Parks and Monuments Association

1992 A Guide to Navajo Rugs. Tucson: Southwest Parks and Monuments Association.

Spears, Beverley

1987 Unpublished Fieldnotes Pertaining to Garcia Trading Post. [Includes annotated site map from Aug. 25 to Aug. 27, 1987, fieldwork and Sept. 10, 1987, interview with Margaret Garcia Delaney, Albuquerque.] On file, U.S. Department of the Interior, National Park Service, Southwest Regional Office, Santa Fe.

Steggerda, Morris, and R. B. Eckardt

1941 Navajo Foods and Their Preparation. American Dietetic Association Journal 17:217–25. [March.]

Stevens, Peggy, T.S.R.

1998 Chinle, Arizona, Help in Healing. [Article about Sister Adelaide Link, S.F.P., of Our Lady of Fatima Church.] Southwest Labor Journal 24(8):11, 13. [August.]

Stewart, Greyeyes

1988 Before Blessingway: An Autobiographical Fragment (as told to James K. McNeley in the early 1970s). Diné Be'iina': A Journal of Navajo Life 1(2):22–33.

Stewart, Irene

1980 A Voice in Her Tribe: A Navajo Woman's Own Story. Doris O. Dawdy, ed. Ballena Press Anthropological Papers 17. Socorro, N.M.: Ballena Press. [Foreword by Mary Shepardson.]

Stewart, Omer C.

1938 The Navajo Wedding Basket. Museum Notes 10(9):25–28. Flagstaff: Museum of Northern Arizona.

Sundberg, Lawrence D.

1995 Dinétah: An Early History of the Navajo People. Santa Fe: Sunstone Press.

Teller, Joanne, and Norman Blackwater

1997 The Navajo Skinwalker, Witchcraft, and Related Phenomena. Spiritual Clues: Orientation to the Evolution of the Circle. Chinle, Ariz.: Infinity Horn Publishing.

Thompson, Gerald

1976 The Army and the Navajo: The Bosque Redondo Experiment, 1863–1868. Tucson: University of Arizona Press.

Thompson, Hildegard

1975 The Navajos' Long Walk for Education: A History of Navajo Education. Tsaile, Ariz.: Navajo Community College Press.

Tohe, Laura

1999 No Parole Today. Albuquerque: West End Press.

Toulouse, Carmie Lynn

1982 Modern Navajo Witchcraft Stories. In Navajo Religion and Culture: Selected Views.

Papers in Honor of Leland C. Wyman. David M. Brugge and Charlotte J. Frisbie, eds. Museum of New Mexico Papers in Anthropology 17:84–88.

Trafzer, Clifford E.

1982 The Kit Carson Campaign: The Last Great Navajo War. Norman: University of Oklahoma Press.

Trennert, Robert A.

1998 White Man's Medicine: Government Doctors and the Navajo, 1863–1955. Albuquerque: University of New Mexico Press.

Trinity Presbyterian Church, Chinle, Ariz. [Before 1959, called Indian Presbyterian Church of Chinle]

  Variety of unpublished church records, including:

    Church Register

    Communicants [first known session records for Chinle start Apr. 20, 1923] and Alphabetical Roll of Communicants

    Minutes of Session

    Register of Deaths and file folder on Funerals

    Register of Marriages

    Roll of Elders

    Roll of Pastors

    Roll of Suspended Members

Trockur, Father Emanuel, O.F.M.

1922 My First Trip to Chin Lee. The Franciscan Missions of the Southwest 10:24–28. [Final vol. of The Franciscan Missions of the Southwest.]

1976 Father Leopold Ostermann, O.F.M. Padres' Trail:14 pp. [but n.p.] [December.]

Tschopik, Harry

1938 Taboo as a Possible Factor Involved in the Obsolescence of Navaho Pottery and Basketry. American Anthropologist 40(2):257–62.

1940 Navaho Basketry: A Study of Culture Change. American Anthropologist 42(3):444–62.

1941 Navaho Pottery Making: An Inquiry into the Affinities of Navaho Painted Pottery. Papers of the Peabody Museum of Archaeology and Ethnology, Harvard University 17(1).

Underhill, Ruth

1953 Here Come the Navaho! United States Indian Service, Indian Life and Customs 8. Lawrence, Kans.: Haskell Institute Press.

1956 The Navajos. Norman: University of Oklahoma Press.

Valette, Jean-Paul, and Rebecca M. Valette

1997 In Search of Yah-nah-pah: The Early Gallegos "Yei" Blankets and Their Weavers. American Indian Art Magazine 23(1):56–69.

Valette, Rebecca M.

1998 Weaving the Dance: Yeibichai Dancers as Depicted in Navajo Rugs, 1900–1940. Paper presented at the Eleventh Annual Navajo Studies Conference, Navajo Nation Museum, Window Rock, Oct. 21–24.

Valette, Rebecca M., and Jean-Paul Valette

2000 The Life and Work of Clitso Dedman, Navajo Woodcarver (1879?–1953). American Indian Art Magazine 25(2):54–67.

Van Valkenburgh, Richard F.

1936 Navajo Common Law I. Museum Notes 9(4). Flagstaff: Museum of Northern Arizona.

1938 A Short History of the Navajo People. Window Rock: Navajo Agency, Mimeograph.

1941 Diné Bikéyah. Window Rock, Ariz.: U.S. Department of the Interior, Office of Indian Affairs, Navajo Service.

1945 The Government of the Navajos. Arizona Quarterly 1:63–73.

Van Valkenburgh, Richard F., edited by Clyde Kluckhohn.

1974 Sacred Places. In Navajo Findings III: Commission Findings. Pp. 9–199. American Indian Ethnohistory: Indians of the Southwest. David A. Horr, comp. and ed. New York: Garland Publishing.

Vestal, Paul A.

1952 Ethnobotany of the Ramah Navajo. Papers of the Peabody Museum of American Archaeology and Ethnology, Harvard University 40(4).

Wagner, Sallie R.

1997 Wide Ruins: Memories from a Navajo Trading Post. Albuquerque: University of New Mexico Press.

Wallechinsky, D., and I. Wallace

1975 The People's Almanac. Garden City, N.Y.: Doubleday and Company.

Ward, Albert E.

1980 Navajo Graves: A Ethnoarchaeological Reflection of Ethnographic Reality. Center for Anthropological Studies, Ethnohistorical Report Series 2.

Warner, Michael J.

1970 Protestant Missionary Activity among the Navajo, 1890–1912. New Mexico Historical Review 45:209–32.

Waxman, Alan G.

1990 Navajo Childbirth in Transition. Medical Anthropology 12:187–206.

Weber, Father Anselm, O.F.M.

1915 Editorial Review. The Franciscan Missions of the Southwest 3:40.

1917 Editorial Review. The Franciscan Missions of the Southwest 5:51.

1919 Editorial Review. The Franciscan Missions of the Southwest 7:39.

1920 Editorial Review. The Franciscan Missions of the Southwest 8:45.

Wheat, J. B.

1974 Navajo Blankets from the Collection of Anthony Berlant. Tucson: University of Arizona Museum of Art.

1975 Patterns and Sources of Navajo Weaving. Denver: The Printing Establishment.

1976a Navajo Textiles. In The Fred Harvey Fine Arts Collection. Byron Harvey, ed. Pp. 9–47. Phoenix: The Heard Museum.

1976b The Navajo Chief Blanket. American Indian Art 1(3):44–53.

1981 Early Navajo Weaving. Plateau 52(4):2–9.

Wheelwright, Mary C., and David P. McAllester

1956 The Myth and Prayers of the Great Star Chant and the Myth of the Coyote Chant. Navajo Religion Series 4. Santa Fe: Museum of Navajo Ceremonial Art.

Wicoff, Mary

1998a Navajos, Friars Hail One Hundred Years. Gallup Independent, Oct. 10:15.

1998b Priest's Family [Family of Anselm Weber, O.F.M.] Sets Up Scholarship. Gallup Independent, Oct. 10:15.

Wilken, Robert

1955 Anselm Weber, O.F.M.: Missionary to the Navaho. Milwaukee: Bruce Publishing Company.

Wilkins, Teresa

1998 Brenda Spencer, Navajo Weaver. Indian Artist:32–36. [Winter.]

Williams, Aubrey W., Jr.

1970 Navajo Political Processes. Smithsonian Contributions to Anthropology 9. Washington, D.C.: Smithsonian Institution.

Williams, Lester L.

1989 C. N. Cotton and His Navajo Blankets. Albuquerque: Avanyu Publishing.

Willink, Roseann S., and Paul G. Zolbrod

1996 Weaving a World: Textiles and the Navajo Way of Seeing. Santa Fe: Museum of New Mexico Press.

Winter, Father Pius, O.F.M.

1961 Religion Boom in Chinle. St. Anthony Messenger 69(6):32–34. [November.]

Wintz, Father Jack, O.F.M.

1994 Hogan Church: Where Navajo and Christian Paths Meet. St. Anthony Messenger 102(4):14–21. [September.]

Witherspoon, Gary

1975 Navajo Kinship and Marriage. Ann Arbor: University of Michigan Press.

1977 Language and Art in the Navajo Universe. Ann Arbor: University of Michigan Press.

1983 Navajo Social Organization. In Handbook of North American Indians, Vol. 10, Southwest. Alfonso Ortiz, ed. Pp. 524–35. Washington, D.C.: Smithsonian Institution.

Wright, H. Diane

1987a Navajo Pottery: Contemporary Trends in a Traditional Craft. American Indian Art Magazine 12(2):26–35.

1987b Revival in Navajo Pottery. Plateau 58(2):8–15.

Wright, H. Diane, and Jan Bell

1987 Potters and Their Work. Plateau 58(2):24–31.

Wyman, Leland C.

1957 Beautyway: A Navaho Ceremonial. Bollingen Series 53. New York: Pantheon Books.

1962 The Windways of the Navaho. Colorado Springs: Taylor Museum.

1965 The Red Antway of the Navaho. Navaho Religion Series 5. Santa Fe: Museum of Navajo Ceremonial Art.

1970a Blessingway [with Three Versions of the Myth Recorded and Translated from the Navajo by Father Berard Haile, O.F.M.]. Tucson: University of Arizona Press.

1970b Sandpaintings of the Navaho Shootingway and the Walcott Collection. Smithsonian Contributions to Anthropology 13. Washington, D.C.: Smithsonian Institution.

1975 The Mountainway of the Navajo. Tucson: University of Arizona Press.

1983 Navajo Ceremonial System. In Handbook of North American Indians, Southwest, Vol. 10. Alfonso Ortiz, ed. Pp. 536–57. Washington, D.C.: Smithsonian Institution.

Wyman, Leland C., and Stuart K. Harris

1941 Navajo Indian Medical Ethnobotany. University of New Mexico Bulletin 3:1–76. Albuquerque: University of New Mexico.

1951 The Ethnobotany of the Kayenta Navajo. Albuquerque: University of New Mexico Press.

Wyman, Leland C., and Clyde Kluckhohn
1938 Navaho Classification of Their Song Ceremonials. American Anthropological Association Memoirs 50.

Yazzie, Alfred W.
1984a Navajo Oral Tradition, Vol. 1 [covers the Beginning part of timeline]. Rough Rock, Ariz.: Rough Rock Demonstration School Navajo Oral Tradition Project.
1984b Navajo Oral Tradition, Vol. 2 [covers from the Emergence into the New Settlement part of timeline]. Rough Rock, Ariz.: Rough Rock Demonstration School Navajo Oral Tradition Project.
1984c Navajo Oral Tradition, Vol. 3 [covers the period of Changing Woman in the timeline]. Rough Rock, Ariz.: Rough Rock Demonstration School Navajo Oral Tradition Project.

Yazzie, Chief Justice Robert
1998 Keynote Address. Presented, by invitation, during Opening Plenary Session at the Eleventh Annual Navajo Studies Conference, Navajo Nation Museum, Window Rock, Oct. 21.

Young, Robert W.
1961 The Navajo Yearbook 8: 1951–1961, A Decade of Progress. Window Rock: Navajo Agency.
1968 The Role of the Navajo in the Southwestern Drama. Gallup: Gallup Independent and Robert W. Young.
1978 A Political History of the Navajo Tribe. Tsaile, Ariz.: Navajo Community College Press.

Young, Robert W., and William Morgan
1980 The Navajo Dictionary: A Grammar and Colloquial Dictionary. Albuquerque: University of New Mexico Press.

Young, Stella
1938 Native Plants Used by the Navajo. Washington, D.C.: Department of Interior, Office of Indian Affairs. Mimeograph.

Zolbrod, Paul
1997 Benally Women: Three Generations of Navajo Weavers. Indian Artist:42–45. [Fall.]
1998 On the Multicultural Frontier with Washington Matthews. Journal of the Southwest 40(1):67–86.

Index

126. *See also* Bitter Water People; Coyote Pass People (Jemez Clan); *Kiyaa'áanii;* Many Goats; Red Bottom People; Red Running into the Water; Salt People; Start of the Red Streak People; Tall Water Flows Together People; *Tó dích'ii'nii;* Towering House People; Two Streams Meet; Water Edge

Clauschee, Norman, 24. *See also* 338 (App. A-2)

Clauschee, Ralph, 24, 389n.37. *See also* 338 (App. A-2)

Clauschees, 389n.37, 466n.5. *See also* 338–39 (App. A-2)

Claw, Charlie, 242, 274

Clay, white, 169, 433n.19, 445n.8

Cliffrose, xxxix, 206, 255, 461n.8; bark of, 88, 255, 419–20n.4. *See also* Buckbrush

Cloth/material, 9, 10, 12, 15, 30, 35, 64, 65, 75, 91, 116, 238, 251, 259, 317, 324, 460n.5.

Clothes, 15, 30, 75, 82, 92, 111, 124, 136, 141, 151, 194, 195, 200, 237, 250, 268, 269, 300, 309, 409n.15, 449n.10, 454n.2; burial in new, 216, 316–17, 318, 485–86n.20; ceremonial/traditional, 188, 383n.18, 404n.14, 469n.9; "dress up," 178, 285 (fig. 40); in mother's time, 15; in own childhood, 30; school, 136, 460n.4

Coal, 213, 222, 224, 254, 450n.11

Code Talkers/code-talking (Navajo), 253, 465n.3, 478n.25

Coffee, 17, 64, 262, 301, 319, 320, 324, 461n.20, 464n.20, 476n.14; pot for, 51

Cohen, Marilyn, 473–74n.12

Cold, 29, 37, 42, 64, 67, 112, 130, 134, 177, 197, 221, 303, 460n.3, 465n.4

Collier, John (Com. of Ind. Affairs), 405n.16, 446n.1, 448n.6, 455n.7

Colorado, 435n.8, 475n.11. *See also* vi (map 1)

Colorado River, Ariz./Colo./Utah, 7. *See also* vi (map 1)

Conflicts (with enemies, before Fort Sumner), 3, 4, 5, 6, 7, 8, 9, 10, 11, 12, 13, 120, 379n.5, 380n.6, 423n.10, 437n.17

Connecticut, 311, 482n.4

Containers, 34, 36, 251, 409n.17; dishes, 9, 51, 208, 237, 483n.7; pans, 9, 51, 249, 251, 309. *See also* Baskets; Buckets; Pots; Pottery-making; Water bags; Water jugs

Cook, The, 289

Cooking, 9, 13, 32, 33, 34, 37, 44, 48, 51, 55, 56, 57, 58, 71, 84, 119, 132, 135, 144, 165, 178, 191, 192, 208, 223, 225, 240, 245–46, 247, 250, 275, 284, 287, 288, 291, 309, 313, 317, 319, 321, 322, 411n.1, 421n.9, 445n.8, 447n.2, 454n.3, 463n.14, 464n.20. *See also* 283 (fig. 38)

Cookshack, 57. *See also* 283 (fig. 36)

Coon Can, 142, 428n.3. *See also* Card playing

Corn, 19, 32, 33, 41, 43, 44, 45, 46, 47, 52, 53, 55, 56, 57, 63, 64, 65, 71, 74, 79, 83, 84, 85, 91, 105, 109, 112, 115, 119, 159, 164, 193, 196, 202, 204, 205, 207, 214, 224, 233, 234, 235, 237, 238, 239,

246, 249, 250, 251, 259, 289, 296, 300, 309, 390n.37, 464n.21, 486n.24; as hominy, 33, 464n.20, 486n.24; four stages of, 250, 463–64n.20

Cornbread, 57, 67

Corn cake baked in ground, 46, 57, 63, 64, 197, 205, 399n.9. *See also* '*Alkaan*

Cornfields, 33, 44, 64, 108, 143, 193, 202, 204, 215, 240, 243, 278, 390n.37, 453n.20, 460n.2

Cornfields, Ariz., 395n.2

Corn grinding, xxvi, 44, 47, 57, 63, 464n.20, 478n.23

Corn husking, 224, 250. *See also* 290 (fig. 41)

Corn husks, 55, 406n.5, 464n.20

Cornmeal, 17, 32, 44, 45, 46, 55, 56, 57, 205, 237, 239, 259, 468n.8; mush, 46, 55, 56, 57, 66, 67, 205, 237, 239, 241, 259, 410n.19, 464n.20

Corn plant leaves, 122, 224, 250, 464n.20

Corn pollen (*Tádidíín*), 47, 58, 90, 195, 204, 205, 236, 240, 249, 289, 410n.19, 468n.8

Cornstalks, 224, 250

Corn whiskey, 453n.23

Corral, 149, 151, 153, 194, 211, 212, 251, 257, 313, 436n.11, 476n.19; brush, 9, 10; for branding, 79, 137, 428n.7; sheep, 29, 42, 112, 114; stone, 98, 99, 100, 104, 105, 106, 289, 290

Corral Dance, 382n.14, 429n.7

Cotton, C. N., 165, 395n.2, 397n.2, 400n.12, 432n.15. *See also* Big House; 165 (fig. 14)

Cottonwood, Ariz., 6, 7, 110, 274, 320, 405n.16, 483n.10; Chapter at, 483n.10. *See also* 28, 80 (maps 2, 3)

Cottonwood trees, xxvi, xxxix, 21, 115, 126, 180, 226, 430n.4, 440n.1, 448n.4, 455n.11. *See also* Man with a Cane/Man with a Cottonwood Tree

Cottonwood Wash, 447n.2

Courts, 261, 262, 268, 275, 294, 408n.11, 418n.8, 471–72n.2, 472n.5; of Indian Offenses, 471n.2; Navajo law in, 472n.2; Navajo system, 471n.2

Cousins, Bill and Jean (Jackson), 445n.5

Cousins, Charles, 397n.2, 418–19n.8

Cousins's Trading Post, Chinle, Ariz., 418–19n.8. *See also* Sam Day's Trading Post/Thunderbird Lodge

Covered with Horses (Horse Blind/Horses on the Edge/Ridge, the), 21, 81, 430n.1. *See also* Horses on the Edge; 80 (map 3)

Cowhide, 100, 403–4n.13. *See also* Moccasins

Cows/cattle, xvii, 21, 24, 37, 48, 54, 59, 66, 79, 82, 98, 99, 100, 102, 114, 124, 129, 137, 138, 139, 141, 147, 148, 211, 212, 226, 244, 246, 423n.10, 426n.3, 428n.7, 447n.2, 448n.4, 450n.10; bull (story about mean), 242; selling, of Man Who Shouts', 138–39, 403n.13. *See also* Livestock

Coyote Pass People (Jemez clan), 129, 382n.13

Coyoteway Ceremony, 382n.14

Cradleboard, 88, 176, 177, 178, 182, 255, 419–20n.4

Cranes. *See* Birds, cranes

Death, beliefs/practices about, 102, 103, 129, 135, 150, 151, 152, 153, 164, 179, 181, 184, 203–4, 216–17, 223, 226–28, 266, 276, 286, 287, 288, 316, 317, 318, 319, 320, 425n.4, 427n.4, 430n.12, 437n.17, 452–53n.20, 453n.23, 457n.18, 467n.5, 479n.36, 479–80n.37; funerals, 319, 484nn.16, 17; 485nn.17–20; 486nn.20–21, 23–25; shelters used during final days, 101, 150, 151, 153, 204, 216, 255, 443n.11, 453n.20. *See also* Burials; Cemeteries; Death; Graves

Dedman, Clitsoi, 420n.7

Deer, 31, 33, 38, 114, 245, 392n.6

Deerskin/buckskin, 30, 31, 58, 288

Deer Springs, Ariz., 474n.2

Deeshchii'nii, 23, 387n.30, 425nn.1, 3. *See also* 335 (App. A-2)

Deities: Changing Woman, 297, 468–69n.8; Dawn, 192, 236; Holy People, xxxvii, 58, 103, 141, 147, 188, 296, 297, 382n.14, 469n.8; Horned Toads, 468–69n.8; Spider Woman, 444n.3. *See also* Spider Rock; Warrior Twins/Twin Warriors/Holy Twins, 146, 468–69n.8; White Shell Woman, 468n.8

Delaney, Margaret Garcia, 396n.2. *See also* Garcia, Camillo and Pauline

Delgadito, 408n.11

Dennehotsoh, Ariz., 450n.11

Depression, The, 185–86, 210, 446n.1

Deschine, Isabel Mitchell, xxviii, xxix, xxxv, 50, 106, 137, 171, 175, 191, 193, 196, 200, 204, 212, 214, 216, 221, 223, 229, 233, 241, 242, 251, 252, 255, 259, 260, 267–69, 274, 275, 277, 278, 289, 309, 310, 311, 315, 316, 317, 318, 319, 320, 433n.18, 436n.12, 443n.11, 453n.2, 454n.4, 460n.3, 461n.8, 462n.14, 469n.9, 473nn.8, 9, 10, 474n.7, 478n.27, 483n.7, 484n.13, 485n.18, 486nn.20, 23; photographs of, 230, 231, 233, 284, 285, 310 (figs. 23, 26, 30, 38, 39, 42). *See also* Deschine, Jimmy; 337, 342, 350 (App. A-2, A-3, A-4)

Deschine, Jimmy, 309–10, 317, 318, 319, 329, 485n.18; wagework, with Isabel, 310. *See also* 342, 350 (App. A-3, A-4)

Deschine, Ralph, 390n.40. *See also* 338 (App. A-2)

"Desert Song" (movie), 435n.9

Diagnosing/diagnosticians, 58, 128, 183, 184, 195, 380n.10, 407n.9, 466n.4, 473n.8, 480n.37. *See also* Hand-trembling; Listeners; Star-gazing

Diłwosh, 384n.8. *See also* Man Who Shouts, names of

Diné, 379n.1. *See also* People, The

Diné College, Ariz./N.Mex., 385n.20. *See also* Navajo Community College

Diné Nééz, 172

Diné Nééz biye', 126, 158, 387n.30, 434n.2. *See also* Son of Tall Navajo; 335–36 (App. A-2)

Diseases/medical problems, 234, 427nn.2,3, 429n.7, 443–44n.12, 457n.17, 458n.22; ailments, some, as listed by Tall Woman, 241; arthritis, 203, 281–82, 309, 322; Bell's palsy, 438n.22; cancer 274, 285, 479n.32, 480n.41, 481n.43, 483n.6, 484nn.14,15; chickenpox, 128, 179, 241, 461n.8; congenital hip, 420n.5; diabetes, 303, 309, 311, 312, 314, 322, 479n.29; fever, 20, 132, 133, 190, 227, 241, 457n.16; flu. *See* flu/influenza epidemic; gallbladder, 111, 276, 278, 285, 322, 479n.29; heart problems, 21, 138, 311, 482n.4, 483n.8; heart problems, stroke, 19, 183, 311, 312, 436n.12, 481n.43; infections, 177, 182, 225, 322, 434n.3, 436n.14, 438n.20, 455n.6, 458n.22; measles, 21, 128, 138, 179, 421n.9, paralysis, 183, 184, 204, 311, 438nn.21, 22, 481n.43; pneumonia, 131, 235, 474n.8, 484n.12; smallpox, 20; sores, 128, 130, 133, 179, 312, 316, 436n.14, 461n.8, 462n.9; spinal meningitis, 443–44n.12, 457n.17; tooth troubles, 64, 225, 266, 434n.3; thyroid, 275–76, 475n.9, 477n.20, 479n.29; trachoma, 225, 455n.6; tuberculosis (TB), 81, 233, 234, 267, 273, 409n.16, 423n.10, 458n.22. *See also* Doctors; Epidemics; Flu/influenza; Hospitals; Illness; Injuries; Medicine, western; Sickness

Disputes, among The People, 60, 123, 151, 262, 265, 267, 277, 303, 442n.5, 466n.5, 472nn.2, 5. *See also* Fighting; Troubles

Ditch, water/irrigation, 34, 36, 61, 246, 247, 249, 252, 446n.1, 447n.2, 463nn.15, 17, 465–66n.4; big, by Mitchells', 160, 162, 202, 203, 215, 237, 238, 443n.11, 445n.5. *See also* 161 (map 4)

Division of labor, 112, 115, 116, 117, 118, 119, 144, 160, 162, 170, 187, 192, 193, 194, 195, 205, 234, 240, 247, 265, 267, 296, 300, 390n.40, 395n.15, 461n.8; in childhood, 37, 38, 44, 46, 47, 53, 62, 63, 65, 93; in learning, 117–19; in Tall Woman's marriage, 296–98; in weddings, 66–67. *See also* Marital relations; Marriage; Wagework; Women's work

Dleesh, 169, 170, 192, 240; kinds of, 433n.19

Dlinasbah, 214, 452n.15. *See also* 335, 350 (App. A-2, A-4)

Doctors, western medical, 19, 143, 151, 177, 182, 226, 227, 235, 254, 274, 275, 276, 281, 285, 286, 303, 316, 456n.13, 458n.22, 460n.24; dentist, 225

Dodge, (Henry) Chee, 163, 226, 253, 261, 408nn.11,12, 417n.7, 420n.7, 426n.7, 431n.11, 448n.6, 456n.15

Dogs, 33, 36, 40, 121, 122, 198, 201, 211, 266, 296, 313, 443n.11

Donkeys, 32, 38, 39, 41, 44, 45, 60, 65, 74, 113, 115, 117, 119, 122, 123, 134, 162, 193, 205, 238–39, 243; as pack animals, 44, 45, 47, 48, 65, 74, 205

Drag the Water Off/Out/Down (Where You), 113, 153

Draper, Henry, 136, 425n.1

Draper, Phillip, 439n.1, 453n.2

Drapers, the, 214

Dreams, bad, 57, 264, 265, 288, 300, 380n.10, 429n.7, 467n.7, 473n.8

292; in Epilogue, 316, 317, 318, 319, 320, 321, 482n.1

Fighting/arguing, 4, 5, 7, 8, 18, 90, 121, 122, 141, 186, 190, 194, 228, 249, 253, 262, 265, 266, 277, 286, 294, 295, 296, 297, 301, 303, 314, 457n.19, 460n.2. *See also* Conflicts; Enemies; Living right

Fingerless Man, 165, 177, 183

Fire Dance, 9, 382n.14, 429n.7

Fire-fighting, 478n.25

Fires, 9, 11, 12, 13, 33, 35, 44, 74, 114, 115, 177, 197, 205, 239, 258, 406n.7, 433n.1, 460n.2, 461n.8, 464n.20, 469n.9

Fish Point, Ariz., 79, 112, 113, 114, 138, 157, 244, 428n.7, 431n.9. *See also* 80 (map 3)

Flagstaff, Ariz., 75, 254, 446n.1, 465n.3. *See also* vi (map 1)

Flats, The (Red Mesa Area), 113, 147, 157, 158, 430n.1, 431n.13, 447n.2. *See also* 80 (map 3)

Flintway Ceremony, xxi, 109, 124, 143, 145, 151, 278, 429n.7; *jish* of, 109–10, 289, 425–26n.2, 426n.3; Lifeway, 143

Flock, 29, 34, 37, 62, 99, 212, 244, 259, 425n.2, 430n.4, 438n.18. *See also* Goats; Sheep

Flood, 43, 55, 453n.22, 476n.19

Flour, 16, 17, 46, 48, 49, 55

Flu/influenza epidemic (1918–19), xxi, 21, 25, 94, 96, 100, 110, 114, 128–39, 140, 143, 144, 179, 328, 383n.16, 385n.18, 421n.9, 421n.10, 426–27n.2, 427n. 3, 431n.9, 434n.1, 435n.8, 437n.17

Fluted Rock, Ariz., 39–40, 41, 42, 43, 53, 54, 55, 64, 74, 79, 96, 97, 98, 107, 114, 116, 118, 255, 474n.4; area, 36. *See also* 28, 80, 161 (maps 2, 3, 4)

Fluted Rock Mountains, Ariz., 27, 41, 42

Foley, John, 451n.11

Food, 6, 9, 10, 11, 14, 15, 16, 17, 32, 33, 34, 42, 44, 46, 47, 48, 50, 53, 59, 60, 61, 65, 66, 67, 83, 84, 90, 91, 92, 103, 111, 114, 117, 118, 119, 123, 135, 136, 152, 157, 158, 159, 164, 188, 189, 192, 195, 201–2, 203, 204, 205, 211, 215, 222, 223, 233, 234, 235, 236, 237, 240, 241, 243, 244, 245, 246, 247, 250, 251, 259, 276, 278, 293, 294, 295, 301, 303, 312, 316, 317, 322, 324, 383n.2, 392n.8, 399n.10, 433n.19, 444n.5, 445n.8, 447n.2, 453n.20, 461n.5, 483n.7; at Tall Woman's funeral, 317, 318, 319, 485n.18, 486n.24; ceremonial, 46, 66, 188, 189, 205, 241, 267, 322; corn, as main, 46, 55, 56, 57; in her childhood, 31, 32, 33; in her mother's time, 14, 15; starting to plant, 43–44; stealing, 4, 15; tomatoes, as a favorite, 444n.2; traditional, xxxi, 119, 169, 205, 223, 241, 267, 310, 311, 313, 322; wasting, 15. *See also* Animals; Bread; Butchering; Corn; Crops; Foods, wild; Hunting; Meat; Milk; Mutton

Foods, wild, xxvi, 33, 34, 118, 125, 157, 205–6, 241; carrots, xxxiv, 119, 240; onions, xxxix, 119, 240; potatoes, xxxix, 119, 240, 433n.19

Footraces, 141, 173, 435n.6, 460n.6. *See also* Ki-naaldá, racing in; Races (daily)

Fort Apache, Ariz., 174, 175, 176. *See also* vi (map 1)

Fort Apache Indian School, Fort Apache, Ariz., 22, 137, 146, 153, 159, 160, 173–74, 179, 181, 182, 186, 189, 193, 195, 201, 202, 204, 208, 210, 255, 425n.1, 430n.4, 435n.8, 444n.4, 450n.10; Mitchells at, 173–74, 189, 438n.18, 441n.3, 450n.10, 461n.8, 473n.11. *See also* 378 (App. C)

Fort Defiance, Ariz., 16, 18, 22, 53, 55, 60, 72, 78, 92, 94, 123, 124, 147, 165, 186, 187, 208, 212, 225, 253, 261, 406n.3, 407n.10, 408n.11, 412n.3, 421n.9, 426n.7, 447n.2, 449n.10, 456nn.12, 15, 471nn.1, 2, 472n.5, 474n.2; agent at, 71, 418n.8; boarding school at, 16, 61, 62, 75, 81, 133, 136, 149, 172, 213, 225, 285, 383n.4, 387n.29, 408n.13, 433–34n.1, 448n.4, 455n.6; cemetery, Veterans at, 482n.4; hospital. *See* Fort Defiance Hospital; missions at (Episcopalian, Presbyterian), 386n.26, 424n.11; sawmill at, 89; stores/trading posts at, 30, 51, 72, 81, 392n.5 (Neale's), 396nn.2, 4, 406n.3 (Manning's); traders in, 395n.2 *See also* vi, 28, 80, 161 (maps 1, 2, 3, 4); 378 (App. C)

Fort Defiance Agency: letterbooks of, 437n.11; schools in, 396n.2, 405n.1, 421n.9; supt. of, 186, 190, 191, 424n.10

Fort Defiance Hospital, 21, 225, 226, 234, 235, 452n.16, 456nn.14, 15, 457n.16, 458n.22, 474n.8, 484n.14; Agnes works at, 455n.6; Mitchells as patients at, 177, 182, 225, 234, 254, 274, 455n.6, 457n.18

Fort Sumner, N. Mex., xvii, 11, 15, 16, 17, 18, 19, 60, 61, 62, 77, 89, 114, 120, 123, 299, 379nn.2, 5, 380n.7, 382n.15, 383n.16, 384nn.5, 6, 391n. 41, 392n.5, 400n.11, 407n.11, 410–11n.1, 436n.13; before the time of, 3, 6, 7; incarceration at, xvii, 6, 17, 384n.6, 385n.14, 448n.4; Man Who Shouts and, 385n.14; release from, 18; Tall Woman's mo.'s experiences at, 16–17. *See also* Long Walk, The; vi (map 1)

Fort Sumner Treaty (Treaty of 1868), 75, 77, 383n.4, 410–11n.1, 414n.5, 417n.7

Fort Wingate, N. Mex., 212, 408n.11, 439n.1, 446n.1, 452n.17, 465n.3; hospital at, 385n.11; store (Stover and Coddington's) at, 392n.5. *See also* vi (map 1)

Fort Wingate-Dutton Plateau, 408n.11

Francis, Ada, 389n.37. *See also* 334, 338 (App. A-2)

Francis, Edward, 456n.12. *See also* 334, 343–44 (App. A-2, A-4)Francis, Ida, xxviii, xxix, xxxv, 214, 215, 328, 389n.37, 457n.18. *See also* Ida; 334 (App. A-2)

Francis, James, 109, 153, 388n.30. *See also* 334 (App. A-2)

Francis Slim Man, 234

Franciscan Fathers, xxxi, xxxv; of St. John the Baptist Province, 459n.23. *See also* Franciscans; individual brothers and priests, indexed under last names

429n.7, 457n.20, 461n.8, 465–66n.4, 473n.9, 478n.25. *See also* Diagnosticians; Diseases/medical problems; Doctors; Epidemics; Health care, Navajo; Hospitals; Illness; Injuries; Medicine people; Medicinal plants/medicine, Navajo; Medicine, western; Singers

Silent Man, 87

Singers (ceremonialists), 21, 24, 29, 63, 64, 65, 87, 88, 101, 109, 111, 118, 122, 123, 124, 141, 142, 148, 150, 151, 152, 160, 176, 177, 182, 183, 184, 186, 187, 188, 189, 196, 197, 198, 203, 226, 233, 244, 258, 265, 266, 268, 269, 289, 304; Blessingway, xvii, xxii, xxviii, 19, 20, 29, 37, 46, 82, 89, 135, 142, 143, 147, 165, 176, 182, 185, 187, 188, 192, 309–10, 441n.5; compensating, 64, 65, 102, 187, 259, 289, 291, 296, 399n.9, 409n.17, 428n.7, 447n.2, 454n.2, 456–57n.15; learning to become, 186, 187, 188; main, 63, 64, 65, 197, 457n.15; no performances over spouses, 57; options of, 394n.14; reputations of, 184, 269, 438n.21. *See also* Childbirth; Man Who Shouts; Mitchell, Frank; Tall Woman, ceremonies for

Singing (ceremonial), 148, 256, 258, 263, 277, 431n.9, 436n.13, 438nn.4, 21, 461n.8, 469–70n.9

Sippel, Fa. Anselm, 215, 383n.1, 415n.6, 447n.2, 450n.11, 451nn.12, 13, 453n.21, 457n.18

Sisters of the Blessed Sacrament, 458–59n.23. *See also* Drexel, Mo. Katharine; Franciscan Fathers; St. Catherine's school; St. Michaels

Skagg, Mr. and Mrs., 395n.2

Skinner, The, 122

Skinwalkers, 262, 381n.11. *See also* Witch/witchcraft

Skirts, 30, 75, 201, 257, 259, 317, 318, 486n.20. *See also* Clothes

Slaves, 4, 15; trading/selling of, 4, 15, 379n.5

Sleep, 10, 38, 144, 146, 150, 176, 177, 182, 195, 196, 197, 203, 204, 229, 240, 259, 263, 265, 266, 268, 301, 311, 319, 429n.10, 460n.2, 463n.19, 476n.14; beds for, 38, 143, 394n.14; on ground, 9, 38

Slim Bottom of the Mountain Man, 177, 178, 184

Slim Curly, 187

Slim Red Running into the Water Man, 126

Slim Woman (Man Who Shouts' second wife), 23, 24, 121, 388nn. 31, 34, 391n.3. *See also* 332, 338 (App. A-1, A-2)

Slim Woman (Tall Woman's half sister, dau. of Slim Woman), xxviii, xxix, 23, 24, 25, 64, 85, 121, 129, 169, 180, 201, 207–8, 214, 223, 227, 229, 244, 255, 256, 257, 281, 312, 313, 316, 320, 321, 328, 388nn.32–34, 391nn. 3, 41, 394n.15, 480n.41; children raised by, 24–25, 387n.30, 389n.37; descendants of, 388–89n.34; funeral/burial of, 389n.37; genealogy of, 322, 338–39 (App. A-1, A-2); intermarriages of Clauschees and Mitchells, 338 (App. A-2); story of own birth, 388n.34, 389nn.36–37, 470n.12. *See also* "Grandma Clauschee"; Old Red Bottom Man

Small Man (Tall Woman's mo.'s bro.), 19, 29, 30,

46, 388n.33, 391n.3. *See also* Hastiin Yázhí; 331 (App. A-1)

Small Man, 21. *See also* Yazzie, Walter; 333 (App. A-2)

Small White Man, 173. *See also* Wilson, Howard

Small Woman (Tall Woman's "real sis."; "Grandma Black"; Woman at the Hard Ground Place), xxviii, xxix, 22, 25, 108, 112, 126, 129, 158, 169, 180, 201, 214, 223, 227, 229, 238, 244, 255, 281, 316, 319, 320, 321, 328, 386n.23, 387n.29, 388n.33, 390nn.38, 40, 391n.41, 475n.13, 486n.23. *See also* "Grandma Black"; *Hastiin łaashi*; Son of Yucca Fruit Man; Woman at the Hard Ground Place; 332, 337 (App. A-1, A-2)

Smith, Eli, 431n.9

Smith, Mr., 405n.1, 421n.9

Smoke Signal, Ariz., 289, 380n.6. *See also* 28 (map 2)

Snake Flat, Ariz., 54

Snakes, 142, 164, 165, 176, 177, 183, 205, 206, 241, 288, 429nn.4, 7, 436nn.11, 13, 438n.22, 447n.2, 482n.2; nonpoisonous (bull, water), 176; poisonous: rattlesnakes, 112, 158, 164, 176, 177, 178, 204; bites by, 112, 164, 176, 177, 183; sidewinders, 164

Snow, 9, 10, 13, 29, 38, 41, 42, 63, 64, 91, 114, 116, 135, 141, 153, 173, 221, 311, 460n.3, 479n.32; sled, 173

Soap/soapweed, 35, 167. *See also* Yucca

Soil Erosion Service, 448n.4

Soldiers/troops, 4, 5, 6, 7, 8, 11, 15, 16, 17, 18, 382n.15; American, 6, 15; Mexican, 4, 6; Spanish, 4

Songs (sacred), 6, 58, 63, 64, 65, 135, 141, 146, 147, 149, 150, 163, 176, 186, 188, 189, 197, 198, 258, 263, 265, 275, 290, 407n.9, 428n.2, 441n.2, 472n.6; practicing, 123, 433n.1; Tall Woman's knowledge of, 263. *See also* Blessingway; Songs: Hogan, Horse, Mountain, Sheep

Songs (secular): "made up," 445n.5 (by Dunaway, Dick); "special," 221–22, 472n.6 (by Mitchell, Frank for own children)

Son of the Late Tall Deschine, 477n.23

Son of Man Who Shouts, 20, 74. *See also* 331, 333 (App. A-1, A-2)

Son of Tall Navajo, 387n.30, 434n.2. *See also* Diné Nééz biye'; 335–36 (App. A-2)

Son of the Late Little Blacksmith, 76–77, 86, 149, 435n.5

Son of Yucca Fruit Man, 23, 25, 144, 152, 158, 181, 197, 227, 229, 256, 387n.29, 430n.3, 437n.15, 456n.12, 457n.18, 458n.21. *See also* 334, 335, 337, 340 (App. A-2, A-3)

Southern Illinois University, Edwardsville, Ill., xxii, xxiii, xxv

Southwest, 312, 411n.1, 479n.30, 481n.43; political control of, through history, 379n.5

Spanish, 4, 13, 15, 120, 379n.5

Spider Rock (in Canyon de Chelly), 238, 241, 269, 444n.3. *See also* 28 (map 2)

Values, 134–35, 141, 193–94, 234, 236, 250, 255, 257, 273, 277, 286, 293, 294, 295, 296, 297, 298, 299, 300, 301, 302, 303, 304, 305, 316, 319, 321, 322, 323, 324, 460n.2, 462n.9; anti-laziness, 255; anti-stinginess 193–94, 234, 277, 302; anti-wasteful-ness, 250, 340. *See also* Helping others; Planning ahead; Respect; Working hard
"Vanishing American," (movie), 436n.10
Vehicles, 71, 74, 75, 90, 216, 222, 261, 287, 291, 314, 411n.1, 447n.2, 474n.5; used as ambulance, 216, 225, 314, 316. *See also* Buggies, Cars, Trucks, Wagons
Video artists, 482n.4, 482–83n.5, 483n.7
Vietnam, 311
Visiting, 42, 50, 72, 78, 99, 103, 130, 132, 137, 157, 169, 172, 197, 200–201, 207, 210, 215, 216, 226, 227, 234, 241, 243, 244, 261, 274, 281, 285, 291, 302, 309, 312, 313, 314, 319–20, 389n.35, 390n.38, 409n.16, 431n.9, 441n.5, 447n.2, 476n.14
Visitors, xxviii, 122, 123, 302, 309, 311, 321
Voice: of Man Who Shouts, 61, 74, 83, 85, 86, 103–4, 118, 125, 134, 206. *See also* Man Who Shouts, names of; of Mitchell, Frank, 193, 263, 298–99; of Old Curly Hair, 224, 442n.5; of Small Woman, 390n.38; of Water Edge Man, 85; preparing, for Yeibichei singing, 466n.4; Tall Woman raises her, 228
Volcanoes, 158, 380n.7
von Hagel, Fa. Davin, 482n.4, 483n.8, 484n.12

Wagework, 90, 142, 175, 185, 186, 247, 253, 254, 259–60, 296, 301, 303, 310, 449n.10, 450–51n.11, 462–63n.14, 477n.22, 483n.10; as boarding school students 435n.8; bootlegging as, 471n.1; during World War II, 253–54, 465n.3. *See also* Bernally, Garnett Scott; Deschine, Isabel and Jimmy; Mitchell: Adelle, David, Frank, Howard, Seya; Sanchez, Agnes; Sandoval, Augusta; Sanishya, Sam; Work/working
Wagons, xxvi, xxviii, 36, 41, 47, 50, 52, 66, 71, 72, 75, 79, 82, 85, 89, 97, 99, 105, 109, 119, 123, 134, 142, 144, 149, 153, 202, 203, 209, 214, 235, 278, 293, 385n.19, 390n.38, 393n.11, 394n.1, 404n.13, 410–11n.1, 421n.9, 431n.9, 444n.5, 445n.7, 450n.11; farm, 55, 72, 74, 91, 98, 99; Frank and Tall Woman's, 90–92, 93, 96, 98, 108, 110, 138, 143, 144, 149, 157, 159, 163, 164, 173, 177, 178, 179, 181, 187, 191, 192, 195, 215, 224, 225, 227, 237, 238, 240, 241, 242, 243, 244, 247, 249, 250, 251, 254, 255, 259, 276, 278, 282, 289, 291, 296, 309, 420n.6, 447n.2, 449n.10, 460n.5, 462n.13, 463n.19; Man Who Shouts', 71, 75; types of, 72. *See also* Buggies; 49, 285 (figs.1, 39)
Walapai Country, Ariz., 18
Walker, Frank, 412n.3
Walker, John, 414n.6
Walker, Raymond, 445n.5
War/warfare, 253, 256, 261, 304, 407n.9. *See also*

Fighting; Raiding; Soldiers; Vietnam; War-riors; World War II
War Dance, 407n.9. *See also* Enemyway Ceremony
Warehouses, 53, 422n.9, 440n.1
Warriors, 4, 7, 8, 19, 20; names of, 21, 209, 381n.13, 385n.17, 440n.2, 484n.13; party of, 3, 13
Wash (dry or running), 36, 216, 217, 238, 438n.18, 447n.2, 451n.12, 467n.5
Washington, D. C., 20, 60, 61, 62, 75, 185, 211, 212, 225, 234, 235, 412n.3, 414n.5, 423n.10, 439n.1, 448nn.4, 6, 455n.8
Water, 9, 10, 13, 32, 34, 35, 36, 38, 39, 53, 54, 55, 61, 79, 103, 109, 113, 114, 130, 131, 147, 151, 158, 183, 196, 202, 242, 245, 247, 264, 267, 309, 436n.11, 447n.2, 465n.4, 469n.9, 476–77n.19; digging for, 34, 35, 36, 53, 54; hauling, xxvi, 34, 35, 36, 38, 54, 62, 75, 113, 135, 146, 152, 153, 192, 202, 204, 216, 221, 222, 223, 226, 228, 237, 238, 239, 240, 243, 249, 254, 278, 393n.11, 406nn.2, 5. *See also* Water belly bags; Water jugs; playing in, 460n.7; running, in homes, 293; sources of, 5, 6, 36, 54, 246. *See also* Ponds; Springs, natural; Water projects, government
Water belly bags/waterbags, 34, 35, 36, 37, 38, 91, 113, 153, 237, 393n.11
Water Edge clan, 452n.15
Water Edge Man (Frank's fa.), 85, 148, 163
Water holes, xxvi, 35, 36, 39, 53, 54, 79, 201, 202, 215, 216, 237
Water jugs (woven), 9, 11, 34, 35, 36, 38, 66, 393–94n.13, 409–10n.17, 410n.19; waterproofing, 35, 393–94n.13
Waterless Mesa (No Water Flat/Mesa), Ariz., 6, 380n.9, 388n.30. *See also* 28 (map 2)
Water projects, government, 54–55, 114, 115, 202–3, 237, 406n.3, 446n.1. *See also* Dams; Ditches, water/irrigation; Water reservoirs/tanks; Wells
Water reservoirs/tanks, 54, 114, 245, 393n.11, 434n.4, 446n.1
Warren, Charlotte, 483n.5
Wauneka, Annie Dodge, xx, xxi, 458n.22
Weaving, xvii, xxviii, 15, 30, 38, 47, 48, 50, 51, 65, 81, 84, 90, 99, 111, 116, 117, 118, 122, 125, 135, 136, 165, 166, 167, 169, 170, 171, 176, 177, 178, 181, 192, 206, 207, 210, 215, 223, 224, 235, 236, 237, 240, 256, 257, 264, 274, 281, 282, 287, 288, 291, 293, 294, 297, 300, 309, 310, 311, 322, 383n.18, 392n.5, 393n.12, 399–400n.11, 400n.12, 401n.13, 421n.9, 423n.10, 432n.17, 432–33n.18, 468n.8; documen-tation of, in Tall Woman's family, 401n.13; im-portance of, for survival, 65, 66, 84, 111, 118, 140, 165, 210, 264, 297, 322; Man Who Shouts' knowledge of, 47, 117, 125, 166, 167, 170, 433n.18; Tall Woman learns, 47, 48. *See also* Chief blankets; Chinle-style rugs; Looms; Rugs; Tall Woman, as weaver; Weaving De-signs; Weaving tools; Wool